"*The Story of Abortion in America* is a tour de force providing a chronicle of the history of abortion that is impeccably documented with near-cinematic realism. The facts are compelling, the human beings—including the unborn—are vividly portrayed, and the interpretations are invariably thoughtful. There is enough in this landmark work to upset easy conclusions about abortion across the full spectrum of opinion. Anyone who wrestles with this topic, as Olasky has done for a lifetime and Savas now follows, must grapple with this account on an issue that will not, and must not, go away."

    Chuck Donovan, President, Charlotte Lozier Institute

"This remarkable and timely book should become the go-to narrative for anyone seeking to understand the tragic history and innumerable human costs of abortion in America. I recommend it enthusiastically."

    Thomas S. Kidd, Research Professor of Church History, Midwestern Baptist Theological Seminary; author, *Thomas Jefferson: A Biography of Spirit and Flesh*

"In this book that is more than just a history of abortion in America, Olasky and Savas have amassed an impressive account through real-life stories of how abortion has impacted everyday people over the centuries. The detailed stories were often tragic and heartbreaking and remind us that, truly, it is everyday people who matter most in the abortion debate. It is astonishing to read how much has changed about abortion over the centuries, but also how much really has not. Those who face unplanned pregnancies and those who seek to help them are the ones who write the real life-and-death stories of abortion and are also the ones who can change the world for the better, one life at a time. This captivating book will certainly help cultivate some of that needed change."

    Anne O'Connor, Vice President of Legal Affairs, National Institute of Family and Life Advocates

"*The Story of Abortion in America* is a big story, a momentous story, that extends to the most consequential of human experiences. The story of the past three hundred and seventy years, told here so clearly and deeply sourced, is largely a tragedy; it is up to us to determine what the rest of the story will be."

    Frederica Mathewes-Green, speaker; author, *Real Choices: Listening to Women, Looking for Alternatives to Abortion*

"A riveting story of the history of abortion by two 'street-level' researchers who tell us real stories of real people who have sought abortions, provided abortions, and lobbied for change in the abortion laws. Spanning nearly four hundred years of abortion history, Olasky and Savas transport us back in time to help us understand that there has always been abortion among women 'seduced by men, money, or the religion of self.' Many of these abortions were coerced, and the chilling narratives of these coercions throughout history are not for the faint of heart. Readers will be moved to tears by the stories, many of them transcribed from published accounts of the very words of the women who have been victims of the abortion industry and those who support it. We meet many of the craven abortion providers on these pages—the infamous Madame Restell, as well as a long list of lesser-known profiteers who have grown rich by ending the lives of unborn children. It is a tragic history, but Olasky and Savas do not leave us bereft of hope."

Anne Hendershott, Professor of Sociology and Director of the Veritas Center for Ethics in Public Life, Franciscan University

"Under the reign of *Roe v. Wade*, abortion became 'normal.' But it wasn't always that way in our nation, as this book explains. Now that the Supreme Court has removed its imprimatur from abortion-on-demand for any reason through all nine months of pregnancy, how do we restore respect for the tiniest among us and care for their mothers? Olasky and Savas provide crucial historical context for this effort, and everyone from the newly minted pro-life student to the battle-worn anti-abortion veteran will glean valuable insight from these pages."

Kristan Hawkins, President, Students for Life Action and Students for Life of America

"What an amazing work! Olasky and Savas have made an important contribution on a topic that is both so controversial and also so essential to the understanding of what America has become and what it will be as a nation in the future. Indeed, this book is a reminder that our nation's abortion history is linked to its destiny, especially if we seek to offer compassion, hope, and help to those at risk for abortion and their vulnerable unborn children."

Roland C. Warren, President and CEO, Care Net; author, *Raising Sons of Promise: A Guide to Single Mothers of Boys*

"Olasky and Savas convey a largely unknown, and as yet unfinished, account of the deep struggle between individual and human rights, worldviews and wickedness. *The Story of Abortion in America* captures the real and raw nature of the battleground over, and for, the unborn. In these pages you'll find selfless servants and the profiteering powerful. Just as other great moral issues have stretched and torn the fabric of America, so has abortion. This work should be read by everyone concerned for the soul of America."

Jor-El Godsey, President, Heartbeat International

The Story of Abortion in America

The Story of Abortion in America

A Street-Level History, 1652–2022

Marvin Olasky
and Leah Savas

Foreword by Robert P. George

WHEATON, ILLINOIS

The Story of Abortion in America: A Street-Level History, 1652–2022
Copyright © 2023 by Marvin Olasky and Leah Savas
Published by Crossway
        1300 Crescent Street
        Wheaton, Illinois 60187

All rights reserved. No part of this publication may be reproduced, stored in a retrieval system, or transmitted in any form by any means, electronic, mechanical, photocopy, recording, or otherwise, without the prior permission of the publisher, except as provided for by USA copyright law. Crossway® is a registered trademark in the United States of America.

Cover design: Jordan Singer

Cover image: "Five Points, 1827," New York Public Library Digital Collections. image id: nypl_grd_415.

First printing 2023

Printed in the United States of America

Unless otherwise indicated, Scripture quotations are from the ESV® Bible (The Holy Bible, English Standard Version®), copyright © 2001 by Crossway, a publishing ministry of Good News Publishers. Used by permission. All rights reserved. The ESV text may not be quoted in any publication made available to the public by a Creative Commons license. The ESV may not be translated into any other language.

Scripture quotations marked NIV are taken from the Holy Bible, New International Version®, NIV®. Copyright © 1973, 1978, 1984, 2011 by Biblica, Inc.™ Used by permission of Zondervan. All rights reserved worldwide. www.zondervan.com. The "NIV" and "New International Version" are trademarks registered in the United States Patent and Trademark Office by Biblica, Inc.™

Scripture quotations marked KJV are from the King James Version of the Bible. Public domain.

Hardcover ISBN: 978-1-4335-8044-4
ePub ISBN: 978-1-4335-8047-5
PDF ISBN: 978-1-4335-8045-1
Mobipocket ISBN: 978-1-4335-8046-8

Library of Congress Cataloging-in-Publication Data

Names: Olasky, Marvin N., author. | Savas, Leah, 1995- author.
Title: The story of abortion in America : a street-level history, 1652-2022 / Marvin Olasky, Leah Savas.
Description: Wheaton, Illinois : Crossway, [2023] | Includes bibliographical references and index.
Identifiers: LCCN 2022016677 (print) | LCCN 2022016678 (ebook) | ISBN 9781433580444 (hardcover) | ISBN 9781433580451 (pdf) | ISBN 9781433580468 (mobi) | ISBN 9781433580475 (epub)
Subjects: LCSH: Abortion—United States—History. | Abortion—Moral and ethical aspects—United States. | Abortion—Religious aspects—Christianity.
Classification: LCC HQ767.5.U5 O44 2023 (print) | LCC HQ767.5.U5 (ebook) | DDC 363.4/6/0973—dc23/ eng/20220414
LC record available at https://lccn.loc.gov/2022016677
LC ebook record available at https://lccn.loc.gov/2022016678

Crossway is a publishing ministry of Good News Publishers.

LB		31	30	29	28	27	26	25	24	23	
15	14	13	12	11	10	9	8	7	6	5	4	3	2	1

For Susan Olasky, founder of the Austin Crisis Pregnancy Center, with thanks for 46 years of marriage, and for CareNet president Guy Condon, who died in 2000 driving home from a pro-life event when a van broadsided his 1990 Honda. Guy, see you again, sometime.

For Stephen Savas, Leah's encourager, and for faithful readers Bonnie Hickman and Janice Main, both young mothers around the time of Roe v. Wade. *Thanks for choosing life and for being my Grandmas.*

Contents

Foreword by Robert P. George *xiii*

Introduction: The Life or Death of Innocent Life *1*

1 Street Level vs. Suite Level *7*

SECTION ONE: UNSAFE, ILLEGAL, AND RARE, 1652–1842

2 Common Law, Common Sense *17*

3 Murder of a Man Child *25*

4 Pressuring the Father *33*

5 Bitter Execrations *41*

6 An Oath for Midwives *49*

7 Double Robbery of Life *55*

8 A Fallen Pro-Life Founder *63*

9 Laws and Scofflaws *71*

10 Insufficient Protection for Women *79*

SECTION TWO: SPECIALIZATION BEGINS, 1838–1878

11 A Fatal Needle *89*

12 The Welfare of Two Patients *97*

13 Madame Restell *103*

14 An Unstoppable Force? *111*

15 A Moral Maelstrom *119*

16 The Unwelcome Child *127*

17 Doctors Push Back *135*

18 Massacres *145*

19 Compassion vs. Abortion *155*

20 Thugs of Society *163*

SECTION THREE: SUPPLY AND DEMAND, 1871–1940

21 A Much Pulverized Reporter *173*

22 The Victims Are . . . *181*

23 So Much Rascality *187*

24 Horror Stories at Century's End *195*

25 Medical Heroines *203*

26 The Erring Women's Refuge *211*

27 Weak-Kneed Enforcement *219*

28 Old-School Abortionists *227*

29 Twentieth-Century Compassion *235*

30 Million-Dollar Hands *243*

SECTION FOUR: SEEING LIFE, 1930–1995

31 Linkages *255*

32 Complicated Lives *263*

33 Losing the Baby *273*

34 Playing the Danger Card *281*

35 The Father of Abortion Rights *289*

36 Eroded Ethic *297*

37 On the Disassembly Line *305*

38 Pro-Life Frustration *313*

39 Pictures Seen and Unseen *323*

40 Cacophony and Compassion *331*

SECTION FIVE: STILL UNSETTLED, 1995–2022

41 Window to the Womb *341*

42 Loving Your Unborn Neighbor *349*

43 Sensational Facts *357*

44 A Sanitized Image *367*

45 Aborting Alone *375*

46 Incremental vs. Radical *385*

47 The Abortion-Industrial Complex *395*

48 A New Enforcement Mechanism *403*

49 Their One Person *415*

50 Egregiously Wrong *425*

Epilogue   *439*
Bibliography   *445*
  Books   *445*
  Selected Journal and Magazine Articles   *461*
Other Books by Marvin Olasky   *467*
General Index   *469*
Scripture Index   *493*

Foreword

MARVIN OLASKY AND LEAH SAVAS tell the story of abortion in America by telling the stories of abortion in America.

These are the stories of people who have over the past 370 years sought abortions; performed abortions—lawfully and unlawfully; were pressured or even coerced to have abortions; pressured or coerced mistresses, daughters, domestic servants, or other women to have abortions; worked to prohibit abortion or strengthen existing prohibitions of abortion; enforced the laws against abortion; sought to circumvent abortion laws, or weaken or overturn them in legislatures and courts; changed their minds about abortion—in one direction or the other; provided alternatives to abortion; made small livings or vast sums of money from abortion; and others.

Olasky and Savas thus provide what they describe, aptly in my view, as a "street-level history" of abortion, in contrast with the formal, academic, and often rather abstract historical (or other) treatments of the subject with which all of us today are more than familiar.

The Story of Abortion in America, then, is the story of abortion as seen through the eyes of a pair of smart, well-informed, independent-minded, truth-seeking journalists—writers who bring to life the flesh-and-blood human beings who made the history. They try sympathetically, and remarkably successfully, to understand not only *what* these people thought, said, and did, but *why* they thought, said, and did it. The authors adopt what the great academic philosopher of law and social science H. L. A. Hart called "the internal point of view"—that is, the perspective of the actors whose behaviors constitute the phenomena they seek to understand and explain.

The success of the volume that you, the reader, hold in your hands does not mean that the work of professional historians and social sciences is irrelevant or unnecessary. Nor do Olasky and Savas claim that it does such a thing. Indeed, in certain important respects Olasky and Savas draw and rely on "suite-level" scholarship for their "street-level" work. But their contribution adds something missing in more formal scholarship—it is not simply the "dumbed-down" version of academic historiography. Indeed, just as Olasky and Savas draw on the work of "suite-level" scholars, I predict that such scholars writing on abortion over the next few decades will draw on their "street-level" history.

Olasky and Savas have a point of view—a moral and political perspective—and they do not try to hide it. They are pro-life, as I myself am. And they recognize that their moral convictions on the question of the sanctity of all human life, including the lives of children in the womb, influence certain of their understandings and judgments even when it comes to the description of historical facts. Admirably, however, they avoid allowing their accounts of the facts to degenerate into propaganda. To the extent possible, they let the facts speak for themselves. Acknowledging, as we all should, that there is not, and can never be, strictly "value free" or "value neutral" historiography or social science, Olasky and Savas at the same time recognize the obligations of the historian or social scientist to provide as refined and accurate an account as possible, uncolored *to the extent possible* by judgments of value, or personal or political morality, on which reasonable people can and do disagree.

As a result, *The Story of Abortion in America* is a book for everyone, and not just a book for people who share the authors' moral convictions on abortion and the sanctity of life. It can and no doubt will be read with profit by people whose moral convictions are quite distant on these matters from those of the authors. And it can and will certainly be read with profit by the many people, in America and beyond, who experience ambivalence on the question of abortion and/or who do not fit neatly into one category or the other when asked, "Are you pro-life or pro-choice?"

One thing is certain. If we are to think well about the question of abortion—and America's future when it comes to the question—we need a sound understanding of the history of abortion in America. Supplementing the good work that has been done on the topic by some suite-level historians (alongside, I regret to say, notoriously shoddy work done by some others), Olasky and Savas's "street-level" story of abortion contributes substantially to meeting that need.

Robert P. George
McCormick Professor of Jurisprudence and Director of the
James Madison Program in American Ideals and Institutions
Princeton University

Introduction

The Life or Death of Innocent Life

LEAH SAVAS AND I WROTE THIS BOOK in anticipation of the 50th anniversary of *Roe v. Wade* on January 22, 2023. Crossway scheduled it for January 3 publication with that date in mind. The 50th anniversary now is likely to be a day of pro-life appreciation rather than lament, and the opposite for abortion supporters.

Roe reversal made the timing of this book moot but increased the need for historical understanding. From 1973 to 2022 pro-life laws could only trim the edges of a beard or the tips of a ponytail. Now legislators can decree a full shave or even a bald head, but will street-level conduct reflect the new judicial reality?

For 370 years, this book shows, laws and their enforcement have depended on public opinion. As Abraham Lincoln said in 1858, "In this country, public sentiment is everything. With it, nothing can fail; against it, nothing can succeed. Whoever molds public sentiment goes deeper than he who enacts statutes, or pronounces judicial decisions."[1]

This book reports on shifting public sentiment over the centuries, and the sentiment in crucial subsets: journalists, pastors, doctors, and others. We also look at records of private opinion, since the views of a woman and her boyfriend or husband are still more influential than any law.

---

1 Abraham Lincoln, *Complete Works* (New York: Century Company, 1907), 1:422.

The Supreme Court majority in the crucial case, *Dobbs v. Jackson*, gave two main reasons for its decision: a re-analysis of the Fourteenth Amendment, and a re-reading of American history.[2]

I'll look at the Fourteenth Amendment issue in chapter 18, but the central question for this book is what Justice Samuel Alito asked, quoting a unanimous Supreme Court opinion from 25 years before: Is a right not mentioned in the Constitution "deeply rooted in this Nation's history and tradition"?[3]

Some thought the answer was an obvious "yes," since in the 1990 lead-up to the Court's *Casey* decision, numerous American historians in an Amicus Curiae brief had said so.[4] And yet, few of those historians had themselves delved into abortion history: I saw in twenty-five years as a professor at The University of Texas at Austin how social pressures influence judgment.

Alito, in his *Dobbs* majority opinion, after disposing of the Fourteenth Amendment contentions, offered fourteen pages of legal history and noted that "*Roe* either ignored or misstated this history. . . . It is therefore important to set the record straight."[5]

He concluded, "a right to abortion is not deeply rooted in the Nation's history and traditions. On the contrary, an unbroken tradition of prohibiting abortion on pain of criminal punishment persisted from the earliest days of the common law until 1973."[6] That's true about the common law that judges and prosecutors applied, but what about common practice outside the courtroom?

---

2   *Dobbs v. Jackson Women's Health Organization*, 597 U.S. ___ (2022).
3   In *Washington v. Glucksberg*, 521 U.S. 702 (1997), 721, the Supreme Court declared 9-0 that the Fourteenth Amendment does not establish a right to assisted suicide. Chief Justice William Rehnquist's opinion acknowledged that the Amendment guarantees some rights not mentioned in the Constitution, but they must be "deeply rooted in this Nation's history and tradition," and assisted suicide is not.
4   "Brief of 281 American Historians as Amici Curiae Supporting Appellees," *The Public Historian* 12 (Summer 1990), 57–75. The brief notes, "Numerous additional historians joined the brief after it was filed, bringing the total number to over 400."
5   *Dobbs v. Jackson Women's Health Organization*, 597 U.S. ___ (2022), 16.
6   *Dobbs*, 25.

National Public Radio in June 2022 stated this as fact about abortion: "In colonial America, it was considered a fairly common practice, a private decision made by women and aided mostly by midwives."[7] True? Other common generalizations: In the nineteenth century, abortion laws were a way for men to put midwives out of business. True? In the twentieth century, coat-hanger and Lysol abortions were frequent. Are those and many other assumptions about the history of abortion true? That's what this book attempts to assess.

Justice Alito dealt with legal history rather than social history, as is proper for a justice, but we should recognize that law is the 10 percent of an iceberg visible from a cruise ship: This book reveals the 90 percent below the ocean's surface. Throughout, Leah and I pay particular attention to what makes this issue different from others the Supreme Court has faced: Abortion is about both the life or death of innocent life and the liberty of young women and men.

The fictional Sherlock Holmes solved a case because a dog did not bark. The 66-page dissent in *Dobbs* was well-written but it skipped one supremely vital matter: Is the creature in the womb human life?[8] That question underlies this book, which makes it unusual among books about abortion history. It's also an unusual book in three other ways.

First, it lays out the history of abortion in America not at "suite level," as a law journal might, but at street level, where human beings make life-or-death decisions.

What difference does that make? A 1976 *New York Times* column by Linda Bird Francke contrasted her abstract thinking during a pro-choice march with her "panic," moments before she was about to abort:

---

7 Sacha Pfeiffer on *All Things Considered*, June 6, 2022, 4:29 p.m. ET.
8 There is no neutral nomenclature for the creature in the womb. "Fetus" is a medical term that became common in news coverage only in 1962, as chapter 33 will show. Some favor the word "preborn," which makes sense because "unborn" now sounds like a horror film term, but since "preborn" is not commonly used it draws attention to itself and away from the facts surrounding it. In this book we'll use the words used throughout most of American history, "unborn child."

"Suddenly the rhetoric, the abortion marches I'd walked in . . . peeled away, and I was all alone with my microscopic baby."⁹

That's the existential moment. Francke's tale ended poignantly: "It certainly does make more sense not to be having a baby right now. . . . But I have this ghost now. A very little ghost that only appears when I'm seeing something beautiful, like the full moon on the ocean last weekend. And the baby waves at me. And I wave back at the baby."

Second, this book favors neither a "Shout Your Abortion" nor a "Shun the Aborting Woman" approach. Abortion is a tragedy that often produces grief, as one recent book of poems about abortion shows. Publicists for *Choice Words* say it will "renew our courage in the struggle to defend reproductive rights."¹⁰ Maybe so, but the bones cry out.

The collection includes the 1945 poem "The Mother," by Gwendolyn Brooks, the first African American to win a Pulitzer Prize for poetry. Brooks wrote that abortions "will not let you forget." She described how she has "heard in the voices of the wind the voices of my dim killed children."¹¹

Two generations later, Teri Ellen Cross Davis told her aborted child, "science tells me / inside my bones / you are still whispering."¹² Many writings regarded as pro-choice reveal pro-life yearnings, and that's one reason partisan books and out-of-context binary polling—"Are you pro-life or pro-choice?"—often oversimplify the issues.

Third, the authors bring to this work diverse experiences. I'm a 72-year-old man who's been through the abortion wars for nearly four decades. Leah reverses my age: She's 27 and has covered *World* magazine's life beat for four years. We each use "I" at times, so you should know that I wrote the first forty chapters, Leah the last ten.

9 Linda Bird Francke, initially writing as "Jane Doe," "There Just Wasn't Room in Our Lives Now for Another Baby," *New York Times*, May 14, 1976, 21.
10 See Annie Finch, ed., *Choice Words: Writers on Abortion* (Chicago: Haymarket, 2020).
11 Gwendolyn Brooks, "The Mother," in *A Street in Bronzeville* (New York: Harper & Brothers, 1945), here quoted from Finch, *Choice Words*, 161.
12 Teri Ellen Cross Davis, "Haint," in *Haint* (Arlington, VA: Gival Press, 2016), 67, here quoted from Finch, *Choice Words*, 226; other poems from *Choice Words* were quoted in *World*, October 9, 2021, 26; and January 29, 2022, 26.

Throughout, we'll look at five considerations affecting views of abortion:
Anatomy: Does that creature in the womb have human characteristics?
Bible: Is its teaching on the sacredness of human life binding on us?

Community: What kind of advice and support do vulnerable women receive from boyfriends or husbands, parents and friends, employers or government, or anyone to whom a woman might look for emotional or financial help?

Danger to women: What is the likelihood of an abortion ending with not just one victim but two?

Enforcement: In what informal and formal ways do those with influence and resources protect the most vulnerable?

Some readers may be familiar with my book *Abortion Rites: A Social History of Abortion in America*, which I researched at the Library of Congress in 1990 and '91: Crossway published it in 1992. My original intent in 2020 was to do a new edition of that work. I quickly learned that many old records and newspaper accounts now available in archives and online throw so much new light on the subject that I needed to write a new book, which Leah's writing and perspective greatly helped.

Readers of the earlier book will recognize some major characters like John McDowall and Madame Restell, but they'll make many new acquaintances as well: Jane Sharp and Anne Orthwood, Sarah Grosvenor and Amasa Sessions, Sarah Cornell and Ephraim Avery, Eliza Sowers and Hugh Hodge, James Jaquess and Andrew Nebinger, Cora Sammis and Jennie Clark, Will Myers and Eliza Levassy, C. H. Orton and Kittie O'Toole, Scott Jackson and Pearl Bryan, Mary Hood and Inez Burns, Frederick Taussig and Robert Dickinson, Edgar Keemer and Ruth Barnett, and others who over the centuries infiltrated dreams and nightmares.

Read on, please.

Marvin Olasky
July 4, 2022

1

Street Level vs. Suite Level

"INDIVIDUALS AND GROUPS *that seek to restrict access to abortion often use sonograms, photos, and plastic models of prenates [unborn children] to play on people's emotional associations with newborn babies.*"¹

Journalists for centuries have wrestled with how much attention to pay to the creature in the womb. Here's a headline at the top of page one of the *New York Times* on the first day of summer, 1883: "TWENTY-ONE MURDERED BABIES." The story showed a detective pushing his shovel through basement dirt and finding tiny skulls, ribs, and leg bones: the remnants of 400–500 unborn children killed by Philadelphia abortionist Isaac Hathaway.²

Was it right for the *Times* to report that, when a district attorney shook the cigar box containing the twenty-one corpses, the bones rattled like "hard withered leaves"? Or how about the specific detail in a Philadelphia newspaper: The bones had "their natural shape." The pieces included "the outer-line of an eye-socket. . . . remnants of arms and hands, shoulder-blades."³

---

1   Rebecca Peters, *Trust Women: A Progressive Christian Argument for Reproductive Justice* (Boston: Beacon, 2018), 42. Peters worries that "a prenate looks like a baby long before it is viable, and our improved technological capacity in the last thirty years has brought prenatal images increasingly into our consciousness."
2   *New York Times*, June 21, 1883, 1.
3   *New York Times*, June 24 and 28, 1883, 1; *Philadelphia Times*, June 28, 1; June 24, 3. See also *Chester Times*, June 21, 4, and June 28, 4; *Philadelphia Inquirer*, June 21, 2, and June 28, 3; *Oil City Derrick*, June 28, 3; *Lancaster Daily Intelligencer*, June 21, 2, and June 23, 3.

Back then a judge exclaimed, "It was murder." Newspapers across America ran with the story, including its specific detail. In Anderson, South Carolina, *The Intelligencer* lamented, "A Philadelphia Golgotha." In St. Louis, the *Globe-Democrat* screamed, "Philadelphia's Ghoul . . . The Men Had Hardly Dug Down Six Inches when They Struck THE SKULL OF A BABE." In Cedar Rapids, Iowa, *The Gazette* front-paged "A Philadelphia Abortionist Makes a Babies' Cemetery in His Cellar." In Mineral Park, Arizona, the *Mohave County Miner* moaned about "A Ghastly Discovery."[4]

And that was not all. In 1883, via the new Associated Press and other press collaboratives, readers across the United States read sensational stories about abortionist Hathaway in colorfully named newspapers like *The Public Reaper* (Farmer City, IL), the *Santa Cruz Surf*, *The Biblical Recorder* (Raleigh, NC), the *Vernon County Censor* (Viroqua, WI), *The True Northerner* (Paw Paw, MI), *The Opposition* (Crete, NE), and *The Whisperer* (Portis, KS).

These newspapers were small but avidly read. Their cumulative circulation of these stories was immense. I traced the Hathaway coverage in 1883 across one state, Kansas, the geographic center of the contiguous United States, and imagined a salesman on a dirt road taking a break from his labors by reading the local newspaper, then jumping up and down, yelling "baby-butcher!" That's what headlines—in the *Garden City Irrigator*, the *Morris County Enterprise*, *The Bronson Pilot*, and *The Pleasanton Herald*—called Hathaway.[5]

A song popular in the 1960s and still broadcast, "I've Been Everywhere," features a rapid-fire "Reno, Chicago, Fargo . . . Boston, Charleston, Dayton . . . Louisville, Nashville, Knoxville . . . Pittsburgh, Parkersburg, Gravelbourg . . . I've been everywhere, man." Try putting to

---

4   *Globe-Democrat*, June 21, 1883, 6; *Gazette*, June 21, 1, and June 22, 1; *Intelligencer*, June 28, 2; *Miner*, July 1, 1. See also *San Francisco Chronicle*, June 21, 3.
5   *Garden City* (KS) *Irrigator*; *Morris County Enterprise* (Parkerville, KS); *Bronson Pilot*: all June 28, 1883, 1; *Pleasonton* (KS) *Herald*, June 29, 1.

that tune the 1883 Kansas abortion stories in Wichita, Salina, Topeka, Oneida... Leon, Atchison, Holton, Hutchinson... Concordia, Emporia, Arcadia... Hays City, Mound City, Elk City, Strong City. That's one state. The message—abortion equals horror—went "everywhere, man."[6]

Some reporters and editors spared readers the grisliest detail, but other newspapers piled on. In Illinois, the *Monmouth Evening Gazette* ran a "BURIED BABIES" headline followed by "Infant Bodies for Dog Meat—A Ghastly Recital." Readers learned about Hathaway's "voracious dogs in the cellar. Sometimes when pressed for time he did not go to the trouble of dismembering the bodies of his little victims, but tossed them into the cellar, where they would be quickly devoured."[7]

---

6   As reported (in chronological order, June and July, 1883), in (JUNE 21) *Atchison Daily Patriot*, 1; *The Daily Commonwealth* (Topeka), 1; *Emporia Weekly Republican*, 1; *The Evening News* (Emporia), 3; *Leavenworth Times*, 1; *Topeka Daily Capital*, 1; (JUNE 22) *The Ottawa Daily Republic*, 1; *The Parsons Daily Sun*, 1; (JUNE 27) *The Elk City Globe*, 3; *Kansas People* (Osage), 2; (JUNE 28) *The Belleville Telescope*, 1; *The Blue Rapids Times*, 4; *Cedarville Telephone*, 4; *Chanute Weekly Times*, 4; *Chase County Leader* (Cottonwood Falls), 4; *Clyde Herald*, 2; *The Great Bend Register*, 4; *The Hays City Sentinel*, 3; *Hepler Leader*, 1; *The Junction City Tribune*, 4; *The Kansas Jewelite* (Mankato), 3; *The Kinsley Graphic*, 4; *Leon Indicator*, 1; *Oberlin Herald*, 4; *Osborne County News*, 2; *Pratt County Press* (Iuka), 4; *The Semi-Weekly Republican*, 2; *The Weekly Herald* (Fort Scott), 1; *The Western Herald* (Girard), 1; *Wichita New Republic*, 2; (JUNE 29) *The Cherokee Sentinel*, 4; *The Douglass Index*, 2; *Erie Record*, 2; *Garnet Republican Plaindealer*, 3; *Greenwood County Republican* (Eureka), 3; *The Hanover Democrat and Enterprise*, 1; *The Lindsborg News-Record*, 4; *Linn County Clarion* (Mound City), 1; *Neodesha Free Press*, 1; *The Sedgwick Pantagraph*, 4; *Washington Weekly Post*, 4; *The Whiting Weekly News*, 1; *The Wilson County Citizen* (Fredonia), 1; (JUNE 30) *The Danville Courant*, 6; *The McCune Times*, 4; *The Oneida Chieftain*, 2; *The Salina Semi-Weekly Journal*, 2; *Western Kansas World* (Wakeeny), 3; *The Wetmore Spectator*, 1; (JULY 3) *The Dodge City Globe*, 1; (JULY 4) *Alma News*, 1; *Ellsworth Messenger*, 2; *Harper County Times*, 6; *Holton Signal*, 2; *The Independence Kansan*, 1; (JULY 5) *The Alliance Herald* (Stafford), 2; *The Alton Empire*, 2; *Anthony Journal*, 6; *The Arcadia Reporter*, 1; *The Beloit Courier*, 2; *Burden Saturday Journal*, 1; *Cawker City Public Record*, 2; *Chetopa Advance*, 2; *Colony Free Press*, 1; *Greenwood County Democrat* (Eureka), 1; *Harper Sentinel*, 2; *Kansas Reporter* (Warnego), 2; *The Kirwin Kansan*, 2; *The Onaga Democrat*, 1; *Topeka Mail*, 6; *The Valley Falls New Era*, 2; *The Wellsville News*, 1; *Westmoreland Recorder*, 6; *Yates Center Argus*, 6; (JULY 6) *Barber County Index* (Medicine Lodge), 2; *Cherryvale Globe and Torch*, 6; *The Courier Tribune* (Seneca), 1; *Delphos Carrier*, 1; *The Frankfort Bee*, 2; *Greenleaf Independent*, 1; *The Grenola Hornet*, 6; *The Iola Register*, 1; *Kansas Kritic* (Concordia), 3; *Labette County Democrat*, 2; *The Lawrence Tribune*, 2; *Strong City Independent*, 1; (JULY 7) *The Cresset* (Clay Center), 3; *Hutchinson Herald*, 1; *The Sun* (Glasco), 2.

7   *New York Times*, June 21, 1; *Monmouth* (IL) *Evening Gazette*, June 21, 2. See also June 21 issues of *Sturgeon Bay* (WI) *Weekly Expositor Independent*, 4; *Janesville* (WI) *Daily Gazette*, 2; *Middletown* (NY) *Daily Argus*, 2; *Norwalk* (OH) *Daily Reflector*, 2 (all 1883).

An angry Mrs. Hathaway said her husband sometimes threw the tiny corpses into their cooking-stove, "preparing the dinner from the heat from the human fuel." She said Hathaway even aborted their own twins and planned to turn them into fuel, but she was "not quite hardened enough to see her own flesh and blood burned before her eyes." They buried the bodies in their yard.[8]

The Hathaway arrest in 1883 received more nationwide attention than any other abortion case in the 1880s. As we'll see, abortions that resulted in the deaths of a mother and a tiny victim received broad attention in 1890, 1893, 1896, 1907, 1910, and other years, but the next discovery of numerous corpses in one place did not come until ninety-nine years after the discovery in Hathaway's basement.

That's when the owner of a Los Angeles pathology lab failed to make payments on a container in which he had stored 16,500 dead unborn children. Workers emptying the container on Thursday, February 4, 1982, discovered the bodies packed in formaldehyde-filled jars stuffed into boxes stacked eight feet high.

Two days later, the *Los Angeles Times* ran on page 27 a headline, "500 Fetuses Found in Metal Container," and reported that "health and safety code violations may be involved." *Times* reporter Judith Michaelson included in her story the reaction of forklift operator Ron Gillett: "I saw one fetus with legs 2½–3 inches long, and the body and head were demolished. I was scared, frightened, and had tears in my eyes."[9]

Was it right that the *Los Angeles Times* and its news service on subsequent days avoided any further description and went up the "ladder of

---

8 *The Ogden Standard*, June 29, 1883, 2; *Montgomery Advertiser*, June 26, 1883, 3. Hathaway himself received vivid description: *The New York Times*, June 24, 1883, 1, called him "a shabby-looking old man, stooping and weak, attired in a very dirty shirt, and with hair and voluminous beard dyed in raven black."

9 Michaelson, on February 6, 1982, also quoted Gillett's boss, Nick Martin, saying "They're just fetuses, but they sure look like bodies to me." A United Press International story the next day ran the same quotation from Martin but included two words at the beginning that gave Martin's words a different twist: "*They say* they're just fetuses, but they sure look like humans to me" (*Pacific Daily News* [Guam], February 7, 9; italics added).

abstraction"? Headlines emphasized the detective aspects: "LA County Tries to Unravel Fetus Mystery," "LA Officials Studying 500 Fetuses to Check whether Crime Occurred," and (on page 54) "Secret Meeting Set in Fetus Discovery Case."[10]

An Associated Press story on February 6—"500 Fetuses Found in Huge Metal Container"—made its way onto page 26 of the *Tacoma News Tribune* and received similar placement in newspapers such as the *Clarion Ledger* in Mississippi and the *St. Cloud Times* in Minnesota. AP stories on subsequent days ran under headlines like those in the *Los Angeles Times*: "Fetuses Are Probed for Abortion Status," "Fetuses to Be Examined," "Fetuses under Guard during Disposal Probe," "Probe Continues in LA Fetus Case," and "Fetus Disposal Probe Continues."[11]

The stories could have been different, as they were in one small newspaper. *The News-Pilot* of San Pedro, California, close to the disposal site, ran its story at the top of page one. Staff writer Rex Dalton, unlike his counterparts in 1883, used the word "fetus," but he humanized the "hundreds of fetuses, some more than five months developed, with expressions on their faces. . . . They varied in development from a few weeks to more than five months, officials said. Larger fetuses—some weighing more than 3 pounds—were in 1-gallon, ice cream-type containers, while smaller ones were in jars marked 'dentures.'"[12]

---

10 *Honolulu Advertiser*, February 7, 1982, 15; *Miami Herald*, February 8, 145; *Los Angeles Times*, February 11, 54. Linguist S. I. Hayakawa developed the "ladder of abstraction" concept in his 1939 book *Language in Thought and Action*. The bottom rung is concrete detail, and every rung higher is more abstract.

11 The initial AP story on February 6, 1982, included a quotation from Mel Grussing of the California Department of Health saying of the workers, "They noticed a foul odor, and what looked to them to be body parts." Further AP stories—*Fresno Bee*, February 7, 16; *Alabama Journal*, February 8, 20; *Burlington Free Press*, February 9, 4; "Probe Continues in LA Fetus Case," *Santa Monica Times*, February 11, 18; *Santa Cruz Sentinel*, February 17, 33—did not include even that small amount of specific detail.

12 Dalton, "Fetuses Found in Wilmington Container," *News-Pilot*, February 6, 1982, 1.

Dalton also quoted Nick Martin, owner of the company that repossessed the container: Martin believed that "abortion is wrong. Anybody seeing what is in that container would, too." But other reporters did not give readers specific detail about what was in the container. Hank Stolk, one of the truck drivers who repossessed the corpse-filled container, later told the author of a pro-life book about the discovery, "We kept trying to get the reporters to talk about . . . these babies that were killed. But they wouldn't listen or ask any questions about that."[13]

In mid-February Nick Thimmesch, a columnist syndicated by the *Los Angeles Times*, wrote about "the ghastly container" and criticized the way some officials and reporters referred to its contents as "medical waste": Thimmesch asked, "But what is medical waste? An amputated leg, a cancerous growth, an unborn child?" The *Times* itself, though, did not run that column, and it apparently appeared only in small newspapers. By the end of February the story seemed dead.[14]

The story had a brief revival late in May, when headlines such as "Caskets Ready for 40 of the 17,000 Aborted Fetuses" appeared, and President Ronald Reagan endorsed the desire of pro-life advocates to have a burial service for them. The *Central New Jersey Home News* quoted Hank Stolk's description of what he saw back in February: "a leg with a little foot on it . . . a hand and part of an arm."[15] But larger newspapers ran neither descriptions nor photographs, and the *Los Angeles Times* quoted abortion advocate Gloria Allred's contention that showing photos of the dead was "a sleazy, callous, and cheap political trick at the expense of women who have already suffered enough."[16]

---

13 Hank Stolk, quoted in S. Rickly Christian, *The Woodland Hills Tragedy* (Westchester, IL: Crossway, 1985), 76.
14 Nick Thimmesch, "A Ghastly Backyard Scene," *Victoria* (TX) *Advocate*, February 16, 4; and *Carlsbad* (NM) *Current-Argus*, February 22, 16; "Life and Death in Woodland Hills," *The Desert Sun* (Palm Springs), February 23, 14.
15 Headline and quotation from *Central* (New Brunswick) *New Jersey Home News*, May 28, 11.
16 Marita Hernandez, "Allred Calls for Probe in Fetus Pictures," *Los Angeles Times*, June 8, 34.

That put the issue well. Was reporting at street level cruel, and an indication of bias? Did abortion advocates have to stay at suite level and push an abstract term: pro-choice?

Not necessarily. Magda Denes was a 42-year-old Holocaust survivor in 1976 when her extraordinary *In Necessity and Sorrow* hit the bookstores. She classified herself as "pro-choice" and apparently remained so until her death 20 years later, but she researched her book for months inside a New York City abortion center because she hated "the evasions, multifaceted, clever, and shameful, by which we all live and die."[17]

Here's one description of how she did not run from reality: "I look inside the bucket in front of me. There is a small naked person in there floating in a bloody liquid—plainly the tragic victim of a drowning accident. But then perhaps this was no accident, because the body is purple with bruises. . . . I lift the fetuses, one by one. I lift them by an arm or leg. . . . I carry on the examination, whose sole purpose by now is to increase the unbearable anguish in my heart."[18]

Denes, in the course of her research, got to know the abortionists (and protected them by changing their names). One said, "You can feel the fetus wiggling at the end of that needle and moving around, which is an unpleasant thing." The director of nursing said her nurses "feel a little repulsed when you get a big fetus. It is very traumatic for the staff to pick this up and put it in a container and say, 'Okay, that's going to the incinerator.'"[19]

Furthermore, Denes empathized with women waiting for abortions: "Their pinched faces are full of determination and terror. Big-eyed,

---

17 Magda Denes, *In Necessity and Sorrow: Life and Death in an Abortion Hospital* (New York: Basic Books, 1976), xv, xvi.
18 Denes, *In Necessity and Sorrow*, 60–61.
19 Denes, *In Necessity and Sorrow*, 141, 144, 154. Denes on 67 quotes one doctor saying, "You have to become a bit schizophrenic. In one room you encourage the patient that the slight irregularity of the fetal heart is not important, everything is going well, she is going to have a nice baby, and then you shut the door and go into the next room and assure another patient on whom you just did a saline abortion, that it's fine if the heart is already irregular, she has nothing to worry about, she is *not* going to have a live baby."

bird-like, pale, hawk-handed in fright, they seem like lost souls before the final judgment." Denes said one patient's "drained face is indistinguishable from the white sheet on which she lies." Denes portrayed women coming out of anesthesia and asking, "Has it been done?" A nurse answered, "It is finished."[20]

20 Denes, *In Necessity and Sorrow*, 136. Denes does not state the Christian reference (Gospel of John 19:30), but says of the patients, "It hardly matters into which eyes I look, which face becomes focal. Only the convent of calvary differs; the stations of the cross remain the same: bewilderment, guilt, helplessness, recurrence, blame, astonishment, shame, and grieving, grieving, grieving" (91).

SECTION ONE

UNSAFE, ILLEGAL, AND RARE

1652–1842

Chapters 2–10 take us from early abortions in Maryland to the early nineteenth century. Knowledge of fetal anatomy was low, but biblical belief and community protection left abortion unsafe, illegal, and rare. While historians still debate what the common law said, juries and midwives tried to offer common sense and sometimes common wisdom.

2

Common Law, Common Sense

CAPTAIN WILLIAM MITCHELL, born in Sussex in 1605 or 1615 (records vary), had a mid-life crisis at mid-century. England's civil war was over: What to do next? Married for eleven years, with one son, he met comely Susan Warren, 21, and said he wanted to marry her. Oh, one inconvenient fact: She, like Mitchell, was already married. Mitchell said she should voyage to America with him.[1]

At this point let's pause for a public service announcement regarding Maryland, where (to quote one typical come-on) "peas grow ten inches long in ten days" and turkeys "whose flesh is very pleasant and sweet" waddle around for the taking. That sounded heavenly, especially when compared to smelly London, where Warren washed clothes in the Thames as men butchered animals and threw offal into the river. London was also a disease center, and America's wide-open spaces were more healthy, weren't they?[2]

Mitchell did not mention "seasoning," the exposure to malaria and various Maryland or Virginia germs that killed about half of all servants within five years. He did not say that 30 percent of infants died in their

---

1 "Capt. William Mitchell," at Geni.com.
2 George Alsop, "A Character of the Province of Maryland" in Maryland State Archives, https://msa.maryland.gov/megafile/msa/library/014300/014309/html/alsop-0001.html.

first year, and almost half of all inhabitants by age twenty.[3] But Warren's husband had heard such talk. He did not want to spend seven weeks in a crowded ship tossed by waves, only to discover the downside on the other side of the Atlantic. So Susan Warren then showed extraordinary independence by deciding to head west without her husband.

She was one of 22 "artificers, workmen, and other useful persons" who embarked with Captain and Mrs. Mitchell. Mitchell had arranged the expedition after Cecilius Calvert of Maryland's founding family offered him 100 acres of Maryland farmland for every person Mitchell paid for. Plus, in Maryland, Mitchell could become a member of the Governor's Council. Plus, Mitchell's wife conveniently died in the middle of the Atlantic, a fact one prosecutor later found suspicious: He said Mitchell "is much Suspected (if not known) to have brought his late wife to an untimely end."[4]

Warren soon developed her own suspicions. Mitchell did not rely on his charms to get her into bed with him. Instead, he claimed she owed him money, probably for the passage to Maryland. He forced her to sign a document stating she would be his servant until she had sweated enough to pay him back. After arrival in Maryland, they lay "in naked bed together" at a colonial inn. Warren became pregnant. Mitchell at first seemed sympathetic to her plight: "She had Suffered much disgrace for his Sake, and now if She pleased he would make her amends." Then he reneged and refused to marry her. She referred to the Bible and said that he, as a Christian gentleman, should make things right. Mitchell laughed it off: Jesus and the Holy Spirit, he said, are only "a man and a pigeon."[5]

Mitchell mixed an abortifacient—a potion that could kill the unborn child—with a poached egg and forced Warren to eat it: "He said if she

---

3 On disease in colonial America, see John Ruston Pagan, *Anne Orthwood's Bastard: Sex and Law in Early Virginia* (New York: Oxford University Press, 2003), 15–16.

4 *Archives of Maryland* (Baltimore: Maryland Historical Society, 1936), III, 151, and CCCCXXVI, 599.

5 *Archives of Maryland*, X, 149, 183, and 176.

would not take it he would thrust it down her throat, so she being in bed could not withstand it." The potion apparently killed the child and caused Warren to lose much of her hair. Her skin erupted into "boils and blains." Mitchell taunted her: "How now hath your God helped you? Ah thou may'st well believe anything that is told you, such a thing as God. . . . O thou art a fool."[6]

A bit of backstory: This was not the first abortion in American history. Before Europeans arrived, Native Americans knew about—and sometimes used—abortifacient plants and other substances. Tribes as varied as the Lenape, Cree, Mohegan, Sioux, Ojibwe, and Chippewa knew of sweet flag, tansy, pennyroyal, and blue cohosh.[7] As Thomas Jefferson later noted, Native American women often accompanied "men in their parties of war and of hunting. Childbearing becomes extremely inconvenient to them. It is said, therefore, that they have learnt the practice of procuring abortion by the use of some vegetable."[8]

Nor was Susan Warren's misery the first of its kind among the colonists. One story tucked into the minutes of the Council and General Court of Colonial Virginia may be America's first written-down abortion saga. In 1629, servant Dorcas Howard told her master, George Orwin, *I'm sick and cannot work.* He suspected she might be pregnant and threatened to beat her. She confessed and told her master the name of the baby's father. He ordered Howard to bed and called "some women to her."

We don't know what those women did, but the next morning the corpse of an unborn child was on the floor. One woman, Elizabeth

---

[6] *Archives of Maryland*, X, 173. Warren's testimony includes a statement of her own faith: "That when she hath been sick calling on God to help her, Captain Mitchell hath replied, 'What was that which I called God, Did I know him, had I ever any conference with him. I said not of his person, but by his works, I was confident that I should have help.'"

[7] Daniel Moerman, *Native American Ethnobotany* (Portland, OR: Timber, 1998), 46–48, 782–801; Virgil J. Vogel, *American Indian Medicine* (Norman: University of Oklahoma Press, 1970), 244.

[8] Thomas Jefferson, *Notes on the State of Virginia*, quoted in Paul Leicester Ford, ed., *The Works of Thomas Jefferson*, Federal Edition, 12 vols. (New York and London: G. P. Putnam's Sons, 1904–1905), vol. 3.

Moorecocke, testified that the child, a boy, was stillborn with a bruised head. We don't know what happened next. That case record and others vanished when Confederate troops burned Virginia's court building on the night of April 2, 1865, as they escaped from Richmond. The fire left us only with tantalizing hints of other abortion tragedies, including a case brought by Thomas Evens, who claimed another woman caused his wife to miscarry.[9]

So, Mitchell's case at a Provincial Court sitting in 1652 is the first abortion for which we have solid records. Mitchell thought his political prominence would protect him—but as the story of his words and behavior spread throughout Maryland, the royal authorities responded. As a prosecutor put it, Mitchell's appointment to the Governor's Council did not allow him to do whatever he pleased: His prominence made his unethical behavior worse because he ought "to have given good example to others."[10]

The prosecutor added that Mitchell's talent, bestowed by God, "should be used to His glory and the publick good." And yet, Mitchell tried "to color over his Villainous Courses, and to mock and deride all Religion and Civil Government." Mitchell tried "to draw others to believe there is no God, making a Common practice by blasphemous expressions and otherwise to mock and deride God's Ordinances, and all Religion." He also plotted "to destroy or Murther the Child by him begotten in the Womb of the Said Susan Warren."[11]

Since Warren was the key witness against Mitchell, the defense called witnesses to raise questions about her honesty. One witness, Mary

---

9 H. R. McIlwaine, ed., *Minutes of the Council and General Court* (Richmond: Virginia State Library Board, 1924), 194 (April 8, 1629). See also the *Virginia Historical Magazine*, XXXI (1923), 210–11, and *County Court Records of Accomack-Northampton, Virginia, 1632–1640*: 1, 43.

10 *Archives of Maryland*, X, 183.

11 *Archives of Maryland*, X, 183. The prosecutor said Mitchell's actions were a natural result of his beliefs: He made "a Common practice by blasphemous expressions and otherwise to mock and deride God's Ordinances and all Religion, thereby to open a way to all wicked lustfull licentious and profane Courses."

Clocker, quoted Warren denying her pregnancy and saying, "If She were with Child it was inspired by the holy Ghost, and not by man." Another witness, Richard Hoskins, quoted Warren saying, "She would damn her Soul but She would be revenged of that Rogue Mitchell."[12]

The messy court record included other charges and nuances, but Mitchell's defense was straightforward: He was innocent unless proven guilty of "Murder Atheism and Blasphemy." His case showed the tensions that would influence abortion law and prosecutions in centuries to come. How could a prosecutor *prove* that an abortifacient or abortionist killed an unborn child? How could a prosecutor know the unborn baby was even alive in the womb? Maybe the child died of other causes. Maybe no pregnancy ever existed. Should an abortion attempt be a crime, regardless of the results?

After all, until quickening—the time after about four months of pregnancy when a woman feels the child moving within her—no one in those days could prove whether a woman was pregnant. One midwife noted that "Diverse Physicians have laid down rules whereby to know when a woman hath conceived with Child," but in a list of fourteen, only one piece of evidence was 90 percent accurate: "Her monthly terms stop at some unreasonable time."[13]

In the absence of pregnancy tests, midwives and others offered uncertain signs of pregnancy like this one: "Her stomach becomes very weak, she hath no desire to eat her meat, but is troubled with sower belchings." Or, her desire for sexual relations was evidence of conception: "The pleasure she takes at this time is extraordinary." Some pointed to a pregnant woman's desire for unusual foods.[14]

We can't read the minds of the Marylanders deciding Mitchell's case, but the evidence for a murder charge was clearly insufficient.

12 *Archives of Maryland*, X, 149, 181.
13 Jane Sharp, *The Midwives Book, or The Whole Art of Midwifry Discovered* (1671; repr., New York: Oxford University Press, 1999), 82–83. Menstrual delays and irregularities can also result from increased exercise, stress, thyroid dysfunction, and other causes.
14 Sharp, *Midwives Book*, 83.

Abortion trials for centuries hinged on whether prosecutors could prove pregnancy. The opinion in the 1348 *Abortionist's Case* in England states regarding the accused, "It is difficult to know whether he killed the child or not." Juries then and now choose not between guilt and innocence, but guilty or not-proven-guilty—and sometimes they seek a compromise.[15]

The legal determinant, theoretically, was English "common law," the cases decided over the centuries. Justice Harry Blackmun in his 1973 *Roe v. Wade* decision asserted that English "common law" accepted abortion. He relied on, and repeatedly cited as authoritative, two law journal articles by Cyril Means Jr., who happened to be the top lawyer of the National Association for the Repeal of Abortion Laws. Surprise! Means cited two English cases but left out numerous others that undermined his contention about abortion's acceptance.

The two cases Means cited are not clear-cut, but even if they were, here are two others. In 1290 a pregnant woman, Alice, slammed a door on "John the Scot," who was chasing her husband, Roger the Spicer. Then came injury: John pushed the door so hard that Alice fell and was severely injured. The twins Alice carried both died. John the Scot ran. The court declared him an "outlaw," a word in those days taken literally: John the Scot was outside legal protection, and anyone who saw him could kill him.[16]

And one from 1530: William Wodlake, "by the instigation of the devil, knowing that a certain Katherine Alaund was pregnant with a child, with dissembling words gave the same Katherine to drink a certain drink in order to destroy the child then being in the said Katherine's body. . . . Katherine was afterwards delivered of that child dead: so that the same William Wodlake feloniously killed and murdered the child

---

15 Anthony Fitzherbert, *La Grande Abridgement* (1516), 268, quoted in Duane L. Ostler, "A Conversation about Abortion between Justice Blackmun and the Founding Fathers," *Constitutional Commentary* 167 (2014): 281, at https://scholarship.law.umn.edu/concomm/281.
16 Philip A. Rafferty, *Roe v. Wade: Unraveling the Fabric of America* (Mustang, OK: Tate, 2012), 140.

with the drink in manner and form aforesaid, against the peace of the lord king." Wodlake escaped punishment by dying in 1531.[17]

In any event, it's unlikely that members of the Provincial Court trying Captain Mitchell had any expertise in the common law concerning abortion. What they did have was common sense. On August 26, 1652, the Council kicked Mitchell off for "scandalous behavior" and banned him from holding any public office in the colony ever again. In a society that emphasized honor and reputation, that was a big hit.

Mitchell also had a pocketbook penalty: The Council freed Warren from whatever service Mitchell said she owed him. The Council gave Mitchell a choice: Take a public, physical whipping to back up the verbal whipping, or pay a fine of 5,000 pounds of tobacco. That's what a worker typically took 3 1/3 years to earn. Mitchell paid up. He received a further warning: Any other poor behavior would cost him even more.[18]

Warren, with no money to pay a fine for fornication, may have received a whipping, although neighbors interceded on her behalf and her final penalty was not recorded. She also received an allowance from Mitchell's wealth and became a free woman. Susan Warren summed up her thoughts about the relation of extramarital pregnancy and abortion: "It was a great Sin to get it, but a greater to make it away."[19]

---

17 Rafferty, *Roe v. Wade: Unraveling the Fabric of America*, 151.
18 *Archives of Maryland*, X, 183–85.
19 *Archives of Maryland*, X, 80, 81, 176.

3

Murder of a Man Child

IN A SMALL COLONY, one life touched another: Maryland's (and America's) next celebrated abortion case began with a business deal between landowner Francis Brooke and the disgraced Captain Mitchell. The year after his heavy fine and requirement to support Susan Warren financially, Mitchell downsized his household. Brooke offered two cows for the remaining indenture of Ann Boulton, one of Mitchell's servants. Mitchell agreed, and the eventual result was the first American court case regarding a pre-quickened child.[1]

Brooke, like Mitchell, arrived in Maryland in 1650, but he came with his father, mother, and nine younger siblings. The household included at least two female servants. Brooke married Ann Boulton, but court records in the Maryland archives show that wedded bliss did not last. Once, when Ann wanted to wash a pail instead of letting a dog lick it, Brooke broke a cane over her. Another time she roasted veal and was about to eat some, but he hit her so hard with an oak board that it broke in two.[2]

---

1 *Archives of Maryland* (Baltimore: Maryland Historical Society, 1936), X, 215, 268, 269, 389, 390. Indentures were the required payback for transportation across the Atlantic.
2 *Archives of Maryland*, X, 464, and http://www.combs-families.org/combs/records/md/stmarys/1633.htm.

A third incident occurred in 1656, when Ann was pregnant. She stewed two sheep's heads and was about to eat one of them. Brooke said no, called her "you whore," chased her outside, and beat her with a large pair of wooden tongs. At that point a brave neighbor, Elizabeth Claxton, intervened. She said Brooke might kill the unborn child and asked if "he longed to be hanged." Brooke said he "did not care if she did Miscarry, if She was with Child it was none of his."[3]

Brooke forced an abortifacient on Ann. Their unborn child died. Midwife Rose Smith described the corpse: "a man child about three months old and it was all bruised one side of it." She suggested that Brooke's beating of Ann caused the death. Neighbor Claxton showed the 3-inch-long corpse to Brooke, accused him of murder, and said he will "dearly answer" for doing evil.

That was no bluff. Smith and Claxton testified at a provincial court trial of Brooke for murder. Justice Harry Blackmun in *Roe v. Wade* will say abortion prior to quickening was not a crime in English or colonial common law. If that's true, why a charge of murder upon the death of an unborn baby merely three months after conception?[4]

Let's pause to ask what people during the 1600s or 1700s knew about the capacities of unborn children at various ages of gestation. Answer: Not much. Much to the frustration of colonial New York doctor Cadwallader Colden, anatomical knowledge had advanced

---

3   *Archives of Maryland*, X, 464. Abortion by assault was not new: Sara Butler's "Abortion Medieval Style: Assaults on Pregnant Women in Later Medieval England," *Women's Studies* 40, no. 6 (2011): 778–99, concludes that "the Christian world, as medieval legislation indicates, was concerned to prosecute abortionists. . . . that courts prosecuted eighty-three abortionists in the late Middle Ages highlights that the English courts were taking their Christian duty seriously."

4   *Roe v. Wade*, 410 U.S. 113 (1973). See Philip Rafferty, *Roe v. Wade: Unraveling the Fabric of America* (Mustang, OK: Tate, 2012), 151. We should distinguish between "quickened" and "quick": the latter means "alive" in the sense of the old expression "the quick and the dead." In that sense an unborn child would already be quick from conception onward. Rafferty, "Roe v. Wade: A Scandal upon the Court, Part I: The Unsettling of Roe v. Wade," appendix 2, 79, at https://lawandreligion.com 5–6, notes that two centuries ago *A Supplement to Johnson's English Dictionary* defined "quick" as "pregnant with a live child."

little during the two millennia since Aristotle (384–322 BC). Colden complained that astronomers were making progress but "Physicians remain Ignorant of the Frame & figure of the Minute parts of the Body."[5]

Aristotle's *History of Animals* and *On the Generation of Animals* included contradictory observations and theories, but one of the oddest was his discussion of how males are "formed" in 40 days and females in 80–90. He wrote, "In the case of a male embryo aborted at the fortieth day . . . all the limbs are plain to see, including the penis, and the eyes also, which as in other animals are of great size. But the female embryo, if it suffer abortion during the first three months, is as a rule found to be undifferentiated."[6]

Aristotle remained influential through medieval times. Two twelfth-century books, Gratian's *Concordance of Discordant Canons* and Peter Lombard's *Sentences*, accepted Aristotle's formed/unformed distinction, as did *De Proprietatibus Rerum* ("On the Property of Things"), which Bartholomaeus Anglicus (Bartholomew the Englishman) wrote between 1230 and 1250.

Bartholomew's book, which some say was the most-read book after the Bible during the late medieval era, claimed that a "child is bred forth . . . in four degrees. The first is when the seed has a milk-like appearance. The second is when the seed is worked into a lump of blood (with the liver, heart and brain as yet having no distinct shape). The third is when the heart, brain and liver are shaped, and the other or external members [head, face, arms, hands, fingers, legs, feet and toes]

---

5 Quoted in "Obstacles to the Progress of Medicine," *Bulletin of the History of Medicine*, 1962, 456–57.

6 Aristotle's *History of Animals*, *On the Generation of Animals*, and *Parts of Animals* are widely available online. Quoted in David Albert Jones, *The Soul of the Embryo* (New York: Continuum, 2004), 27. Aristotle was a step back from Hippocrates (460–370 BC), whose followers saw the formation of limbs and organs among all humans as complete in about 40 days, or six weeks. (As it turns out, that's the furthest extent of legal abortion in today's pro-life "heartbeat bills.") The Hippocratic Oath famously stated, "I will give no sort of medicine to any pregnant woman, with a view to destroy the child."

are yet to be shaped and distinguished. The last degree is when all the external members are completely shaped."[7]

Bartholomew did not accept Aristotle's male-female distinction. He offered specific numbers: "In the degree of milk it remains seven days; in the degree of blood it remains nine days; in the degree of a lump of blood or unformed flesh it remains twelve days; and in the fourth degree, when all its members are fully formed, it remains eighteen days. . . . So from the day of conception to the day of complete disposition or formation and first life of the child is forty-six (46) days."[8]

Thomas Aquinas followed Aristotle's male/female differentiation but added a twist of his own: He contended that an unborn child is first a vegetative soul (nutritiva), then an animal soul (sensitiva), and finally—only near the end of the developmental process—a human soul (intellectiva). He followed Aristotle's schema by accepting the 40- or 80-day formation concept and adding the idea of ensoulment at that time, but he also said abortion at any time violates natural law and is wrong.[9]

We might think of Aristotle and Aquinas as food for intellectuals, but the most popular seventeenth-century guide to pregnancy and fetal anatomy, *The Midwives Book*, showed their thinking was more broadly applied. Author Jane Sharp probably became a midwife west of London in the 1640s and melded her experience with medical tradition. She quoted Aristotle, employed his 40-80 day male-female differentiation, and echoed Aquinas's threefold charting of fetal development: "first the life of a Plant, then of a Beast, and lastly of a Man."[10]

---

7   On the Properties of Things: John Treviso's Translation of "Bartholomaeus Anglicus De Proprietatibus Rerum": A Critical Text (Oxford: Oxford University Press, 1975), 296.
8   On the Properties of Things, 297.
9   John Haldane and Patrick Lee, "Aquinas on Human Ensoulment, Abortion, and the Value of Life," Philosophy 78, no. 304 (April 2003): 255–78.
10 Sharon Jansen, "Jane Sharp: Midwife," July 21, 2015, online at https://www.monstrousregiment ofwomen.com/2015/07/jane-sharp-midwife.html. Originally published in 1671, *The Midwives Book* is now most readily available in a paperback edition published by Oxford University Press in 1999. My favorite *Midwives Book* comments are on 83, 89, 100, 105, 106, 111, 114, 122, 134,

Sharp described the womb in terms familiar to Aquinas readers: as home for "the Infant conceived, kept, formed, and fed until the rational Soul be infused from above, and the Child born." She added her speculations to theirs: "that the seed of the male is more active than that of the Female in forming the creature, though both be fruitful, but the female adds blood as well."[11]

Sharp, like others at that time, added myth and whimsey to ancient anatomy: *The Midwives Book* included an account of a woman who at age 40 had at one birth 365 children, 182 of them boys all named John and 182 girls all named Elizabeth, with the odd child "partly male, partly female." Sharp relied on astrology and like many others emphasized the importance of thinking high thoughts at the time of conception and during pregnancy: "Imagination ofttimes also produceth Monstrous births, when women look too much on strange objects."[12]

Enough background. The basics to keep in mind: Seventeenth-century people knew little about human development within the womb. The common wisdom, from Aristotle, Bartholomew, and others, was that maybe at six weeks, or by three months at the latest, an unborn child was human life, and those who killed him or her committed murder most foul. That's why Smith and Claxton could take Brooke to court for killing an unborn child only three months after conception.

For colonial Americans, the common wisdom trumped the common law, whether it imposed a four-and-a-half-month "quickening" divide

---

135, 178, 216, 246, 255, 263, 275. Sharp jabbed at men for relying on ancient theory rather than observation: She did the same, but was able to write, "The stones [ovaries] of a woman for generation of seed are white, thick, and well concocted, for I have seen one . . . and that is more by one than many Men have seen." Men, though, also produced books for midwives: See James Guillimeau's *Childbirth, Or the Happy Delivery of Women* (1612); Jacob Rueff's *The Expert Midwife* (1637); and Nicholas Culpeper's *A Directory for Midwives* (1651).

11 Jane Sharp, *The Midwives Book, or The Whole Art of Midwifry Discovered* (1671; repr., New York: Oxford University Press, 1999), 63, 68, 105. Sharp wrote, "The blood hath no active quality in this great work, but the seed works upon it. . . . The cause why the child is a boy or a girl is the heat of the seed, if the man's seed prevail in mixing above the woman's it will be a boy, else a girl."

12 Sharp, *Midwives Book*, 113, 135.

or not. When Marylanders examined Francis Brooke's action in the light of testimony from Claxton and Smith about the unborn child he allegedly killed, here was the result: "Being Conceived that there is Cause of Suspition of Murther, the Court doth therefore Order that the Said Francis Brooke Shall Stand Committed in the Sheriffes Custody untill he give Sufficient Securitie for his personall appearance at the next Provincial Court to be held at Putuxent the 20th of March."[13]

This meant six months in jail unless Brooke could produce a bond to guarantee his appearance. Happily for him, he could: 10,000 pounds of tobacco. At the next court session in March, Ann Brooke changed her story: In the new version, the unborn child's death followed a fall from a tree, not a beating or an abortifacient. Her changed testimony saved her husband. Officially, the testimony of neighbors about Ann's complaints counted as hearsay. Francis Brooke was publicly embarrassed but officially not guilty.

What to make of this strange outcome? Volumes of the *Archives of Maryland* have impressed upon me the common sense with which many cases ended. Few if any Marylanders were familiar with Sir Edward Coke's four-volume *Institutes of the Laws of England*, with initial publication in London in 1628 but no immediate distribution across the Atlantic. Another four-volume work that became widely used, William Blackstone's *Commentaries on the Laws of England*, was still a century away. The "common law" that governed Captain Mitchell and Susan Warren, or Mr. and Mrs. Brooke, was not available for consultation in a book. It was gut feeling, the common sense of neighbors.

---

13 *Archives of Maryland*, XVII, 279–80, 283, 325–26; and X, 464–65. In the 1963 movie *The Great Escape*, American pilot Hilts, played by Steve McQueen, provokes the German prison camp commandant to ask, "Are all American officers so ill-mannered?" Hilts responds, "Yeah, about 99 percent." Were all colonial Americans insubordinate toward the common law? Many. Even a county court clerk, Swithen Wells, was churlish: When a judge told him to increase his knowledge by reading a law book, Wells called the justice an "ignorant fool" and threw the book at him, saying *read it yourself*. See Raphael Semmes, *Crime and Punishment in Early Maryland* (Baltimore: Johns Hopkins University Press, 1938), 5.

The neighbors probably concluded that Ann Brooke's new statement was a lie. They did not know whether she gave her husband an alibi out of love or out of fear of another beating. But six months had gone by since the initial testimony, with no reports of new beatings within that time. Maybe Brooke was a changed man. If not, he certainly knew he was being watched, and that further rages could lead to imprisonment. Perhaps the Brookes, and their neighbors, wanted to preserve the marriage.

Whatever the reality, Ann Brooke deserves our sympathy. Neighbor Claxton deserves the last word: She told Brooke "that although he Scaped in this world, yet in the world to Come he Should Answer for it."[14]

---

14 *Archives of Maryland*, X, 465, 488.

4

Pressuring the Father

IN 1656, as Francis Brooke caused an abortion, immigrant Jacob Lumbrozo arrived from Lisbon and Amsterdam. He was a middle-aged doctor, lawyer, planter, innkeeper, wolf-hunter, and lone wolf. He was also Jewish but thoroughly secularized, with no indication that he read the Bible, prayed, or respected the commandment not to commit adultery.

Other Marylanders may have respected the Bible theoretically, but the *Archives of Maryland* are full of charges and insinuations of adultery. Doctor Thomas Ward, for instance, called Henry Clay's wife "a burnt arse whore." The *Archives* describe how John Hammond wanted legal services from Lumbrozo but did not want to pay for it, so (according to Lumbrozo) Hammond offered Lumbrozo sex with his wife in exchange for the help, but then reneged on the deal. Hammond sued Lumbrozo for defamation and won.[1]

Many other Maryland cases involved claims and counterclaims of sex. In 1662, two of Lumbrozo's bondservants, John and Margaret Gould, sued Giles and Elizabeth Glover for defamation after Mrs. Glover allegedly called Mrs. Gould a "whore." Lumbrozo served as the Goulds' attorney, and they called him "our trusty and well beloved friend," but

---

1 *Archives of Maryland* (Baltimore: Maryland Historical Society, 1936), X, 234; and IL, 590–91.

comity did not last. The Goulds sued Lumbrozo for allegedly demanding sex from Margaret Gould as payment for his legal representation. He countersued for defamation. Both sides eventually dropped their suits and the Goulds gained freedom from Lumbrozo's employ, which may have been their objective all along.[2]

The following year, Lumbrozo was in another controversy with a servant, Elizabeth Weales, twenty-two. She confided to a neighbor that she had sex with Lumbrozo but retained her virtue because "before shee coold Consent to ly with him, hee tooke a booke in his hand and swor many bitter oaths that hee woold marry me." Pledges of that sort were not unusual in colonial America. One advice manual for young women said celibacy is good but exceptions were allowed if a man gave a woman a signed statement pledging marriage. Elizabeth Weales said yes before getting Lumbrozo's word in writing. When he reneged on his marriage vow, she told her neighbors.[3]

Weales might have thought she could use a county jury, aware of Lumbrozo's reputation, to force him into marriage. But her neighbors asked probing questions and elicited sensational testimony from two women: Lumbrozo gave Weales an abortifacient and there "came sumthing downe as big as her hand from her bodie." Two male neighbors were more specific: When Weales was "with Child," Lumbrozo gave her "a strong purge to take away her swelling ... the Phisick that the doctur did give her did kill the Child within."[4]

Without determining whether the unborn child had quickened or not, authorities jailed Lumbrozo on a murder charge. When Weales saw the situation getting out of control, she walked back her account. Under oath on June 29, 1663, she said, "what I have said Concerning Lumbrozo it is false." She claimed miscarriage and said Lumbrozo merely

---

2 Raphael Semmes, *Crime and Punishment in Early Maryland* (Baltimore: Johns Hopkins University Press, 1938), 224–26.

3 *Archives of Maryland*, LIII, 387–90. The records sometimes spelled Weales as Weale, Wile, or Wieles.

4 *Archives of Maryland*, LIII, 387–89.

gave her a drink when she complained of aches in her stomach and her heart. According to Weales, Lumbrozo said the drink "will Cleare the poison from you." She pleaded with the jury to clear Lumbrozo "from the scandal that I rise upon him for what I said came out of my own head."[5]

The jurors must have wondered which story was true: Abortion? Lies? The last witness, Margaret Oles, testified that Weales asked her for advice on how to testify: "best for her to clear him or no?" All twelve jurors apparently found her original testimony more convincing: They believed Weales's "owne publick Confession that she was with Child by Lumbroso and that hee did give her phisick to destroy it."[6]

After the Mitchell and Brooke precedents, the jurors probably knew the Provincial Court would be unlikely to take tough action against Lumbrozo without Weales's testimony. Nevertheless, they charged Lumbrozo with a felony and sent the case to the higher court for further review. We can't discount the possibility of anti-Semitism, but officials had been similarly serious about the actions of Mitchell and Brooke. Why?

To understand why abortion was so rare in early America, we need to spend less time debating obscure "common law" cases and more time entering the stream of church-going colonists walking to common worship on a Sunday morning, with the father carrying the family Bible. That was the one book in most homes. In an era of frequent Bible reading, few missed God's creative involvement in human life from its beginning. Colonists read in Psalms, Job, Isaiah, Jeremiah, Luke, Galatians, and other books not only that we are made in God's image, but that he "knitted me together in my mother's womb," "formed me in the womb," and "formed you in the womb."[7]

Picture those townsfolk walking to a typical church: Not fancy like many in England, but barn-like buildings with plain walls and wooden

---

5 *Archives of Maryland*, LIII, 390.
6 *Archives of Maryland*, LIII, 391.
7 See Ps. 139:13; Job 31:15; Isa. 44:24 and 49:1, 5; Jer. 1:5; Luke 1:15; and Gal. 1:15.

pews. In New England, a high pulpit was usually front and center. The pastor, often dressed in a black gown, stood and called the congregation to worship. In some churches he turned over an hourglass and explained at length a passage from the Bible.

Churchgoers not only lacked distraction during that hour but read and heard sensational detail about what evildoers did to unborn children. Syrians attacked Israelites and "ripped up their women with child." When an Israelite town did not surrender to an evil king, "all the women therein with child he ripped up." Hosea prophesied that "Samaria shall become desolate. . . . their women with children shall be ripped up." God will severely punish the Ammonites because "they have ripped up the women with child of Gilead, that they might enlarge their borders."[8]

Volumes other than the Bible, like *The Midwives Book*, featured the sacred and secular overlapping seamlessly. Jane Sharp quoted from or alluded to the Bible at least thirty times. She twice referred to Psalm 139's "knitted me together," but also noted Genesis chapters 1, 2, 3, 4, 17, 29, and 30, as well as other passages from Exodus, Leviticus, Deuteronomy, 1 and 2 Samuel, 1 Chronicles, Psalms 113 and 127, Matthew, John, Acts, and Hebrews. Sharp frequently referred to "the law of God," "the laws of God," and "the blessings of God."[9]

Preachers often had educated audiences: New England by 1660 had 236 well-schooled men, most of them with Oxford or Cambridge degrees, many with knowledge of Hebrew. That affected the way they read

---

8 See 2 Kings 8:12 and 15:16; Hos. 13:16; Amos 1:13 (all KJV).
9 Jane Sharp, *The Midwives Book, or The Whole Art of Midwifry Discovered* (1671; repr., New York: Oxford University Press, 1999), 16, 44, 51, and 76. Pastors sometimes explained that the Bible does not deal with every exigency or even every major controversy. The Bible is full of verses with pro-life implications, and has a very clear "Do not murder" sentence, but it does not include a specific "Do not murder unborn children" verse. That did not signal acceptability: Even without laws specifying forgery, perjury, attempted burglary, attempted murder, or abortion as offenses, juries considered those actions wrong and prescribed penalties. A present-day pastor, Tim Keller, has noted that few books today explicitly say "the world is round." Some things are so well understood by a contemporary audience that writers and speakers don't spell them out.

passages like Genesis 9:6 and 7: "Whoso sheddeth man's blood, by man shall his blood be shed, for in the image of God made he man. And you, be ye fruitful and multiply" (KJV). Many then and now viewed that as a general ban on murder of both the born and the unborn, but some saw a specific prohibition of abortion: The Hebrew *ha-Adam v-Adam* can be read as "sheds the blood of humans by humans," but also as "sheds the blood of human-in-human"—namely, an unborn child.[10]

College students learned that abortion is wrong. Benjamin Wadsworth, who became president of Harvard College, declared that those who "purposely endeavor to destroy the Fruit of their Womb" were "guilty of Murder in God's account." Those who read John Calvin learned that "the unborn, though enclosed in the womb of his mother, is already a human being, and it is an almost monstrous crime to rob it of life which it has not yet begun to enjoy."[11]

We might think *that's Massachusetts*, but historian James Truslow Adams pointed out in 1927 how colonists both northern and southern were Bible-centric, with their populations "drawn originally from the same reservoir of sober, God-fearing people in the home country." He said the idea of a more godly New England, with Virginia and Maryland backboned by "gay Cavaliers," arose from "prejudice, ignorance, and abounding conceit" on both sides.[12]

Colonists in Virginia had access to the Book of Common Prayer and different catechisms. They read the King James Version of the Bible rather than the Geneva Bible, which was popular in New England, but they were equally familiar with the rule in chapter 21 of Exodus that

---

10 That variant reading of Gen. 9:6 also has Talmudic support: R. Yishmael, in the Babylonian Talmud, Sanhedrin 57b, asks, "Who is the human-in-human? It refers to the fetus in the mother's womb." See discussion in David Jones, *The Soul of the Embryo* (London: Continuum, 2004), 45–46.
11 Benjamin Wadsworth, *The Well-Ordered Family* (Boston, 1712), 45. Calvin's commentary on Gen. 25:1–4 declares, "If it seems more horrible to kill a man in his own house than in a field, because a man's house is his most secure place of refuge, it ought surely to be deemed more atrocious to destroy the unborn in the womb before it has come to light."
12 James Truslow Adams, *Provincial Society 1690–1763* (New York: Macmillan, 1927), 150.

"If men strive, and hurt a woman with child, so that her fruit depart from her, and yet no mischief follow: he shall . . . pay as the judges determine. And if any mischief follow, then thou shalt give life for life" (vv. 22–23, KJV).

That came right after chapter 20's listing of the Ten Commandments. The King James word "mischief" might now suggest playful misbehavior, but in the 1600s it denoted distress in line with its derivation from the Old French verb *meschever*, from *mes* (adversely) and *chever* (come to an end). In other words, "yet no mischief follow" means "yet no one comes to an end"—that is, no one dies, as in an abortion.[13]

In the twentieth and twenty-first centuries, such a discussion came to seem esoteric to many, but a moment within U.S. Senate debate shows its relevance. In 1981, the Senate by a 52-43 vote forbade the use of federal funds to pay for an abortion unless continuing the pregnancy endangered a woman's life. The measure's proponent, Sen. Jesse Helms (North Carolina), said, "We're talking about the deliberate termination of human life." Sen. Bob Packwood (Oregon), complained: "There is growing in this country a Cotton Mather mentality." Helms replied, "If there's a Cotton Mather mentality, so be it. There is a set of instructions that came down from Mount Sinai about that."[14]

That's the answer a Mather would have given. In the seventeenth and eighteenth centuries, settlers throughout the thirteen colonies saw a pro-life river running through the Bible. Anatomical knowledge did not send a clear message about the creature in the womb, but the Bible did. That means Lumbrozo had one way out: No one other than he

---

13 Some defenders of abortion today choose to interpret the verse to require "life for life" only if the woman dies, but the verse defines the incident not as one fatal to her but as one in which "her fruit depart"—the child comes out. The meaning was clearer four centuries ago: If the delivery is premature but the child lives, the miscreant must pay a fine ("as the judges determine"). If the child dies, it's murder.

14 "Cotton Mather Politics," *New York Times*, May 24, 1981, E19. The 1981 debate included the rejoinder from Connecticut Senator Lowell Weicker that, "We're not running this country from divine commandments or instructions from Mount Sinai." *New York Times* columnist Anthony Lewis said amen to that: "Most Americans do not want this country run by divine commandments."

and Weales had seen the dead unborn child. All the other testimony was hearsay. He proposed marriage, and she accepted. Wives cannot be forced to testify against their husbands. The case of *Commonwealth v. Lumbrozo* had no witnesses. The felony charge disappeared.

The *Archives of Maryland* show that Lumbrozo married Weales within five months of the trial: On a bill of sale dated November 16, 1663, she was Elizabeth Lumbrozo. A will dated September 24, 1665, noted that Lumbrozo was "in perfect and sound health" but was aware of the "transitory nature of all things," so he intended to leave almost everything (including thousands of pounds of "well-conditioned tobacco") to "my Dearly beloved wife" Elizabeth Lumbrozo, and make her his executrix. By then she was probably pregnant, and this time there was no abortion.[15]

I'd like to say that Mr. and Mrs. Lumbrozo lived happily ever after. Not so. Lumbrozo died the following year, 1666, before their son John was born. Elizabeth, now with property, soon married a wealthy second husband, but he died a few months later. Elizabeth died several years later, at about age 30.

We do not know what happened to John, now an orphan. We do know that abortion was rare in seventeenth-century America. We have records of only a handful—but three in a row in one colony from 1652 to 1662 showed that the death of an unborn child, at whatever age of gestation, was a serious matter.

---

15 *Archives of Maryland*, IL, 30, 52, 53, 76, 84, 104, 222, 223, 142, 145, 147, 156, 161, 354, 455.

5

Bitter Execrations

THE CRUCIAL DATE is Saturday, November 28, 1663, five months after Jacob Lumbrozo's trial. The life-changing place was John Webb's inn on Virginia's eastern shore, 70 miles north of the courthouse where Lumbrozo had learned that his choice was marriage or jail.

On that day Anne Orthwood was a single, twenty-four-year-old indentured servant from Bristol, England. She was also born to a single mom, as only about 1 or 2 percent of babies in England and America were in the seventeenth century. After a rough childhood and adolescence, she decided life in the New World would be better than bare survival in England—but first she had to endure a six-week passage on a crammed, wind-buffeted ship full of seasickness.[1]

In Virginia, Anne entered indentured life: essentially short-term slavery, typically requiring five years of service. She arrived amid a crisis in Virginia's economic system. In 1663 nine servants plotted to acquire weapons, march to the home of royal governor William Berkeley, and demand release from their indentures. Berkeley sniffed out the plot and hanged four of the conspirators.

---

1   Danger did not end at the shoreline. Malaria and other diseases in Maryland and Virginia killed thousands. About 34,000 people (10% of them black) came to Maryland between 1634 and 1680, but the total population in the latter year was only 20,000.

Anne had a brief indenture to a wealthy landowner, Lieutenant Colonel William Kendall. There she met his nephew, John Kendall, a man in his twenties with opportunities for a financially advantageous marriage. Perhaps out of worry that young John had eyes for Anne, the older Kendall sold her indenture to tenant farmer Jacob Bishopp.

Anne Orthwood's new habitation was a come-down from life with the wealthy Kendalls. Now she lived in a two-room house with Mr. and Mrs. Bishopp, their child Jacob Jr., a male servant, and perhaps another female servant. She slept on a blanket on a dirt floor. Bugs, damp, and light seeped through cracks in the chinking that held together the unpainted planks of the walls.[2]

Not a charming existence: Archeologists Barbara and Cary Carson say the typical mid-Atlantic household was made up of "a wife, husband, two children, and perhaps a servant gathered together in the perpetual dusk of their sheltered cottage . . . their dinner is cornmeal mush boiled in an iron pot. . . . They drink milk or water from a common cup, tankard or bowl passed around. . . . The room grows completely dark except for the glow of embers on the hearth." Then all slept around edges of the room, covering themselves with canvas sheets or bed rugs.[3]

On Saturday, November 28, 1663, the Northampton, Virginia, County Court met at John Webb's inn. Jacob Bishopp attended and took along Anne. William Kendall, there to conduct business, brought his nephew, John. As the elders socialized during the evening, the twenty-somethings apparently shared pints, then found a private spot—a loft, a storeroom, or an outbuilding. He hinted at marriage down the road and, to use the language of a notable case in Portsmouth, England, had "carnal knowledge of her body."[4]

2 Merril D. Smith, *Women's Roles in Seventeenth-Century America* (Westport, CT: Greenwood, 2008), 34.
3 James Horn, *Adapting to a New World: English Society in the Seventeenth-Century Chesapeake* (Chapel Hill: University of North Carolina Press, 1994), 314–15. See also Barnard Bailyn, *The Barbarous Years: The Peopling of British North America: The Conflict of Civilizations, 1600–1675* (New York: Vintage, 2012), 172.
4 John Pagan, *Anne Orthwood's Bastard* (New York: Oxford University Press), 5.

John Kendall then reneged. Anne realized she was pregnant and hoped he would do the right thing. Community pressure on young men meant that pregnant, unmarried women could generally count on marriage before going into labor. If young men hesitated, older men intervened. They rarely needed shotguns, but every father had one. To be married under shotgun pressure carried no disgrace, and most marriages were by (at least informal) parental arrangement anyway. But Anne Orthwood had no father or brothers. Her mother was 3,000 miles away.

At that point, others in the community were supposed to step up. But Jacob Bishopp—perhaps suspecting that Anne was pregnant—sold her indenture to another landowner, Lieutenant Colonel William Waters. Bishopp thus avoided any need to come to her aid. When Waters learned that Anne was pregnant, he tried to sell her back. Meanwhile, John Kendall still refused to take responsibility.

Anne's original master, William Kendall, did not help, even after John told his uncle he had impregnated her. The older Kendall, instead of suggesting public confession and acceptance of responsibility, did damage control: no acknowledgment of his unborn grandchild. The older Kendall had started out as an indentured servant himself. He had gained wealth through astute business dealings, two advantageous marriages, and the work of indentured servants and two slaves. But instead of helping others climb out of poverty, he pulled up the ladder.[5]

Kendall's behavior was particularly grievous because he had used his financial success to gain a plum position as parish churchwarden. That meant he was to counsel and discipline those who "offend their brethren, either by Adulterie, Whoredome, Incest, or Drunkennesse, or by Swearing, Ribaldries, Usurie, or any other uncleannesse and wickedness of life." Kendall wielded that power in the case of John Wills and Mary Reddy, fining them a thousand pounds of tobacco for

---

5 Pagan, *Anne Orthwood's Bastard*, 86.

fornicating. Regarding his nephew, though, he looked the other way, abandoning Anne at her time of great need.[6]

Our last three chapters have reported on abortions that husbands or masters forced on women, and how the legal system reacted. Anne's is a story of one woman left all alone who bravely continued her pregnancy. For many months she refused to name the father of her child, hoping that John Kendall (or at least his uncle) would act responsibly. Finally, as she delivered twins, she screamed John's name with "bitter Execrations." One baby was stillborn. The other, Jasper, lived. Anne died soon afterward. The midwife, Ellinor Gething, faced a charge of bias against an unwed mother that led her to be lackadaisical in doing her duty to keep her maternal patient alive.[7]

Too late for poor Anne, John Kendall partially stepped up. He paid for a wet nurse to suckle Jasper. He found a 41-year-old farmer and his wife who took in Jasper: Kendall probably provided funding until Jasper became a teenager and an indentured servant. When Jasper turned 22 in 1686, he became free with an award of 600 pounds of tobacco. John Kendall soon married an heiress and died 13 years later, still in his thirties.[8]

Susan Warren, Ann Brooke, Elizabeth Lumbrozo, Anne Orthwood—all standard English first names, but not standard stories. The first three were notable not only as principals in the few recorded abortion sagas we have from seventeenth-century America, but also because in each case juries or officials ruled against the men who pushed abortion. Anne Orthwood's story is notable because she did not have an abortion,

---

6   Pagan, *Anne Orthwood's Bastard*, 34.
7   *County Court Records of Accomack-Northampton, Virginia, 1640–1645*, ed. Susie M. Ames (Charlottesville, VA: University Press of Virginia, 1973), 129, cited in Pagan, *Anne Orthwood's Bastard*, 82. For midwife obligations, see the *British Journal of Midwifery*, December 2002, 757; and Linda Pollock, "Embarking on a Rough Passage: The Experience of Pregnancy in Early-Modern Society," in Valerie Fildes, ed., *Women as Mothers in Pre-Industrial England* (London: Routledge, 2013), 39–67.
8   Pagan, *Anne Orthwood's Bastard*, 134. I haven't found in any records what Jasper did after 1686.

although she was exactly the type of solitary and poor person whom we might think would.

Her tragedy also illuminated a hole in colonial customs and law. Young men who were sexually active outside of marriage were supposed to take responsibility. But what if they did not? "Family" is central in seventeenth-century colonial American order: Parents were supposed to educate, direct, and protect children and young adults. Bondservants were supposed to receive protection from masters functioning as fathers. Every pregnancy was first an extended family responsibility, then a community one, even when the woman was "disreputable." But what if the community failed the young woman?

Anne Orthwood did not receive the help she needed. Her lack of parents was no excuse. Colonial families were often unlike the nuclear ones common in mid-twentieth-century America. The father figure in a typical household might be an uncle, the mother figure a second or third wife, the children a mix of half brothers and stepsisters. The oldest male, not necessarily the father, was always supposed to step up.[9]

Despite the community failures at times, abortion in colonial times remained rare. Historians for nearly half a century have failed to bulwark Justice Blackmun's surmise that abortion then was common, legal, and acceptable, at least until quickening. Perhaps the Civil War destruction of records erased traces of some Virginia abortions—but other colonial records are sparse as well. Delaware authorities gave Agnita Hendricks 27 lashes in 1679 for an attempted abortion. Rhode Island's lone case ended with 15 lashes.[10]

---

9 One child, Agatha Vause, had by her tenth birthday lost a father, two stepfathers, a mother, and a guardian uncle. Her household in 1666 included children from four marriages along with two live-in servants. The situation of slaves in colonial America was different. They typically did not have extended households and official marriages. Sales broke up unofficial ones. See Russell R. Menard, "The Maryland Slave Population 1658 to 1730," *William and Mary Quarterly* 32, no. 1 (January 1975): 48.

10 Newport County General Court Trials, 1671–1724; Court Records of New Castle on Delaware, 1676–1681; cited in Joseph W. Dellapenna, *Dispelling the Myths of Abortion History* (Durham, NC: Carolina Academic Press, 2006), 220. The infrequency of cases could mean no one cared

It's not that Puritans were pure. British scholar Roger Thompson's *Sex in Middlesex* emerged from his thorough look at records in the Middlesex County courthouse in Cambridge, Massachusetts. The county justice system registered 221 cases of alleged sexual misbehavior from 1649 to 1699, but only one involved the death of a child through abortion: Hannah Blood of Groton, Massachusetts, used savin, a potent abortifacient, and lost "her great belly." That's it. One.[11]

Anne Orthwood did not abort her twins, and other women were similarly reluctant. One young Middlesex woman, Sarah Crouch, testified in January 1669 that Christopher Grant pushed her for sex and promised that "no hurt should come of it," because if she became pregnant he would marry her. When she did become pregnant, though, his marriage proposal became conditional: "He said he would marry me if I would make away with the child, which I did refuse to do, for which I bless my God."[12]

---

enough to prosecute abortionists, but that's unlikely given attitudes toward abortion that are on the record. The better surmise is that abortion was rare. To refer to Sherlock Holmes once more, the dog did not bark. But it's important to point out something that goes beyond the scope of this book: Two good record-keeping colonies, Massachusetts and Connecticut, had 66 infanticide convictions during the 137 years from 1670 to 1807, almost one every two years. Infanticide, a hanging offense when prosecutors had proof of a child murdered, was something done in secret and alone. One popular ballad in England, "The Cruel Mother," described a woman "All alone, alone and aloney,/ She fell in love with her father's clerk/ Down by the greenwood siding." The clerk did not take responsibility, so the mother "alone and aloney" had twins as Anne Orthwood did. This mother, though, "took her penknife keen and sharp/ And pierced those babies tender hearts" (quoted in Peter Hoffer and N. E. H. Hull, *Murdering Mothers: Infanticide in England and New England 1558–1803* (New York: New York University Press, 1981).

11 Roger Thompson, *Sex in Middlesex: Popular Mores in a Massachusetts County, 1649–1699* (Amherst: University of Massachusetts Press, 1986), 25. The occasional abortion did not stun Massachusetts residents, who realized that sin cannot be abolished but *can* be contained. The twentieth century's preeminent scholar concerning colonial New England, Edmund Morgan, described how Puritans and Pilgrims passed laws concerning sex but had "no misconceptions as to the capacity of human beings to obey such laws." See Edmund Morgan, "The Puritans and Sex," *The New England Quarterly* (December 1942): 594.

12 Thompson, *Sex in Middlesex*, 42: Sarah Crouch reported Grant saying a man who has sex without promising marriage is "a Rogue in his heart.... If she was not good enough to make his wife she was not good enough to make his whore." One man who met resistance to his sexual advances

Why did she refuse? Thompson noted that colonial "standards of living were meager and discomfort endemic, [but] the great majority of men and women encountered in the court records were, quite literally, God-fearing." They did not know much about anatomy, but they read the Bible and sat through sermons based on it. They, like Anne, had an internal sense that abortion was wrong.[13]

---

stopped because "God smote him with a trembling." Community standards and expectations supported popular piety.

13 Thompson, *Sex in Middlesex*, 196.

6

An Oath for Midwives

ELIZABETH WELLS emigrated from England to Massachusetts in the 1660s and bragged to her New World friends about her adventures in the Old. One wide-eyed twenty-two-year-old, Samuel Blunt, recalled in court her story about fooling her father, who locked her in her bedchamber to keep her from heading out on the town and did not know that another young woman and three young men were already in the room. Elizabeth became pregnant, gave birth, and then abandoned her son to come to New England. It isn't clear whether her son was one of "four Bastards" she buried in a garden, pulling "a verie good handkerchief from her neck to bury one of them in."[1]

In America, Wells continued her wayward ways. She became pregnant in 1668 and mixed into beer some oil of savin. It did not work, and she gave birth several months later. She named as the father a young man, James Tufts, whose grandmother objected, saying Wells was "addicted to lying with conviction." In court, the grandma recounted Elizabeth's boast that if pregnant she would name a man "rich enough able to maintain it whether it were his or no." Nevertheless,

---

1 Roger Thompson, *Sex in Middlesex: Popular Mores in a Massachusetts County, 1649–1699* (Amherst: University of Massachusetts Press, 1986), 25–26.

the official records listed, "James the child of James Tufts and Elizabeth Wells."[2]

Wells gained child support from Tufts for two reasons. First, she and Tufts did have intercourse in a barn during harvest time. Second, Wells gave birth just after Massachusetts enacted a law about "reputed fathers." The law stipulated that midwives should ask unwed mothers during labor to name the father. Legislators believed that women, facing the travails of childbirth, would not lie about such an important fact, so the man named became the "reputed father" with an obligation to pay support. With "trust the woman" as official policy, Middlesex County in Massachusetts had only a single case of abortion in 50 years but 96 cases of men cited as the father for purposes of child support.[3]

This pattern continued into the eighteenth century. In Maine, then part of Massachusetts, unmarried Bathsheba Lydston in 1724 accused Daniel Paul Jr. of fathering her child. He denied it. Two women testified that she during labor named Paul as the father. Three witnesses said they had seen her and Paul in "familiar" activity. Three other witnesses said she had also been "familiar" with three other men. Paul's possible fatherhood was enough to allow Lydston to claim him as the reputed father, the one who would have to pay child support until the child reached the typical apprenticeship age of twelve or thirteen.[4]

Such arrangements were common in Massachusetts. Virginia and other colonies developed similar statutes to provide for children

---

2 Deloraine Corry, *History of Malden* (Malden, MA: self-published, 1898), 327; Thompson, *Sex in Middlesex*, 20, 24, 46.

3 Thompson, *Sex in Middlesex*, 21, 183. The law specified that "the Man charged by the Woman to be the Father, she holding constant in it (especially being put upon the real discovery of the truth of it in the time of her Travail) shall be the reputed Father, and accordingly be liable to the charge of maintenance as aforesaid (though not to other punishment) notwithstanding his denial." The law could not guarantee happiness: Elizabeth died in 1674 and James Sr. died in King Philip's War (also called "the first Indian War") the following year. But at least orphan James Jr. received financial support out of the Tufts estate.

4 Court of General Sessions, April 7, 1724, in *Province and Court Records of Maine*, 250. See also *Virginia Antiquary: Princess Anne County*, X, 83, 116, 119, 149, 254, 171–73.

born out of wedlock—and to make it less likely that poor women would feel driven to abortion or infanticide. Children born outside of marriage had a hard life but they did not go hungry (unless a drought left everyone hungry).[5] But Francis Makemie, a Presbyterian church planter who helped to form congregations in the mid-Atlantic colonies during the 1680s and '90s, was one of many pastors who emphasized that private passions had public consequences: "How expensive a darling sin and vice has proved to many families.... It is justly sin and disobedience which blasts our names and stains our reputations."[6]

A graduate of the University of Glasgow, Makemie emphasized the role of community order in fighting vice and supporting marriages: In small towns, many eyes saw who was "keeping company" with whom. Makemie noted the importance of pastors and governmental leaders leading by example: "To whom much is given, of them much is required ... the higher our Station or Calling is, the more shining and exemplary should our lives be.... When rulers and magistrates give evil example ... it is no wonder to see people trace their evil steps."[7]

Makemie made that last statement in 1707 during a sermon in New York City that offended New York's royal governor, Lord Cornbury. According to eighteenth-century historian William Smith, Cornbury often dressed in women's clothes. He sometimes called it a tribute to his cousin, Queen Anne, who had given him the gubernatorial appointment, but Cornbury created "general dismay" as he "paraded in

---

5 Thompson, *Sex in Middlesex*, 195.
6 L. P. Bowen, *The Days of Makemie: Or, The Vine Planted, A.D. 1680–1708* (Philadelphia: Presbyterian Board of Publication, 1885), 290–91. Makemie warned, "It is a hard thing to lead righteous lives in the midst of multiplied and repeated evil precedents; as it is to touch pitch and not be defiled therewith, or to put coals into our bosoms and not be burnt. Lot found it no easy matter to maintain his righteousness in the midst of an unrighteous Sodom."
7 Francis Makemie, *Life and Writings*, ed. Boyd S. Schleither (Philadelphia: Presbyterian Historical Society, 1971), 38; Bowen, *Days of Makemie*, 376. See also Marshall Page, *The Life Story of Rev. Francis Makemie* (Grand Rapids, MI: Eerdman's, 1938).

such a manner on all the great Holidays and even in an hour or two after going to Communion."⁸

This becomes important in the history of abortion because Cornbury threw Makemie into jail, charged him with preaching without a license, and called him a "strolling preacher . . . prone to bid defiance to Government." Cornbury had already fought with local legislators over taxes, expenditures, thefts of land, and his personal behavior. The persecution of Makemie was the final upset. Complaints flowed to London: Makemie gained his freedom, Cornbury lost his governorship, and Robert Hunter replaced him.⁹

In Maryland and Virginia, reliance on social pressure to prevent abortion had mixed success. In New York, the first attempts to use governmental pressure emerged after the switch of officials. Hunter came from a middle-class background and as a teenager was an apprentice to an apothecary, where he likely learned about abortifacients. He ran away to join the British army and rose to the rank of general. Raised in a devout Presbyterian home, he apparently took seriously this instruction from London: "You are to take especial care that God Almighty be devoutly and duly served throughout your Government."¹⁰

---

8   William Smith, *History of the Province of New-York* (London: Thomas Wilcox, Bookseller at Virgil's Head, 1757; repr., Cambridge, MA: Harvard University Press, 1972), 130. For more about Cornbury, see Marvin Olasky, *Fighting for Liberty and Virtue: Political and Cultural Wars in Eighteenth-Century America* (Wheaton, IL: Crossway, 1995).

9   Smith, *History of the Province of New-York*, 482–83; and Francis Makemie and William Livingston, *A Narrative of a New and Unusual American Imprisonment, of Two Presbyterian Ministers, and Prosecution of Mr. Francis Makemie One of Them, for Preaching One Sermon in the City of New-York* (New York, 1755).

10 John Brodhead, ed., *Documents Relative to the Colonial History of the State of New York* (Albany, NY: Weed, Parsons, 1855), 125, 132, 135, 136. London's instructions on December 27, 1709, emphasized rebuilding a sense of community: "Whereas the inhabitants of our said Province have of late Years been unhappily divided and by their enmity to each other our service and their general welfare have been very much obstructed, you are therefore . . . to use such moderation as may best conduce to our service, by quieting the minds of the people and reconciling all differences amongst them." London told Hunter he should allow "no inhumane severity" toward servants and slaves, and noted that "willful killing of Indians and Negroes may be punished by death." He was also to "encourage the conversion of Negroes and Indians." In 1703 about two of five New

As Hunter settled into his new position, he learned of problems concerning pregnancies among New York's unmarried population and those without the usual family support networks. Any policy needed to recognize the crucial role midwives played in colonial society, both in guiding inexperienced women through the birth process and in learning the identity of the father, who would then be responsible for child support.

In England, the Church of England organized and licensed midwives, who were usually financially comfortable wives and widows of good standing in their communities. Bishops administered oaths with fifteen items including this stipulation: "You shall not give any counsel, or minister any Herbe, Medicine, or Potion, or any other thing, to any Woman being with Childe whereby she should destroy or cast out that she goeth withal before her time." That oath dates from 1649. A license issued in 1686 by the Bishop of London contained the same items.[11]

This prohibition was also standard in popular books. One, written by a person who called himself "Aristotle," instructed midwives to refuse "to give directions for such Medicines as will cause abortion." Doing so was "a high degree of wickedness, and may be ranked with Murther."[12] Botanist Nicholas Culpeper, writing about drugs useful for some ailments, told midwives, "Give not any of those to any that is with Child, lest you turn Murtherers. Wilful Murther seldom goes unpunished in this World, never in that to come."[13]

Governor Hunter, the former apothecary apprentice, understood the temptations surrounding unwed pregnancies. He could have asked

---

York City households included slaves, used as domestic servants and laborers, and sometimes as artisans.

11 Doreen Evenden, *The Midwives of Seventeenth-Century London* (Cambridge: Cambridge University Press, 2000), 169, 206. See also Thomas Forbes, *The Midwife and the Witch* (New Haven, CT: Yale University Press, 1966), 246–47; James Hitchcock, "A Sixteenth Century Midwife's License," *Bulletin of the History of Medicine* 41 (1967): 75–76; and Ann Oakley, *The Captured Womb: A History of the Medical Care of Pregnant Women* (Oxford: Basil Blackwell, 1984).
12 *Aristotle's Masterpiece, Or, The Secrets of Generation Displayed in All the Parts* (London, 1684), 101.
13 Nicholas Culpeper, *A Directory for Midwives* (1651; repr., London, T. Norris, 1724), 69.

the Church of England to organize the colony's midwives, but Hunter and Rector William Vesey of Trinity Church, located where Broadway met the wall that gives Wall Street its name, did not get along. Hunter did not direct church authorities to instruct midwives about abortion. Instead, he turned to the New York City Common Council (which over the centuries became the Board of Aldermen and now the current New York City Council).[14]

While historians normally say the first American law against abortion emerged in Connecticut in 1821, New York City took action 105 years earlier: In 1716, the Common Council forbade midwives to aid in or recommend abortion. All midwives had to swear an oath not to "Give any Counsel or Administer any Herb Medicine or Potion, or any other thing to any Woman being with Child whereby She Should Destroy or Miscarry of that she goeth withall before her time." That's almost word-for-word a segment of the oath administered by British clergy, including the Bishop of London—but in New York City the power of law was behind it, and other colonies adopted similar policies.[15]

---

14 "Letter to Lords of Trade, August 13, 1715," in Brodhead, *Documents*, 420. Hunter, a friend of Jonathan Swift, had a literary flair and in 1715 wrote the first play known to have been published in colonial America, *Androboros* ("man-eater," in loose Greek). In it Hunter satirized political and religious opponents, saying their "Long Robes" covered "Poyson prepared for the Innocent." See Robert Hunter, *Androboros: A Biographical Farce in Three Acts* (New York, 1715; repr., Franklin Classics, 2018), 24; and Peter Davis, *From Androboros to the First Amendment: A History of America's First Play* (Iowa City: University of Iowa Press, 2015).

15 *Minutes of the Common Council, New York City*, III, 22, July 27, 1716, quoted in Dennis Horan and Thomas J. Marzen, "Abortion and Midwifery: A Footnote in Legal History," in Thomas W. Hilgers, Dennis Horan, and David Mall, *New Perspectives on Human Abortion* (Frederick, MD: University Publications of America, 1981), 199. See also William Waller Hening, *The New Virginia Justice* (Richmond, VA: T. Nicolson, 1795).

7

Double Robbery of Life

AS EZRA STILES founded Brown University, his hobby was keeping records of deliveries of newborns in Newport, Rhode Island: 1,600 births from 1760 to 1764, he noted, and only ten maternal deaths. On Long Island, a midwife reported two maternal deaths in 1,300 deliveries. Late in the century, Maine midwife Martha Ballard recorded in her diary four maternal deaths among the 996 women whose babies she delivered from 1785 to 1812. *Childbirth* was an ordeal in the eighteenth century but not a dangerous one for most women.[1]

Abortion in colonial times, on the other hand, was always dangerous. Ingesting an abortifacient was playing Russian roulette: Place a bullet in a revolver, spin the cylinder, point the muzzle at your head, pull the trigger. Letting an abortionist invade a uterus was the equivalent

---

[1] F. Apthorp Foster, ed., *New England Historical and Genealogical Register* 62 (1908): 283–91, 352–63; and 63 (1909): 51–58; Richard and Dorothy Wertz, *Lying-In: A History of Childbirth in America* (New Haven, CT: Yale University Press, 1989), 9; Laura Ulrich, *A Midwife's Tale: The Life of Martha Ballard Based on Her Diary, 1785–1812* (New York: Random House, 1990). We don't have good records of the maternal mortality rate in the South among either whites or blacks, but among northern white women the maternal mortality rate was probably about 1 percent. Given the typical six or seven births in a lifetime, about one of every sixteen women would eventually die in childbirth. The possibility of death from normal disease or during an epidemic was much greater: The 1677–1678 smallpox epidemic in Boston probably killed one-fifth of its inhabitants. But odds of surviving a surgical abortion were worse than that.

of two bullets in the cylinder. Only utter desperation, or unrelenting pressure from a lover, would lead a woman to accept a one-third possibility of death.

That's what Sarah Grosvenor, 19 and unmarried, did in 1742. She and Amasa Sessions, 27, lived in Pomfret, Connecticut, which now advertises itself as the "quintessential New England community." But the community let Sarah down when Sessions persuaded her to have sex with him by promising to marry her. She became pregnant. He reneged on his promise, giving this reason, according to court documents: "afraid of parents."[2]

Nathaniel Sessions, Amasa's father, may indeed have been scary. The town constable and a lieutenant in the militia, he had in 1721 ramrodded completion of a road to Providence, Rhode Island, twenty-nine miles east of Pomfret, and had shown that it worked by bringing in himself the first shipment of goods from the Caribbean. Sarah's father, Leicester Grosvenor, was also a leader, serving as a justice of the peace and member of the Connecticut General Assembly. But in this crisis they were either passive, which seems unlikely, or unaware. The older women of Pomfret—Sarah's stepmother and two widowed aunts—also were either unintentionally or deliberately uninvolved.[3]

That's not the way New England society was supposed to operate: Its assumption was that parents and churches would disciple the young, protect them from temptation, and rescue them if they slipped. Parents and churches were supposed to help the young be more passionate about the Bible than about sex, but that was hard—and it was easy to fall into rule-making that attempted to control behavior from the outside in rather than from the inside out.

Members of the younger generation knew about Sarah's pregnancy. Her older sisters, Zerviah Grosvenor and Anna Wheeler, knew. Her

---

2   Cornelia Hughes Dayton, "Taking the Trade: Abortion and Gender Relations in an Eighteenth-Century New England Village," *William and Mary Quarterly* 48, no. 1 (1991): 19–49.

3   Dennis Partridge, "Early Residents of Pomfret Connecticut," https://connecticutgenealogy.com/windham/early_residents_pomfret.htm.

married friend Abigail Nightingale and her cousins and cousin-in-law John, Ebenezer, and Hannah Grosvenor, knew. Amasa's brother and sister-in-law, Alexander and Silence Sessions, knew. Historian Cornelia Dayton's summary seems apt: "These sisters, brothers, cousins, courting couples, and neighbors . . . had managed to create a world of talk and socializing that was largely exempt from parental supervision."[4]

Instead of going to his parents, Amasa Sessions solicited help from rascally doctor John Hallowell, who had already shown his untrustworthiness by counterfeiting currency. Hallowell obtained an abortifacient, and Amasa told Sarah to swallow it. She did. The potion sickened her but did not kill their unborn child, apparently in his or her sixth month. Hallowell then doubled down, ending one life and gambling with another by performing surgery: He used his fingers and an instrument of some kind to abort the baby.

New England records do not describe Hallowell's surgical method, but we do have this description from a trial in Derby, England, ten years earlier: Eleanor Beare received a three-year prison sentence for "destroying the foetus in the womb [by] putting an iron instrument into the body" of Grace Belfort, one of her employees. Belfort testified that "I laid me on the bed, and my mistress brought a kind of instrument, I took it to be like an iron skewer, and she put it up into my body a great way, and hurt me. . . . The next day . . . I had a miscarriage."[5]

Dr. Hallowell in Connecticut likely poked and scraped until the unborn child came out, dead. The danger was evident, especially since the

---

[4] Dayton, "Taking the Trade," 34.
[5] "The Tryal of Eleanore Beare of Derby," *Gentleman's Magazine* (1732), 933–34. The prosecutor described Beare's crime as "of a most shocking Nature; to destroy the Fruit in the Womb carries something in it so contrary to the natural Tenderness of the Female Sex, that I am amazed how ever any Woman should arrive at such a degree of Impiety and Cruelty. . . . It is cruel and barbarous to the last degree." Beare also had public humiliation: Neighbors, "to show their Resentment of the horrible Crimes wherein she has been charged, and the little Remorse she had shown since her Commitment," threw eggs, turnips, and other vegetables at her.

tools of the abortionist's trade hadn't changed much in two millennia. Around AD 200 the theologian Tertullian described how an abortionist inserted into the uterus "an annular blade, by means of which the limbs within the womb are dissected," along with a blunt gripper "wherewith the entire foetus is extracted by a violent delivery," and "a copper needle or spike, by which the actual death is managed in this furtive robbery of life."[6]

The surgical trauma was bad enough, but then infection arrived. Without antibiotics, that were two centuries in the future, Sarah Grosvenor died. Amasa Sessions continued to be irresponsible. It fell to Sarah's sister Zerviah and their cousin Hannah to walk into the forest and bury the dead infant, whom Zerviah later described as "a pretty child, a perfect child. . . . Took it and buried it." Most people today have seen photos of babies in the womb. We know about fetal development, but Zerviah had no knowledge of that sort. The burden was heavy. The memory of death and burial haunted her.[7]

That was particularly true because Connecticut was going through theological changes during the early 1740s. The Great Awakening was enlivening Pomfret and its surroundings: Evangelist George Whitefield had preached through Connecticut in 1740 and taught that the right biblical response after sin is confession, not cover-up. Pastors and church members looked for "remarkable providences" that could indicate God's

---

6 Quintus Tertullian, *Treatise on the Soul*, trans. Peter Holmes (Whitefish, MT: Kessinger Legacy Reprints, 2010), 75.

7 Testimony by Zerviah Grosvenor in the Windham County Superior Court Files (1726–1908), Box 172, Record Group 3, Archives, History, and Genealogy Unit, Connecticut State Library, Hartford, CT; identified and brought from obscurity by Cornelia Hughes Dayton. See also Ellen Larned, *History of Windham County Connecticut, 1600–1760* (self-published, 1874; repr., London: Forgotten Books, 2018), 363. That history, originally published in 1880, said townspeople still whispered 140 years later about what eventually pushed Zerviah to tell many neighbors about the death and burial: "Night after night, in her solitary chamber, the surviving sister was awakened by the rattling of the rings on which her bed-curtains were suspended, a ghostly knell continuing and intensifying till she was convinced of its preternatural origin; and at length, in response to her agonized entreaties, the spirit of her dead sister made known to her, 'That she could not rest in her grave till her crime was made public.'"

displeasure. In 1742, the year Sarah died, lightning struck a barn filled with hay and stacks of grain: It burned down. The following summer, winds during a violent hailstorm blew down a house and barns, and a wolf devastated sheepfolds.[8]

Gradually, word of the abortion reached the older generation, and investigation began. Jonathan Trumbull, a former speaker of the Connecticut House, presided over two days of hearings in November, 1745. Zerviah Grosvenor testified that Sarah "had been Taking Medicines of Doctor Hollowell to make her Miscarry ... my Sister was loath to Take it, & Thot it an Evil.... I thot It a Sin." Abigail Nightingale said her close friend Sarah worried whether "her Sins would ever be pardoned." Hannah Grosvenor said she saw "The Child, which was not half So large as Children commonly are when Born.... We took The child wrapped it up & conveyed it away and Buryed it."[9]

A jury took into account both victims, finding that Hallowell "by actual force and violence" destroyed Sarah Grosvenor's "health & Soundness ... and ye fruit of her womb to destroy & cause to perish." Hallowell's sentence: Two hours standing in the gallows on April Fools' Day "with a rope visibly hanging about his neck," plus 29 lashes "on his naked back," plus six months of imprisonment. But Hallowell broke out of jail and made it to Providence over the road Nathaniel Sessions had built. Hallowell never returned, and Rhode Island never forced him out.[10]

One reason the Sessions/Grosvenor abortion was so unusual is that, in most communities of that era, three of the four usual determinants of

8 Partridge, "Early Residents of Pomfret Connecticut," https://connecticutgenealogy.com/windham/early_residents_pomfret.htm. For the excitement that greeted Whitefield in Connecticut, see the description by Nathan Cole in *The William and Mary Quarterly*, 3rd ser., 7 (1950): 590–91.
9 Testimony of Zebulon Dodge, Rebeckah Sharp, and Alexander Sessions (Amasa's brother), November 5 and 6, 1745. Abigail Nightingale said she told Sarah, "if she humbled herself on her Knees to her Father, he would take her & her Child home."
10 Dayton, "Taking the Trade," 19–49. Jonathan Trumbull went on to become governor of Connecticut in the 1770s. He was the only governor to join the Patriot cause when the Revolutionary War began.

attitudes toward abortion would have pointed strongly toward having rather than killing a baby: Anatomy was still a mystery, and those who thought unborn children early in the pregnancy were unformed lumps might think that killing them was not killing a human being—but Bible knowledge would guide young men and women away from abortion. Danger for the mother was certainly also a deterrent.

So was community pressure, with Pomfret an exception. If Amasa had come through on his marriage promise to Sarah, their child would have been considered fully legitimate, even though conceived outside of marriage. One of six colonial brides in the late eighteenth century had a child within six months of marriage. Four of five children conceived outside marriage in one Massachusetts county during the 1760s had a married father and mother listed at birth.[11]

When men refused to marry, women took them to court and were usually successful. Elizabeth Wells in 1668 and Bathsheba Lydston in 1724 had advantageously made use of the "trust the woman" standard. That pattern continued throughout the eighteenth century in many areas: Nineteen paternity suits in Lincoln County, Maine, between 1761 and 1799, resulted in only three acquittals. Women called off lawsuits when men gave in. For example, Mary Crawford of Bath, Maine, certified that "Samuel Todd of said Bath hath agreed to make me satisfaction for getting me with child by promising to marry me, therefore, I wish that the prosecution I commenced against him for so doing may be squashed."[12]

That system worked because the woman's testimony in small towns had backup from eyewitnesses in the neighborhood. A theological emphasis on the importance of confession also influenced behavior: Since Bible readers knew that "all have sinned and fall short of the glory of God" (Rom. 3:23), a man who committed adultery and then confessed would not be shunned. But during the eighteenth century that internal

11 Robert V. Wells, *Revolutions in Americans' Lives* (Westport, CT: Greenwood, 1982), 353.
12 Ulrich, *Midwife's Tale*, 155.

pressure may have diminished while the growth of cities increased the opportunity for hidden dalliance. An early men's movement pushed back against automatically accepting a woman's declaration. A double standard began to emerge.[13]

---

13 Cornelia Hughes Dayton, *Women before the Bar: Gender, Law, and Society in Connecticut, 1639–1789* (Chapel Hill: University of North Carolina Press, 1995), 158–61.

8

A Fallen Pro-Life Founder

SLAVERY WAS BRUTAL, legal, and common in colonial America, so almost all of those who signed the Declaration of Independence and the Constitution spoke out about it. Abortion was unsafe, illegal, and rare, so it was not a subject of controversy, but one of the six men who signed both documents did attack it—and left a story for his descendants of what to do, and what not to do.

James Wilson grew up in Scotland, six miles from a famous three-centuries-old university, St. Andrews. He entered it in 1757 at age 15 as a scholarship student of the third rank: sons of aristocrats were first rank, sons of "gentlemen commoners" second, and sons of poor parents third. His breakfast was a half loaf of oat bread and a pint of beer "of the meanest quality," his supper a loaf of wheat bread and another pint.[1]

Wilson emigrated to America in 1765 and entered legal studies in Philadelphia. He married and had six children. Starting in 1774 he became widely known amid the political upheaval of the day. Wilson also wanted to be rich. Land speculation was the means to that end. During the Revolutionary War and for nearly twenty-five years thereafter he borrowed money to plunge into deals in Pennsylvania, Virginia,

---

1   Page Smith, *James Wilson, Founding Father, 1742–1798* (Chapel Hill: University of North Carolina Press, 1956), 12–14.

and other areas. After his wife, Ruth, died in 1786, his financial crises became more frequent, as did his desperate attempts to survive them through more speculation.[2]

Get-rich schemes were only part of Wilson's professional life. He was a frequent flyer of ideas and compromises at the Constitutional Convention in 1787. Wilson gave the major oration at Philadelphia's July 4 celebration in 1788, although a crash of cannon salutes from ten ships in the harbor (one for each state that had ratified the Constitution at that point) made most of Wilson's words inaudible. Five months later, he and 44 other members of the St. Andrews Society met to sing ballads (with bagpipe accompaniment), eat haggis, and go through 73 bottles of wine as they drank toast after toast.[3]

In April 1789, Wilson asked George Washington to make him chief justice of the new Supreme Court. Washington instead appointed John Jay, perhaps because Wilson's speculations and debts raised questions of character. No one doubted his intellect, though, so Wilson became an associate justice and lectured in 1790 and thereafter at the school that became the University of Pennsylvania. The goal was to define "a new *American system* of jurisprudence," one in which American common sense would eventually supplant British common law. George Washington, John Adams, and other top officials attended the first lecture.[4]

Wilson was not trying to impose biblical law, nor was he known as one of early America's Christian leaders, but in his law lectures he emphasized the natural law of natural birth. Abortion was not a subject for argument but something the Founders perceived to be wrong through

---

2 Smith, *James Wilson*, 163–68 and 212: Wilson would make a small down payment to secure a preliminary warrant, and then hire a surveyor. Since speculators were "searching out choice lands like bloodhounds," an unscrupulous surveyor could "choose lands for his own employer that were not the best, leaving choice sections for a rival survey and in this way doubling his fee" (Robert McCloskey, "Introduction," *The Works of James Wilson*, 2 vols. [Cambridge, MA: Harvard University Press, 1967], 1:17–19). McCloskey writes, "Land was his passion, and he plunged [into] his land speculations with the rashness, optimism, and growing desperation of a compulsive gambler."
3 Smith, *James Wilson*, 205.
4 Smith, *James Wilson*, 205–6, 309; McCloskey, "Introduction," 28–29.

their own experience: Most were not only the fathers of their country but the fathers of many children. Every parent, when he or she held a baby, knew that abortion was wrong: That was common sense, and perhaps even common wisdom.[5]

Wilson's lectures included these lapidary lines: "With consistency, beautiful and undeviating, human life, from its commencement to its close, is protected by the common law. In the contemplation of law, life begins when the infant is first able to stir in the womb. By the law, life is protected not only from immediate destruction, but from every degree of actual violence, and, in some cases, from every degree of danger."[6]

We can't say for sure whether Wilson meant objectively "stirring" (soon after conception) or subjectively in the consciousness of the mother, which, as we have noted, is "quickening," typically after four months. Wilson knew well the work of England's William Blackstone, published in the 1760s in London, and practically quoted Blackstone's statement that life "begins in contemplation of the law as soon as an infant is able to stir in the mother's womb."[7]

Wilson also knew the standard work of the previous century, Edward Coke's *Institutes of the Laws of England*, with its declaration of "a great misprision" whenever a woman is "quick with child" and she, or a man, kills the child. Some jurists later thought "quick" meant quickened, but it probably meant having a live child, as in the old differentiation (noted earlier) of "the quick and the dead." "Misprision" fell short of

---

5   M. E. Bradford, *A Worthy Company: Brief Lives of the Framers of the United States Constitution* (Marlborough, NH: Plymouth Rock Foundation, 1982), ix, 81–87. When University of Dallas professor Mel Bradford looked at the Constitutional Convention delegate by delegate in an attempt to prove the Christian influence in America's founding, he counted 53 of the 55 delegates as orthodox Christians, leaving out Hugh Williamson (who thought men live on comets) and Wilson, whom Bradford calls "probably a free thinker in the privacy of his study." John Eidsmoe, in *Christianity and the Constitution: The Faith of Our Founding Fathers* (Grand Rapids, MI: Baker, 1987), calls Washington, Hamilton, and Madison "strong Christians" but ignores Wilson.

6   *Collected Works of James Wilson*, ed. Kermit L. Hall and Mark David Hall, 2 vols. (Indianapolis: Liberty Fund, 2007), 2:749.

7   William Blackstone, *Commentaries on the Laws of England*, 4 vols. (1765; repr., Chicago: University of Chicago Press, 1979), 1:129.

murder but was still a serious crime, not just a misdemeanor: Misprision meant criminal neglect and was used especially in connection with treason, so an aborting mother in England was a traitor to both the king and the unborn child.[8]

Such a concept of abortion was not controversial, especially since the Founders also read about defending life in the Bible and in the writings of the popular theorist Charles-Louis de Secondat Montesquieu, who noted "the cruel practice of abortion."[9] Some Founders were also familiar with a seventeenth-century German thinker largely forgotten now, Samuel Pufendorf: He said parents should not "destroy by abortion the offspring conceived within their flesh."[10]

As some of the Founders moved from British subject to American citizen, popular English writers still had cultural influence. Thomas Browne, from the 1740s until his death in 1782, was a favorite poet on both sides of the Atlantic. Had printed greeting cards been popular in the eighteenth century, Browne's sentiments like this would have graced them: "The created world is but a small Parenthesis in Eternity." But Browne also wrote "Satire upon a Quack," which labeled one British abortion-pusher a "graveyard pimp" who used "pointed darts" and a "murdering quill" to leave behind "unborn infants murder'd in the womb." Such a killer was condemned to hear forever "the screams of infants."[11]

Scottish doctor William Buchan's *Domestic Medicine* (1769) sold more than 80,000 copies, including some in America. This medical

8   Edward Coke, *The Third Part of the Institutes of the Laws of England: Concerning High Treason, and Other Pleas of the Crown and Criminal Causes* (London: M. Flesher, 1648; repr., London: The Lawbook Exchange, 2001), 50.
9   "Founding Fathers' Library," https://oll.libertyfund.org/pages/founding-father-s-library. See Charles-Louis de Secondat Montesquieu, *The Persian Letters* (1721; repr., Shrewsbury, MA: Garland, 1972, trans. John Ozell), 1:218.
10 Samuel Pufendorf, *Two Books of the Elements of Universal Jurisprudence*, trans. William Abbot Oldfather (1660; repr., Oxford: Clarendon, 1931), 2:283, cited in Duane Ostler, "A Conversation about Abortion between Justice Blackmun and the Founding Fathers," *Constitutional Commentary* 167 (2014): 281, at https://scholarship.law.umn.edu/concomm/281.
11 Thomas Browne, *Religio Medici* and sequels, 194, 200; "A Satire upon a Quack," in *Works Serious and Comical in Prose and Verse* (London 1760, and NYRB Classics reprint, 2012, 62–65), quoted in Kate Lister, "Bringing Down the Flowers," at www.academia.edu/28203855.

guide to the perplexed warned, "Every mother who procures an abortion does it at the hazard of her life.... It is surely a most unnatural crime." Those who proffer abortion, Buchan wrote, are "wretches who ... deserve in any opinion, the most severe of all human punishments."[12]

So abortion was not unknown, but it rarely received newspaper coverage. Dozens of American newspaper articles from 1760 through 1800 included the word "abortion," but almost all of them meant it metaphorically: Unethical proposals were "abortions in the moral world," bad ideas "abortions of the brain," dictatorships were "abortions." In what was probably a nonmetaphorical use, one writer urged women to wear wool, for, "with the flimsy importations of Asia and of Europe, they are continually exposed to all the diseases caused by cold, perhaps to abortion." Non-metaphorically, "abortion" was apparently a synonym for miscarriage.[13]

The earliest American newspaper story I've found about aborting a child appeared in the *Maryland Gazette* in 1752. It reported on a man who became "too familiar" with his servant. She "let him know she was with Child by him, which made him uneasy for fear it should come to the Knowledge of his Wife." The man consulted "with two idle Fellows of the Town, and they procured him an Herb, which they said would cause an Abortion. He administered the Dose, but it proved ineffectual."[14]

The desperate adulterer then asked "a Person whose Reputation in Physic was more famed." Having attained a stronger potion, the man gave it to his servant. She took it and went to milk the cows, but "was seized so violently that she could not return. She found Means of acquainting her Master with it, he fetched her, but she was not brought home many Hours before she died." The man "endeavoured to destroy

---

12 William Buchan, *Domestic Medicine* (London, 1769; repr., Sagwan Press, 2015), 531.
13 *Virginia Gazette*, February 10, 1774, 2; *Freeman's Journal*, September 15, 1784, 2; *Hartford Courant*, August 22, 1771, 2; *Aurora General Advertiser*, July 9, 1796 (general conclusions based on reading newspapers.com and newspaperarchives.com entries).
14 *The Maryland Gazette* (Annapolis), December 21, 1752, 2.

himself," but did not go through with it: He ran off and was apparently not apprehended.[15]

Nor could I find any record of arrest following a Brattleboro, Vermont, story that appeared in 1800. *The Federal Galaxy* noted "the dead body of an infant ... dug out by dogs. The body appeared to be produced by abortion." The reporter noted that some thought the baby had been born alive, but he drew no line between death before birth and after: "The perpetrators of the murder if convicted will suffer the punishment which they richly deserve."[16]

The lack of references to abortion did not mean that newspapers were squeamish: One Philadelphia newspaper noted that "of all the Diseases incident to human kind, none has perhaps so much taken up the attention of the physicians as the Venereal Disease."[17] The absence of abortion in news coverage suggests little abortion news to report.

Nor did hospital records often show any abortion cases, even those described euphemistically as "obstructed menses." The Pennsylvania Hospital reported in 1794 a year's worth of charitable help that included sixty-seven cases of "lunacy," thirty-seven of venereal disease, thirty-five of fevers, and thirteen of scurvy, yet only one of "obstructed menses" (along with one for "drinking cold water"). In 1798, the number of "lunatics" had jumped to 108 but the "obstructed menses" category still listed only one. The hospital's list of outpatients included thirty-two smallpox inoculations and only two cases of obstructed menses.[18]

---

15 *The Maryland Gazette* (Annapolis), December 21, 1752, 2.
16 *Federal Galaxy* (Brattleboro, VT), September 13, 1800, 1.
17 *Philadelphia Inquirer*, May 5, 1795, 2. Although some academics and pundits follow the Supreme Court in assuming that abortion was acceptable, legal, and not uncommon in the seventeenth and eighteenth centuries, some have a better grip on reality. See, for example, Jillian Overstake's straightforward statement that abortion "rarely occurred" in early America (Jillian Overstake, *A Most Earnest Plea: Pregnant Women Facing Capital Punishment in the American Colonies* [Department of History, Wichita State University, 2010], 22).
18 *Philadelphia Inquirer*, March 12, 1795: The report for the fiscal year ending on April 27, 1794, also notes that the hospital had used 3,794 gallons of milk, 523 pounds of butter, 636 pounds of veal, 1,140 pounds of pork, 119 gallons of rum, 300 pounds of chocolate, and 1,081 pounds of

James Wilson could have written more about protecting unborn life, but that was not a hot topic and, following his lectures on law in 1790, he apparently spent more time on land speculation than on his Supreme Court calling. Wilson gave gossips a gift in 1793 when he proposed to beautiful and well-connected 19-year-old Hannah Gray ten days after meeting her—and she accepted.[19] When John Jay became governor of New York in 1795, Wilson hoped to move from associate to chief justice, but John Adams wrote, "Wilson's ardent speculations had given offense." Washington looked elsewhere.[20]

Wilson kept speculating and borrowing large sums, such as $80,000 (the equivalent of $1.6 million today) from Baltimore merchant John Young. Friends and one son twice extricated him from jail for nonpayment of debts. By 1798, as some spoke of impeaching Wilson, he hid out at the bleak Horniblow Tavern in Edenton, North Carolina, home of Associate Justice James Iredell: "Gaunt, listless, his clothes ragged and stained, Wilson sat staring interminably out of the window." Then came malaria and what Iredell called "a distress of the mind" that left Wilson raving "deliriously about arrest, bad debts, and bankruptcy." He died on August 21, 1798.[21]

In Philadelphia, lawyer Jacob Rush wrote to his brother, Dr. Benjamin Rush, the only other signer of the Constitution to lay out a pro-life position, "What a miserable termination to such distinguished abilities."[22]

---

coffee. The report on the fiscal year ending on April 28, 1798, appears in the *Gazette of the United States and Philadelphia Daily Advertiser*, February 18, 1799.

19 Natalie Wexler, "The Case for Love," *The American Scholar*, June 1, 2006, https://theamericanscholar.org/the-case-for-love/.

20 John Fabian Witt, *Patriots and Cosmopolitans: Hidden Histories of American Law* (Cambridge, MA: Harvard University Press, 2007), 72.

21 Smith, *James Wilson*, 374–86; Witt, *Patriots and Cosmopolitans*, 75–80.

22 Smith, *James Wilson*, 386–88; Witt, *Patriots and Cosmopolitans*, 80. Benjamin Rush was pro-life both theoretically and personally: He and his wife Julia had 13 children. See also Mark David Hall, *The Political and Legal Philosophy of James Wilson, 1742–1798* (Columbia: University of Missouri Press, 1997), 18.

9

Laws and Scofflaws

NORWICH, CONNECTICUT, thirty miles south of Pomfret, was supposed to be an agricultural community north of where the Thames River begins. Settlers planned a community three miles long and three miles wide on which sixty-nine founding families could grow crops. By 1800, though, shipping at the harbor was more important to community wealth than farming, and the city hall, the post office, and other central buildings were along the waterfront.

That wasn't the only change. Norwich had been used to scholarly and aloof Puritan preachers, but Ammi Rogers, a Yale graduate and Episcopal Church clergyman born in 1770, had personal conversations with teenaged female congregants. In 1817 he paid particular attention to Asenath Smith, the twenty-one-year-old granddaughter of a dying church member. Word on the street was that they would be married, despite an age difference almost as great as that between James Wilson and Hannah Gray. Then came rumor: Was Asenath pregnant?

Rogers could lose his ministry if it became known that his counseling had become too intimate. He procured an abortifacient for Asenath, but it didn't end the pregnancy. Next step was his use of a "tool" of some kind, which caused bleeding, intense pain, and then delivery of a dead child. That led to Rogers's arrest and, in 1820, a trial summarized this way by *The Norwich Courier*: "The county never witnessed a trial in which so much baseness and cold calculating depravity of heart were disclosed, and where so black a deed was attempted to be smothered by the Culprit by so much subornation and falsehood."[1]

Rogers's primary defense was that Puritan descendants were out to get him. He said Asenath testified about the abortifacient only because "conspirators" had threatened her with a public whipping: "that she would be stripped naked and sit upon the gallows with a rope around her neck." Then, he said her pregnancy wasn't proven: She merely had a "supposed child," and if so the death might "have been produced by sickness, infirmity, or accident in the mother."[2]

Jury members did not need a specific anti-abortion law: Everyone knew abortion was wrong. Books by doctors had begun to notice, and attack, abortion. Dr. John Burns criticized those who view "abortion as different than murder, upon the principle that the embryo does not possess of life [for] it undoubtedly can neither think or act, but upon the same reasoning we should conclude it to be innocent to kill the child in birth."[3] Dr. John Broadhead Beck described a young woman "betrayed by the arts of a base seducer, and . . . reduced to a state of pregnancy." Hoping to avoid disgrace, she "may stifle the birth in the womb."[4]

Jurors in the Rogers trial, like their predecessors in Maryland and in Pomfret, did not have clear evidence for a verdict of murder, which was a hanging offense. They did find Rogers guilty of causing an abortion through "the use of pernicious drugs." Rogers received a two-year

---

1 *Norwich Courier*, October 11, 1820, 3; Ammi Rogers, *Memoirs of the Rev. Ammi Rogers* (Schenectady, NY: G. Ritchie, 1826), 120.
2 *Norwich Courier*, October 11, 3, and several different *Memoirs*, one self-published in Troy, New York (1836), see 80; and one in Schenectady, see 149.
3 John Burns, *Observations on Abortion* (New York: Collins & Perkins, 1809), 34. Burns adds, "Whoever prevents life from continuing, until it arrives at perfection, is certainly as culpable as if he had taken it away after that had been accomplished."
4 J. B. Beck, "An Inaugural Dissertation on Infanticide," *Medical Dissertations and Theses* (New York: J. Seymour, 1817), 84.

sentence in Norwich's jail, not the much-feared Newgate prison. Some legislators thought he was getting off easy: Rogers, after all, was a member of the clergy whose violation of public trust could lead some to scorn Christ.[5]

The Rogers verdict led to the first state law against abortion. The Connecticut General Assembly approved punishment for administering "any deadly poison, or other noxious and destructive substance, with an intention . . . to murder, or thereby to cause or procure the miscarriage of any woman, then being quick with child." Imprisonment would be in Newgate, not in a local jail. Politicians responded to the news: Within six years, state legislatures in Missouri and Illinois passed their own laws that explicitly criminalized pushing abortion-inducing potions at any stage of pregnancy. That these laws did not explicitly prohibit surgical abortions shows how rare such abortions were.[6]

The Ammi Rogers case received press attention in Connecticut but very little outside it: abortion did not seem a major threat to social stability. But if a pastor could not be trusted, who could be? If a young woman could be groomed and victimized in Norwich, still a small city where community supervision was supposed to offer some protection, what would happen 135 miles down the coast in New York City, with its population of 120,000 in 1820—and half a million in the 1840s?

Some Manhattan residents were wealthy, with walnut and mahogany furniture and Duncan Phyfe cabinets. They drank Rhenish and Moselle wines, or Madeira and claret, in parlors stacked with bronze busts, vases, cigar stands, alabaster candlesticks, and gift books bound in velvet. But from those homes came tales of domestic servants turned into sex toys, often unwillingly. A woman's family was not present to press for marriage when extramarital activity led to pregnancy. New York City

5   Daniel Phillips, *Griswold: A History of the Town of Griswold Connecticut from the Earliest Times to the Entrance of Our Country into World War in 1917* (New Haven, CT: Tuttle, Morehouse, & Taylor, 1929), 115–16.
6   *Public Statute Laws of the State of Connecticut, 1821* (Hartford, CT: S. G. Goodrich, & Huntington & Hopkins, 1821), 152–53.

had America's first large society of unsupervised young people, with their own sources of income and the opportunity to live with complete disregard for their parents' morality.

In the eighteenth century, servants were often the children of friends and neighbors. That changed in the nineteenth century, when big city servants were often migrants from rural areas or immigrants from England or Ireland. Numerous historians have documented the tragic results. Typical tale: a young woman lived "some months in a family, conducting herself with perfect propriety.... Then, in an unfortunate hour," she fell for a man who pledged marriage. He effected "her ruin" and then absconded.[7]

Most New Yorkers were poor and lived in disease-riddled neighborhoods. A lack of trash collection turned some Manhattan streets into final resting-places for dead cats. Broken pieces of furniture became rat hotels. One magazine, the *Constellation*, asked whether "between the citizens and swine, to which the streets do most belong?" A bull gored a man walking down Hester Street on the city's east side. Prostitutes awaited strangers on mattresses of straw, cotton, hair, or husks in rooms sporting rusty tin basins on bare tables. Many had multiple abortions.

New York legislators responded in 1829 with the first law in the nation to punish abortion by any means. Proving pregnancy before the fifth month remained a problem. Legislators who did not want jurors to rebel made the penalties light: "Imprisonment in a county jail"—not the state prison opened in Auburn in 1819—for up to one year, and/or a fine of up to $500. The law was also the first to include an exception for those unusual situations in which at least two physicians saw abortion as "necessary to preserve the life" of the mother.[8]

---

[7] Faye Duden, *Serving Women: Household Service in Nineteenth-Century America* (Middletown, CT: Wesleyan University Press, 1983), 215. See also Timothy Gilfoyle, *City of Eros: New York City, Prostitution, and the Commercialization of Sex, 1790–1920* (New York: Norton, 1992); and Allen Horlick, *Country Boys and Merchant Princes: The Social Control of Young Men in New York* (Lewisburg, PA: Bucknell University Press, 1975).

[8] *Revised Statutes of New-York . . . 1828 to 1835 Inclusive* (Albany, NY: Packard & Van Benthuysen, 1836), 1:578.

Laws could reduce the supply of abortionists. What about the demand for abortion? One year after the New York legislature acted, John McDowall—a Yale graduate and young pastor—began working on the demand side. He saw that "legislative enactments exist against those who administer drugs to do this wicked work," but abortion was increasing "in defiance of penalties." McDowall organized a "Society for the Moral and Religious Improvement" of the poorest Manhattan neighborhood, Five Points, and reached out to young women "allured by the desire for fine clothing—others by the hopes of wealth, luxury, and ease."[9]

McDowall carried a black umbrella and wore a black broadcloth coat and pants supported by suspenders. He walked the street offering street-walkers sympathy and challenge. His clothing differentiated him from the New York "dandies" who carried canes with ivory heads, or blue-and-white striped silk umbrellas with handles carved in the shape of animal heads. Women told him of a potion-providing doctor who escaped punishment because the witness against him was "esteemed to be impure." McDowall was shocked to find "a member of a Christian church criminal in procuring abortions. Truly, the depravity of human nature is complete."[10]

Ammi Rogers, during the 1830s, lived in disgrace, bitterly writing and rewriting his memoirs: He came out with six different editions. McDowall, though, wrote about the plight of others in his monthly *McDowall's Journal*. One of his subjects: an unmarried eighteen-year-old mother cast out by her family. McDowall found an older woman who took in the young woman and her baby. He lamented alongside abandoned, pregnant women who thought "it is better for

---

9 Phoebe McDowall, ed., *Memoir and Select Remains of the Late Rev. John P. McDowall* (New York: Leavitt, Lord, 1838), 101. McDowall at street-level did what Alexis de Tocqueville generalized about in his famous *Democracy in America* (book 2, ch. 6) in 1835: Americans "constantly form associations. . . . If it is proposed to inculcate some truth or to foster some feeling by the encouragement of a great example, they form a society."

10 John McDowall, in *Memoir and Select Remains*, 251.

their offspring to die thus early than to be born to an inheritance of shame and poverty."[11]

McDowall was well aware that the New York legislature had just passed a law banning abortion—"severe legislative enactments exist against those who administer drugs to do this wicked work"—but he saw that reducing supply only worked if demand also decreased. Since new suppliers would arise, unborn children would not be saved by laws alone. McDowall particularly praised those who offered challenging, personal, and spiritual help. He found a physician to give medical care to a woman seduced into a brothel: "The doctor eventually takes her into his own family." McDowall and his wife welcomed despairing young women into their home as well.[12]

McDowall mapped out the boundaries of the youth culture and the growth of seduction, prostitution, and abortion that accompanied it. He interviewed young women who acknowledged doing "the criminal deed . . . abortion." McDowall recorded reports by ex-prostitutes "that in some houses of prostitution it is a common practice every three months to use means preventive of progeny. One says she has destroyed five of her own offspring. Another says she has killed three."[13]

McDowall particularly criticized older men like Ammi Rogers who used their prominence or money to attract the young. McDowall described "a case of premature birth, produced, as supposed, by improper means. . . . the mother, a young woman of hitherto unblemished character [who] finally acknowledged that the physician (a married man) who attended her was the father of the child." He noted that some New Yorkers blamed women for abortion, but it's usually men who "offer physicians large sums of money [to fix] the problem."[14]

---

11 John McDowall, *McDowall's Journal*, February 1833, 9; John McDowall, in *Memoir and Select Remains*, 124.
12 *McDowall's Journal*, March 1833, 18; April 1833, 27.
13 *McDowall's Journal*, May 1833, 37. See also *First Annual Report of the New York Magdalen Society* (New York: John T. West, 1831), 23.
14 *McDowall's Journal*, February 1833, 9; May 1833, 36; September 1833, 65.

McDowall complained that ministers rarely preached against sex outside marriage, so "it is not a matter of surprise" that men should call prostitution and abortion necessary evils. He said pastors were "specially charged to lift up their voice" against sin: "Are not the lascivious criminals condemned in the Bible, in plain bold and decisive terms?" McDowall complained that many church attenders didn't care: They go to church "to be seen and heard, to whisper and laugh, to ruffle their books."[15]

McDowall received criticism from such influential men, and from some female church members, who claimed that offering "fallen women" second chances might make others see their fall as not so terrible. McDowall wrote, "We are denounced and condemned as traitors, for . . . visiting lanes, alleys, cellars, garrets, and yards, in New York, to rescue unprotected women from barbarous insult, extreme poverty, starvation, disease, despair, and loathsome death."[16]

But McDowall was a good reporter of fact and friction. He criticized male church members who lived by a double standard: "Saturday night on the town and Sunday morning in church." He described a "Reputably Pious Merchant" who walked a woman home "in a friendly manner" and said he needed to stop by his store for a moment: "He requested her just to step in; she did so, and the door was locked. By persuasions and promises and presents, he effected his base designs." Soon the woman was left "shunned and despised, while her unprincipled seducer still retains his standing."[17]

City leaders attacked McDowall for "defaming New York's good name" by running stories of young women heartlessly played by powerful men. A grand jury called *McDowall's Journal* "a nuisance . . . degrading to the character of our city." Supported by six church groups

15 *Magdalen Facts*, no. 1 (New York: January 1832), 74; Joel Ross, *What I Saw in New York* (Auburn, NY: Derby & Miller, 1852), 259.
16 *Magdalen Facts*, no. 1, 69.
17 *McDowall's Journal*, April 1834, 27. See also Lewis Tappan, *The Life of Arthur Tappan* (New York: Hurd & Houghton, 1870), 196.

that came to his defense, McDowall argued that members of the grand jury and their friends kept mistresses, owned brothels, and wanted to do so without criticism that could drive up rents or drive out customers. One newspaper, the *Christian Advocate*, defended him: "It is indeed mortifying to a virtuous mind to be under the necessity of believing that so much licentiousness exists. But must it be concealed for fear of offending the ears of delicacy?"[18]

McDowall's Journal gained readers among reformers in Massachusetts, Vermont, Rhode Island, Ohio, Virginia, and South Carolina. Newspapers including the *Nashville Republican*, *Rochester Enquirer*, *Baltimore Working Men's Advocate*, and *New Orleans American* kept readers posted on the battle of New York. But advertisers boycotted his journal. McDowall ran out of money and had to stop publishing. Then he came down with typhoid fever. His wife asked, "Are you not afraid to die?" He replied, "Afraid, no. Legions are waiting to conduct me through and Jesus will go with me." He died, and New York's strongest pro-life voice was gone.[19]

---

18 *McDowall's Journal*, April 1834, 32.
19 *McDowall's Journal*, May 1834, 10; June 1834, 13, 14, 16. Sarah Bennett, *Woman's Work among the Lowly* (New York: American Female Guardian Society, 1877), 17: "He prayed fervently for his enemies and expressed only sentiments of forgiveness toward them."

10

Insufficient Protection for Women

THIS FIRST SECTION CONCLUDES with three early-nineteenth-century cases that illuminate the difference between common law and common sense—and also show the early stages of community breakdown that would leave more women and children at risk.

The first criminal abortion case in the newly constituted United States came in Massachusetts, where Isaiah Bangs in 1810 beat up pregnant Lucy Holman and forced her to consume an abortifacient—but it did not kill their unborn child. A jury found Bangs guilty of a series of interrelated offenses: assaulting Holman and "administering to her a certain dangerous and deleterious draught or potion, against her will, with intent to procure the abortion and premature birth of a bastard child, of which she was then pregnant, and which the defendant had before that time begotten of her body."[1]

The jury was murky on which charge was most important. Common sense said Bangs needed to be punished because battering a woman and killing a baby were "against good morals and good manners, an evil example to others in like case to offend."[2] The Massachusetts Supreme Court in 1812, though, overlooked colonial cases from Maryland and

[1] *Commonwealth v. Isaiah Bangs*, October Term, 1812, 9 Mass. 387.
[2] *Commonwealth v. Isaiah Bangs*, October Term, 1812, 9 Mass. 387.

other jurisdictions outside New England and relied more on earlier cases from Old England. The jurors had ignored the old "quickening" distinction and decided a baby was a baby, no matter how small, but the Supreme Court delivered Bangs from large liability because there was no proof that the unborn child had quickened. Second, the Court oddly concluded that Holman, an abused woman, willingly consumed the poison: Banks went free.

A second case, where a jury and a chief justice disagreed, came in Rhode Island in 1832, when Sally Burdick died at the hands of abortionist Frances Leach. His attorneys dragged Burdick's character through the mud, and Dr. Cyrus James exposed her insides to the world: He "found the sides in a gangrene state, very green, the back of florid red . . . the opening was large enough to receive my fist without much resistance."[3]

Reporters and pamphleteers quickly published that description, equivalent to a giant warning sign: DON'T GET AN ABORTION! If some found that description insufficiently gruesome, there was more: Dr. James "found seven perforations or holes all separate; it appeared as though an unskillful hand had attempted to produce an abortion." He was also specific about what he found in Burdick's stomach: "about half a pint of thick dark matter, resembling fetid matter, almost as thick as tar, smell very offensive, probably produced by violent vomitings."

James contrasted that horror with what he found in Burdick's womb: "The finger and toe nails of the child were perfect—child about 12 or 13 inches in length—female child—short hair on the head . . . from 6 to 7 months from gestation." Another doctor, Thomas Carpenter, similarly reported that "the deceased came to her death by inflammation and internal bleeding," but inside her was "a perfect female child."[4]

---

3 Thomas Wilson Dorr, *A Report of the Examination of David Gibbs, Fanny Leach, and Eliza P. Burdick, for the Alleged Murder of Sally Burdick, at Coventry, R.I. on the 18th Feb. 1833* (Hartford, CT: Hanmer & Comstock, 1833), 8, 9.
4 Dorr, *Report of the Examination*, 10, 22.

Leach's lawyers responded with a defense that showed how hard it was to put an abortionist behind bars: "the death was not sufficiently proved to have resulted from the wounds, seven in number; the prisoner was not conclusively shown to have inflicted them." The prosecution could not provide a living witness, so someone other than Leach could have made those holes. Other causes of the fatal contamination could not be ruled out.[5]

Rhode Island was a small state, and this was a big crime, so Chief Justice Samuel Eddy presided over the trial: Apparently appalled by the descriptions, Eddy explained to the jury that murder is an intentional act and manslaughter was an act resulting from a sudden quarrel or done in the heat of passion. Since abortion was intentional and planned out, not something done in passion, the jury could not bring in a verdict of manslaughter: It was murder (a capital crime) or nothing. He pressed the jury to come to a decision, not a compromise.

But jurors were reluctant to impose a death sentence when the evidence was not clear beyond the shadow of a doubt. It returned the compromise verdict against which Chief Justice Eddy had warned: voluntary manslaughter. The sentence was two years' imprisonment and a $1,000 fine. Eddy "expressed his regret," but given the difficulty of proof it was a commonsense verdict. The jail time and narrow escape from death apparently convinced abortionist Leach to stop the killing—and the story made the front pages of newspapers as far away as North Carolina.[6]

The most highly publicized case during the first third of the nineteenth century also came in Rhode Island, just on its side of the border with Massachusetts: A farmer in December 1832 discovered the corpse of Sarah Cornell, an unmarried thirty-year-old millworker, hanging on a stake, with a rope around her neck. Suicide? Maybe, but the placement of the knot on the rope suggested murder, and the corpse of a

---

5   *Niles National Register* (St. Louis), November 30, 1833, 12.
6   *Tarboro* (NC) *Press*, November 8, 1833, 1.

three-month-old unborn child inside the corpse of Cornell, along with bruises on her abdomen, suggested a motive.[7]

Cornell had a troubled family history. Her mother was the daughter of a rich manufacturer who abandoned and disinherited her when she ran away with James Cornell. He deserted his family soon after the birth of Sarah, the youngest of their three daughters. Sarah lived with relatives until she became a tailor's apprentice at age 15. That didn't work out, and at age 19 she became a seasonal weaver and machinist, working with cotton and wool in factories (such as those in Fall River) dependent on water power.[8]

Parents and brothers were the natural protectors of young women, so reporters made a point of quoting several letters from Cornell to her mother showing estrangement from family: "Almost two years have lapsed since I have written a letter. . . . Perhaps you have long since forgotten you have a daughter. . . . nearly six months have again elapsed since I have heard from you." Her loneliness and despondency is evident as she writes that friends are not sending mail either: "Sometimes I think they have lately forgotten me, but I have no reason to complain."[9]

In the thirteen years since leaving her Vermont home, Cornell had worked in nine different mill towns. Dozens of newspaper stories and eight short books recounting her travels and travails emphasized the danger facing young women, especially if (like Cornell) they were "very pretty" and "had the curse of beauty." Catherine Williams, who wrote a popular book on the killing and trial, criticized "that baneful disposition

---

7 Catherine Read Williams, *Fall River, an Authentic Narrative* (Providence, RI: Cranston & Hammond, 1833). Williams glowingly described that New England locale as notable for "the salubrity of its air" and the "charms of its landscape. . . . It requires no great effort of imagination to go back a few years, and imagine the Indian with his light canoe sailing about in these waters, or dodging about among the rocks and trees" (7–8).

8 Judith Barbour, "Letters of the Law: The Trial of E. K. Avery for the Murder of Sarah M. Cornell," *Law, Text, Culture* 2 (1995): 119.

9 Williams, *Fall River*, 124–33. Williams offered sympathy: Had Cornell found a "respectable connexion and decent settlement in life, she would have made a very respectable figure in society" (75).

to rove, to keep moving from place to place, which has been the ruin of so many." Williams saw her work "as a salutary and timely warning to young women in the same situation in life."[10]

Newspaper articles and quickly written books were cautionary tales. They taught that women should be on guard, especially when they gained the admiration of men who liked "amusing themselves at the expense of young women. . . . The young and the beautiful [should] read the warning against the wiles of man." Stories offered "lessons of prudence and caution, which of all other lessons the youthful heart is most apt to revolt at, the youthful mind to forget." Cornell's life as a rolling stone, though, left her "without friends and natural protectors," and a proper outlet for her "affectionate and confiding disposition. . . . Be warned, by the fate of one."[11]

Who was guilty? Cornell had told people that Ephraim Avery, a thirty-three-year-old married Methodist minister, was the father of her baby. Witnesses said Avery had been with Cornell at a Methodist camp meeting that featured numerous sermons but sex on the edges. Prosecutors brought up possibly incriminating evidence. An autopsy revealed vaginal penetration and internal hemorrhage, indicating an attempt at surgical abortion.[12]

Mill owners and agents wanted jurors to find Avery guilty. Fall River business leaders and their counterparts in Lowell, Lawrence, and other New England towns had claimed their facilities were safe for young women. Boardinghouse mothers, curfews, and required attendance at religious services would stand in place of parental supervision. The

---

10 Williams, *Fall River*, 17. See also Ian Pilarczyk, "The Terrible Haystack Murder: The Moral Paradox of Hypocrisy, Prudery, and Piety in Antebellum America," *American Journal of Legal History* 41 (1997): 25–60.
11 Barbour, "Letters of the Law," 131; David Richard Kasserman, *Fall River Outrage: Life, Murder, and Justice in Early Industrial New England* (Philadelphia: University of Pennsylvania Press, 2010), 51–74; Karen Halttunen, *Confidence Men and Painted Women: A Study of Middle-Class Culture in America, 1830–1870* (New Haven, CT: Yale University Press, 1982), 12–13.
12 Barbour, "Letters of the Law," 121, 131.

population of Fall River had jumped in 20 years from 100 to more than 5,000, mostly unmarried females. Many, like Cornell, hopped from job to job. If the environment was not safe for her, it wasn't safe for many others—and if mommas didn't let their babies grow up to be millworkers, the whole New England economy would falter.[13]

On the other hand, if Avery was the culprit . . . well, it was hard to guard against a snake in the grass, a pastor who (as one writer put it) "converted the temple of the most high God into a detestable brothel." Writers passed along gossip that wasn't true: Avery had been a pirate in the Caribbean; he had a previous wife who had died from his abuse; he had broken Cornell's arm. New England was going through an industrial and social revolution that the rest of the country would eventually follow. Thousands were moving from farms to cities. If the jury absolved Avery and implicitly blamed the new economy, all of that progress could be jeopardized.[14]

Mill owners wanted the spotlight just on Avery: "Heaven will reap its vengeful curses on the wretch," one Rhode Island reporter wrote. The rapidly growing Methodist denomination had a different perspective. Methodists said New England's Calvinist churches appealed largely to the mind, with ministers refraining from emotional involvement with congregants—but Methodists were willing to hug, and some young women misinterpreted the intentions of caring pastors like Avery.[15]

After sixteen hours of deliberation, the jury found Avery not guilty. Cornell had confessed "unlawful intercourse with several men," and the jury ended up believing the praying pastor rather than the woman

---

13 Elizabeth A. DeWolfe, "Storytelling, Domestic Space, and Domestic Knowledge in the Murder of Berengera Caswell, *Storytelling: A Critical Journal of Popular Narrative* 6 (Winter 2007): 123: "Mill agents soliciting new workers made great efforts to establish that their facilities presented a safe environment for the daughters of New England farmers."

14 Kasserman, *Fall River Outrage*, 51–74, 130–31; Williams, *Fall River*, 3; Luke Drury, *A Report of the Examination of Rev. Ephraim K. Avery, for the Murder of Sarah Maria Cornell* (self-published, 1833), 55.

15 *Pawtucket Chronicle*, December 28, 1832, quoted in Kasserman, *Fall River Outrage*, 112 and 136.

prosecutors had said was Avery's prey. What the evidence did suggest, in one recent historian's words, was that the "patriarchal family [was losing its] power to shape the lives of its children." Depending on the ideology of the writer, that may appear as a good or bad thing, but it did create a hazardous situation for unborn children.[16]

The small-town supervision of relationships that was common before the 1830s meant that unplanned pregnancies would not go unnoticed by parents and neighbors. As noted in chapters 6 and 7, communities (and courts, if necessary) held "reputed fathers" responsible for their probable progeny. Pregnant women would usually get married. If the men in their lives refused, which was unusual, at least the mothers would receive child support. The deaths of Burdick, Cornell, and their unborn children made headlines because they were unusual—but they were also heralds of a new era in which the rare became common and only spectacular abuses received a second look.

---

16 See Ephraim Avery and Richard Hildreth, *A Report of the Trial of the Rev. Ephraim K. Avery* (Boston: David H. Ela, 1833), which views Cornell as a troubled and unreliable young woman.

SECTION TWO

SPECIALIZATION BEGINS

1838–1878

Chapters 11–20 move from the 1830s to the 1870s, years in which most states passed anti-abortion laws but enforcement was sporadic. Doctors knew more about creatures in the womb but parents did not. Specialized abortion businesses, pro-abortion ideologies, and media inducements grew: So did knowledge of how human lives began.

11

A Fatal Needle

THE FOUNDER OF *USA TODAY*, Al Neuharth, told editors that when they had a photo of a beautiful woman to decorate page one, be sure her chest was visible on the top half of the page: He thought potential buyers viewing a stack of folded newspapers in a vending machine would be more likely to make the purchase. Publications with a similar philosophy in 1839 gave front-page attention to the tragedy of twenty-one-year-old Eliza Sowers, who had "personal charms of more than ordinary attraction."[1]

Sowers worked at a paper mill in Manayunk, eight miles from downtown Philadelphia. In 1838, engaged to marry a local railroad superintendent named Charles Corman, she fell for mill superintendent William Nixon, a handsome married man with two children. In May she left the mill and moved to Nixon's house with the task of helping Mrs. Nixon. She quickly learned that part of her job was "helping" Mr. Nixon as well, and she later told a confidant, "Leaving the mill has been the ruin of me."[2]

By the end of May, Sowers was pregnant. In July she gave Nixon the crisis news. A fellow servant, Hannah Beersley, shared a bed with Sowers at Nixon's house, and Nixon's little girl sometimes slept with

---

1 *Atkinson's Saturday Evening Post*, January 26, 1839, XVIII, 913.
2 *Atkinson's Saturday Evening Post*, 913.

them, three in the bed—not unusual in that era. Beersley heard Sowers weeping through the night and told her she could get a fix from Henry Chauncey, a scholar and Philadelphia "botanical doctor" who offered herbal remedies. Near the end of July, Beersley made for Sowers some pennyroyal tea: The ancient Greeks had identified pennyroyal as an abortifacient.[3]

When the pennyroyal didn't work, either Beersley or Nixon obtained for Sowers bottles of oil of tansy and other substances. Nothing worked, except to make Sowers sick. Next, she tried sitting over a pot of steam, only to scald her feet so badly on August 21 that she had to go home for two weeks. Increasingly depressed as summer became fall, she went back and forth between Nixon's house and her family home but told no one in her family that she was getting desperate.[4]

Sowers needed what today we would call a crisis pregnancy center, a place where she could get informed counseling and practical help on getting through the next few difficult months. Instead, four months into the pregnancy, she talked with Nixon for two hours: He said that when his brother "had a disease on his head, Dr. Chauncey gave him medicine which cured him in a week's time." Neither Beersley nor Nixon had anything to say about Chauncey's surgical skills. When Sowers took a streetcar to Chauncey's office in Philadelphia on October 3, she was still hoping for a pharmaceutical cure.[5]

---

3 Anonymous, *The Life of Eliza Sowers, Together with a Full Account of the Trials of Dr. Henry Chauncey, Dr. William Armstrong, and William Nixon for the Murder of That Unfortunate Victim of Illicit Love: Containing the Examination of Witnesses, Verdict, &c. &c. at the Court of Oyer and Terminer, January Session, 1839* (Philadelphia: P. Augustus Sage, 1839), 1, 27; John M. Riddle, *Eve's Herbs: A History of Contraception and Abortion in the West* (Cambridge, MA: Harvard University Press, 1997), 46–47; Sarah Cousins, "Abortion in the 19th Century," *National Museum of Civil War Medicine*, February 9, 2016. Aristophanes, in his play *Lysistrata*, describes a beautiful pregnant woman "trimmed and spruced with pennyroyal."

4 Anonymous, *Life of Eliza Sowers*, 27–28; and "History of Abortion" at Biounity.com. Some Jewish immigrants to America became known for trying to bring on an abortion in that way. An eighth-century Sanskrit text instructs women wishing to induce an abortion to sit over a pot of steam.

5 "Report of the Trial of Henry Chauncey for Murder," *The* (Philadelphia) *Medical Examiner* 2, no. 5 (February 2, 1839): 72; Anonymous, *Life of Eliza Sowers*, 10.

With Nixon paying, Chauncey gave Sowers more abortifacients—ergot and savin—and took her to a cheap boarding house. Chauncey told Sowers she'd be better in five days. He told the proprietor, Mary Kingsley, that Sowers had a bowel problem and would stay for three or four days. The next morning, though, Sowers told Kingsley, "I won't take any more of that doctor's medicine: It will kill me."[6]

Sowers became worse, and Chauncey returned to the boarding house. Kingsley eventually testified about what came next: "He told her to get up, and sit on the edge of the bed; he told her to sit out as far as she could. He told her to lean on me. He did to her what doctors do to women when they are confined." Sowers screamed. Kingsley recalled that Chauncey then "washed his hands. He picked up something off the washstand, which shined and looked like a knitting needle, and wiped it." Chauncey poked, Sowers screamed some more, and Kingsley "put her to bed."[7]

Chauncey was way beyond his knowledge of medicine. It isn't clear whether he even washed his hands before his initial probe of Sowers, but it's highly unlikely that he proceeded antiseptically, since germ theory and the consequent need for utter cleanliness was not understood until later in the nineteenth century. The next day, Sowers hemorrhaged. Chauncey returned in the evening, saying "he had not gotten the placenta" and that Sowers "was the most difficult person he had ever operated on."[8]

Chauncey was already blame-shifting and planning a coverup. Kingsley testified that he wouldn't let her see the aborted baby, and "said I must not tell any of the neighbors that she had been confined." Sowers remained at the boarding house for a week "in a good deal of pain. . . . She wanted to see her mother." She asked regarding Nixon, "Why don't William come?" After several more days of agony for Sowers and panic for Chauncey, he took her away in a carriage: "Said he was going to take her home."[9]

But Chauncey did not. Instead, he took her to another boarding house, run by Elizabeth Hubbard, who had little confidence in him.

---

6 "Report of the Trial," 73.
7 "Report of the Trial," 73.
8 "Report of the Trial," 73.
9 *Atkinson's Saturday Evening Post*, January 26, 1839, 914.

The next morning, when Sowers asked if another doctor could examine her, Hubbard summoned Dr. James Rush, a son of Declaration of Independence signer (and pro-life doctor) Benjamin Rush. James Rush saw that Sowers was dying. He later described her "wild, staring eye, great restlessness . . . and difficult respiration; sighing, moaning, and exclamations of agony; her abdomen was very much swollen, and hard and tender to the touch; her extremities cold."[10]

On October 13, ten days after her arrival at Chauncey's office, Sowers died. Rush told Chauncey, "This will be a serious matter, doctor." When Chauncey replied, "There's nothing herein that will criminate me," Rush said, "This may undergo a judicial Investigation. If it does I shall feel called upon to tell all I know."[11]

Chauncey obtained from a compliant official a death certificate giving the cause of death as abdominal pain rather than abortion. He had Sowers quickly buried and then sent her family an elaborate fictional account regarding a complaint about bowels, medicine that cured it, the patient visiting friends and then shopping for wood stoves, then staying in Philadelphia because it was raining.[12]

Isaac Sowers, Eliza's older brother, did not accept that tale. Mary Kingsley, the rooming house proprietor, disregarded Chauncey's command not to talk with neighbors. Chauncey, making light of the rumors of pregnancy, considered himself safe after several days: "She'd been buried so long, that, with inflammation and mortification, her insides were so much decayed, they could make nothing out of it." His backup, if officials did catch him in a lie: "He had done this to save her character."[13]

---

10 Dorothy Schullian, "Notes and Events," *Journal of the History of Medicine and Allied Sciences* 19 (October 1964): 419: James Rush was "able, intelligent, and accomplished," one medical journal editor observed, but also "peevish and prickly." Those characteristics stopped Chauncey's cover-up and turned a Philadelphia story into a national event.
11 Anonymous, *Life of Eliza Sowers*, 25.
12 Anonymous, *Life of Eliza Sowers*, 23–24.
13 Anonymous, *Life of Eliza Sowers*, 19–21.

But Chauncey wasn't safe. Officials disinterred Sowers's body a week after her death. Physician W. M. Egbert said Sowers had undergone "abortion by external mechanical violence . . . the greater part of the internal surface of the uterus exhibited a bluish black appearance, similar to that of gangrene in the first stage of mortification." (This paralleled the post-mortem look at Sarah Cornell several years earlier.) Cause of death was peritoneal inflammation, the natural consequence of a laceration Egbert spotted.[14] Today, prompt intravenous antibiotics would have helped. Then, surgery to remove infected tissue would have helped, but also probably would have produced more infection.

Once the inexperienced Chauncey picked up a sharp implement, Sowers was a dead woman. At the trial, his lawyers brought forward witnesses to challenge Kingsley's testimony regarding "the knitting needle," but the laceration was hard evidence. Once James Rush, with his reputation for honesty, refused to whitewash a fellow physician, Chauncey was on his way to a conviction.

Rush testified he had told Chauncey, "If you are an innocent man—act as if you were one. Go and inform the family of everything you know about—of every and any thing. . . . You will have to tell sometime. You had better go even now and tell them." Chauncey did not. The jury found him guilty. The judge sentenced him to prison for five years.[15]

Journalists covered the Sowers story as melodrama. She became the subject of quickly produced books like *The Life of Eliza Sowers*, which called her "the beautiful, innocent, and unfortunate victim of a fatal passion." Readers could learn that "grief appeared to take possession of her soul, the gay dreams of life vanished from her sight—the society of her friends appeared to be painful—employment brought her no relief—the days seemed to her to pass gloomily. . . . The dreadfulness

---

14 "Report of the Trial," 74–76, 78. Official cause of death: an infection "resulting from a laceration of the uterus caused by an instrumental abortion."
15 "Report of the Trial," 75.

of her situation became to her every day more and more apparent, and she felt herself a miserable desolate outcast."[16]

That became the formula for publishing success. Two years later another twenty-one-year-old, "beautiful cigar girl" Mary Rogers, became another highly publicized victim. Her good looks had attracted into a Manhattan cigar shop customers who looked, lingered, purchased smokes, and sometimes published poems about her starry eyes and heavenly smile. In July 1841, she disappeared. Three days later passersby spotted her corpse in the Hudson River.[17]

For months the story was a murder mystery, with newspapers speculating about individual suspects and gang violence. In 1842 a witness claimed Rogers was an abortion victim. A new newspaper started by Horace Greeley, the *New York Tribune*, pushed that theory and claimed, "Thus has this fearful mystery, which has struck fear and terror in so many hearts, been at last explained away."[18]

That theory explained wrinkles in the story such as a reported comment by the mother of Mary Rogers that she never expected to see her daughter again. Mary was supposedly visiting a nearby aunt, but the mother supposedly knew that an abortion was coming. Edgar Allen Poe transposed the Rogers tragedy to Paris and published a 20,000-word novella, *The Mystery of Marie Roget*.[19]

Eliza Sowers, like Sarah Grosvenor in Connecticut a century before, relied on a general practitioner without much experience in abortion. Mary Rogers may have done the same. A question lingered in both New York and Philadelphia, two of the four largest U.S. cities in 1840:[20] When the men in their lives proved irresponsible, and parents were either unknowledgeable or unaware, did Eliza Sowers or Mary Rogers

---

16 Anonymous, *Life of Eliza Sowers*, 1.
17 Daniel Stashower, *The Beautiful Cigar Girl* (New York: Dutton, 2006), 16–30, 52–59, 77–79.
18 Stashower, *Beautiful Cigar Girl*, 215.
19 Stashower, *Beautiful Cigar Girl*, 209–23, 250–51, 289–91. See also Amy Srebnick, *The Mysterious Death of Mary Rogers* (New York: Oxford University Press, 1995).
20 Baltimore was second in population, New Orleans third.

have alternatives? How much did they know about the creature stirring inside them, and when did they know it? Or, if they were determined to abort, how would they find someone who would not be guessing about abortifacient dosages or using tools better suited to knitting or dentistry than to surgery?

The age of specialization was coming.

12

The Welfare of Two Patients

IN 1818 HUGH HODGE, a graduate of Princeton College and the University of Pennsylvania School of Medicine, sailed from New York on a merchant ship, the *Julius Caesar*, looking for adventure.

Hodge's job: ship surgeon on a voyage to India and back. At first he found the day-to-day changes on the ship enthralling: "now sailing pleasantly and with delightful breezes," and the next day "strained in every timber by a violent tempest." The sailing ship did not proceed on a timetable: "hot suns, no winds, calm after calm, for nearly forty days." Moving from the Atlantic to the Indian Ocean, the ship rolled, dipped, rose, fell. Fierce wind made "every rope a whistle."[1]

In India Hodge witnessed poverty and a deadly cholera epidemic. He also saw the "burning of a widow with her dead husband" atop a funeral pyre: She did not resist when the fire was lit, and he hoped she suffocated from smoke before feeling the flames.

Hodge saw the effect of religious belief on life and death. He almost died when the ship nearly sank on the way back to America. After a

---

1 Hugh Hodge, *Memoranda of Family History* (Philadelphia: privately printed, 1903), 43. During his last years, with diminished vision, he dictated that history "upon the earnest solicitation of his daughter, Harriet Woolsey Hodge," and looked back upon "many anxieties and labors" while emphasizing "years of usefulness to the profession, and also to the public."

year, he was home but no longer seeking a placid existence doctoring the wealthy. He became a doctor in the poorest part of Philadelphia and once again almost died, this time from typhoid.[2]

For most of the 1820s Hodge served as doctor of the Philadelphia Almshouse Hospital, where sometimes all went well and at other times typhus raged: "Few escaped the poison.... The mortality in the house was great." He married, became a father in 1829, and survived another serious illness in 1830. He recovered and joined the Second Presbyterian Church, a legacy of the teaching of George Whitefield almost a century before. Hodge and his wife had seven children, but the firstborn, "active, cheerful, intelligent," suffered in his ninth year a "perforation of the bowel" and suddenly died.[3]

In the 1830s Hodge built a private practice, with 1832 "rendered memorable by the invasion of cholera." Hodge in his memoir only slightly mentioned the epidemic, but city officials gave him a vote of thanks and a silver pitcher "as a more lasting memento of their respect." Leaders at the University of Pennsylvania were also impressed: They made him Professor of Obstetrics and the Diseases of Women and Children, a post at which he remained until retirement at age 67 in 1863.[4]

Each fall Hodge presented an introductory lecture on obstetrics. He did not examine abortion in his first four lectures, from 1835 to 1838, but in 1839 the Eliza Sowers tragedy was a major topic in Philadelphia drawing rooms and classrooms. Hodge spoke up, and a memoir writer thirty-five years later remembered that "the bold and uncompromising stand which he took against criminal abortion made a deep impression upon his students."[5]

Hodge began by noting that obstetrics differs from other fields of medicine because "the welfare of two individuals is involved." The un-

---

2 Hodge, *Memoranda of Family History*, 44, 53.
3 Hodge, *Memoranda of Family History*, 62, 64, 68, 71, 72, 87–88, 91, 93.
4 Hodge, *Memoranda of Family History*, 83–84.
5 William Goodell, *Biographical Memoir of Hugh L. Hodge* (Philadelphia: Collins, 1874), 13.

born child "from the moment of its conception . . . although retained within the system of its mother [has] an independent existence. . . . It forms its own fluids, and circulates them. . . . It daily gains strength and grows."[6]

Hodge did not see quickening as the dividing point: "What, it may be asked, have the sensations of the mother to do with the vitality of the child? Is it not alive because the mother does not feel it? Every practitioner of Obstetrics can bear witness that the child lives and moves and thrives long before the mother is conscious of its existence."[7]

Hodge emphasized pre-birth and post-birth continuity: "The child unborn absorbs nourishment from its parent through the medium of the uterus. After birth, it imbibes the materials for nutrition by means of the mammae, or breasts. There is essentially no difference in its physiological properties, or as to the independent character of its existence."[8]

Hodge's lecture, quickly published with the title *Foeticide*, drew attention to the endangered unborn child, not just the endangered mother: "There can be no reasonable doubt that human existence . . . commences not with the birth of the foetus and the first inspiration, but at conception." Knowing that, physicians "must be regarded as the guardians of the rights of infants."[9]

Hodge left biblical exegesis to his younger brother, Reformed theologian Charles Hodge, but expressed his belief in life before birth and after death: "The existence commenced in the ovary of a woman, mysterious and wonderful as it may be, is but the commencement of a series of changes, each more wonderful and glorious than its predecessor,

---

6 Hugh Hodge, *Foeticide, or Criminal Abortion: A Lecture Introductory to the Course on Obstetrics and Diseases of Women and Children. University of Pennsylvania, Session 1839–40* (Philadelphia: Lindsay & Blakiston, 1869), 12, 15.
7 Hodge, *Foeticide, or Criminal Abortion*, 21. Hodge saw quickening as a scientifically useless consideration, arguing that at conception "not only physical existence, but intellectual, moral, and spiritual existence commences" (16).
8 Hodge, *Foeticide, or Criminal Abortion*, 22.
9 Hodge, *Foeticide, or Criminal Abortion*, 17, 28–29, 35.

to which the *same identical human being* will be subjected, even for eternity." Death is not the end but the time "when changes will be effected infinitely greater and more mysterious than occur at conception and during gestation."[10]

Here's an example of how a biblical worldview—double-transition, womb to walking-on-earth, and tomb to walking-in-heaven—underlay a concern with abortion. Other doctors concentrated on the human beings in front of them and disregarded the pre-birth or after-death beings not seen. Some opposed abortion out of concern for mothers rather than concern for both mothers and unborn children.[11]

Hodge's two-patient emphasis differed from that of a rival, Alexander Draper, a member of the Medical and Chirurgical (the old word for surgical) Faculty of the State of Maryland. They had competed for the University of Pennsylvania professorship; Hodge won. As Hodge gave his lecture on foeticide, Draper published a book, *Observations on Abortion . . . Together with Advice to Females*. Three of its forty-one pages described fetal anatomy, but most of the book was a how-to: Draper emphasized the difficulty of abortion with an implicit message that if a woman chose to endanger herself, she should place herself in the hands of an experienced doctor.[12]

Draper listed the most popular abortifacients: "The oil of tansy is a powerful stimulant . . . but it is attended with great danger—as inflammation, mortification, and death may result." He had similar

---

10 Hodge, *Foeticide, or Criminal Abortion*, 30.
11 Hodge died in 1873 at age 77. See R. A. F. Penrose, *Commemorative of the Life and Character of Hugh L. Hodge* (Philadelphia: Collins, 1873), 26: "His faith in the simple fundamental principles of the Christian religion was as firmly fixed as his conviction of the truth of a demonstrated problem in mathematics."
12 Anonymous, *The Life of Eliza Sowers*, 34 (for full reference, see ch. 11, note 3). Membership in the Maryland Faculty, created by the Maryland General Assembly in 1798, became a seal of approval for itinerant medical lecturers. Draper had testified at the trial following the death of Eliza Sowers, defending Dr. Chauncey and calling him "a good Classical, Latin and Greek scholar"—as if a knowledge of ancient languages would improve the odds of having an abortion that would kill one but not two patients.

reservations about pennyroyal and savin but praised ergot, since it could "exercise a direct and specific action over the womb. . . . Ergot in a large proportion of cases produced [abortion. It is] the only article which appears to act in a special manner on the uterus, without at the same time, causing a general perturbation of the system."[13]

Draper said he believed that after women "have carefully perused these pages, they will be cautious how they attempt to procure abortion. . . . Medicine taken to produce that effect must be regarded as an experiment of danger." Dosage was crucial: Sometimes, one ounce of tansy killed the unborn child but two killed the mother as well. Readers could infer that they should pay for both the ergot and the experience of a licensed physician, since amateurs might not realize that the power of a substance like ergot (a fungus that grows on rye) could vary from season to season.[14]

Draper's preference for ergot received backing from a medical journal article by male midwife Thomas Wardleworth. He explained that ergot in large doses was overkill, but "I give small doses of the drug, say from two to three grains every three or four hours," and "the ergot manifests its wonderful powers over the functions of the uterus." Wardleworth added triumphantly, "if the patient be of a low or phlegmatic temperament [and] the uterine action becomes again suspended," the medical expert should give "half a dram to two scruples of the ergot . . . to arouse the uterus to complete its purpose in the animal economy."[15]

---

13 Alexander Draper, *Observations on Abortion . . . Together with Advice to Females* (Philadelphia: self-published, 1839), 17–22.
14 Draper, *Observations on Abortion*, 3–5, 23, 41. Draper was careful to put on the record his dislike for "the degeneracy of the times" that led men to push women into danger. He wrote, "All appear to be more or less contaminated by the polluting doctrines of the day," and blamed "the facilities which are afforded in all our large cities for seduction, and its consequent frequent occurrence, both by single as well as married men." He said it was hard for women to say no "in the moment of excitement—alone with her lover—safe from interruption."
15 "Effects of Ergot in Producing Abortion," *Provincial Medical and Surgical Journal* 8 (May 8, 1844): 78–79. These were small measures: three drams made a scruple, eight scruples added up to an ounce.

Draper, Wardleworth, and mid-century medical textbook author Amos Dean stressed that a surgical abortion is a violent intrusion "for the purpose of rupturing the membranes": The result could be a mother's life "either sacrificed or greatly endangered." One slip, and an often-fatal laceration would result. Do everything accurately and a septic infection, usually fatal to the mother in pre-penicillin days, would still often result. Unlike Hodge, who emphasized that an abortion involved two patients, Draper and others focused on the larger one.[16]

When the only issue is women's health, "safe" abortionists can be heroines, as in a well-written recent novel, *My Notorious Life*. Author Kate Manning gives a blow-by-blow description of her nineteenth-century heroine doing a first-trimester abortion: "Pass the two fingers of the left hand within [to] enlarge the portal. With the right hand you will pass along the instrument . . . through the opening you will push but not forcefully, and maneuver the instrument upward around a bend. . . . Whatever you do don't go back straight or use a sharp probe. If you do you will perforate the woman and she will die. . . . The walls are firm but delicate. You will scrape gently two or three times. . . . Like cleaning the guts of a pumpkin."[17]

But in Hugh Hodge's understanding, an abortionist who pretended to be cleaning the guts of a pumpkin was both self-deluded and deluding others. The road to a surgical abortion was often step-by-step: powders, then pills, then a visit to an abortionist to take under supervision a more powerful drug, and only then "the use of mechanical means." Abortionists took small steps to groom young women, as sexual predators do today. It was hard to know whom to trust. How could women willing to risk their lives maximize their survival prospects?

---

16 Amos Dean, *Principles of Medical Jurisprudence* (Albany, NY: Gould, Banks, 1850), 136.
17 Kate Manning, *My Notorious Life* (New York: Scribner, 2013), 225.

13

Madame Restell

A SHORT BOOK PUBLISHED in 1847 reported a conversation between a doctor and a young woman seeking an abortion. He insisted on parental notification, saying, "I fear to commit a crime . . . to destroy a human being, whose existence has now begun." The doctor then learned that the mother wanted her daughter to abort so as to save herself from "disgrace . . . and society from a bad example." He asked how they would choose an abortionist. The young woman picked up a copy of the *New York Herald* and pointed to an ad.[1]

That was a big change from Philadelphia nine years earlier, when abortion-seeking Eliza Sowers went to a general practitioner who apparently had little abortion experience but, according to a character witness, knew Greek and Latin. The ad was for America's most famous abortion entrepreneur ever, Madame Restell.

Her story begins with the brutal murder in 1836 of Helen Jewett, a young woman who had transitioned from teenaged servant in Maine to fashionable prostitute in Manhattan—until someone murdered her with a hatchet. The lead suspect was clerk Richard Robinson, one of Jewett's regular customers. A recent start-up, the *New York Herald*,

---

1 Anonymous, *Madame Restell, With an Account of Her Professional Career, and Secret Practices* (New York: Charles, 1847), 10, 14.

became the most popular, profitable, and powerful newspaper in the United States by covering the murder and trial the way a sensational cable news network would today.[2]

Helen Jewett's story resonated because her short career in prostitution was not unusual except in its ending. Robinson's defense was also typical: "I was an unprotected boy without female friends to introduce me to respectable society, sent into a boarding house, where I could enter at what hour I pleased—subservient to no control after the business of the day was over." Early in the nineteenth century, clerks often lived with their employers and saw them as second fathers. By the 1840s they typically lived in boarding houses with other clerks and without any parental supervision. Had the jury found Robinson guilty, it would also be condemning the new New York City. The jury found him not guilty.[3]

Herald printer Charles Lohman saw how the coverage of Jewett made *Herald* sales leap. Among the new readers were young women and men who might be seeking a relatively safe abortion. Lohman urged his new wife, twenty-five-year-old Anna, to learn about drugs and potions from a doctor who lived next door. Until the Lohmans came along, the *Herald* and its main competitor, the *New York Sun*, were largely running small, whispering ads for abortion, but Charles Lohman saw an opportunity to sell a product and an idea to tens of thousands. Anna Lohman adopted the trade name Madame Restell, for Americans considered the French to be the most up-to-date in anything related to sex.[4]

The Lohmans wrote ads thinly veiled in two ways. Instead of pointing to their major customer demographic, those involved in extramarital sex, they spoke of a woman's love for her "hard-working" husband who—if she kept having children—would be "tugging at the oar of incessant labor, toiling but to live and living but to toil." Instead of

---

2   For the *Herald*'s ascent, see James Crouthamel, *Bennett's New York Herald and the Rise of the Popular Press* (Syracuse, NY: Syracuse University Press, 1989).
3   Timothy Gilfoyle, *City of Eros: New York City, Prostitution, and the Commercialization of Sex, 1790–1920* (New York: Norton, 1992), 97.
4   Mitchell Stephens, *A History of News* (New York: Viking, 1988), 202–5.

using the word "abortion," the ads referred to "an attempt to remove female blockages" or "a cure for stoppage of the menses."[5]

Those expressions were accurate in one sense, because pregnancy *is* the leading cause of menstrual stoppage among women of childbearing age. The abortifacients were purportedly "female monthly regulating pills," with the pretense that the only goal was regulation of the monthly cycle. Restell ads were like our modern advertorials or storytelling infomercials. They showed editorial-like concern for wives dying in childbirth or from overwork, leaving "young and helpless children" without "those endearing attentions and watchful solicitudes, which a mother alone can bestow." The pills would stop the "melancholy of mind and depression of Spirits that make existence itself but a prolongation of suffering and wretchedness, and which alas! not infrequently dooms the unhappy victim to the perpetration of suicide."[6]

The Lohmans functioned like journalists, selling not just a product but a worldview. In connection with that pretense, and to reduce criticism from those opposed to publicizing abortion, Restell's ads specified that her pills "must not be taken when * * * * * * * *." Even in those days before *Wheel of Fortune*, "every schoolgirl" in New York—according to one doctor—knew the asterisks were placeholders for "pregnant." Pills worked for "suppression," "irregularity," or "stoppage of the menses." Pregnancies that continued after pill use were "Obdurate," "obstinate," or "persistent" cases that might require a desperate surgical visit to Madame Restell, who could "be consulted with the strictest confidence on complaints incident to the female frame."[7]

---

5 *New York Herald*, March 6, 1840, 1; April 13, 1840, 8; August 26,1841, 3; Marvin Olasky, *The Press and Abortion, 1838–1988* (Hillsdale, NJ: L. Erlbaum, 1988), 3–13. See also Michael Schudson, *Discovering the News* (New York: Basic Books, 1978),18; E. S. Turner, *The Shocking History of Advertising* (New York: E. P. Dutton, 1953), 135; and Frederic Hudson, *Journalism in the United States, from 1690 to 1872* (New York: Harper & Brothers, 1872), 286.

6 *New York Sun*, September 27, 1840, 4; *New York Herald*, November 3, 1839, 4; February 15, 1842, 4; September 22, 1843, 4; January 17, 1845, 4.

7 *New York Sun*, May 9 and 18, June 12, August 17, September 11, all 1839 and p. 4; Ely van de Warker, "The Criminal Use of Proprietary Advertised Nostrums," *New York Medical Journal*,

The asterisks and euphemisms showed abortion was not socially accepted, but it leaped the minimal hurdle: Police and prosecutors could overlook offenses (often taking bribes) without getting fired. Had Madame Restell's surgery regularly killed women, police would have had to act, but she evidently had the "touch," unlike Dr. Chauncey in Philadelphia, and avoided lacerating her adult patients.

Profits for the Lohmans soared. "Restellism" became a common descriptor for pro-abortion ideology and practice. When smaller competitors tried to gain pieces of the action, the Lohmans called them dangerous fakes. The Lohmans created seven outlets in New York City and Newark that sold boxes of pills with quality guaranteed by Madame Restell's signature. The Lohmans established branch offices in Boston, Providence, and Philadelphia.[8]

New York and Connecticut had anti-abortion laws, and other states would soon add theirs, but they were rarely enforced. The *Herald* even reported that "The office of the pretty Madame Restell is crowded every day, morning and night, by young damsels in distress. . . . Madame Restell has increased her issues of paper, recipes, prescriptions, discounts, &c. to a large extent; and as a natural consequence, the portion of the community dependent on her for assistance, have been greatly relieved from the pressure of their sufferings."[9]

The warnings implicit in coverage of the Sowers and Rogers tragedies were intermittent. Advertisements for purportedly safe abortifacients

---

January 1873, 23–25; New York *Herald*, March 6, 1840, 1; August 26, 1841, 3; September 22, 1843, 4; December 13, 1843, 4; April 13, 1844, 4; January 11, 1845, 4; *New York Sun*, October 21, 1841, 4; February 24, 1842, 4; August 6, 1842, 4; *New York Herald*, July 15, November 26, and December 3, 1841, 4; September 22, 1843, 4; January 26, 1845, 4.

8 Other doctors also used euphemisms. Dr. Bell promised to cure "irregularity of females," Dr. Ward treated "suppression, irregularity, and female obstructions," and Dr. Vandenburgh contended that his "Female Regeneracy Pills" were "an effectual remedy for suppression, irregularity, and all cases where nature has stopped from any cause whatsoever" (*New York Herald*, January 6, February 25, and August 21, 1841, all 4; *New York Sun*, September 14, 1840, 4).

9 *New York Herald*, November 2, 1839, 2. See also Charles Meigs, *The Philadelphia Practice of Midwifery* (Philadelphia: James Kay, 1842), 134.

were daily. Newspapers that profited from abortion ads also profited from sensational stories that would increase street sales. They did not create dedicated abortion beats to track the unpublicized small deaths and remind newspaper readers about tiny victims. Sometimes publicists even put out stories of young women who not only survived but thrived: "Her constitution recovers from the shock, she pursues her round of gayeties and pleasures."[10]

Gayeties and pleasures: New York and other large cities starting in the 1830s had the first youth culture in American history. Although Pomfret, Connecticut, was an exception, in "eighteenth-century American society . . . crude housing, crowded sleeping arrangements, and the watchful eyes of family and church members were unlikely to foster sexual experimentation." In the nineteenth century, however, big cities with their rooming houses, brothels, saloons, "concert halls," and theater "third tiers" (the upper reaches, taken over by prostitutes), were a strange new world.[11]

Once pregnant, young New York women needed a crisis pregnancy center, not tut-tutting. Young New York men needed personal accountability, but what they often got were advice books like *Lectures to Young Men*, a best-selling collection of advice from Hartford pastor Joel Hawes. Hawes's table of contents shows his direction: "Early Rising and Rest—He Who Would Rise Early, Must Retire Early. . . . On Forming Temperate Habits—Drunkenness and Gluttony. Indulgences Very Expensive. . . . On Lotteries, the Worst Species of Gaming. They Are a Species of Swindling."[12]

That book by Hawes showed some self-awareness: "Most persons, as they grow old, forget that they have ever been young themselves. This

---

10 Anonymous, *Madame Restell*, 10, 14.
11 Gilfoyle, *City of Eros*, 26; Claudia Johnson, "That Guilty Third Tier: Prostitution in Nineteenth-Century American Theaters," in Daniel Howe, ed., *Victorian America* (Philadelphia: University of Pennsylvania Press, 1976), 111–20.
12 Joel Hawes, *Lectures to Young Men on the Formation of Character* (Hartford, CT: W. J. Hamersley, 1851, 9–18, 41; repr., San Francisco: Palala, 2015).

greatly disqualifies them for social enjoyment." Nevertheless, Hawes counseled the young "to draw forth from the old the treasures of which I have been speaking. Let them even make some sacrifice of that buoyant feeling which, at their age, is so apt to predominate. Let them conform, for the time, in some measure, to the gravity of the aged, in order to gain their favor, and secure their friendship and confidence."[13]

Blah, blah, hems and Hawes. He wanted to do what Pittsburgh Pirates pitching coach Ray Miller gave as his task in 1993: "put old heads on young bodies." But that required the challenging and personal counseling that few gave or received. Instead, many young people in New York took guidance from "the flash press," four weeklies that included sexually oriented articles plus "pictorial representations calculated to excite the imaginations and passions of the young." One opined that "man is endowed by nature with passions that must be gratified," so sexually available women are "as necessary as bread or water."[14]

One result was an enormous expansion of prostitution. William Sanger, a public health doctor who surveyed prostitution at mid-century in New York City, Buffalo, Louisville, Newark, New Haven, Norfolk, Philadelphia, Pittsburgh, and Savannah, concluded that there were about sixty thousand prostitutes nationwide. Sanger (no relation to twentieth-century birth controller Margaret) surveyed two thousand

---

13 Hawes, *Lectures to Young Men*, 28–32, 88, 272–73. He gave good advice on how to select a newspaper to read: "Do not take a paper which dwells on nothing but the details of human depravity. It will indeed, for a time, call forth a sensibility to the woes of mankind; but the final result will probably be a stupidity and insensibility to human suffering which you would give much to remove. Avoid those papers which, awed by the cry for short and light articles, have rendered their pages mere columns of insulated facts or useless scraps, or what is still worse, of unnatural and sickening love stories. Lastly, do not take a paper which sneers at religion."

14 Patricia Cline Cohen, Timothy Gilfoyle, and Helen Lefkowitz Horowitz, *The Flash Press: Sporting Male Weeklies in 1840s New York* (Chicago: University of Chicago Press, 2008), 17–22. One newssheet popular among men in their 20s and 30s, the *New York Sporting Whip*, editorialized against madams enticing 9 to 13-year-old girls into prostitution, then listed the girls' names and the addresses where they could be found. The age of consent in New York was 10. Social historians have shown that most nineteenth-century working-class young women did not menstruate until they were about 15, so young prostitutes often earned the most money for brothel-owners: They were less likely to have venereal diseases and less likely to become pregnant.

prostitutes who received medical help at New York's main public hospital: He found that "one of the most deplorable results of prostitution was the sacrifice of infant life." One guidebook to Manhattan, *Sunshine and Shadow in New York*, noted that many prostitutes die "by the hand of the criminal practitioner."[15]

In Paris, where regulated prostitution was legal, the leading public health researcher of the 1820s and 1830s, Dr. Alexandre Jean-Baptiste Parent-Duchatelet, concluded, "If these prostitutes rarely bring their pregnancies to term, it is because they almost always abort them, whether these abortions take place through criminal acts or whether they can be attributed to the exercise of their occupation." We have no solid U.S. statistics, but New York detective John Warren linked prostitution and "the business of the abortionist" as he complained that abortionists "flourish and grow rich from prostitution as a source of income."[16]

---

15 William Sanger, *The History of Prostitution* (New York: Harper Brothers, 1858), 482, 586; Matthew Hale Smith, *Sunshine and Shadow in New York* (Hartford, CT: J. B. Burr, 1868), 378–79. See also William Acton, *Prostitution, Considered in Its Moral, Social, and Sanitary Aspects* (London: J. Churchill, 1857), 206.

16 Alexandre-Jean-Baptiste Parent-Duchatalet, *De la prostitution dans la ville de Paris* (Paris: Balliere, 1837), 232; John H. Warren, Jr., *Thirty Years' Battle with Crime* (Poughkeepsie, NY: A. J. White, 1874), 37–38. Three decades ago, I went through all the source material I could find deep inside the Library of Congress and estimated that prostitutes between 1830 and 1860 averaged 1.8 abortions per year. That was one reason the life expectancy of New York prostitutes was four years. Prostitutes with low self-esteem took huge risks more readily, since many felt they had little to live for—and some had no choice. A prostitute in the second half of her pregnancy sacrificed desirability, so madams and pimps insisted on abortions and scheduled regular abortionist visits to brothels (Olasky, *Abortion Rites: A Social History of Abortion in America* [Wheaton, IL: Crossway, 1992], 50–57).

14

An Unstoppable Force?

SOME NEW YORKERS cared little about the ABCs—fetal anatomy, Bible, community—that kept others from procuring abortion. For them, danger to self was the main impediment to abortion—and Restell's expertise made that barrier inches high rather than unscalable. By 1845, women in elegant carriages lined up outside her office in lower Manhattan, where Restell was open for business from 9 a.m. to 9 p.m. An assistant screened customers and sent some to Restell's study, furnished with anatomical plates, specimens, and other medical displays. The furnishings and exhibits cried out: Not a butcher. Not a quack. An accomplished professional.[1]

Restell had on her side the *New York Herald* and the city's other major newspapers, which benefited greatly from her advertising. *The New York Express*, "never an outstanding newspaper" in the view of one press historian, bravely assessed Restell's power: "Those who are most guilty are bound by their fears to protect her.... Names, and dates, and circumstances are all recorded, and her downfall would shake society to its very centre.... In a word, Madame is a woman of genius, who understands her position and knows how to use its advantages." She

---

1 Clifford Browder, *The Wickedest Woman in New York* (New York: Archon, 1998), 25.

had "in her keeping" the secrets of leading officials, and knew enough to keep quiet as long as she was not bothered. Rumors had her also bribing key members of the police.[2]

On September 13, 1845, though, a new newspaper entered the arena with an editor deemed unprincipled by many but adamant about abortion. George Wilkes filled three of the eight pages of his *National Police Gazette* with ads for patent medicines and other dubious goods and services, but he refused abortion ads at considerable cost to himself. Two months after starting publication he ran an article by Dr. Gunning Bedford that reached well beyond Bedford's earlier attacks in medical journals: Restell, Bedford wrote, was "a monster who speculates with human life with as much cruelness as if she were engaged in a game of chance." He described a Restell abortion in which the aborted baby "kicked several times after it was put into the bowl."[3]

On Valentine's Day in 1846, Wilkes explained why he opposed abortionists so strongly: They are "child destroyers.... Restell still roams at large through the influence of ill-gotten wealth and will probably still continue until public indignation drives her and her associates from our midst." Wilkes stated his hope: "Full expositions of the infamous practices of abortionists will tend to present these human fiends in a true light before the eyes of those who may become their dupes." Wilkes proposed tough action, including police establishment of "a night-and-day watch at the doors of the slaughterhouses of the murderous abortionists of this city."[4]

---

2 Richard Schwarzlose, *The Nation's Newsbrokers*, vol. 2, *The Rush to Institution, from 1865 to 1920* (Evanston, IL: Northwestern University Press, 1990), 89; *New York Express* quoted in *The Louisville Daily Courier*, January 30, 1847, 1; Anonymous, *Madame Restell, With an Account of Her Professional Career, and Secret Practices* (New York: Charles, 1847), 47; Browder, *Wickedest Woman in New York*, 107.

3 *National Police Gazette*, November 15, 1845, 100 (the *Gazette* numbered its pages consecutively, issue after issue). Bedford complained that Restell's "advertisements are to be seen in our daily papers.... She tells publicly what she can do; and without the slightest scruple, urges all to call on her who might be anxious to avoid having children."

4 *National Police Gazette*, February 14, 1846, 205. Some Americans had exchanged handmade valentines early in the nineteenth century, but in the 1840s Esther Howland, the "Mother of the Valentine," began selling mass-produced ones with lace, ribbons, and colorful pictures.

Other newspapers remained silent as long as they saw only one victim, not two, so the *Gazette*, one week after Valentine's Day, hit harder: It said a "day of vengeance" would arrive for Restell and other "fiends who have made a business of professional murder and who have reaped the bloody harvest in quenching the immortal spark in thousands of the unborn." The *Gazette* called "Restell, the murderess paramount in the dark scheme of professional destruction, openly defying decency and the statute, and proclaiming to the world to stifle human life at so much per deed." The *Gazette* did not see abortion as a victimless crime simply because the corpses were small: Restell "might be drowned in the blood of her victims, did each but yield a drop."[5]

Wilkes had a tool: New York's legislature had followed Massachusetts and passed a new law that made it a crime in New York to "administer, prescribe, advise, or procure for any pregnant woman any medicine, drug, or substance for the purpose of causing a miscarriage, or to use any instrument or other means for that purpose."[6] But would the new law be enforced? On February 21, Wilkes was direct: "We call for action from the authorities in relation to this woman. She has been for nearly ten years involved in law, and her money has saved her, as yet."[7]

The next day, a local activist put up flyers across Manhattan castigating police for their "neglect of duty before the face of Heaven," and calling for a demonstration. On February 23, several hundred New Yorkers gathered in front of Restell's house, calling her a "wholesale female strangler," shouting, "Hanging is too good for the monster," and asking, "Where's the thousand children murdered in this house?" They cheered when forty policemen arrived—but instead of arresting Restell, they surrounded her house to protect her, and rumors flew that bribes were more influential than protests.[8]

---

5   *National Police Gazette*, February 21, 1846, 218.
6   Act of May 13, 1845, ch. 260, 1845, *New York Laws*, 285–86.
7   *National Police Gazette*, February 21, 1846, 218.
8   *New York Tribune*, February 24, 1846, 2; *New York Morning News*, February 24, 1.

The New York Herald, flush with abortion advertising, editorialized: "We hope that nothing will be done to endanger the peace of the city." Wilkes, irate, escalated the journalistic pressure: He said police were engaged in "neglect of duty before the face of Heaven," since abortion is "murder... strangling the unborn." Out-of-town newspapers picked up the story and were not so polite: The *New Orleans Times-Picayune* reported on "The Infamous Restell."[9]

In 1847, Charles Lohman published *The Married Woman's Private Medical Companion*. He ignored the effects of abortion on the small patient and claimed that abortion when "undertaken with great care [brought] no danger, especially in the earlier stages of pregnancy."[10] The Lohmans drove up and down Manhattan avenues in a glistening carriage pulled by four fine horses—two bays, a chestnut, and a gray. *The New York Tribune* printed in August a letter noting the parade of illicit wealth and complaining about Restell "driving in such state through our midst," and then published her response: "Can we not drive in public with two or four horses without spiteful comments from a bystander?"[11]

In September 1847, police not on Restell's payroll finally found a woman willing to testify. At the trial, poor, uneducated Maria Bodine gained sympathy with a vivid account of pain: "She hurt me so that I halloed out and gripped hold of her hand; she told me to have patience, and I would call her 'mother' for it." James T. Brady, Restell's expensive lawyer, went all out to find a favorable jury—the *voir dire*

---

9 *New York Herald*, February 24, 1846, 1; *National Police Gazette*, April 25, 1846, 284; *Times-Picayune*, March 10, 1846, 2.
10 Lohman published under the name Dr. A. M. Mauriceau (see Browder, *Wickedest Woman in New York*, 74–75).
11 *The North-Carolinian*, in Fayetteville, North Carolina, commented that Madame Restell had become too well known for her own good: "Before her time no person will deny that abortions were produced, but then it was done in some dark corner of the city and but few knew that such things were done. When this woman undertook to amass wealth by destroying the human race, she proclaimed it from the house tops, and those who were living in comparative ignorance in these matters were for the first time made acquainted with them" (November 27, 1847).

process eliminated 102 jurors—and then to discredit Bodine. Restell faced five counts that could have meant five years in prison, and one for a misdemeanor that would jail her for only one year. Jurors compromised and agreed to the minor charge.[12]

Restell spent a year in the prison on Blackwell's Island in the East River. For a while, it seemed as if community pressure had won out over advertising clout. According to later accounts, however, political connections preserved Restell from any great misery. She put aside the lumpy prison mattress and brought in her own fancy new featherbed, along with her own easy chairs, rockers, and carpeting. Visiting hours changed so that Charles Lohman could visit at will and "remain alone with her as long as suited his or her pleasure," according to Warden Jacob Acker. When Restell left prison in 1848, she proclaimed that the trial and imprisonment were easily worth $100,000 to her in advertising.[13]

As Restell had, at age thirty-five, her "enforced vacation," inexpensive biographies of her appeared. One anonymous work described her as possessing "the beauty of a good complexion, and a full formed English shape. Her figure is of the medium height, and of fine proportions . . . she has a profusion of dark brown hair, which she dresses tastefully; regular, and rather intelligent features; a handsome bust." The author's verdict: "Is she detestable? On the contrary, she is charming; her short sleeve exposes a round, plump arm, that looks remarkably white and enticing." Oh, have we mentioned that she had "a bust of faultless development"?[14]

During Restell's year off, other abortionists tried to grab some of her business by claiming their abortion pills were "never attended with any distressing operation, are always certain, and therefore pregnant

---

12 Browder, *Wickedest Woman in New York*, 75–94; Alan Keller, *Scandalous Lady: The Life and Times of Madame Restell, New York's Most Notorious Abortionist* (New York: Atheneum, 1981), 32–64.
13 Browder, *Wickedest Woman in New York*, 95–102; Keller, *Scandalous Lady*, 65–69.
14 Anonymous, *Madame Restell*, 4, 18.

women should not take them." They used Br'er Rabbit's reverse psychology technique in the tar baby folktale: The wily bunny said, *Don't throw me into that briar patch*, when that's what he wanted, to get the tar off him.[15]

It's possible that some women believed the pills merely destroyed "menstrual blockages," not unborn children, but abortionists including "Dr. Bell," "Dr. Ward," "Dr. Vandenburgh," "Madame Vincent," "Mrs. Bird," "Madame Costello," and others used the doublespeak ads to inform pregnant women that they *should* use the pills when they wanted an abortion. Contemporary observers noted that the "no distress" claims were clearly untrue, in that the point was to distress the unborn child, but as long as people perceived that pills or surgery were fatal to only one human, not two, business grew. When Restell's prison year was up she moved to larger and better offices and was soon spending $20,000 per year on advertising (the equivalent of $600,000 now).[16]

As demand continued, so did supply, and so did a lack of enforcement. An abortionist in the novel *My Notorious Life* gives a true-to-life summary of New York City life: "The police don't bother with the law. . . . They leave us alone. Nobody who comes to me complains. . . . Secondly, who can prove anything? . . . If there's trouble, you just pay a bit here and there and they leave you alone." Later, the protagonist, modeled after Restell, says about New York's anti-abortion law, "So what? . . . How could they prove anything? Certainly it was legal to advertise a Lunar Remedy for Relief of Obstruction, for not all obstructions was due to the Delicate Condition. . . . Officials lived in a world of smoke and pronouncements, rooms full of throat clearings and whiskey breath."[17]

15 For the whole story, see https://americanfolklore.net/folklore/2010/07/brer_rabbit_meets_a_tar_baby.html.
16 For more detail on advertising, see Marvin Olasky, *The Press and Abortion, 1838–1988* (Hillsdale, NJ: Lawrence Erlbaum, 1988), 6–9.
17 Kate Manning, *My Notorious Life* (New York: Scribner, 2013), 151, 155, 209, 258.

In 1853, five years after Restell left prison, New York Mayor Jacob Westervelt performed the wedding ceremony for her daughter. When popular pressure led to a Restell re-arrest in 1856, her political connections were so strong that she was released at once. By the 1860s, 61 percent of ads in the "Medical" column of the *New York Herald* were for abortion. Throughout the 1860s, all the way to 1878, Restell did not even have a whiff of prison.

New York's abortion law raised the bribery cost of doing business for abortionists, but even when an arrest occurred prosecutors were almost always unable to prove guilt to the satisfaction of all twelve jurors.[18] *The New York Herald* emphasized "the insuperable legal difficulties in the way of obtaining a conviction. The professional abortionist is able to command the most eminent legal talent that money can secure to interpose technical objections, which often befog juries and thus lead to a disagreement, which is tantamount to an acquittal."[19]

Across the land, by the late 1850s abortion was common enough to make newspaper stories repetitious. In Massachusetts, Emma Post, 20, and her child were abortion fatalities: A reporter wrote, "Our city was yesterday astounded by the development of another of those hellish acts." In Chicago, an unborn child and an 18-year-old with "the fatal gift of beauty" died, and it seemed like more of the same: "Another of those startling incidents took place yesterday."[20]

A supply-side policy by itself did not do the job as long as demand for abortions continued. The rarity of convictions, however, did not mean laws were useless: In 1857, Wisconsin physician Dr. Henry

---

18   Horatio Storer, *On Criminal Abortion in America* (Philadelphia: Lippincott, 1860); Janet Brodie, *Contraception and Abortion in Nineteenth-Century America* (Ithaca, NY: Cornell University Press, 1994), 254.
19   *New York Herald*, January 27, 1871, 4. See also Michael Grossberg, *Governing the Hearth: Law and the Family in Nineteenth-Century America* (Chapel Hill: University of North Carolina Press, 1985), 166.
20   *Boston Traveler*, June 12, 1857, 1; *Chicago Tribune*, December 7, 1859, 1. See also *New-York Evangelist*, February 21, 1856, 3; *Buffalo Courier*, June 15, 1857, 2; and *Detroit Free Press*, December 9, 1857, 1.

Brisbane wrote concerning abortion, "It is not probable that any law could be enforced, [yet] the existence of a law making it criminal, would probably have a moral influence to prevent it to some extent." But the most-used medical jurisprudence textbook in 1855 was pessimistic about curtailing abortion through legal action: It is "easier to pass laws against abortion than to make them work."[21]

---

21 Henry Brisbane to Horatio Storer, April 6, 1857 (Storer Papers, quoted in James Mohr, *Abortion in America: The Origins and Evolution of National Policy, 1800–1900* [New York: Oxford University Press, 1978], 140); Francis Wharton and Moreton Stille, *Treatise on Medical Jurisprudence* (1855; repr., Arkose Press, 2015), 267–77. See also Francis Wharton's *A Treatise on the Criminal Law of the United States* (Philadelphia: James Kay, Jun. and Brother, 1846; repr., Charleston, SC: Nabu, 2011), section 1220, for a definition of generally understood law in the middle of the nineteenth century: Destruction of any unborn infant is "deemed murder," and legitimizing it before quickening was "neither in accordance with the result of medical experience, nor with the principles of the common law."

15

A Moral Maelstrom

AT CHRISTMAS TIME IN 1849, New England millworker Catherine Louisa Adams died during a surgical abortion. Dr. Moses Clark allegedly cut up her unborn child and picked the pieces out of Adams's uterus. She screamed and then died not from the abortion itself but by suffocation: "The deceased, while undergoing the operation, made outcries, and fearing a discovery, the doctor put a folded cloth over her mouth, and was finally obliged to kill her." The story made headlines even on the Minnesota frontier: "Murder of a Young Girl" and "Horrible Developments."[1]

Newspaper readers could also learn that "Miss Adams, the victim of this most sickening tragedy . . . possessed much personal beauty," but her body was "shockingly mutilated . . . with a cord tied so tightly around her neck as to produce strangulation itself, and with marks of violent blows upon her head." Newspapers described other "inhuman evidences of secret foul practice," as "the foetus of about four or five months, had apparently been dissected with a sharp instrument, and parts of it taken away by piece-meal."[2]

1   *The Minnesota Pioneer*, March 20 and 27, 1850, 1; *Luzerne Union* (Wilkes-Barre, PA), February 20, 1850, 2. See also *The Buffalo Courier*, February 18, 1850, 2; *Sandusky* (OH) *Register*, February 22, 1850, 2; *The Williamsburgh* (Brooklyn) *Daily Gazette*, March 5, 1850, 2; *Buffalo Evening Post*, March 9, 1850, 2; *Baltimore Sun*, March 8, 1850, 1.
2   *Sandusky Register*, February 23, 1850, 2. See also *Boston Evening Transcript*, March 2, 1850, 2; *Enterprise and Vermonter* (Vergennes, VT), 1850, 1; *Vermont Journal*, March 15, 1850, 2; *Milwaukee*

And yet, abortionist Clark went free. One reason: key witness Darius Taylor was also the impregnator, and, as the *New York Tribune* reported, he "was found to contradict himself so much in his testimony as to render it utterly unreliable, and as no part of it was sustained by other evidence, the Court ordered the Jury to find for the prisoners, which they did."³ Such outcomes were common.

Soon, newspapers across America ran another story of disaster. Berengera Caswell, born in 1828, began work at a Lowell, Massachusetts, textile mill in 1848. In 1849 she moved to Manchester, New Hampshire, felt lonely, and became sexually involved with a machinist, William Long. She traveled for an abortion in nearby Maine by James Smith, who knew her only by a code name, Mary Bean. He punctured the amniotic sac, killing the baby, but also left behind in his adult patient a four-inch gash. Then came infection and death. Smith tied Caswell's corpse to a board and slid it into the river—on its way to the Atlantic Ocean, he hoped—but amid snow and ice it got caught in a culvert.⁴

The spring thaw in April 1850 offered newspapers a fresh story: "Excitement in Saco! Dead Body Found . . . Young and Beautiful Female." Newspapers vividly exploited the death of "a woman among the most beautiful of her sex, her character excepted. . . . The body when found was almost in a state of nudity . . . flesh eaten off by rats. . . . the principal part of the nose, the right eye and right ear, the whole mouth and chin gone." Readers learned that, with so much missing, a witness

---

Daily Sentinel, March 2, 2; *Bangor Daily Whig and Courier*, June 29, 2. The *Poughkeepsie Journal*, March 2, 1850, 1, added, "The evidence before the Coroner upon this point we forbear to give. It is too horrible to contemplate." Horace Greeley's *New York Tribune* merely said, "A further examination of the body brought to light practices surpassing in inhuman barbarity [evidence] too horrible to contemplate" (quoted in the *Sandusky Register*, February 23, 1850, 2).

3 *New York Tribune*, June 28, 1850, 6. See also *Wayne County Herald* (Honesdale, PA), July 3, 1850.

4 Elizabeth A. DeWolfe, "Storytelling, Domestic Space, and Domestic Knowledge in the Murder of Berengera Caswell," *Storytelling: A Critical Journal of Popular Narrative* 6 (Winter 2007): 121–22.

could still identify Caswell "by the extraordinary length and beauty of the hair." Smith was allegedly "instrumental in procuring an abortion [with] intent to destroy, and which did destroy, a child."[5]

The story appealed to editors interested in both sensation and sociology: They noted "the intense and all-pervading interest felt by all classes of our citizens in the discovery and punishment of the crime, but also the "perceived dangers of women's . . . increasing physical distance from the domestic circle." As in the Cornell case seventeen years earlier, the deaths of a woman and an unborn child were due to "participation in a workforce beyond the reach of parental control," and a "yielding to the temptations of the seducers and the power of [their] own passions. . . . Once isolated from the protection of home and proper guardians, young women faced grave danger alone."[6]

A jury, after two hours of deliberation, found Smith guilty of murder. His sentence: life imprisonment at hard labor. But Maine Chief Justice John Tenny said the prosecutor had not proven that Smith had "intent to destroy" the unborn child, who had not yet quickened, because only the existence of a quickened infant would prove that the abortionist knew his victim was pregnant. The Supreme Court overturned the murder verdict and freed Smith, since he had already been imprisoned for the year that a manslaughter sentence required.[7]

---

5 "Dead Body Found," *Saco* (ME) *Union*, April 19, 1850, 2; *Augusta* (ME) *Age*, April 25, 1850, 1; April 26, 2 and 3; May 10, 2; January 24, 1851, 2; January 31, 2 and 3; DeWolfe, "Storytelling," 122.

6 DeWolfe, "Storytelling," 123–24; *Augusta* (ME) *Age*, April 25, 1850, 1; *Boston Medical and Surgical Journal* 43 (October 9, 1850): 206; *Boston Evening Transcript*, April 18, 1850, 2; April 19, 2; April 23, 2; April 25, 2; September 21, 2; *Hartford Courant*, April 29, 2; *Buffalo Daily Republic*, May 13, 2; *Brooklyn Eagle*, January 30, 1851, 2; *Woodstock Mercury*, January 30, 2; *New York Daily Herald*, April 21, 1850, 4.

7 Michael Grossberg, *Governing the Hearth: Law and the Family in Nineteenth-Century America* (Chapel Hill: University of North Carolina Press, 1985), 165–66. Smith died three years later of tuberculosis, probably contracted in prison. See also http://www.murderbygaslight.com/2010/05/mary-bean-factory-girl.htm. Doing legal work to free an abortionist was not a career-killer: The lawyer who won Smith's appeal, Nathan Clifford, was a former U.S. Attorney General and future U.S. Supreme Court justice.

Jurors were frustrated, and others wondered: If some abortion providers were briefly jailed, wouldn't they come back, or wouldn't others replace them? With enforcement largely unsuccessful in reducing the supply of abortionists, what about decreasing demand? As specialist providers of abortion emerged, what about specialist providers of ways for young men to spend time in evening pursuits other than pressuring women for sex?[8]

Such thinking contributed to the advent of the Young Men's Christian Association, which began when Pastor Isaac Ferris spoke to 300 young New Yorkers at a May 1852, meeting in a Presbyterian church. He said an apprentice or clerk a generation earlier lived with his employer's family, "but now it is sadly altered. The lad is left on the wide world—he is surrounded by the mercenary and the callous, and is happy if he escapes unhurt." Apart from a community that would encourage self-sacrifice rather than self-indulgence, a young man was in a "moral maelstrom" and would be led "by persuasion to all manner of indulgences, step by step until the end is reached."[9]

Ferris told young Christians that they could help themselves and non-Christians as well: Old merchants and pastors did not understand members of the 1850s generation, but "you will be his natural counselors." Ferris exhorted his audience to action, not just words, and 173 of the 300 signed up for the first YMCA, which rented its own meeting space on the third floor of a building on Broadway.

At the YMCA's opening, lawyer Daniel Lord spoke of a youth who grew up within a "little circle where he had a character well known,"

---

8   Christians such as William E. Dodge, one of Wall Street's "merchant princes" at mid-century, supported prayer meetings, city missions, anti-alcoholism gatherings, and church-building at or near his business enterprises—but not programs specifically aimed at young men and women. See D. Stuart Dodge, *Memorials of William E. Dodge* (New York: Anson D. F. Randolph, 1887; repr., Wentworth Press, 2019), 22, 208–60.
9   Isaac Ferris, *Address Delivered at a Meeting of Young Men, Convened for the Formation of the Young Men's Christian Association. Held in the Lecture Room of the Mercer-St. Presbyterian Church* (New York, 1852), quoted in Allan Horlick, *Country Boys and Merchant Princes* (Lewisburg, PA: Bucknell University Press, 1975), 231.

and was not prepared for an urban "attack of worldly excitement and sensual allurements." His employer was busy running the business, "his time too much absorbed in it for him to bestow sympathy on his humble assistant." Lord got personal: "You may die in your boarding house, and scarcely any but your landlady, the doctor, and perhaps the parson know it." He asked YMCA leaders to make up for loss of community: "May not this want of a home be, in a degree at least, supplied? Can you not, finding your associate worthy of your friendship, take him into the society, the families of your friends?"[10]

The idea spread throughout the United States. The Boston YMCA gave details of its goal: to "meet the young stranger as he enters our city, take him by the hand, direct him to a boarding house where he might find a quiet home pervaded by Christian influences, introduce him to the Church and Sabbath School, bring him to the rooms of the Association, and in every way throw around him good influences, so that he may feel he's not a stranger, but that noble and Christian spirits care for his soul."[11]

The Indianapolis YMCA in 1855–1856 provided lectures "to amuse, interest, and instruct our whole people [and] to purify our intellectual and social atmosphere." The Pittsburgh YMCA saw itself in opposition to "one of the great enemies of the young—the Theatre—with its small fry of inevitable accompaniments, the gin shop and gaming salon." (That opposition to theaters seems over-the-top now, but most theaters in the 1850s were hangouts for prostitutes.)[12]

---

10 Daniel Lord, *Address Delivered on the Opening of the Rooms of the New York Young Men's Christian Association* (New York: Theo. H. Gray, 1852), quoted in Horlick, *Country Boys and Merchant Princes*.

11 Charles Howard Hopkins, *History of the YMCA in North America* (New York: Association Press, 1951), 18. The Newark YMCA in 1854 similarly aimed to reach the "thousands of youth and young men, many of whom are from the country, unacquainted with the city, desirous of securing good friends and associations and anxious to pursue a course of rectitude and virtue."

12 Hopkins, *History of the YMCA*, 31. *The Young Man's Guide*, a book of advice authored by William A. Alcott (1798–1859), spoke of theaters the way public health officials during the COVID-19 era have spoken of super-spreader events: "Respiration contaminates the air; and where large assemblies are collected in close rooms, the air is corrupted" (Boston: Perkins & Marvin, 1835; repr., Avon, MA: F+W Media, 2013; the quotation is on page 93 in another edition of the book).

YMCA libraries were also important at a time when reading rooms were mostly for the rich: Most cities did not have public libraries until Andrew Carnegie funded the construction of 1,689 in the United States between 1883 and 1929. The Boston, New York, Brooklyn, Buffalo, and Charleston YMCAs all hired librarians, and many others also made librarians their first employees. Librarians were to care about people as much about books: In Boston, librarian Levi Rowland "called upon young men in stores and offices and shops . . . introduced them into some church connection."[13]

The Philadelphia YMCA in 1857 was the first to hire a corresponding secretary, nineteen-year-old John Wanamaker. He helped to add two thousand members via "tireless visitation of those who dropped in . . . or whose names were sent by pastors in hometowns." YMCAs benefited "a class of our young men who have hitherto been debarred from the pleasure of social intercourse and intellectual improvement." Every evening spent in a library that allowed quiet talking and social intercourse was one fewer evening spent in hustling for sexual intercourse, and potentially attempting to eradicate its consequences.[14]

The YMCA movement flourished in 1857–1858 alongside a massive national revival. It began in New York City in 1857 with the decision by evangelist Jeremiah Lanphier to schedule a downtown noontime prayer meeting. Only six people came to the first meeting. Twenty came the next week and forty the following week. Wednesday, October 14, brought the worst financial crash in America's history to that point. Banks and companies failed. Thousands were suddenly poor. Soon, three thousand came to pray amid downtown sounds: "the bells of the horse cars, the shouts of carmen, the noise of artisans, the hammer and saw of the carpenter, the whistle of the

---

13 Hopkins, *History of the YMCA*, 30, 36. To help young men from the countryside stay in contact with events in their hometowns, the Boston YMCA subscribed to 40 New England newspapers and 35 magazines.

14 Hopkins, *History of the YMCA*, 36, 43–45. Wanamaker became famous in Philadelphia for his department store and philanthropies.

steam-engine. . . . Seats are hard, crowded together to make room, and are very uncomfortable."[15]

Newspapers found news in their backyards, as the *New York Herald* substituted glowing headlines for its usual macabre ones: "Great Revival of Religion in New York. . . . Remarkable Conversions among the Unrighteous. Sinners Brought to the Way of Grace." Then the revival spread to other cities. A Philadelphia prayer meeting that started with 40 participants had more than 3,000 day after day. Most Yale students began attending prayer meetings, and "among the converts are some who have been very bitter scoffers, and who were tolerably well armed with the philosophy of the infidel."[16]

Revivals worked alongside expansion of the YMCA movement. University of Virginia and University of Michigan students formed local Christian associations and witnessed "deep and solemn thoughtfulness . . . strong revivals of religion." In 1858, New York City women formed the Ladies Christian Association, which two years later established its first boarding house for female students, teachers, and factory workers. That was the beginning of the Young Women's Christian Association. YWCAs later established employment bureaus, low-cost summer resorts for employed women, medical services for the sick, Travelers' Aid programs designed to protect women traveling to cities alone, and bilingual instruction to help immigrant women.[17]

---

15 "Revival Born in a Prayer Meeting," *Knowing and Doing* (C. S. Lewis Institute), Fall 2004, 1–6. Participants were wary of "high-sounding phrases, pompous words." William C. Conant, *Narratives of Remarkable Conversions and Revival Incidents* (New York: Derby & Jackson, 1858), 364, shows how other meetings soon began for "mechanics who work in the vicinity, and . . . come into the meeting blackened with smoke and dust of the forge and anvil. See also Matthew Hale Smith, *Sunshine and Shadow in New York* (Hartford, CT: J. B. Burr, 1868), 237, 239.

16 Kathryn Long, *The Revival of 1857–58: Interpreting an American Religious Awakening* (New York: Oxford University Press, 1998), 26, 62, 64; Conant, *Narratives*, 367–80. See also Robert Tribken, "The Fulton Street Prayer Meetings and the Revival of 1857/58: The Workplace Connection," *Center for Faith and Enterprise*, March 26, 2019. *The New York Times* reported on March 20, 1858, "The great wave of religious excitement which is now sweeping over this nation, is one of the most remarkable movements since the Reformation."

17 Long, *Revival of 1857–58*, 62. See also "About YWCA USA–HISTORY," www.ywca.org/about/history.

Headlines in Chicago, St. Louis, and Omaha showed how the movement headed westward. From 1857 to 1860 membership in major Protestant denominations increased by 474,000 people, twice the increase from 1853 to 1856. Conversion narratives had headlines such as "Conversion in a Rail Road Car," "Met Christ at the Wheel," "Found Christ in the Parlour," and "The Man That Found Christ at the Lamp Post."[18]

By 1860, the 205 local YMCAs had 25,000 members. They listed "respectable" boarding houses that were not adjacent to brothels. They served as employment bureaus. They distributed "the charities of the citizens among the destitute poor," implemented plans "for the relief of the sick," and mobilized against yellow fever. When a church worried that a local YMCA would be a competitor, "the YMCA sought to allay ecclesiastical fears by stressing the association's function as a surrogate family."[19]

Then as now, some who professed faith in Christ would still feel desperate and seek out abortionists. It's oversimplifying history to state that, as more people were born again, this automatically resulted in more endangered children being born. But those who embraced or re-embraced the Bible were less likely to fall for a new revelation that swept through the United States in the 1850s and left many men and women in an abortion frame of mind.[20]

---

[18] Long, *Revival of 1857–58*, 48, 50.
[19] Hopkins, *History of the YMCA*, 29–30.
[20] Long, *Revival of 1857–58*, 140; Talbot W. Chambers, *The New York City Noon Prayer Meeting* (New York: Dutch Reformed Church, 1858; repr., Colorado Springs: Wagner, 2002), 48.

16

The Unwelcome Child

FORTY YEARS BEFORE the revival that began in 1857, nineteen-year-old hat-making apprentice Henry Wright professed faith in Christ during an upstate New York religious upsurge. He headed to Andover Seminary in Massachusetts, taught for a year, continued his ministerial training, and in 1823 married Elizabeth Stickney, a wealthy widow 17 years older than he with four children. Wright became pastor of an affluent congregation and lambasted Unitarians, Jacksonians, and "busy Reformers who break up our Parishes & interrupt the peace & harmony of our social intercourse [with] new-fangled notions about Religion."[1]

In 1828, five years before the deaths of millworkers Sarah Cornell and Sally Burdick in Rhode Island made headlines, Wright criticized the state's new factories for purportedly debasing New England morality and ruining farm families. In 1832 he raised money for Amherst College, which he viewed as a biblical alternative to Harvard infidelity. The next year he blasted school textbooks that didn't sufficiently recognize God and urged parents to scrutinize what their children were reading. In 1835 he continued his defense of everything conservative and lamented "a strong propensity to try new

---

1 *Essex Gazette* (Haverhill, MA), October 10, 1829, 1.

measures in civil governments & in religious matters. . . . changes are dangerous."[2]

In 1836, though, Wright started consorting with non-conservatives, first with the American Peace Society, then with the American Anti-Slavery Society, then with radical pacifists in the New England Non-Resistance Society, then on his own as an itinerant lecturer on a variety of social evils. He was a sought-after speaker throughout the northern states, with funding largely from his wife's wealth. Wright spent little time at home and began writing in his diary lines like these: "My wife feels that I neglect her—that I don't love her nor the children—that I feel no interest in them." A biographer reports that Wright's wife and stepchildren found his long absences on speaking tours "agreeable," and his occasional visits home were "politely and formally received." Wright blamed "Orthodoxy, Hell-born Calvinist Orthodoxy" for his poor relationship with his family.[3]

Wright, in an intimate 1843 diary entry, also blamed his wife: "No marriage love is between us. She was past child-bearing when I first knew her—we have not had intercourse as husband and wife for 15 years—it is many years since we have slept in the same bed." Wright observed that many women who came to his lectures developed at least intellectual crushes on him. That year he wrote about an Englishwoman he had met, Elizabeth Pease, "My personal acquaintance & intercourse with E.P. have formed an era in the history of my spirit. No mortal ever had that influence over me." In 1846 he wrote about another woman, Maria Waring, "in whom & for whom I have lived the past few weeks . . . mingling our entire natures into one."[4]

These words do not necessarily mean what they suggest today. Wright's biographer does not know whether in each case the "affair was explicitly

---

2 Lewis Perry, *Childhood, Marriage, and Reform: Henry Clarke Wright, 1797–1870* (Chicago: University of Chicago Press, 1980), 5, 7, 10, 12.
3 Perry, *Childhood, Marriage, and Reform*, 37, 50–59, 172–80.
4 Perry, *Childhood, Marriage, and Reform*, 181, 190, 193.

sexual." Later came another woman, Esther Lukens, and gossip in 1857 that Wright was living "out of marriage bonds." Whatever was happening personally certainly had an effect on his affiliations and writing. The conservatism of his first forty years vanished. He became radically anti-slavery but also radically anti-marriage. His crowds swelled and so, apparently, did his self-esteem. In 1858 Wright published a book about what to do with the small by-products of what he then saw as accidents.[5]

The term "unwanted child" became popular with the advent of Planned Parenthood in the 1940s, but nine decades before that, Henry Wright wrote *The Unwelcome Child: The Crime of an Undesigned and Undesired Maternity*. He said an "unwelcome child" would be addicted "to drunkenness, to lying, to revenge," and would become "a miser, a warrior, a slaveholder, a robber, murderer, a pirate, or an assassin." Wright praised one woman who had killed three unborn children after deciding it was wrong to have a child "when her own heart loathes its existence." Abortion was a defense against "a sacrilegious intruder into the domain of her life; an invader of the holy of holies of her being."[6]

Wright praised the way another pregnant woman dealt with her unplanned pregnancy: "My own soul, and the God whose voice was heard within, repudiated its existence. [A friend] told me it was not murder to kill a child any time before its birth. . . . God and human laws would approve of killing children before they were born, rather than curse them with an undesired existence." Wright's central message: A merciful mother should save herself from "enforced, repulsive maternity [by] killing her unborn babe to save it from a worse doom." Frequent abortion was fine, because a woman should be brave enough to declare, "I cannot consent to have the woman, *the real soul-and-spirit woman* in me, obliterated."[7]

5   Perry, *Childhood, Marriage, and Reform*, 195, 204; Henry Clarke Wright, *The Unwelcome Child: The Crime of an Undesigned and Undesired Maternity* (Boston: Bela Marsh, 1858).
6   Wright, *Unwelcome Child*, 21, 36, 40, 80.
7   Wright, *Unwelcome Child*, 82, 102, 108: A child's "first claim is, to a designed existence, if it is to exist at all."

Wright was honest in using the words "killing" and "unborn babe," but he defined abortion as a mother "killing her unborn babe to save it from a worse doom" and herself from "enforced, repulsive maternity." He claimed many women "would gladly strangle their children, born of undesired maternity, at birth, could they do so with safety to themselves." Wright did not explicitly advocate such strangling either before or after birth, but he was sympathetic to women who made that choice: "It is no matter of wonder that abortions are purposely procured; it is to me a matter of wonder that a single child . . . reluctantly conceived, is ever suffered to mature in the organism of the mother. Her whole nature repels it. How can she regard its ante-natal development but with sorrow and shrinking?"[8]

American history textbooks tend to treat the 1850s largely as a run-up to the Civil War, but while many southerners dug in on slavery, many northerners embraced aspects of spiritism and "free love." Radical-turned-conservative Orestes Brownson observed, "There are some three hundred circles or clubs in the city of Philadelphia alone. [Spiritism] seizes all classes, ministers of religion, lawyers, physicians, judges, comedians, rich and poor, learned and unlearned. The movement has its quarterly, monthly, and weekly journals, some of them conducted with great ability." Dr. Benjamin Hatch described how "women who have abandoned their husbands and who are living in adultery with their paramours, produce abortion, and arise from their guilty couches and stand before large audiences as the medium for angels."[9]

Dr. Thomas Nichols claimed sales of 250,000 for his book *Esoteric Anthropology*, which praised a wealthy woman who "six times had

8 Wright, *Unwelcome Child*, 35.
9 Orestes Brownson, *The Spirit-Rapper: An Autobiography* (Boston: Little, Brown, 1854), 138, 236; Benjamin Hatch, *Spiritualists' Iniquities Unmasked* (New York: Hatch, 1859), 50–51; Slater Brown, *The Heyday of Spiritualism* (New York: Hawthorn, 1970), 151; Grace Adams and Edward Hutter, *The Mad Forties* (New York: Harper & Brothers, 1942); *Boston Medical and Surgical Journal* 51 (October 4, 1854): 224; and 52 (November 26, 1855): 245. John Greenleaf Whittier, Henry Wadsworth Longfellow, Harriet and Calvin Stowe, Horace Greeley, Henry Ward Beecher, Ralph Waldo Emerson, William Lloyd Garrison, and Charles Sumner all attended seances, at least out of curiosity.

abortion procured, and by her family physician, too." Nichols argued that "the Woman alone has the right to decide whether her ovum shall be impregnated [and] must also have the privilege of determining the circumstances which justify the procurement of abortion." Later, he wrote of "the marked effect of spiritism upon American fact, feeling and character. Nothing within my memory has had so great an influence. It has broken up hundreds of churches and changed the religious belief of hundreds of thousands."[10]

Americans who retained faith in the Bible saw adultery as sin, but those who worshiped their own spirit felt free, temporarily. Popular speaker Andrew Jackson Davis called marriages "legalized adultery and bigotry" unless they were true spiritual marriages with "affinity-mates." He asserted euphemistically, "The female has the right to control all the manifestations of love." Diarist George Strong in New York City described the growth "of the 'free love' league . . . 'passionate attraction' its watchword, fornicating and adultery its apparent object." Abortion often was the outcome: "Unintended" children were "children of chance, children of lust" and "abortions [with] no right to existence."[11]

Newspapers took notice. The *Cincinnati Daily Times* reported in 1854 an "astonishing" expansion of spiritism, whose adherents were now found "on every street and corner of the city."[12] The next year *The New York Times* said of spiritism, "Judging from its rapid extension

---

10 Thomas Nichols, *Esoteric Anthropology* (New York: Nichols, 1853), 172: He saw "no reason why anyone should be compelled to bear children who wishes to avoid it." Nichols later changed his mind about basics: See his *Forty Years of American Life*, 2 vols. (London: John Maxwell, 1864), 2:40, 49. Hiram Knox Root, *The Lover's Marriage Lighthouse* (New York: Root, 1858), 8, 194, 348, is amusing: Root associated "deistical free spiritualism" with free love, and claimed that "in the eye of the female who has sexual intercourse out of marriage . . . there is a look of mildness and confidence." When pregnancy occurred, he had the solution: the "French Instrumental Uterine Regulator," which he would sell and mail for ten dollars. According to Root, his Uterine Regulator "will bring on contractions, and produce evacuation of the contents of the womb, commonly known as miscarriage, no matter at what period of gestation."

11 Allan Nevins and Milton Thomas, eds., *Diary of George Templeton Strong: The Turbulent Fifties: 1850–1859* (New York: Macmillan, 1952), November 26, 1855, 245.

12 Quoted in Emma Hardinge Britten, *Modern American Spiritualism* (New York: Britten, 1870), 351.

and widespread effects, it seems to be the new Mahomet, or the social Antichrist, overrunning the world."[13] The *Times* in June 1858 gave most of its front page to coverage of a Rutland, Vermont, gathering of three thousand spiritists and abortion proponents.[14]

That gathering was one of many in the late 1850s: New railroad companies profited by scheduling special trains. Within a giant tent conventioneers considered resolutions: "That the sacred and important right of woman is her right to decide for herself how often, and under what circumstances, she shall assume the responsibility and be subjected to the sufferings and cares of maternity.... That nothing is true or right, and nothing is false or wrong, because it is sanctioned or condemned by the Bible; therefore the Bible is powerless to prove any doctrine to be true, or any practice to be right, and it should never be quoted for that purpose."[15]

Henry Wright gave the convention keynote speech. He advocated abortion, condemned those who thought it wrong, and pushed another resolution: "That the authority of each individual soul is absolute and final, in deciding all questions as to what is true or false in principle, and right or wrong in practice. Therefore, the individual, the Church, or the State, that attempts to control the opinions or the practice of any man or woman, by authority of power outside of his or her own soul, is guilty of a flagrant wrong."[16]

Popular speaker Julia Branch emphasized a woman's "right to bear children when she will." Respondent Eliza Farnham echoed her and Wright's eugenic idea that it was unfair to a child to let him live if the

---

13 *New York Times*, September 8, 1855, 2.
14 *New York Times*, June 29, 1858, 1.
15 *Proceedings of the Free Convention* (Boston: J. B. Yerrington, 1858), 9, 10.
16 The *Proceedings of the Free Convention* reported that one of the convention's celebrities, former Liberty Party presidential candidate William Goodell, challenged the resolution: Suppose someone "should stand up and plant himself on the ground that he knew no rule but his own will, which God has revealed in him, and that he believed in the divinity of slavery?" Goodell asked if that person could grab a child in the audience and enslave him? The convention transcript includes this reaction: "Voices—No." Wright had no immediate response.

mother was unhappy, given "the monstrous evils which grow out of the wrong and wicked generation of human beings." Many would be criminals or impoverished, and it was a "sinful waste" to work "for the reform of such persons, after we have idly suffered this irreparable and greatest wrong to be done against them."[17]

Spiritism's emphasis on each person being a god unto himself or herself went along with the emphasis on freedom to abort. At the Rutland gathering, Unitarian pastor Amory Dwight Mayo announced that "scientific interpretation" made belief in a God-inspired Bible "as dead as the Ptolemaic system of Astronomy." Mayo spoke of "a great army who sincerely hate the Bible and believe the world would be better off without it." Like Wright and others, he dumped God's instructions in favor of the "direct presence of the Infinite Spirit in every human soul." Speaker Helen Temple of Bennington advised, "Look within yourself to find the breath of God." Speaker A. W. Sprague added, "Though no God ever thunders on Sinai or walks in the garden, to tell me his law, I will do my duty nobly, because I see its truth and nobleness in my own spirit."[18]

Justice Anthony Kennedy famously wrote in 1992 that "At the heart of liberty is the right to define one's own concept of existence, of meaning, of the universe, and of the mystery of human life."[19] That was a common view at the Rutland Convention, and it reflected the spiritist acceptance of abortion in the 1850s. Medical journals in Boston and Atlanta, and doctors throughout the still-United States, reported mature and married women, not just unmarried young ones, seeking abortions.[20]

---

17 *Proceedings of the Free Convention*, 55, 67.
18 *Proceedings of the Free Convention*, 44–45, 49–50, 78–184. See also Marvin Olasky, "Abortion and Spiritism," in *Abortion Rites: A Social History of Abortion in America* (Wheaton, IL: Crossway, 1992), 61–82.
19 *Planned Parenthood of Southeastern Pennsylvania, et al. v. Robert P. Casey, et al.*, 505 U.S. 833, 112 S. Ct. 2791.
20 *Boston Medical and Surgical Journal* 51 (October 4, 1854): 224; "Foeticide," *Atlanta Medical and Surgical Journal*, II, 257–58; *Boston Medical and Surgical Journal* 55 (March 17, 1859): 249.

17

Doctors Push Back

SIXTEEN YEARS AFTER Hugh Hodge's widely distributed lecture on abortion, Dr. David Storer, Dean of the Harvard Medical School, offered a few words on abortion. Storer said in a November 1855 lecture that he "should be unworthy of the confidence or esteem of my brethren did I refrain . . . to enter my solemn protest against the existing vice. . . . The moment an embryo enters the uterus a microscopic speck, it is the germ of a human being, and it is as morally wrong to endeavor to destroy that germ as to be guilty of the crime of infanticide."[1]

Storer said doctors treating a pregnant woman had two patients, not one. He complained that "the press is silent" on abortion (except when a woman dies). Ironically, after saying in his lecture that he would be unworthy should he refrain from commenting, he did refrain: in the published version of his lecture, Storer deleted his words about abortion. The *Boston Medical and Surgical Journal* noticed: "Professor Storer has omitted the very paragraphs which, in our judgment, should have been allowed to go forth." The *Journal* opined that people ignorant about "intra-uterine murder" needed education by "some bold and manly appeal."[2]

---

1   David Storer, quoted in Frederick Dyer, *The Physicians' Crusade against Abortion* (Sagamore Beach, MA: Science History Publications, 2005), 5.
2   *Boston Medical and Surgical Journal* 53 (December 1855): 409–11.

Storer had reason to fear the reaction of his medical peers. Dr. W. C. Lispenard wrote in 1854 that abortion "is exclusively the affair of the mother. She alone has a right to decide whether she will continue the being of the child she began. Moral, social, religious obligations should control her, but she alone has the supreme right to decide." Dr. Ferdinand Rattenmann would write in 1858 about the "doubtful life of the embryo" and the "mere possible life of the child."[3]

But David Storer's son Horatio, who idolized his professorial dad and also became a doctor, complained to a friend that his father "show[ed] the white feather" of cowardice when he dropped from publication his words about abortion. Storer the younger tried to make up for that in April 1857 by presenting a report on abortion to the Suffolk [Boston] District Medical Society. His message: Current law views abortion as an offense against women but "utterly ignores the existence of the living child, though the child is really alive from the very moment of its conception, and from that very moment is and should be considered a distinct being."[4]

Storer argued that a doctor's duty regarding abortion should be to "declare its true nature, its prevalence, and its deplorable consequences; to denounce it in unmeasured terms, and, where possible, to point out and enforce efficient means for its suppression." But another local doctor, Charles Buckingham, fiercely opposed him, saying—in anticipation of many twentieth-century arguments—that a woman who cannot purchase abortifacients will operate on herself. He said doctors "will fail to convince the public that abortion in the early months is a crime, and a large proportion of the medical profession will tacitly support the view of the subject."[5]

---

[3] William C. Lispenard, *Private Medical Guide* (Rochester, NY: J. W. Brown, 1854), 194; Ferdinand Rattenmann, *Induced Abortion* (Philadelphia: Rudolph Stein, 1858), 10.

[4] Frederick Dyer, *Champion of Women and the Unborn: Horatio Robinson Storer, M.D.* (Canton, MA: Watson, 1999), 113. Horatio Storer was born in 1830.

[5] Dyer, *Physicians' Crusade against Abortion*, 39, 40.

Time for some backstory: While New Age fervor and Christian revival spread around the country during the late 1850s, a new understanding of fetal anatomy was spreading among scientists and then physicians. A century and a half had passed between the identification of sperm in 1677 and publication in 1827 of a book by Karl Ernst von Baer documenting his discovery of mammal eggs. During the next three decades scientists realized that cells form the structure of life, and that sperm and the egg are cells.[6]

That new knowledge undercut Preformationists. Whether they thought sperm or eggs were most prominent, Preformationists agreed that what began at conception might for a while be only half a person: for example, the sperm might not trigger the blood in the uterus for six weeks. But if both sperm and eggs were cells that combined to form a new person at conception, an abortion anytime after conception was killing a human being. The "new embryology" understood that human life begins at conception and develops "without the decisive ontological transition that had once been a part of every theory of delayed animation."[7]

Rhode Island physician John Leonard was in line with this new understanding when he complained in 1851 about "physicians who, Herod-like, have waged a war of destruction upon the innocent."[8] In 1853, Dr. Stephen Tracy's *The Mother and Her Offspring* laid out the implications: "If examined three to four weeks from the commencement of pregnancy, the embryo will be found to have about the size of a grain of wheat. . . . It is a Human Being. It is one of the human family as really and truly as if it had lived six months or six years; consequently, its life should be as carefully and tenderly cherished."[9]

---

6   Karl Ernst Von Baer, *Ovi Mammalium et Hominis Genesi*, available online at https://openlibrary.org/books/OL24429704M/De_ovi_mammalium_et_hominis_genesi.
7   *The American Journal of Legal History* 49, no. 3 (July 2007): 296.
8   John Preston Leonard, "Quackery and Abortion," *Boston Medical and Surgical Journal* 43 (January 1851): 477–81.
9   Stephen Tracy, *The Mother and Her Offspring* (New York: Harper & Brothers, 1853), 108.

Tracy said science had shown that life begins "at the moment of conception; and no person has any right to destroy it by any means whatever." He opposed abortion "even in those lamentable and distressing cases where conception has taken place unlawfully, [for] the life of this new human being is sacred, and no one but God himself either has, or can have, the least shadow of a right or liberty to take it away. To destroy its life, for the sake of saving one's self from exposure and mortification, is but to add a greater to a lesser crime."[10]

Tracy wanted his readers to visualize specifics: "At forty-five days, the form of the child is very distinct, and it is not termed a fetus. The head is very large; the eyes, mouth, and nose are to be distinguished; the hands and arms are in the middle of its length—fingers distinct . . . at two months, all the parts of the child are present . . . the fingers and toes are distinct. At three months, the heart pulsates strongly, and the principal vessels carry red blood." Tracy thus saw no conflict between his religious beliefs and what was scientifically established: "The investigations of physiologists have established them as incontrovertible TRUTHS." But his book did not sell well and did not make much of an impact on public understanding.[11]

Other doctors tried to raise the alarm. The *Boston Medical and Surgical Journal* editorialized that abortion "is murder, and the perpetrator of it cannot expect to escape the vengeance of offended heaven."[12] Hugh Hodge repeated his 1839 lecture and added a new twist: "Married women also . . . have solicited that the embryo should be destroyed by their medical attendant. [Doctors must] let her know, in language not to be misunderstood, that she is responsible to her Creator for the life of the being within her system."[13] The *New York Medical Gazette* thought several abortionists should "be

10 Tracy, *Mother and Her Offspring*, 109.
11 Tracy, *Mother and Her Offspring*, 109; Dyer, *Champion of Women and the Unborn*, 113.
12 "Procuring Abortion," *Boston Medical and Surgical Journal* 51 (October 4, 1854): 224–25.
13 Hugh L. Hodge, *Introductory Lecture to the Course on Obstetrics and Diseases of Women and Children: Delivered in the University of Pennsylvania, November 5, 1846* (Philadelphia: Collins, 1854), 18.

hanged together ... as a warning against this fiendish and awfully frequent crime."[14]

Horatio Storer saw that he had support and pushed on, circulating nationally his 1857 report to the local medical society. When Tracy read Storer's report, he voiced his compliments. So did the *New-Hampshire Journal of Medicine*, which reported that Storer had started a "war" on abortion that would be "participated in by physicians of other States." At first nothing much happened. Many doctors were reluctant to criticize their colleagues. The big news in March 1857 was the U.S. Supreme Court's Dred Scott decision that animated Abraham Lincoln and many others.[15]

But in 1858–1859, the medical mood seemed different. Storer had successfully pushed the American Medical Association to form a Committee on Criminal Abortion. Committees are often ways to slow down or kill initiatives, but this time, with Christian revival in the air, more doctors showed concern for their smallest patients. They listened to Storer's demand that doctors become educators, fighting "a widespread popular ignorance of the true character of the crime"—a belief, even among mothers themselves, "that the foetus is not alive till after the period of quickening." Leaders of the young AMA supported Storer's attack on "the grave defects of our laws, both common and statute, as regards the independent and actual existence of the child before birth, as a living being."[16]

The Committee on Criminal Abortion strongly backed Storer's view that abortion should be seen "as no simple offence against public morality and decency, no mere misdemeanor, no attempt upon the life of the mother, but the wanton and murderous destruction of her child." The AMA, in a dramatic change from the mixed signals earlier in the

---

14 "Criminal Abortionist," republished in *Boston Medical and Surgical Journal* 50 (March 8, 1854): 128.
15 Dyer, *Champion of Women and the Unborn*, 112–13, 119.
16 *Transactions of the American Medical Association* 12 (1859): 73–78.

decade, unanimously passed three resolutions on May 3, 1859, with the last calling for "zealous co-operation of the various State Medical Societies in pressing this subject upon the legislatures of their respective states."[17]

Why did the doctors take this stand? Some historians view it through the perspective of what I'd call Critical Abortion Theory (CAT), a subset of the critical theory perspective that most of life is a pursuit of power, with ideals acting as only a spoonful of sugar to make the poison go down. CAT contends that mid-nineteenth-century AMA physicians opposed abortion out of a desire to monopolize medicine, put midwives and other doctors out of business, and support nativism at a time when immigration was growing.[18]

CAT, though, does not take into account the overall pro-life views that transcended any particular advantage. Horatio Storer is a good punching bag because he and other doctors mistakenly connected postpartum psychosis to reproductive organs and in some cases suggested ovariectomies.[19] Storer also made several nativist statements, advocating that women of northwestern European ancestry should have more children. Unlike twentieth-century population control proponents, though, he did not say or suggest that immigrants or minority members should have abortions. Later in life Storer publicly criticized racism in

---

17 *Transactions of the American Medical Association* 12 (1859): 27–28, quoted in Dyer, *Champion of Women and the Unborn*, 150.
18 Nicola Beisel and Tamara Kay, "Abortion, Race, and Gender in Nineteenth-Century America," American Sociological Review 69 (August 2004): 499. See also Michael Omi and Howard Winant, Racial Formation in the United States (New York: Routledge, 1994), 23–24, 102.
19 See contention on NPR, June 6, 2022, that Storer "was really hostile to women." Compare with Nancy Theriot, "Diagnosing Unnatural Motherhood: Nineteenth Century Physicians and 'Puerperal Insanity,'" *American Studies* (Fall 1989): 76: "much of the medical discourse on puerperal insanity seems to have been influenced very little by male doctors' concepts of femininity, but instead reflected the state of medical knowledge about insanity. . . . Throughout the nineteenth century physicians asserted that mental illness in general, not just women's mental illness, reflected a connection between mind and body; if the mind was unbalanced, a brain lesion was responsible, and the 'exciting' cause of the brain lesion could be physical or emotional. . . . From the general assumption of a mind/body link as part of the nature of mental disease, it was logical to conclude that puerperal insanity was in some way caused by the physical state of pregnancy, parturition or lactation."

books and movies, and received letters from black leaders appreciating his support. To accept CAT, we have to conclude that thousands of pro-life statements and actions by Storer and his colleagues were all smokescreens—and that "gotcha" historians know best.[20]

In 1859–1860, many legislatures responded to Storer's invitation. Connecticut upgraded its 1821 statute and declared any surgical or medical abortion a felony. Pennsylvania's legislature in 1860 removed any ambiguity in its law by criminalizing every abortion. Other states acted, and more legislators laid plans—but in 1861 came war. The effect of massive death on army doctors is hard to quantify: Piles of corpses could have a brutalizing effect on some and a deepening of the tragic sensibility in others. Still, it was moving to read, in the Library of Congress, letters by Civil War doctors who literally bound up the nation's wounds—and to trace what they did after the war.[21]

Joseph C. Stone became a doctor in 1854, served in the First Iowa Cavalry, and then joined state and county medical societies. Elected to Congress, he called abortion, like slavery, a "violation of every natural sentiment, and in opposition to the laws of God and man. [The] fertilized human ovum is not like the seed that has been wrapped in some old mummy, and left to await for ages the conditions for its development. Its growth is steady and progressive, physiological and positive."[22]

Maine's Dr. Oren Horr in 1863 did what many other white physicians would not do: He became assistant surgeon to the 114th (Colored) Regiment, U.S. Army. He served with that regiment until the close of the war, then went to Texas with it, and returned to Maine

---

20 Leslie Reagan, *When Abortion Was a Crime: Women, Medicine, and Law in the United States, 1867–1973* (Berkeley: University of California Press, 1997), 11, says "Regular physicians won passage of new criminal abortion laws because their campaign appealed to a set of fears of white, native-born, male elites about losing political power to Catholic immigrants and to women." On racism, see Dyer, *Champion of Women and the Unborn*, 474 and 491.
21 Connecticut Public Acts, LXXI, 65 (1860); letters in the Library of Congress Manuscript Division.
22 J. C. Stone, "Report on the Subject of Criminal Abortion," *Transactions of the Iowa State Medical Society*, 1867 (Davenport, IA: Griggs, Watson, 1871), 27, 31.

and became president of his local medical society. He became an expert on autopsies and at age 57 died of septicemia contracted while making a post-mortem examination probably connected to a doubly fatal abortion.[23]

Dr. Alexander Semmes, a physician with Charity Hospital in New Orleans, foresightedly believed abortion needed to be stopped before it became "a characteristic feature of American 'civilization.'" He was a brigade surgeon during the war, resumed his position at Charity Hospital after it, and published a paper entitled "Vaccination: It's important." After his wife died in 1872, he became a Catholic priest and president of Pio Nono, a Catholic college in Macon, Georgia.[24]

Meanwhile, the revival that began in 1857–1858 continued to ripple during and after the war among Union soldiers, Confederate armies, and Horatio Storer himself (who had heart problems and did not serve). He acknowledged that he had a spiritual heart problem as well and had pushed forward his pro-life statements based solely on medical knowledge: He could not believe "that the contents of the womb, so long as manifesting no perceptible sign of life, were but lifeless and inert matter: in other words, a mere ovarian excretion" until quickening. Nevertheless, he had found himself "in the midst of a conflict with uncertainties, doubts & downright disbelief." Then he had come to Christian belief: "Compelled humbly to surrender to the Master my life had denied, I find a peace of which before I had had no conception."[25]

Many doctors were both anti-slavery and anti-abortion. Dr. P. S. Haskell of Maine argued that both slavery and abortion were sins that bring penalties: "If abortion continues, we shall all suffer, as a people,

---

23 William Atkinson, *Physicians and Surgeons of the United States* (Philadelphia: Charles Robinson, 1878), 112; Joshua Taylor Bradford diary, March 6, 1862, Toner Collection, Library of Congress manuscript division.
24 Dumas Malone, ed., *Dictionary of American Biography* (New York: Scribner, 1935), 578.
25 Horatio Storer and Franklin Heard, *Criminal Abortion: Its Nature, Its Evidence, and Its Law* (Boston: Little, Brown, 1868), 8; Dyer, *Champion of Women and the Unborn*, 156, 294–95.

as a profession and as individuals, just as we all have suffered and are now suffering for the curse of American slavery."[26]

These doctors influenced their churches. To choose just one example, a Congregational church conference in 1868 declared that because of abortion, "full one third of the natural population of our land, falls by the hand of violence; that in no one year of the late war have so many lost life in camp or battle, as have failed of life by reason of this horrid home crime. We shudder to view the horrors of intemperance, of slavery, and of war; but those who best know the facts and bearing of this crime, declare it to be a greater evil, more demoralizing and destructive, than either intemperance, slavery, or war itself."[27]

---

26 P. S. Haskell, "Criminal Abortion," *Maine Medical Association Proceedings* 4 (1873): 465–73. He and others argued that abortion defenders treated unborn children as the property of their mothers, liable to being killed without penalty. Unborn children were unable to speak for themselves or fight for their own liberty. Their owners could dispose of them in the way that maximized the owners' advantages, without any regard for the welfare of the person considered inferior.
27 August 4, 1868, quoted in George Grant, *Third Time Around: A History of the Pro-Life Movement from the First Century to the Present* (Brentwood, TN: Wolgemuth & Hyatt, 1991), 99.

18

Massacres

IN MAY AND JUNE 1865, Union Colonel and Methodist minister James Jaquess sat in Nashville with the remains of "the preachers' regiment" he had organized three years before. Robert E. Lee had surrendered on April 9. Union soldiers captured the fleeing Jefferson Davis on May 10. The last Confederate general still in the field, Kirby Smith, surrendered in Galveston on May 26.[1]

But Jaquess did not merely sit. With his wife and two children at home in Quincy, Illinois, 440 miles away, Jaquess at age 46 had a 29-year-old mistress in Nashville, Louisa C. Williams. When the U.S. Army mustered out his regiment near Springfield, Illinois, on June 27, 1865, Jaquess was not there. That day he had hand-delivered to General Clinton B. Fisk (appointed to head the Freedmen's Bureau in Kentucky and Tennessee) a letter laying out the great desire Jaquess had to help former slaves in those two states. Jaquess was so committed to that task that he was willing to spend more time away from his family.[2]

---

1 Patricia Burnette, *James F. Jaquess* (Jefferson, NC: McFarland, 2013), 63–64, describes the formation of the 73rd Illinois Infantry Volunteers, which Jaquess recruited with the help of nine other Methodist ministers.

2 W. H. Newlin et al., Regimental Reunion Association, *A History of the Seventy-Third Regiment of Illinois Infantry Volunteers* (1890; various reprint eds. available); 1860 U.S. Census accessed through Ancestry.com.

Fisk offered Jaquess a position at a freedmen's refugee camp near Lexington, Kentucky. It just so happened that Louisa C. Williams moved to Louisville, which was on a direct train line from Lexington to Quincy, Illinois. Since her economic goal was to become a sewing machine saleswoman, Jaquess had the charitable heart to ship her nine sewing machines that he happened to purchase. He also visited several times: On September 11 he asked Fisk for permission to be absent because he needed to go home immediately to Quincy.[3]

Jaquess apparently got only as far as Louisville. On September 22 he was at the bedside of Williams when she died after an abortion by a doctor Jaquess apparently had hired. The next day, Jaquess was under arrest and arraigned for "procuring the death" of Williams and "procuring the death of the child" within her. Newspapers across the United States reported his arrest because Jaquess had gained some fame by serving as a special agent for Abraham Lincoln during 1863–1864. Furthermore, a Methodist minister's involvement with abortion was a scandal reminiscent of Ephraim Avery's three decades before (ch. 10).[4]

The trial, delayed several times because of illness and the absence of crucial witnesses, began on May 14, 1866, four days after the House of Representatives in Washington had voted on the Fourteenth Amendment to the Constitution. It concluded on May 16, 1866, one week before Senator Jacob Howard introduced the amendment to his Senate colleagues. As Congress debated, southern newspapers criticized the Union ex-colonel, but so did the *Chicago Tribune*, which reported in a page one headline the "testimony of a large number of witnesses" who saw Jaquess with Williams. The *Tribune* said the "evidence shows strong against the prisoner."[5]

3 Burnette, *James F. Jaquess*, 100–109; Richard D. Sears, *Camp Nelson, Kentucky* (Lexington: University Press of Kentucky, 2002), 239–40; National Park Service, *Camp Nelson*, at nps.gov. *Chicago Tribune*, September 26, 1865, 1.

4 *New York Times*, August 26, 1864, 3; *Louisville Daily Courier*, May 17, 1866, 3; *Chicago Tribune*, September 28, 1866, 1; *Lancaster* (PA) *Intelligencer*, October 4, 1866, 3; *New York Daily Herald*, June 22, 1870, 8.

5 Jaquess scandal coverage: *Louisville Courier Journal*, April 4, 1866, 3; May 16, 3; May 17, 3; May 24, 1; *Richmond Dispatch*, April 10, 1866, 3; *Illinois Daily State Journal*, April 13, 1;

The *Daily National Republican* (Washington, DC) on its front page mourned that Jaquess was "in disgrace." As Republicans pushed for the Fourteenth Amendment, journalists criticized Jaquess and also the "demons of society known as abortionists." Given such widespread anti-abortion belief, were unborn children among the "persons" the Amendment protected? Or, should the words "liberty" and "equal protection of the laws" in the Amendment include freedom for women to abort? Do either of those positions reflect an unlikely stretch?[6]

The stakes were and are high. Both sides in *Roe v. Wade* oral arguments agreed with what Justice Harry Blackmun acknowledged in his majority ruling: "If this suggestion of personhood is established, the appellant's case, of course, collapses, for the fetus' right to life would then be guaranteed specifically by the Amendment." If unborn children are persons, they cannot be denied the same legal protection that born persons have.[7]

Would unborn children have been seen as persons in the 1860s? The 1864 edition of Noah Webster's *American Dictionary of the English Language* defines "person" as relating "especially [to] a living human being; a man, woman, or child; an individual of the human race." The entry for "human" includes all those belonging to "the race of man." (The *Oxford English Dictionary* defines "person" similarly: "A human being.")[8]

Alton (IL) *Telegraph*, April 20, 1; *Chicago Tribune*, May 14, 2; *Lansing* (MI) *State Republican*, May 30, 7.

6 Here's the crucial first section of the Amendment: "All persons born or naturalized in the United States, and subject to the jurisdiction thereof, are citizens of the United States and of the State wherein they reside. No State shall make or enforce any law which shall abridge the privileges or immunities of citizens of the United States; nor shall any State deprive any person of life, liberty, or property, without due process of law; nor deny to any person within its jurisdiction the equal protection of the laws." Those words have figured prominently in some of the Supreme Court's most important decisions, but the *National Republican* (established in 1860 as a pro-Lincoln newspaper) mocked them as "generalizations about personal rights, all of which are sufficiently guaranteed [by the Constitution and by federal and state laws]. It is therefore surplusage, and of no real value" (May 1, 1866, 2).

7 Even ardent abortion proponents have criticized Blackmun's use of the Fourteenth Amendment to procure abortion liberty, as ch. 38 will show.

8 Noah Webster and Associates, *An American Dictionary of the English Language* (Springfield, MA: G & C Merriam, 1864), 974, 643; *Oxford English Dictionary* at www.lexico.com/en/definition

Jacob Howard, the Fourteenth Amendment's sponsor on the Senate side, said the Fourteenth Amendment would "disable a state from depriving not merely a citizen of the United States, but any person, whoever he may be, of life, liberty and property without due process." Howard emphasized that even the weakest and "most despised of the [human] race" would have equal protection.[9]

Other Amendment supporters displayed similar understandings of "person" and "human being." Rep. James Brown saw "person" as "a simple allusion to the existence of the individual."[10] Rep. Thaddeus Stevens stressed "the perfect equality of every human being before the law."[11] Sen. Lyman Trumbull, who chaired the Senate Judiciary Committee, equated "person" with "human being." He said any law "which deprives any human being in the land of those great rights of liberty will be in defiance of the Constitution."[12]

So why didn't Congressional debates during May 1866, the action month for passage of the Fourteenth Amendment, include any discussion of offering protection to unborn children? Just as Connecticut's 1821 abortion law can't be understood without reference to a news item just prior to it (the Ammi Rogers case), so also the Congressional debate in May owes much to the Memphis massacre of May 1–3, 1866.

This highly publicized tragedy started when white policemen and black Civil War veterans fought. It ended with mobs of white residents killing forty-six African-Americans and burning down every black church and school in Memphis—twelve in all. State and local officials, instead of trying to stop the violence, led mobs. The attorney general of Tennessee encouraged his forty-man posse not to defend the innocent

---

/person. See Joshua J. Craddock, "Protecting Prenatal Persons: Does the Fourteenth Amendment Prohibit Abortion?" *Harvard Journal of Law and Public Policy* 40, no. 2, 539–71.
9 *Congressional Globe*, 39th Cong., 1st Session, 2766.
10 *Congressional Globe*, 38th Cong., 1st Session, 1753.
11 Thaddeus Stevens, address at Bedford, Pennsylvania (September 4, 1866), reprinted in the *Sacramento Daily Union*, October 3, 1866, at 1.
12 *Congressional Globe*, 39th Cong., 1st Session, 77.

but to burn and murder. Memphis Mayor John Park did nothing: a Freedmen's Bureau report said "his friends offer in extenuation of his conduct that he was in a state of intoxication." City Recorder John Creighton took action, though: He urged a crowd of whites to "go ahead and kill every damned one of the [black] race and burn up the cradle."[13]

Later, U.S. Attorney General James Speed said prosecution against rioters was a state matter. The Tennessee state legislature responded to the massacre not by punishing the perpetrators but by passing two laws that local authorities could use against blacks: one intensified penalties used to "Punish all Armed Prowlers," and the other established execution as a potential punishment for theft. Officials did not invoke a grand jury or take any other action to punish the killers during the massacre.[14]

Senator Jacob Howard's May 23 speech, three weeks after the massacre, displayed Washington's tight focus on the recent news. Howard emphasized "the injustice of subjecting one caste of persons to a code not applicable to another." Howard was probably referring to Tennessee's new laws when he said the Fourteenth Amendment "prohibits the hanging of a black man for a crime for which the white man is not to be hanged."[15]

The U.S. Senate on June 8, 1866, voted 33-11 for the Fourteenth Amendment. Later that month it went to the states, three-fourths of which needed to ratify the Amendment for it to become law. That effort received powerful reinforcement from another massacre: On July 30, a white mob attacked New Orleans blacks meeting in the Mechanics

---

13 Art Carden and Christopher Coyne, "An Unrighteous Piece of Business," Mercatus Center Working Paper No. 10–40, July 2010, 19; Charles Johnson and T. W. Griffith, "Report of an Investigation of the Cause, Origin, and Results of the Late Riots in the City of Memphis," National Archives Microfilm Publication M999, roll 34; *The American Citizen*, May 23, 1866, 1.
14 James Ryan, "The Memphis Riots of 1866," *The Journal of Negro History* LXII (1977): 250–51; Beverly Forehand, "Striking Resemblance: Kentucky, Tennessee, Black Codes, and Readjustment, 1865–1866" (Masters Thesis, Western Kentucky University, 1996), 71–73 (paper 868, accessed at http://digitalcommons.wku.edu/theses/868).
15 *Congressional Globe*, 39th Cong., 1st Session, 2766.

Institute: "Policemen smashed the institute's windows and fired into it indiscriminately until the floor grew slick with blood.... Some leapt from windows and were shot dead when they landed. Those lying wounded on the ground were stabbed repeatedly, their skulls bashed in with brickbats. The sadism was so wanton that men who kneeled and prayed for mercy were killed instantly, while dead bodies were stabbed and mutilated."[16]

The Fourteenth Amendment's primary framer, Ohio Rep. John Bingham, had given a prophetic speech in February when he said the Amendment was "essential to the protection of the Union men of Tennessee," outnumbered in their state and without "security except from the armed presence of the United States Government there."[17] The Memphis Massacre angered him. Then came the New Orleans massacre. In Ohio three weeks later, Bingham gave a fiery speech urging ratification of the Amendment because "no state in the Union should deny to any human being . . . the equal protection of the laws."[18]

Bingham had gotten his political start in 1846 as district attorney of Tuscarawas County, eighty-seven miles south of Cleveland, so he was certainly aware of abortion tragedies over the years. The most recent local victims were Flora Jones and her unborn child: The *Cleveland Daily Leader* described the gruesome crime and concluded, "The fiends in human form who would commit it or wink at it, deserve the utmost penalties of the law."[19]

Bingham wasn't a winker, nor were Ohio state legislators. In January 1867 they took two big steps: They ratified the Fourteenth Amendment and took up a bill to toughen the state's pro-life law passed in 1834.

16 Ron Chernow, *Grant* (New York: Penguin, 2017), 574–75.
17 *Speech of Hon. John A. Bingham of Ohio, Feb. 28, 1866* (privately printed, 1866), 6.
18 John Bingham, address at Bowerston, Ohio (August 24, 1866), reprinted in "The Constitutional Amendment Discussed by Its Author," *Cincinnati Commercial*, September 11, 1866, 19, quoted in Craddock, "Protecting Prenatal Persons."
19 *Cleveland Daily Leader*, April 16, 1864, 4. See also *Cincinnati Enquirer*, December 21, 1865, 3; *Cleveland Daily Leader*, March 7, 1866, 3; *Ashtabula Weekly Telegraph*, June 29, 1867, 1.

Following the Jones abortion and others, an Ohio Senate committee noted that doctors "have now arrived at the unanimous opinion that the foetus in utero is alive from the very moment of conception. . . . The willful killing of a human being, at any stage of its existence, is murder.'" The bill became law in April.[20]

Other state legislatures from 1866 to 1868 debated both abortion and the Fourteenth Amendment. Solons in Florida, Illinois, and Michigan passed pro-life laws within two months of their ratification of the Fourteenth Amendment. The Ohio, Kansas, Missouri, Nebraska, New Jersey, Oregon, and Vermont legislatures all bulwarked their pro-life laws quickly before or after their ratification votes.[21]

By the end of 1868, 30 of the 37 states (including 25 that ratified the Fourteenth Amendment, and 27 that criminalized abortion before as well as after quickening), had pro-life statutes. They referred to the fetus as a "child" and/or "person." Twenty of them punished equally killing an unborn child at six weeks or six months. Laws in 17 of the states called abortion manslaughter, murder, or assault with intent to murder, and classified abortion as a crime against a person.[22]

The 1860s did not bequeath us public opinion polling, yet judging by newspaper accounts, medical society reports, and state legislative action, most Americans were in favor of protecting unborn children. Although racism was rampant not only in the South but in the North as well, most Americans were not in favor of murdering blacks. But, given the evidence of the Memphis and New Orleans massacres, freedmen needed federal protection against state-level politicians out for

---

20 *Ohio Senate Journal* (1867), 233, quoted in Craddock, "Protecting Prenatal Persons."
21 James Witherspoon, "Reexamining *Roe*: Nineteenth-Century Abortion Statutes and the Fourteenth Amendment," *St. Mary's Law Journal* 17 (1985): 29–70. See also John D. Gorby, "The 'Right' to an Abortion, the Scope of Fourteenth Amendment Personhood, and the Supreme Court's Birth Requirement," *Southern Illinois University Law Journal* 4 (1979): 9–49.
22 Witherspoon, "Reexamining *Roe*," 34–36, noted the variety of states without a quickening distinction: Alabama, California, Illinois, Indiana, Iowa, Louisiana, Maine, Maryland, Massachusetts, Missouri, Nevada, New Jersey, Texas, Vermont, and Virginia.

blood. Most unborn children did not need federal protection: They were gaining rights at the state level.

Furthermore, abortion had long been a state-by-state issue, not a federal one with constitutional antecedents, nor one that had just pushed the nation into civil war. Besides, some politicians may not have talked about abortion publicly because it was not considered a subject for public discussion: When Congregational minister E. Frank Howe preached in Indiana a "Sermon on Ante Natal Infanticide," he said "It is with extreme reluctance that I touch the subject," for "some will be disgusted."[23]

Here's what is clear: After the Memphis and New Orleans outrages, concern about protecting southern blacks, and not negating the results of the Civil War, was so prominent among Republican leaders that other issues had no heft. Had the Fourteenth Amendment debate occurred following sensational abortion coverage in 1871 and thereafter, personhood for the unborn could have become explicit, but that had no chance in 1866.[24]

The irony is that the Supreme Court did stretch the Amendment in the late nineteenth century to consider corporations as persons, and in the late twentieth century to turn unborn children into nonpersons nationwide.

---

23 E. Frank Howe, *Sermon on Ante-Natal Infanticide* (Terre Haute, IN: Allen & Andrews, 1869). Howe said he would try to get out the message about destroying human beings as best he could: "In the ears of the thoughtless I would sound the cry of MURDER! so clearly that henceforth they cannot fail to think." One more possible reason abortion went unmentioned: Ratification of the Amendment by three-fourths of the states was not a sure thing, and addition of another issue might have complicated the process. The Ohio and New Jersey legislatures rescinded their ratifications, largely for reasons of racism, and Secretary of State William Seward adroitly substituted ratifications by Alabama and Georgia (required to ratify so as to rejoin the Union) before certifying the Amendment's adoption on July 28, 1868. But I doubt that Republicans were thinking much about abortion: They heard the cry of MURDER down south, and the focus on protecting freedmen was intense.

24 For more understanding of the "persons" issue, see Michael Paulsen, "The Plausibility of Personhood," *Ohio State Law Journal* 74, no. 14 (2012): 13–73; and *Brief of Amici Curiae Scholars of Jurisprudence John M. Finnis and Robert P. George in Support of Petitioners*, No. 19-1392 (2021) re. *Dobbs v. Jackson Women's Health Organization*.

And James Jaquess? The Louisville prosecutor wanted to give immunity to the abortionist who killed Louisa Williams so as to prosecute the man who apparently paid him, Jaquess. The judge, though, said no. Witnesses testified to the adultery of Jaquess, but without an eyewitness to Jaquess doing the actual "procuring," the jury declared him not guilty. Mrs. Jaquess left him and he didn't want to show his face in Illinois again, so Jaquess went south and failed at growing cotton. He then went to England and became involved in a scam that led to a twenty-month British prison sentence. Jaquess died in Minnesota in 1898.[25]

---

25 *Boston Evening Transcript*, June 2, 1885, 4; *The* (London) *Standard*, July 11, 1894, 2; *Old Bailey Proceedings Online*, November 1894, trial of JAMES FRASIER JAQUESS, June 24, 1898, 5; Burnette, *James F. Jaquess*, 111–64.

19

Compassion vs. Abortion

FROM 1865 THROUGH 1876, many Americans focused on the attempt to enforce equal rights for ex-slaves in the South. Northern cities, though, also had their racism. Blacks in Philadelphia could not ride on the horse-drawn streetcars that began operating in 1858. After agitation, the Ridge Avenue Passenger Railway Company started running a special car for African-Americans, designated by a sign reading, "Colored Persons Allowed to Ride on This Car." The segregation plan led to renewed protests, with some Philadelphians writing "one man is as good as another" and "equal rights the world over."[1]

On March 22, 1867, the Pennsylvania legislature seemed to settle the debate by passing a bill permitting blacks to ride on all streetcars. Three days later a twenty-one-year-old schoolteacher, Caroline LeCount, tried to board a streetcar, as she had several times previously, each time being ejected. The streetcar conductor snarled at her and uttered a racial slur. LeCount complained and won. The conductor paid a $100 fine, and all eighteen streetcar companies saw they must stand for equal rights or fall into legal trouble.[2]

1 Winnifred MacKay, "Philadelphia during the Civil War, 1861–1865," *The Pennsylvania Magazine of History and Biography* 70, no. 1 (January 1946), 36–37.
2 Center for Black Educational Development, "Caroline LeCount, Black Educator Hall of Fame," *Philly's 7th Ward*, February 3, 2021. https://phillys7thward.org/2021/02/caroline-lecount-black-educator-hall-of-fame/.

It was supposed to work the same way regarding abortion: Protect the unborn child or be penalized. The Pennsylvania legislature in 1860 had taken a firm stand: Since abortionists could contend regarding a pre-quickening abortion that the woman was never pregnant, one section of the new law said any abortion attempt was an offense, whether a woman was pregnant or not. "This section," the reformers said, "will put a stop to a crime of too frequent occurrence."[3]

Not so. One physician, Andrew Nebinger, saw up close the lack of enforcement. Nebinger knew about demand for abortifacients from his ten years as an apothecary before he graduated in 1850, at age thirty-one, from the Medical Department of Hugh Hodge's University of Pennsylvania. He knew about demand for surgical abortions because he had built a medical practice among some who were wealthy but also among the poor of south Philadelphia.

Rich and poor knew of Nebinger's charitable work. During the Civil War he served as surgeon-in-charge at a hospital for wounded soldiers and did not take a salary, but earned comments like these: "God bless you for your faithful efforts to relieve the sufferings of, and restore my dear, my oldest son," and, "His kindness to the sick, and his untiring zeal for their comfort, proves him to be a philanthropist of the first order."[4]

Nebinger also believed in both educating—he gave free lectures at the Mechanics' Institute—and castigating. He protested lack of city action in flushing culverts and cleaning up cesspools and slaughterhouses that contributed to a cholera epidemic in 1866. He pointed to sufferers and reminded officials of "the long and weary hours of

---

3   Pa. Laws No. 374, §§ 87, 88, 89 (1860); reprinted in Eugene Quay, *Justifiable Abortion: Medical and Legal Foundations* (Washington, DC: Family Life Bureau, 1961), 507.
4   Fannie W. Overton, in James Moore, ed., *The History of the Cooper Shop Volunteer Refreshment Saloon* (Philadelphia: J. B. Rogers, 1866), 57–58; C. E. Hill, in *House Divided: The Civil War Research Engine at Dickinson College*, hd.housedivided.dickinson.edu; MacKay, "Philadelphia during the Civil War, 1861–186," 22.

agony, the wasting of the forms and strength of each of these victims of public neglect."[5]

A constant opponent of abortion, Nebinger was effective in his warnings because neighbors saw his compassion. Manuscripts in the Library of Congress show the regard for him "particularly in the lower [poorer] section of the city, where he gave advice, medicine and pecuniary assistance to those who stood in need. It is said that during his long professional life he never asked or accepted a fee from a poor orphan or widow." He never married and became a "kindly and considerate friend to the sick poor. He followed the teachings of the Divine Master, 'In so much as ye have done it unto one of the least of these, ye have done it unto me.'"[6]

Nebinger was for eighteen years a member of Philadelphia's Board of Public Education. He aided directly those leaning toward abortion because of poverty: He abandoned his paid medical practice and volunteered "to relieve the sufferings of the sick poor who had not the means to engage a physician." He became a manager of the St. Joseph Orphan's Asylum and a doctor at two charity-oriented hospitals. No one could accuse him of being "pro-life only up to birth."[7]

Nebinger's frustration with callousness toward "the least of these" appears in the transactions of the Medical Society of Pennsylvania for 1876. When the Society asked Nebinger and several associates to research abortion, he wrote a short book, *Criminal Abortion: Its Extent and Prevention*. His survey of fifty-nine doctors from all parts of Philadelphia showed that "'the murder of the innocent' is now in our day of such magnitude as to 'out-Herod Herod.'" Nebinger did not give specific numbers but estimated a quadrupling of the abortion rate during the previous sixty years: "The crime is rapidly marching on,

---

5   *Public Ledger* (Philadelphia), March 6, 1860, 2; Andrew Nebinger, "On the Prevention of Cholera," *Saturday Evening Post*, May 12, 1866, 5. For background on cholera in Philadelphia, see Charles Rosenberg, *The Cholera Years: The United States in 1832, 1849, and 1866* (Chicago: University of Chicago Press, 1987), 59–60, 145.

6   Nebinger folder, Toner Collection, Library of Congress Manuscript Division.

7   *The Philadelphia Inquirer*, January 25, 1878, 3; April 13, 1886, 2; and April 29, 1886, 2.

gathering annually blood-stained recruits to its murderous ranks, and promising . . . to render itself defiant by the number of its devotees."[8]

Nebinger expected little from enforcement of Pennsylvania's law as long as the number of abortion devotees increased. His survey showed abortion to be "more frequent in the better classes of society than among the poor"—and those better classes were well-connected politically. One colleague told Nebinger, "I have been often called upon by ladies of the most undoubted character, who very innocently suppose that it cannot be wrong to produce abortion, as long as there is no quickening." Nebinger largely ignored the question of supply of abortionists and emphasized the need for education that could reduce demand.[9]

Nebinger also complained about "ignorance of the true physiology of gestation. [A woman lets] the little being within to be ruthlessly destroyed, mainly because she does not comprehend the immoral enormity of her conduct. . . . The embryo is a living being from the moment of its conception. . . . A wide-spread diffusion of the necessary information among women, by those in whom they have confidence as moral and religious instructors, will in a brief cycle very perceptibly diminish, and finally almost entirely prevent, the commission of the crime of abortion."[10]

Nebinger became president of the Medical Society of Pennsylvania in 1880. Colleagues said Nebinger was effective because he was "the guide, philosopher, and friend of all," not only "a man of strong opinions" but one of the "tender helpers to the distressed of every sort

---

8   Andrew Nebinger, *Criminal Abortion: Its Extent and Prevention* (Philadelphia: Collins, 1876), 4, 5, 10. See also Laurie A. Wilkie, *The Archaeology of Mothering: An African-American Midwife's Tale* (Milton Park, UK: Taylor & Francis, 2003), 150.
9   Nebinger, *Criminal Abortion*, 13.
10 Nebinger, *Criminal Abortion*, 11, 12, 19, 21. Nebinger praised Episcopal bishop Arthur Cleveland Coxe's criticism of "murder of the unborn human" and Coxe's statement that science was on his side: "No physiologist doubts the ovum an instant old [has] existence and individuality." Nebinger also quoted Catholic Bishop John Bernard Fitzpatrick of Boston about human life "beginning the very instant conception has taken place." (See A. Cleveland Coxe, *Moral Reform Suggested in a Pastoral Letter with Remarks on Practical Religion* [Philadelphia: J. B. Lippincott, 1869], 103–5).

and condition." When he died in 1886 at age 67, a biographer called him "a brave man who struck with no uncertain hand at a crime that still remains a blot upon our civilization. Would that there were more men of his stamp among us, ready to brave everything for the truth."[11]

Nebinger was not the only pro-life doctor known also for helping the poor. The disgraced James Jaquess stayed away from Quincy, Illinois, but Dr. Addison Niles helped that city's impoverished for years. He told fellow doctors and pregnant patients, "The Creator has provided the foetus with a house in which to live, with a temperature suited to its wants, with expanding walls to accommodate its increasing development, and a fountain from which to imbibe his nourishment."[12]

When Niles died in 1875 at age 63, the *Chicago Medical Examiner* noted, "To his patients, and especially to those of the poorer class, among whom he had many, he was ever kind and tender." Other obituaries also called Niles "admired by his enemies, loved by his patients, especially the poor."[13]

Some pastors after the Civil War risked backlash by speaking of slavery and abortion as twin evils. Minister and bestselling author John Todd told a reporter, "We have rid ourselves of the blight of Negro slavery, affirming that no man may be considered less than any other man. Now let us apply that holy reason to the present scandal." The General Assembly of the Presbyterian Church in the United States of America came to a similar conclusion, declaring that it viewed "the destruction by parents of their own offspring before birth with abhorrence."[14]

---

11 *Philadelphia Times*, April 18, 1866, 4; *Medical and Surgical Reporter* 54 (April 24, 1886): 544; and 57 (October 29, 1887): 582; *Philadelphia Inquirer*, April 29, 1886, 2. Nebinger left behind bequests for the orphan asylum, a shelter for women in trouble, a hospital, and a soup kitchen colorfully named the Southwark Soap Society.
12 Addison Niles, "Criminal Abortion," *Transactions of the Twenty-First Anniversary Meeting of the Illinois State Medical Society, Held at Peoria, May 26, 1871* (Chicago: Fergus, 1872), 96–101.
13 Toner Manuscript Collection, Library of Congress.
14 "Criminal Abortion," *Northwestern Christian Advocate*, March 13, 1867; *Christian Monitor*, July 18, 1868, 2; *Minutes of the General Assembly of the Presbyterian Church in the USA* (Northern), vol. 18 (Philadelphia: Presbyterian Publications Committee, 1869), 937. Todd was 67 and finishing

Most pastors during the last quarter of the nineteenth century were not so clear. Doctors noticed: Niles criticized the "lack of proper religious teaching" about protecting the unborn, listed several cases of clerical cover-up, and demanded, "The clergy should speak out from the pulpit, [with] discipline of the Church brought into action."[15] Dr. Winslow Ayer's book on "the great crime of the nineteenth century" charged cowardice regarding abortion: Pastors thought "a plain sermon upon it from the sacred desk would strike directly at many professed Christian members, and give such mortal offence that the offender would preach to slim audiences ever after, if at all."[16]

One exception to this silence of the shepherds came in 1891 at Old South First Presbyterian Church in Newburyport, Massachusetts. That church's pastor, Brevard Sinclair, preached an entire sermon against abortion, and the *Boston Globe* reprinted it. The next year, Sinclair published it along with the reactions it generated. His major point: American pastors who dodge the abortion issue constitute "the Church asleep." His goal was to wake it up and oppose those who claim "life only begins at birth. . . . When they make this claim they lie! I know that the best biological science of the 19th century says they lie!"[17]

---

out 30 years as the pastor of a Congregational Church in Pittsfield, Massachusetts. His *Lectures to Children* sold 200,000 copies, but he chose the unpleasant subject of abortion for one of his last works, *Serpents in the Doves' Nest*, and began it, "Nothing but an imperative sense of duty could induce me to pen what I am about to write." Todd described abortion as "deliberate, cold murder," and said, "If we continue to do what we are doing, the wrath of God will burn towards our land" (Boston: Lee & Shepherd, 1867), 3, 14, 24. The Presbyterians said those guilty of abortion were excommunicating themselves: "except they repent, they cannot inherit eternal life." The General Assembly asked ministers to be "no longer silent or tolerant" regarding abortion, but to "endeavor by all proper means to stay the flood of impurity and cruelty."

15 Niles, "Criminal Abortion," 98–101.
16 Winslow Ayer, *The Great Crime of the Nineteenth Century and Perils of Child Life* (Grand Rapids, MI: Central Publishing, 1880), 5.
17 Brevard Sinclair, *The Crowning Sin of the Age: The Perversion of Marriage* (Boston: H. L. Hastings, 1892), 16. The most famous eighteenth-century evangelist, George Whitefield, is buried in a tomb under Old South's pulpit. Historians estimate that four out of five Americans heard him preach at least once from 1738 to 1770, when Whitefield died in Newburyport.

Sinclair contended that many churchgoers "would be astonished to hear that they are not Christians," given their lackadaisical attitude toward abortion and sometimes their emergency patronage of abortionists. He said those "who perhaps with great pretentions pray for a revival in the church, and for the out-pouring of God's Holy Spirit, are often the guilty parties. . . . Let me say then to hypocritical Pharisees that smoking a cigar may be a filthy habit, but that abortion is murder! And not even the mask of self-righteousness . . . will save them from the wrath of God."[18]

The reaction to Sinclair's gambit proved his point about fearfulness among ministers. Some ministers thought his sermon should have been "toned down." James Mitchell, pastor of First Presbyterian Church in New Bedford, Massachusetts, told Sinclair he "recently treated the same subject in a part of a discourse which I preached to my people. I was not able then, nor am I at any time, to present it with the pointedness and boldness which you have done." Frank Barton, pastor of a Newton, Massachusetts, Methodist church, said he knew "what it means to stand before a cultured, refined and conservative audience and proclaim the bold, uncompromising and unflinching truths of God"—but most do not, since "many pulpits are but empty or ornamental."[19]

After seeing the reaction, Sinclair concluded that "euphemism is . . . the bane of the modern sermon," yet "a sermon against sin, which does not like a quivering spear hit the mark of some guilty soul, is as great a failure as Satan might himself desire." He said ministers are "too often afraid to handle the delicate matters," so they could safely refer to "the sins of Pharaoh and Nebuchadnezzar, or the Slaughter of the Innocents . . . but [not] assail the sins of today."[20]

After 1900, more pastors spoke out about the plight of the poor but were still quiet about abortion. Some theological conservatives

---

18 Sinclair, *Crowning Sin of the Age*, 22.
19 Sinclair, *Crowning Sin of the Age*, 43.
20 Sinclair, *Crowning Sin of the Age*, 29.

preached about life after death and outsourced preaching about life before birth to pro-life doctors. Dr. E. E. Hume told a Kentucky medical meeting that when a church member couple asked him to do an abortion, he was the one who needed to explain: "This is a life, as soon as impregnation occurs."[21] Dr. Walter Dorsett, at an American Medical Association convention, complained that "the clergy do not seem to be at all concerned. Few sermons are preached from the pulpit for fear of shocking the delicate feelings of a fashionably dressed congregation."[22]

---

21 *Kentucky Medical Journal* 2 (September 1904): 100, quoted in Leslie Reagan, *When Abortion Was a Crime: Women, Medicine, and Law in the United States, 1867–1973* (Berkeley: University of California Press, 1997), 83.

22 Walter Dorsett, "Criminal Abortion in Its Broadest Sense," *Journal of the American Medical Association* 51, no. 12 (1908): 957–61.

20

Thugs of Society

IN 1871, a gentleman walking down Fifth Avenue in his heavy black suit and white linen shirt would pass by billboards advertising new consumer items: hair tonic, Pear's soap, and tobacco. One tobacco ad showed a horse-drawn bus driver smoking his pipe as a passenger sniffed and said, "If that's Honest Long Cut, blow the smoke this way!"[1]

A half mile away, between Eighth Avenue and the Hudson River, sat impoverished blocks that received their name when one policeman supposedly said, "This place is hell itself," to which the other replied, "Hell's a mild climate. This is Hell's Kitchen."[2]

A New York legislative committee reported, "Cattle were better housed than human beings in Hell's Kitchen." The neighborhood's street names—Rag Picker's Row, Cat Alley, Rotten Row, Bummer's Retreat, Cockroach Row—announced its squalor. Residents drank at colorfully named taverns—Paddy the Pig's, the Star and Garter, McElroy's Pig's Head—and formed gangs: Dead Rabbits, Gorillas, Gophers. But on Manhattan's finest street, the Fifth Avenue Hotel

---

1 Alexander B. Callow Jr., *The Tweed Ring* (London: Oxford University Press, 1965), 50.
2 Richard O'Connor, *Hell's Kitchen* (New York: Alvin Redman, 1958), 12–14.

sported a public elevator publicized as a "perpendicular railway intersecting each story."³

How could New Yorkers move up from Hell's Kitchen or other poor neighborhoods to Fifth Avenue? Some did it by years of hard work. Others saw sudden openings, seized legitimate entrepreneurial opportunities, and became rich. But the two most famous Fifth Avenue homeowners in 1871 had millionaire incomes gained illegally. They lived nine blocks apart: "Boss" William Tweed, at the corner of Fifth Avenue and 43rd Street, and Madame Restell (whom we met in ch. 13) at the corner of 52nd.

They set the pattern by which abortionists would stay in business for the next century, until abortion became legal in New York in 1970 and nationwide in 1973: Send bribes and donations to political machine leaders, and those officials will not send police to break up the killing fields.

Restell's house was the gaudier. James McCabe, author of an 1868 guide to New York City, marveled over her first-floor grand hall, made of marble and lined with mirrors, and the three large dining rooms furnished in bronze and gold. The next three floors had bedrooms with blue brocade satin and gold-and-ebony bedsteads, along with a picture gallery. The fifth floor boasted a billiards room and dance hall. Throughout stood statuettes, paintings, ornamental and valuable clocks, and candelabra.⁴

Restell supplemented her income with blackmail. McCabe wrote, "It may be one or ten years after her services were rendered, but at what she considers the proper time she . . . will startle [former customers] with a call, or a note regarding the events that they would gladly forget. . . . The appeal is generally made to the man, and is sustained by such strong proofs that he dares not refuse to comply."⁵

3 Callow, *Tweed Ring*, 50. Temporarily, Trinity Church's 284-foot tower remained the highest structure in the city.
4 Edward Martin [James McCabe], *The Secrets of the Great City* (Philadelphia: Jones Brothers, 1868), 430.
5 McCabe, *Secrets of the Great City*, 430.

Another impressed observer, Ferdinand Longchamp, walked readers through Restell's home. He noted costly furniture "imported from France and Italy, China and Japan, some inlaid with gold.... Throughout the house, made bright as day by hundreds of gaslights, one walked on soft, smooth carpets of the best manufactures in Europe. They alone were worth a fortune."[6]

Longchamp brought along to a Restell soiree a foreign friend: Unaware of the owner's reputation, he thought the house must be that of an ultra-rich merchant or manufacturer. Longchamp told him the hostess "practices infanticide every day," and "all of the furniture ... has been purchased with the money received for the murder of a child."

The friend asked, "Must I infer from this that the laws of America do not punish infanticide, that fearful crime of getting rid of children before or after their natural birth?" Longchamp replied, "The law often remains a dead letter. This thug of society holds in her hands the honor of hundreds of families and it would be dangerous to arouse her resentment."[7]

In 1871 Restell rode up Fifth Avenue in a carriage pulled by matched grays. So what if children called her "Madame Killer"? In 1871 a district attorney denounced abortionists generally and the best-housed one, Restell, specifically: "Every brick in that splendid mansion might represent a little skull, and the blood that infamous woman has shed might have served to mix the mortar." But bribes to politicians and police kept her in business: As one historian noted, "a single word from Tweed would have closed this human abattoir.... But Madame knew too much. Tweed did not want to bring down her wrath upon his friends."[8]

William M. Tweed was eleven years younger than Restell and probably 180 pounds heavier: In 1871 he weighed more than 300 pounds.

6   Ferdinand Longchamp, *Asmodeus in New York* (New York: Longchamp, 1868), 19.
7   Longchamp, *Asmodeus in New York*, 19.
8   *New York Times*, September 3, 1871, 8.

He grew up poor and left school at age eleven to learn the chairmaking trade from his father. He clawed his way up the political ladder and as New York City's commissioner of public works learned how to add millions of dollars to city budgets. The 15 percent he typically raked off the top went into his mansion, his stable on 40th Street where he kept carriages and sleighs, a country mansion in Greenwich, Connecticut, and upkeep on a steam yacht named "The Wm. M. Tweed."[9]

As mentioned in chapter 15, Restell showed her political power in 1853 by having Mayor Jacob Westervelt preside at her daughter's wedding. Tweed used *his* daughter's wedding on May 31, 1871, to flash his money during the post-wedding reception at his city mansion. A *New York Sun* reporter was tongue-tied: The parlor, "lighted up with the utmost brilliancy . . . beggared description." The Tweed family resembled "a Christmas tree of diamonds."[10]

The wedding presents showed how officials and corporate heads pledged allegiance to Tweed: Forty sets of sterling silver, one of which had 240 pieces. A cross of eleven diamonds from a state senator. "Diamonds as big as filberts" from a judge. A 60-diamond representation of wheat sheaves from a city contractor. A huge sterling silver bowl for ice cream from businessman Jim Fisk, soon to be shot dead. Diamond bracelets of "fabulous magnificence": One gift of jewelry carried a $45,000 appraisal. Total value of wedding presents: $700,000 or so, the equivalent of more than $15 million today.[11]

Unlike Restell, politician Tweed spread the wealth. The Young Men's Democratic William M. Tweed Club had its headquarters at 105 East Broadway. The first floor featured a parlor with a grand piano, a gold and bronze chandelier, rosewood furniture, a "sumptuous" carpet, and a bar and billiard room. Tweed supporters at one party consumed

---

9   Kenneth Ackerman, *Boss Tweed* (New York: Carroll & Graf, 2005), 47–52.
10 M. R. Werner, *Tammany Hall* (New York: Doubleday, 1928), 190–93. Callow, *Tweed Ring*, 250–51. Tweed's daughter was particularly sparkly, with diamonds on her ears, neck, arms, bosom, and even her white satin shoes.
11 *New York Times*, June 1, 1871; Ackerman, *Boss Tweed*, 145–46. See also Werner, *Tammany Hall*.

one hundred kegs of beer, fifty cases of champagne, twenty gallons of brandy, ten gallons of gin, a barrel of whiskey, two hundred gallons of chowder, fifty gallons of turtle soup, thirty-six hams, and 4,000 pounds of corned beef.[12]

But Tweed, like Restell driving down Fifth Avenue, could not help showing off. He wore a large diamond on his vested chest. His followers wore smaller diamonds on theirs. Less than two months after the wedding reception, *New York Times* editor Louis Jennings used records from a weary, insubordinate Tweed appointee to publish "The Secret Accounts: Proofs of Undoubted Frauds Brought to Light."[13]

The records showed how "the Tweed Ring" siphoned off millions from projects and bond issues. From 1869 through 1871 New York City's debt tripled and city taxes soared. Analysts said one-third of the city budget went to those who lacked real jobs and did no work. The payroll included twelve manure inspectors.[14]

Facts in the *Times*, along with cartoons by Thomas Nast in *Harper's Weekly*, turned public opinion against Tweed. That complicated life for Madame Restell. While she apparently did not directly bribe Tweed, she sent new gold pieces to many of his allies. But she, like Tweed, was overly ostentatious, and the *Times* emphasized that the perpetrators of both abortion and political corruption lived in splendor: "Great mansions on grand avenues are occupied by disgusting 'practitioners' who continue to escape prosecution."[15]

With the *Times* and other newspapers pushing, the New York legislature in 1872 created easier rules regarding evidence of abortion and raised the maximum penalty to twenty years' imprisonment.[16] Meanwhile, prosecutors went after Tweed, but his first trial, in January 1873, ended with a hung jury amid rumors of bribery. At a second trial

12 *New York Times*, October 24, 1871, 1.
13 Callow, *Tweed Ring*, 247; *New York Times*, July 22, 1871, 1.
14 *New York Times*, October 3, 1871, 4.
15 *New York Times*, January 12, 1872, 4.
16 Act of April 6, 1872, ch. 181, 1872, *New York Laws*, 509–10.

later that year, the jury convicted Tweed on 204 of 220 counts. A judge sentenced him to twelve years in prison. Once Tweed entered prison, Restell's political protection decreased. She hunkered down, still selling abortifacients but avoiding surgery that could send her to prison.[17]

While Restell rested in her gilded cage, Tweed languished behind bars. When a judge in December 1875 allowed him a pre-Christmas visit to his family, Tweed escaped to Florida and Cuba, then boarded a ship to Spain. U.S. officials pursued him and made a deal with Spain that led to Tweed's arrest and return to a New York prison. Depressed and ill, he disclosed in 1877 details of his Tweed Ring thefts, hoping to trade confession for release from prison, but the deal broke down. The Ring was broken, and many who depended on its protection faced prosecution.[18]

One of them was Madame Restell. In 1878 she sold some abortive drugs to undercover federal agent Anthony Comstock. The *Times* reported her arrest and noted, "The residence of Mme Restell is one of the best known in New York. Her wealth is entirely the proceeds of her criminal profession. Her patrons are said to belong to the wealthiest families."[19] This time, though, Restell's patrons were not able to protect her from arrest or from reporters who followed every detail of her arraignment and trial.

Some of the developments were low comedy. Since Restell could not immediately turn her investments in bonds and real estate into cash for bail, she had to rely on bondsmen. But they, aware that public opinion had turned against Restell, agreed to put up sufficient funds only if the judge ordered newspapers not to print their names. The judge refused and the bondsmen refused.

Restell's lawyer turned to one and asked him to help out, saying, "Will you not allow a Christian feeling to govern you?" The bonds-

---

17 Dennis Tilden Lynch, *"Boss" Tweed: The Story of a Grim Generation* (New York: Boni & Liveright, 1927), 178, 183. Reprinted in 2017 by Routledge (London).
18 Lynch, *"Boss" Tweed*, 292–344. See also Oliver E. Allen: *The Tiger: The Rise and Fall of Tammany Hall* (Reading, MA: Addison-Wesley, 1993). For a sympathetic look at Tweed, see Leo Hershkowitz: *Tweed's New York: Another Look* (Garden City, NY: Anchor/Doubleday, 1977).
19 *New York Times*, February 14, 1878, 8.

man replied, "I've got a wife and a family of girls, and I'll be hanged if I'm going to have my name in the papers as a bondsman for an abortionist."[20]

Restell eventually left jail while awaiting trial, but she could not leave behind newspaper attacks. She had lived by the press and was now dying by it. Her lawyers failed in their attempt to suppress the newspaper accounts and complained that the press was "without standards" in criticizing a "poor old woman." Restell, still blind to the humanity of the unborn, said she did not understand why she faced judgment: "I have never injured anybody. Why should they bring this trouble upon me?"

The New York Times described Restell as "driven to desperation at last by the public opinion she had so long defied." At night she paced her mansion halls like a latter-day Lady Macbeth, looking at her hands and bemoaning her situation. Finally, early in the morning of April 1, 1878, the day Restell's trial was to begin, a maid discovered her in the bathtub, throat cut from ear to ear. The *Times* headline at the top of page one announced, "END OF A CRIMINAL LIFE. MME RESTELL COMMITS SUICIDE." Some at first thought it a grotesque April Fool's Day joke, but police confirmed her death and newspapers throughout the United States reported it.[21]

The next day, undertakers buried her at the Sleepy Hollow Cemetery: Hers was the largest monument in that part of the cemetery, and it included a carved figure of a sleeping infant. Ten days later Boss Tweed died of pneumonia at age fifty-five. Mayor Smith Ely refused to fly the City Hall flag at half-staff.[22]

---

20 *New York Times*, February 14, 8. For more on the *Times* coverage of this story, see Marvin Olasky, *The Press and Abortion, 1838–1988* (Hillsdale, NJ: L. Erlbaum, 1988), 29–33.
21 *Indianapolis People*, April 13, 1878, 6; *Cincinnati Weekly Enquirer*, April 3, 1878, 4; *Philadelphia Inquirer*, April 2, 1878, 3.
22 Eric Hornberger, *Scenes from the Life of a City* (New Haven, CT: Yale University Press, 1994), 139.

SECTION THREE

SUPPLY AND DEMAND

1871–1940

Section 3 examines supply-side and demand-side opposition to abortion through the early twentieth century. Newspapers sensationally exposed abortionists, and police rounded up the usual suspects. Women became doctors and led compassionate organizations. New-schoolers with antiseptic procedure began to replace old-school abortionists, who sometimes killed not one but two patients.

21

A Much Pulverized Reporter

THE MOST SENSATIONAL WEEK in American abortion history began on August 23, 1871. On that day the *New York Times* published a long and vivid story headlined "THE EVIL OF THE AGE. Slaughter of the Innocents... Scenes Described by Eyewitnesses." Reporter Augustus St. Clair wrote of "human flesh, supposed to have been the remains of infants, found in barrels of lime and acids, undergoing decomposition." He described the affluence of an abortionist couple, Dr. and Madame H. D. Grindle: "The parlors are spacious, and contain all the decorations, upholstery, cabinetware, piano, book case, &c., found in a respectable home."[1]

St. Clair quoted Madame Grindle about "the class of people that come to us. We have had Senators, Congressmen and all sorts of politicians bring some of the first women in the land here." He named abortionist names: Restell, Mauriceau, Ascher, Selden, Franklin, Van Buskirk, Maxwell, Worcester. He emphasized the constant cover-up, since "All the parties have the strongest motives to unite in hushing the scandal."

Reporters from the 1830s onward had generated reader involvement by emphasizing the beauty of abortion seekers and adult victims.

---

1 *New York Times*, August 23, 1871, 6.

St. Clair's story lacked only a description of a woman coming for an abortion—say, someone "about twenty years of age, of slender build, having blue eyes, and a clear, alabaster complexion . . . long blonde curls, tinted with gold." The face and figure of that particular woman are relevant because, three days after the publication of St. Clair's big story, a train station baggage handler smelled a horrible odor emanating from a trunk to be shipped to Chicago. He opened it and found the corpse of that twenty-year-old, long blonde hair and all. The autopsy verdict: abortion.[2]

Newspapers throughout the United States ran stories about the "trunk murder." Here's the lead of a semi-prurient story the *Louisville Ledger*, the *Ottawa* (Canada) *Daily Citizen*, and many other small newspapers ran, erroneously making the dead woman a teenager: "NEW YORK—The body of a lovely girl of seventeen, evidently the victim of an abortionist, was found entirely naked and thrust into a trunk. . . . The affair is causing intense excitement, and promises to become a *cause celebre*. Bystanders were horrified at the sight of a nude girl, lying cramped up at the bottom. . . . The body was ruthlessly bent double and crammed into the trunk."[3]

An odd vaccination mark and two dental fillings helped police identify the dead woman as Alice Bowlsby, 20. On August 30 a St. Clair follow-up story included a full description of the young woman he had purportedly seen at an abortion office but strangely neglected to mention the week before. He finished the new story with a flourish, in italics: "*I positively identify the features of the dead woman as those of the blonde beauty, and will testify to the fact, if called to do so, before a legal tribunal.*"[4]

Was that true? A third of a century ago I wrote about the long-forgotten St. Clair and made him a pro-life hero, but with archives

2 *New York Times*, August 27, 1871, 1; August 30, 8.
3 *Louisville Ledger*, August 27, 1; *Ottawa* (Canada) *Daily Citizen*, August 30, 4. See also *Chicago Tribune*, August 28, 1871, 3, and August 31, 1871, 1; *New Orleans Daily Picayune*, August 30, 1871, 8; *Galveston Daily News*, August 30, 1871, 1, and September 6, 1871.
4 *New York Times*, August 30, 1871, 8.

of small newspapers and small towns now available online, I've taken another look and learned about a scandalous past that had led him in 1867 to change his name officially from William Augustus Doolittle Jr. to Augustus St. Clair.[5]

Born in New York City in 1839, Doolittle/St. Clair at age 19 married a beautiful woman, Mary Byington, also 19. At 20 he became the rector of an Episcopal church in Yonkers but fought with the congregation. The vestry demanded that the bishop remove him. The bishop complied. Doolittle was bitter and became a Congregational minister. He avoided Civil War service and had three daughters by the time he and his wife were 26, in 1865.[6]

In 1867 Doolittle headed 150 miles north and was pastor for a half year at First Baptist Church in Hoosic Falls, New York, near the Vermont border. He did not last long because, as he eventually confessed, he became sexually involved with a deacon's wife. That's when he legally changed his name and became a newspaper reporter in Troy and then Newburgh, New York, in 1870–1871. According to court documents, he then became sexually involved with another woman, Mrs. Jenny Erkenbrach, whom the *New York Sun* described as "a woman of unusual personal attractions."[7]

Let's review: Fired from at least two pastoral jobs, caught in at least two adulteries, he hung around the *New York Times* office during the extraordinarily busy summer of 1871. The *Times* was battling Tweed and covering the aftermath of a July 12 clash between Protestant and Catholic immigrants in which more than 60 New Yorkers died.[8]

---

5   Marvin Olasky, "Opposing Abortion Clinics: A New York Times 1871 Crusade," *Journalism Quarterly* (Summer 1986); *St. Louis Globe-Democrat*, September 10, 1875, 7.
6   Episcopal Diocese of New York church records, 1767–1970; Mount Vernon (Eastchester) St. Paul's records, 1856–1896.
7   *Rutland* (VT) *Weekly Herald*, November 4, 1869, 6; *The Evening Gazette* (Port Jervis, NY), July 14, 1870, 1; *Mobile Weekly Tribune*, October 19, 1872, 5; *New York Sun*, May 1, 1872, 1; *Vermont Gazette*, January 11, 1873, 4.
8   Dennis Tilden Lynch, *"Boss" Tweed: The Story of a Grim Generation* (New York: Boni & Liveright, 1927), 367–69. Reprinted in 2017 by Routledge (London).

The background of *Times* editor Louis Jennings does not suggest much interest in abortion. He produced one editorial about abortion that criticized "talk of such matters with bated breath, or . . . the veil of a false delicacy. . . . From a lethargy like this it is time to rouse ourselves."⁹ But Jennings did not even mention abortion in a book about America he wrote just before becoming editor—even though abortion was rampant. During the summer of 1871 he was looking for another way to poke at the corruption of Tweed's associates. His regular reporters were busy. But look—here's Augustus St. Clair, hungry for work. Sure, let him spend a couple of weeks visiting abortionists. See if he can produce a story with all the right elements: human interest, crime, vulnerable women, death.¹⁰

St. Clair came through: "The Evil of the Age" was his one shining moment in journalism.

But his artful reporting made him a public figure, and some reporters learned of the difference between his day job, which led to jail sentences for some abortionists, and his "night work" in Hoosic Falls and elsewhere, which could have *caused* some abortions. Seven months after his stellar work, he publicly defended a corrupt government official, and other newspapers attacked him, suggesting bribery. The *Times* threw him under a horse-drawn bus: "He is the father of more misstatements than any other twenty correspondents put together."¹¹

St. Clair's shaky reputation plummeted in October 1872 after famed entrepreneurs/finaglers Jim Fisk and Edward Stokes quarreled over a girlfriend: Stokes shot and killed Fisk outside a New York hotel. St. Clair testified that he saw a pistol in Fisk's hand, so Stokes purportedly had fired in self-defense. Others saw no pistol. The *Brooklyn Eagle* called St. Clair "eccentric" and a "much pulverized reporter." The *Charleston*

9   "The Least of These Little Ones," *New York Times*, November 3, 1870, 4.
10 Louis Jennings, *Eighty Years of Republican Government in the United States* (1868; repr., San Francisco: Palala, 2015).
11 *New York Times*, March 9, 1872, 4; *Chicago Tribune*, March 18, 3; *Buffalo Commercial*, March 23, 2.

Daily News said, "St. Clair's story bears the strongest evidence of having been manufactured."[12]

Other newspapers agreed that St. Clair was a liar. They reported that four men from Hoosic Falls were ready to swear "that they would not believe St. Clair under oath." The *Boston Globe* declared, "Those who claim to know [him] say that he is not a man worthy of belief," and suggested bribery once again: "He would not hesitate to swear to more than he knew, for a consideration."[13] His career as an investigative reporter was over.

In 1874 St. Clair snagged a public relations job for the Liquor Dealers Protective Union of Brooklyn. In 1875 he was a toastmaster at a Long Island hotel. During the rest of the decade he wrote advertising booklets for hotels, with gushing words like these: "Visitors will experience complete satisfaction not only in respect to the refreshments they obtain, but in the charges they pay, and the handsome treatment they will invariably receive." It was a long way down from his investigative journalism.[14]

In 1884 St. Clair received a "severe thrashing" when traveling salesman Henry Van Bunckle found his wife with St. Clair at a hotel. Over the next fifteen years, St. Clair picked up some short-term editing and public relations jobs in Elmira, New York City, and St. Joseph, Missouri. Census reports show him as still married in Mount Vernon, New York, but his wife often appeared as "head of household." When she died in 1906, her obituary (as Mary C. Doolittle) said she "was at one time considered one of the most beautiful women in Westchester

---

12 *Brooklyn Daily Eagle*, October 2, 1872, 2; *Charleston Daily News*, October 21, 1; *Washington Evening Star*, October 1, 1.

13 *Wisconsin State Journal*, October 16, 1872, 1; *New York Times*, October 16, 2; *Muscatine* (IA) *Evening Journal*, October 19, 1; *Chicago Tribune*, October 17, 1; *Nashville Union and American*, October 17, 1; *Boston Globe*, October 17, 5.

14 *Brooklyn Daily Eagle*, July 2, 1874, 8; August 8, 1874, 2; August 25, 1874, 2; October 10, 1874, 3; *Boston Post*, August 28, 1875, 3; Augustus St. Clair, *Guide to Rockaway Beach, with Illustration of the New Rockaway Beach Hotel, the Largest and Grandest Structure of Its Kind in the World* (New York: Garland, 1880); *Mount Vernon Chronicle* (New York), July 23, 1880, 3.

County," and "four daughters survive her." The obituary said nothing about a husband. St. Clair was still alive, though: He died in 1915 in Brooklyn and is buried in Greenwood Cemetery.[15]

The facts of St. Clair's life make me doubt the truthfulness of the dramatic ending to his second story, cited earlier: "*I positively identify the features of the dead woman as those of the blonde beauty, and will testify to the fact, if called to do so, before a legal tribunal.*" When police arrested Jacob Rosenzweig, the abortionist whose operation led to the young woman's death, prosecutors trying to prove her presence in Rosenzweig's house did not call upon St. Clair to offer crucial testimony. It seems they did not consider him a credible witness.

Nevertheless, St. Clair's story led to others. Horace Greeley's *New York Tribune* ran a hard-hitting editorial entitled "THE ROOT OF THE EVIL," in obvious homage to the *New York Times*'s "EVIL OF THE AGE" theme of abortion as big money-maker. Newspapers that had avoided the topic in Chicago, New Orleans, Galveston, and other cities began using the words "abortion" and "abortionists."[16]

As New Yorkers demonstrated in front of abortionist offices, including those belonging to Madame Van Buskirk, Thomas Evans ("the ghoul of Chatham Street"), the Grindles, and Ann Burns, it looked like protest by press and populace would work: Police arrested all those abortionists. But in January 1872, the Van Buskirk trial ended in a deadlocked jury and the Madame went free. In April 1872, the Court of Appeals said Evans needed a new trial because of judicial

---

15 *New Orleans Times-Picayune*, December 3, 1884, 2; *Pittsburgh Daily Post*, March 2, 1887, 1; *The Catholic Tribune*, November 29, 1890, 8; *The Courier* (Waterloo, IA), February 17, 1891; *Iowa State Reporter*, February 29, 1891, 10; *Star-Gazette* (Elmira, NY), October 1, 1892, 4; *New York Times*, October 17, 1906, 9.

16 *New York Tribune*, August 30, 1871, 1; *Chicago Tribune*, August 31, 1871, 1; *New Orleans Daily Picayune*, August 30, 1871, 8; *Galveston Daily News*, August 30, 1871, 1; and September 6, 1871, 1. *The New York Tribune* attacked "an infamous but unfortunately common crime—so common that it affords a lucrative support to a regular guild of professional murderers, so safe that its perpetrators advertise their calling in the newspapers, and parade their spoils on the fashionable avenues. The editorial concluded with a flat statement: "Abortion at any period is homicide."

error: Prosecutors said they were too busy and witnesses were unavailable, so Evans went free.[17]

That month, the district attorney decided he had insufficient evidence to put the Grindles on trial: They went free. Ann Burns, convicted of manslaughter and sentenced to seven years in prison, gained a new trial on a technicality. In May 1872, the chief witness for the prosecution disappeared. Burns went free.

Rosenzweig hired some of New York's best lawyers to appeal his conviction. The state Supreme Court agreed and ordered a new trial, but they argued successfully that he could not be convicted under the old law now that the New York legislature in 1872 had passed a new one. Rosenzweig went free after just two years in prison, much to the chagrin of journalists from Vermont to Iowa.[18]

---

17   *New York Times*, October 30, 1871, 1; December 8, 1871, 2; December 15, 1871, 1.
18   *Consolidated Laws of New York* (Brooklyn: Edward Thompson, 1917), 591; *Chicago Tribune*, November 14, 1873, 1; *Chicago Evening Mail*, November 14, 1; *Rutland* (VT) *Weekly Herald*, November 20, 2; *Quad-City Times* (Davenport, IA), November 13, 4.

22

The Victims Are . . .

EXCITEMENT CONCERNING "the trunk murder" showed editors that readers wanted such life-and-death stories. Newspapers that had been skittish about printing unpleasant words such as "abortion" and "abortionist" would now report on the what, when, and where—but they still were uncertain about the "who."

The *Chicago Tribune* announced in 1878, "A horrible death by abortion took place this morning in this city, the victim being Maggie Gibbons, a pretty young girl 18 years of age."[1] But weren't there two victims? In 1901, former Secretary of State John W. Foster wrote that in the nineteenth century normal usage changed from "the United States are" to "the United States is." Did abortion bring a parallel question: When a woman died following an abortion, was the story "the victim is" or "the victims are"? Let's look at three tragedies in 1879.[2]

New York, February: Cora Sammis, twenty-one, "a sweet, innocent, lovely country girl," lived with her parents "in a beautiful little cottage in a village on Long Island." She was "one of the handsomest and best educated girls in the village. . . . of a gentle and amiable disposition

---

1 "Special Dispatch," *Chicago Tribune*, January 3, 1878, 1.
2 John W. Foster, "Are or Is?" *New York Times*, May 4, 1901, BR7. Novelist/historian Shelby Foote made that formulation famous in *The Civil War*, the 1990 Ken Burns/PBS series.

... much beloved by all with whom she came in contact.... luxuriant brown hair ... one of the prettiest as well as one of the most exemplary girls in the village. ... a member of the village Methodist church and a teacher in the Sunday school."[3]

One neighbor called Sammis "the last girl in the village ... that I would have supposed could be tempted." But here comes the wolf, Frank Cosgrove, "a gay, fashionable butterfly, entertaining an exceedingly high opinion of himself. ... In an evil hour she listened to the tempter, and under the sacred promise of immediate marriage, he lured her to her ruin. ... Instead of marrying her at once, and endeavoring to hide her shame, and to make some atonement for his crime, he brought her to a famous New York abortionist."[4]

That's where she died. *New York Herald* reporters were probably the best at paint-by-numbers sentimental abortion stories: "The words from a dying girl's lips yesterday revealed a sad, sad tale of human weakness and depravity and tore the veil from the secrets of an abode in which she had sought death as a shield from the world's dishonor. It was away upstairs, in a dismal little room ... ill-furnished, ill-ventilated, with only the blank, dismal walls to greet the patient's eye."[5]

But with all that sympathy for beautiful and dead young women, some newspapers did not forget the dead unborn children, even though few people then knew what they looked like. The *Herald* in essence said, "the victim is," but *The Brooklyn Eagle* noted that each child is "an immortal being," so that every slain pregnant woman signifies "a double

---

3 *Boston Globe*, February 13, 1879, 1; *Brooklyn Daily Eagle*, February 12, 8; February 13, 4; February 20, 4; *Marion* (SC) *Star*, May 13.
4 *New York Herald*, March 29, 1879, 9; *Brooklyn Daily Eagle*, April 2, 2; *New York Times*, April 3, 8; *New Orleans Daily Democrat*, July 8, 1.
5 The *Herald* (March 29, 1879, 9) continued: "Honest, God-fearing, simple-minded folks were the girl's parents." Cora's father, sixty-five-year-old Henry Sammis, a coal and lumber dealer on Long Island, learned she was suffering, rushed to the metropolis, and heard the news of his daughter's death: "I was almost paralyzed with horror, and could not believe the story to be true." Viewing his daughter's body, "he stooped and kissed her forehead, and, controlling himself, arose and looked at her for a long time in silence."

murder—that of the mother and of the child in her womb." The *Eagle* used the Sammis deaths to reflect on "The Great American Crime" and the police, prosecutors, and judges who enabled it: Abortion "is murder, and the official who complacently permits the perpetration of a murder, becomes an accomplice."[6]

The Brooklyn Eagle also recommended compassionate alternatives to abortion: maternity homes, foundling hospitals, and adoptive homes. It noted that abortion was often the result of illicit sex but stressed the importance of hospitals and then homes for unwanted children: Providing such facilities will not "eradicate unchastity [but] will assuredly remove the motive for murder." Cosgrove should have married Sammis, but if he refused, the other recourse was "to pay the young woman money enough to leave home for a long period and be delivered of her child naturally."[7]

The second tragedy of 1879 came in March: "Jennie Clark Killed by Abortionists and Her Body Disfigured." As in the trunk murder of 1871, the Jennie Clark story featured a corpse crammed into a trunk, this time one floating down a river north of Boston. For newspapers across the country it was a circulation gift that kept on giving, as readers from late March through early November learned of (1) a corpse disposed of and found, (2) attempts to identify the disfigured woman, (3) detective work revealing the guilty, (4) a trial ending with a hung jury, and (5) a second trial ending in conviction.[8]

The Boston Globe used specific detail: "Decomposition had so far advanced that recognition was impossible. . . . horribly mangling her poor body before death had made it cold forever. . . . the genitive organs bore signs of recent inflammation." The victim's looks again were

---

6   *Daily Eagle*, February 13, 1879, 4; *Sunday Eagle*, February 16, 1879, 2. The *Eagle* that year claimed it had "the Largest Circulation of any Evening Paper published in the United States." Later, newspapers owned by Joseph Pulitzer in the 1880s and William Randolph Hearst in the 1890s outpaced it.
7   *Sunday Eagle*, February 16, 1879, 2.
8   *Fort Wayne Sentinel*, July 16, 1879, 1.

important, with newspapers presenting a sketch and commenting, "with such a face Jennie Clark should have won the sympathy and kind regard of all who knew her. A sad contrast to . . . the mutilated body."[9]

Then came detective work, "Searching for the Villains Who Brought Poor Jennie Clark to Her Shame, Ruin, and Most Cruel Death." Alleged abortionists and killers Caroline C. Goodrich and Daniel F. Kimball had cut off Clark's hair and her nose to make identification of the corpse more difficult. Kimball had looked for a river into which to dump the trunk, but most of the streams were frozen, so he finally chose the small Saugus River. Newspapers around the country emphasized one victim, the mother, and noted only in passing that a child was also dead.[10]

Reporters made sure "the sensation caused by the discovery of the mutilated body will not soon be forgotten." Fall brought a trial and a hung jury: As frequently happened, one juror held out. Then came a second trial, during which reporters were getting bored or impatient, as one *Boston Globe* headline indicated: Then came an unusual ending: The jury unanimously found the defendants guilty, with the two abortionists getting sentences of ten years (Goodrich) and eight years (Kimball), far longer than usual.[11]

---

9 *Boston Globe*, March 20, 1; Mar 21, 8; March 24, 1; March 25, 2; March 26, 1; March 27, 1; April 4, 4; April 7, 5. To guarantee sympathy for Jennie Clark, it was important that the pregnancy resulted from a single misstep rather than a repeated lack of chastity. A typical headline was, "Most Emphatic Testimony to the Pure Character of the Murdered Jennie" (*Globe*, March 21, 8).

10 *Boston Globe*, June 29, 1; *Boston Post*, July 17, 3; *New England Farmer*, July 26, 2; *Fall River Daily Evening News*, July 18, 2; *Arizona Daily Star*, July 18, 2; *Topeka State Journal*, July 16, 1; *Lawrence (KS) Daily Journal*, July 17, 1; *Detroit Free Press*, July 17, 7; *Nebraska State Journal*, July 18, 3; *Cincinnati Enquirer*, July 17, 5; *Wheeling (WV) Daily Register*, July 17, 1; *Oshkosh Northwestern*, July 16, 1; *Watertown (WI) News*, July 23, 2.

11 *Boston Post*, July 17, 3; *Boston Evening Transcript*, September 22, 1879, 8; September 23, 8; September 24, 1; *Boston Globe*, October 22, 4; *Fitchburg Sentinel*, October 30, 1879, 3; *New England Farmer*, November 8, 2. I do not know whether they served their whole sentences. If Kimball received time off for good behavior, he could be the Daniel Kimball convicted of larceny in 1884. Caroline C. Goodrich, in 1889, her year for leaving prison if she had served her full time, sold a building in Boston for $10,500 ($318,000 now) (*Boston Globe*, July 1, 1884, 1; and July 13, 1889, 5).

The third tragedy, in Greensburg, Indiana, a quiet city of three thousand located halfway between Cincinnati and Indianapolis, received coverage in those cities and in the weekly *Greensburg Standard*. Its November 21, 1879, issue had a normal news roundup: "The Christian church is being repaired.... Rev. Deshiell and G. W. Crawford had quite a debate, as to whether temperance was on the decrease or increase." Will Myers Jr., a young entrepreneur, from one of the city's leading families, ran an ad for "THE FAVORITE BRAND OF FLOUR. WE SELL IT."[12]

Suddenly the quiet city found itself split into factions on a sensational story: Entrepreneur Myers had captivated Eliza Frances Levassy, "a good-looking country girl... considered quite a belle in her neighborhood.... She yielded to his mellifluous tones and submitted to his embraces.... In due time fruits of her illicit love became so plain that Eliza called in her alleged seducer."[13]

Myers and Levassy went to the dental office of Dr. C. C. Burns, who allegedly aborted their unborn child. Levassy survived but the couple broke up, as is typical after abortions: Animosity became both personal and legal. Lawyers on Levassy's side brought four civil suits against Burns and Myers along with two criminal ones: the first against Burns and Myers for procuring an abortion, the second against Burns for killing the unborn child.[14]

Burns, described as one of Greensburg's "oldest and most respectable citizens," struck back, saying, "the girl's character was bad... it is a blackmailing scheme." Subpoenas went to ninety-seven witnesses who could provide alibis for Burns and Myers or character references for Levassy and the two defendants. Residents packed the Decatur County courthouse day after day, with "the best legal talent" in Greensburg

---

12 Ad in the *Greensburg Standard*, July 11, 1879, 5; *Greensburg Standard*, November 21, 1879, 5. The 1880 census recorded a population of 3,198. Interstate 74 now runs by Greensburg.
13 *Cincinnati Commercial*, November 24,1879, 4.
14 *Cincinnati Commercial*, November 24, 4, and November 26, 2. Some stories gave the unborn child's gestational age as three months. Others said five.

engaged on both sides. Jurors met for twenty-eight hours and could not agree. The judge dismissed the jury and the lawyers settled up, giving Levassy $1,500 and agreeing to no jail time for Burns or Myers.[15]

Burns continued to advertise his dental practice in a *Greensburg Standard* ad showing teeth and announcing, "THE OLD RELIABLE DENTAL OFFICE. . . . No cheap operation performed." *The Greensburg Standard* reported in 1884 that Will Myers Jr. was "building a new frame wagon shop" and grinding "large wagon loads of wheat." Five years later Myers became a founding member of the Decatur County Fiddlers' Association. Meanwhile, Eliza Levassy disappeared from the newspaper records and probably moved away.[16]

The Greensburg story received attention in Cincinnati, sixty miles away, but no further, probably because Levassy survived. To gain national attention, a story usually needed the death of a pretty woman, such as the "very beautiful" Annie J. Curtis, whose voice had "surpassing sweetness, compass, and power." The villain was "Benjamin Gregory, a man of great inherited wealth. His ruling passion is music, and he made a vacancy for her in the choir of the Church of the Atonement, of which he is organist."

The story practically wrote itself. "The intimacy began three months ago," and the pregnancy was a "death blow . . . to her musical aspiration." But journalists at some point had to choose: write about one victim, or two? In this story, readers learned that Curtis chose "foeticide. . . . The story of her sorrow and death is peculiarly sad." True, but except for the passing mention of "foeticide," readers did not learn about what made it even sadder: two victims.[17]

---

15 *Greensburg Standard*, November 28, 1878, 5, and June 25, 1880, 3; *Cincinnati Commercial*, December 1, 1879, 1; *Indianapolis Journal*, December 11, 1879, 2.
16 *Greensburg Standard*, February 3, 1882, 5; *Versailles Republican*, August 7, 1884, 4; *Greensburg Standard*, June 14, 1889, 1.
17 "A Sad Story: The Fatal Folly of a Gifted Woman," *The Perry County Democrat* (Bloomfield, PA), March 24, 1875, 2.

23

So Much Rascality

DURING THE 1870S AND '80S, newspapers regularly reported that abortion was arousing "intense feeling." *The Boston Post* stated, "Intense feeling has been manifested in regard to . . . the crime of abortion." The *Wisconsin State Journal* reported an arrest "on the charge of seduction and abortion made by the parents of a girl 14 years old. . . . The arrest causes intense feeling." But with all the intensity, it was still hard to lock up abortionists.[1]

In Newark, New Jersey, for example, alderman and doctor Herman Gedicke was used to getting his way. He received the largest majority of anyone ever elected alderman from Newark's fourth ward. Residents learned not to upset him. In July 1880, corset manufacturer Edward Leonard told Gedicke that his bill of $8 for medical services was too high. Gedicke, according to *The New York Times*, "applied an insulting epithet to Leonard, and while the latter's head was turned aside, raised his chair and struck him with it over the head."[2]

Four months after that unpenalized assault, Gedicke—coincidentally the chairman of the aldermen's police oversight committee—went to court for killing the unborn child of Sadie Severance, who survived to

---

1 *Boston Post*, April 27, 1874, 3; and April 28, 3; *Wisconsin State Journal*, April 26, 1882, 1.
2 *The Boston Globe*, November 17, 1880, 1; *New York Times*, July 19, 1880, 8.

testify against him. As was typical, the Newark district attorney gave her immunity from prosecution in exchange for testimony. Severance's testimony moved the jury, so Gedicke made his move: He paid $2,000 (the equivalent of $54,000 today) to bribe the jurors. When the bribes came to light, Gedicke ended up with a two-year sentence for criminal abortion, which one judge called "a most signal triumph of the law over power and influence."[3]

Not so fast: Gedicke gained release from prison after serving only five months when the New Jersey Supreme Court threw out the verdict on a technicality. Five years later two doctors sued Gedicke for malpractice, but a grand jury did not indict him. Political power had its privileges.[4]

Let's go to September 1882, when a steamboat employee fished up a cigar box containing "the body of a female child of about five months development." Police dried out the piece of water-soaked brown paper wrapped around the crushed corpse and saw pencil marks with a name: "Geo. L. Davidson." They arrested Davidson, "a man of wealth and high position" who had married twenty-year-old Mamie Baldwin six weeks earlier.[5]

Davidson, twenty-three, confessed, saying his wife "threatened that if he did not assist her in getting rid of her unborn offspring she would contrive to accomplish the act herself." He said he contacted Dr. Theodore Kinne and promised $2,000 if Kinne would "relieve his wife from her dilemma." Kinne gave her "medicine" that killed the child. He also suggested the cigar box as a way to dispose of the corpse. Davidson

---

3 Prosecutors offered immunity for the same reason their modern counterparts sometimes let drug sellers walk in return for their testimony about kingpins. Prosecutors also knew that men often pushed women into aborting: women frequently were victims rather than primary perpetrators (*New York Times*, November 6, 1880, 8; November 7, 2; November 12, 2; November 13, 2; November 14, 2; January 4, 1881, 8).

4 *New York Times*, April 12, 1881, 1; *State v. Gedicke*, February Term, 1881, 93. *Archives of Dentistry* 4 (1887): 426.

5 *New York Times*, September 7, 1882, 5.

boarded a ferry and in midstream dropped the box over the side. Alas, Davidson had not sufficiently weighted the box: the *Times*, as if to explain his incompetence in crime, emphasized that "He is possessed of wealth and lives on his income."[6]

Police also arrested Kinne, who denied any malpractice. He said Baldwin, an invalid for the past two years and the daughter of a former New Jersey county judge, had been his patient since she reached puberty. After Davidson summoned him, "I found her feverish, with great thirst, and then felt something must be done. I applied remedies." Kinne said he was not aware of an offer of $2,000. The jury accepted Kinne's statement that he was merely attempting to alleviate Mamie's suffering. Both he and Davidson went free.[7]

The *Wisconsin State Journal* in February 1883 ran a clear statement of "the victims are" rather than "the victim is." Here's the news bulletin: "Dr. C. H. Orton of Milwaukee was found guilty yesterday afternoon by the coroner's jury of a double murder in performing an abortion on ... O'Toole, and thereby causing the death of the woman."[8]

Charles Orton, age around sixty—newspaper accounts varied widely—was half a year removed from the death of his wife, "a leading society lady and a very wealthy woman." He lived "at the Metropolitan hotel. Kittie, waited on me and I learned to like her as a daughter.... We became intimate." News of Orton's peculiar definition of parenting twenty-eight-year-old Kittie "caused a profound sensation," particularly because Orton "for many years was the acknowledged leader of the Democracy" in Wisconsin and had "held many public offices."[9]

Orton, a former Milwaukee mayoral candidate and chairman of the Democratic County Committee, had also committed crimes including selling liquor without a license in 1876 and counterfeiting in 1877, for

6 *Times*, September 7 and September 8, 8.
7 *Times*, September 10, 7.
8 *Wisconsin State Journal*, February 22, 1883, 1.
9 *Fort Wayne Sentinel*, February 23, 1883, 3; *The Southern Standard* (Arkadelphia, AR), March 3, 1883, 1.

which he spent a year in prison. He claimed he had planned to marry O'Toole, but she had died of an epileptic fit. The jury did not accept that: "In view of the statement sworn to by said Orton and others, that he was engaged to marry soon said Kittie O'Toole, we consider his double crime of abortion and murder more than ordinarily brutal and deserving the severest sentence of the law."[10]

Orton, though, had political connections. When he received his sentence of a year in prison for counterfeiting, he told a reporter, "I expect to be pardoned before long. I have influence enough for that." Fifteen "old friends of the prisoner, gentlemen occupying the highest positions in social, professional, and mercantile life," asked U.S. District Judge Charles Dyer to release him, saying, "the disgrace already suffered is a sufficient penalty." Dyer did not agree, but Orton did receive a presidential pardon in 1878.[11]

Five years later, in 1883, "influence" appears again to have worked. Physicians who examined O'Toole post-mortem testified that "the condition of the womb . . . indicated pregnancy and harsh usage. . . . abortion," but municipal court judge James Mallory ignored the jury's decision and dismissed all charges against Orton. One headline succinctly showed dismay concerning Mallory's decision to release a serial criminal: "Turned loose to prey."[12]

In 1886, a Michigan jury convicted Dr. Nathan J. Aikin of aborting the unborn child of Mary Noel and giving her negligent care afterward. Aikin had long been a scofflaw: The Illinois State Board of Health in 1878 had made Aikin the first doctor to have his license revoked by a state medical board. But the Michigan Supreme Court freed Aikin on a technicality and made clear the distinction between what the public wanted and what the justices would allow, "no matter how firmly the

10 *Janesville* (WI) *Daily Gazette*, December 6, 1877, 1; *Saint Paul Globe*, February 21, 1883, 3.
11 *Daily Milwaukee News*, December 6, 1877, 4; *Superior* (WI) *Times*, May 12, 1883, 1; *Wisconsin State Journal*, April 7, 1883, 1; *Daily Milwaukee News*, October 16, 1878, 4.
12 *Wisconsin State Journal*, February 21, 1883, 1; *Daily Memphis Avalanche*, April 29, 1883, 2; *The Gazette* (Cedar Rapids, IA), April 30, 1; *Superior* (WI) *Times*, May 12, 1883, 1.

public prosecutor and the community at large may be satisfied of the guilt of the accused, and even though in fact he may be guilty." In 1887 the Maryland Court of Appeals in *Lamb v. State* similarly overturned a jury's abortion verdict.[13]

These resolutions parallel those of recent libel law, where juries have wanted to punish reckless publications but appeals courts have overturned verdicts. In both the seventeenth and the nineteenth centuries juries convicted with their hearts, showing their opposition to abortion, but Maryland and Michigan justices differentiated popular desires and judicial demands. Meanwhile, newspaper stories continued to highlight the humanity of preborn life. In 1887 railroad workers found "three decayed bodies of infants. . . . One was a female . . . of about six months gestation. . . . A successful abortionist has been plying his craft in the neighborhood."[14]

In 1887 as well, New York reporter Nellie Bly became famous for writing a series about her undercover experiences ("Ten Days in a Madhouse") and the increasing sales of Joseph Pulitzer's *New York World*. Newspapers had begun hiring "girl reporters" to do other investigative work, and it seemed only a matter of time before one did Bly-like investigative work concerning abortion. The most likely newspaper could be one unafraid of sensationalism, perhaps one infamous for headlines like "Suicide by Swallowing a Red-Hot Poker" or "The Remorseless

---

13 *People v. Aiken* 66 Mich. 460, 480–81; Samuel Hinds Thomas, "Court of Appeals of Maryland. *Lamb v. State*," *The American Law Register* 26 (October 1887): 641–54. Aiken moved to California but ran afoul of state laws against extortion and soliciting abortion by mail. Sentenced to prison, he committed suicide in 1894. "Dr. Nathan Aikin's Last Resource. POISON BEFORE A PRISON. He Preferred Death to Five Years' Solitude," *The Morning Call* (San Francisco), June 10, 1894, 1.

14 "Three Dead Babies," *The Evening Bulletin*, Maysville, KY, July 18, 1887, 1. Michael Grossberg, in *Governing the Hearth: Law and the Family in Nineteenth Century America* (Chapel Hill: University of North Carolina Press, 1985), 179–81, describes how "judges repeatedly overturned convictions." For example, in 1875 an Illinois judge freed Trevlar Slattery, charged with causing an abortion by beating his wife: The judge said the law in question was "aimed at professional abortionists," not amateurs who produce such a result. See also F. A. Harris, "A Case of Abortion with Acquittal," *Boston Medical and Surgical Journal* 104 (1881): 346–50.

Murder of Three Husbands. A Story of Arsenic, Arsenic, Arsenic. A Constant, Itching Temptation Which She Was Powerless to Resist."[15]

That was the style of the *Chicago Times*, purchased in 1887 by James J. West, who moved from the advertising department to editor in chief by putting together a syndicate that purchased the newspaper. The *Kansas City Times*, half-mocking and half-admiring, called West "a commercial Napoleon [who] bears a striking resemblance to the accepted pictures of "The Little Corporal." (West wore a black slouch hat and a black cape "with an eye for the picturesque.")[16]

Before 1888, West had shown little interest in abortion, and the *Chicago Times* early in 1888 ran ads for "Chichester's English Pennyroyal Pills" and other abortifacients. But just as *The New York Times* in 1871 had covered "The Evil of the Age" partly as a way to jab at Tweed Ring corruption, so the *Chicago Times* from December 12 to Christmas 1888 investigated abortion not because it was pro-life but because it was pro-circulation—and willing to become feared. "I have few friends," West bragged: "My wife says those I have are friends because they fear me."[17]

West chose a female writer who never got a byline and remains unidentified by historians to this day. The woman, identified only as "girl reporter," said she spent three weeks visiting 200 doctors. She named those who agreed to perform "infanticide" and "child-murder" for fees of $40–250 (about $1,100 to $6,800 today). One of her interviews was with Dr. John Chaffee, who urged her to have an abortion immediately, saying, "Thousands are doing it all the time." Chaffee was arrested several days later for performing an abortion that produced two deaths.[18]

---

15 *Chicago Times* headlines quoted in Marvin Olasky, *Prodigal Press: Confronting the Anti-Christian Bias of the American News Media* (Wheaton, IL: Crossway, 1988), 47.
16 *The Kansas City Times*, September 20, 1891, 12.
17 Kim Todd, "These Women Reporters Went Undercover to Get the Most Important Scoops of Their Day," *Smithsonian Magazine*, November 2016, Smithsonianmag.com; *Kansas City Times*, September 20, 1891, 12.
18 Todd, "These Women Reporters."

The series was a sensation, in part because "girl reporter" voiced her frustrations: "Tonight as I write this I am sick of the whole business. I did not suppose there was so much rascality among the 'reputable' people." She also showed spunk: "I felt that there was some big ruffians to be brought down yet, and I was anxious to have a composed mind and a strong heart."[19]

West won readers and created fear among doctors and pastors: He called for stricter certification requirements and more courage in preaching. But, like St. Clair, West had only one shining moment. One year later, on Christmas Eve 1889, a jury found him guilty of theft by fraudulently over-issuing and selling stock in the *Chicago Times*. Sentence: Five years.[20]

Some groups pushed for not only "intense feeling" but intense attempts to educate men into a greater sense of responsibility. Organizations such as the White Cross Society, influential in the 1880s, pressed men to "treat the law of purity as equally binding on men and women." Thousands of men signed pledges promising chastity and affirming "the unity of the moral law for both sexes." The Women's Christian Temperance Union tried to teach men about self-control in sexual as well as alcoholic pursuits.

One partial legislative success toward the end of the nineteenth century is worth noting. A magazine influential among charity leaders, *The Philanthropist*, urged federal and state legislators to penalize seduction and "defilement" of anyone under eighteen. The drive to raise the "age of consent"—the age at which a girl was "regarded by the law as competent to consent to her own seduction"—turned into a major campaign, as *The Philanthropist* criticized "the statute book in its present low estate, with its flagrantly unjust discrimination against unprotected girlhood and womanhood."[21]

19 Todd, "These Women Reporters."
20 That was the end of West's journalistic career: He did his time, moved to California, and died in 1926 (*Fresno Bee*, January 29, 1926, 11).
21 *The Philanthropist*, January 1886, 4; and May 1886, 4.

The details are devastating. In 1894, the age of consent was seven years in Delaware, ten or twelve in fifteen other states, and thirteen or fourteen in twenty more. *The Philanthropist* provided sensational stories concerning the need for a higher age of consent. One article described how two teens, thirteen and fourteen, were taken to bed by "two of the popular beaux of the town," ages twenty-eight and thirty. The men pleaded consent, and despite conclusive proof that the men had gotten the girls drunk, they escaped punishment. The movement to raise the age of consent gained traction. By 1900 only two states or territories had an age of consent below fourteen, and twelve had raised the age to eighteen.[22]

---

22 *Philanthropist*, July 1886, 4; and February 1891, 5. When families were intact, *The Philanthropist* editorialized, legal protection usually was not so vital, but life was different for "the orphaned or worse than orphaned, the homeless, penniless working girls continually made the prey of sensual, unscrupulous men, who, if able to plead consent, even on the part of the child who just passed her tenth birthday, may evade legal punishment." Then some would say these children should not be bearing children, so abortion is the solution (*Philanthropist*, December 1886, 4). See also Robert South Barrett, *The Care of the Unmarried Mother* (Alexandria, VA: Florence Crittenton Mission, 1929), 85.

24

Horror Stories at Century's End

DURING THE 1890S local newspapers continued to remind readers that sin surrounded them. A small Ohio newspaper in August 1890 ran a story of "fiendishness and heartlessness" that featured a woman confessing to "having cut two of her babies in slices and boiling them in a kettle." Other newspapers did not run with that horrific tale, but from July to October 1890 a different abortion story ran nationwide: the three main characters were pretty Annie Goodwin, the man who betrayed her, and the "vulture" who operated on her.[1]

The stories typically started with Goodwin, "a handsome girl, possessing to a marked extent the fatal gift of beauty." At age eighteen she fell for Gus Harrison, son of a wealthy builder and possessor of "plenty of money and a smooth tongue." He gave her fine clothes and jewelry. When her parents urged caution, she left home and soon was pregnant: "Her condition became such that with Harrison's consent she called Dr. Henry McGonegal. . . . He is 70 years of age, has been arrested twice for similar offenses, and has been watched closely by the police for a long time."[2]

---

1 "MOWER THE BRUTE," *Wooster* (OH) *Republican*, August 21, 1890, 3; *New York Times*, July 23, 1890, 8.
2 *Union-Leader* (Wilkes-Barre, PA), October 6, 1890, 2.

McGonegal almost got away with an abortion that killed first a child, then the mother. He arranged for Goodwin to be buried under a false name, but a policeman overheard two young women on a streetcar discussing her disappearance. An investigation led to the coroner's exhuming of Goodwin ten days after burial: she was already in an "advanced state of decomposition."

The New York Times added, "far more terrible than the terrors of decomposition were the evidences of the brutality with which the poor creature had been consigned to the earth. The only shroud she had was the ragged, filthy bed quilt . . . which Dr. McGonegal had thrown about the body in the stillness of the night when he stole it away from the loathsome east-side tenement."[3]

The *Times* made McGonegal the perfect villain, with "the appearance of a vulture. . . . His sharp eyes glitter from either side of his beaked nose, and cunning and greed are written all over his face." McGonegal's accomplice, Fannie Shaw, was similarly "repulsive in appearance, [with] vice and disease having made her a disgusting object." A reporter interviewed McGonegal's neighbors: "To the good people of Harlem, and especially to the poorer class, this grizzly old physician had long been an object of intense hatred. They were certain of his unholy practices, although he had escaped conviction, and when he drove through the streets in his old-fashioned, ramshackle gig, they hooted and jeered at him, in derision."[4]

On October 4, 1890, Joseph Pulitzer's *Evening World* dramatically reported the climax of two weeks of jury selection and trial testimony: It was not just a dark and stormy night but "a dreary, dismal night in New York's streets. Rain came down in torrents. Muddy water bubbled in rushing streams. . . . The buildings were dark and dimly outlined against the sickly flicker of the gas lights and the pale glare from the electric lamps. But one corner of the brown stone Court-House shone brilliantly through

---

3 *New York Times*, July 24, 1890, 2.
4 *New York Times*, July 23, 1890, 8; July 24, 2; July 25, 8; July 26, 2; July 27, 13; July 28, 8; July 29, 8; July 30, 8; July 31, 8; September 19, 8; September 23, 8; September 24, 9; September 25, 3; September 26, 2; September 27, 8; October 1, 8; October 2, 9; October 3, 3; October 4, 1.

the surrounding gloom. The chamber of the Court of General Sessions was brightly illuminated. Every gas jet was lighted in the room where patient Judge Fitzgerald has sat for two long weeks an arbiter between the law and the ancient destroyer of woman's life—an assassin of lives not yet begun."

The jury at "a quarter of an hour past midnight" rendered the verdict convicting McGonegal of first-degree manslaughter. Fitzgerald thanked the jury, saying any other verdict would have been erroneous, and "many mental but fervent amens were said." The *Evening World*'s story showed the difficulty of putting away abortionists, even those with blood on their hands and curses from their neighbors. The foreman said the jury took four ballots. The first: nine to three for conviction. After discussion, a second ballot was ten to two, and a third eleven to one. The last holdout, Bernard Heinrich, said he had no "doubt of the guilt of Dr. McGonegal . . . but he is such an old man." Others finally convinced Heinrich that age was no excuse.

The story was well cast: "Annie Goodwin, the pretty cigarette maker," killed by a buzzard: McGonegal "looked defiant at first, and his arms swung by his sides. But there came a change. The cold, hard light faded out of those little steely eyes, and there came an anxious look, almost pitiful, and he reached out his hand and supported himself by the table."[5]

McGonegal at age 70 faced 14 years of hard labor at Sing Sing, New York's most infamous state prison. When a judge reduced his bail from $20,000 to $5,000, McGonegal paid up and became a fugitive, but he seemed unable to lie low. In 1892 police arrested him for another abortion, and a headline read, "Only what he deserves. The Notorious Career of Dr. McGonegal is at an end." That was true: New York's Court of Appeals affirmed the verdict and the 14-year sentence. He died after serving six of them.[6]

---

5   *Journal* (Meriden, CT), October 3, 1890, 1. See also *Philadelphia Times*, October 16, 2; and (Allentown, PA) *Morning Call*, October 5, 1; *The Sunbury* (PA) *Gazette* (July 25, 1) and other newspapers initially headlined Goodwin as a "pretty typewriter," the original job title for those who typed.

6   *Union Leader* (Manchester, NH), July 28, 1892, 1; *Tribune* (Scranton, PA), November 30, 1892, 1; *St. Louis Globe Democrat*, November 30, 3; *The Standard Union* (Brooklyn), February 25, 1898, 1.

In 1893 another horror story arose in a town 100 miles northeast of Indianapolis: "Jack Roush, a huckster of Bluffton, has been criminally intimate with one Tibby Liby, a comely young woman. . . . About fifty persons accompanied the [coroner] to the graveyard and saw the grave opened. A horrible sight presents itself to their gaze. The corpse has become bloated, had turned black, while with it in the casket was the body of a child which had been born in the grave."[7]

That horrific sight made for a headline in *The Times and News* of Eufaula, Alabama: "BABY BORN IN THE COFFIN. Singular Find in the Grave of a Girl Who Was Betrayed and Poisoned." Neighbors who had seen Roush give Liby an abortifacient became suspicious following a hasty burial. They summoned a coroner, who determined that she had died "in terrible agony" following her expulsion of the aborted baby, who had a gestational age of eight months. But journalists did not know what to call the smaller victim. He wasn't an unborn child because he was born, so one reporter called him "an eight-months-old baby" and another said "the foetus of an eight-months-old baby which was born in the casket."[8]

Not only local newspapers but ones in Virginia, North Carolina, Florida, and other states described the reaction of eyewitnesses: "A mob of 100 angry farmers [went after] Jack Roush, over whose head hangs the charge of murder by poisoning." The two deaths became "the theme of conversation everywhere in the city today. The arrest is the outcome of intense feeling on the part of neighbors near the Liby home. . . . Three hundred persons from the Liby neighborhood [are] loud in their threats to lynch the prisoner." Liby was only sixteen. Police moved Roush to another town, where he disappeared from the news.[9]

7 "LYNCHING," *Fort Wayne Weekly Sentinel*, August 23, 1893, 8; "Babe Born in Coffin," *St. Louis Globe-Democrat*, August 22, 4; *Indianapolis News*, August 22, 6; *Elwood* (IN) *Daily Press*, August 22, 3; *The Republic* (Columbus, IN), August 22, 1.
8 *Memphis Commercial*, August 23, 1893, 3; *Times and News* (Eufaula, AL), August 31, 1; *Staunton* (VA) *Spectator*, August 30, 3; *Mecklenberg Times* (Charlotte, NC), August 31, 3.
9 *Cincinnati Enquirer*, August 22, 1893, 1; *The Republic* (Columbus, IN), August 22, 1; *Elwood* (IN) *Daily Press*, August 22, 3; *Indiana State Sentinel*, September 6, 5; *Pensacola News*, August 25, 3; *Indianapolis News*, August 22, 6.

Three more years went by before a new horror story, with a long-lasting aftermath, originated in another small Indiana town: Greencastle, forty miles southwest of Indianapolis. Pearl Bryan, twenty-two, had "bright blue eyes," blonde hair, and "the flawless complexion of an unspoiled country girl," along with "an attractive personality, a jolly disposition, and a confiding manner." She was "a Sunday school and church worker, sprightly and vivacious, and a social favorite in her home."[10]

Pearl Bryan also became the subject of quickly published books with titles like *The Mysterious Murder of Pearl Bryan*, *The Headless Horror*, and *Headless, Yet Identified*. Cincinnati reporter Joe Doran a generation later summarized the reasons the story had legs: "Mystery, love, tragedy, and pathos. Its brutality was enraging and its inhumanity sickening."[11] George Stimson wrote in *The Cincinnati Crime Book*, "There was the image of a young country girl meeting her tragic end in the big city ... and there was a missing head."[12]

Pearl Bryan did not die of an abortion. Her lover-turned-hater, dental student Scott Jackson, sent abortion pills to her in Greencastle, but she didn't take them. She traveled to Cincinnati early in 1896 with a plan to marry Jackson, but his plan was to abort their baby using dental tools. When she resisted, Jackson slipped cocaine into her drink and butchered her. With his roommate Alonzo Walling, Jackson took Bryan—bleeding and disoriented but still alive—across the Ohio River into rural Kentucky. There they cut off her head and left the remaining corpse in a field with all identification removed—they thought.[13]

The headless corpse stimulated gossip. When Dr. Robert Carothers conducted an autopsy and found Bryan had been pregnant with

10 *Cincinnati Commercial Gazette*, February 19, 1896, 2; March 7, 1896, 1; May 12, 1896, 1 and 2.
11 *Cincinnati Post*, April 26, 1930, 1.
12 Paul Slade, *Pearl Bryan*, at http://www.planetslade.com/pearl-bryan-01-03.html.
13 *Cincinnati Commercial Gazette*, February 19, 1896, 2; March 7, 1896, 1; May 12, 1896, 1 and 2; *Columbus* (IN) *Herald*, May 1, 1896, 9.

a five-month-old unborn male, interest skyrocketed. Carothers sent a message to his friend John Youngblut, who owned a nearby drugstore: Did Youngblut have a container suitable for storing an unborn child? Youngblut picked up a jar, emptied its peppermint sticks on the counter, and handed the jar to a messenger. Carothers put the dead child in the jar, added a preservative, and sent it back to Youngblut, who placed the jar on his counter.[14]

Within a few hours, Youngblut's sales of soda water rose "to enormous heights." In those days before fetal photography and ultrasound, people came to see and stare with fascination. They mourned Pearl Bryan's death but the tiny corpse in a jar forced them to think about abortion's second victim. Some newspaper stories noted both: The coroner "found a healthy foetus, which must have been alive up to the time of the mother's death."[15]

Following a month-long investigation, detectives solved the mystery of Bryan's death by researching a footprint left at the scene. They traced it to an unusual shoe that Jackson wore. Detectives focused their suspicions on dental student Jackson and roommate Walling, who confessed. After trials and unsuccessful appeals, Kentucky officials hanged Jackson and Walling in 1897, with headlines proclaiming, "The Necks of Neither Broken, and Both Struggle Hard in the Process of Strangulation." But that wasn't the end of the story. Musicians recorded Pearl Bryan ballads in 1926, 1927, 1928, 1940, 1944, 1954, 1962, 1965, and 2001.[16]

---

14 Indiana newspapers covering this news included *Osgood Journal*, April 30, 1896, 7; *Mitchell Journal*, April 30, 3; *Brownstown Banner*, April 30, 1; *Columbus Weekly Herald*, May 1, 9; *Indianapolis Journal*, April 23, 1; and *Connersville Daily Examiner*, April 23. See also *Ceredo* (WV) *Advance*, April 28, 1896, 2; *Norwalk* (OH) *Daily Reflector*, April 23, 1; 1896, 2; *Savannah Morning News*, April 23, 2; *Maysville* (KY) *Daily Public Ledger*, April 23, 5; and *Lincoln* (NE) *State Journal*, April 23, 1.

15 Personal memoir by Carothers quoted in Slade, *Pearl Bryan*, ch. 1, p. 3, at http://www.planetslade.com/pearl-bryan-01-03.html; *Cincinnati Commercial Tribune*, December 9, 1896.

16 *Cincinnati Commercial Gazette*, February 1, 1897, 8; and March 21, 1897, 7; *Cincinnati Commercial Tribune*, March 7, 1897, 1; and March 21, 1897, 1; *The Record-Union* (Sacramento), March 21, 1897, 1. Cable episodes of *Ghost Adventures* and *Most Terrifying Places in America* have retold the

Alongside the extraordinary Goodwin, Liby, and Bryan deaths came the ordinary ones: "Pretty Waitress Mamie Shannon Dies after Butchery"; "Coroner Hoeber Takes Six Men to the Bedside of Pretty Loretta Hannigan"; "Miss Perkins Was a Young Woman Who Was almost Worshipped. By Reason of Her Beauty and Charming Manner She Was Much Sought After." The emphasis was still on the dead woman and her looks, with the never-to-be-born child part of the background.[17]

Nevertheless, extreme cases plus the drip, drip, drip of everyday tragedy affected public opinion, according to contemporary observers. That probably had an effect on judicial opinion. The New York Court of Appeals in 1892 upheld McGonegal's conviction despite defense claims that biased jurors heard questionable testimony and saw inadmissible evidence. The justices unanimously agreed that a juror who had an opinion regarding the guilt of an abortionist could still serve if he "believed that he could render an impartial verdict according to the evidence."[18]

With witnesses hard to find and evidence of pregnancy before quickening still disputable, appeals court judges began giving prosecutors a better shot at success. The Massachusetts Supreme Court in 1892 accepted the uncorroborated testimony of a woman involved with an abortion. In 1898 the Florida Supreme Court said the conviction of an abortifacient pusher did not depend on whether a woman was pregnant: "It is unnecessary to allege or prove such fact."[19]

Nevertheless, in an 1896 issue of the *American Medico-Surgical Bulletin*, attorney Robert Taylor still asked a key question: "Why Do Abortions Go Unpunished?" He answered it: "Every person involved in the affair . . . is, for his or her own sake, pledged to secrecy." Even in the

---

story. Websites include "Pearl Bryan Murder" and "The Chilling Case of Pearl Bryan—and Her Missing Head."
17 *New York World*, March 10, 1895, 1; March 21, 1895, 1; September 16, 1898, 3.
18 *People v. McGonegal*, 136 NY., 62 (N.Y. 1892) in *Casetext*, 70.
19 *Commonwealth v. Follansbee*, 155 Mass. 274, in *Casetext*, 277; *Eggart v. State* in 25 So. 144 (Fla. 1898), 40 Fla. 527.

relatively small number of cases involving maternal death, prosecutors faced a "practical impossibility of securing convictions [due to] the secrecy with which this crime in its very nature is committed.... Such proofs as are attainable rarely do more than cast a strong suspicion of guilt upon the person charged with the offense."[20]

But Taylor and others did not see laws as useless, for even laws that did not put or keep abortionists in jail could restrict their practice. Statutes designed to protect unborn children sent a message: Abortion is wrong. Laws cut into the wages of abortionists, who had to spend part of their earnings hiring lawyers and bribing police and politicians. Laws did not end abortion but they could reduce the casualties, similar to how laws against drunken driving today cannot end the practice but can save lives.

The absence of legal panaceas meant that the supply of abortionists was likely to continue as long as demand for their services stayed strong. Doctors and others in the late nineteenth century kept coming back to the need for demand-side pro-life work, or what some today call a "culture of life": Instead of interdicting a toxic substance or activity, was it possible to reduce the yearning for it?

---

20 Robert Taylor, *American Medico-Surgical Bulletin* 9 (1896): 453–54: Even dying declarations often received "little weight" because defense attorneys could claim that the dying woman's reason was clouded and her willpower gone.

25

Medical Heroines

THE COMMON SUPPOSITION in almost every abortion story during the 1880s and '90s is that women were putty in the hands of manipulative men. For women challenging that assumption, the heroine of Sarah Orne Jewett's *A Country Doctor* was a role model. Nan Prince, slim and pretty, grows up an orphan with a kind doctor as her guardian. She wants to be a healer as well: "The thought entirely possessed her, and the glow of excitement and enthusiasm made her spring from the cedar boughs and laugh aloud. . . . God had directed her at last [to] something to work for with all her might as long as she lived. People might laugh or object. Nothing should turn her aside."[1]

Later, frumpy Mrs. Fraley is aghast: "I warn you, my dear, that your notion about studying to be a doctor has shocked me very much indeed. I could not believe my ears,—a refined girl who bears an honorable and respected name to think of being a woman doctor!" Nan "looked at Mrs. Fraley frankly, with a beautiful light in her clear eyes. 'I believe that God has given me a fitness for it, and that I never could do anything else half so well.' Her whole heart

---

1 Sarah Orne Jewett, *A Country Doctor* (Boston: Houghton, Mifflin, 1884; repr., New York: Penguin, 2005), 236, www.gutenberg.org/ebooks/15294.

had been stirred and claimed by the noble duties and needs of the great profession."[2]

The novel ends with Nan firmly on a God-led medical track: "The warm wind that gently blew her hair felt almost like a hand, and presently she went closer to the river, and looked far across it and beyond it to the hills. The eagles swung to and fro above the water, but she looked beyond them into the sky. The soft air and the sunshine came close to her; the trees stood about and seemed to watch her; and suddenly she reached her hands upward in an ecstasy of life and strength and gladness. 'O God,' she said, 'I thank thee for my future.'"[3]

Mary Gould Hood, born in 1850, was a real-life equivalent. The daughter of a country pastor, she graduated in 1874 with seventeen others from Women's Medical College of Pennsylvania. Four years later she went into private practice in Minneapolis, but her work always had a public face. She was a founding doctor at the Bethany Home for Unwed Mothers and also practiced at the Northwestern Hospital for women and children, which had an all-woman medical staff and an all-woman board of fifty directors.[4]

Those institutions emerged as in one decade the population of Minneapolis more than tripled, soaring from 46,887 in 1880 to 164,738 in 1890, which made it the eighteenth largest U.S. city. Most of the 118,000 new residents were immigrants either from the Midwest countryside or from northern Europe. As in New York City or in New England mill towns during the 1830s, most were away from their families and prey for those who wanted to take advantage of them.[5]

---

2 Jewett, *Country Doctor*, 394–95, 467.
3 Jewett, *Country Doctor*, 490. Some other late-nineteenth-century novels with women doctors as main characters: Rebecca Harding Davis's *Kitty's Choice; or, the Story of Berrytown* (1874); Elizabeth Stuart Phelps's *Doctor Zay* (1882); William Dean Howells's *Dr. Breen's Practice* (1886); Annie Nathan Meyer's *Helen Brent, M.D.* (1892).
4 "Sweet Charity," *Minneapolis Star Tribune*, January 1, 1887, 10.
5 Don Hoffsommer, *Minneapolis and the Age of Railways* (Minneapolis: University of Minnesota Press, 2005), with census numbers at biggestuscities.com.

Mary Hood jumped in at Bethany, "where any erring woman, no matter what may be her past history, is received for care and instruction, the only requirement or pledge being a promise to obey the rules of the house and to remain one year's time unless sooner discharged by the managers." Bethany's president, Charlotte Van Cleve, was all in: She gave birth to twelve children and fostered ten more born to "erring women" who had entered Bethany pregnant, sometimes escaping from brothels.[6]

As Minneapolis grew, other new institutions included the Woman's Boarding House, where "those trying to earn their own living, can find the comfort and protection of a Christian home." The Woman's Christian Association also aimed to "relieve, as far as possible, the temporal and spiritual wants of the poor." The Maternity Hospital offered free care. Children who needed care and education could stay at the Newsboy Home, the Washburn Home, or the Sheltering Arms, and other homes for orphans and destitute children.[7]

Mary Hood was one of many women physicians who believed that knowledge of what their unborn children were like, plus the assurance that they would be cared for following birth, would leave women unwilling to have abortions. The woman-to-woman educational effort began in the 1850s when Dr. Elizabeth Blackwell, the first female to receive a medical degree in the U.S., included in her book, *The Laws of Life*, a plea to "look at the first faint gleam of life, the life of the embryo. . . . The cell rapidly enlarges. . . . Each organ is distinctly formed. . . . It would be impious folly to attempt to interfere directly with this act of creation."[8]

---

6 *Minneapolis Star Tribune*, January 1, 1887, 10. The City of Minneapolis, instead of enforcing laws against prostitution, began fining brothels and giving Bethany two-thirds of the monthly revenue. The American Medical Association in those years supported legalization of prostitution as a way to fight venereal disease through regular medical inspection, but Van Cleve (and female leaders in other cities) pushed back: When a reporter asked her about the integrity of former prostitutes, Van Cleve said he should interview "the men who make these girls what they are" (Hennepinhistorymuseumblog.wordpress.com/2019/03/26/the-bethany-home-for-unwed-mothers-fighting-for-the-fallen).
7 *Minneapolis Star Tribune*, January 1, 1887, 10.
8 Elizabeth Blackwell, *The Laws of Life, With Special Reference to the Education of Girls* (New York: Putnam & Sons, 1852), 70–72. Blackwell wrote in her memoir, "The idea of winning a doctor's

Blackwell said female doctors bridged public and private, "occupying positions which men cannot fully occupy, and exercising an influence which men cannot wield at all." In the 1860s Dr. Anna Densmore French gained permission from the New York City Board of Education to use school property to teach schoolteachers about fetal anatomy. Densmore said "women would rarely dare to destroy the product of conception if they did not fully believe that the little being was devoid of life during all the earlier period of gestation." She showed, step-by-step, that "life processes were going on from the very beginning of embryonic development."[9]

In the 1870s Dr. Rachel Gleason directly addressed statements such as, "quickening is not till the four-and-a-half month, and so abortion before that time is no sin." She responded, in lectures and in *Talks to My Patients*, "True, that is about the time that the mother becomes conscious of motion, but [the child] lives, moves, and grows just as truly before as after, only the motions are so slight as not to be appreciated. . . . An attack with intent to kill is crime, whether the victim be large or small." Gleason described post-abortion syndrome: "Remorse for the deed drives women almost to despair."[10]

---

degree gradually assumed the aspect of a great moral struggle. . . . The moral aspect of the subject was increased by a circumstance which made a very strong impression on me. There was at that time a certain Madame Restell flourishing in New York. . . . The gross perversion and destruction of motherhood by the abortionist filled me with indignation, and awakened active antagonism." See Elizabeth Blackwell, *Pioneer Work in Opening the Medical Profession to Women* (London and New York: Longman's, Green, 1895), 29.

9 "A Teacher," writing in *The Revolution*, March 19, 1868, excerpted in Mary Krane Derr, Linda Naranjo-Huebi, and Rachel MacNair, eds., *ProLife Feminism: Yesterday and Today* (New York: Sulzburger & Graham, 1995), 22.

10 Rachel Brooks Gleason, *Talks to My Patients: Hints on Getting Well and Keeping Well* (New York: M. L. Holbrook, 1882), 158–59. The book, first published in 1870, went through eight editions. Elizabeth Evans reported in *The Abuse of Maternity* (Philadelphia: Lippincott, 1875) her interviews with women still troubled years later by their abortions. One woman said her "thoughts were filled with imaginings as to what might have been the worth of that child's individuality; and especially, after sufficient time had elapsed to have brought him to maturity, did I busy myself with picturing the responsible posts he might have filled. . . . [I never] read of an accident by land or by water, or of a critical moment in battle, or of a good cause lost through lack of a brave defender, but my heart whispered, 'He might have been there to help and save.'"

In the 1880s, Dr. Alice Bunker Stockham shot down the quickening doctrine in *Tokology: A Book for Every Woman*. She wrote, "Many women have been taught to think that the child is not viable until after quickening. [But] when the female germ and male sperm united, then is the inception of a new life." She challenged abortionist logic in frequent lectures: "The life of the babe in her arms is to the mother more precious than all else. . . . By what false reasoning does she convince herself that another life, still more dependent upon her for its existence, with equal rights and possibilities, has no claim upon her for protection?"[11]

In the 1890s, Dr. Prudence Saur hit the lecture circuit with her new book, *Maternity: A Book for Every Wife and Mother*. She said female physicians had a particular role in convincing women to avoid sex (and possible pregnancy) outside of marriage: "How much more God-like, to *prevent* as well as *cure*!" But once a woman is pregnant, Saur said she must remember that "the embryo is alive and hence quick from the moment of conception, [as] modern science has abundantly proven. It follows, then, that this crime is equally great whether committed in the early weeks of pregnancy or at a more advanced period in the life of the foetus."[12]

In the 1900s, Dr. Jennie Oreman spoke of her "firm determination not to tolerate abortion." She argued for challenging patients and not despairing if they nevertheless have abortions: Doctors could "control a part of the evil, though not by any means banish it. . . . Our duty as physicians is to be strong and firm in our 'no.' Practical moral sympathy

---

11 Alice Bunker Stockham, *Tokology: A Book for Every Woman* (Chicago: Sanitary Publishing, 1883 and 1887), 245. Stockham gave copies to poor women in Chicago for door-to-door selling. Each book included a certificate entitling the purchaser to a free Stockham gynecological exam.

12 Prudence B. Saur, *Maternity: A Book for Every Wife and Mother* (Chicago: L. P. Miller, 1889), 150. Saur noted that abortion has "existed among pagan nations from the earliest times. . . . The influence of Christianity has ever been to banish the practice. . . . As Christianity becomes weakened or destroyed, the fearful evil in question reappears and extends." Saur was one of the first four women admitted to the Ohio State Medical Society. Her office was in her husband's Saur Drug Store in Napoleon, Ohio: for 140 years a large gold color mortar and pestle on top of the building was visible for several miles.

is what the world needs, and not a flimsy sensual sympathy which is not altruism."[13]

In the 1910s, Dr. Mary Ries Melendy lectured frequently and published her thinking in the ambitiously titled *The Ideal Woman: A Book Giving Full Information on All the Mysterious and Complex Matters Pertaining to Women*. She wrote, "Intentional abortion is to all purposes a murder," and echoed what Saur had said: "The embryo is alive and hence quick from the moment of conception. Modern science had abundantly proven this to be a fact. It follows, then, that this crime is equally as great whether committed in the early weeks of pregnancy or at a more advanced period."[14]

The culmination of this series of books was Mary G. Hood's *For Girls and the Mothers of Girls: A Book for the Home and the School concerning the Beginnings of Life* (1914). She had moved to Boston and joined the executive committees of Boston Baptist Hospital and Vincent Memorial Hospital, both of which provided medical services for the poor: Vincent Memorial was particularly devoted to wage-earning women. Hood kept teaching and lecturing and turned her talks into the most delightful of the explanatory genre.

Here's how she introduced the first moments of fetal anatomy: "The two cells unite, and become one, much as two drops of water, when they come into contact, merge into each other and become one drop. Thus the two cells, which in their origin come from two different beings, unite to form the new cell, which will result in a completely new

---

13 Jennie Oreman, "The Medical Women's Temptation and How to Meet It," *Woman's Medical Journal* 3 (March 1901): 87–88. In Philadelphia, at the Woman's Medical College, women studied anatomy, chemistry, and other subjects. One student in 1893 noted her schedule for one day: four hours in the laboratory, three hours of classroom instruction, three hours with her cadaver. But they also gained training lower on the ladder of abstraction than men received: Female students made house calls to pregnant patients, collected urine samples, and performed pelvic exams (Jessica Leigh Hester, July 26, 2019, https://www.atlasobscura.com/articles/women-doctors-1800s-philadelphia-embroidery).

14 Mary R. Melendy, *The Ideal Woman for Maidens, Wives, Mothers* (Chicago: J. R. Peper, 1911), excerpted in Derr et al., *ProLife Feminism*, 126.

and different human being. . . . What experience can be more sacred, or more marvelous, than that of the mother who understands that a new human has begun within her?"[15]

Hood, like other doctors, pushed back against the idea that life begins at quickening: "This phrase gives undue importance to the first feelings of the mother, for life has been present for eighteen weeks. . . . The mother does not recognize the presence of this life until she feels the movement of the child within her body."[16]

Hood particularly tried to reduce the demand for abortion by describing how children quicken the mother: "Only yesterday there came to me a letter from a young mother who has two babies—one very young, and the other not able to walk. She writes, 'There is always something to do for one or the other baby—but I was never so happy in my life.' Motherhood brings with it cares and responsibilities, but it also brings the greatest of earthly joys."[17]

Sadly, the influence of pro-life female doctors decreased through much of the twentieth century. In 1890 the United States had 14 women's medical colleges, and Boston alone had 210 women doctors (18% of all physicians in the city). Formerly all-male medical schools were going co-ed: In 1893, 19 percent of students at the University of Michigan Medical School were female. Ironically, the opening of those doors in Michigan and elsewhere contributed to the closing of 11 of the 14 women's schools by 1904. Then came backlash, as medical schools shunted women into nursing, and only after 1970 did the number of female doctors increase once again.[18]

---

15 Mary G. Hood, *For Girls and the Mothers of Girls: A Book for the Home and the School Concerning the Beginnings of Life* (Indianapolis: Bobbs-Merrill, 1914), 68.
16 Hood, *For Girls and the Mothers of Girls*, 77.
17 Hood, *For Girls and the Mothers of Girls*, 69.
18 Joseph Dellapenna, "You're So Vain, I'll Bet You Think This Song Is about You" (2006), *Working Paper Series* 43, https://digitalcommons.law.villanova.edu/wps/art43, 57–59. See also Dellapenna, *Dispelling the Myths of Abortion History* (Durham, NC: Carolina Academic Press, 2006).

26

The Erring Women's Refuge

FROM THE CIVIL WAR through the Great Depression, women managed and volunteered at a huge variety of pro-life organizations that helped pregnant women and children without parents. The names of some of the groups in just one city, Chicago, are in the footnote below, and each large city in the United States had similar offerings of compassionate help.[1]

---

1 Chicago groups that helped mothers and children included: Babies' Nursery, Boys Manual Training School, Catholic Orphans Asylum, Chicago Industrial School, Chicago Orphan Asylum, Children's Home and Aid Society, Church Home for Orphans, Deaconess' Home, Deaf and Dumb Asylum, Englewood Nursery, Episcopal Home for Orphans, Epworth Children's Home, Foundlings Home, Friendly Aid Society, Florence Crittenden Mission, Glenwood Industrial School, Guardian Angel Orphan Asylum, High Ridge Orphan Asylum, Hinsdale Fresh Air Home, Home for Destitute and Crippled Children.

Also: Home for the Friendless, Home for Self-Supporting Women, Home of Industry, House of the Good Shepherd, House of Providence, Infant Asylum, International Girls' School, Jewish Orphan Home, King's Daughters and Sons, Ladies Christian Home, Maternity Infant Asylum, Maternity Home and Training School for Nursery Maids, Hull House, Masonic Orphans Home, McCowen Oral School for Young Deaf Mutes, Newsboys' Home, Nursery and Half Orphan Asylum, Margaret Etter Creche, Orgel School for the Deaf, Protective Agency for Women and Children.

Plus: Protestant Orphan Asylum, Relief and Aid Society, Roman Catholic Orphan Asylum, St. Mary's Society, St. Mary's Training School, St. Peter's Day Nursery, Sisters of Charity, Sisters of Mercy, Swedish House of Mercy, Uhlich Orphan Asylum, United Hebrew Charities, Visitation and Aid Society, Women's and Children's Protective Agency, Waifs' Mission, Waifs' Training School, Working Boys' Home, Working Girls' Home. See *The Inter-Ocean*, November 30, 1883, 3;

This chapter tells the story of one with a frank and feisty name, the Erring Women's Refuge. The *Encyclopedia of Chicago* says, "the philosophy of the home was revolutionary for its time, stressing the reformability of prostitutes and the transforming spiritual power of women."[2] The Refuge began in 1863 when twenty-four women from Protestant churches agreed to create a home for women seeking to leave prostitution or in the middle of crisis pregnancies. Women comprised the Refuge's board of managers, but they drafted men to be trustees responsible for raising the money, saying males were in large part responsible for the problem.[3]

The feisty choice of name was deliberate. Through 1880 the Erring Women's Refuge sheltered more than 1,000 women who at least said they wanted to move from a "dishonorable to an honorable manner of life, who are animated by a wish to reform, and who need friends to help them through the struggle." Many young women willing to admit they were erring still fought the requirement to reform: until 1881 superintendents and matrons became exasperated and quickly quit. A copy of that year's Refuge annual report in the Library of Congress shows a line through one name and "Mrs. Woods" written in.[4]

Helen Mercy Fish was born on December 14, 1831, in Williamstown, an upstate New York town 35 miles east of Lake Ontario. She had six sisters along with an older brother who owned boats that plied the Gulf of Mexico. When visiting him in Indianola, Texas, she met Leonard Woods. They married in 1853. When the Civil War began they moved to upstate New York, where Helen in the 1870s

---

February 18, 1896, 1; November 24, 1898, 2; January 24, 1899, 5; June 24, 1900, 7; June 13, 1901, 5; June 16, 1901, 8; December 25, 1901, 2; November 28, 1904, 3.

2 "Erring Women's Refuge," Encyclopedia.chicagohistory.org/pages/434.html.
3 Erring Women's Refuge, *Third Annual Report* (1866), 28. The initial meeting was on February 13, 1863. The Refuge, like the other organizations, was donor-supported, but it had one special source of support: It and the Catholic-based House of the Good Shepherd split the fines brothels paid the city. In 1899 each group received $1,329.50, the equivalent of $48,000 in 2022.
4 Erring Women's Refuge, *Third Annual Report*, 8–9; *Eighteenth Annual Report* (1881), 1.

became superintendent of the Onondaga County Orphan Asylum in Syracuse—a tough assignment, but one that prepared her for the even tougher one she began in 1881, mostly with teenagers who had often erred by trusting men.[5]

Her personal history was also preparation. Helen and Leonard Woods divorced in 1873 and Leonard died in 1875. It isn't clear who initiated the then-rare divorce, but the monthly newsletters Helen sent to Erring Women's Refuge volunteers and donors for 21 years often showed a skepticism about male intentions and trustworthiness: "J. B., a very pretty, bright girl, 17 years of age, [who] has been more sinned against than sinning. . . . Katie H., brought by her mother, a young, pretty girl, out to service and betrayed. . . . E. L., nineteen [and] anxiously looking each day for the young man who has promised to come and marry her."[6]

In the mid-1880s Woods was in charge of more than a hundred young women and their babies. She supervised a daily routine that began with singing, Bible reading, and prayer. All residents sewed during the day and had two to four hours of schooling, along with training in dressmaking, cooking, nursing, and other skills. Woods recorded comings and goings: "M. W. has been in this country only long enough to learn that friendless girls are the prey of the designing men and women who are watching for them. . . . M. L. came because she is friendless and alone. She expects to become a mother. . . . One child was adopted. Little Earl has found a home with a kind-hearted and lonely woman."[7]

---

5 *Camden Advance-Journal*, Camden, New York, May 22, 1902, and in https://www.findagrave.com/memorial/214529959/helen-mercy-woods.

6 *Refuge Journal*, April 1886, 1; May 1886, 1; July 1886, 2; August, 1886, 2; September 1886, The *Journal* (actually a newsletter) was monthly from 1886 to 1891 and quarterly for the rest of the century. I encountered the reports at the Chicago Historical Society. We know about the good works of wealthy philanthropists because they received "the gratitude of society" and often had biographers recording their benevolence. The name of frontline leader Helen Woods, though, is missing from late-nineteenth-century Chicago directories of "important" community leaders. It's also not in *Bio-Base*, an index to five hundred biographical dictionaries.

7 *Refuge Journal*, March 1886, 2; May 1886, 3; June 1886, 1; May 1887, 2; June 1887, 2.

When the *Chicago Tribune* interviewed her, Woods emphasized the importance of job skills: "Not long ago a girl came to us from a western town. She was heartlessly betrayed, and if she had not found shelter under our roof she probably would have sunk into a vicious life of helplessness but she stayed with us several months, learned the dressmaking trade, and has now gone back home and is practicing it there." Woods worried about justice: "L. E. came a long distance from her home to find refuge and to hide her shame from her friends. Are the men never punished, who bring all this sorrow and disgrace on these young, trusting girls?"[8]

Woods was most sympathetic to "young girls who have been betrayed by promise of marriage and have fled from home to avoid exposure and disgrace." She understood that lack of support during crisis pregnancies led to abortion: "Frequently unmarried mothers are destroying themselves and destroying born or unborn babes." Such danger showed why each newcomer needed personal attention: "Each has a sad history to relate. How to comfort, how to instill courage and patience, God helping us, we will do our best."[9]

Woods understood the problems of those who had "lost their mother when very young, been allowed to have their own way, or lacked discipline. . . . B. T. and child, three weeks old, were admitted. E. B. is a betrayed girl. Parents dead. Says she has no friends." Those without protectors were at great risk: "Thrown upon the world and compelled in many cases to seek at the hands of men some employment to support themselves, and having that most dangerous endowment of nature—personal beauty—they soon find that they are valued more for their attraction than for their services, and become a victim of man's cruel lust."[10]

8 Reprinted in *Refuge Journal*, July 1887, 2; October 1887, 6.
9 *Refuge Journal*, September 1886, 3, from her report to the Thirteenth National Conference of Charities and Corrections, St. Paul, Minnesota.
10 *Refuge Journal*, April 1887, 5; November 1887, 2; December 1887, 2. Woods attacked "artful and unscrupulous men" who posed as "patrons and benefactors" and then demanded sexual repayment "for favors bestowed in securing positions or furnishing employment."

Month after month, in crowded conditions throughout the 1880s, Helen Woods prayed for God's grace and then did her best. Materially, the Refuge became better off in the 1890s as it moved into a new building that featured Roman red brick, stone trimmings, octagonal rotunda lined with mahogany paneling, a slate roof, and wings radiating in the shape of a Maltese cross. More room meant more teenagers: E. C., seventeen and pregnant. P. H., fifteen and four months pregnant. J. T., sixteen, and H. P., eighteen, [both] sent from an Indiana school and pregnant. The Refuge was integrated, rare in those days: "L. M. is a colored girl brought by her mother. She is 16."[11]

Woods gained satisfaction in finding adoptive homes for children born at the Refuge. "Two infants were adopted last month, good homes being provided for them. A good home is provided for C. S.'s child, Jane." She relished meeting Refuge alumni like "L. G. with her little child, now a fine handsome boy in his third year." But even joy came rarely without sadness tagging along: "F. K. was married to the man who would have been the father of her child had it lived. It was stillborn the day after the marriage."[12]

At the turn of the century Helen Woods was still at her post after twenty years, still writing about her "family" of over one hundred women and babies and a half-dozen assistants. She never wrote about herself, but she did explain that compassion began with realism: "This home of ours has been to many of those whose steps have begun to slide like a ledge of rock midway in the slope of a precipice." Residents were still on a precipice, and a rulebook did not get them off: "A fallen woman, to be saved, must come in contact not with a system, or rule, but with another woman."[13]

Woods added, "Not only Christlike charity must go out to meet her, but careful, shrewd sagacity and knowledge of human nature." She did

---

11 *Refuge Journal*, September 1899, 7; November 1899, 6; April 1902, 6.
12 *Refuge Journal*, January 1899, 6; and November 1899, 6.
13 *Refuge Journal*, April 1902, 6; March 1886, 4; *Eighteenth Annual Report* (1881), 6.

not shy away from examining personal responsibility—"Love of whiskey has been her ruin"—and requiring work: "That nobody shall be idle is an inflexible rule." She emphasized the need for "industrial training for practical success" along with the spiritual healing that testimonies printed in the *Journal* emphasized: "Ah the beauty and joy of living with Christ and of being pure and true to yourself and others. Jesus can and does save even me."[14]

Only when personal concern was present were women likely to take personal challenges to heart. Woods cared for a young woman, Mabel, who later wrote that the Refuge was "the first place I ever lived that any person cared enough about the salvation of my soul to make it a matter of interest to me." Making such concerns a priority was central to the Refuge's task of "changing utterly the physical, mental and moral status of the women."[15]

The newsletters from Woods included specific detail, but for her audience of volunteers and donors she left out hard parts that occasional news stories about the Refuge illuminated. Item: "Maggie Hogan, the dissolute character so well known in police circles . . . sought to enrich herself by pilfering various articles." Item: A woman says she'll kill her younger sister, a Refuge dweller at age seventeen, if the sister comes home. Item: A fourteen-year-old comes to the Refuge after arrest in a brothel. The madame gave her half of what she earned, minus $3 for food. Item: A twelve-year-old is abused by her sixty-year-old stepfather, who had "flowing hair and beard as white as snow."[16]

---

14   Erring Women's Refuge, *Fifteenth Annual Report* (1878), 10–11; *Refuge Journal*, September 1887, 3. The *Refuge Journal*, May 1886, 3, summarized three vital changes: "Morbid tendencies must give way to wholesome ones, mental activity take the place of inert lethargy in the mind, religious sentiments give rise to good thoughts and insights as to duty."

15   *Refuge Journal*, April 1886, 2. Compassion was effective only if it included a willingness to suffer *with* those being helped: "the seeking shepherd shares largely in the lot of the lost sheep; if its fleece is torn, so are his garments; if . . . it has strayed away into dank and deadly places, he must breathe the fatal air."

16   *Inter-Ocean*, October 25, 1881, 7; November 26, 1893, 5; October 29, 1896, 11; February 3, 1888, 7; March 23, 1901, 4; November 9, 1901, 5; January 9, 1897, 7.

Back in 1884 the annual report had noted that the residents most likely to cause trouble "are the girls sent to the refuge from the police courts," often after arrests for prostitution. In February 1902 two teens at night set fire to their beds in the third floor dormitory room, figuring the doors would open and they'd run away. The *Minneapolis Journal* covered the outcome: "While they clamored for the doors to be opened, Mrs. Helen M. Woods, chief matron, stood them at bay, and with the keys in her hand refused to let them out. Her firmness cowed the boldest . . . the crowd stood huddled in the main hallway, completely subdued, until the fire department had extinguished the blaze."[17]

Incidents like that were probably hard on a seventy-year-old. Three months after the fire gambit, on May 18, 1902, Woods died of a cerebral hemorrhage during a Refuge chapel service. Like similar leaders in other cities, Woods realized she could not save the world, but she could help save some. As the Penitent Female's Refuge in Boston acknowledged, "We cannot purify a whole city—would that we could! But each of these changed lives is a center of influence. Who can estimate how far and wide may extend the purifying influence of one redeemed life?"[18]

Hope for redeemed lives triggered the founding of some national organizations. When four-year-old Florence Crittenton died of scarlet fever in 1883, her grieving father, Charles, who had made a fortune in pharmaceuticals, went to prayer meetings, became born again, and hoped others would find grace. He created in New York City the first Crittenton Home: It and the 70 that followed offered shelter, vocational training, and spiritual help.[19]

---

17 *Inter-Ocean*, February 10, 1884, 6; *Minneapolis Journal*, February 12, 1902, 13.
18 Penitent Female's Refuge, *Annual Report*, 1884, 15. This small refuge noted, "Although the numbers received here at any one period may seem not very large, the aggregate, when years are taken into account, is by no means small. And when the unquestioned good results are considered—the large proportion of changed lives which results, under the blessing of God, from the influences here exerted—the work must be regarded as anything but small."
19 Otto Wilson, *Fifty Years' Work with Girls, 1883–1933* (Alexandria, VA: National Florence Crittenton Mission, 1933), 144. Regina G. Kunzel, "The Professionalization of Benevolence," *Journal*

By the early twentieth century the Salvation Army had thirty-four homes for unmarried mothers and the Women's Christian Temperance Union's Department of Rescue Work had at least five. The Protestant Episcopal Church had twelve "Homes of Mercy." The "Door of Hope" group had forty homes "for fallen girls [built] in hopes of not simply sheltering and furnishing them with employment, but through love and sympathy to lead them to a Christian life. None desirous of reforming are refused admission day or night."[20]

---

of Social History 22 (Fall 1988): 21–23. For more on Crittenton Homes, see Marvin Olasky, *Abortion Rites: A Social History of Abortion in America* (Wheaton, IL: Crossway, 1992), 247–48.

20 *New York Charities Directory* (New York: Charity Organization Society, 1899), 229.

27

Weak-Kneed Enforcement

RUDOLPH HOLMES, the only child of Dr. Edward Holmes, followed in his distinguished father's footsteps. The senior Holmes, the first specialist in eye and ear disease west of the Appalachians, was president of the faculty of Rush Medical College. Rudolph Holmes graduated from Harvard and Rush, specialized in obstetrics, and in 1904 told the Chicago Medical Society, "Education is absolutely indispensable to a proper realization of the heinousness of destroying the unborn child. . . . As infanticide is murder, so should feticide be murder."[1]

At age thirty-four, Holmes was respectable and on his way to affluence: He would buy a house in Chicago's "Gold Coast" neighborhood close to Lake Michigan and next door to William Wrigley, the chewing gum magnate who became the principal owner of the Chicago Cubs. Holmes's concern with abortion alienated some Chicagoans, but he successfully urged the Chicago Medical Society to create a Committee on Criminal Abortion. Holmes became chairman and pushed his colleagues to try "influencing the daily press to discontinue criminal advertisements."[2]

---

1 "Chicago Medical Society," *Medical News*, January 28, 1905, 191.
2 Minutes of the Chicago Medical Society, vol. 16, 1903–1904, at the Chicago Historical Society. The committee grew out of a special "Symposium on Criminal Abortion" at which Holmes read his paper, "A Brief Consideration of Criminal Abortion in Its Relation to Newspaper Advertising."

Holmes gained support from another Chicago doctor, Charles Bacon, who complained that few of his colleagues put up with "the many disagreeable annoyances attendant upon fighting abortion: the loss of time resulting from attendance at the Coroner's and the Grand Jury and finally at the trial . . . attacks to be expected from the defendant's attorney . . . the enmity of the friends of the accused midwife or physician is a factor that will cause many to hesitate to do anything that promises no return except loss of time and money, and worry and annoyance." Bacon cajoled his fellow doctors to try harder.[3]

Some did. In 1905 the *Chicago Tribune*, visited by Holmes's committee, agreed to ban ads for "female irregularities or female ailments." Holmes then tried "to influence other papers to follow the lead of the *Tribune*." His committee visited eight other newspaper editors and demanded they give up abortion advertising in any form, or face public attack and eventual prosecution by the Medical Society. Four agreed. Four disagreed.[4]

To rope in the recalcitrant, the Medical Society hired a detective agency to gain proof that ads in those four newspapers were for abortion. Female detectives visited advertisers and requested an abortion: Almost all agreed. The Medical Society confronted the newspapers with that evidence and also informed postal authorities, who issued a stop order against mail delivery of the publications containing abortion ads.[5]

---

3 Charles Bacon, "The Duty of the Medical Profession in Criminal Abortion," symposium before the Chicago Medical Society, November 23, 1904, *Illinois Medical Journal* 7 (1904): 18. Bacon added, "Ordinarily it is very difficult to get satisfactory evidence against a professional abortionist. The relatives or others interested in the case are generally very anxious to prevent any publicity for obvious reasons, and even in case of the death of the mother it is frequently impossible to get any member of the family to take action in the matter."

4 Minutes of the Chicago Medical Society, vol. 16, 1903–1904, at the Chicago Historical Society. Holmes said one newspaper lost $50,000 per year by banning ads. Two newspaper editors said their newspapers did not run ads for abortion. They did not respond when Holmes sent clippings from their publications as proof: "Representatives of the two remaining papers heaped upon us the most vituperative insults."

5 Minutes of the Chicago Medical Society, vol. 16, 1903–1904.

Holmes's strategy worked for a time. The *Tribune* in March 1905 had seventeen abortion ads promising to take care of "all difficult female complaints" or "all diseases and complications peculiar to women." By the end of the year, the *Tribune* had zero. Other newspapers acted similarly. Holmes offered congratulations all around and said his committee must be vigilant "to see that they are kept out; in the course of time they undoubtedly will reappear in a new guise."[6]

In 1908 Holmes was still a whistle-blower. He described three kinds of abortionists: the young doctor who needs money, the established physician who is largely ethical but "systematically relieves his patients in order that he may hold his families," and the full-time abortionist recruited by established doctors to handle their "dirty work." Holmes said doctors in good standing in medical societies performed abortions but their colleagues were "too weak-kneed to take aggressive action for their expulsion." He also complained that complicit politicians took donations from abortionists.[7]

By 1910, though, Holmes was despairing. He noted in a medical journal that abortionists, denied newspaper advertising space, printed more business cards and distributed them through brothels and rooming-house landlords. He said Chicago abortionists had their own legal department, with witnesses on tap and ready to swear that "the young woman had an operation elsewhere and the doctor was merely performing a life-saving operation."[8]

---

[6] Minutes of the Chicago Medical Society, vol. 17, October 1905–June 1907, at the Chicago Historical Society.

[7] Rudolph Holmes, in Walter Dorsett, "Criminal Abortion in Its Broadest Sense," *Journal of the American Medical Association* 51, no. 12 (1908): 960. Holmes in 1908 extended his pro-life work to born children by educating parents with "ignorance of what good milk is. There is dirty milk, and old milk, and adulterated milk, but after these are eliminated there is still the fact that cow's milk is not a proper food for babies unless properly modified . . . to correspond to mother's milk" ("Open Talks on Summer Maladies: Says Bad Milk Is Foe to Babies," *Chicago Tribune*, July 23, 1908, 8).

[8] Rudolph Holmes, "The Methods of the Professional Abortionist," *Journal of Surgery, Gynecology, and Obstetrics* 10 (May 1910): 542.

Holmes described the working methods of abortionists who managed to stay out of jail year after year: "The cardinal principle of their actions is never to perform an operation with a witness present; her companion is rarely if ever allowed in the room. If discovery is made it is her word against his; if she dies he stands alone." Holmes told how "two or more operators . . . work in harmony; one will make all the arrangements for the procedure, and then when all is ready another will slip in to do the work."[9]

A sense of being almost all alone pushed Holmes toward giving up. He concluded "that the public does not want, the profession does not want, the women in particular do not want, any aggressive campaign against the crime of abortion. I have secured evidence." He spoke of doctors who knew of crimes not showing up for trials, while some "so-called reputable members of our Chicago Medical Society regularly appear in court to support the testimony of some notorious abortionist."[10]

Juries were also a problem: "It is not possible to get twelve men together without at least one of them being personally responsible for the downfall of a girl, or at least interested in getting her out of her difficulty." Holmes concluded that new "legislation is not needed, at least, in Illinois. We have as good a law as perhaps can be made. It is the enforcement of law that is needed."[11]

The statistics over the long run bore out Holmes's pessimism. Yes, a short-lived rise in arrests followed the 1888–1889 investigative series in the *Chicago Times*. Yes, another brief surge came after the Chicago Medical Society's efforts in 1905, and another peak followed U.S. Post

---

9 Holmes, "Methods," 542–43: "In Boston, a coterie of some four or five abortionists adopted this method—the operator would enter the room masked. One of these men confided in a lawyer that he and his associates were doing like 800 to 1,000 a year."
10 Holmes, "Methods," 542–43.
11 Holmes, "Methods," 543. Later in 1910, Holmes was driving slowly when three-year-old Valerie Poocas ran into the street from behind some bushes. He hit her and took her to a nearby hospital, where she died. A police captain said, "he witnessed the accident and he believed it to have been unavoidable" (*Chicago Tribune*, August 4, 1910, 3).

Office raids on illegal mailings in 1912—but permanent improvements did not arrive. During the first third of the century, Chicago averaged sixty investigations per year and twenty-five arrests but only a handful of criminal prosecutions and only one or two convictions each year. The level of legal action against abortion increased decade by decade but the number of convictions did not.[12]

Doctors in other cities shared Holmes's pessimism about enforcement. They often wrote in academic prose, but one doctor, M. S. Iseman, offered in 1912 an acidic city-by-city tour of how laws were not working at street level. During five years in Washington, DC, thousands of abortions led to "only nine indictments for abortion and three convictions—not enough to do more than to slow down slightly the traffic to abort." In New York City, abortion was rampant but "in some years not a single indictment follows.... It is difficult to say which is the stronger attraction for the lady visitors to the metropolis—the horseshow, the opera, or the gynecologist." In Atlanta, "After years of suspended animation, the police made a solitary arrest for the crime of abortion."[13]

Those were big-city generalizations, so here's a typical case in a smaller community: On January 12, 1902, Ella Stehman of Manheim, Pennsylvania (north of Lancaster), died after having an abortion. Her last action was to write out a notarized statement, in the presence of a doctor and family members, that Dr. J. H. Seiling performed it. At the trial, jurors saw the statement and heard evidence, but Ella's boyfriend, Monroe Todd, said Ella had told him she had done it herself. The jurors found Seiling not guilty.[14]

12 Leslie Reagan, *When Abortion Was a Crime: Women, Medicine, and Law in the United States, 1867–1973* (Berkeley: University of California Press, 1997), 116, 298. Carolyn Frazier and Dorothy Roberts, "Victims and Villains in Murder by Abortion Cases from Turn-of-the-Century Chicago," *Triquarterly* 124 (2006): 72, noted that the number of coroner's office charges increased from an average of two per year (1894–1903) to ten per year from 1904 to 1913, the decade of those two surges. During those two decades, grand jury indictments went from .7 to 5.5 per year.
13 M. S. Iseman, *Race Suicide* (New York: The Cosmopolitan Press, 1912), 158, 199, 230.
14 *Lancaster New Era*, April 30, 1902, 1; *Lancaster Inquirer*, May 3, 1902, 1; *Philadelphia Inquirer*, August 22, 1890, 5.

What was going on? Poor Ella credibly described Seiling's instruments and quoted Seiling's description to her of what an abortion involved: Since when would the testimony of an impregnating young man outweigh credible deathbed testimony? But a look at local newspapers suggests why Seiling went free. A reporter dubbed him "a physician of high standing and an historian of more than local note. . . . A highly-esteemed physician of Manheim [known for] the active interest he manifested in the annual 'Festival of Roses,' an event that attracts widespread attention." Seiling was the president of choral unions involving seven hundred vocalists. If one of those seven hundred vocalists was serving on a jury, how likely was he or she to find Seiling guilty?

Seiling had much more going for him. Here's one local newspaper account: "Wesley J. Fink, aged four years, residing on Company Street, fell down the front steps yesterday knocking out his upper front teeth, cutting his upper lip badly. He was taken to Dr. Seiling's office, who rendered professional aid." Other stories: "Dr J. H. Seiling was called upon yesterday to dress wounds for three persons who received severe injuries." A thirteen-year-old had his left hand caught in a corn sheller "and was fearfully lacerated." Seiling gave him thirty stitches. A fifteen-year-old working at the York Card and Paper company entangled his hand in the cog wheels of a machine. The machine badly mangled his fingers, but Seiling dressed the wound.[15]

Here are three more incidents: An adult walking down Market Street and carrying a knife turned to look at a car, stumbled over a porch, and fell. The knife slashed his left wrist and "severed a number of nerves, tendons, and an artery." Seiling patched him up. Mrs. Franklin W. Strausbaugh, "a paralytic, fell down a long flight of steps at her home yesterday and was seriously injured." Dr. Seiling rushed to her aid. George Buck got his left hand stuck in the gears of an elevator, which pulled him up two stories "until the ends of the fingers gave way." Buck

15 *The York Dispatch*, November 20, 1903, 6; and March 7, 1903, 5.

lost the end of every finger, including the nails, but who was there to dress the wound? Dr. Seiling.[16]

It took the jurors only ten minutes to decide they did not want their beloved doctor to spend years in prison, when he otherwise could be helping everyone from four-year-olds to old, paralyzed women.

Another big problem for enforcement: Much of the press had a short attention span. In 1905, Boston police raided the offices of more than fifteen "alleged malpractitioners," many of them downtown on Tremont and Boylston Streets. *The Boston Globe* gave the raid large initial coverage, for the places had "been known to the police and the prosecuting authorities for a long time, and public interest [was] aroused to such a high pitch." But the Boston police themselves downplayed the importance of the raids: They said their goal was not to arrest abortionists but to "harass the operators into putting an end to the illegal traffic themselves." That could have worked, except that the police raid became a one-hit wonder and Boston newspapers did not push for more.[17]

Although frustrated on abortion enforcement, Dr. Rudolph Holmes kept trying. Addressing in 1918 a conference of the American Association for the Study and Prevention of Infant Mortality, he said the coroner's office investigated not more than 1 percent of abortion deaths in Chicago: "The persons who perform the operations find it easy to cover up their tracks, and it is difficult to get witnesses to testify in cases of this kind." But the only specific proposal Holmes made was vague: "It is important that societies should take up this question and see that something is done to remedy the conditions."[18]

---

16 *Dispatch*, March 7, 1903, 5; *The Gazette* (York, PA), December 16, 1905, 1; and September 26, 1905, 1.
17 *The Boston Globe*, November 12, 1905, 1.
18 "THOUSANDS OF BABIES SLAIN IN YEAR," *Chicago Tribune*, December 7, 1918, 5. Holmes went on to other battles. Holmes introduced to U.S. obstetrics scopolamine, which combined with morphine sent moms during the birth process into a "twilight" sleep with amnesia, unable to push during delivery and usually not remembering anything about it afterward. Obstetricians without the active help of the mother often used forceps to deliver babies. Holmes, seeing forceps as overused, said about his introduction of scopolamine, "I wish to God I hadn't done it." He

Holmes remained a professor at Rush for thirty years and then taught for ten more years at Northwestern before retiring in 1943 and dying ten years later. His wife was already deceased, and they had no children: He bequeathed his entire estate to a trust for the reduction of maternal mortality.[19]

---

concluded, "The basic error has crept into the obstetric field that pregnancy and labor are pathologic entities, that childbearing is a disease, a surgical malady which must be terminated by some spectacular procedure. There is too insistent preachment by those who are defending a reign of terror of promiscuous operative furor" (L. F. Vernon, "A Brief Overview of How Male Medicine Co-Opted the Birth Process," *Women Health International* 1, no. 2 [December 27, 2015]: 110). Half a century later, many women (including my wife) insisted on being fully awake during the birth process.

19 *Chicago Tribune*, April 26, 1953, 41.

28

Old-School Abortionists

WHILE AMERICANS FOUGHT in the Civil War, Louis Pasteur in France advanced his theory that bacteria caused diseases. British surgeon Joseph Lister in 1865 applied Pasteur's finding to transform surgery at the Glasgow Royal Infirmary. When Lister used carbolic acid (now known as phenol) to sterilize surgical instruments and soak post-surgery dressings for wounds, he saw much lower infection rates. Lister's surgeons used clean gloves and washed their hands in a carbolic acid solution.

That made a huge difference. News of the innovation spread to the United States, where doctors still thought miasma—"bad air"—caused infections. Surgeons did not wash their hands before examining patients' wounds, and even were proud of stains on unwashed hospital gowns: "surgical stink" showed a doctor was experienced. In the 1880s, T. Gaillard Thomas, a professor of obstetrics and gynecology at Columbia University, and probably America's leading expert on miscarriage and abortion, criticized "charlatans" who aborted pregnancies "in the roughest and most unscientific manner."[1]

Thomas identified septicemia and peritonitis as key problems, since "the finger of the physician may convey . . . a minute portion of septic

---

[1] T. Gaillard Thomas, *Abortion and Its Treatment, from the Standpoint of Practical Experience* (New York: Appleton, 1890), 43, 45.

material." He opposed abortion but instructed students in reducing risks to their adult patients should they perform one: "You must be thoroughly aseptic yourself. . . . Your clothes, hands, instruments, sponges, and tampon (if you use the latter) should all be aseptic. . . . The nurse should be thoroughly aseptic as to her clothes, her hair, her hands, and especially her finger-nails. . . . Next, the patient should be rendered aseptic herself," with private parts "thoroughly bathed with some aseptic fluid."[2]

The Maryland Court of Appeals in 1901 recognized the move to antisepsis in abortion when it declared, "Death is not now the usual, nor, indeed, the always probable, consequence of an abortion. The death of the mother, doubtless, more frequently resulted in the days of rude surgery." The Maryland justices praised operations now performed "by skillful and careful men without danger to the life of the patient."[3]

The choice of words was significant: one patient, not two, and "skillful men." Early in the twentieth century midwives still performed some abortions, and the Chicago Medical Society's Committee on Midwives complained that the typical midwife is "filthy beyond description . . . lax in her methods . . . by her carelessness or overconfidence, [a threat to] the lives of hundreds of mothers and their babes." Such statements reeked of male chauvinism, according to some recent historians, but abortionists unaware of the importance of antisepsis, or unable or unwilling to spend extra time and money in the pursuit of safety, clearly threatened the lives of their adult patients.[4]

---

2   Thomas, *Abortion and Its Treatment*, 72–74. More subtle is "putrid intoxication," when absorption of part of "the product of conception" occurs. "The effect is the same as that which would be produced on any one by making an opening in the arm and inserting within it, so that it will come in contact with the issues, a piece of flesh. As the latter undergoes putrefaction the whole system will become more or less infected, as indicated by headache, pains in the back and limbs, quickened pulse, high temperature, and a general feeling of malaise."
3   *Worthington v. State*, 48 A (Md. 1901), 355, 356–57.
4   Charles Bacon et al, "The Midwives of Chicago," *Journal of the American Medical Association* 50 (1908): 1346–50; Carolyn Frazier and Dorothy Roberts, "Victims and Villains in Murder by Abortion Cases from Turn-of-the-Century Chicago," *Triquarterly* 124 (2006): 74.

As understanding of the danger of sepsis grew, abortionists began forming two camps. The old-school abortionists did not follow what T. Gaillard Thomas and others taught. They would sometimes end up with two corpses rather than one. (Experienced and specialized abortionists usually did better than general practitioners who had done only a few.) "New-school" abortionists, who understood the importance of antisepsis, though, probably averaged fewer than 1.01 deaths per abortion, which meant almost all women would survive physically (but often suffer psychological damage). In this chapter, we'll look at two multicity, old-school abortionists, and in chapter 30 a new-school leader.

Old-school Lucy Hagenow began her practice in San Francisco, with Louise Derchow as her first adult victim. The *San Francisco Examiner* headlined the "PATHETIC HISTORY" of Derchow, "a young and pretty fraulein" recently immigrated from Germany. In August 1887 she went to Hagenow's home, located in "a quiet and secluded spot . . . hidden from the gaze of the ordinary passers-by." The reporter called it "just such an establishment as a novelist would select . . . as the scene of a sensational crime or dark mysterious deed." When Derchow died, police arrested Hagenow but a hung jury freed her. She then killed by abortion Annie Dories, Alice Richards, Emma Depp, and their unborn children.[5]

Other hung juries allowed Hagenow to go free despite charges of abortion and of "instigating a witness to give false testimony." She hightailed it to Chicago, used aliases such as "Dr. Sucy" and "Ida Von Schultz," and advertised herself as a "licensed physician . . . all difficult female complaints; new, successful, scientific method." Her real success was in avoiding imprisonment: In 1896 and 1898 she gained acquittal on four abortion deaths. The deaths of Marie Hecht and her unborn child in 1899 earned Hagenow only a year in prison. Out she came

---

5 Her newspaper ads said, "Mrs. Dr. S. Hagenow graduated from Germany and America; diploma in office," but Missouri Medical College, her claimed alma mater, announced that she never went there ("Poor Louise Derchow," *San Francisco Examiner*, November 29, 1887, 6; *Los Angeles Herald*, August 26, 1888, 5).

and killed May Putnam and her child: "Several testified against her," but a judge ruled the evidence insufficient.[6]

Hagenow's neighbors called her home "the house of mystery" and said they would like her to move. Cause of death in one operation: peritonitis, which antiseptic procedures would almost certainly have prevented. Chicago Coroner Peter Hoffman announced "he will begin a crusade against practitioners of illegal obstetrics." Hagenow's victims in Chicago included Lola Maddison, Minnie Deering, Sophie Kuhn, Emily Anderson, and Hannah Carlson, along with their unborn children.[7]

Dr. Rudolph Holmes and other members of his Criminal Abortion Committee put a watch on Hagenow, the way dentists put a watch on a threatening tooth. When Hagenow in 1907 killed another mother and unborn child, a quick burial seemed to dispose of the evidence, but Holmes had Chicago Coroner Peter Hoffman order the body disinterred. A Medical Society detective extracted from Hagenow a confession that yes, she performed abortions. Holmes did a postmortem examination and then testified against Hagenow. His expertise sufficiently convinced all twelve jurors to send Hagenow to the state prison in Joliet on a twenty-year sentence.[8]

Even then, enforcement faced more hurdles: Hagenow's lawyers appealed to the Illinois Supreme Court and almost freed her on the argument that the trial judge allowed prosecutors to report that Hagenow was guilty of other abortions: The vote to uphold her sentence was only 4-3.[9]

Newspaper headlines called Hagenow a "TERRIBLE OLD WOMAN," one "Who Defied Police for Years." A subhead, adding in the children among her victims, counted "one thousand victims of

---

6   *Chicago Tribune*, March 17, 1905, 3. RealChoice.blogspot.com, June 2, 2013, and other dates, lists Hagenow victims.
7   *Chicago Tribune*, October 2, 1904, 50; *Tribune*, March 17, 1905, 2; *The Inter-Ocean* (Chicago), March 4, 1906, 6. Hagenow's ad was one of those that Dr. Holmes's campaign the following year extinguished.
8   Frazier and Roberts, "Victims and Villains," 71.
9   *The Inter-Ocean*, October 28, 1908, 1.

Chicago midwife." Readers learned that Hagenow had paid hush money to "a regularly organized clique of politicians and police." In Nebraska, the *Lincoln Star* showed its pro-life colors by specifying that Hagenow "caused the death of 1,000 infants and mothers." Reporters noted that a twenty-year sentence meant she would be unable to do more damage until she was in her seventies.[10]

Not so. Released after serving less than half her sentence, Hagenow started doing abortions again. When abortee Pauline Albrecht ended up in the hospital, Hagenow told reporters, "Yes, I've served time in Joliet—why do you blame me for these things? If these fool girls would take care of themselves they wouldn't have these things done, would they?" In 1925, five young women who purportedly had not taken care of themselves—Lottie Lowy, Nina Pierce, Jean Cohen, Bridget Masterson, and Elizabeth Welter—died at the hands of seventy-seven-year-old Hagenow, as did their children. Her overall score at that point was seventy-five arrests, eight trials, three convictions.[11]

In 1927 a jury found Hagenow guilty of murder and gave her a 14-year sentence. One indication of Hagenow's experience was a story told by undertaker W. J. Freckleton, who had trouble getting the corpse of one woman down a narrow staircase. Hagenow said the usual undertaker had no problem doing it. Amazingly, the Illinois Supreme Court in 1929 ordered a new trial that ended with Judge Comerfield setting her free, saying, "You had better make your peace with God." Hagenow muttered something, shambled "laboriously from the room," and died in 1933 at age 84.[12]

10 *The Dispatch* (Moline, IL), November 30, 1907, 1; *Tucson Citizen*, November 30, 1907, 1; *Salt Lake Telegram*, May 23, 1907; *Omaha Daily Bee*, December 1, 1907, 1; *Lincoln Star*, November 30, 1907, 1; *New York Times*, December 1, 1907, 6. See also two headlines from November 30, 1907: "Human Monster Is Behind Bars" (*Bellingham* [WA] *Herald*); and "Old Woman Kills Ten Thousand Persons" (*Seattle Times*).
11 "Lucy Hagenow," Cemetery of Choice Website, at http://cemeteryofchoice.com/2020/09/25/lucy-hagenow-2/.
12 *Sedalia* (MO) *Weekly Democrat*, November 23, 1927, 3; *Jefferson City* (MO) *Post-Tribune*, June 20, 1929, 8.

The other multi-city abortionist, Robert Thompson—alias Dr. Grant, Stanton Hudson, or Robert Malcolm—was active for three decades. Early in the twentieth century, calling himself "Dr. Grant," Thompson advertised in the *San Francisco Examiner* that he was a "graduate physician" and "female specialist" who would "GUARANTEE to cure the longest and most obstinate female cases in 24 hours by STRICTLY up to date, ANTISEPTIC, SAFE and painless METHODS without delay from home or work. TRAVELERS can be treated and return home the same day. We have never had a failure."[13]

A failure in 1910 made the ad disappear and graduated Thompson to the front page. The *Examiner* on September 24 described how he gave schoolteacher Eva Swan an abortion, "packed the body of the girl in a trunk," and buried her in his San Francisco cellar. Accompanying the main articles and outraged headlines—"Buried Like an Animal"—were large pictures of Swan and Thompson, and specific detail about her "hacked and acid-eaten body."[14]

The *Examiner* said Thompson spent lots of money, owned a big automobile, and appeared heartless: booked for murder, Thompson "squeezed a puffed cheek with pudgy hand . . . never blinked an eyelid . . . chew[ed] gum as he heard the charge read against him." *The Los Angeles Times* played up a nurse's testimony of witnessing Thompson "saw off the young woman's legs with a common wood saw, and then jam her mutilated and blackened body into the trunk."[15] Thompson himself had "the appearance of a vulture . . . his cruel mouth twisted into a cynical smile."[16]

Jurors also viewed Thompson as devilish and gave pro-life forces a rare legal victory: He served nine years in San Quentin. Thompson then

---

13 *San Francisco Examiner*, multiple dates, typically on page 5: this particular ad ran in September 1910.
14 *San Francisco Examiner*, September 24, 1, 2, 3.
15 *San Francisco Examiner*, September 24, 1; September 26, 1; September 27, 1.
16 *San Francisco Examiner*, September 24, 2; and September 27, 1; *Los Angeles Times*, September 28, 1910, 1.

moved to Boston and did abortions as Stanton A. Hudson: He also married or promised to marry six women ranging from stenographers to society ladies. Arrested three times, he lawyered up, spent only three months in jail, and moved to New York City.[17]

There he struck it rich. Using the alias "Robert Malcolm," Thompson arranged with thirty doctors to send him patients for abortions "in return for generous commissions." *The New York Daily News* in 1928 was the rare newspaper still interested in exposing abortionists through front-page investigations. Police, pushed by public opinion and the board of health, eventually raided Thompson's office. They botched the raid, probably intentionally, with the *Daily News* saying policewomen were "bribed by Thompson to destroy evidence of the clinic's criminal operations."[18]

Thompson's nurse said, "My God, some of these women are too sick to be moved." Policewomen assisted "the quack doctor in spiriting away his semi-conscious women patients," and helped these key witnesses into taxicabs. Thompson said he was confident about avoiding more jail time: If officials indicted him, he pledged "to spill everything and the thought of it makes them sick." He bragged about keeping $5,000 to $15,000 of cash on hand to "make a fix" when arrested.[19]

The *Daily News* played up Thompson's long history: "The ghost of Eva Swan, whose carefully dissected body was found 18 years ago, [faced] the head of Manhattan's criminal surgery ring." But Thompson wore an expensive suit and smoked a cigar while handcuffed to a police officer, "relaxed and confident like he was taking a Sunday stroll in the park instead of the walk to and from the courthouse." Thompson received only a one-year prison sentence and a $500 fine.[20]

---

17 *The Boston Globe*, November 5, 1910, 3.
18 *New York Daily News*, May 17, 1928, 6.
19 *Daily News*, June 13, 1928, 2; March 22, 1931, 6.
20 *The San Francisco Call*, September 29, 1910, 1.

29

Twentieth-Century Compassion

I'VE READ HUNDREDS of accounts of young unmarried women moving from farm to big city early in the twentieth century and then facing a crisis pregnancy. Rather than pick one, here's a composite: Call her Debbie, and meet her as she steps off the train with a plan to become a shopgirl or a stenographer. She is likely to receive a courteous greeting from a well-dressed man who asks if she needs help to find a job or a place to live. Confused and nervous, she's about to accept his offer, until a matron from a Traveler's Aid Committee steps in. The older woman explains what the man really wants: He's a sex-trafficker. She offers Debbie a clean and safe room.

The next day, Debbie rents a bed in a family-style lodging house or a YWCA-type boarding house where decent rooms are available for $1.50 per week. She scrutinizes *Help Wanted* newspaper ads and plans to head out the next morning to visit potential employers. But that evening, in her rooming house, several young women meet with a volunteer from the Girls' Protective League. The volunteer notes the importance of spurning "improper proposals when applying for positions through newspapers and employment agencies." The volunteer shows Debbie a "blacklist of dangerous places." It includes an address of one of the places she was planning to visit.

Debbie navigates early difficulties. She gets a low-paying, entry-level job and gains the initial buzz of making it on her own. Then boredom sets in and temptation grows. A friend makes good money for "massage parlor" work, with top tips for sex. Debbie resists that, but she goes out evenings with a "gentleman caller." He takes her to restaurants and theaters and pushes for sex in return. She says no, not for moral reasons but pragmatic ones: What if she gets pregnant? The gentleman says he'll marry her, but when she gets pregnant he turns ungentle and says only that he'll pay for an abortion.

Debbie has a choice. She could follow the path taken by a young woman in Eugene O'Neill's first play, *Abortion*, which he wrote while a Harvard student in 1914. The main character, a college sports star, shows little concern for the woman he has impregnated but focuses on the consequences to his reputation. When the woman's brother tells the sports star that the woman he impregnated has died from an abortion and that he will tell the world about it, the star shoots himself. The situation is extreme but believable.

Let's say Debbie does not get an abortion. Marriage is also not an option: in big cities, the absence of fathers with shotguns leaves many young women adrift. Suddenly she is called upon to be a heroine. As Reverend Peter O'Callaghan told doctors in 1904, "The woman who in conscious knowledge of the obstacles before her, calmly faces the world with her illegitimate child, is a heroine. Her path is beset by daily perils and pitfalls that demand all the resourcefulness of her intellect and courage."[1]

Let's say Debbie wanted to face the world with her child. Working women in the United States on average earned wages half that of men. A 1908 study of Chicago's store and factory workers found more than half of the women living alone earned less than a subsistence wage. Let's say Debbie wanted to gain financial support from the father of their

---

[1] *Illinois Medical Journal* 7 (1904): 27–28.

child. Women a century ago often had a hard time winning paternity suits. Since lawyers for male defendants often called plaintiffs unchaste, many women preferred to go it alone rather than "brave the notoriety and unpleasant experiences which they must endure in court trials," as the Chicago Vice Commission reported. One woman recalled, "The men looked at each other and smiled at what I said, that was what made me get nervous and jerk so."[2]

Furthermore, when an abandoned woman was able to bring a successful suit for child support, amounts obtained were almost always inadequate. In Illinois in 1910, if a judge gave the father of a child "the highest sentence the law of the state imposes"—and that was rare—he would pay child support of $100 the first year, $50 for each of the next nine years, and nothing afterwards: In today's dollars, $2,900, $1,450, and zero. Clifford Roe, a Chicago prosecutor known for his efforts to fight prostitution and the trafficking of women for sex work, called the outcome of a case that ended with the maximum "a travesty. . . . That father came and went as so many fathers do. He was free of all care for a paltry five hundred and fifty dollars . . . she the victim of the double standard of morals."[3]

Other states were worse. In Delaware, a father had to pay ten dollars for confinement expense, ten dollars to the attending physician, and between five and twenty-five dollars to the mother or custodian of the child. Florida set a maximum of fifty dollars per year. Maryland was a little better, offering a maximum monthly payment at fifteen dollars a month. Unwed mothers no longer had the economic safety net present in colonial times.[4]

Given those realities, Debbie was more likely to place her child for adoption. As historian Joan Brumberg noted following her study

[2] Vice Commission of Chicago, *The Social Evil in Chicago* (Chicago: Vice Commission, 1911), 227.
[3] Clifford Roe, *The Great War on White Slavery: Or, Fighting for the Protection of Our Girls* (Chicago: Roe & Steadwell, 1911), 66.
[4] Robert South Barrett, *The Care of the Unmarried Mother* (Alexandria, VA: Florence Crittenton Mission, 1929), 84.

of a refuge in Elmira, New York, "Recovery from the multiple crises posed by an unmarried pregnancy was possible so long as the birth remained covert and the baby properly disposed of. A proper disposition meant adoption—either through a private family or through a welfare agency, generally a county orphanage." More than two-thirds of the babies born between 1890 and 1907 at the home Brumberg studied were adopted.[5]

Work on the demand side required promotion of adoption as an option that was good for most children and gave mothers some peace of mind that the child they had borne would not be abused. Organizations like the New York Children's Aid Society placed four thousand children into homes each year. Late in the nineteenth century, a Chicago study of adoption groups such as the Children's Aid Society and the Foundlings' Home concluded, "the children generally remain at the homes but a few weeks, there being more calls for their care and adoption than the supply can meet." It remained that way early in the twentieth century.[6]

Doctors saw the importance of compassionate approaches. *The Illinois Medical Journal* asked Americans to "found and support homes and places of refuge for the woman awaiting confinement." Female physicians like Rosalie Ladova emphasized the need to create more "homes for the care of unfortunate girls and women, so they can be delivered from the physical as well as moral burden." But such efforts received little press attention. By the 1920s reporters often treated abortion and compassionate alternatives as old news, with kidnapping stories getting more attention than kid-killing.[7]

---

5 Joan Brumberg, "'Ruined' Girls: Changing Community Responses to Illegitimacy in Upstate New York, 1890–1920," *Journal of Social History* 18 (Winter 1984): 260.
6 Marvin Olasky, *The Tragedy of American Compassion* (Washington, DC: Regnery, 1992), 34–41, 151.
7 *Illinois Medical Journal* 7 (1904): 29, 43. Medical Society leader Charles Bacon concluded, "The only means that we can regard as efficient is the erection of a sufficient number of obstetrical asylums in which the unmarried can be protected."

For example, in 1923 someone abducted three-month-old Lillian McKenzie from a baby carriage outside a Manhattan department store: Her mother, who had dashed in to pick up an item, screamed when she came out and Lillian was gone. One hundred police officers plus hundreds of Boy Scouts and Girl Guides searched for the baby, to no avail. The story became news nationwide.

The snatching was still a mystery when, two years later, investigators thought a Henry L. Mottard, alias Dr. H. L. Green, might have been indirectly involved. Newspapers across the United States on April 9 and 10, 1925, played up Mottard's potential kidnapping connection. *The New York Journal* ran the story at the top of its front page, with pictures and text showing the walls of Mottard's home filled with "countless photographs of pretty women—some of them known on the stage—who ventured to inscribe their pictures with various terms of affection, such as to 'our dear benefactor and friend.'" But as soon as investigators absolved Mottard of kidnapping and arrested him only for abortion, newspapers dropped coverage, as if the unborn were insignificant.[8]

The director of a New York City crisis pregnancy refuge was unable to gain much press publicity, so after twenty years she published an account herself. Annie Kennedy filled her pages with stories: "A young American girl, 17 years old, who because of her trouble has been abandoned by her mother, has nowhere to go—no home—no work. She remains in the home and is now being trained for a good position." Or, "She loved a young man and he ruined her and left her. . . . She came to our home through a member of church; she did not know what it meant to be 'born again.' She knows now."[9]

For Annie Kennedy, as for Helen Woods a generation earlier, the goal with each young woman was to "work from the inside out. [Christ]

---

8 *New York Journal*, April 10, 1925, 1 and 2; *The Ogden Standard-Examiner*, April 10, 3; *The Nebraska State Journal* (Lincoln), April 10, 13; *Medford* (OR) *Mail Tribune*, April 10, 8; *The Oneonta* (NY) *Star*, April 10, 1; *Montpelier Evening Argus*, April 9, 7; *The Brattleboro* (VT) *Reformer*, April 9, 1; *The Bristol* (TN) *News*, April 9, 1; *Los Angeles Evening Express*, April 10, 5.
9 Annie Kennedy, *The Heartsease Miracle* (New York: Heartsease Publishing, 1920), 51, 62.

alone can relieve them of their burden of sin." Journalists often unimpressed with religious sentiments were impressed with Heartsease's results. Jacob Riis wrote of Heartsease, "No work that I ever came across seems to go nearer the heart of things than that of these devoted women. Heartsease deserves the enthusiastic support of all our people."[10]

The Heartsease emphasis on "family" led to an emphasis on adoption: "Every child, whenever possible, should grow up in a home with both a father and a mother . . . adopted into families where they will have the love and care for which they are entitled. . . . Many babies are adopted. We have a long list of prospective foster parents waiting . . . to give a child a chance." When a mother decided to keep the baby, Heartsease emphasized reconciliation between the mother and *her* mother.[11]

Kennedy wanted young women to recognize their dependence and not assert a false independence. She wrote of a young southern girl who joined a touring vaudeville act, slept around, and became pregnant: "When her employer discovered her condition, she was practically abandoned in New York and was sent to us from a hospital. When she came to the door she was literally without funds, clothing and alone. We have since written her mother and she will care for the girl and her baby. They are very poor but respectable people. The girl has been led to see the folly of her way."[12]

Kennedy pushed back against the common way of describing a woman seduced and abandoned as "ruined": "I will give you a few cases.

10 Kennedy, *Heartsease Miracle*, 58, 65, 42. Endorsements from Riis and others helped, because Heartsease always relied on food and other necessities arriving just on time, as recorded in letters: "One of our good friends sent us vegetables during last summer in such a quantity that we were able to can enough for our winter supply."

11 Kennedy recalled a pregnant fifteen-year-old who gave birth: "May and the boy stayed with us nearly six months. . . . We also taught her stenography. Her whole life and nature changed, due to her fellowship with her Lord." Kennedy then described a recent visit with May, May's mother, and May's child, now seven: "The boy came in from school while I sat there. The first thing he did was to get a book and sit down and read. . . . His school card bears the highest marks. The old mother said to me over and over again with tears running down her cheeks, 'May is my good girl, my good girl'" (*Heartsease Miracle*, 76).

12 Kennedy, *Heartsease Miracle*, 50.

No. 2681, student-teacher, engaged, betrayed. Her beautiful child was adopted. . . . No. 2748, young American girl 19 years, seduced under promise of marriage, well-educated and wellbehaved girl, was cast out, but through prayer she went home with her baby. She is doing nicely; she writes that God is leading."[13]

Compassionate help of this kind required perseverance. Kennedy headed Heartsease for decades, and southerner Lem Odom could legitimately title his memoir, *Fifty Years in Rescue Work*. Odom emphasized that lives were not "ruined": He recommended that unmarried mothers place their children for adoption and said 85 percent of the girls and women he helped were able to marry or to be restored to "homes, gainful occupations, and positions of trust."[14]

Odom, after his half century in Montgomery, Jacksonville, and Shreveport, wrote about Ida, whose father died when she was small, and how at age sixteen Ida "capitulated to the blandishments of a young man" and became pregnant. Odom sent her to a Christian home in St. Louis, where the baby was born and adopted: Ida then returned to school. He portrayed Eudora, daughter of a widow and pregnant at eighteen, arriving at Odom's Montgomery rescue home, where she gave birth to a boy who was then adopted by a farmer: Later, Eudora married a railroad engineer and had other children. Odom described how Delenia, daughter of a minister, came to Montgomery five months pregnant. She gave birth there, and her parents received her and their grandchild. Odom visited the family ten years later and found them all well: Delenia had become a nurse.[15]

Two more stories: Josephine, eight months pregnant and sick with malaria and a venereal disease, gave birth to a healthy boy who was adopted and became the chief engineer of a steamship company and the father of five children. Josephine became a nurse and married a

---

13 Kennedy, *Heartsease Miracle*, 61.
14 Lem Odom, *Fifty Years in Rescue Work* (Cincinnati: Revivalist Press, 1938), 50, 72.
15 Odom, *Fifty Years in Rescue Work*, 99, 141, 174.

minister. Delilah, sixteen and an orphan, eloped with a young man who delayed marrying her when his car supposedly broke down on the way to the county courthouse. While they waited for the car to be repaired, she agreed to "show him" her love. He then abandoned her: She went to Odom's shelter in Jacksonville, where she bore a child, who was then adopted.[16]

Odom kept going for half a century because he saw live babies who otherwise would probably have died before birth. More and more women were on their own: the U.S. female labor force outside the home increased from 2.6 million to 10.8 million between 1880 and 1930. Exposed to many new ideas about behavior, those millions had many opportunities to act on the ideas but were also subject to moral expectations that young men could evade.

16 Odom, *Fifty Years in Rescue Work*, 160, 180.

30

Million-Dollar Hands

IN 2016 A RETROSPECTIVE FEATURE about Robert Thompson in the *San Francisco Examiner* concluded, "Abortion in San Francisco continued to be a risky business until improvements in medical practice and the appearance of the legendary Inez Burns." It stayed risky for unborn children, but Burns became the first major "new-school" abortionist.[1]

Her story begins with old-school abortionist Eugene F. West, who in 1902 advertised that "my method of curing female disorders is always reliable. Irregularities from any cause successfully overcome in one visit. Consultation is free. Confidential office and private entrance." But West was not reliable. His hand was not always steady and his operating room rarely spotless. One visit might be all it took to produce two deaths.[2]

West was implicated in several adult abortion deaths but became notorious in 1893 when charged with cutting into pieces the body of a dead patient and throwing her remains in San Francisco Bay. Headlines included, "WOMAN'S HEAD. Thought to Be That of Addie Gilmour." Then came more certainty: "MUTE EVIDENCE OF GUILT. More

---

1 Paul Drexler, "The Crimes of Dr. Grant," *San Francisco Examiner*, February 28, 2016, https://www.sfexaminer.com/news/the-crimes-of-dr-grant/.
2 Stephen G. Bloom, *The Audacity of Inez Burns* (New York: Regan Arts, 2018), chs. 3–4; *San Francisco Call*, October 19, 1902, 10.

Evidence of Addie Gilmour's Dismembered Body Found Floating in the Bay," followed by "HER SAD FATE: ADDIE GILMOUR FOULLY BUTCHERED. DR. WEST ARRESTED."[3]

A jury convicted West but the California Supreme Court said the judge had erred in ruling out some pro-West testimony. West received a new trial, and with top legal help along with a claim that Gilmour died as he tried to remedy the injuries another abortionist had inflicted on her, he gained acquittal. He said prejudice against altruists like himself, who just wanted to help young women, made necessary his unorthodox disposal of the body.[4]

West "helped" many young women by paying for their company: One of them, seventeen-year-old Inez Ingenthron, became infamous as Inez Brown Burns, taking the last names of two of the four men she married. Growing up poor, she received her first steady income as a teenaged manicurist and then a provider of other services to smitten gentlemen like West. She was destitute following the San Francisco earthquake in 1906: When West took her on as his assistant, she watched and learned. Then West watched her doing abortions and was amazed: She had "the touch."[5]

Indeed she did. She was a "good" abortionist by the standards of abortion defenders: 50 percent of those she operated on survived. (Mothers lived, unborn babies died.) Burns bragged about her "million dollar hands." West loved her surgical steadiness—but, once trained, Burns spent no more time loving him. An insomniac, during the 1920s and '30s Burns typically slept for only three or four hours each night. So much to do, so little time: Buy tanks of nitrous oxide for anesthesia, pay

---

3   *San Francisco Morning Call*, September 20, 1893, 10; *San Francisco Examiner*, September 28, 12; *San Francisco Chronicle*, September 29, 10.
4   *San Francisco Morning Call*, February 6, 1894, 12; and December 11, 1895, 8; *Examiner*, December 27, 1895, 9.
5   Lisa Riggin, *San Francisco's Queen of Vice* (Lincoln: University of Nebraska Press, 2017), 13–15. I visualize her, following the earthquake, like Vivian Leigh playing Scarlett O'Hara in *Gone with the Wind*, vowing she'll never go hungry again.

off police and politicians, rubber-band another load of cash and hide it in a secret compartment, buy Egyptian cotton sheets for all her beds.[6]

The Burns abortion business at 327 Fillmore Avenue in San Francisco was "spick-and-span sterile and hygienic," according to one of Burns's admiring biographers, Stephen Bloom.[7] At a trial in 1946, Burns employee Madeline Rand explained Burns's painstaking directions on cleaning the tables with antiseptic and rinsing the rubber surgical pads into buckets that contain "mucus, blood, and the eyes of the fetus."[8]

Burns also had an aesthetic: Her office resembled "an elegant ladies' tearoom." The entrance through an arched entryway led to two waiting rooms with tannish-white stucco, a bank of bay windows facing east, maroon velvet drapes, crystal chandeliers, velvet-upholstered sofas, Chippendale chairs, and oil paintings on the walls. Other rooms included Tiffany lamps and Persian rugs on a waxed parquet floor.[9]

For almost a quarter-century, starting in 1922, Burns ran her business with little interference from the authorities, who viewed her as offering what biographer Bloom called "a kind of public service.... Most juries, at least in San Francisco, didn't convict defendants, especially women, charged with what many considered a victimless crime." She had an "excellent reputation as an efficient and safe abortionist," and substantial press support from those who ignored the small victims: "The prevailing standard in San Francisco and other American cities ... was that if the woman undergoing the procedure didn't die, the police looked the other way."[10]

---

6   Riggin, *San Francisco's Queen of Vice*, 20–23 Bloom, *Audacity of Inez Burns*,167.
7   Bloom, *Audacity of Inez Burns*, 159. Another writer, June Morrall, also noted that Burns's "facilities were antiseptic and she was said to be a 'perfect abortionist' (with no fatalities)" (halfmoonbaymemories.com/category/inez-burns). That comment also reveals how differences in worldview lead to different corpse counts.
8   Riggin, *San Francisco's Queen of Vice*, 103.
9   Bloom, *Audacity of Inez Burns*, 159.
10 Bloom, *Audacity of Inez Burns*, 176.

Nonenforcement allowed Burns over the years to perform about fifty thousand abortions herself in San Francisco and in a satellite Oakland office. She also loosely supervised a hundred thousand more. Cash rolled in. She avoided a paper trail by building a home at 274 Guerrero Street with sliding panels, hollow banisters, liftable floorboards, and secret compartments in which to hide cash. She also had enough clout to get the number she wanted for her street address: Section 274 in the California penal code banned abortion.

The Guerrero Street home had a master bedroom with a wall of mirrors built for self-admiration and a walk-in closet with slots for 320 hats. Burns paid cash for a mansion on fashionable Mulholland Drive in Beverly Hills, next to the home of conductor Xavier Cugat. She owned another home with a view of the Golden Gate Bridge, a third home in Oakland, and two more along with an 800–1000-acre ranch in San Mateo County, forty miles south of San Francisco, where she boarded horses.[11]

Half a century after Madame Restell flaunted her wealth, then finally crashed and committed suicide, Burns was a West Coast equivalent. A jeweler's best friend, with an open account at Shreve and Company. An antique dealer's best friend, creating smaller versions of William Randolph Hearst's castle. She bought for herself ermine, seal, mink, fox, and beaver coats and hoped for weather cold enough in San Francisco to wear them. She filled her closet with designer hats and high-heeled shoes, and purchased jewel-studded, custom-made collars for her two pet Pomeranians, Foxy and Theda Bara (named after a vampish silent movie actress). Like Madame Restell riding down Fifth Avenue in her carriage a half century before, Burns traversed San Francisco in her chauffeured Pierce-Arrow.[12]

Gangsters at one point tried to get a piece of the action. Nick DeJohn, running from Chicago after skimming profits from an Al Capone en-

---

11 Riggin, *San Francisco's Queen of Vice*, 25–28, 31–32, 29–40, 64–65, 71, 90–91, 107, 160–64, 181–82, 190.
12 Bloom, *Audacity of Inez Burns*, 168; Riggin, *San Francisco's Queen of Vice*, 31.

terprise, tried to shake down Burns. She did not like him or his musky cologne, anchovy breath, and seven-caret diamond pinkie ring. Burns bouncer Joe Hoff pointed a snub-nosed 38 at DeJohn's chest, then at his right temple. Burns asked, "You wanna leave alive through the front door or dead through the back? . . . I got an incinerator in the back and I can make you, all of you, disappear just like that." She snapped her fingers. DeJohn left.[13]

In the 1930s, Burns decided she had enough money to mingle with high society. To be comfortable in high heels, she had her little toes surgically removed. She bought expensive season tickets at the new opera house next to City Hall and made a prime appearance on November 1, 1935, at the San Francisco debut of Richard Wagner's *The Ring of the Nibelung*. She strode down the red carpet wearing an ostrich-feather hat, a form-fitting Madeleine Vionnet gown, a Barguzin sable stole, and a diamond brooch.[14]

Society page photographers popped their flashbulbs but could only guess at the intimate connections between Burns and some tiara-wearing women upon whom she had operated. But Burns broke the prime rule for new-school abortionists who want to continue their killing: low profile. Public opinion forced the police to do a halfhearted raid in 1936, but no one came forward to testify. Meanwhile, Burns maintained both her volume and her star clients, including Sonja Henie, the Norwegian figure skater turned U.S. movie box office sensation.[15]

In 1938 two *San Francisco News* reporters, Mary Ellen Leary and Joe Sheridan, masqueraded as a married couple and wrote an undercover exposé headlined "San Francisco Mill operates openly." Local officials did not follow up, but the IRS sniffed around for income tax evasion: thirty to forty abortions a day at Fillmore at $75 to $350 each ($900 to $4,200 in today's dollars), ka-ching! Burns, though, claimed a minimal

---

13 Bloom, *Audacity of Inez Burns*, 241.
14 Bloom, *Audacity of Inez Burns*, 170; Riggin, *San Francisco's Queen of Vice*, 22.
15 Riggin, *San Francisco's Queen of Vice*, 53.

income, and complained privately that her payoffs cost $20,000 per month. Another required bribe: Buy 10,000 tickets ($1 each) for the annual policeman's ball.[16]

In 1939 IRS agents settled with Burns for a mere $10,000. During World War II the heat was off and the money kept coming. Friendships as well as payoffs yielded protection: Burns and her fourth husband, Joe, played poker at their home every Wednesday night with a police inspector, a fire captain, local doctors, and city supervisor Warren Shannon. Shannon's wife, Gloria, described meeting Burns in the dining room of the swanky Fairmont Hotel in 1944: Burns suddenly stopped talking, glanced around distractedly, then said in a hoarse whisper, "Good God, where's my purse? My day's receipts are in it—$5,000." Burns found the purse under a heap of furs and said, "Thank God."[17]

With war's end and abortionists bribing hundreds of police officers, District Attorney Edmund "Pat" Brown cracked down on abortionists not to reduce baby-killing but to fight government corruption. Brown's deputy, Norman Elkington, agreed that abortion by itself was not scandalous: the problem was "police corruption," and politicians also, "corrupted from the highest level down to the lowest. The queen of abortions in San Francisco was Inez Burns." Brown said, "Everyone thought she was a necessary evil, but . . . her business had become flagrant."[18]

In September 1945, police raided Burns's office and home. Homicide inspector Frank Ahern, forty-five, led the raid and startled Burns by turning down a $350,000 bribe. She told him, "You ain't gonna git another offer like this in your lifetime. You better think long and hard about this, Inspector." Ahern responded, "I don't gotta think long and

16 Riggin, *San Francisco's Queen of Vice*, 39–40, 54, 136–37, 160–67, 174–75, 191–92.
17 The equivalent of $75,000 today; *San Francisco Examiner*, January 20, 1946, 14.
18 Interview by Amelia Fry in the Earl Warren Oral History Project, quoted in Bloom, *Audacity of Inez Burns*, 227 and 434; Elkington interview in the Regional Oral History Office, the Bancroft Library, University of California, Berkeley, quoted by Bloom, *Audacity of Inez Burns*, 228.

hard about nothing. You're getting charged with bribing a cop. And a lot more."

Burns countered, "I can count on one hand the number of cops I haven't paid off. . . . You're a damn fool! That's what you are. You'll never have to work another day in your life! Take the money for Christ's sake! What the hell's wrong with you?" Ahern responded, "Tell it to the judge."[19]

With Burns about to go on trial, Gloria Shannon—wife of the poker-playing city supervisor—drafted a book about her and sold the *San Francisco Examiner* on publishing daily excerpts. The first article ran under a front-page banner headline: "Shannon Exposes Inez Burns' House of Horrors." Shannon said Burns "sits on a stool before the narrow table and for six hours every day butchers the unborn," then boasts, "I am the greatest abortionist in the United States!"[20]

Shannon's critique seemed more personal than principled, though, when she said in her second article that laws should leave the abortion decision up to the woman and "a skilled surgeon," thus keeping women from having to submit to "brutality." Brutal toward unborn children, yes, but not true in regard to women, according to reporter Jerry Flamm: "Inez was the place to go if you wanted it done right." Brown, whose prosecution of Burns helped him become California's attorney general and then governor, later affirmed Burns's "good reputation" as a killer of small humans but not large ones.[21]

The second story's last line was in boldface, "Continued tomorrow." But *Examiner* owner William Randolph Hearst heard complaints on two grounds—"good taste" and accuracy. Without explanation from

---

19   Bloom, *Audacity of Inez Burns*, 252.
20   *San Francisco Examiner*, January 20, 1946, 1.
21   Riggin, *San Francisco's Queen of Vice*, 37; Jerry Flamm, *Hometown San Francisco* (San Francisco: Scottwall Associates, 1994), 33. Police Lieutenant Michael Mitchell, leader of the raid on Burns's office, called her operating room "scrupulously clean and completely outfitted as a hospital," with white tiles from floor to ceiling, two large surgical beds, and stainless steel surgical equipment (*San Francisco Examiner*, January 21, 1946, 7).

the editors, the series disappeared. Nevertheless, Pat Brown used the newspaper publicity to gain praise for arresting Burns.[22]

Burns's defense attorney, Walter McGovern, put on a populist defense. He said she was "operating a public utility. If she is punished, I say the overwhelming majority of the people of San Francisco are equally guilty. [Burns is] running wider open than the City Hospital. . . . Laws are enforced by public demand." McGovern asked jurors to deliver a "protest" verdict as a way of showing disapproval of the California law making abortion a felony.[23]

The first trial, after eighty-five ballots, was eleven to one for conviction, but juror twelve did not budge. The second trial also ended with a hung jury, but during trial number three a Burns nurse, Lavinia Queen, testified. That jury on September 26, 1946, convicted Burns. She served two years and seven months at Tehachapi Women's Prison, southeast of Bakersfield.

In 1949, back in San Francisco, Burns began aborting babies again and earning hundreds of thousands of dollars. She had to invest nearly half of her revenue in payoffs and bribes: $6,000 per week to downtown officials, $12,000 per month to San Francisco police, $5,000 "to every politician running for office."[24]

In 1951 Burns visited plastic surgeon Albert Davis, who gave her a facelift that made her think she looked ten years younger. But legal troubles escalated, and that year she headed to a brief prison sentence for tax evasion. (Her attorney pleaded for delay: "Next Sunday is Mother's Day.") In 1952, as part of a 1950s crackdown on many abortionists, she was back to prison for another twenty-four months for performing

---

22 "To San Simeon's Taste," *Newsweek*, February 4, 1946, 86; "Mrs. Burns Blasts Abortion Mill Tale," *Nevada State Journal*, January 22, 1946, 1. For a recent story sympathetic to Burns, see transcript of an April 22, 2018, NPR *Morning Edition* segment at https://www.npr.org/2018/04/22/604702064/inez-burns-abortion-clinic-was-one-of-san-franciscos-worst-kept-secrets.

23 *San Francisco Chronicle*, March 8, 1946, 1; *San Francisco Examiner*, March 8, 1946, 3; *Oakland Tribune*, March 7, 1946, 7.

24 Bloom, *Audacity of Inez Burns*, 9, 80, 234, 238, 253, 348, 412.

an abortion. In 1955 she settled with the IRS by paying it $745,325 (about $8 million in today's dollars).[25]

In the 1950s, imprisoning abortionists was still popular. As mentioned, Brown used the positive press he received to become California's attorney general and then governor. A mayor praised the integrity of homicide inspector Ahern and promoted him over dozens of other police officers to make him chief of police.

Burns lived on but retired from the abortion business. Biographers described her as bitterly staring out the window of her Guerrero Street home, intimidating neighbors with an angry glare. A statue of a little boy stood in front of the house. She left instructions that upon her death her medical instruments should be put in the casket with her: "I relied on them. . . . They're what got me everywhere in my life."[26]

She was right: Old-school abortionists were sloppy, new-school abortionists were precise, and attacks on them as "dangerous to women" did not work well. Burns died in bed in 1976 at age eighty-nine.

---

25 Riggin, *San Francisco's Queen of Vice*, 160–64.
26 Bloom, *Audacity of Inez Burns*, 431.

SECTION FOUR

SEEING LIFE

1930–1995

Chapters 31–40 show how abortion moved from anathema in the 1930s to triumph in the early 1990s, with help from journalists, judges, and a contraception connection. Medical committees that assessed individual needs gave way to disassembly-line work. Antibiotics virtually eliminated maternal danger, and everyone could see what unborn children looked like. Abortion advocates and opponents sometimes inadvertently empowered their foes.

31

Linkages

WHEN DR. FREDERICK TAUSSIG wrote *The Prevention and Treatment of Abortion* in 1910, he criticized the "wholesale slaughter of the innocents" and "the myth that life does not begin until fetal movements are felt." He said, "Almost daily the physician hears the story that the woman did not think it was wrong to stop pregnancy in the early months before the child was alive." What to do? Don't *tell* women that abortion even early in pregnancy is killing: *Show* them "how early the fetal heart begins to pump blood through its vessels."[1]

Taussig had his nurse *show* women an enlarged photo of a six-week-old unborn child with "eyes, ears, nose, mouth and extremities already crudely formed." He said pictures "of the six weeks' embryo will keep many women from having an abortion done," and that's more effective than legal action against abortionists: "In St. Louis it is only a few times a year that a case comes up for trial and then the chances are ten to one against conviction."[2]

---

1 Frederick J. Taussig, *The Prevention and Treatment of Abortion* (St. Louis: C. V. Mosby, 1910), 7, 79.
2 Taussig, *Prevention and Treatment of Abortion*, 80. Taussig's enthusiasm about the results seems similar to what pro-life counselors now have as they show ultrasound pictures: He said women display "much amazement." He proposed a loosening of the rules regarding testimony: "The fault

During the next two decades, though, Taussig changed his views. His wife, Florence, led battles for women's suffrage and international disarmament. Their daughter Mary became a social worker and activist. Through them, Taussig came to appreciate "the spread of the Woman's Suffrage Movement throughout the world and the newer economic independence of women.... There can be no question that more consideration must be given to the right of women to control their own bodies."[3]

Taussig's Judaism crumbled, and he became a member of the Ethical Society of St. Louis, which advocated the separation of not only church and state but theology and morality. Taussig came to advocate "freedom from religious bias.... Our ethical ideas of right and wrong are not absolutely fixed. They have changed with the evolution of our social structure." He also heard much that was positive about the Soviet Union, which had a reputation on the left not yet marred by Josef Stalin's purges, so he journeyed to Moscow in 1930 to see for himself.[4]

Journalist John Reed titled his book on the Russian revolution *Ten Days That Shook the World*. It took ten minutes in a Soviet "abortarium" to shake Taussig. He wrote that each abortion took only ten minutes: one minute getting on and off the table, three minutes preparation, six minutes of "actual curettement." The women groaned as they underwent abortions without anesthesia, but "the ability of the Slavic people patiently to endure pain" impressed him. Besides, a government translator told him the women said "it wasn't so bad." Taussig wrote that Russians were poor, and abortion was the best way to keep them from becoming poorer.[5]

---

lies primarily in the difficulty of obtaining the admission of evidence.... It is to be hoped that before long laws will be enacted that will more effectually protect the community."
3   *St. Louis Jewish Light*, October 10, 2019, 1. See also Colin Campbell, *Towards a Sociology of Irreligion* (London: MacMillan, 1931).
4   Frederick J. Taussig, *Abortion, Spontaneous and Induced* (St. Louis: C. V. Mosby, 1936), 400, 417.
5   Taussig, *Abortion, Spontaneous and Induced*, 400 and 417: "Nevertheless," he also admitted, "there was ample evidence of severe suffering by many of the women in the process of dilating the cervix and their groans sent shivers down our backs."

That pragmatism made sense to Taussig. He told a Congressional committee that "families who are on relief rolls cannot welcome additional children." He flipped on abortion: He had urged tough laws in 1910, but in 1934 he attacked "ridiculous, ofttimes incomprehensible, and harsh statutes on our books." He proposed that abortion be legal when "the mother is physically depleted by childbearing and poverty, [or] any condition that produces bodily exhaustion," including having several young children. He even said abortion might be justified when a pregnancy interrupted the careers of women with "unusual ability in artistic, intellectual, and administrative fields."[6]

Taussig's new definition of "therapeutic abortion" opened the door for millions of deaths, although he still maintained that "science has swept away" earlier ideas of unborn children at first existing in a "vegetative" state, and that they are not "part and parcel of the mother's body, to be disposed of as she sees fit."[7] Taussig said abortions should take place only after two licensed physicians have made "a careful survey of the facts," and should be done only in licensed hospitals: That would "prevent the establishment of small private hospitals designed especially for the care of abortion cases."[8]

Taussig's *Abortion, Spontaneous and Induced: Medical and Social Aspects* (1936) was hugely influential during the third of a century that led to *Roe v. Wade*. Taussig planted the idea of radically revised laws concerning abortion, but he did not envision abortion as a woman's choice: No, doctors would make sure that those who needed an abortion got one, and that those who did not, did not. No nonessential killings. A full-page review in *Time* pronounced the book "authoritative" and relayed Taussig's encouragement of doctor-approved abortions when there were "eugenic reasons," "suicidal tendencies," or "economic reasons in women of high fertility."[9]

---

6 *St. Louis Post-Dispatch*, January 18, 1934, 1.
7 Taussig, *Abortion, Spontaneous and Induced*, 390, 400, 448.
8 Taussig, *Abortion, Spontaneous and Induced*, 400–401, 443–45.
9 *Time*, March 16, 1936, 52.

Another strand of social change contributed to the idea of wise doctors as gate-keepers. For that we need some backstory starting in 1865, when Senator Jacob Collamer, who had been Zachary Taylor's postmaster general, complained that "Our mails have been made the vehicle for the conveyance of great numbers and quantities of obscene books and pictures." Congress that year made mailing any "obscene book, pamphlet, picture, print, or other publication" a misdemeanor punishable by a fine of up to $500 or a prison sentence of up to one year.[10]

Meanwhile, young Anthony Comstock moved from the countryside to New York City, as John McDowall had thirty-five years earlier. Both of them reacted to flagrant vice—but their reactions were opposite. McDowall emphasized personal compassion toward those enmeshed in prostitution or poverty. Comstock came to believe that reducing the incitement to sin would reduce sin. He gained support from YMCA leaders encouraged by the success of their one-to-one evangelistic work with young men and looking for a way to reduce the competition from pornography.[11]

Comstock and those leaders created the New York Society for the Suppression of Vice. He headed to Washington in November 1872, with the goal of extending the 1865 law. Comstock's timing proved exquisite. Abortion was in the headlines. Congress and the Grant administration were in trouble, with corruption and rumors of corruption flooding Pennsylvania Avenue. Politicians were looking for a way to improve their public standing and to seem on the side of angels.

Comstock convinced Supreme Court Justice William Strong, Vice President Henry Wilson, and lawyer Benjamin Abbott to help him draft an "Act for the Suppression of Trade In, and Circulation of, Obscene

---

10 *Congressional Globe*, February 8, 1865, 661. For an extended history, see James C. N. Paul and Murray Schwartz, *Federal Censorship: Obscenity in the Mail* (New York: Free Press, 1961).
11 Janet Brodie, *Contraception and Abortion in Nineteenth-Century America* (Ithaca, NY: Cornell University Press, 1994), 256–62.

Literature and Articles of Immoral Use." Abbott knew how Congress worked: Then as now, senators and congressmen sometimes voted on bills without having read them. Abbott took three anti-obscenity bills already introduced in the House of Representatives, consolidated them with Comstock's specific concerns, and connected Comstock with key legislators who would make it seem that the new bill was nothing new.[12]

But the bill did have something new: a prohibition on selling, giving away, or mailing "any article or medicines for the prevention of conception or for causing abortion." Most states had already passed legislation against abortion but not against contraceptives. Comstock linked the two. Contraception had two primary uses: facilitating sex within marriage when parents already had as many children as they wanted or thought they could care for, and facilitating adultery. The bill amalgamated the two uses and linked them to the life-or-death issue of abortion.[13]

One powerful Republican senator, Roscoe Conkling of New York, had a well-deserved reputation for philandering and was probably familiar with contraceptives. He complained several times that he and other senators did not have legible copies of the bill under discussion. He said, "The indignation and disgust which everybody feels in reference to the acts which are here aimed at may possibly lead us to do something [unwise]." Others who saw it as a free vote for virtue rammed through the legislation. President Ulysses S. Grant signed it and appointed Comstock a special agent able to seize illegal items or mail and arrest offenders.[14]

Linking contraception and abortion became common. New York passed stringent legislation against manufacturing, selling, or advertising contraceptives. In Connecticut, P. T. Barnum moved from promoting circuses and "freak shows" to successful lobbying for a ban

12 Brodie, *Contraception and Abortion in Nineteenth-Century America*, 263–64; for confusion about the legislation, see *Congressional Globe*, February 18, 1873, 1437.
13 "An Act to Revise, Consolidate, and Amend the Statutes Relating to the Post-Office Department," known popularly as The Comstock Act, 17 Stat. 598.
14 Brodie, *Contraception and Abortion*, 265–66.

on contraceptives. During the rest of the century twenty-two other state legislatures said information or products related to abortion and contraception could not be distributed within their states. In 1909, a federal act extended the ban beyond the U.S. Post Office to deliveries by any common carriers, including railroads.[15]

This is a book about abortion, not contraception, but linking the two had three eventual twentieth-century effects. The linkage made it seem to many liberals that the debate on such matters was about sex, not killing. It weakened the nineteenth-century connection of feminist and pro-life views: When a new wave of feminism rolled in during the 1960s, the battle for contraception (seen as a liberating instrument for women) turned into a campaign for abortion. Finally, court decisions on contraceptives and privacy—first within marriage, and then between unmarried men and women—paved the way to *Roe v. Wade*, which some portrayed as one more case about liberty, rather than an assault on the voiceless.[16]

Comstock's last highly publicized success came 40 years after his 1873 Washington lobbying victory. Margaret Sanger wrote for the *New York Call* a weekly sex education column, "What Every Girl Should Know." Comstock used his postal authority to ban it, and the editor pushed back the following week by running a blank space headlined, "What Every Girl Should Know—Nothing! By Order of the Post Office Department."

Then came 1914 and Margaret Sanger's declaration of war: Instead of digging a trench, she went on offense with her own magazine, *The*

---

15 Michael Grossberg, *Governing the Hearth: Law and the Family in Nineteenth Century America* (Chapel Hill: University of North Carolina Press, 1985), 177. The linkage of contraception and abortion, as if the issue was sex rather than life, was evident at a 2021 rally of pro-abortion activists at the Texas State Capitol: One sign said, "Keep your filthy laws off my silky drawers" (aljazeera.com, September 20, 2021). The history of legislation banning use of mail or express services for abortifacient delivery is relevant once again. *The New York Times* in April 2022 counted nineteen states that prohibited abortion pills from being prescribed by telemedicine or delivered through the mail.

16 Some contraceptives may function as abortifacients, but contraception cases such as *Griswold v. Connecticut* in 1965 involved barrier methods such as diaphragms and condoms that clearly do not cause abortion.

Woman Rebel. The Post Office seized the first issue and the police seized Sanger, indicting her for indecency: She voyaged to Europe to avoid a potential prison term.[17]

Sanger herself emphasized contraception and tried to avoid abortion advocacy, but the second issue of *The Woman Rebel* was not so demure. A column by Dorothy Kelly labeled abortion "a weapon to keep poor people ignorant, stupid, and miserable," and said it would "soon come to be regarded as useful, necessary, and humane."[18] French anarchist Victor Meric wrote that a woman "must recognize her absolute right . . . to suppress the germ of life. . . . Only a ridiculous idea of love and of the act of reproduction, an idea handed down from the infamous Christian religion, could have led women to forget that she alone has the right to decide."[19]

Sanger returned from Europe after Comstock died in 1915, and his followers declined to make her a martyr. But in the 1920s she changed her tactics. Instead of attempting to repeal anti-contraceptive laws, she decided to create medical allies by advocating "doctors-only" bills: Contraceptive use could be agreed upon by a woman, a doctor, and her God.[20]

Europe offered America two opposite pathways. In August 1930, Anglican prelates at their once-every-decade conference in Lambeth Palace approved contraceptive use when there is "a morally sound reason for avoiding complete abstinence."[21] Four months later, Pope Pius XI

---

17 R. Marie Griffith, *Moral Combat: How Sex Divided American Christians and Fractured American Politics* (New York: Basic Books, 2017), 6–7.
18 Dorothy Kelly, "Prevention and the Law," in *The Woman Rebel*, April 1914, 10.
19 Victor Meric, "The First Right," in *The Woman Rebel*, April 1914, 9.
20 Margaret Sanger, "The War against Birth Control," *American Mercury* (June 1924), 233. For battles about contraception in Connecticut, see *Bridgeport Telegram*, February 14, 1923, 1; and *The Journal* (Meriden, CT), February 14, 7. Sanger also allied with eugenicists hoping to reduce birth rates of "foreign" and "unfit" groups that threatened Anglo-Saxon ascendency. Criticized by Roman Catholic bishops and arrested at one speech by an Irish policeman, she skillfully used Catholic leaders as punching bags and claimed they "worked miracles of publicity that would have been impossible to a regiment of press-agents."
21 *New Blackfriars* 11 (December 1, 1930): 726.

declared that contraceptive use is "an offense against the law of God and of nature, and those who indulge in such are branded with the guilt of a grave sin."[22]

Four months after that, the Committee on Marriage and the Home of the Federal Council of the Churches of Christ in America, which represented 21 million Protestant church members, took an opposite position. The FCC committee stated in April 1931 that contraceptive use within marriage is "valid and moral," allowing for spacing of children, protection from poverty, and sexual intercourse between husband and wife that is good even when it is not procreative.[23]

The contraception battle was on, with fundamentalist and Catholic churches opposed in most areas but united against contraceptive use: Most mainline Protestant churches accepted it and, at least by the end of the 1930s, aligned with the American mainstream. By 1940, Gallup polls regularly showed about three-fourths of Americans favoring "the distribution of birth-control information to married persons by government health clinics." That wording, emphasizing medicine and marriage, reflected the work of Taussig and Sanger.[24]

In 1936, the same year Taussig's second abortion book went to press, the U.S. Court of Appeals for the Second Circuit overrode the Comstock Act by legalizing doctors' distribution of contraceptives to patients for medical reasons. The book and the court decision, which the U.S. Supreme Court let stand, had in common a desire to allow doctor-authorized exceptions to rules that had been in place for two generations. The moderate-sounding proposal had some unanticipated side effects.[25]

---

22 Pius XI, *Casti Connubii* encyclical ("Of Chaste Wedlock"), § 56.
23 "Birth Control: Protestant View," *Current History* 34 (April 1931): 97–100. Three of the twenty-eight committee members publicly dissented, and three others did not sign the statement.
24 Griffith, *Moral Combat*, 45.
25 *United States v. One Package*, 86 F. 2d 737 (1936). In 1936 also the newly constructed Boulder Dam became operational, with an unanticipated side effect just down the road: Cheap hydroelectricity powered the flashing facades of the giant casinos that crime syndicates would build in Las Vegas during the next three decades.

32

Complicated Lives

OBSTETRICIAN/GYNECOLOGIST Robert L. Dickinson defended abortion, hid a camera in a flowerpot to photograph his patients' private parts without their consent, and was a patron of sexologist Alfred Kinsey. He also made a huge contribution to popular pro-life understanding at the 1939 World's Fair in New York City.

Born in 1861, Dickinson was a practicing physician for four decades and headed at various times the American Gynecological Society, the New York Obstetrical Society, the American Medical Association's obstetrical section, and the American College of Surgeons. He was also a fine artist and a liberal Episcopalian who in 1931, at age seventy, put out the first editions of a book, *Control of Conception*, that started with information about contraceptive techniques and the creation of birth control centers, and then described how and when to do abortions, with pages of illustrations.[1]

---

1 Among Dickinson's book titles: *Control of Conception: An Illustrated Medical Manual*; *Human Sex Anatomy*; *Thousand Marriages: A Medical Study of Sex Adjustment*; *The Single Woman: A Medical Study in Sex Education*; *Techniques of Conception Control*; and *Atlas of Human Sex Anatomy*. Dickinson's "Control of Conception, Present and Future," *Bulletin of the New York Academy of Medicine* V (1925), 413–34, gives a good sense of his thinking and style. See also James Reed, *From Private Vice to Public Virtue: The Birth Control Movement in American Society Since 1830* (New York: Basic Books, 1978).

In 1936 he wrote the foreword to Taussig's second abortion book, calling it a contribution to "fearless inquiry" and promising an "era of fewer and better abortions," when we're more concerned with the woman than with "theological doctrine." He also wrote but did not publish a personal essay, "Blessed Be Abortion," that called abortion a "blessing" for bringing relief from "intolerable" burdens like "added maternal care, or freedom from life-long shame, or the stigma of bastardy."[2]

But here's the twist: Much as Augustus St. Clair, a reporter committed to adultery and lying, brought home to many the danger of abortion through his "Evil of the Age" stories, so Dickinson, with all his pro-abortion tendencies, helped millions of Americans to contemplate the humanity of unborn children by helping to create sculptures showing what they looked like at every stage of development.

That story begins in 1933 with a booth and an article. That year the Chicago World's Fair included a booth that presented information about how to choose a doctor and set up a nursery. The booth's sponsor, the Maternity Center Association, decided to invest in another booth for the 1939–1940 New York World's Fair, and hoped for one that would make a bigger splash. Meanwhile, an article by Dickinson in the *American Journal of Cancer*, focused on how pictures were worth thousands of words: "For sheer definitiveness, no record of physical findings competes with the diagram or picture made to scale. Words cannot equal pictures for visualizing conditions."[3]

Dickinson's pictures-better-than-words perspective, like Taussig's, made sense. Since the 1990s, ultrasound images have helped millions see an unborn child. A century ago, almost no one knew what an unborn child midway through gestation looked like. So Dickinson had little trouble convincing a splash-seeking Maternity Center Association plan-

---

2   Frederick J. Taussig, *Abortion, Spontaneous and Induced* (St. Louis: Mosby, 1936), 8; Rose Holz, "The 1939 Dickinson-Belskie Birth Series Sculptures," *Journal of Social History* 51, no. 4 (2018): 1005.

3   Robert L. Dickinson, "Life Size Outlines for Gynecological Cancer Case Records," *American Journal of Cancer* 17 (1933): 784.

ning committee to appropriate funds for sculptures that would illustrate how humans developed during their nine months of invisibility.[4]

Dickinson had doctors in East Coast hospitals take x-rays of pregnant women so he could be accurate about dimensions.[5] Dickinson then sketched, and thirty-two-year-old Abram Belskie carved, the most realistic—and beautiful—sculptures of unborn children ever created.

The result was spectacular. More than 2 million people viewed the Birth Series sculptures at the World's Fair in Queens, New York: "All summer people stood in line [with] wonder on their faces for hours to see the marvelous plaster models of the beginning of life." The sculptures combined scientific accuracy with artistic beauty to depict development as a romance beginning with conception and unfolding all the way to birth.[6]

The Gerber Products Company handed out at the World's Fair a pamphlet that explained, "A baby's life begins not when he puts in his squalling appearance but at the moment the sperm (from the father) meets the egg (from the mother) in the Fallopian tube." The pamphlet pointed readers to the sculpture showing fertilization and used the term "fertilized egg." In subsequent pages it used only one word to describe the creature in the womb: "baby."[7]

The pamphlet that Gerber later distributed added a warning: "Abortions Are Dangerous! . . . Frequently women become seriously ill from infection. Many of them seem to feel no ill effects, but may find that when they do want babies later in life they are sterile, they do not conceive; or they may have one 'miscarriage' after another. So they live with unhappy memories of what might have been. If you are thinking about an abortion—stop! Go to your family doctor. Talk it over with

---

4   Holz, "1939 Dickinson-Belskie Birth Series Sculptures," 989–90.
5   Not until 1956 did physicians come to understand that x-rays could endanger the development of unborn children.
6   Holz, "1939 Dickinson-Belskie Birth Series Sculptures," 990.
7   Maternity Center Association, *How Does Your Baby Grow?* (Florham Park, NJ: Gerber Products Company, 1939); Holz, "1939 Dickinson-Belskie Birth Series Sculptures," 1001.

him. Remember, some women get pregnant only once in life. Don't make a move you'll regret."[8]

After the Fair, the sculptures traveled to medical and public health institutions in Cleveland, Chicago, and many other cities. The Dy-Dee Wash diaper company and numerous stores asked to borrow them for openings. Then came mass reproduction and photographs of the series in books with names like *Birth Atlas*.[9]

In the nineteenth century Hugh Hodge, Stephen Tracy, Horatio Storer, and many other doctors had said what Dr. James Whitmer of Illinois summarized in 1874: the doctor sees "in the embryo the rudimentary foetus, and in that, the seven-months viable child and the prospective living, moving, breathing man or woman."[10] In 1939 and thereafter, everyone could see what only doctors before had visualized. Early in the century, doctors wished that mothers could see how "abortion is the destruction of a living body, the murder of a defenseless life, whether the deed is committed six months or six minutes after conception has taken place."[11] Dickinson, despite his personal sentiments, had granted that wish.

Dickinson's secret photographing of patients became public only after his death. In the 1940s he was a Planned Parenthood senior vice president and director, and a backer of Alfred C. Kinsey, who became famous in 1948 upon publication of his *Sexual Behavior in the Human Male*. Kinsey, in a 1941 letter to Dickinson, bragged about recording 2,100 sex histories by personal interviews of adults and junior high school students. In 1948 Kinsey wrote to Dickinson, "We still look to you as the great inspiration which started our whole business, and one

---

8   Holz, "1939 Dickinson-Belskie Birth Series Sculptures," 1002. Maternity Center Association statement added after the World's Fair to *How Does Your Baby Grow?*
9   Holz, "1939 Dickinson-Belskie Birth Series Sculptures," 992; Robert L. Dickinson and Abram Belskie, *Birth Atlas*, 3rd ed. (New York: Maternity Center Association, 1953).
10 James S. Whitmer, paper read before the Woodford County Medical Society and published in the *Chicago Medical Journal* 31 (1874): 392.
11 E. F. Fish, "Criminal Abortion," *Milwaukee Medical Journal* 17 (1909): 106–9.

who has given most abundant help." Twenty days before Dickinson died in 1950, Kinsey complained in a letter to him about the "moralistic thinking" of many marriage counselors.[12]

And yet, Dickinson stayed married to one woman for forty-eight years. He also showed how popular visualizing unborn children could be. Four years after Dickinson's death, Swedish photojournalist Lennart Nilsson, during a visit to New York, told editors of *Life* magazine that he wanted to photograph unborn children. The editors were technically skeptical but supportive: That partnership led to a *Life* cover in 1965 featuring a "Foetus 18 Weeks" photo of an unborn child floating within an amniotic sac. The issue was *Life*'s all-time fastest seller at checkout counters.[13] Nilsson's *A Child Is Born* became one of the top-selling illustrated books of all time.[14]

It was good for the pro-life side that public understanding of fetal anatomy grew from the 1930s to the 1960s, because the personal danger concerns that kept some women from obtaining abortions dropped steadily during those decades. New-school abortionists emphasized antiseptic operating conditions and, after World War II, had antibiotics as backup in case something did go wrong. Some were just in it for the money, but others sympathized with desperate women and defined "compassion" as meeting the requests of the visible patient, even though that meant death to the hidden one. Some of the most prominent new-schoolers were open about their ideological commitments—atheistic, Darwinian, or socialist.

One now-honored abortionist, Robert Spencer of Ashland, Pennsylvania, was "a kindly old man" with a "spotless" office, according to feminist Susan Brownmiller, who visited Spencer shortly before he died in 1969 at age 80. She wrote, "The public image of an abortionist,

---

12 Copy in 1990s Fieldstead Forum archives housed in Austin, Texas.
13 Charlotte Jansen, "Foetus 18 Weeks: The Greatest Photo of the 20th Century?" *The Guardian*, November 18, 2019, at https://www.theguardian.com/artanddesign/2019/nov/18/foetus-images-lennart-nilsson-photojournalist.
14 Lennart Nilsson, *A Child Is Born*, first American ed. (New York: Delacorte, 1967).

through books, plays, movies, articles, or whatever, was of an evil, leering, drunken, perverted butcher at worst, and a cold, mysterious, money-hungry Park Avenue price-gouger at best. And then there was Spencer . . . on the main street of a small American town, who charged fifty dollars, who believed in abortions, and who was kind."[15]

Biographer Vincent Genovese described Spencer dilating a young woman's cervix and then moving to the second step of dilation and curettage ("D-and-C"), but using instead of a curette "his index finger. His hands were small and extremely tuned to the touch of a uterus. Using this method greatly reduced the possibility of internal damage and bleeding. . . . He simply inserted his finger and moved it deftly against the uterine wall, causing both fetus and placenta to break free." Spencer would then "gently remove the seven-week-old embryo. It was discarded without any sense of loss into a basin which already held two others from this morning's work."[16]

Spencer felt no sense of loss because, as a student at Penn State, he had become a confirmed Darwinist, later writing that "Zoologists look upon an embryo as a parasite. . . . murder is the basis for life, for one form of life eats another. . . . I am an evolutionist, hence I am an atheist. . . . The basic structure of all matter is electrical." He may have leaned in that direction ever since he was six and his older brother at age eight contracted diphtheria. His parents told him to pray for his brother's recovery and he did, ardently, but his brother died.[17]

Spencer's wife burned his records, so it isn't clear how many children he aborted during a half-century career: Estimates range from forty thousand to a hundred thousand. In Ashland, with a population of five thousand in 1960 and about half that now, some residents had friendly relations with Spencer. Others depended on

15 Susan Brownmiller, "Dr. Spencer, 1889–1969: Last Trip to Ashland," *Village Voice*, January 30, 1969, https://www.villagevoice.com/2010/06/21/when-an-abortionist-dies.
16 Vincent J. Genovese, *The Angel of Ashland: Practicing Compassion and Tempting Fate: A Biography of Robert Spencer, M.D.* (Amherst, NY: Prometheus, 2000), loc. 62, Kindle.
17 Genovese, *Angel of Ashland*, locs. 102, 480, 499, 582.

him economically, since the thousands of abortion seekers who came to Ashland from across the United States patronized local hotels and other businesses.

Once, when the local Knights of Columbus chapter pledged to stop Spencer's abortion business by tracking and then accosting out-of-state visitors, Spencer "received word that the heat was on and temporarily shut down his illegal activity. After weeks of uneventful stakeouts, the state police left empty-handed." It appears that Spencer killed only one of the tens of thousands of women for whom he performed abortions during his fifty-year career. When he was brought to trial, a jury that included at least one former Spencer patient found him not guilty: His record of careful technique and cleanliness made jurors believe that some other abortionist must have made the fatal blunder.[18]

Another ideological abortionist, Dr. Edgar Keemer, was born in 1913 and grew up in a middle-class home desiring to follow in the profession of his father, who rose from a poor rural background to become a pharmacology professor. Keemer, an African American, received his MD from Meharry Medical College in Tennessee and quickly turned down a request to perform an abortion, but then reconsidered and went to New York City to learn the technique from a top abortionist there, "Dr. G."[19]

Keemer tried to develop a well-paid practice in Indiana, but the local medical society denied him membership on racial grounds and the local hospital refused him admitting privileges. He considered New York City and Chicago but found underpaid black doctors there moonlighting as railway porters. He settled in Detroit, where blacks had entered the auto industry at good wages and Wayne County's welfare system paid for doctors' visits.

---

18 Genovese, *Angel of Ashland*, loc. 593.
19 Leslie Reagan, *When Abortion Was a Crime: Women, Medicine, and Law in the United States, 1867–1973* (Berkeley: University of California Press, 1997), 156. Keemer wanted to avoid emulating his great uncle, who was lynched in 1875.

Keemer let other black physicians know that he would do abortions. His initial patients were their relatives. As others became aware of his maternal safety record better than that of old-school abortionists, referrals increased. As the Reproductive Health Access Project stated, his practice was "far different from the stereotypical 'back alley abortion.' ... Keemer took medical histories, explained the procedure, performed the abortion, sent patients home with printed instructions on post-abortion care, and conducted follow-up visits."[20]

When the United States entered World War II, Keemer tried to enlist in the Navy as a doctor but encountered racial slurs and suggestions that he work in the kitchen or mop floors. The Army then drafted him and Keemer said no: "I will not be drafted as a private since I have been turned down as an officer in the navy because of my color. I'll go to jail first." The NAACP and the Communist Party, each trying to show patriotism, pressured him to relent.[21]

Keemer later said only one person "came not to lecture me but to help me win my struggle. He was a member of the Socialist Workers Party," the Communist offshoot that supported Leon Trotsky in his battle against Joseph Stalin. Keemer joined the SWP in 1943, committed to replacing "capitalism with socialism wherein every man and every woman would be guaranteed a satisfying function in society." He wrote in the SWP newspaper, *The Militant*, that "the segregated, second-class, Jim Crow army 'for Negroes' is a dead giveaway to the hypocritical character" of the U.S. war effort.[22]

In 1946 Keemer proposed that the SWP create an independent organization for radical blacks who wanted to make fighting racism

---

20 Reproductive Health Access Project, February 16, 2018, https://www.reproductiveaccess.org/2018/02/black-history-month-dr-edgar-bass-keemer-jr.

21 Ruth Ryan, "Tribute to Black Socialist and Abortion Doctor," *Workers Vanguard* 1138, August 24, 2018, at icl-fi.org/print/english/wv/1138/ed_keemer.html.

22 Ryan, in *Workers Vanguard* 1138, reported Keemer's "racial equality" response to the charge that aborting black babies meant supporting a eugenics agenda: "If a sister chooses to defer her family until later, she goddamned well has a right to the same safe and legal treatment as a middle-class white woman."

their primary goal. When party leaders said no, Keemer resigned, still asserting that he was a "sympathizer with international socialism." He kept aborting children—probably about thirty thousand in all—and in 1946 remarried. When his second wife learned about his affairs with two other women, she divorced him. In 1948 Keemer bought mistresses Mrs. Fannie Bulkley a dress shop and Mrs. Mildred Mason Ballard a $42,000 ($468,000 now) home.[23]

Keemer's other expensive tastes included trophy-hunting around the world in Africa, Canada, Europe, Russia, and South America: He used rare animal hides to decorate his uptown Detroit office. Despite the absence of maternal deaths, police began to take notice. In 1956 four of Keemer's former patients testified against him. Police said they had nabbed the kingpin of "the most prolific abortion ring yet uncovered in Detroit." Keemer received a thirty-month sentence, spent fourteen months in prison, and reportedly performed an abortion on the daughter of "a high prison officer," at the officer's request. That got him out of prison early. He avoided more Michigan jail time by moving to New York, where he died in 1980.[24]

23 *Detroit Free Press*, January 19, 1949, 21.
24 *The Detroit Tribune*, June 9, 1951, 7; *Detroit Free Press*, May 7, 1973, 3B; *Jackson* (MS) *Free Press*, May 22, 2019, at jacksonfreepress.com; *The Detroit Tribune*, November 21, 1959, 3; *Detroit Free Press*, March 4, 1980, 6.

33

Losing the Baby

A THIRD NEW-SCHOOL ABORTIONIST, Ruth Barnett, differed from Spencer and Keemer both in background and expressed motivation. Although she was not a doctor, she was as competent in abortion as the best. A close friend of Planned Parenthood founder Margaret Sanger, Barnett performed about forty thousand illegal abortions from 1918 to 1968 in Portland, Oregon, with at least two-thirds of the women coming to her by referral from established doctors.[1]

Barnett's self-appraisal seems accurate: "I have never lost a single patient. . . . I have a light touch. . . . In the movies, they always depict the fallen women sneaking up a dirty, rickety stairway to a dismal room—or making her way, furtively, into a dark alley where some alcoholic doctor or untutored butcher performs the abortion. A clinic such as mine was not that way at all."[2] Her biographer, Rickie Solinger, describes Barnett as "clean and careful and very highly skilled. . . . The operating rooms were antiseptic."[3]

Barnett's memoir and biography suggest she became an abortionist partly out of revenge. An early sexual experience with "Frank" left

---

[1] Ruth Barnett, *They Weep on My Doorstep* (Beaverton, OR: Halo, 1969); Rickie Solinger, *The Abortionist: A Woman against the Law* (New York: Free Press, 1994).
[2] Barnett, *They Weep on My Doorstep*, 9, 36, 39, 40, 46, and 70.
[3] Solinger, *Abortionist*, 15, 30.

her pregnant: "He was not to blame, he said. What kind of a little fool had I been to be so careless? . . . 'You got yourself that way, now get yourself out of it.' Seeing the look of amazement on my face, he added a thrust that I've heard second-hand a thousand times since. 'How do I know I'm responsible anyways? You've been going around with other guys.'"[4]

Years later Barnett recalled, "He turned and hurried away. I never saw him again. In the years that followed, I have observed many 'Franks.' . . . For years I hated Frank. So it was no surprise to me to find many of my patients had the same implacable hatred for the man responsible." Early in Barnett's career, a nineteen-year-old came to her office and said her boyfriend had pledged "to be married at noon, but he said to come here first." Barnett asked, "Is your husband-to-be the father?" When the young woman said yes, Barnett told her, "Then you have nothing to worry about." Soon the young woman learned "the marriage is cancelled. Edward left her standing at the altar, the son of a bitch."[5]

Barnett raged not only against men who snubbed her but against those who snubbed her daughter: "Maggie" entered the University of Oregon in 1932 and tried to pledge a sorority, Alpha Chi Omega, but members rejected her because of her mom's occupation: Barnett was "screaming and crying in rage," but then told her daughter, "For every fraternity ring or pin I take in off these girls trying to pay for their abortions, and for every sorority girl that comes in my office, you'll get a new dress!"[6]

Maggie recalled, "That's what happened. I was the most fashionable and best outfitted girl at the university that season. And also the wildest, wickedest, drunkenest, most daring, and most

[4] *Spokane Chronicle*, April 25, 1989, A1.
[5] Barnett, *They Weep on My Doorstep*, 32–37.
[6] Solinger, *Abortionist*, 50–51: "Ruth's formulation was instinctively, pointedly vengeful: the sorority girls who snubbed their noses at her daughter would pay. Ruth would see to it that *their* secret shame—their abortions—paid Maggie back for the public humiliation of being blackballed."

promiscuous."[7] Barnett aborted Maggie's children, her own grandchildren, six times.[8]

Barnett also liked earning at least $9 million (much more than $100 million today), buying "jewelry, expensive bric-a-brac, minks," and telling her daughter, "Buy yourself a man, a husband, a lover. What can't money buy? . . . She had the most gorgeous fur coats, always had one draped over her shoulders when she came strolling in the room. We had about four or five fur coats apiece. . . . She loved jewelry. She had some gorgeous pieces. A canary diamond . . . with jaguar and square-cut diamonds on the side—white, but flames of ultraviolet in them."[9]

Money came in but also went out for bribes. Until the 1950s, Portland detective Barney Shields reminisced, "We never bothered any abortion clinics. Everybody knew of them." That was typical not only in Oregon but throughout the United States: Doctors "were not able to convince district attorneys or police chiefs to enforce the laws they'd hammered out in state capitals." Abortionists had "an 'unwritten agreement' with the cops that set a very broad limit on how and where and by whom the abortion clinics were run: no prosecution unless there was a death."[10]

To put it another way, much of the United States had a 2-C policy toward abortion: corruption and containment. Ambitious district attorneys like Brown in San Francisco or John Amen in New York sometimes put abortion on the front burner as part of an anti-corruption campaign. The emphasis was on corruption, not the deaths of unborn children. As Portland's leading newspaper, *The Oregonian*, editorialized, "The practice of abortion on a large scale almost inevitably leads to corruption of law enforcement . . . and perversion of justice and government."[11]

7 Solinger, *Abortionist*, 51.
8 Jann Mitchell, "My Mother, Ruth Barnett," *The Oregonian*, October 27, 1987.
9 Solinger, *Abortionist*, 37, 41.
10 Solinger, *Abortionist*, 11, 14.
11 Solinger, *Abortionist*, 182.

In the late 1940s a new word became prominent in international policy discussions: containment. George Kennan, in his famous 1947 *Foreign Affairs* article, stressed that the United States should avoid war with the Soviet Union and concentrate on the "long-term, patient but firm and vigilant containment of Russian expansive tendencies."[12] But the U.S. cities already had a containment policy in place regarding prostitution and pornography: Allow it in a few unsavory areas—Boston, for example, had its "combat zone"—but do not allow it to spread.

Abortion had also been "contained." Entrepreneurial reporters sometimes forced police to pay attention until the headlines receded. Generally, though, the policy in regard to desperate mothers and their unborn children during the 1930s and '40s was *live and let die*.[13]

That changed during the 1950s. Leslie Reagan's *When Abortion Was a Crime* is a credible history from a pro-abortion perspective: She did street-level research and described a "newly aggressive level of the state's suppression of abortion" in which prosecutors "worked to shut down the trusted and skilled abortionists, many of them physicians, who had operated clinics for years with little or no police interference.... The attack on these established practices meant the destruction of a system that... had created a space in which thousands of women obtained safe abortions from skilled physicians in an environment nearly identical to that of any other medical practice."[14]

The safety, of course, was for the woman, not her baby, but it's true that "thousands of women obtained abortions from physicians in con-

---

12 George Kennan, "The Sources of Soviet Conduct," *Foreign Affairs* 25 (1947): 575–76. Kennan wrote, "Soviet pressure against the free institutions of the Western world is something that can be contained by the adroit and vigilant application of counterforce at a series of constantly shifting geographical and political points, corresponding to the shifts and maneuvers of Soviet policy, but which cannot be charmed or talked out of existence."

13 Chapter 30 details the prosecution of Inez Burns. For John Amen's campaign, see my book *The Press and Abortion, 1838–1988* (Hillsdale, NJ: L. Erlbaum, 1988).

14 Leslie Reagan, *When Abortion Was a Crime: Women, Medicine, and Law in the United States, 1867–1973* (Berkeley: University of California Press, 1997), 160-61.

ventional medical settings and suffered no complications afterwards," at least no physical ones. In city after city, some physicians "specialized in abortion and had open, busy practices.... They were not located on back alleys, but on main streets. Dr. Gabler [Josephine, Chicago] had a business card; Dr. Timanus [George, Baltimore] was listed in the phone book and his office had a sign in front."[15]

In 1950 Baltimore police raided Timanus. The following year, after *The Oregon Journal* published an expose of Barnett, police raided her office and she spent several months in prison. As with Inez Burns, Barnett's tax avoidance led to jail time in 1952 and '53, followed by new arrests and sentences in 1957 and '58. The arrests saved some unborn lives but had unexpected consequences: the creation of new concerns about maternal safety and class inequality.[16]

Reagan writes, "It was not until the postwar period, quite late in the history of illegal abortion, that women's descriptions of illegal abortions included meeting intermediaries, being blindfolded, and being driven to a secret and unknown place where an unseen and unknown person performed the abortion." Maternal deaths were down due to the availability of antibiotics, but infections that required hospital visits apparently increased as some abortions took place in old-school, non-antiseptic conditions. The number of women arriving at Chicago's Cook County Hospital for complications following miscarriages or (more often) abortions quadrupled from 1940 to 1960.[17]

Money continued to play a role in safety, as it had in the days of Madame Restell: in general, the higher the cost, the lower the danger. A new twist by the 1950s was the creation in most hospitals of "therapeutic abortion committees": They gave affluent women who

15 Reagan, *When Abortion Was a Crime*, 161.
16 *Statesman Journal*, February 7, 1952; *News-Review* (Roseburg, OR), May 6, 1952, 7; *The Coos Bay* (OR) *Times*, January 14, 1953, 5; *Statesman Journal*, February 11, 1954, 20; *News-Review*, October 22, 1957, 7; *Statesman Journal*, March 13, 1958, 2.
17 Reagan, *When Abortion Was a Crime*, 197, 209–10.

could afford to see specialists, and knew what to say, the opportunity to get legal abortions. As Reagan learned, "Physicians and their private-paying female patients together made psychiatric reasons the primary indication for therapeutic abortion," and the result was "class inequality."[18]

Problem: When mental health became a common reason for abortion, few knew what the boundaries were. Enforcement of laws protecting unborn children had been erratic because of corruption, but at least the principle seemed right to most. That changed in 1962, the last year of Communist China's disastrous "great leap forward" and the first year of American abortion's great leap. One piece of evidence: An episode of CBS's drama *The Defenders* portrayed abortionists as kindly but victimized public servants who risked their freedom for the sake of many.[19]

A second piece: When newspapers across the country reported how an abortionist who killed the mother as well as the unborn child cut up the woman and stuffed her down a sewage line that became clogged, the gory details may have seemed like traditional sensationalism. This time, though, reporters portrayed the problem not as abortion but as *illegal* abortion. They implied that if abortion were legalized such things would not happen.[20]

The year's largest abortion story had as its heroine Sherri Finkbine, twenty-nine, the "pretty mother of four healthy children" and the wife of a high school history teacher. As Miss Sherri, she starred in the Phoenix version of *Romper Room*, a nationally syndicated program for children. She seemed to have an all-American life. But she had unwittingly taken the drug thalidomide, then surfacing in Europe as

---

18 Reagan, *When Abortion Was a Crime*, 200–201, 205.
19 Telecast on April 28, 1962.
20 The abortionist evaded American police but their counterparts in France captured and then extradited him. See "Queens M.D. Admits Girl's Abortion Death," *New York World-Telegram-Sun*, September 12, 1962, 1; and "Runaway M.D. Is Indicted in Death of Coed," *New York Journal-American*, September 26, 1962, 1.

the reason why some children were born with phocomelia (flipper-like limbs) or without any limbs at all.[21]

On July 16, 1962, Sherri Finkbine read a newspaper story about babies born in Europe with serious birth defects after their mothers had taken thalidomide. She called her doctor to ask about her tranquilizers, and the doctor found out she had been taking thalidomide. He suggested abortion, legal at that time in Arizona when the mother's life was in danger. On July 23, a rule-stretching committee of three doctors approved an abortion, scheduled for July 25 or 26, on the grounds of psychological danger to the mother. Finkbine told her story to a Phoenix reporter so as to "alert others" to thalidomide dangers.[22]

Once the story hit the front page, hospital administrators feared protest and possible legal action and refused to authorize the abortion that the doctors already had approved. Sherri Finkbine was the heroine. The system designed to limit abortion was villainous. Newspaper readers learned that abortion was not merely the refuge of the seduced and abandoned but the goal of "pretty Sherri Finkbine," suburban housewife and mother, a "deeply tanned brunet [sic] wearing a sleeveless dress of white linen who tapped the toe of an orange spike heeled pump."[23]

During July and August 1962, hundreds of newspaper reporters hung on the Finkbines' words as they arranged for travel to Sweden: Reporters said Sherri Finkbine had to go there "to find a more civilized attitude toward her plight," and Americans "ought to have a look at their abortion laws in light of what they did to her."[24]

21 *Washington Post*, August 3, 1962, A4; *Newsweek*, August 13, 1962, 52. Starting in 1958, European mothers used thalidomide, which became known in England as "The Sleeping Pill of the Century," to relieve the nausea of early pregnancy. Distributed to children as a pacifier, some called thalidomide "West Germany's Baby-Sitter." But doctors soon learned that women who took thalidomide during their second month of pregnancy ran a 20 percent chance of bearing a deformed child, according to Dr. Frances Kelsey of the Food and Drug Administration.
22 *Arizona Republic*, July 23, 1962, 1; July 24, 1; August 21, 1.
23 *Los Angeles Times*, August 4, 1962, 1.
24 *Atlanta Constitution*, August 18, 1962, 30.

Although many people throughout the United States offered to adopt the child if born, reporters accepted the Finkbine contention that the "operation" would be performed for the good of the baby. A *Washington Post* reporter told Finkbine of one such offer and said she burst into tears, because adoption "wouldn't be fair to the child."[25]

Sherri Finkbine referred to the being in her womb as a "child" or "baby," as did most journalists, at first. Headlines used the word "baby" and came up with euphemisms for abortion. *The New York Times* reported, "Couple May Go Abroad for Surgery to Prevent a Malformed Baby." A *Los Angeles Times* headline said the Finkbines planned "Baby Surgery." *The New York Journal-American* described an operation to "lose the baby."

Since the Finkbines did not seem like murderers, reports disassociated them from abortion, and soon the word "fetus"—which previously had been used only when reporters focused on the medical aspects of the situation—began to replace the words "unborn child."[26]

On August 18 the Finkbines' unborn child died from abortion in Sweden, and coverage dribbled off with some final praise for Sherri Finkbine's assumedly compassionate decision. Soon after, a question on abortion was included for the first time in a Gallup poll. The poll asked whether Sherri Finkbine did right or wrong "in having this abortion operation." Some 52 percent of those responding thought she had "done the right thing," 32 percent felt she had done wrong, and 16 percent had no opinion.[27]

---

25 *Chicago Tribune*, August 4, 1962, 5; and August 5, 1; *Atlanta Constitution*, August 18, 30; *New York Journal-American*, July 25, 1; *Washington Post*, July 31, A-3.

26 *New York Times*, August 1, 1962, 19; *Los Angeles Times*, August 1, 1962, 1; *New York Journal-American*, August 18, 1962, 1. Three decades before, anthropologist Herbert Aptekar, in *Anjea: Infanticide, Abortion, and Contraception in Savage Society* (New York: William Godwin, 1931), 131, had proposed changes in vocabulary since "the word abortion used in Western Civilization carries with it the connotations of the word murder. Mention of the word always brings up the feeling-tones connected with a host of other terms designating despicable and dishonorable acts."

27 George Horace Gallup, *The Gallup Poll, Public Opinion 1935–1971* (New York: Random House, 1972), 1984.

34

Playing the Danger Card

CAITLYN FLANAGAN is a good reporter and a poetic writer whose articles show a mind at work, not a propagandist on the prowl—so when she says "we need to face the best arguments" from both sides of the abortion debate, and then presents what they are, people should listen. The best pro-life argument, she says, "is a picture." She looks at photos of unborn children and writes, "these images made me anxious. They are proof that what grows within a pregnant woman's body is a human being," and it takes "a profound act of violence to remove him from his quiet world and destroy him."[1]

Flanagan thought a first-trimester photo would not prompt that response, "until it occurred to me to look at one of those images taken at the end of the first trimester. I often wish I hadn't. . . . I think: *Here is one of us; here is a baby*. She has fingers and toes by now, eyelids and ears. She can hiccup—that tiny, chest-quaking motion that all parents know. . . . These are human beings, the most vulnerable among us, and we have no care for them. How terrible to know that in the space of an hour, a baby could be alive—his heart beating, his kidneys creating

---

1 Caitlyn Flanagan, "The Dishonesty of the Abortion Debate: Why We Need to Face the Best Arguments from the Other Side," *The Atlantic*, December 2019, https://www.theatlantic.com/magazine/archive/2019/12/the-things-we-cant-face/600769.

the urine that becomes the amniotic fluid of his safe home—and then be dead, his heart stopped, his body soon to be discarded."

The best argument for abortion, Flanagan says, is women's health: "Here is one truth: No matter what the law says, women will continue to get abortions. How do I know? Because in the relatively recent past, women would allow strangers to . . . poke knitting needles and wire hangers into their wombs, to thread catheters through their cervices and fill them with Lysol."

Lysol? The cleaner we now use on countertops? While anyone who's been to an abortion advocacy march is familiar with the wire hanger symbol, Flanagan tells the less-known story of Lysol, the household product that women readily purchased and sometimes used from the 1930s through the 1960s (in diluted form, with disputable results) as a form of birth control. But to understand why that happened, we have to go back to the 1890s.

That's when (as ch. 29 explains) doctors realized the importance of being earnestly aseptic. That was all very well as a principle, but how would doctors put it into practice? In 1892 the *Medical and Surgical Reporter* complained about "washing and brushing with soap and water, rinsing with 80 percent alcohol, and the subsequent scrubbing" with a bichloride of mercury solution: It was all "very inconvenient . . . three wash basins are required besides the necessary solutions."[2]

What doctors needed: "an antiseptic easily soluble in water. . . . Even in weak solutions it must act as a speedy and positive germicide. It must be very slightly if at all poisonous to the human organism. Its price must be reasonable enough to permit of its general and free use. It should have freedom from offensive odor." But who had such a semi-miraculous concoction like that? Look: It's a bird, it's a plane, it's a super substance—Lysol, "a near approach to an ideal antiseptic

---

2 "Lysol in Gynaecology and Obstetrics," *Medical and Surgical Reporter* 66 (June 18, 1892): 983–84.

for gynecological and obstetrical practice." It's also 95 percent cheaper than a carbolic acid solution.[3]

Lysol? The *Medical and Surgical Reporter* recommended not only "scrubbing arms, hands, and nails in a 1 per cent. warm solution of Lysol for four minutes," and not only bathing previously sterilized instruments in Lysol, but also using a Lysol solution to wash the patient's genitalia: Lysol provides "relative freedom from danger, easy solubility . . . cheapness, and remarkably convenient applicability."[4]

Other medical publications similarly lauded Lysol: "Lysol, the new disinfectant and antiseptic, is recommended as promptly arresting the development of micro-organisms. It can be mixed readily with water, and . . . is only as poisonous as carbolic acid, and cheaper." *Scientific American* in 1892 called Lysol "the ideal soluble disinfectant. . . . Admirably adapted for use in surgical operations."[5]

Cheap and poisonous . . . what could go wrong? Stories from 1898 to 1911 in even one newspaper in one city alone, the *San Francisco Examiner*, suggest an answer to that question: Accidental poisonings, sometimes deadly. Suicide attempts ("piqued bride takes Lysol"), sometimes successful. The "pretty abortion victim" genre expanded to "A very pretty girl . . . swallowed a bottle of Lysol and laid down to die, with a white rose in her mouth . . . From being the plaything of one careless man she became the plaything of the careless many." Headlines included, "Drinks Lysol when Love Is Spurned," with an important element of the story: "Mrs. Melswinkel is exceptionally pretty."[6]

---

3 "Lysol in Gynaecology and Obstetrics," 984.
4 "Lysol in Gynaecology and Obstetrics," 985.
5 "Lysol," *The Dental Register* 46 (February 1892): 91–92; *Scientific American* 67 (December 10, 1892), 369. See also *The Hospital* (London), December 13, 1890, 179.
6 *Examiner* articles: poisoning: April 7, 1906, 4; December 19, 1909, 25; accidental deaths: June 9, 1903, 11; July 14, 1903, 12; January 4, 1906, 5; July 2, 1907, 4; July 14, 1903, 12; suicide attempts: October 10, 1898, 2; October 25, 1906, 10; April 15, 1909, 3; November 25, 1909; "Piqued Bride Takes Lysol," May 28, 1911, 3; "Pretty Rosa Reaves Is Saved from Death—for What?" April 14, 1900, 14; "Mrs. Melswinkel," August 19, 1910, 3. See also "Lysol and Kreolin Poisoning," *The Hospital* (London), March 5, 1910, 656–58.

Lehn & Fink, the company that produced Lysol, saw its sales decline around 1910 as doctors reported instances of adverse physical effects, particularly internal burning, after patients received treatment with Lysol. In 1912, with the American Medical Association saying doctors should not use it, Lehn & Fink began looking for other markets. In the 1920s the company launched one campaign advertising Lysol as a household cleaner and another promoting it as a contraceptive douche. Ads in magazines such as *Ladies Home Journal* used "feminine hygiene" as a euphemism for birth control.[7]

Lysol was not particularly effective in contraception, but used in a mix of 1 percent Lysol and 99 percent water, it was also not particularly dangerous. Given the blurring between contraception and abortion that was commonplace, though, some women thought it made sense to increase the percentage of Lysol, and that's when tragedy came. From the 1930s through the 1950s medical journals had articles with titles like these: "Intrauterine Injection of Lysol as an Abortifacient; Report of a Fatal Case Complicated by Oil Embolism and Lysol Poisoning," "The Use of Oral Procaine in a Case of Lysol Poisoning," and "Lysol-Induced Criminal Abortion."[8]

A day's foray into this medical literature is a miserable experience that shows the desperate misery of some women in those decades. Here's case three in a *New England Journal of Medicine* article: a woman with "severe abdominal pain and vaginal bleeding a few hours after a 'Lysol douche' during the 4th month of pregnancy." Here's case four: "Seven

---

7   Kristin Hall, "Selling Sexual Certainty? Advertising Lysol as a Contraceptive in the United States and Canada, 1919–1939," *Enterprise and Society* 14, no. 1 (March 2013): 71–98.

8   Louis Pancaro, "Poisoning from Compound Solution of Cresol [Lysol ingredient] Following Uterine Injection," *Journal of the American Medical Association* 104 (1935): 2387; B. M. Vance, "Intrauterine Injection . . . ," *Archives of Pathology* 40 (November–December 1945): 395–98; A. D. Silk and S. J. Stempien, "The Use of Oral Procaine . . . ," *Gastroenterology* 23 (February 1953): 301–3; J. A. Presley, W. E. Brown, "Lysol-Induced Criminal Abortion," *Obstetrics and Gynecology* 8 (September 1956): 368–70; Karl Finzer, "Lower Nephron Nephrosis Due to Concentrated Lysol Vaginal Douches," *Canadian Medical Association Journal* 84 (March 11, 1961): 5649.

days previously an alleged nurse had given the patient an intrauterine injection of Lysol during the 3d month of her 1st pregnancy."[9]

This was largely a forgotten aspect of medical history until Andrea Tone's *Devices and Desires* (2001), and numerous journalists used her research to produce magazine articles: "When Women Used Lysol as Birth Control," "The Secret Life of Vintage Lysol Douche Ads," "When Lysol Was Used as Birth Control," and "Lysol Was Once Used as Birth Control—and Poisoned a Lot of Women." Their common indictment: Social and legal restrictions on abortion pushed women into hazardous activity during the bad old days, and those days could come again if new restrictions arise.[10]

That is the question: Will those dangerous days come again now that the Supreme Court has discarded *Roe v. Wade*? What do we know about maternal danger from the 1940s to the 1960s? In 1942, just before antibiotics became widely available, Taussig estimated 5,000 adult abortion deaths per year. In 1948 Christopher Tietze, who with his wife Sarah Lewit would receive a Planned Parenthood award for research, said abortion deaths were rapidly declining because penicillin and sulfa drugs had become available: "The outstanding fact about mortality from abortion is the steady and sometimes precipitous decline which has been observed almost everywhere." Tietze estimated 2,677 deaths from abortion in 1933 and 888 in 1945.[11]

Planned Parenthood medical director Mary Calderone wrote in 1960 that for women, "Abortion is no longer a dangerous procedure." For

---

9   Robert Bartlett and Clement Yahia, "Management of Septic Chemical Abortion with Renal Failure," *New England Journal of Medicine* 281 (October 2, 1969): 747–53.
10 Andrea Tone, *Devices and Desires: A History of Contraceptives in America* (New York: Hill & Wang, 2001), 170–73. Nicole Pasulka, "When Women Used Lysol as Birth Control," *Mother Jones*, March 8, 2012; Lisa Wade, "The Secret Life of Vintage Lysol Douche Ads," *Sociological Images*, September 27, 2013; Kyrie Gray, "When Lysol Was Used as Birth Control," *Medium*, August 17, 2020; Aimee Lamoureux, "Lysol Was Once Used as Birth Control—and Poisoned a Lot of Women," *All That's Interesting*, July 11, 2021. See also Flanagan, "Dishonesty of the Abortion Debate."
11 Regarding the difficulty in developing accurate numbers concerning what for decades occurred in secret, see Tietze's paper in Mary Calderone, ed., *Abortion in the United States* (New York: Hoeber-Harper, 1958), 180.

example, New York City went from 144 abortion deaths in 1921 to only 15 in 1951. Calderone attributed the decline to antibiotics plus better training among the licensed physicians who did 90 percent of abortions. She took into account the possibility of misreporting on death certificates but noted that autopsies revealed causes of death, doctors uninvolved in the cases filled out death certificates that went to the Bureau of Vital Statistics of the U.S. Public Health Department, and doctors who favored legalization of abortion wanted those deaths recorded, since they were ammunition for those favoring abortion law reform or repeal.[12]

In the 1960s, though, both sides of the abortion debate used a flashing fluorescent DANGER sign to buttress their positions. A key argument for legalization: DANGER. A key reason not to have an abortion: DANGER. Tietze guessed the number of abortions annually might be anywhere from 200,000 to 1,200,000, and said greater precision was impossible. Pro-abortion doctor Harold Rosen guessed 330,000 annually. Others guessed 100,000, and the book *Criminal Abortion* guessed one million.[13]

The crucial questions when evaluating potential deaths in a post-*Roe* environment: How many deaths occurred during the years immediately preceding *Roe*, and how might a post-*Roe* environment be similar or

---

12 Mary Calderone, "Illegal Abortion as a Public Health Problem," *American Journal of Public Health and the Nation's Health* 50, no. 7 (July 1, 1960): 948–54.

13 Harold Rosen, ed., *Therapeutic Abortion: Medical, Psychiatric, Anthropological, and Religious Considerations* (New York: Julian Press, 1954); republished as *Abortion in America* (Boston: Beacon, 1967), 267; Jerome Bates and Edward Zawadzki, *Criminal Abortion: A Study in Medical Sociology* (Springfield, IL: Charles C. Thomas, 1964), viii, 5–6; the coauthors said, "four major independent studies . . . agree that, at this writing, about one million criminal abortions are performed annually in the United States." Present tense in 1964: "are performed." Yet two of the studies were based on interviewing patients at Margaret Sanger's Birth Control Clinical Research Bureau in New York City from 1925 through 1929. They were hardly a cross-section of America, and the most recent cases were thirty-five years old. The other two studies were also flawed. See Marie Kopp, *Birth Control in Practice* (New York: Robert McBride, 1934), 222; Regine Stix, "A Study of Pregnancy Wastage," *Milbank Memorial Fund Quarterly* 13 (October 1, 1935): 347, 364; Paul Gebhard, Martin Wardell, Clyde Martin, and Cornelia Christenson, *Pregnancy, Birth, and Abortion* (New York: Harper & Brothers, 1958), 136–37.

different? Tietze estimated the illegal pre-*Roe* maternal abortion death rate to be not more than one maternal death for each 1,000 fetal deaths. Tietze's estimated death rate for *illegal* abortions in the United States was like that for *legal* abortions in European countries where abortions took place in antiseptic conditions, which suggests that most U.S. abortions took place in similarly clean environments.[14]

Many abortion supporters admit that their movement exaggerated the maternal danger of abortion in the 1960s, but one reporter said the "image of tens of thousands of women being maimed or killed each year by illegal abortion [was] so persuasive a piece of propaganda that the movement could be forgiven its failure to double-check the facts."[15] That was then, but Planned Parenthood has continued to predict that an overturn of *Roe v. Wade* will mean "thousands of women" annually will die. *The Washington Post* strongly backs abortion, but the chief writer for its Fact Checker feature, Glenn Kessler, gave Planned Parenthood's numerology a "four Pinocchios" rating (its sign of maximum displeasure, reserved for "whoppers").[16]

What's a more realistic story? Stanley Henshaw, who from 1979 to 2013 researched abortion statistics at the Guttmacher Institute, predicted that "if *Roe v. Wade* were overturned, women would turn to relatively safe medications that can be purchased over the Internet." Michele Landeau of the Gateway Women's Access Fund told NPR in 2019 that a post-*Roe* future will not be a replay of the 1960s: "the Internet has happened since then, and a lot of advances in medical

---

14 Christopher Tietze in Calderone, "Illegal Abortion as a Public Health Problem," 180; Christopher Tietze and Stanley K. Henshaw, *Induced Abortion: A World Review* (New York: The Population Council, 1986, 6th ed.), 107.
15 Marian Faux, *Roe v. Wade: The Untold Story of the Landmark Supreme Court Decision That Made Abortion Legal*, quoted in *National Review*, July 22, 1988, 45.
16 Dr. Leana Wen on WFAA-Dallas and MSNBC's *Morning Joe*, and tweeting on April 24, 2019; Glenn Kessler, "Planned Parenthood's False Stat: 'Thousands' of Women Died Every Year before Roe," *The Washington Post*, May 29, 2019. Kessler said the best comparison would be to the years just before *Roe* when both California and New York had liberalized their abortion laws and became abortion havens.

science have happened since then. . . . it's not going to look the same as it did pre-*Roe*."¹⁷

I'll come back in the epilogue to what post-*Roe* could be. Caitlyn Flanagan said the best argument on one side is an ultrasound of a baby, and the best on the other side is that women would use Lysol or something like that, and some would die. She wrote, "the best argument on each side is a damn good one."¹⁸ Considering what we've seen in this chapter, abortion advocates will need to come up with a better one.¹⁹

---

17 Sarah McCammon, "With Abortion Restrictions on the Rise, Some Women Induce Their Own," *All Things Considered* (National Public Radio), September 19, 2019.
18 Flanagan, "Dishonesty of the Abortion Debate."
19 Pro-abortion groups are promoting abortion pills: see https://shoutyourabortion.com/abortion-pills/. Some say restrictions will scare hospitals away from treating women with ectopic pregnancies and miscarriages. Abortion advocates say innocent girls and young women will have to travel for abortions resulting from rape. Some say it's time to ditch the coat hanger symbol since it might lead women to equate self-administered abortions with that approach rather than with abortion pills (https://jezebel.com/please-stop-using-coat-hangers-to-protest-abortion-bans-1848820926).

35

The Father of Abortion Rights

LAWRENCE LADER enrolled at Harvard in 1937. He moved to the left politically and hosted U.S. Communist Party leader William Z. Foster on a campus radio station, later explaining that "with all Stalin's sins, the revolution stood as an island of socialist hope in a disintegrating world." He set up radio relays in the South Pacific during World War II, then added to his radical resume by advising socialist U.S. Congressman Vito Marcantonio.[1]

Lader ran for a seat in the New York State Assembly as a socialist and lost, but he gained success as a magazine writer with *Esquire*'s mini-magazine *Coronet*. Bylines in *The Saturday Evening Post*, *Parade*, and other publications gained him entry to New York magazine offices he described as overflowing "with seduction. . . . In the glittering crescendo of those postwar years, I moved from affair to affair."[2]

Lader's articles often had grabby headlines: "One Way to Live Longer," "Landing a Jet without Looking," "We Can Stop Sadism in Our Mental Hospitals." He became president of the Society of Magazine

---

1 Douglas Martin, "Lawrence Lader, Champion of Abortion Rights, Is Dead at 86," *New York Times*, May 10, 2006, 23.
2 Elizabeth Mehren, "Champion of Choice: Lawrence Lader's 1966 Book Launched a Crusade for Reproductive Rights. Now 76, He's Backing an Abortion Drug for the U.S. Market," *Los Angeles Times*, November 30, 1995, E1.

Writers, held memberships in select Manhattan clubs (The Harvard, Century, and Lotos), and later owned an apartment on Fifth Avenue in Greenwich Village.[3]

Lader wanted to move beyond short profiles and light features to write a book "that would involve meaningful currents of social change." More specifically, a book about "a new type of woman, one who would break out of all the prejudices and molds of the past." He found his perfect subject in Margaret Sanger, who was historically significant and still living, which would allow him to do first-person research. Sanger agreed but set one condition: She'd have final say over the manuscript.[4]

When they met, Lader was thirty-four and Sanger seventy-four. For three years he spent days with her in Tucson, part researcher and part squire. Although not sexual, the relationship between Lader and Sanger had romantic overtones. It cooled when Sanger wanted to make changes to the final manuscript—she preferred a younger birthdate for herself—but Lader said *The Margaret Sanger Story* "shaped my future writing and campaigns on birth control and abortion."[5]

Lader credited Sanger with stirring his thinking by giving him a medical text about abortion. He became convinced that "contraception

---

3 Some Lader articles: "The Road from Buchenwald," *The New Republic*, September 20, 1948; "Fit Yourself to a Lasting Job," *Coronet*, September 1946, 83–88; "He Makes Checks Talk," *Coronet*, March 1948, 139–42; "One Way to Live Longer," *Coronet*, June 1946, 3–6; "Lunt and Fontanne: First Family of the Theater," *Coronet*, June 1948, 123–32; "Childhood's Crippled Minds," *Collier's Weekly*, July 15, 1950, 9–11; "Landing a Jet without Looking," *The Saturday Evening Post*, February 15, 1964, 64–65; "We Can Stop Sadism in Our Mental Hospitals," *Look*, April 24, 1951; "The Bail Scandal," *Parade*, March 1, 1964.

4 According to the Margaret Sanger Papers Project at NYU, "the enthusiastic and charming Lader promised Sanger a detailed and uplifting biography over which she would have the final say" ("Writing Sanger's Life," Newsletter 14 [Winter 1996/1997], at https://web.archive.org/web/2021 0507162326/https://www.nyu.edu/projects/sanger/articles/writing_sangers_life.php).

5 Lawrence Lader, *The Margaret Sanger Story: And the Fight for Birth Control* (Garden City, NY: Doubleday, 1955). He explained his writing process in "Margaret Sanger: Militant Pragmatist Visionary," *On the Issues Magazine*, Spring 1990, 10–12, 14, 30–31, 34–35: "During the months I spent interviewing her in Arizona, California, New York and Washington, DC, we would start work at 9 a.m. and often continue through the evening, breaking only for lunch and cocktails. Her favorite drink was champagne, and I spent far more than I could afford buying it for her."

alone could never handle the problem of unwanted pregnancies." Lader shared with Sanger the belief that "women must have complete control over their own bodies and childbearing." He wrote in 1990, "When I published the first book calling for legalization of abortion in 1966, and became overnight a campaigner rather than a writer, it was as though every step I made was with Margaret's ghost at my side directing my strategy."

Starting in the late 1950s, Lader wanted to write mainstream magazine stories about abortion, but editors rejected his queries until Sherri Finkbine's story in 1962 changed popular understanding of what was allowable. The following year German measles, which can also lead to babies being born with birth defects such as heart, liver, and spleen damage, swept the United States. A prestigious legal group, the American Law Institute, advocated reform of state abortion laws. In New York, the Association for the Study of Abortion—made up of 250 leading doctors, lawyers, professors, and pastors—was studying the issue. People were talking, at least in elite circles, about changing abortion laws, but few were pressing for total repeal. Lawrence Lader was.[6]

In 1965 pollsters found 88 percent of women supporting abortion when the mother's health was threatened, but only half approving it when a child was likely to be born deformed or when pregnancy resulted from rape. Only 8 percent approved of abortion for any reason. That year Lader landed an article in the *New York Times Sunday Magazine* that laid out his major arguments. The danger concerns were dead: Anti-abortion laws existed to protect maternal health, but modern abortion was safer than childbirth. Enforcement of those laws forced women into the hands of untrained and unfit abortionists. Lader gave hero status to several doctors who risked arrest by performing abortions despite their illegality.[7]

---

6   Lader said 82,000 women contracted German measles in the first trimester of their pregnancies, with up to 15,000–20,000 of those pregnancies resulting in babies born with birth defects. Lader advocated aborting unborn children when their mothers contracted German measles early in pregnancy.
7   Charles F. Westoff, Emily C. Moore, and Norman B. Ryder, "The Structure of Attitudes toward Abortion," *Milbank Memorial Fund Quarterly* 47, no. 1 (January 1969): 12; Lawrence Lader, "The Scandal of Abortion—Laws," *New York Times Sunday Magazine*, April 25, 1965, 32.

In 1966 Indianapolis-based Bobbs-Merrill put out Lader's radical book, *Abortion*.[8] The publisher, best known for *The Joy of Cooking* and *The Childhood of Famous Americans* biography series for kids, was hardly an avant-garde publisher. *Abortion* received positive reviews in the *Los Angeles Times*, *The Washington Post*, and other newspapers. It included the dubious statistic of one million abortions a year, which became the standard number in pro-abortion propaganda.[9]

An excerpt from the book in *Reader's Digest*, known for its Main Street conservatism, reached millions of ordinary Americans with Lader's pro-abortion interpretation of history. Publisher Dewitt Wallace was a longtime supporter of Margaret Sanger and population control.[10] Lader later acknowledged the role Wallace played: He "digested my strongly pro-choice book *Abortion* in 1966, and helped me promote the subject in a national tour that *Reader's Digest* paid for."[11]

The tour, during which Lader spoke one hundred times, marked his transformation from writer to campaigner—a role he played for the next forty years. He helped to transform abortion from crime story to civil rights issue. At every stop Lader argued that abortion laws were "a total evil" demanding obliteration, not moderation. He compared the frequency of legal abortion among affluent women (who paid doctors to provide legal reasons for "therapeutic abortion") with its relative infrequency among poorer patients: "INEQUALITY," Lader thundered. He also gave abortion a utopian focus by calling it "The Final Freedom" on the road to female autonomy.[12]

Lader laid out principles and also developed the tactics that would enable abortion advocates to overwhelm their opposition during the late 1960s. "The best chance to build a movement," he argued, was to make abortion a battle against a villain: "every revolution has to have

8   Lawrence Lader, *Abortion* (Indianapolis: Bobbs-Merrill, 1966).
9   Meryle Secrest, "New Book Is Provocative," *Washington Post*, July 29, 1966, D2.
10 Lawrence Lader, "Let's Speak Out on Abortion," *Reader's Digest*, May 1966, 82.
11 Lawrence Lader, *New York Times*, September 12, 1993, 43.
12 Lader, *Abortion*, 29, 167–75.

its villain . . . it really doesn't matter whether it's a king, a dictator, or a tsar, but it has to be *someone*, a person, to rebel against. It's easier for the people we want to persuade to perceive it this way. [But] a single person isn't quite what we want, since that might excite sympathy for him. Rather, a small group of shadowy, powerful people."[13]

Lader, because of his own prejudice and careful calculation, made "the Catholic hierarchy" the designated villain: "That's a small enough group to come down on, and anonymous enough so that no names ever have to be mentioned, but everybody will have a fairly good idea whom we are talking about." Catholics were also useful punching bags because they connected and opposed both birth control and abortion, and Lader "was trying to make the jump from birth control to an abortion right that not only didn't exist but was an underground, abhorrent topic." Church leaders had already done the heavy lifting to link contraception and abortion in the public mind.[14]

Lader decided to escalate his campaign for repeal of all anti-abortion laws only after he found reporters sympathetic and developed the "reasonable assurance that repeal could stir some excitement in the press." When Lader founded the National Association for the Repeal of Abortion Laws (NARAL) and saw the support he was receiving from journalists, he "was sure we could ignite the country." The press, he found, was on his side and eager to cover NARAL demonstrations: "The press turned out strongly in every city and NARAL had suddenly become a national force."[15]

Lader also needed bodies willing to march in the streets. He turned to old friend Betty Friedan, a relative latecomer to abortion advocacy:

---

13 Lawrence Lader, *Abortion II: Making the Revolution* (Boston: Beacon, 1973), ix. Quoted by Bernard Nathanson in *Aborting America* (Garden City, NY: Doubleday, 1979), 51.

14 Nathanson, *Aborting America*, 52; Elaine Woo, "Lawrence Lader, 86," *Los Angeles Times*, May 14, 2006, B14.

15 Lader, *Abortion II*, 92, 97. Following *Roe v. Wade*, NARAL kept its initials by changing its name to the National Abortion Rights Action League. It now advertises itself as "NARAL Pro-Choice America."

She neither mentioned it in *The Feminine Mystique* nor focused on it when founding the National Organization for Women in 1966. Lader convinced her that no woman could be free unless she had absolute control over her fertility. That meant making abortion the centerpiece of feminism. Friedan sold NOW on abortion advocacy and joined with Lader and others in forming NARAL.[16]

Lader, Friedan, and abortionist Bernard Nathanson organized NARAL's first national conference—on Valentine's Day, 1969—and recruited those advocating complete repeal to show up. Debate among the 360 delegates from fifty organizations pitted those who wanted merely to change the laws against those who wanted to repeal them. The "moderates" cited public opinion polls: one from Gallup showed 40 percent of adults supporting the legalization of abortion, but only during the first twelve weeks of pregnancy. Lader and his allies, though, argued that anything less than total repeal was worthless. Since they had stacked the conference with like-minded people, the repealers won and chose Lader to be chairman of the new organization.[17]

In 1969, abortion advocates had supporters in the political heights, including numerous Republicans. Richard Nixon, who became president in 1969, combined some politically useful anti-abortion comments with pro-abortion appointments. Abortion supporter John Ehrlichman became domestic chief of staff. Louis Hellman, a director of the Association for the Study of Abortion, took the key spot for abortion policy in the Department of Health, Education, and Welfare. Reimert Ravenholt headed the Population Affairs section of the Agency for International Development. John D. Rockefeller III chaired a feder-

---

16 Betty Friedan, *The Feminine Mystique* (New York: Norton, 1963). NOW's 1970 Strike for Equality in New York and cities across the country made repeal of abortion laws its number one demand. See David M. Dismore, "When Women Went on Strike: Remembering Equality Day, 1970," *Ms.* Magazine blog, August 26, 2010, https://msmagazine.com/2010/08/26/when-women-went-on-strike-remembering-equality-day-1970.

17 Lader, *Abortion II*, 86–97; R. Sauer, "Attitudes to Abortion in America, 1800–1973," *Population Studies* 28, no. 1 (March 1974): 63.

ally financed "Commission on Population Growth and the American Future." Of Nixon's twenty appointees to the commission, sixteen were pro-abortion. The commission predictably recommended abolition of all abortion laws.[18]

Abortion advocates, though, did not have broad popular support. In 1972, although Detroit newspapers heavily supported a Michigan referendum to legalize abortion on demand through the first five months, 61 percent of Michigan voters said no. In North Dakota, 77 percent of voters turned down a similar referendum. Overall, despite overwhelming press sentiment, thirty-one states in 1972 still resisted any abortion liberalization. Fifteen more kept most abortion illegal but allowed it in cases of fetal deformity, rape, incest, or "mother's health" (defined in various ways). A Gallup poll in 1972 asked, "Do you think abortion operations should be legal where the parents simply have all the children they want although there would be no major health or financial problems involved in having another child?" Two-thirds of respondents said no.[19]

---

18 Reimert Ravenholt, in *Population and the American Future* (Washington, DC: Government Printing Office, 1972), 5–6, 161. A dissenting member of the commission, Grace Olivarez, wrote, "To talk about the 'wanted' and the 'unwanted' child smacks too much of bigotry and prejudice. ... Those with power in our society cannot be allowed to 'want' and 'unwant' people at will. ... The poor cry out for justice and equality, and we respond with legalized abortion." John Noonan discusses the Nixon administration's role in abortion in *A Private Choice: Abortion in America in the Seventies* (New York: The Free Press, 1979), 41–45.
19 Judith Blake, "The Supreme Court's Abortion Decisions and Public Opinion in the United States," *Population and Development Review* 3 (1977): 45–62.

36

Eroded Ethic

LAWYERS LIKE CYRIL MEANS and Harriet Pilpel (a Planned Parenthood board member) agreed with Lawrence Lader's push for total repeal of state abortion laws, but they did not expect to win at the ballot box. It seemed likely that radical change could occur faster through the courts than through the legislative process. They began looking for the right test case and ultimately found it in Texas. Emphasizing courts allowed them to avoid experiences like that in Maryland: Legislators debating abortion legalization in 1971 gasped when a pro-life doctor showed photos of aborted unborn children, and then voted down the bill.[1]

Journalist and humorist Finley Peter Dunne invented a character with a thick Irish brogue, Mr. Dooley, who said in 1901, "The Soopreme Court follows the illiction returns." That's often quoted, sometimes without the brogue, but on abortion the Court followed pastors and journalists—and then, in an amazingly arbitrary last-minute reach, went beyond what medical associations wanted into the total repeal that Lader had envisioned.[2]

---

1 Daniel K. Williams, *Defenders of the Unborn: The Pro-Life Movement before* Roe v. Wade (New York: Oxford University Press, 2016), 133, 140. Williams summarized the pro-life hope: "Instead of simply rehashing the philosophical and constitutional arguments against abortion legalization, the pro-life movement would use the power of fetal photography to convince the public that every abortion killed a human baby."
2 *Political Science and Politics* 38 (October 2004): 839.

Pro-life doctors from the 1870s through the 1950s were often grumpy about a lack of support from the pulpit—but at least they knew that pastors, despite their general silence, were not abortion advocates. Some retained the abortion and slavery analogy: In both, one human treated another human like property that could be disposed of at will. Starting in the 1920s, Protestant pastors increasingly supported contraceptive use by married couples, but they remained opposed to abortion. In the 1960s, though, many came to support some abortion.

In the beginning, theological liberals led the way: In Lawrence Lader's words, "We needed a breakthrough. . . . So it was tremendously important when the clergy, the cloth, came to help. I cannot overestimate this." Lader in 1966 talked with activist New York pastor Howard Moody about channeling women to abortionists. They began meeting once a month with like-minded ministers and rabbis. After six months Lader, impatient, forced the issue by speaking publicly about forming a "Clergy Consultation Service on Abortion."[3]

Moody, worried about pastors aiding and abetting what was still a crime, puzzled over "how to announce what the clergy were about to do, publicly and officially." He knew most reporters were with him, but "the media, even if sympathetic, could, by incorrectly stating our purpose or using the wrong language, state our case in an unhelpful way." Besides, if Moody held a press conference, it was possible that an unsympathetic reporter might show up: "One determined, antagonistic reporter can make any group look very bad if he wants to . . . we were unwilling to be questioned by one who was anti-abortion."[4]

---

3 Joshua Wolff, *Ministers of a Higher Law: The Story of the Clergy Consultation Service on Abortion* (New York: Self-published, 1998), 41, http://classic.judson.org/MinistersofaHigherLaw. Moody pastored Judson Memorial Baptist Church in Greenwich Village. See also Marvin Olasky, *The Press and Abortion, 1838–1988* (Hillsdale, NJ: L. Erlbaum, 1988), 108–9.

4 Arlene Carmen and Howard Moody, *Abortion Counseling and Social Change, from Illegal Act to Medical Practice* (Valley Forge, PA: Judson Press, 1973), 18.

Moody decided to give the "religion editor" of *The New York Times* a scoop. His strategy worked perfectly: The *Times* article, in Moody's words, was "a superb media interpretation of our aims and goals.... It made our actions acceptable to many people who otherwise might have thought this to be the work of wild-eyed radicals breaking the law."[5] Lader called abortion referrals "the most valid symbol of resistance." Regional newspapers favorably covered Clergy Consultation Service launches of new chapters, introducing a new part of America to support of abortion among prominent religious leaders.[6]

Moody then heard that the *New York Post* was planning a piece that would not have the right slant: "We asked a friend to intercede with the publisher of the *Post*. The inner counsels of that newspaper finally decided that the story would be detrimental to what the clergy were trying to do and so it was killed. We were very grateful to the *New York Post* and hoped that it viewed the situation as the working of a responsible newspaper rather than the suppression of freedom of the press."[7]

After the mainline churches came the evangelicals. They had no pope or college of cardinals but they did have *Christianity Today*, the leading evangelical voice. The magazine ran a neutral article on abortion in 1966.[8] In 1968 a cover story declared that a "consensus of 25 evangelical scholars" said, "The Christian physician will advise induced abortion only to safeguard greater values sanctioned by Scripture. These values may be individual, familial, or societal.... Each case should be considered individually, taking into account the various factors involved and using Christian principles of ethics." The twenty-five approved of "therapeutic abortions [amid] serious risk for health," with

5 Carmen and Moody, *Abortion Counseling and Social Change*, 18. For the article itself, see Edward Fiske, "Clergymen Offer Abortion Advice: 21 Ministers and Rabbis Form New Group—Will Propose Alternatives," *New York Times*, May 22, 1967, 1.
6 Lawrence Lader, *Abortion II: Making the Revolution* (Boston: Beacon, 1973), 28.
7 Carmen and Moody, *Abortion Counseling and Social Change*, 45.
8 Jerome Politzer, "Abortion at Issue," *Christianity Today*, September 22, 1966, 51–53.

attention paid to "the patient's total environment, actual or reasonably foreseeable."[9]

Those sentiments opened wide the abortion door. The twenty-five may have changed their view of "therapeutic abortion" had they known how California's 1967 Therapeutic Abortion Act was working out. Some scholars had predicted that many doctors "will tend to liberally construe the terms of the statute." That's exactly what happened, as legal abortions in California in five years soared from 518 in 1967 to 65,000 in 1970 and (with further liberalization) at least 116,000 in 1972, the year before *Roe v. Wade*.[10]

Lawyer Harriet Pilpel summarized the pro-abortion victory: "By 1968, almost all the major religious groups in the United States except the Roman Catholic Church were on record in favor of abortion-law reform or repeal." Lader, with press support, managed to turn Catholic durability to propagandistic advantage: One church trying to dictate to others![11]

---

9 "A Protestant Affirmation on the Control of Human Reproduction," *Christianity Today*, November 8, 1968. This "consensus of 25 evangelical scholars" is readable at https://www.christianitytoday.com/ct/1968/november-8/protestant-affirmation-on-control-of-human-reproduction.html. The same *Christianity Today* issue also featured an article by influential seminary professor Bruce Waltke, who interpreted Exodus 21:22–23, which describes the criminal punishment for someone who hits a pregnant woman and causes a miscarriage, as indicating that "the fetus is not reckoned as a soul." Waltke was serving as president of the Evangelical Theology Society in 1975 and at that time repudiated his 1968 position, as chapter 38 will show.

10 Brian Pendleton, "The California Therapeutic Abortion Act: An Analysis," *Hastings Law Journal* 19, no. 1 (November 1967): 242–55. See also E. W. Jackson, M. Tashiro, George C. Cunningham, "Therapeutic Abortions in California," *California Medicine* 115, no. 1 (July 1971): 28–33; Paul Kengor and Patricia Doerner, "Reagan's Darkest Hour," *National Review*, January 22, 2008; Jonathan Vankin, "Abortion Rights in California, Explained: State Has Led the Way in Establishing Woman's Right to Choose," *California Local*, December 7, 2021; Wm. Robert Johnston, *Historical Abortion Statistics*, http://www.johnstonsarchive.net/policy/abortion/ab-unitedstates.html.

11 Harriet Pilpel, "The Right of Abortion," www.theatlantic.com/magazine/archive/1969/06/the-right-of-abortion/303366/. The *Dallas Morning News* (November 16, 1970) followed the Lader line in arguing, "Does the Catholic Church, a powerful political as well as religious force, have the right to impose its beliefs on the rest of society?"

Dr. Robert Hall, a professor of obstetrics at Columbia Presbyterian Medical Center in New York, also practiced masterful public relations. He founded the neutral-sounding Association for the Study of Abortion: it published pro-abortion materials and helped abortion advocates develop higher profiles. Hall, in a *Playboy* interview, said abortion was controversial only because of "theological metaphysics" rather than medical science. Hall made John D. Rockefeller III the keynote speaker at an Association conference in 1968: Rockefeller urged repeal of all abortion laws and backed up words with his dollars and organizational influence.[12]

That was the establishment. Reporters wanting a walk on the wild side interviewed Pat Maginnis, founder and head of the San Francisco-based Society for Humane Abortion. She spoke of how she had twice administered abortions to herself by using her fingers to irritate her own uterus to bring on contractions and eventual miscarriage. Maginnis received respectful coverage from *The Washington Post* and made Lader seem moderate in comparison. Abortion advocacy in the era of "radical chic" could be both "radical" and "establishment," ideal fodder for newspapers that catered to power but wanted to appear as tribunes of the people.[13]

The New York Times in a 1969 article described "the Protestant position" as one tending toward "total repeal of abortion laws." The *Times* as early as 1965 developed a new euphemism in claiming that "civilized compassion demands a liberalization of abortion law."[14] One doctoral dissertation found that 90 percent of *Times* articles and editorials from

---

12 Lawrence Lader, *Abortion* (Indianapolis: Bobbs-Merrill, 1966), 248; *Playboy*, September 1970, 112–15, 272–76. Rockefeller was chairman of the Population Council, which in February 1969 devoted an entire issue of its magazine to "Beyond Family Planning." Articles proposed the full legalization of abortion and noted, "More extreme or controversial proposals tend to legitimate more moderate advances, by shifting the boundaries of discourse."

13 Lader, *Abortion*, 39; and *Abortion II*, 32 and 34; *Washington Post*, September 7, 8, 9, 1967; Tom Wolfe, *Radical Chic and Mau-Mauing the Flak-Catchers* (New York: FSG, 1970).

14 *New York Times*, December 29, 1968, VI-10; and April 7, 1965, 42.

1965 through 1972 that expressed a position on abortion clearly favored it. The other 10 percent had a bit of ambivalence.[15]

The *Times* also downplayed stories that could hurt the abortion movement. Lader worried that the arrest of an allied abortionist "threatened the whole [illegal abortion] referral system."[16] Members of NARAL's board of directors were deeply divided on whether to continue breaking the law, according to Lader, until they saw the *Times* reaction: The *Times* quoted an anonymous woman saying, "the conditions were antiseptic and sanitary,"[17] and for the *Times* in 1969, that just about ended the discussion.

Many other newspapers similarly protected abortion advocates. The *Chicago Sun-Times* in 1969 lovingly quoted Howard Moody and complained that Chicago "has nothing like" Moody's abortion referral group. Later that year a similar organization started up in Chicago, and the *Sun-Times* gave it free publicity. The newspaper also ran a glowing profile of Dr. Lonny Myers, "a woman, a mother and a physician . . . these qualities combined uniquely suit her to lead the fight in Illinois for abortion law repeal." The *Sun-Times* did not mention Myers's other interests, later chronicled in the pages of *Playboy*: Myers owned a "sex therapy" business that played clients a song (to the tune of *Jimmy Crack Corn*) filled with four-letter words for intercourse.[18]

Other newspapers displayed a treacly tendency to make abortion seem easy. The *Omaha World-Herald* quoted "Betty" describing her abortion experience: "I had to stay quiet for 15 minutes. When I got

---

15 Nguyenphuc Buutap, "Legislation, Public Opinion, and the Press: An Interrelationship Reflected in the New York Times Reporting of the Abortion Issue" (doctoral dissertation, University of Chicago, 1979), 117.
16 *New York Times*, May 3, 1969, 96.
17 *New York Times*, May 26, 1969, 12.
18 "No Help Here for Woman in Trouble," *Chicago Sun-Times*, February 23, 1969, 4-1; December 14, 1969, 4-1, 22; February 9, 1969, 4-1; *Playboy*, July 1974, 164: "As the song was played over and over, therapist Myers danced to the music, kicking up her heels."

up, I felt like a brand-new woman. I felt so happy."[19] The *Long Island Press* quoted "Susan" telling the abortionist when the operation was over, "Oh, thank you, thank you." The reporter added, "Within the next half hour she will have some cookies and a soft drink in the recovery lounge, fill out a few forms, pay a fee of $200 and be on her way back home"—probably skipping, the article seemed to suggest.[20]

The *San Francisco Chronicle* called unborn children "products of conception" and—ignoring the second patient—proclaimed that "abortions can now be performed safely, efficiently and economically." The *Chronicle* told how a typical young woman "came back from the abortion smiling and saying, 'I feel fine.'" The reporter portrayed the woman putting on "a bright scarf over her hair" and telling her mother, "I'm starved. Let's go to lunch." The reporter added that the abortion "procedure is so simple and over so quickly that [aborting women] have no feelings of guilt."[21] The *Memphis Commercial Appeal* ran a headline "Hand of Mercy Extends in Abortions."[22]

Compare those journalistic accounts with what San Francisco poet laureate Diane di Prima expressed as she imagined a child she had aborted, at successive stages of life. One of the wished-for looks: "your ivory teeth in the half light / your arms / flailing about. that is you / age 9 months, / sitting up & trying to stand . . ."[23]

A few newspapers did not fall in line. The *Indianapolis Star* published a diagram showing the growth of unborn children within the womb.[24] The *Buffalo Evening News* used public documents to tally death totals that included unborn children as well as maternal fatalities: One of its

---

19 *Omaha World-Herald*, October 4, 1970, D12.
20 *Long Island Press*, December 20, 1970.
21 *San Francisco Chronicle*, May 5, 1970, C10; April 11, 1970, B8; November 6, 1950, B10.
22 *Memphis Commercial Appeal*, October 3, 1970, C10.
23 Diane di Prima, *Brass Furnace Going Out: Song, After an Abortion* (Buffalo, NY: Pulpartforms Unlimited, Intrepid Press, 1975), here quoted from Annie Finch, ed., *Choice Words: Writers on Abortion* (Chicago: Haymarket, 2020), 210–15.
24 *Indianapolis Star*, September 13, 1970, C2.

stories began, "A total of 877 fetal deaths, the majority due to abortions induced by physicians under the new liberal state law, were reported by Erie County hospitals to the County Health Department in July and August. There were no maternal deaths."[25] The *Cincinnati Enquirer* quoted one doctor saying, "when you're in the operating room and look down into the gauze and see the little hands there, you think, 'I've just killed something.' It's awful."[26]

---

25 Mildred Spencer, "877 Fetal Deaths Are Reported," *Buffalo Evening News*, September 29, 1970, E7.
26 Lynn Sherr, "Abortion Law Reforms Still Leave Some Problems," *Cincinnati Enquirer*, September 27, 1970, B4.

37

On the Disassembly Line

ABORTIONIST MICHAEL FREIMAN had what colleagues called "the touch . . . his wonderful feel for the precision of a good abortion, his ability to visualize solely with fingers and instruments." But he did only first-trimester abortions, and the director of a St. Louis center wanted him to do second-trimesters as well. So in 1979 Freiman was in Washington, DC, watching an abortionist skilled at D-and-E, dilation and evacuation, which meant extracting a fifteen-week unborn child piece by piece. Freiman stood over the abortionist's "left shoulder, studying the doctor's technique, listening to his moment-by-moment explanation."[1]

It was a great opportunity to learn the technique—"and then a small arm with a hand on it dropped into the surgical pan. A hand. It had fingers." Freiman felt like someone had punched him hard in the stomach. He suddenly thought about Nazi Germany. Then came a leg or the other arm. With his first-trimester abortions, a mush of mangled tissue was in the petri dish, and he did not have to look closely. Now he had to think about "the most efficient maneuver for using forceps to reach inside a woman's uterus and twist off a fetal arm." He said, "I don't know whether I can do this."[2]

---

1 Cynthia Gorney, *Articles of Faith: A Frontline History of the Abortion Wars* (New York: Simon & Schuster, 1998), 300.
2 Gorney, *Articles of Faith*, 300.

But, *The Washington Post*'s Cynthia Gorney wrote, "He did know." He couldn't do it. To readers of medical literature, his reaction was no surprise: "The visual impact of the fetus compels some to withdraw from participation." Others asked, "How could he be emotionally capable to doing it at twelve weeks but not at sixteen weeks?" At suite level, Freiman was OK with abortion: He did not think D-and-E was morally wrong, and he was not "a deeply religious man." At street level, he just was "not going to do" second-trimester abortions.[3]

During the 1950s Justice-to-be Harry Blackmun was "resident counsel" at the Mayo Clinic in Rochester, Minnesota. The day after Chief Justice Warren Burger in 1972 assigned him the task of writing the majority opinion in the *Roe v. Wade* case, Blackmun wrote to Thomas Keys, the Mayo Clinic librarian, and said he wanted to learn more about abortion. As both pro-life lawyer Clarke Forsythe and abortion advocate David Garrow relate, Blackmun spent two quiet July weeks in the Mayo library. He read about the history of state abortion statutes, attitudes toward abortion among medical and professional groups, and speculation concerning the history of the Hippocratic Oath.[4]

Blackmun is a hero to some and a villain to others, but both sides of the abortion debate agree that he did not understand how the abortion industry was changing. Forsythe of Americans United for Life noted, "When Justice Blackmun thought of abortion providers, he thought of his [Mayo] friends and colleagues. . . . He assumed that doctors just like them would step in to do abortions."[5] Abortion-supporting historian David Garrow said Blackmun thought of abortion "in the medical framework of Rochester, Minnesota. He imagined abortions would be performed by a family physician or in a hospital."[6]

3 Gorney, *Articles of Faith*, 301.
4 Clarke Forsythe, *Abuse of Discretion: The Inside Story of* Roe v. Wade (New York: Encounter, 2013), 48; David Garrow, *Liberty and Sexuality: The Right to Privacy and the Making of* Roe v. Wade (Berkeley: University of California Press, 1994), 558–59.
5 Forsythe, *Abuse of Discretion*, 220.
6 David Garrow, quoted in David G. Savage, "Roe Ruling: More Than Its Author Intended," *Los Angeles Times*, September 14, 2005, 1A.

Anyone who had played a *Roe* drinking game that included a toast to every mention of "physician" would soon have been staggering. Justice Blackmun listed psychological and physical "factors the woman and her responsible physician necessarily will consider in consultation." He noted decision-making by "the woman and her responsible physician . . . the attending physician in consultation with his patient . . . the medical judgment of the woman's attending physician," and so on. That's what Frederick Taussig in 1936 had hoped for.[7]

It's too bad Blackmun didn't break away from his library research for even a day to visit an abortion center in a state that had already legalized widespread abortion. For example, he could have visited the Center for Reproductive and Sexual Health (CRASH) in a converted townhouse on Manhattan's upper east side. New York's liberal abortion statute went into effect on July 1, 1970, and six months later the center was doing 120 abortions a day. Dr. Bernard Nathanson was CRASH director: He initially called his medical staff "deplorable, consisting of an extraordinary variety of drunks, druggies, sadists, sexual molesters, just plain incompetents, and medical losers."[8]

If Blackmun had visited the Center in July 1972, he would have seen personnel turnover: Nathanson "hired and fired physicians until I had a clean, competent, industrious medical staff." Industrious it was: "The physicians, who performed ten or fifteen abortions daily, were paid at the rate of $70 to $90 per hour. One obstetrician-gynecologist would practice his specialty in Lexington, Kentucky, from Monday to Friday, then fly up to New York City, work five shifts of eight hours each at the clinic over the weekend, and then fly back to resume his practice on Monday morning. He earned $185,000 in the one year he worked at the clinic."[9]

---

7 *Roe v. Wade*, 410 U.S. 113 (1973), 72, 84, 96, 101, 106.
8 Bernard Nathanson, *The Hand of God: A Journey from Death to Life by the Abortion Doctor Who Changed His Mind* (Washington, DC: Regnery, 1996), 104.
9 Nathanson, *Hand of God*, 107.

The street-level reality: Abortion centers resembled what Taussig had seen in Moscow in 1930, rather than the doctor's office quiet that Blackmun imagined. Yes, abortions in Manhattan used anesthesia so women were unconscious, but the process made a mockery of the language in Blackmun's opinion: "responsible physician . . . attending physician. . . . exercising proper medical judgment." Doctor-patient consultation? Typically, zero. Consideration of psychological factors? What percentage of abortionists knew about the psychology of the women they first saw with their feet in stirrups?

On January 22, 1973, the day the Supreme Court unveiled its ruling, Chief Justice Warren Burger said, "Plainly, the court today rejects any claim that the Constitution requires abortion on demand." Blackmun's written statement to accompany the decision stipulated that the Supreme Court was not creating "an absolute right to abortion," but the *Los Angeles Times* noted, "In reality, the court did just that." Blackmun's opinion concluded, "The decision vindicates the right of the physician to administer medical treatment according to his professional judgment. . . . The abortion decision in all its aspects is inherently, and primarily, a medical decision."[10] No: at street level it was an assembly-line (actually, a disassembly-line) decision.

Georgetown University law professor Mark V. Tushnet, in 1973 a clerk for abortion-supporting Justice Thurgood Marshall, said the justices "were not thinking long-term with an overall vision." But all they needed was the willingness to leave the library and see what was already occurring at street level: "Few women sought abortions from their family or personal physician and most sought abortions from high-volume abortion providers whom they had never seen before."[11]

Blackmun said the American Medical Association was on his side—but it had also operated at suite level. In 1970 it said abortion should be

---

10 Quoted in Savage, "Roe Ruling."
11 Quoted in Forsythe, *Abuse of Discretion*, 346; and Garrow, *Liberty and Sexuality*, 908: Garrow quotes Tushnet saying in 1983, "It seems to be generally agreed that, as a matter of simple craft, Justice Blackmun's opinion for the Court was dreadful."

allowed only when the abortionist and two other physicians concurred, only when it was done in a hospital, and only on the basis of "'sound clinical judgment,' and 'informed patient consent,' in contrast to 'mere acquiescence to the patient's demand.'"[12]

There's no need to dissect further Blackmun's decision, since even abortion supporters have eviscerated his logic and prose (while agreeing with the result).[13] Two historical fallacies and one irony, though, are worth shout-outs.

First, Blackmun stated, "It is undisputed that at common law, abortion performed before 'quickening'—the first recognizable movement of the fetus in utero, appearing usually from the 16th to the 18th week of pregnancy—was not an indictable offense." A Maryland jury in the 1650s was ready to indict, and many indictments did occur early in the nineteenth century. It was undisputed only by Cyril Means, Lawrence Lader, and other propagandists.[14]

Second, Blackmun's most famous paragraph was this: "We need not resolve the difficult question of when life begins. When those trained in the respective disciplines of medicine, philosophy, and theology are unable to arrive at any consensus, the judiciary, at this point in the development of man's knowledge, is not in a position to speculate as to the answer."[15] But at least those trained in medicine had clearly resolved the question.

The irony: *Roe v. Wade* came on the 100th anniversary of the federal Comstock law that in 1873 wrapped together contraception and abortion. As noted in chapter 31, *Griswold v. Connecticut*, a 1965 Supreme Court decision that paved the road to *Roe*, dealt specifically with that state's 1879 law, which echoed the federal statute.[16] The contraception

---

12 AMA House of Delegates 220 (June 1970). The AMA Judicial Council rendered a complementary opinion (*Roe v. Wade*, 56).
13 See Jack Balkin, ed., *What* Roe v. Wade *Should Have Said* (New York: New York University Press, 2005). See also Anne Hendershott, *The Politics of Abortion* (New York: Encounter, 2006).
14 *Roe v. Wade*, 40, 47.
15 *Roe v. Wade*, 91.
16 *Estelle T. Griswold et al. Appellants, v. State of Connecticut*, 381 U.S. 479 (1965).

issue is complicated: Contraception affects attitudes both inside and outside marriage, and some contraceptives may be abortive. But it's easy to see the logic of viewing contraception as a privacy issue, whereas abortion is "private" only if we assume the unborn child is not a live human being—and that's resolving what Blackmun said he "need not resolve."

Many liberals in 1966 did not think *Griswold* would lead to abortion victory. That year Marshall Krause of the Northern California Civil Liberties Union said at an abortion advocacy conference, "Those people who attempt to say that there is a constitutional right to have an abortion are stretching the Constitution beyond bounds which it has ever gone and ever will go for a long time."[17] But in 1966 Lawrence Lader, at the end of *Abortion*, mused that Justice William O. Douglas's newly established "right to privacy" could go much further than contraception. Later that year, California lawyer Zad Leavy and law professor Herma Kay contended, "The striking similarity of the anti-abortion laws and the Connecticut anti-contraceptive statute is too patent to be overlooked. Both statutes invade the intimate realm of marital privacy."[18]

By the time the Association for the Study of Abortion met in 1968, more abortion advocates saw *Griswold* as their ticket to ride: It was "quoted increasingly frequently as a manifesto which points to the right of the individual woman to decide against pregnancy even though abortion is involved."[19] The Catholic Church had fought for decades to link contraception and abortion, and abortion advocates now linked the two. Had contraception and abortion been kept separate, the Court majority may have found a different way to orchestrate abortion liberty, but the sound would have been even more cacophonous.

So Blackmun cited *Griswold* in decreeing in 1973 that abortion was part of sexual privacy. He wasn't exactly sure where the Constitu-

---

[17] Garrow, *Liberty and Sexuality*, 104, 310.
[18] Lawrence Lader, *Abortion* (Indianapolis: Bobbs-Merrill, 1966), 57.
[19] Talk by Ned Overstreet at ASA conference, quoted in *New York Times*, November 24, 1968, 77; and in Garrow, *Liberty and Sexuality*, 358.

tion said that but asserted that "the right of privacy, however based, is broad enough to cover the abortion decision."[20] That was reasonable, if unborn children are not human beings: If they are, the distinction between contraception (which allows individuals to make choices) and abortion is that abortion ends the life of a person not making the choice.

Editorial writers, though, said the decision "wisely avoids the quicksand of attempting a judicial pronouncement on when life begins" and is "remarkable for its common sense." Some wiped off their crystal balls, said goodbye to "emotion-charged hearings" on abortion, praised the Court for a "bold and unequivocal decision" that would virtually end the abortion wars, and declared that "politicians and policemen and judges" would no longer be busy with the "distractive" issue.[21]

Some news pages were unrealistic: One headline, "Mechanics More Than Morality Main Concern," suggested ethical issues would now be put to rest. But when the *Milwaukee Journal* descended the ladder of abstraction, reporter Nina Bernstein wrote a street-level report that described first the women in crowded abortion business waiting areas, and then the men: "About 30 men stood or sat against the walls, looking worried, guilty, or just stony eyed. 'The casket faced brigade,' an assistant at the clinic called them. The air was hot and thick with smoke. 'It's like cattle,' one girl said as she left after her abortion."[22]

20 *Roe v. Wade*, 82.
21 *New York Times*, January 24, 1973; *St. Louis Post-Dispatch*, January 28; *Des Moines Register*, January 23; *Louisville Courier-Journal*, January 24; *Milwaukee Journal*, January 24, reprinted in Lauren R. Sass, ed., *Abortion: Freedom of Choice and the Right to Life* (New York: Facts on File, 1978), 3, 4, 8, 9, 10. Some of these statements sound like those in several Southern newspapers following the Dred Scott decision in 1857. Then, the *Memphis Appeal* on March 9 called the Supreme Court ruling "The most important decision, accompanied by the most learned and interesting opinion that has probably ever emanated from . . . the only tribunal which could settle the question permanently and satisfactorily to the great mass of the people." The *Charleston Daily Courier* predicted on March 10, 1857, that the decision "will exert the most powerful and salutary influence throughout the United States." The *Little Rock True Democrat* on March 24 ran the headline, "Momentous Question Settled."
22 *Dallas Morning News*, January 23, 1973, 1; *Milwaukee Journal*, January 23, 1973, C12; and February 11, 1973, F4.

A few editorialists objected to the Court's decision. The *Indianapolis News* called the decision "a shocking inversion of fact" and a "grim Orwellian reversal of the simplest ethical values. . . . If this opinion were all there was to go on, you would scarcely know that what is being talked about is the cold and deliberate extermination of life." The *Omaha World-Herald* raised constitutional questions: abortion is a concern of "legislators, not of would-be legislators and sociologists on the nation's highest court." The *Orlando Sentinel* said the Court's "devaluation of morality" will hurt American families and leave parents with "the haunting memory of a child that might have been."[23]

23 *Indianapolis News*, January 26, 1973; *Omaha World-Herald*, January 28, 1973; *Orlando Sentinel*, January 28, 1973. Columns reproduced in Sass, *Abortion: Freedom of Choice and the Right to Life*, 3, 4, 6.

38

Pro-Life Frustration

JANUARY 22, 1973, was a busy news day. The top *New York Times* headline the next morning was "LYNDON JOHNSON, 36TH PRESIDENT, IS DEAD." Below that came "High Court Rules Abortions Legal the First 3 Months. . . . Cardinals shocked."[1]

One Catholic, Nellie Gray, immediately set out to get the flawed Supreme Court decision recalled. Gray was a liberal feminist and civil rights activist who worked for the federal government, so she began knocking on the Capitol Hill doors of Ted Kennedy and other Catholic senators she admired. Gray assumed they would say, "We've got to fix this." She assumed Kennedy and others would share her horror about people being deprived of personhood. They did not. A 1971 Kennedy letter stated, "human life, even at its earliest stages, has a certain right which must be recognized—the right to be born, the right to love, the right to grow old." In 1973, he slammed the door on Gray.[2]

---

1 The *Times* misreported the ruling: as some Americans realized, *Roe*—with its companion case, *Doe v. Bolton* (410 U.S. 179 [1973])—meant unrestricted abortion for the first six months of pregnancy, and only slight restrictions during the last three.
2 At "Fieldstead Forum" meetings of pro-life organizations in Washington, DC, from 1989 to 1992, I had many conversations with Nellie Gray; Kennedy letter quoted in https://www.ncregister.com/blog/the-story-behind-kennedy-s-pro-life-letter.

Others at least opened their doors. Another Catholic Democrat from Massachusetts, Rep. James Burke, introduced an explicit Human Life Amendment: "The word 'person' . . . applies to all human beings, including their unborn offspring at every stage of their biological development, irrespective of age, health, function, or condition of dependency." Burke's proposal allowed abortions only when "continuation of pregnancy would cause the death of the mother."[3]

The proposed amendment went nowhere. Seven other Democratic representatives also introduced Human Life Amendments in 1973. So did fourteen Republicans. That opened Gray's eyes to other opportunities. Nevertheless, a savvy pundit in 1973 would have predicted that the Democrats, with their Catholic base, would become the pro-life party, while Republicans, with their elite connections, would join John and Nelson Rockefeller in supporting eugenics-flavored "population control."[4]

Rep. Richard Gephardt, who became the Democratic leader in the House of Representatives, wrote in 1977, "Life is the division of human cells, a process that begins with conception. . . . The [Supreme Court's abortion] ruling was unjust, and it is incumbent on the Congress to correct the injustice."[5]

That same year, civil rights leader Jesse Jackson wrote, "It takes three to make a baby: a man, a woman, and the Holy Spirit." He said, "What happens to the mind of a person, and the moral fabric of a nation, that accepts the aborting of the life of a baby without a pang of conscience? What kind of a person, and what kind of a society will we have 20 years hence if life can be taken so casually?" He noted, "Failure to answer that question affirmatively may leave us with a hell right here on earth."[6] Then Jackson ran for president.

---

3 House Joint Resolution 769, introduced on October 12, 1973, and referred to the House Committee on the Judiciary, where it died.
4 Conversations with Nellie Gray.
5 Richard Gephardt, quoted in Mark Collette, "Pangs of Conscience," *World*, January 17, 1998, 18.
6 *World*, January 17, 1998, 18. Jackson also opposed "those who argue that the [woman's] right to privacy is of a higher order than the right of life. That was the premise of slavery. You could not

As Kennedy, Gephardt, Jackson, and other ambitious Democrats abandoned earlier pro-life positions, Nellie Gray formed an alliance of the willing. She started by organizing a 1974 Washington march, on the *Roe* decision's first anniversary, with the goal of putting pressure on Congress. The first march was small, but Gray's March for Life became bigger every year. Conservatives noticed. The pro-life issue pushed Democratic voters to vote Republican—and "Reagan Democrats" made the difference in the 1980 election. Republicans and the pro-life movement became allies.[7]

The other big change involved evangelical churches. On February 16, 1973, a *Christianity Today* editorial stated that "the majority of the Supreme Court has explicitly rejected Christian moral teaching and approved the attitude of what it calls 'ancient religion' and the standards of pagan Greek and Roman law."[8] One month later, *Christianity Today* ran an article taking to task evangelicals who five years earlier had said verse 22 in chapter 21 of Exodus justifies abortion: "Absolutely no linguistic justification" for that, author Jack Cottrell insisted. He said the verse refers to a child born prematurely but healthily, with no harm to either mother or child. If a person harms either, the penalty should be severe: "There is absolutely no warrant for concluding the fetus is not reckoned as a soul."[9]

Theologian Bruce Waltke had come to that conclusion in 1968 but seven years later thought differently. Even more influential having become president of the Evangelical Theological Society, he declared in his presidential address "that the body, the life, and the moral

---

protest the existence of slaves on the plantation because that was private [property] and therefore outside of your right to be concerned" (quoted in Nat Hentoff, "My Controversial Choice to Become Pro-Life," *Human Life Review*, Summer 2009, republished after Hentoff died at https://humanlifereview.com/9680-2.0).

7 Conversations in Washington, DC, with Nellie Gray, 1990, and Connie Marshner, 2020.
8 Editorial reprinted in Timothy D. Padgett, ed., *Dual Citizens: Politics and American Evangelicalism* (Bellingham, WA: Lexham, 2020), 357–62.
9 Jack Cottrell, "Abortion and the Mosaic Law," *Christianity Today*, March 16, 1973, https://www.christianitytoday.com/ct/1973/march-16/abortion-and-mosaic-law.html.

faculty of man originate simultaneously at conception. . . . The fetus is human and therefore to be accorded the same protection to life granted every other human being. Indeed, feticide is murder, an attack against a fellow man who owes his life to God, and a violation of the commandment, 'You shall not kill.'"[10]

Later during the 1970s another evangelical intellectual leader, Francis Schaeffer, moved thousands of Christians from pews into pro-life activities with two books made into two films, *How Should We Then Live?* and *Whatever Happened to the Human Race?* Schaeffer showed how *Roe* was an "arbitrary ruling medically and legally." Schaeffer films received viewing in Madison Square Garden, the Republican Club in Washington, DC (with an audience of more than 70 U.S. senators and representatives), and in hundreds of civic and church venues.[11] Dallas Cowboys quarterback Roger Staubach screened segments to an audience of six thousand, including half of his teammates.[12]

The National Right to Life Committee was largely Catholic-led, so evangelicals created the Christian Action Council (CAC) to push for pro-life legislation. A twenty-nine-year-old pastor, Curtis Young, became the CAC's executive director and traveled the nation to plant local CACs. Typical newspaper account in 1982: "Curtis Young talks with all the confidence of a poker player standing pat with a full house."[13]

Young did not have a full house—Democrats retained their majority in the House of Representatives—but the Senate, starting in 1981, had

---

10 Bruce K. Waltke, "Reflections from the Old Testament on Abortion," *Journal of the Evangelical Theological Society* 19 (Winter 1976): 3–13 (at 13). In a footnote to this published text of his address, Waltke said the Exodus 21 analysis he had presented in 1968 "is less than conclusive for both exegetical and logical reasons." He self-criticized his "illogical conclusion . . . the purpose of the decision recorded in this debated passage was not to define the nature of the fetus but to decide a just claim in the cases of an induced abortion that may or may not have been accidental."
11 Francis Schaeffer, *How Should We Then Live?* L'Abri 50th Anniversary Edition (Wheaton, IL: Crossway, 2005), 223. Schaeffer noted "some of our ancestors' cruel viewing of the black slave as a non-person," and now "unborn babies of every color of skin are equally by law declared non-persons."
12 Ken Kersch, *Conservatives and the Constitution: Imagining Constitutional Restoration in the Heyday of American Liberalism* (London: Cambridge University Press, 2019), 279.
13 *Lincoln Journal Star*, January 19, 1982, 6.

twelve additional Republican senators, creating a GOP majority with fifty-three. Given that House Democrats still had a sizeable pro-life faction, it looked like a pro-life bill could get through Congress if Ronald Reagan made it a priority. Some politicians were already jostling: Who would be in the front row and gain a souvenir pen when Reagan signed into law the big statement that Congress would produce?

It never happened. Two pro-life senators went to war. Jesse Helms of North Carolina proposed a Human Life Statute that would ban all abortions—but by itself would save no unborn lives, because the Supreme Court was likely to declare it unconstitutional. Orrin Hatch of Utah proposed a Human Life Federalism Amendment to the Constitution that would nullify *Roe* and return abortion decisions to the states—but it was unlikely to pass and by itself it would not provide safety for unborn children, because states could decide to maintain the status quo.[14]

Each side insisted the other was cowardly: The Human Life Statute would still leave the Supreme Court in charge, and the Human Life Federalism Amendment would allow all kinds of state-level compromises. The Catholic Conference of Bishops endorsed the Hatch approach. The Christian Action Council was for Helms. The Reagan administration's two prime goals were tax reduction and ending the Cold War successfully. Keeping pro-life groups happy was a bonus, and given the opportunity to alienate one or the other faction of the pro-life movement, Reagan chose neither. Both gambits, Helms and Hatch, failed.

With legislative action stalled, the legislative-judicial sector of the pro-life movement concentrated on the composition of the Supreme Court. Sam Ericsson, executive director of the Christian Legal Society, calculated that the median age of the U.S. Supreme Court was seventy-six, making it one of the oldest Courts in U.S. history—and several

14 Cynthia Gorney, *Articles of Faith: A Frontline History of the Abortion Wars* (New York: Simon & Schuster, 1998), 352–65.

justices had been seriously ill. Ericsson said two appointments would make the Court pro-life. Curt Young said, "It's amazing to think that the abortion issue could be decided around actuarial tables."[15]

Reagan's first Supreme Court pick was a bust from a pro-life perspective. Sandra Day O'Connor made it because Reagan, during the 1980 campaign, pledged to nominate a woman—but she turned out to uphold *Roe v. Wade*. Reagan's second appointee, Antonin Scalia, became a solid pro-life justice for thirty years, but since he was replacing William Rehnquist, one of the *Roe* dissenters, his appointment did not change the Court's composition.

In 1986 Republicans lost control of the Senate, so pundits expected a contest regarding a nominee to replace Court swing vote Lewis Powell—but Joe Biden and Ted Kennedy turned it into a massacre. Less than an hour after Reagan nominated pro-life Robert Bork, Kennedy delivered his prepared assault: "Robert Bork's America is a land in which women would be forced into back-alley abortions, blacks would sit at segregated lunch counters, rogue police could break down citizens' doors in midnight raids, and schoolchildren could not be taught about evolution." Bork lost the Senate vote, fifty-eight to forty-two.[16]

Reagan's second try, Douglas Ginsburg, withdrew when NPR revealed that Ginsburg smoked marijuana "on a few occasions" as a Harvard student and then assistant professor. The third try brought in Anthony Kennedy, who won ninety-seven to zero, as pro-life conservatives hoped for his support—but so did liberals who studied Kennedy's libertarian instincts. Although Kennedy said he was brought up to think of abortion as a "great evil," and although he once denounced the *Roe* decision as the "*Dred Scott* of our time," the right was wrong, and the left proved right.[17]

---

15 Fieldstead Forum archives.
16 Ilya Shapiro, *Supreme Disorder: Judicial Nominations and the Politics of America's Highest Court* (Washington, DC: Regnery, 2020), 137–49.
17 *Los Angeles Times*, December 13, 1992, 1; Shapiro, *Supreme Disorder*, 151–58.

Overall, the Court during the 1980s regularly strode to the plate, heard eleven abortion cases, and—from a pro-life perspective—repeatedly struck out or bunted. Major cases came up every three years. In *Harris v. McRae* (1980), the Court on a five to four vote upheld the Hyde Amendment, which since 1976 had restricted federal funding of abortions. But in *City of Akron v. Akron Center for Reproductive Health* (1983), the Court that gaveth also tooketh away: the justices invalidated requirements for informed consent and a twenty-four-hour waiting period. They axed requirements that all abortions after the first trimester be performed in a hospital and that a parent consent to a minor's abortion.

Then in 1986's *Thornburgh v. American College of Obstetricians and Gynecologists* case, the Court ruled five to four against a Pennsylvania law that required informed consent, instructed abortionists to use the method most likely to preserve the life of a viable unborn child, and required a second physician to be present during a post-viability abortion. In 1989, though, the Court gave babies a break: in *Webster v. Reproductive Health Services*, justices upheld a Missouri law that prohibited the use of government personnel or facilities to perform abortions, and required ultrasound tests in pregnancies of twenty weeks or more.

Meanwhile, pro-life support among Democratic politicians narrowed. Bill Clinton flatly told his state's Right to Life committee in 1986, "I am opposed to abortion." Clinton's position flipped as his presidential ambitions grew. Rep. Al Gore eight times voted for the Hyde Amendment. In 1984 he stated, in a letter to a constituent, his "deep personal conviction that abortion is wrong," and voted to amend the Civil Rights Act to define the term "person" to "include unborn children from the moment of conception." In 1988, though, Senator Gore ran for president and even denied casting that vote: "I have not changed.... I have always been against anything that would take away a woman's right to have an abortion."[18]

18 https://www.ontheissues.org/Al_Gore_Abortion.html.

In 1990 the number of abortions in the U.S. hit a record 1.6 million. Pro-life hope regarding judicial appointments remained, however, despite frustration regarding appointees by Republican presidents. George H. W. Bush's first nominee, David Souter, was an unmarried and little-known New Hampshire Supreme Court judge who had made it to the federal bench only six months before his nomination. White House Chief of Staff John Sununu said Souter would be "a home run for conservatives," and National Organization for Women head Molly Yard said confirming him would "end freedom for women in this country."[19]

As New Hampshire's attorney general, Souter had opposed the use of public funds to finance what he called "the killing of unborn children." Souter had opposed repeal of the state's protective abortion laws, even though *Roe* had invalidated them. Bush's second nominee, Clarence Thomas, also looked to be a strong and consistent Court opponent of abortion. A last-minute sexual harassment charge almost derailed Thomas, but when he survived the Senate vote, fifty-two to forty-eight, pro-life leaders in Washington thought the political and judicial strategy might finally pay off.

Many of them placed their hopes in a Supreme Court reversal of *Roe v. Wade*. The first half of 1992 brought lots of waiting. On June 29, 1992, the Court finally announced its decision in *Planned Parenthood v. Casey*. As expected, the vote was five to four. Not expected: it was five to four essentially approving *Roe*, with Souter and Anthony Kennedy (in the seat Robert Bork would have held) joining the abortion defenders.

Kennedy wrote that on abortion "choices central to personal dignity and autonomy are central to the liberty protected by the Fourteenth Amendment." He did not count the unborn child as a person whose dignity also counted. What came next from Kennedy was more ex-

---

19 *Dayton Daily News*, September 14, 1990, 4; *Durham* (NC) *Morning Herald*, September 28, 1990, 12.

traordinary: "At the heart of liberty is the right to define one's own concept of existence, of meaning, of the universe, and of the mystery of human life."[20] U.S. Court of Appeals Judge Robert Beezer called that sentence "so broad and melodramatic as to seem almost comical in its rhetorical flourish."[21]

At street level, *Casey* went beyond *Roe* in creating a high bar for state laws protecting unborn children: laws cannot impose an "undue burden . . . a substantial obstacle in the path of a woman seeking an abortion before the fetus attains viability," the ability to live on his or her own. Pro-lifers were shocked. Definitions of viability varied, but twenty-four weeks—down from twenty-eight weeks a half century ago—was a common marker. The overwhelming majority of abortions occur before then.

Legislators in many states had passed laws precisely to save unborn children's lives, which meant placing obstacles in the path of women who believed their only way out of a difficult situation was to have an abortion. The Court essentially locked the pro-life movement in a prison camp: *You can pass any law you want, as long as it doesn't have much effect.* Pro-life leaders, like some of the women at the center of abortionists' attention, had been seduced and abandoned. Gary Thomas of the Christian Action Council said, "Every pro-life organization I know was talking about post-*Roe* America."[22] Then came the *Casey* decision.

Some of the leaders maintained their optimism until November 3, 1992, hoping George H. W. Bush would gain a second term and not nominate another Souter—but Bill Clinton won the election, with support from abortion advocates. He came through for them. He reversed the rule by which counselors were not to push abortion at federally funded clinics. He reversed the Mexico City Policy that withheld funds

---

20 *Planned Parenthood v. Casey*, 505 U.S. 833 (1992).
21 *Chicago Tribune*, June 4, 1989; Fieldstead Forum archives.
22 *The Courier* (Waterloo, IA), March 24, 1993, 1.

from abortion programs overseas and reversed the ban on abortion at military hospitals overseas. He made two nominations for the Supreme Court in 1993 and 1994, when Democrats held a Senate majority. Ruth Bader Ginsburg and Stephen Breyer became two reliable votes to maintain the essence of *Roe*.

39

Pictures Seen and Unseen

NEW ENGLAND PRO-LIFERS thought they had a path to public education in 1975 when a Boston jury found Kenneth Edelin guilty of manslaughter after he botched an abortion and killed the just-born child. Mildred Jefferson, a Massachusetts doctor who chaired the National Right to Life Committee, had testified effectively about the child's humanity. The prosecutor told juror members to look at a photo of the victim: "You tell us what it is. Look at the picture. Show it to anybody. . . . Are you speaking about a blob, a big bunch of mucus, or . . . an independent human being . . . ?" But New England's major newspaper, *The Boston Globe*, never published the photo.[1]

In 1978 the *Chicago Sun-Times* culminated a five-month investigation with a two-week series on "The Abortion Profiteers." No major metropolitan newspaper had spent such resources on an abortion exposé since the *New York Times* and the *Chicago Times* in 1871 and 1888. The *Sun-Times* included specific detail about an abortionist's dog licking blood off the floor, and abortionists using "every trick in the book to

---

[1] William Nolen, *The Baby in the Bottle* (New York: Coward, McCann & Geoghegan, 1978), 179. For more about the Edelin affair, see *Boston Globe* page one stories on January 21, 1975, and February 6, 7, 9, 11, 13, 14, and 16, 1975; and see Marvin Olasky, *The Press and Abortion, 1838–1988* (Hillsdale, NJ: L. Erlbaum, 1988), 124–30.

peddle abortions to confused and frightened women, [with] dozens of abortion procedures performed on women who were not pregnant."[2]

During the second week of the series, though, *Sun-Times* schizophrenia reigned. A story in one column included evocative detail: An abortion operation stops when the woman begins hemorrhaging, and afterward she gives birth "to a baby girl—apparently normal except the infant is missing a piece of scalp about the size of a 50-cent piece." No evocative pictures, though—and a story in the next column reminded readers that abortion is a boon to women and merely involves removing "tissue."[3]

Pictures changed the attitudes of men otherwise unlikely to oppose abortion. I talked with three born in the mid-1920s. Nat Hentoff (1925–2017) was a creator in the 1950s of *The Village Voice*, the iconic New York City weekly. He was an atheistic radical, but then he saw "multi-dimensional ultrasound sonograms of infants waiting to be born: their eyes, the moving, outstretched fingers and hands." He did not see why abortion should be only a conservative issue: he wanted to protect the weak and helpless, and saw unborn children as those most in need of protection.[4]

Bernard Nathanson (1926–2011), the Lader ally introduced in chapters 35 and 37, directed in 1971 and '72 the largest abortion center in the Western world. There he saw how "mass-scale efficient abortion technology" using vacuum suctioning of wombs allowed for the creation of "assembly-line abortion clinics." In 1973 he became chief of obstetrical services at St. Luke's Hospital in New York City

---

2 *Chicago Sun-Times*, November 12, 1978, 1 and 5; and November 13; and Olasky, *Press and Abortion*, 133–37.
3 *Chicago Sun-Times*, November 21, 1978, 3.
4 Nat Hentoff, "My Controversial Choice to Become Pro-Life," *Human Life Review*, Summer 2009. In 1990 I waited to interview Hentoff in the brightly-lit *Village Voice* city room where a 45-year-old editor in Dockers trousers was haranguing seven 25-year-olds about the "blow-dried fascism of the Reaganitemare." Then, from a dim hallway, a bent-over 65-year-old in gray slacks shuffled in. The young staffers had jobs because of Hentoff's creativity, but no one said hello to him or smiled at him: attacking abortion was treason. See Marvin Olasky, "The Village's Prolife Voice," *Christianity Today*, June 24, 1991, 24–27.

just as "we began moving a marvelous new technology into the hospital. It was ultrasound. . . . For the first time we could really see the human fetus." Nathanson "had for the first time in years a little time and space to think."⁵

After studying ultrasound video, Nathanson in 1974 wrote in *The New England Journal of Medicine*, "There is no longer serious doubt in my mind that human life exists within the womb from the very onset of pregnancy. . . . We must courageously face the fact—finally—that human life of a special order is being taken [in abortion]. Denial of this reality is the crassest kind of moral evasiveness."⁶

Nathanson's *The Silent Scream*, a 1984 documentary using ultrasound video and showing the moment an unborn child dies, fostered a national debate. Nathanson traveled the country showing it and describing how and why he had come to believe in both the humanity of the unborn and the reality of God.⁷

Joe Scheidler (1927–2021) was an account executive with a Chicago public relations firm when he saw a pamphlet titled "Life or Death." On the back cover was a photo of aborted babies in a garbage bag. One looked like Scheidler's young son, Eric. That night, Scheidler couldn't sleep. In 1974 he became director of the Illinois Right to Life Committee. He wanted to show photos of aborted children, but his committee thought that medicine too strong, so after several years he formed his own organization, the Pro-Life Action League.

Scheidler eagerly read the *Chicago Sun-Times* series, "The Abortion Profiteers," but also noted how the newspaper caved. In *Closed: 99*

---

5   Bernard Nathanson, *The Hand of God, A Journey from Death to Life by the Abortion Doctor Who Changed His Mind* (Washington, DC: Regnery, 1996), 125.
6   Bernard Nathanson, "Deeper into Abortion," *The New England Journal of Medicine* 291 (November 28, 1974): 1189–90.
7   Nathanson, *Hand of God*, 140–46, 187–96. I met Nathanson while facilitating meetings of pro-life leaders in 1990 and observed that he still had a deer-in-the-headlights look facing Nellie Gray and other pro-life veterans. But Nathanson found comfort in "the special role for forgiveness" within the Christian understanding that all of us are sinners. In 1996 he converted to Roman Catholicism.

Ways to Stop Abortion (1985), Scheidler proposed ways to push past journalistic blackouts: Sidewalk conversations with women on their way into abortion businesses. Filing complaints about abortion facilities with local departments of health. Abortion center sit-ins that allowed for conversation with patients—until police arrived. *Closed* included a chapter called "Violence: Why It Won't Work."[8]

Some in the next generation took Scheidlerism a step further, going from sit-ins to blocking the doors of abortion centers. In the process Randall Terry (1959–) became the most-publicized pro-life leader of the late twentieth century. Pictures made a huge difference once again. Reporter Cynthia Gorney summarized the problem as seen through the eyes of lifetime pro-life activist Sam Lee: "When Sam watched the Terry videotapes he felt a curious chill: the man was as repellent as one of the hostile feminist leaders from the National Organization for Women, Sam thought, looking so angry all the time, goading people for not being angry enough. . . . Terry lent himself to caricature, how precisely his carriage and language suited every secular cliché of the heavy-breathing right-to-lifer."[9]

As a young man Terry sold used tires and cars—a detail reporters thereafter would almost always mention. His first wife, Cindy, led him into pro-life activities that culminated with his "Operation Rescue" vision: Protesters would block entrances to abortion businesses. Police would haul them away. Massive press coverage with video of the arrests

[8] The book was still too aggressive for some. When Scheidler brought a box of copies of *Closed* to a right-to-life conference where Mother Teresa appeared, the organizers did not give him permission to promote them. The books did not go to waste, however: when the five-foot-tall nun began speaking and the audience couldn't see her behind the podium, Scheidler placed a box of the books behind the podium, and she stood on it. The National Organization for Women fought Scheidler in a case that began in 1994 and went on for nearly two decades, like a bleak tale out of Dickens. Scheidler appealed a lower court ruling that his own home be seized. I visited him there a third of a century ago and saw it was nothing fancy, but it was home. The Supreme Court finally ruled 9-0 that protesters not making money through their protests are not racketeers.
[9] Cynthia Gorney, *Articles of Faith: A Frontline History of the Abortion Wars* (New York: Simon & Schuster, 1998), 462.

would let pro-lifers gain sympathy similar to what civil rights activists in the 1960s received.[10]

Press coverage of the 1988 "Siege of Atlanta," at which police arrested more than 1,300 Terry followers who blocked the entrances to abortion businesses, was predictably hostile. During the next several years television producers enjoyed putting Terry on interview shows across from Faye Wattleton, the demure black president of Planned Parenthood. His typical rhetoric—*God will avenge innocent blood and wipe out this country. Severe economic crisis during the 1990s. Incredible internal turbulence!*—fit the "angry white man" stereotype.

In 1991 well-intentioned Operation Rescuers briefly delayed abortion-minded women in Wichita. Police made about 2,600 arrests. Pictures bulwarked by words were important. *CBS Evening News* combined video of carried-off demonstrators with anxious narration by reporter Scott Pelley: "four weeks of chaos" as "radical anti-abortion" forces used "intimidation at the door." CBS included a clip of U.S. District Court Judge Patrick Kelly calling Operation Rescue leaders "hypocrites" and did not include any response from the leaders. Pelley later gained promotion to anchor. Local television stations told the story from the police perspective: protesters "carried off by tired and hot officers."[11]

One station said the protests cost Wichita taxpayers $500,000 and were "putting Wichita in a bad light across the nation." A poll by the local *Wichita Eagle* and television station KAKE asked city residents, "How do you feel about Operation Rescue's tactics?" One in five was positive, four in five were negative. Of those who said Operation Rescue

---

10 Conversation with Randall Terry in 1990. I asked whether he saw himself as John Brown and expected him to deny it, but he offered an enthusiastic *Yes!* I pushed on: "Do you want to start a civil war?" *Yes!* Flip Benham, Terry's deputy until they fell out and Terry called him "a Judas," said Terry at the Dallas Convention Center in 1989 mesmerized thousands of preachers by issuing "a flat-out call to war. . . . We were getting up and jumping." For more about Terry and the action he inspired, see Marvin Olasky, *Abortion at the Crossroads: Three Paths Forward in the Struggle to Protect the Unborn* (New York: Post-Hill, 2021), 80–84.
11 *CBS Evening News*, August 19, 1991; Gorney, *Articles of Faith*, 463.

changed their views of abortion, two-thirds said it had made them more "in favor of abortion rights."[12]

When Operation Rescue did not achieve what pro-life activists had hoped for, a few turned from nonviolence to killing. In 1993 Michael Griffin murdered David Gunn in Pensacola, Florida, and Shelley Shannon wounded George Tiller in Wichita. *The Los Angeles Times* reported, "The killing of Dr. David Gunn, on top of legal setbacks and political reversals, has flattened the anti-abortion movement." In 1994 Paul Hill in Pensacola murdered John Britton and Britton's bodyguard. Matt Waters of CareNet, the umbrella group for pro-life pregnancy centers, said Hill's action was "absolutely negative" for the pro-life cause and positive for abortion advocates who "raise money off of bulletproof vests. It's a fundraiser for them—a tragedy for us."[13]

The difference between Operation Rescue's nonviolence and these killings was huge, but conservative activist Connie Marshner witnessed media lumping them together as extremist activity: "Operation Rescue, combined with shootings that were happening at the same time, gave the pro-life movement such a black eye that many people became afraid to be pro-life." Congress passed the Freedom of Access to Clinic Entrances Act (FACE) that turned into a federal crime any interference with an abortion center's normal operations.[14]

The U.S. Supreme Court also let stand an injunction that kept demonstrators at least thirty-six feet away from an abortion center. Sidewalk counseling and other nonviolent interventions became almost impossible. Public opinion polls showed increasing support for abortion, with the highest percentage of Americans ever (34 percent)

---

12 Mike Taylor, TV 10 *Nightside*. Video compiled by KMUW-Wichita. Terry left Operation Rescue and eventually ran for Congress but lost. He divorced his wife and married his assistant. He moved to Nashville but failed to gain traction as a country music artist.
13 Lynn Smith, "Bowed but Unbroken?," *Los Angeles Times*, March 22, 1993, 1. Griffin received a life sentence. Shannon gained prison release in 2018. Florida executed Hill in 2003. For a biblical view of taking vengeance, see Deut. 32:35, Rom. 12:19, and Heb. 10:30.
14 *World*, January 30, 2021, 32–33.

saying every abortion should be legal, and 56 percent calling themselves pro-choice, compared to 33 percent describing themselves as pro-life.[15]

Popular fiction reflected the negative press portrayals. In 1994 Stephen King's *Insomnia*—initial printing, 1.5 million copies—featured an abortion opponent, Daniel Dalton, speaking on a television news show with "dour, jut-jawed determination." Dalton is "a few sandwiches shy of a picnic." A second abortion opponent, wife-beater Ed, believes flatbed trucks are carrying thousands of infant corpses out of town: "How many times a week do you see one of those big flatbeds tooling down the road? A flatbed with a tarp stretched across the back? Ever ask yourself what those trucks were carrying? Ever wonder what was under most of those tarps?"[16]

A third major character, anti-abortion Charlie Pickering, has eyes that float "like strange fish . . . disconnected and oddly frightened." King called him a man "who would see signs in the sky and perhaps hear voices whispering from deep in the closet late at night." As Pickering pricks the book's hero with a knife, he says "Ohboy ohboy ohBOY!" and sprays "flecks of spittle."[17]

When the hero sprays pepper-gas in Pickering's face, he screams, "I can't see and my skin is melting! I can feel it melting!" Pickering is not only a wicked witch but a killer who sets fire to an abortion center and murders its workers, plus state troopers who try to stop him. He screams, "Barbecue! Barbecue! Holy cookout! . . . God's fire! God's holy fire!" When one "Friend of Life" sees "her own daughter among the pro-choice people," the mother charges the daughter and claws a young man who gets in the way: "Mom opened his face with her fingernails."[18]

---

15 Gallup, In Depth: Topics A to Z, "Abortion," at https://news.gallup.com/poll/1576/abortion.aspx.
16 Stephen King, *Insomnia* (New York: Scribner, 1994), ch. 5, ebook loc. 2140; ch. 3, loc. 1100.
17 King, *Insomnia*, ch. 7, locs. 2854 and 2900.
18 *Insomnia*, ch. 6, loc.. 2441; ch. 7, loc. 2953; ch. 21, loc. 7392.

40

Cacophony and Compassion

IN *ARTICLES OF FAITH*, the best-reported book about 1990s abortion battles, *Washington Post* reporter Cynthia Gorney noted that "all the Operation Rescue blockaders put together" added up to "a tiny fraction of the right-to-life volunteers across the United States."[1]

Many reporters missed, and others criticized, a growing compassion movement that took root in the 1970s and '80s among both Catholics and Protestants. Young women in a crisis, often abandoned by boyfriends and parents, needed a new family of helpers—and groups that became known as crisis pregnancy centers or pregnancy resource centers provided one.

One of the first centers opened in Toledo in 1971, two years before *Roe v. Wade*. OB/GYN John Hillabrand, who had delivered more than eight thousand babies without a maternal death, operated it out of his office. Other likeminded doctors, nurses, and social workers—many of them Catholic—came together in Chicago in 1971 to form Alternatives to Abortion, which later became Heartbeat International. They hoped to provide a "safety net" for women who might otherwise feel pressured to have an abortion.[2]

---

1 Cynthia Gorney, *Articles of Faith: A Frontline History of the Abortion Wars* (New York: Simon & Schuster, 1998), 463.
2 "The Ground Is Tilled and the Seed Is Planted by the 'Greatest Generation,'" Heartbeat International, accessed May 30, 2022, https://www.heartbeatinternational.org/heartbeat-history.

The largely evangelical Christian Action Council initially sent out instructors to teach local chapters how to write letters and buttonhole legislators. Before long, as board member Melinda Delahoyde recalled, the CAC board started to receive stacks of letters "from grassroots evangelicals around the country. They all say the same thing: 'We get the politics. We're in front of our state capitols. But what do we do to help the woman who's facing abortion in our community?'"[3]

In 1981 the CAC established its first crisis pregnancy center in Baltimore. By 1993 hundreds of centers were helping tens of thousands of women, and spokesman Gary Thomas told the *Los Angeles Times* the CAC was shutting down its "program of boycotting corporate sponsors of Planned Parenthood" and instead focusing on building up crisis pregnancy centers: "For 20 years, pro-life said what it's against. We want to say what we're for: caring for women, for unborn children. . . . We can save a lot of women from abortion regardless of what the law is."[4]

The CAC soon changed its name to CareNet, reflecting the new emphasis on compassion rather than political lobbying. Guy Condon personified the trend as he moved to CareNet from heading an organization that drafted legislation: Condon told colleagues the pro-life side was "losing miserably the battle for perception and public conviction. . . . We have engaged in a top-down strategy, concentrating on litigation, legislation, and scholarship to influence the policy elites through the intellectual argument."[5]

Feminists for Life leader Frederica Mathewes-Green had a similar personal realization after she worked for a Maryland pro-life referendum that lost, despite the expenditure of $2.5 million: "That's a lot of money to lose, but perhaps the defeat was a blessing. . . . Perhaps we

---

3 Susan Olasky interview with Delahoyde, 2020.
4 *Los Angeles Times*, March 22, 1993, 1. Although each center was locally governed and funded, they all operated according to standards set by the CAC, which also provided a start-up guide for local volunteers that laid out the ABCs of setting up a nonprofit organization.
5 Guy Condon, *A Strategic Proposition for Advancing the Public Campaign for Life*, Americans United for Life Outline for Discussion, October 23, 1991.

have been putting too much faith in working to elect legislators to pass laws that would compel people to agree with us. Now we are realizing the need to put first things first and help people to come to agree with us, before we can pass and sustain pro-life laws."[6]

Fueled by such realizations, the pregnancy center movement grew throughout the 1980s. In 1991, abortion advocates complained that hundreds of crisis pregnancy centers (a.k.a. "bogus clinics") were counseling women about abortion alternatives. Some journalists reported their activities accurately. Wanda Kohn, during the 1990s a volunteer counselor at the Pregnancy Care Center in Leesburg, Florida, impressed *Orlando Sentinel* columnist Lauren Ritchie, who called Kohn "Leesburg's version of Mother Teresa.... She is passionately anti-abortion, but tempers it with practicality that provides a place to live and diapers."[7]

Across the country, *Tucson Citizen* editor Peter Bronson supported legal abortion but still reported accurately the free services that city's crisis pregnancy center offered: Women "get free counseling, a place to stay, job assistance, help obtaining prenatal care, even diapers, cribs, and baby clothes if that's what they need. They also get spiritual support. The organization is supported by 25 local churches. Make no mistake: It is very pro-religion, very anti-abortion.... But I'm sure of one thing: There's something truly good about people who are willing to back up their moral beliefs by helping women who decide to save their babies."[8]

Bronson then asked the journalistic question: "Why isn't that story being told? ... I looked in our newspaper clipping library and found 22 stories about Planned Parenthood in the past year, including two announcements and a column publicizing its annual fund-raiser on

---

6 *Baltimore Sun*, June 27, 1991, June 30, 1992.
7 Lauren Ritchie, quoted in Olasky, "Frontline Dispatches," *World*, December 15, 2007, 20.
8 *Tucson Citizen*, October 3, 1991, 13. Bronson attended in 1991 a pregnancy center banquet and described seeing "a dozen moms and their kids—little guys in baby ties, little girls with their hair just right, bright bows, clean white shirts, shiny shoes, shy smiles and fidgeting fingers.... Each would have been erased—aborted—without the help, guidance, support and, yes, love of the Crisis Pregnancy Center."

September 20. It drew about 75 people. The Crisis Pregnancy Center file had just two clips: a tiny item announcing a workshop . . . and a story ('Guilt called the price at anti-abortion centers'). The clip file contained no announcement for Sunday's annual fund-raiser by the Crisis Pregnancy Center. It drew 1,400 people."[9]

Modern versions of the late-nineteenth-century refuges (see ch. 26) also emerged. Outside Baltimore a three-story Victorian was home to Sparrow House, a modern maternity home where a pregnant woman could live, continue her education, and plan for her baby's future, whether adoption or single-parenting. Halfway across the continent in the Kansas City metro area, The LIGHT House occupied a renovated convent with the capacity to shelter sixty young women. Some attended school and others learned vocational skills.[10]

Further west, the Christian Family Care Agency in Phoenix also helped both the unborn and their moms. It provided in-depth counseling, shepherd homes for pregnant women, foster care for parenting teens and their children, and support groups for pregnant and parenting teens, as well as for those choosing adoption. CFCA's foster care program for parenting teens allowed a young mother and her new baby to live in a group home under the supervision of house parents. The foster home's goal was to combine a lesson about reality with protection for the child.[11]

Housemothers did not assume infant care nor offer to baby-sit: if a teen was desperate, a housemother would take over for a short time, but only in exchange for the new mother doing laundry for the household or mowing the lawn. "We're trying to avoid those situations where a

---

[9] The *Tucson Citizen* printed positive responses to Bronson's column: October 8, 9; October 10, 23; October 12, 11; October 19, 11; October 23, 7; October 25, 17; October 26, 9; November 9, 11; November 15, 17. Later, some newspapers refused to print any letters about abortion, pro or con.

[10] Susan Olasky and Marvin Olasky, *More Than Kindness: A Compassionate Approach to Crisis Childbearing* (Wheaton, IL: Crossway, 1990), 81–84, 93–94.

[11] Olasky and Olasky, *More Than Kindness*, 89–91.

teen and her baby are indulged by parents or foster parents for three, six, or nine months, until the teen is spoiled, the parents are exhausted, and a break occurs," CFCA director Kay Ekstrom said. "The girls we get here are usually not very open to suggestion until the reality of parenting comes home to them."[12]

Although usually founded by social entrepreneurs responding to local needs, the groups formed networks like the Christian Maternity Home Association, which represented family-style maternity homes with six to eight women at a time in residence. Some residents chose these maternity homes because they felt uncomfortable at home or were pushed out by parents angry or embarrassed about their pregnancy. Others sought a supportive environment in which to explore adoption and gain the friendship of women in similar situations.[13]

Pro-abortion public relations professionals repeatedly struck back against pro-life efforts. One of the earliest attacks came in 1986, when William Schulz, president of the Unitarian Universalist Association, called pro-life centers "new and insidious. . . . Like spiders, they lure their victims into their webs and then apply psychological terror." Later that year *USA Today* ran a story about "brainwashing techniques and the lies." Every few years thereafter the National Abortion Federation, a trade association for abortion businesses, began a new campaign along the lines of "right to life is right to lie."[14]

---

12 Interview by Susan Olasky, 1989.
13 Olasky and Olasky, *More Than Kindness*, 87–88. All CMHA homes were open to non-Christian women, but the program stressed spiritual as well as material needs. Loving and Caring, a group in Lancaster, Pennsylvania, offered training for maternity home leaders and decision-making workbooks for young women to use as they thought through their parenting choices.
14 My interviews of abortion public relations advocates on January 29, February 25, and February 27, 1987; press statements provided by the Religious Coalition for Abortion Rights; *USA Today*, July 23, 1986, ID, 4D. For more detail, see Marvin Olasky, *The Press and Abortion, 1838–1988* (Hillsdale, NJ: L. Erlbaum, 1988), 144–47. See also Jane Gross, "Pregnancy Centers: Anti-Abortion Role Challenged," *New York Times*, January 23, 1987, B1 (late edition); Dawn Stacey, "History of Crisis Pregnancy Centers," Crisis Pregnancy Center Watch, accessed May 30, 2022, https://www.motherjones.com/files/cpchistory2.pdf; Pamela Wong, "Attracting Clients and Controversy," *Christianity Today*, September 18, 1987, 32.

Pro-life support for adoption also came under attack. *People* in 1992 portrayed a mother accused of beating her adopted son with a broom and saying she would "trade him in." The *Austin American Statesman* in 1993 reported on adopted children who "set fires, snuck out of the house at night, tried to hang the family dog," with the result that, "As bliss turns to heartache, parents seek to end adoption." *Time* in 1993 headlined one story, "The Ties That Traumatize." Adoption opponents portrayed adoption as class struggle (poorer birthmother vs. middle-class adoptive parents), racial struggle (black vs. white), and sexual struggle (liberated vs. married).[15]

Every happy adoptee was a reminder to aborting parents of the road not taken. Joss Shawyer began *Death by Adoption* by shouting her preference for abortion over adoption, which she called "a violent act, a political act of aggression toward a woman who has supposedly offended the sexual mores by committing the unforgivable act of not suppressing her sexuality."[16] Negative depictions of adoption affected pro-life volunteers and birth mothers. Studies in the late 1980s showed that pregnancy center volunteers were reluctant to suggest adoption to pregnant women. Some popular Christian teachers also discouraged adoption.[17]

Since playboys have been major beneficiaries of *Roe v. Wade*, it was not surprising to find in *Playboy* one of the most extreme anti-adoption short stories. In T. C. Boyle's "King Bee," two infertile adoptive parents, Ken and Pat, sit in "the plush, paneled conference rooms of Adopt-a-Child," where a man with "the voice of a seducer" gives them the good news that they can adopt Anthony, "a sunny, smiling towheaded boy." Fictional Anthony, of course, broils a puppy in the oven, rapes a fifth-

---

15 Marvin Olasky, "The War on Adoption," *National Review*, June 7, 1993, reprinted in Kathryn Lopez, ed., *Standing Athwart a Culture of Death* (New York: National Review Institute, 2018), 2–8.
16 Joss Shawyer, *Death by Adoption* (New York: Cicada, 1979), 1.
17 For a discussion of adoption complexity in the late 1980s see Olasky and Olasky, *More than Kindness*, 121–35; and "Bethany Christian Services Responds to Bill Gothard," *More Than Kindness*, appendix A, 183–91.

grade girl, eats so much that Pat "could barely make out his eyes, sunk in their pockets of flesh," and sends them thirty-two death threats.[18]

Overall, in the early 1990s the pro-life movement was losing the battle for public sentiment. Columnist Tony Snow summarized the condition of a movement purportedly made up of "finger-wagging prudes, fanatics, and clinic bombers": Pro-lifers were "getting smashed politically."[19]

The publishing industry also piled on. In 1995 lawyer J. Stanley Pottinger came out with his first novel, *The Fourth Procedure*, which also featured crazy pro-lifers. Hero Jack MacLeod literally wrestles with an anti-abortion activist subtly named Graves: "Just as Jack thought he had the upper hand, a man standing over him with a sign reading STOP VIOLENCE TO THE UNBORN! lifted his stick in both hands, like Excalibur, and rammed it straight down. Into Jack's eye."[20]

Former senator and Democratic presidential frontrunner Gary Hart panned the book in *The New York Times* but said its treatment of abortion is "as cogent and balanced as you will ever find." Such "balance" is hard to discern when a character looks into the eyes of a second pro-lifer and sees "two empty craters, the eyes of a man whose soul had already departed." But Random House gave first-time author Pottinger a $500,000 advance, at least in part for what Hart discerned: The novelistic screed is "a soap opera conducted on the front lines of the abortion wars." Random House's expenditure of $250,000 for marketing the book propelled it onto top ten *Los Angeles Times* and *Wall Street Journal* lists.[21]

18 *Playboy*, March 1989. After Ken and Pat quit their jobs and move without leaving a forwarding address, Anthony tracks down and tries to kill Pat by trapping her amid thousands of swarming bees. The short story has a happy ending of a sort: the bees turn on Anthony and sting him to death.
19 Tony Snow, comment at Fieldstead Forum, 1991.
20 Stanley Pottinger, *The Fourth Procedure* (New York: Ballantine, 1995), 331.
21 Gary Hart, "One Damn Thing after Three Anothers," *New York Times*, April 9, 1995, section 7, 8; Pottinger, *Fourth Procedure*, 337; Ann Costello, "Powerful Lawyer's Path to Hot Author," *New York Times*, January 7, 1996, section 13WC, 17.

One by one and even thousands by thousands, pro-life people in 1995 were helping to save and change lives. But characterized by both journalists and novelists as awful rather than awesome, the pro-life movement in 1995 hit bottom.

SECTION FIVE

STILL UNSETTLED

1995–2022

The spread of ultrasound technology opened a window to the womb and made visible the developing baby, a boon to the compassion wing of the pro-life movement. Abortion advocates countered by celebrating abortion as a spiritual act. Meanwhile, advocates on both sides of the issue pushed new legislation either to enshrine *Roe* at the state level or to challenge its status as settled law—and both sides avidly watched the Supreme Court.

41

Window to the Womb

GEETA SWAMIDASS stood on a stool behind the surgeon and looked eagerly over his shoulder to watch him work. The twenty-two-year-old had just finished her medical studies in India and was working at the Christian Medical College and Hospital in Vellore. It was 1973. She loved surgery. When another doctor asked her to accompany the patient to this procedure, she quickly accepted, expecting to enjoy watching the intricate process. But in a 2021 interview, she said the physician shocked her when he opened the woman's uterus and out popped a baby, probably about twelve to thirteen weeks along.[1]

"I could see the heart beating through the tiny chest wall," Swamidass said: After the procedure, the baby lay on a tray with all the operating instruments. She said she watched as the baby moved, struggling to breathe with underdeveloped lungs.[2]

That was her first exposure to abortion. Swamidass, a Christian college graduate, knew about anatomy but had not learned about elective abortions or seen a baby yanked from her mother. "It totally devastated me," she said in the 2021 interview: "I felt like the blood of that baby was on my hands."[3]

---

1 Geeta Swamidass, interview with author, June 4, 2021.
2 Swamidass interview.
3 Swamidass interview.

Swamidass thought of that moment a decade later, after she and her husband moved to California with their three young children. In her early thirties at the time, she hoped to land a medical residency position that would help pay the family bills, but a handful of businessmen and doctors from her prayer group wanted her to direct a new pregnancy center in Orange, California, that would be the first pro-life medical pregnancy center in the country. She said no, deterred by the prospect of little pay to help support her family.

Her husband disagreed. In India, Swamidass had worked as a physician at an orphanage that often dealt with crisis pregnancies and adoptions—not much different from the work of a pregnancy center. He thought she'd be perfect for the position. *Do you believe abortion is wrong? Do you remember what you saw?* he asked one day. Of course she remembered that dying baby. *Then what are you going to do about it?* he urged.[4]

The LivingWell Clinic opened in April 1985 with Swamidass at the helm. It became the first U.S. pregnancy center to use ultrasounds to confirm pregnancies and allow clients to see their unborn babies. A second pregnancy center added medical services in 1989 and a third in 1991. At least fifty medical pregnancy centers were open by March 1998.[5]

Pro-lifers first recognized the benefits of ultrasounds for tiny unborn humans when a tall, redheaded English OB/GYN in the 1950s began using the technology in obstetrics. Dr. Ian Donald developed an interest in sonar while serving as a medical officer for the Royal Air Force during World War II. When the war ended, he returned to civilian employment as an obstetrician and gynecologist. He wanted to help solve the breathing problems of premature infants with underdeveloped lungs, which led him to design respirators for neonatal patients. But Donald struggled to identify the cause of these respiratory problems.[6]

---

4   Swamidass interview.
5   Mai Bean et al., *A Legacy of Life and Love: Pregnancy Centers Stand the Test of Time* (Arlington, VA: Charlotte Lozier Institute, 2020), 6–7, 9; Lois Cunningham, email to author, January 12, 2022.
6   S. Campbell, "A Short History of Sonography in Obstetrics and Gynaecology," *Facts, Views, and Vision: Issues in Obstetrics, Gynaecology, and Reproductive Health* 5 no. 3 (2013): 213–16, https://

In 1954 Donald began exploring ultrasound—similar to the sonar technology used during the war—as a way to learn about the development of unborn babies. Four years later, he and a group of clinicians and engineers became the first to publish ultrasound images of an unborn baby. In a 1978 lecture, Donald showed an audience of nonmedical people one of the first real-time films of an unborn baby moving around inside of his mother: "Here's the baby. See how he jumps. . . . This baby is about a 12 week pregnancy . . . [the mother] has only missed two periods. She does not even know she is pregnant. She certainly cannot feel these movements but there is no doubt about the reality."[7]

While working at the Queen Mother's Maternity Hospital in Glasgow, Scotland, Donald used ultrasound images to help change the minds of women considering abortion. He strongly opposed abortion and thought his legacy clear: "If I have done nothing else in my life, I have killed that dirty lie that the foetus is just a nondescript meaningless jelly, disposable at will, something to be got rid of."[8]

Swamidass saw the effects of the technology at her own pregnancy center: "Obviously it was so effective because when you show a woman her baby's heartbeat at, you know, six to eight weeks, she knows it's life, and now it's not just telling her that's life. You know, she's seen it."[9]

Swamidass tells of one patient in her late teens who came to the center in 1985: The girl was a youth ministry leader at a local church and had sexual intercourse only once, but that one time left her pregnant. Swamidass said the girl told her she needed an abortion because she

---

www.ncbi.nlm.nih.gov/pmc/articles/PMC3987368/; Nicole Erjavic, "Ian Donald (1910–1987)," The Embryo Project Encyclopedia, published January 30, 2018, https://embryo.asu.edu/pages/ian-donald-1910-1987.

7 Erjavic, "Ian Donald (1910–1987)"; Malcolm Nicolson, "Ian Donald, Diagnostician and Moralist," Royal College of Physicians of Edinburgh, published 2000, http://www.rcpe.ac.uk/heritage/ian-donald-diagnostician-and-moralist.

8 Donald made an exception to his standard refusal to perform abortions in cases of severe fetal deformity. He was willing to consider aborting children who are "so mentally defective" as to be "incapable of spiritual development." See Nicolson, "Ian Donald, Diagnostician and Moralist."

9 Swamidass interview.

didn't want others at church to know what she had done. She wanted Swamidass to give her a biblical okay to get an abortion, but Swamidass told her *killing your baby would be sin no matter what circumstance under which your baby was conceived.* The young woman cried during the ultrasound: "She saw a baby—a perfectly formed little baby—and she could not get away from that fact." Swamidass said the girl eventually confessed what she had done in front of her church and placed her baby for adoption.[10]

Ultrasound images shocked even women who had been pregnant before. Swamidass remembers one who came to the center in the late 1990s after having ten abortions but having never seen an ultrasound of her babies. She was amazed: *Wow, it is a baby. Nobody told me this before.* Swamidass said the woman still had abortion number eleven—and regretted it immediately: When she got pregnant again, she married her boyfriend and kept baby twelve.

But Donna Ezell, in the late 1980s, did have an abortion. She remembers the day a pro-life sidewalk counselor outside an Arkansas center told her the baby she was about to abort already had arms and legs. Ezell, then nineteen, momentarily stopped, shocked that she hadn't considered how developed the baby inside of her was. But she said a family member ushered her inside. Later, after becoming the clinical director at the Arkansas Pregnancy Resource Center, Ezell described her teenaged self as well-educated: a good student who had even visited a doctor to receive prenatal care—but she had never seen an ultrasound of her baby, and knew nothing about fetal development.[11]

She didn't find out until later that the flicker of a heartbeat is visible three weeks after conception, that the buds of arms and legs appear at five weeks, and that fingers and toes become identifiable seven weeks out. She said in 2021 that many women still don't know that, even though technology has only improved since her teen years: "I witness

---

10 Swamidass interview.
11 Donna Ezell, interview with author, March 31, 2021.

daily women who are amazed at just how developed their unborn baby is at six weeks, eight weeks, ten weeks."[12]

Ezell listed those stages of development when testifying before an Arkansas legislative committee in support of a bill that strengthened the state's existing ultrasound requirement. The original law passed in 2003 and required physicians who perform ultrasounds for abortions to offer women a look at the image before aborting.[13] Even though that law did not *mandate* showing ultrasounds before all abortions, opponents such as Rep. Jay Bradford complained—but he inadvertently touched a deeper issue: "You really want them to have that image, to take that with them forever? . . . I don't know that the guilt involved in that is something we should be promoting." Bradford knew guilt would be involved because "that image" would show a tiny human baby.[14]

In 2002, Alabama became the first state to require abortionists to perform an ultrasound and offer women a peek at the image. Eight years later, the owner of a Birmingham abortion facility estimated about half of the women said they wanted to see the ultrasound but she had never seen a patient leave because of what she saw.[15] A study following patients at an urban abortion provider in 2011 found that almost 43 percent of all women at the facility that year chose to view the ultrasound but 99 percent of the total still chose to abort.[16]

12 Statement of Donna Ezell, RN, regarding the *Right-to-Know-and-See Act: Hearings on S.B. 85, Before the Arkansas House Committee on Public Health, Welfare and Labor*, 93rd General Assembly (2021), https://sg001-harmony.sliq.net/00284/Harmony/en/PowerBrowser/PowerBrowserV2/20210318/-1/21384?viewMode=1#info_.
13 Andrew DeMillo, "Arkansas Senate OKs Ultrasound Requirement for Abortions," Associated Press, March 8, 2021, https://apnews.com/article/arkansas-abortion-legislation-ultrasound-bills-6e9065aac70da2b6604d0e2032468102.
14 "Arkansas: Bill Requires Abortion Providers to Offer Ultrasounds," *Feminist Majority Foundation Blog, Feminist Majority Foundation*, April 9, 2003, https://feminist.org/news/arkansas-bill-requires-abortion-providers-to-offer-ultrasounds/.
15 Kevin Sack, "In Ultrasound, Abortion Fight Has New Front," *New York Times*, May 27, 2010, https://www.nytimes.com/2010/05/28/health/policy/28ultrasound.html.
16 Mary Gatter, MD et al., "Relationship between Ultrasound Viewing and Proceeding to Abortion," *Obstetrics and Gynecology* 123, no. 1 (January 2014): 83, https://doi.org/10.1097/AOG.0000000000000053.

One Birmingham woman who looked at the ultrasound before aborting her baby told *The New York Times* in 2010, "It was really the picture of the ultrasound that made me feel it was O.K." She said her eight-week-old baby "looked like a little egg, and I couldn't see arms or legs or a face." Another woman at the facility for her second abortion shared her tactic for having a less emotionally fraught procedure: "You almost have to think of it as an alien."[17]

Pro-life centers, though, have seen ultrasound make a difference. A 2019 internal report at CareNet found client "no-abort" rates after ultrasounds were close to 90 percent for women who were "at risk for abortion based on their life circumstances," but that percentage was not significantly higher than for women who received no ultrasound. For women "actively pursuing an abortion," however, the percentage that chose not to abort increased from 26 percent to 45 percent after they had seen the ultrasound images and to 55 percent when they had the father with them during the ultrasound. The National Institute of Family and Life Advocates surveyed its nationwide affiliates in 2014 and found 78 percent of women at risk for an abortion who saw an ultrasound image chose not to abort. The percentage of pro-life decisions by all clients was even higher.[18] Such a stark difference between the effectiveness of ultrasounds at abortion facilities and at pregnancy

---

17 Sack, "In Ultrasound."
18 CareNet Chief Outreach Officer Vincent DiCaro, email to author, September 16, 2021. CareNet separated the data between "abortion-minded" and "abortion-vulnerable" women. Focus on the Family, in a 2009 document for pregnancy centers, defined "abortion-minded" as "one who appears to be planning or intending to obtain an abortion" and "abortion-vulnerable" as "one who by continuing her pregnancy faces obstacles that she may feel incapable of handling or unwilling to experience. This category might also include women who state that they are pro-choice but are uninterested in aborting at this point." See "Excellence of Care: Standards of Care for Providing Sonograms and Other Medical Services in a Pregnancy Medical Clinic," Focus on the Family, last modified June 5, 2009, https://media.focusonthefamily.com/heartlink/pdf/standardsofcare.pdf; Thomas Glessner, "The NIFLA Survey: The Effectiveness of Ultrasound Confirmation of Pregnancy," *National Institute of Family and Life Advocates Legal Tips, Clinic Tips* 22, no. 2 (February 2015): 1–2. A Baton Rouge, Louisiana, pregnancy center director reported in 2000 that 98 percent of women who had ultrasounds at her facility chose not to abort. A Providence, Rhode Island, center in 2004 reported 24 out of 25 ultrasound viewers chose life. See Lynn Vincent,

centers makes sense: Women who are already at an abortion facility are more invested (perhaps even financially) and more likely to feel like it's too late to back out, no matter what they see on the screen. Meanwhile, ultrasounds at pregnancy centers generally cost the patient nothing and take place in environments where the woman faces no pressure to abort.[19]

By 2022, twenty-eight states had passed some sort of ultrasound requirement for abortionists. In March 2021, Arkansas became one of six states that require abortionists to show the woman the ultrasound image and also describe what she is viewing. As pro-life states have passed these laws, the number of medical pregnancy centers like the one Swamidass opened in the 1980s have continued to grow to meet the increased demand for a window into the womb. By 2009, 52 percent of CareNet's 1,113 affiliates offered ultrasounds. A decade later, that number had grown to 77 percent of that year's 1,055 affiliates.[20]

Since beginning her career as an OB/GYN in the 1980s, Dr. Sandy Christiansen, national medical director for CareNet, has performed hundreds of obstetrical ultrasounds. She knows the drill: "We try to explain what we're seeing." At her Frederick, Maryland, pregnancy center, she applies transducer gel to the patient's abdomen and talks the

---

"Window to the Womb," *World*, August 19, 2000, 27–28; and Alisa Harris, "Bittersweet Success," *World*, August 15, 2009, 54–55.

19 Pregnancy center data has flaws. CareNet affiliates base a "choice for life" on the "last stated intent" of the woman. So, if a center last heard that a client planned to abort, that's what would appear in the report, even if the woman later changed her mind. The outcome could also go the other way (DiCaro, email to author, September 17, 2021). NIFLA did not record how participating centers determined a choice for life (Anne O'Connor, email to author, September 17, 2021). But even a 2021 study funded by the University of California San Francisco found women are less likely to abort and more likely to carry a pregnancy to term after visiting a pregnancy center (Alice F. Cartwright et al., "Pregnancy outcomes after exposure to crisis pregnancy centers among an abortion-seeking sample recruited online," *PLoS ONE* 16, no. 7 (July 2021): 1–14, https://doi.org/10.1371/journal.pone.0255152). For many, the ultrasound image is key, and pregnancy center staffers regularly see how it affects women and their families.

20 "Requirements for Ultrasound," Guttmacher Institute, accessed February 9, 2022, https://www.guttmacher.org/state-policy/explore/requirements-ultrasound; CareNet Vice President of Center Services and Client Care Cynthia Hopkins, email to author, June 2, 2021.

woman through the ultrasound procedure: *Here you can see the uterine wall, and inside the uterus is the gestational sac, which appears black. Can you see the white bean-shaped structure? That is the embryo. Do you see the flickering? That's the baby's heart beating.* She points with her finger or the monitor's arrow to the pixelated grays and whites on the screen.[21]

During these fifteen- to twenty-minute show-and-tells, reactions vary from shocked silence to tears: "I've had dads faint . . . crumple to the ground." Even the ultrasound footage that can't show the embryo in detail but only depicts the flickering light representing a heartbeat is enough to help some frightened mothers and skeptical fathers connect with their unborn children.[22]

"For the person who feels this [pregnancy] is just the worst thing that's happened to them . . . it's a terrible shock," said Christiansen: "We desperately want them to understand that, yes, you're in this crisis moment, this moment where this feels impossible, but we want to try to help you see a bigger picture . . . to be able to look back on that decision and say, 'Yes . . . it was tough, but I am so glad that I had this child.'"[23]

Some women see the baby and still decide to abort—a choice that can weigh heavily on counselors: "We feel so responsible if somebody doesn't choose to carry. At the end of the day, I'm not in control of that. . . . We do what we can . . . and then God will do the rest."[24]

---

21 Sandy Christiansen, interviews with author, April 30 and May 25, 2021.
22 Christiansen interviews.
23 Christiansen interviews.
24 Christiansen interviews.

42

Loving Your Unborn Neighbor

IN 1988, Pastor John Piper of Bethlehem Baptist Church in Minneapolis sat in a Pizza Hut watching a TV news report about a pro-life demonstration in Atlanta. Events unfolding on the screen struck a chord with him. He told his wife, *That's just plain right.*[1]

He didn't see spectacular visions that day in Pizza Hut, just plain stuff that was right, "seeing other people taking it seriously and then beginning to check my own soul. . . . God just mercifully taking away some blind spots, showing me in the Scriptures all kinds of reasons for standing up and defending these little ones." Piper had written an article against abortion in 1982 and had given his first Sanctity of Life Sunday sermon in 1987, but this moved him to action: in 1988, police arrested him and seven other Bethlehem pastors and members for sitting in front of the door of a St. Paul Planned Parenthood facility.[2]

---

1 Joe Maxwell and Steve Hall, "Still-Silent Shepherds," *World*, January 25, 2014, 40; John Piper, "Planned Parenthood: Invitation, Explanation, Indignation," Desiring God, August 21, 2015, https://www.desiringgod.org/articles/planned-parenthood-invitation-explanation-indignation.
2 Maxwell and Hall, "Still-Silent Shepherds," 40; Piper, "Abortion, Father's Day, and Infant Doe," Desiring God, June 15, 1982, https://www.desiringgod.org/articles/abortion-fathers-day-and-infant-doe; Piper, "Why Would Three Pastors from Bethlehem Get Arrested?" Desiring God, January 9, 1989, https://www.desiringgod.org/articles/why-would-three-pastors-from-bethlehem

Piper preached more than twenty sermons on abortion before retiring from the Minneapolis pulpit in 2013. He acknowledged that some of the women listening may have had abortions themselves. He offered them gospel hope: "No one is cut off from Christ because of past sin—any past sin. What cuts a person off from Christ and the fellowship of his people is the endorsement of past sin. For the repentant there is forgiveness and cleansing and hope." He called upon women who had been through abortion and found forgiveness and healing: "There is a great work to be done, and we await your help."[3]

He also used his sermons to call the entire congregation to action. In the sermon "Love Your Unborn Neighbor," he connected "America in the 21st century, stained with the blood of millions of unborn babies," to teaching in chapter 24 of Proverbs: "Hold back those who are stumbling to the slaughter. If you say, 'Behold, we did not know this,' does not he who weighs the heart perceive it? Does not he who keeps watch over your soul know it, and will he not repay man according to his work?'"[4]

Thirty-five years later, David Michael, a former Bethlehem pastor, remembered Piper's first Sanctity of Life Sunday sermon in 1987 and how Piper called abortion "an assault on the unique person-forming work of God."[5] Michael said the understanding that "abortion is an assault against God's glory" spurred on the pro-life work at Bethlehem: "The horror of babies being slaughtered three blocks away was motivating, but what motivated us more was the glory of God . . . there was just

---

-get-arrested. See also Justin Taylor, "'Abortion Is about God': Piper's Passionate, Prophetic Pro-Life Preaching," in *For the Fame of God's Name: Essays in Honor of John Piper*, ed. Sam Storms and Justin Taylor (Wheaton, IL: Crossway, 2010), 328–50.

3 Maxwell and Hall, "Still-Silent Shepherds," 40; John Piper, "Rescuing Unborn Children: Required and Right," Desiring God, January 15, 1989, https://www.desiringgod.org/messages/rescuing-unborn-children-required-and-right.

4 Piper, "Love Your Unborn Neighbor," Desiring God, January 22, 2006, https://www.desiringgod.org/messages/love-your-unborn-neighbor.

5 John Piper, "Abortion: You Desire and Do Not Have, So You Kill," Desiring God, January 18, 1987, https://www.desiringgod.org/messages/abortion-you-desire-and-do-not-have-so-you-kill.

this inner spiritual passion for the glory of God that was underneath all of our activity that we were doing."[6]

The preaching bore fruit in the church: Bethlehem financially supported local crisis pregnancy centers. Members and attendees counseled outside of abortion centers and demonstrated at the Minnesota state capitol. In the 1990s, the Pipers adopted a child, as did others in the church: one couple started a fund to help facilitate adoptions of minority children. The fund by 2001 had helped with 195 adoptions both inside and outside the church.[7]

The Southern Baptist Convention (SBC), the nation's largest Protestant denomination, also went through a transformation. In 1971 the denomination had said abortion should be legal when there is "carefully ascertained evidence of the likelihood of damage to the emotional, mental, and physical health of the mother."[8] (Already at that time, however, California had shown that abortionists would legally expand their practice without careful ascertainment, as we noted in our chapter 36.)

The SBC stood by its 1971 statement even after *Roe*, calling it "a middle ground between the extreme of abortion on demand and the opposite extreme of all abortion as murder." But in 1976 the denomination acknowledged that every abortion decision "must necessarily involve the decision to terminate the life of an innocent human being." By 1980 the SBC advocated "legislation and/or a constitutional amendment prohibiting abortion except to save the life of the mother." Two years later the denominational transformation was complete. The SBC resolved that "biblical references indicate that human life begins at conception."[9]

---

6 David Michael, interview with author, March 17, 2022.
7 Michael, interview; Brad Nelson and Kenny Stokes, interview with author, March 10, 2022; Delsie Baxter and Wayne King, interview with author, March 16, 2022; Kenny Stokes, email to author, March 10, 2022. See also Piper, "Talitha Ruth Piper," Desiring God, December 19, 1995, https://www.desiringgod.org/articles/talitha-ruth-piper.
8 "Resolution on Abortion," Southern Baptist Convention, June 1, 1971, https://www.sbc.net/resource-library/resolutions/resolution-on-abortion-2/.
9 "Resolution on Abortion and Sanctity of Human Life," SBC, June 1, 1974, https://www.sbc.net/resource-library/resolutions/resolution-on-abortion-and-sanctity-of-human-life/; "Resolution

Baptist churches in the South often spread pro-life seeds on well-watered soil. Seed-sowers had a harder task in Manhattan, where Tim Keller, founder and longtime pastor of Redeemer Presbyterian Church, explained in a 2008 sermon that Christian opposition to abortion relied not just on many verses of Scripture but also on the overwhelming biblical emphasis on *imago Dei*, the image of God (e.g., Gen. 1:26–27). In preaching on Genesis, Keller asked, "What happens when you have a secular society in which most of the cultural elite say, 'well, we don't believe in God anymore, and therefore we don't believe human beings were made in the image of God, we just evolved'?"[10]

Keller said those who don't see humans as made in God's image "ground human rights in what they call capacities. . . . the capacity to reason . . . to make moral choices, they know right from wrong, they have the capacity for what some professors call 'preferences.'" Keller cited one of those professors, Princeton's Peter Singer, who said, "human rights are grounded in capacities, [and] the Supreme Court was right when it said abortion was alright."[11]

Keller continued, "Now everyone gets so quiet here. Because the life in the womb doesn't have capacities. They can't make choices. They can't reason, they can't tell right from wrong, they can't live apart from the mother. They don't have capacities and therefore they don't have rights. And here's what Peter Singer says, yes, he agrees with that. But if that's true let's keep something in mind. Born infants don't have those capacities either. They can't reason; they have no preferences yet. They can't make moral choices and neither can senile old people. And neither can very mentally handicapped people. And therefore, none of them.

---

on Abortion," SBC, June 1, 1976 and 1980, https://www.sbc.net/resource-library/resolutions/resolution-on-abortion-3/ and https://www.sbc.net/resource-library/resolutions/resolution-on-abortion-6/; "Resolution on Abortion and Infanticide," SBC, May 1, 1982, https://www.sbc.net/resource-library/resolutions/resolution-on-abortion-and-infanticide/.

10 Tim Keller, "In the Image of God," BaylyBlog, November 30, 2008, http://www.baylyblog.com/blog/2009/01/tim-keller-addresses-abortion.

11 Keller, "Image of God."

... if you believe abortion is alright, then you really can't protect the rights of any of these other people."[12]

One way abortion-friendly denominations and ministries challenge that logic is by weaponizing confusing Bible verses. Michele Hendrickson, a regional coordinator for Students for Life, said she heard one of those arguments while standing in front of the Supreme Court during an annual Washington, DC, March for Life in the late 2010s. A young man clad in pink and holding a Planned Parenthood sign approached her: *Are you a Christian?* he asked. Hendrickson responded yes. The man shot back, *Well then, what do you have to say when your God supports abortion?* He quoted Numbers 5:27.[13]

To understand the young man's point, we have to get into the weeds for a bit. The Numbers passage describes what a man in ancient Israel should do if he suspects his wife has committed adultery but has no proof. The man should bring his wife to the priest, who will mix into water dust from the tabernacle floor and tell her to drink the concoction.

The passage is obscure, and no one knows quite what it means. But the 2011 New International Version (NIV) translates the passage to say that if the wife has been unfaithful, the drink "will enter her, her abdomen will swell and her womb will miscarry."

In trying to make clear what is confusing, the 2011 NIV went beyond what the Hebrew says. Other translations, including the 1984 NIV, stick to a more word-for-word translation of the Hebrew: the guilty woman's "thigh will fall." It isn't clear what that meant in ancient Israel or today, but Wayne Grudem, general editor of the *ESV Study Bible*, notes that there are two Hebrew words for miscarriage and Numbers 5:27 doesn't use either of them: "If it meant miscarriage, why not use the common words for miscarriage?" In fact, says Grudem, according to the Hebrew there's no confirmation that the wife is even pregnant.[14]

---

12 Keller, "Image of God."
13 Michele Hendrickson, interview with author, March 12, 2021.
14 Wayne Grudem, interview with author, October 21, 2020.

But some abortion advocates have used the 2011 NIV translation for political purposes. During a South Carolina House Judiciary Committee hearing in February 2021, a Democratic opponent of the state's heartbeat bill quoted the verse. Sitting with the other legislators around an oblong desk, Rep. Justin T. Bamberg urged others to set aside their personal beliefs when voting on the legislation: "There are those who say . . . abortion shouldn't happen because the Bible doesn't allow them. . . . Well, it depends on which version of the Bible you read." He pointed to Numbers 5:27 in the 2011 edition of the NIV and its "miscarriage" translation.[15]

Viva Ruiz, a former stripper who has had multiple abortions, approached abortion in a different way. In 2015 she started an art collective called "Thank God for Abortion" to broadcast her belief that "the Christ message is unconditional love and made in God's image." Her group's primary product was a Thank God for Abortion T-shirt. In 2020 Ruiz told a *Jezebel* reporter that people who have had abortions "are more holy," and that "abortion providers are doing Jesus-work." After Texas in 2021 passed a law protecting unborn babies with a detectable heartbeat, Ruiz said it's "a blasphemy to force childbirth on a person," adding, "abortion is about self-love and is actually sacred."[16]

That approach would not appeal to many Bible-oriented Christians, so Planned Parenthood has tried to find its way into churches by creating a Clergy Advocacy Board that also appeals to *imago Dei*: The board says humans are "created in God's image" and have the "right

---

15 *Fetal Heartbeat Protection from Abortion Act: Hearings on S. 1, Before the Full South Carolina House Judiciary Committee*, 124th General Assembly (2021) (statement of Representative Justin T. Bamberg). https://www.scstatehouse.gov/video/archives.php?key=10808&part=1.
16 Viva Ruiz talks about her experience as a dancer and sex worker in an interview with Matthew Rodriguez, "Viva Ruiz Wants You to Thank God for Your Abortion," Spirituality and Religion Interviews, The Body, February 10, 2020, https://www.thebody.com/article/viva-ruiz-thank-god-for-abortion. See also Shannon Melero, "A Vision of God That Wants People to Access Abortion," *Jezebel*, October 13, 2020, https://jezebel.com/a-vision-of-god-that-wants-people-to-access-abortion-1845325539; Shout Your Abortion (@shoutyourabortion), "Hi! Amelia with SYA Here . . ." Instagram, September 6, 2021, https://www.instagram.com/p/CTfT1W0htrc/.

to self-determination," so any policy that denies that right is morally objectionable.[17] Baptist minister Katey Zeh, a member of the board, said she "discovered my call to ministry within a Planned Parenthood," where she volunteered as an abortion doula—giving emotional support to aborting women—while in seminary.[18]

Christians throughout history have said the developing baby in the womb is also made in the image of God—but some pastors have been reluctant to say so. For years, theologian R. C. Sproul produced pro-life materials for pastors to use with their congregations but often received a discouraging response. He said in 2014, "It was like a broken record. Pastors said, 'I can't use this material. It'll split our church.'" That year, a survey of forty pastors from denominations in the National Association of Evangelicals found all agreed that life begins at conception and that pastors should preach against abortion, but five had never preached that and almost half hadn't broached the subject in the past year.[19]

But Piper in Minnesota marched onward with his Sanctity of Life Sunday sermons, choosing passages from Job, the Psalms, Matthew, Luke, Romans, and 1 Peter as texts for the annual message. And he reminded listeners of the priority behind their convictions on the issue of abortion: "The most important thing that could happen this morning in this room is not that anyone become pro-life, but that everyone be justified before God by faith alone in Jesus Christ, the Son of God, crucified and risen."[20]

Meanwhile, Keller in Manhattan grounded his preaching about abortion historically by explaining how "in the Greco-Roman world

---

17 "Religious Pluralism and Women's Health," Clergy Advocacy Board, Planned Parenthood, accessed March 22, 2022, https://www.plannedparenthood.org/about-us/our-leadership/clergy-advocacy-board/our-values/religious-pluralism-and-womens-health.
18 Jack Jenkins, "Planned Parenthood Announces New Clergy Advocacy Board Members, Many from Red States," Religion News Service, April 13, 2021, https://religionnews.com/2021/04/13/planned-parenthood-announces-new-clergy-advisory-board-members-many-from-red-states/.
19 Maxwell and Hall, "Still-Silent Shepherds," 42.
20 Piper, "God at Work in Every Womb," Desiring God, January 21, 2001, https://www.desiringgod.org/messages/god-at-work-in-every-womb.

you had slavery, you had terrible poverty, you had lots of abortion . . . you had infanticide, it was perfectly legal, especially girl babies died of exposure. And you took the elderly and sick poor people and just let them die. And that was all legal; and it was done all the time." Keller said Christians who "believed in the image of God . . . were totally against abortion, from the beginning. . . . They were champions of women; they were champions of orphans; they were champions of the weak; they were champions of the poor. And they were against abortion."[21]

When Piper delivered the annual Sanctity of Life message at one of the Bethlehem campuses in January 2021, almost a decade after retiring, he again reminded the congregation that "Jesus Christ crucified for sinners and risen and reigning is the only reality in the world that gives pardon to the agents of death and power to the agents of life—all to the praise of the glory of the grace of God."[22]

Into 2022, Christians at Bethlehem Baptist Church continued to volunteer at and donate to their local pregnancy centers and do sidewalk counseling outside of local abortion facilities. Delsie Baxter, a leader of Bethlehem's pro-life ministry, said her convictions on abortion began before she started attending the church—but she didn't act on them until Bethlehem helped her put beliefs into action. Before attending Bethlehem she had never heard a sermon about the sanctity of life—but Piper's preaching "resonated. It was just like, okay, I'm not alone. Somebody else gets it, and he's got the pulpit, he's got the mic."[23]

---

[21] Keller, "Image of God."
[22] Piper, "Doing the Right Thing Never Ruins Your Life," Desiring God, January 28, 2021, https://www.desiringgod.org/messages/doing-the-right-thing-never-ruins-your-life.
[23] Delsie Baxter, interview with author, March 16, 2022.

43

Sensational Facts

IN JUNE 1995, Congress began debating a proposal to ban a particularly graphic type of abortion known as "intact dilation and extraction" or "partial-birth abortion." Brenda Pratt Shafer, a nurse who had witnessed that type of abortion, described how "the baby's body was moving. His little fingers were clasping together. He was kicking his feet. All the while his little head was still stuck inside." The abortionist then stuck scissors into the back of the baby's head, used a suction tube to extract the baby's brains, and "threw the baby in a pan."[1]

Many news outlets claimed only 500 partial-birth abortions actually happened in a year—a number based on statements from abortion lobbyists. NBC's Matt Lauer called the procedure "rare" or "little-used" five times in thirteen stories between November 1 and December 8, 1995. The day after the ban passed the House in March 1996, Troy Roberts on CBS *This Morning* reported "about 500" happened each year and claimed two times that it was "often chosen by mothers who discover serious birth defects in the fetus." A CBS report didn't even explain the procedure, and another CBS

---

1 "Former Clinic Worker Brenda Shafer," ClinicQuotes, posted September 10, 2012, https://clinicquotes.com/former-abortion-provider-brenda-shafer/.

report on President Bill Clinton's veto of the legislation called "so-called partial-birth abortions" rare.[2]

In September 1996, though, abortionists at a facility in Englewood, New Jersey, told reporter Ruth Padawer with the *Bergen-Hackensack Record* that they performed more than 1,500 partial-birth abortions per year at the facility. The same month, *Washington Post* reporters found in interviews and published documents that most partial-birth abortions were not due to medical emergencies.[3]

The next year, *The New York Times* quoted lobbyist Ron Fitzsimmons, executive director of the National Coalition of Abortion Providers, saying he "lied through my teeth" when he said in an earlier interview that the procedure was rare and was used only on endangered mothers and damaged children. He confirmed that the procedure was common and that abortionists usually performed it on healthy mothers and babies. The Media Research Center noted that, despite the new information, NBC's Tom Brokaw still said, "What anti-abortionists call partial-birth abortions—that's a provocative and mostly inaccurate statement."[4]

Six years later, President George W. Bush finally signed the Partial-Birth Abortion Ban into law. Abortion proponents challenged its constitutionality. At one of its days in court in 2004, an abortionist given

---

2 "Roe Warriors: The Media's Pro-Abortion Bias," Media Research Center, July 22, 1998, https://www.mrc.org/roe-warriors-medias-pro-abortion-bias.

3 Barbara Vobejda and David Brown, "HARSH DETAILS SHIFT TENOR OF ABORTION FIGHT," *The Washington Post*, September 17, 1996, https://www.washingtonpost.com/archive/politics/1996/09/17/harsh-details-shift-tenor-of-abortion-fight/c65611f7-0ae2-4ef7-821d-2e5149f701e4/; Douglas Johnson, "Discredited Myths about Partial-Birth Abortion—and Some Journalists Who Won't Let Go of Them," National Right to Life, September 15, 2003, https://www.nrlc.org/abortion/pba/pbamythsmemo01303/.

4 "Roe Warriors," Media Research Center. Fitzsimmons's earlier interview was a taped one with ABC's *Nightline*. His claim about the numbers of partial-birth abortions didn't make the final cut and never aired, but Fitzsimmons said the lie still "made me physically ill." According to the *Times* article, he also admitted that abortion is "a form of killing . . . you're ending a life," although he still said he supported the procedure. See David Stout, "An Abortion Rights Advocate Says He Lied about Procedure," *New York Times*, February 26, 1997, A-12; Diane M. Gianelli, "Abortion Rights Leader Urges End to 'Half Truths,'" *American Medical News*, March 3, 1997, 3, 54–56; "The Numbers Racket," *World*, March 22, 1997, 7.

anonymity testified about the precise techniques used in partial-birth abortions: "They delivered the fetus intact until the head was lodged in the cervix. Then they reached up and crushed it. They used forceps to crush the skull."[5]

Judge Richard C. Casey asked, "Like a cracker that they use to crack a lobster shell?"

The abortionist clarified: "Like an end of tongs you use to pick up a salad, except they are thick enough and heavy enough to crush the skull."

Casey replied, "Except in this case you are not picking up a salad, you are crushing a baby's skull."[6]

World magazine reported on this and other exchanges from the Casey trial but found that only one daily newspaper, in Lancaster, Pennsylvania, ran the Associated Press report detailing the judge's probing questions. Besides reports on the first day, CBS and ABC did not cover the trial. NBC reported only on the ruling, which came that summer.[7]

More mis-coverage and non-coverage of news about abortion occurred throughout the next decade. One example: Abortionist Kermit Gosnell's 2013 murder trial in Philadelphia. When *Philadelphia Inquirer* police courts reporter Joseph Slobodzian entered the courtroom on the first day of testimony on March 18, 2013, he was surprised to find it mostly empty, including three rows of benches set aside for "press." That was a big contrast to standing-room-only crowds at other high-profile cases.[8]

Slobodzian thought covering Gosnell's trial would be a "no-brainer": it was a major prosecution involving a doctor who had illegally aborted

---

5 Lynn Vincent, "THE UGLY TRUTH," *World*, April 17, 2004, 16–18.
6 Vincent, "UGLY TRUTH."
7 Vincent, "UGLY TRUTH." I based the information about the TV networks on a search of the Vanderbilt Television News Archive. The Media Research Center found in 2003 that, in a study of 217 stories on ABC, CBS, and NBC that mention partial-birth abortion, only eighteen of those stories included medical basics about the procedures, and only three of those stories ran after 1998. See Tim Graham and Rich Noyes, "Censoring the Partial-Birth Abortion Basics," *Media Research Center*, October 27, 2003, http://archive.mrc.org/realitycheck/2003/fax20031027.asp.
8 Joseph Slobodzian, interview with author, February 17, 2022.

infants past twenty-four weeks and had killed others born alive. Slobodzian saw the Gosnell case as an example of the state's failure to enforce its own laws: "There was no question in my mind that this would be a case that . . . I'd want to cover because it was an important case, a big case, and it would certainly have been at high interest."[9]

Slobodzian attended almost every session of the roughly ten-week trial, sitting each day in his preferred seat—not in the benches marked off for press but the seat closest to the witness stand and jury box, where he could still hear the occasional mumbling witnesses and catch reactions from jury members. Also at the front of the courtroom were dirty beds, chairs, and medicine cabinets taken from Gosnell's facility. Each day he sat through testimony that "ranged from black humor to just horrifying. It was impossible to make it up."[10]

Slobodzian's coverage of the trial did not reflect any pro-life commitment: In a 2022 interview, he described himself as pro-choice. He reported because he was a reporter. Slobodzian reported the testimony of one teenager who interned for Gosnell and saw aborted babies moving, breathing, and sometimes "screeching." She saw Dr. Gosnell "snip" the necks of babies still moving after abortions. Also chilling was the jury reaction to that account after already hearing "a four-week parade of horrible testimony." They received it "calmly," Slobodzian wrote.[11]

Despite the sensational facts revealed during the trial, the story was largely absent from national news. Democratic political analyst and columnist Kirsten Powers opened an April *USA Today* column by succinctly describing "Infant beheadings. Severed baby feet in jars. A child

---

9 Slobodzian interview.
10 Slobodzian interview. He observed that one of those jurors during jury selection had a fashionable stubble beard that by the time the verdict came out in May was long and black—a detail you wouldn't catch unless you were in the courtroom.
11 Slobodzian interview; Joseph Slobodzian, "Teen Intern at Gosnell Clinic Recalls Hearing Aborted Fetus 'Screeching,'" *The Philadelphia Inquirer*, April 12, 2013, https://www.inquirer.com/philly/news/20130412_Teen_intern_at_Gosnell_clinic_recalls_hearing_one_aborted_fetus__quot_screeching_quot_.html.

screaming after it was delivered alive during an abortion procedure." She called out other journalists for failing to cover the story: "Let me state the obvious. This should be front-page news . . . a major human rights story if there ever was one." But instead, her Lexis-Nexis search revealed that the top three national TV networks hadn't brought up the trial in the past three months—except for an unplanned mention on *Meet the Press*.[12]

Powers's call-out worked for a time. Her op-ed came out on a Thursday. The next day, CNN's Jake Tapper interviewed Slobodzian about the case, presenting it as a follow-up to his previous 25 seconds of coverage.[13] On the following Monday, reporters from the *Washington Post*, *New York Times*, *Wall Street Journal*, and Fox News showed up—but that afternoon bombs went off near the finish of the 2013 Boston Marathon, and many reporters left the courtroom and didn't come back the next day.[14]

Some news organizations covered the Gosnell trial as a media story rather than a crime story. *Mother Jones* reported that the conservative *Washington Times* devoted only one article to the case and seven articles to the lack of coverage from other outlets.[15] According to theories *The Atlantic* listed, the lack of coverage reflected mainstream

[12] Kirsten Powers, "Philadelphia Abortion Clinic Horror: Column," *USA Today*, April 11, 2013, https://www.usatoday.com/story/opinion/2013/04/10/philadelphia-abortion-clinic-horror-column/2072577/. *The New York Times* covered the case the first day of the trial, but Powers noted that the article was on page A-17 and that the outlet hadn't followed up since. See Jon Hurdle, "Abortion Doctor's Murder Trial Opens," *New York Times*, March 18, 2013, https://www.nytimes.com/2013/03/19/us/philadelphia-abortion-doctors-murder-trial-opens.html.

[13] Noah Rothman, "Not All of Cable News Ignored Kermit Gosnell," *Mediaite*, April 12, 2013, https://www.mediaite.com/tv/not-all-of-cable-news-ignored-kermit-gosnell-cnns-jake-tapper-first-covered-house-of-horrors-on-march-21/; Joseph Slobodzian, "Kermit Gosnell Trial Reveals 'House of Horrors,'" interview by Jake Tapper, CNN, YouTube video, April 12, 2013, https://youtu.be/JZmoj1vjfAw.

[14] Steve Volk, "After National Outcry for News Coverage, This Was the Scene at the Gosnell Trial on Monday," *Philadelphia Magazine*, April 16, 2013, https://www.phillymag.com/news/2013/04/16/national-news-coverage-abortion-trial-philadelphia-gosnell/.

[15] Kevin Drum, "Kermit Gosnell: A Case Study in Working the Refs," *Mother Jones*, April 15, 2013, https://www.motherjones.com/kevin-drum/2013/04/kermit-gosnell-case-study-working-refs/.

media bias or the kinds of victims: poor, minority women, and tiny babies.[16] The *Washington Post* executive editor said he simply hadn't heard about the story.[17] Slobodzian pointed out that both the *New York Times* and the Associated Press ran stories when testimony began and that perhaps the prohibition of cameras in Pennsylvania courtrooms deterred TV networks from covering the trial.[18]

One other explanation: While interviewing Slobodzian, CNN's Tapper mentioned that many of the details were "too graphic" for television.[19] Slobodzian also appeared on MSNBC's *Morning Joe* program, where host Joe Scarborough said some of the details were too horrible to outline. (He said the disturbing facts meant reporters *should* pursue the story.)[20]

Network journalists had no "bloody" excuse, however, for mostly ignoring the annual March for Life in Washington, DC. A study of ABC, CBS, and NBC coverage from 2013 through 2016 showed the huge marches received less than one minute across all networks each year until 2017, when Vice President Mike Pence appeared at the march, earning that year's twenty-two minutes of coverage from networks. That year, the abortion-friendly Women's March got more than an hour of screen time.[21]

---

16 Conor Friedersdorf, "14 Theories for Why Kermit Gosnell's Case Didn't Get More Media Attention," *The Atlantic*, April 15, 2013, https://www.theatlantic.com/politics/archive/2013/04/14-theories-for-why-kermit-gosnells-case-didnt-get-more-media-attention/274966/.
17 Paul Farhi, "Is Media Bias to Blame for Lack of Gosnell Coverage?" *The Washington Post*, April 14, 2013, https://www.washingtonpost.com/lifestyle/style/is-media-bias-to-blame-for-lack-of-gosnell-coverage-or-something-far-more-banal/2013/04/14/473e6668-a536-11e2-a8e2-5b98cb59187f_story.html.
18 Joseph Slobodzian, interview with author, February 17, 2022.
19 Tapper, "Kermit Gosnell Trial Reveals 'House of Horrors.'"
20 "Gosnell Murder Case Inside Media Coverage," interview by Joe Scarborough, MSNBC, April 15, 2013, video, https://archive.org/details/MSNBCW_20130415_100000_Morning_Joe/start/5400/end/5460.
21 Katie Yoder, "5-Year Study: Nets Spend Fewer than 24 Minutes on March for Life," *MRC Culture*, January 17, 2018, https://www.newsbusters.org/blogs/culture/katie-yoder/2018/01/17/5-year-study-nets-spend-fewer-24-minutes-march-life; Yoder, "CBS Ignores, ABC, NBC Give under 3 Minutes to March for Life," *MRC Culture*, January 19, 2018, https://www.newsbusters.org

And yet, sometimes major newspapers did write stories featuring sympathetic pro-life people. In 2021 the *Washington Post* published an article by Casey Parks about Tere Haring, a woman who directs a San Antonio pregnancy center and believes "abortion is the lack of an option." Parks reported how Haring had handed out 45,569 diapers and $71,000 in rent assistance during the COVID-19 pandemic to pregnant women in need. Although the piece took swipes at the religious priorities of pregnancy centers and highlighted the reputation of using "dishonest tactics," Parks moved past knee-jerk criticism of pro-lifers to profile fairly Haring, a nonpolitical person who believes abortion is murder and used to be a sidewalk counselor outside abortion facilities.[22]

Some readers commenting on the story admired Haring's generosity. Others complained that her work wasn't enough and that abortion was the only real solution. Melanie L. Mason wrote, "Advertising yet another misguided anti-abortionist is a disservice to your readers. Tiresome, repetitious, and something that might be more appropriate for a church bulletin."[23]

Three days later, *Post* reporter Stephanie McCrummen profiled Aubrey Schlackman, a Dallas mother in her thirties who in 2020 had the idea to start a "'maternity ranch' . . . a place for struggling pregnant women who decide to have their babies instead of having abortions, a Christian haven where women could live stress-free during their newborn's first year of life." *Post* editors allowed McCrummen more than four thousand

---

/blogs/culture/katie-yoder/2018/01/19/cbs-ignores-abc-nbc-give-under-3-minutes-march-life. The March for Life organization calls the event "the largest annual human rights demonstration in the world." See "National March for Life," March for Life, accessed March 10, 2022, https://march forlife.org/national-march-for-life/. The March is one of the few annual marches on Washington and probably the most long-standing one: The Memorial Day weekend Rolling Thunder demonstration, organized to demand the U.S. government account for prisoners of war and soldiers missing in action, began in 1988. The annual Women's March began in 2017.

22 Casey Parks, "What Happens when People in Texas Can't Get Abortions: 'Diapers Save a Lot More Babies Than Ultrasounds,'" *The Washington Post*, November 13, 2021, https://www.washington post.com/dc-md-va/2021/11/13/san-antonio-pregnancy-center-texas-abortion-ban/.

23 Melanie L. Mason, November 15, 2021, comment on Parks, "Diapers Save," *The Washington Post*, November 13, 2021, https://www.washingtonpost.com/dc-md-va/2021/11/13/san-antonio-pregnancy-center-texas-abortion-ban/.

words to tell of Schlackman's fundraisers outside coffee shops, her belief that abortion is the "genocide of children," her modern-rustic home with a farmhouse table and an extra room for a pregnant mother, her baby showers and Bible studies for pregnant women in need, and her vision for "15 to 20 mother cottages on 60 to 100 acres" of Texas farmland.[24]

McCrummen, a history major with a master's in journalism from Columbia University, spent ten years with the *Post*, four in East Africa, before moving to long-form journalism in 2012: "I like to go deep with one person, whoever that is, or a moment." When she got the idea in 2021 of writing about the political engagement of evangelical Christians, including one story about young women who "are supportive of restricting abortion rights," her editor gave her a green light: "His reaction and his guidance was the same as it always is with any subject, which is report deeply, understand, and describe."[25]

When McCrummen came to Dallas and visited the Village Church, she heard about Schlackman, a member there. McCrummen contacted her, and they met to talk about what Schlackman was doing. Schlackman was hesitant: would the story be positive or negative? McCrummen said neither. Her goal was to make it true and thorough: "I think I told her . . . 'I think it's interesting what you're doing but I also want to understand your whole worldview and how you came to this moment and how you see the world.'"[26]

McCrummen said her own position on abortion doesn't and shouldn't matter: "People deserve to be treated fairly and people deserve to be understood and people get to be whoever they are. And my job as a reporter is to understand people."[27]

McCrummen shadowed Schlackman for two weeks—attending church, sitting in coffee shops while Schlackman worked, running

---

24 Stephanie McCrummen, "A Maternity Ranch Is Born," *The Washington Post*, November 16, 2021, https://www.washingtonpost.com/nation/2021/11/16/evangelical-women-texas-abortion/.
25 Stephanie McCrummen, interview with author, February 19, 2022.
26 McCrummen interview.
27 McCrummen interview.

errands, joining her Bible studies with pregnant moms—so she could understand and describe Schlackman's worldview: "her view on [abortion] is so much bigger than just an issue, a stand . . . it has to do with a larger worldview about how life and the universe is organized."[28]

Some *Post* readers complained on Twitter: "irresponsible journalism," or that the article "turned my stomach," or that it was "too appealing to the religious right," or it was "horrific," "really weird," and a "disaster of a story." McCrummen said she also received "the best kind of emails" from people who effectively said *I completely disagree but this story helped me understand something*, or, *Thank you for not condescending*. She noticed it was the most-read story on the website for some time, and she said that did not surprise her, given the controversy of the topic.[29]

The criticism spread to other publications: Slate writer Dahlia Lithwick called the articles "another example of what can go wrong when a publication apparently believes there are 'two sides' to human rights atrocities and rape." Amy Hagstrom Miller, CEO of the abortion provider Whole Woman's Health, told Lithwick, "As a progressive Christian abortion provider I am appalled by what these organizations are doing and how they frame Christianity, and I am stunned that the *Washington Post* would cover these organizations as if this is normal, sensible activity."[30]

28 McCrummen interview.
29 McCrummen interview; Paige Schneider (@PLSCHNEID), "Without mentioning . . ." Twitter, November 17, 2021, 12:12 a.m., https://web.archive.org/web/20220311015952/https://twitter.com/PLSCHNEID/status/1460838213732478978; Words Matter (@radseg_cs), "I couldn't even read . . ." Twitter, November 17, 2021, 11:45 a.m., https://twitter.com/radseg_cs/status/1461012692961947650; Vicki Z (@vickiwhofan), "I suggest you . . ." Twitter, November 17, 2021, 12:06 p.m., https://twitter.com/vickiwhofan/status/1461017845345701889; Maureen Flatley (@moflatley), "Talk about soft ball . . ." Twitter, November 18, 2021, 7:44 p.m., https://twitter.com/moflatley/status/1461495547496439813; Ella (@EllalovesEles), "This is horrific . . ." Twitter, November 17, 2021, 12:12 p.m., https://twitter.com/EllalovesEles/status/1461019430897340417; Moira (@moiraeve1), "I found this story . . ." Twitter, November 17, 2021, 6:50 p.m., https://twitter.com/moiraeve1/status/1461119535415808004; Henry Belanger (@henrypbelanger), "What a credulous disaster . . ." Twitter, November 18, 2021, 11:08 a.m., https://twitter.com/henrypbelanger/status/1461365719577337856.
30 Dahlia Lithwick, "The Problem with the Washington Post's Glowing Coverage of 'Maternity Ranches,'" Slate, November 17, 2021, https://slate.com/news-and-politics/2021/11/washington-post-pregnancy-center-coverage-texas.html.

44

A Sanitized Image

MANY MOVIEMAKERS, like many journalists, contributed to the abortion cause. The 1996 HBO movie *If These Walls Could Talk* featured an abortionist, played by Cher, who has to force her way into her abortion facility through a crowd while protesters shout "baby killer." Inside her office, the character removes her bulletproof vest before performing an abortion. Just as she finishes, a tall young man bursts into the room and fires six bullets into her chest. The scene ends with the crying patient cradling the abortionist's dead body as blood pools on the floor. The film won four awards and praise from *The New York Times* for its unapologetically pro-abortion stance.[1]

Nevertheless, advances in ultrasound technology, teaching in some churches, the facts about partial-birth abortion, and the end of large-scale attempts to block entrances to abortion centers contributed to a pro-life rebound in opinion polls. By December 2002, almost one-third of Americans said they had changed their minds about abortion since the early 1990s—and two times as many had grown more

---

1 *If These Walls Could Talk*, segment 3, "1996," directed by Cher, written by Marlene King and Nancy Savoca, featuring Cher, Anne Heche, and Jada Pinkett Smith, aired October 13, 1996, on HBO; Claudia Dreifus, "A Case for Abortion Rights. No Apologies," *New York Times*, October 13, 1996, section 2, 41.

negative about abortion than those who had grown more positive. Most Americans at that time said they would urge women not to abort their unborn babies.[2]

In 2004, though, the Democratic Party hardened its abortion stance: the platform committee added a section scolding Republican pro-life efforts and removed a section urging "respect" for "the individual conscience of each American on this difficult issue," referring to abortion. These decisions set the Democratic Party against a large minority of its own voters: 43 percent of Democratic voters in a January 2004 Zogby poll said "abortion destroys human life and is manslaughter."[3]

Democratic presidential candidate John Kerry failed to take the White House from incumbent George Bush in the 2004 election, and the party began to reconsider its platform. The week after Thanksgiving, Kerry advised party loyalists in a closed-door meeting to welcome more pro-life candidates into the party and to make sure voters knew Democrats didn't like abortion. The audience gasped.[4]

By early 2005 party officials were finally returning phone calls to Democrats for Life president Kristen Day. "This election was a wake-up call for a lot of people," Day said.[5] Her group drafted an initiative that Rep. Lincoln Davis (D-Tenn.) introduced on the House Floor in April. It proposed things like grants for purchasing ultrasound machines and funding for toll-free numbers in every state that would tell women where to find pregnancy help and adoption centers. The goal: to provide avenues to dissuade women from having abortions with the goal of cutting abortions by 95 percent.[6] In 2008, the Democratic party platform called for policies to "reduce the need for abortions,"

---

2 Bob Jones, "30 Years' War," *World*, January 18, 2003, 19.
3 Lynn Vincent, "Aborted Language," *World*, August 7, 2004, 22.
4 Vincent, "Climate Change," *World*, January 14, 2005, 32.
5 Vincent, "Climate Change," 33.
6 Mark Bergin, "The New Pro-Choice," *World*, May 14, 2005, 25.

and primary candidate Hillary Clinton expressed "respect" for those who opposed abortion.[7]

By 2010, a Gallup poll showed the drastic shift in public opinion after the debate over partial-birth abortions: Those who called themselves "pro-life" increased from 33 percent in 1995 to 44 percent in 2008 and 51 percent in 2009.[8] Chris Kan, twenty-eight years old in 2010, was one of those whose view had shifted. From his vantage point in the New York financial world, he had seen the "pro-choice" side as the civilized and intellectual position. All that changed when he saw a video depicting fetal development followed by an abortion and its aftermath: "mangled limbs . . . on a surgical counter," a "severed head in . . . gloved hands." In 2009, Kan trained to be a counselor at the Midtown Pregnancy Support Center near Grand Central Station.[9]

One problem for abortion advocates: Moviemakers often depicted abortion as serious and dramatic or gave examples of women changing their minds. The main character in the popular 2007 movie "Juno" decides against abortion after a pro-life sidewalk counselor tells her the baby has fingernails.[10]

Planned Parenthood assigned senior field organizer Caren Spruch, a petite woman with a "long face and dark bangs," to organize Hollywood actors for abortion advocacy. After years of attending film festivals and movie screenings and awkwardly starting conversations with celebrities, Spruch's breakthrough came in the form of *Obvious Child*, a 2014 rom-com about a young woman who gets an abortion and doesn't second-guess the decision or have any guilt.[11]

---

7   "2008 Democratic Party Platform," Democratic Party Platforms, The American Presidency Project, accessed March 3, 2022, https://www.presidency.ucsb.edu/documents/2008-democratic-party-platform; Paul Kengor, "Choice Language," *World*, November 17, 2007, 25.
8   Gallup, In Depth: Topics A to Z, "Abortion," accessed March 3, 2022, https://news.gallup.com/poll/1576/abortion.aspx.
9   Alisa Harris, "Eyewitnesses," *World*, January 30, 2010, 46.
10 Lynn Vincent, "The Plots Thicken," *World*, January 12, 2008, 59.
11 Nora Caplan-Bricker, "Planned Parenthood's Secret Weapon," *The Washington Post Magazine*, September 23, 2019, https://www.washingtonpost.com/news/magazine/wp/2019/09/23/feature/planned-parenthoods-woman-in-hollywood/.

In 2016, researchers at the University of California San Francisco (UCSF) counted thirteen abortion plotlines in American TV shows.[12] The Democratic National Convention that year went more liberal than ever on abortion by calling for the repeal of the Hyde Amendment, the once-bipartisan budget rider that since 1976 had kept taxpayer money from directly funding abortion.[13]

By 2019, the number of abortion plotlines had ballooned to forty-three shows—"more than we've ever observed in a single year," wrote UCSF researchers—and three movies. Not all depicted abortion favorably: the UCSF report that year bemoaned that none of the characters who obtain abortion pills online have complete abortions, and one character on NBC's *Law and Order: SVU* tells a pregnant rape survivor her baby is "innocent" and "deserves to be loved." "[A]nother incidence of . . . providing shaming morality tales," wrote the researchers.[14]

But other plots fit better in the abortion advocacy narrative. The 2019 report noted "a continuing trend of plotlines that address the predatory practices of [pro-life pregnancy centers]" as characters seeking abortions end up at the centers, where staff try to convince them to keep their babies. The report also praised episodes in Netflix's *13 Reasons Why*, HBO's *Euphoria*, and Hulu's *Shrill* that depict abortions as opportunities for a character to "prioritize her well-being."[15] "We've seen pop culture change views around LGBTQ issues, for example, and

---

12 "Abortion Onscreen in 2016," Advancing New Standards in Reproductive Health, accessed March 3, 2022, https://www.ansirh.org/sites/default/files/publications/files/abortion_onscreen_in_2016_0.pdf.
13 Molly Redden, "Clinton Leads Way on Abortion Rights as Democrats Seek End to Decades-Old Rule," *The Guardian*, July 26, 2016, https://www.theguardian.com/us-news/2016/jul/26/abortion-rights-clinton-hyde-amendment-federal-funds.
14 "Abortion Onscreen in 2019," Abortion Onscreen, Advancing New Standards in Reproductive Health, accessed March 3, 2022, https://www.ansirh.org/sites/default/files/publications/files/Abortion%20Onscreen%20Report%202019.pdf; "Abortion Onscreen in 2020," Abortion Onscreen, Advancing New Standards in Reproductive Health, accessed March 3, 2022, https://www.ansirh.org/sites/default/files/field/page-files/abortiononscreenreport2020final.pdf.
15 "Abortion Onscreen in 2019."

pop culture has the power to challenge abortion stigma, too," Planned Parenthood's Melanie Roussel Newman said.[16]

Donald Trump's presidential administration took executive actions that pro-lifers praised—especially his Supreme Court appointments that would later prove crucial in overturning *Roe*. But some regretted his association with the pro-life movement because of his polarizing personality and degrading comments toward women. Weeseetsa Maeding, a staff member at a Sacramento, California, pregnancy center, said, "We get lumped in with Donald Trump, and I don't know if that is going to have a positive, long-lasting effect for people who are going to outlast Donald Trump for fighting for the pro-life movement."[17]

As Trump entered his last year in office, NBC's *The Blacklist* aired an episode premised on a common pro-abortion trope often attributed to feminist Gloria Steinem: "If men could get pregnant, abortion would be a sacrament." In the episode, a female doctor kidnaps male pro-life politicians and transplants impregnated uteruses into them. She then keeps them captive until it's too late for them to get abortions. One governor she kidnaps violates a pro-life law he wrote in his attempt to get an abortion. It's payback for the doctor's own experience: she was raped and then thrown in jail for attempting to get an abortion past her state's legal limit. She gave birth to a daughter in jail.[18]

Despite the stereotype, polling shows the abortion issue isn't a man versus woman struggle: a 2021 Pew Research Center survey found that, although women have been trending more favorable to abortion, the statistical difference is still small, with 35 percent of women and 41 percent of men agreeing that abortion should be illegal in all or

---

16 Caplan-Bricker, "Planned Parenthood's Secret Weapon."
17 Weeseetsa Maeding, interview with author, June 30, 2020. See also Leah Savas, "Calling on a Fighter to Fight," *World*, October 10, 2020, 52–57.
18 "Abortion Onscreen in 2019." According to Steinem's 1983 memoir, she first heard the trope from a taxi driver in Boston. Information from "If Men Could Get Pregnant, Abortion Would Be a Sacrament," Quote Investigator, accessed March 25, 2022, https://quoteinvestigator.com/2013/09/11/men-pregnant/.

most cases.[19] A 2021 Gallup poll also showed 50 percent of men and 43 percent of women calling themselves "pro-life."[20] Women leaders also head up many of the nation's pro-life organizations, including the Susan B. Anthony List, Americans United for Life, and numerous pregnancy centers.

In 2020, thirty-one television shows and thirteen feature films included abortion as a central plot device. In 2021, the year the Supreme Court agreed to reconsider a central holding of *Roe* in the *Dobbs v. Jackson Women's Health* case, forty-two television shows had abortion plotlines. "Abortion access in the United States is at a critical point, with the Supreme Court poised to erode the right to abortion rooted in *Roe v. Wade*," wrote the UCSF researchers in that year's report. "Yet, even as legal precedents precariously stand and state legislatures subversively undermine access, our ability to tell stories remains unhindered."[21]

Some polls showed the abortion advocacy camp gaining support: The month after oral arguments in the *Dobbs* case, a CNN poll found 69 percent of Americans opposed overturning *Roe v. Wade* while 30 percent supported the idea. But other studies suggested public opinion on abortion was more nuanced. A 2021 AP-NORC poll surveyed 1,125 Americans and found support for abortion varied depending on stage of pregnancy. Sixty-one percent supported legal abortion in the first trimester but only 34 percent supported legal abortion in all or most cases in the second trimester.[22]

---

19 "Public Opinion on Abortion," Fact Sheet, Pew Research Center, posted May 17, 2022, https://www.pewforum.org/fact-sheet/public-opinion-on-abortion/.
20 "'Pro-Choice' or 'Pro-Life,' 2018–2021 Demographic Tables," Politics, Gallup News, accessed March 25, 2022, https://news.gallup.com/poll/244709/pro-choice-pro-life-2018-demographic-tables.aspx.
21 Caplan-Bricker, "Planned Parenthood's Secret Weapon"; "Abortion Onscreen in 2020"; "Abortion Onscreen in 2021," Abortion Onscreen, Advancing New Standards in Reproductive Health, accessed March 3, 2022, https://www.ansirh.org/sites/default/files/2021-12/Abortion%20Onscreen%202021.pdf.
22 Ariel Edwards-Levy, "CNN Poll: As Supreme Court Ruling on Roe Looms, Most Americans Oppose Overturning It," *CNN*, January 21, 2022, https://www.cnn.com/2022/01/21/politics/cnn-poll-abortion-roe-v-wade/index.html; "Public Holds Nuanced Views about Access to Legal

"There has never been majority support for what *Roe v. Wade* and *Doe v. Bolton* actually did," David O'Steen, executive director of the National Right to Life Committee, said about polling results: Most people don't realize that *Doe*'s broad health exception allows for abortion up to birth in cases where keeping a baby alive could cause emotional and familial stress. "You want to find out how people feel relative to what they're going to hear from the press or the other side," O'Steen said. "But you also want to find out how they're going to feel if the question is framed absolutely accurately."[23]

Polls initiated by National Right to Life sometimes include starker questions that make people think. Survey results released by the Knights of Columbus in 2019 showed 59 percent of respondents supported a "ban on abortion after 20 weeks, except to save the life of the mother." O'Steen said a later poll conducted on behalf of National Right to Life, in November 2020, found 71 percent of respondents strongly or somewhat supported such laws when the question pointed out that unborn babies can feel pain at about twenty weeks of gestation.[24]

"We try to stick very closely to how is the public hearing about this issue from leaders, from the news media," said Lydia Saad, director of U.S. social research at Gallup. "We're trying to understand, how do Americans feel just sitting out there in their homes on this issue without being given any additional information than what they have or they're hearing on the news?"[25]

But to O'Steen, that's just the problem: Many Americans don't know crucial information that could help them see the problems with

---

Abortion," AP-NORC Center for Public Affairs Research, June 24, 2021, https://apnorc.org/projects/public-holds-nuanced-views-about-access-to-legal-abortion/.

23 David O'Steen, interview with author, June 30, 2021.
24 O'Steen interview; NRLC Press Secretary Laura Echevarria, emails to author, July 2, 2021; "Marist Poll Finds 3 in 4 Americans Support Substantial Abortion Restrictions," KofC-Marist Polls, Knights of Columbus, posted January 15, 2019, https://web.archive.org/web/20190122232233/https://www.kofc.org/en/news/polls/abortion-restrictions-supported.html.
25 Lydia Saad, interview with author, June 30, 2021.

supporting legal abortion, and they won't get it from mainstream culture. As soothing pictures on some Planned Parenthood walls distract attention from the violence unborn babies experience, so Hollywood influence sanitizes the image of abortion on television screens.[26]

---

26 O'Steen interview.

45

Aborting Alone

LAWRENCE LADER'S proudest moment came when the *Roe v. Wade* decision cited his book eight times. But Lader always pushed for more. After his big *Roe* triumph he founded a new organization, the Abortion Rights Mobilization, which became his vehicle to sue the Catholic Church and orchestrate a campaign to bring RU-486 abortion pills to the United States.[1]

In the 2000s, the success of that campaign began to return America to a version of what abortion was like two centuries before, when abortion by ingesting a substance was more common than surgical abortion. Lader's success also changed the life of Leslie Wolbert, who in 2005 was in her twenties and suspected she might be pregnant. She didn't have a doctor, so she went to Planned Parenthood. In her mind it was a safe place, where "women go for womanly services." Wolbert told the counselor she opposed surgical abortions because she knew that surgically aborting unborn babies was murder.[2]

The Planned Parenthood counselor told Wolbert she could take a pill. Wolbert thought the pill was like the morning-after pill or Plan B, which she had used before: "I just thought it made you get your period, and if

---

1 *Los Angeles Times*, May 14, 2006, B14.
2 Leslie Wolbert, interview with author, May 6, 2021.

you have your period, you can't be pregnant." She assumed this pill was similar, "a thing that isn't an abortion." She took the first pill at Planned Parenthood. They sent her home with instructions to take another set of pills, which they sent home with her in a little brown paper bag.[3]

The counselor warned Wolbert she would experience cramping and bleeding, like a heavy period. But the reality was much worse. Hours after she took the second set of pills, "It came on violently." Wolbert sat on the toilet, vomiting and passing diarrhea at the same time. Alarmed, she called Planned Parenthood. As she recalls, the staff person on the phone reassured her that her symptoms were normal but that if they worsened she should go to the ER.[4]

Later, in the shower, Wolbert passed a mass of blood that clogged the drain. Not knowing what else to do, and suspecting it was her baby, she picked up the mass and flushed it down the toilet.

Unlike many stories of chemical abortions from colonial days, Wolbert's abortion story ended with one death instead of two. Centuries of abortion practice had mostly eliminated danger to the mother. But no amount of specialization could spare Wolbert from the emotional and mental turmoil she experienced during and after the abortion. Horrible images from those agonizing hours stuck with her.

Wolbert became a Christian, married, and, after two miscarriages, gave birth to a baby boy. His birth brought back "with a vengeance" guilt over her abortion and fear that she might hurt her son: "I was afraid, like something inside of me kept saying, 'You're going to go stab your baby.' And I didn't want to . . . but there was always this memory of, 'Of course you would, you killed your first baby. Why wouldn't you kill this next baby?'"[5]

Years later, after counseling had helped Wolbert heal from the abortion, she testified by video in favor of a law the Montana House of

---

3 Wolbert interview.
4 Wolbert interview.
5 Wolbert interview.

Representatives was considering to regulate distribution of the abortion pill. Wolbert gave emotional testimony about her abortion pill experience: "The home where all this took place that was once a refuge for me became a murder scene. . . . What I felt, saw, and touched that day can never be removed from my memory."[6]

Wolbert's abortion in 2005 came just five years after the U.S. Food and Drug Administration (FDA) gave its stamp of approval to RU-486 (also known as mifepristone, the first pill in the two-drug regimen with misoprostol).[7] Although the FDA considered medical abortion safe for women, problems appeared soon after approval.

In 2002, the mifepristone's distributor, Danco Laboratories, issued a letter informing doctors that six women had become seriously ill after taking mifepristone and two had died, one from a ruptured ectopic pregnancy that had been masked by the abortion pill, and another from a bacterial infection that developed after taking the drug.[8]

In 2003, cemetery workers in San Francisco, California, buried eighteen-year-old Holly Marie Patterson, another abortion pill victim. Seven days after taking mifepristone, the blonde high school graduate and Macy's employee died from septic shock resulting from an incomplete abortion. A friend said Patterson and her boyfriend had researched the pill on the internet: "They were told no one in the country had died of this. But we later found out that's not true."[9]

By December 2021 the official toll of adult female deaths associated with mifepristone was twenty-six. The FDA had reports of 4,207

---

6 See also Leah Savas, "Pro-Lifers Fight to Protect Women from Dangerous Drugs," *World*, May 10, 2021, https://wng.org/roundups/pro-lifers-fight-to-protect-women-from-dangerous-drugs-1620677758.
7 Mifepristone blocks the effects of the hormone progesterone, essentially cutting off nutrients to the unborn baby. The second drug, misoprostol, induces contractions that expel the dead baby from the mother's body.
8 "Killer Pills?" *World*, May 4, 2002, 7.
9 Lynn Vincent, "Legal, but Not Safe," *World*, October 4, 2003, 37–38. "Teen Dead after Abortion Pill," *The Washington Times*, September 22, 2003, https://www.washingtontimes.com/news/2003/sep/22/20030922-105418-2823r/.

adverse events for mothers. It estimated 4.9 million women had taken mifepristone since its approval in 2000.[10]

Some pro-lifers were skeptical about those numbers. Since 2018, U.S. women have been able to buy abortion pills online from the European website Aid Access. That group and other international sources are unlikely to report to a U.S. government agency the number of abortion pills sold. Aid Access and the FDA have a rocky relationship: In 2019 the FDA ordered Aid Access to cease selling abortion pills to U.S. women. Lack of reporting from Aid Access and similar groups disguises the abortion pill's true number of unborn victims.[11]

Aid Access also gives customers advice that could be obscuring the number of adult victims. The website tells women who end up in the ER, "You do not have to tell the medical staff that you tried to induce an abortion; you can tell them that you had a spontaneous miscarriage. ... The symptoms of a miscarriage and an abortion with pills are exactly the same and the doctor will not be able to see or test for any evidence of an abortion, as long as the pills have completely dissolved." Other abortion websites give the same advice.[12]

[10] "Questions and Answers on Mifeprex," Food and Drug Administration, last modified December 16, 2021, https://www.fda.gov/drugs/postmarket-drug-safety-information-patients-and-providers/questions-and-answers-mifeprex; "Mifepristone U.S. Post-Marketing Adverse Events Summary through 06/30/2021," Food and Drug Administration, accessed February 25, 2022, https://www.fda.gov/media/154941/download. The FDA reported that some of those deaths were homicides, suicides, or drug overdoses, but it acknowledged other causes of death commonly linked to chemical abortion, including sepsis from a bacterial infection, hemorrhage, and ruptured ectopic pregnancies. The FDA report notes that seven of the eight women who died from sepsis took the second drug, misoprostol, vaginally. That is also the method that Holly Patterson reportedly used during her chemical abortion and is considered off-label usage. At the time, the FDA recommended taking the drug orally. Today, both the FDA and Danco recommend taking it buccally, letting it dissolve inside the mouth. See "How to Take Mifeprex," Danco, accessed February 25, 2022, https://www.earlyoptionpill.com/what-can-i-expect/how-to-take-mifeprex/.

[11] "Warning Letter: Aidaccess.org," Food and Drug Administration, last modified March 12, 2019, https://www.fda.gov/inspections-compliance-enforcement-and-criminal-investigations/warning-letters/aidaccessorg-575658-03082019.

[12] "How Do You Know If You Have Complications and What Should You Do?" AidAccess, accessed February 25, 2022, https://aidaccess.org/en/page/459/how-do-you-know-if-you-have

Some women are following that advice. In 2021 the Charlotte Lozier Institute analyzed Medicaid data from 1999–2015, tracking the emergency room visits of women within thirty days of their chemical abortions. Lozier found that ER staff miscoded abortion-related complications as miscarriages more than half of the time in 2015.[13]

In 2016 the FDA stopped requiring abortion facilities to report complications associated with mifepristone, except those resulting in death.[14] Four years later, the administration removed all requirements for in-person visits to get the abortion pill.[15] That opened the floodgates to mail-order abortion businesses and furthered the patient-provider gap. One online abortion pill provider in 2022 said half of her patients didn't respond to follow-up calls, texts, or emails, although she called the follow-up rate "pretty high compared to what I remember in clinics."[16]

The psychological and emotional effects of abortion on women are just as difficult to track. In 2012, researchers from the University of California San Francisco's Bixby Center rushed out preliminary findings from the Turnaway Study, a survey of women who have abortions compared to those denied abortions: "One week after receiving or being denied an abortion, women denied an abortion had significantly higher

---

-complications-and-what-should-you-do. See also "The Plan C Guide to Abortion Pills," Plan C, accessed February 25, 2022, https://www.plancpills.org/guide-how-to-get-abortion-pills.

13 The study also found that the rate of Medicaid patients ending up in the ER within thirty days of a chemical abortion increased 507 percent from 2002 to 2015, much higher than the increase for surgical abortions. Compared with surgical abortions, the risk of a chemical abortion patient needing to go to the ER for specifically abortion-related reasons was 53 percent higher. See James Studnicki et al., "A Longitudinal Cohort Study of Emergency Room Utilization Following Mifepristone Chemical and Surgical Abortions, 1999–2015," *Health Services Research and Managerial Epidemiology* 8 (November 2021): 4, https://doi.org/10.1177/23333928211053965.

14 Mifeprex Clinical Review, Medical Reviews, Center for Drug Evaluation and Research, Reference ID 3909590, March 29, 2016, https://www.accessdata.fda.gov/drugsatfda_docs/nda/2016/0206 87Orig1s020MedR.pdf, 49.

15 Tessa Longbons, "Analysis: FDA Decision Ignores Data on Complications, Puts Women at Risk," Charlotte Lozier Institute, December 16, 2021, https://lozierinstitute.org/analysis-fda-decision-ignores-data-on-complications-puts-women-at-risk/.

16 Carrie N. Baker, "Online Abortion Provider Julie Amaon of Just the Pill Is 'Making Abortion as Easy as Possible for People,'" *Ms.* magazine, January 26, 2022, https://msmagazine.com/2022/01/26/online-abortion-provider-julie-amaon-just-the-pill/.

anxiety than women who received the abortion. . . . [R]eceiving an abortion does not increase the incidence of mental health disorders compared to having an unwanted birth."[17]

Data from the study turned up in more than fifty scientific, peer-reviewed journal articles, each championing results amplified by the press. *The Washington Post* headlined further results in 2015: "95 percent of women who've had an abortion say it was the right decision." In 2016 a *New York Times* headline about another study read, "Abortion Is Found to Have Little Effect on Women's Mental Health."[18]

Some women who have had abortions expressed skepticism about the claims. "Ask in five more [years] and see where they stand," said ProLove Ministries director Pamela Whitehead in 2020, referring to the findings of another journal article about the Turnaway Study released that year, which said women feel more relief than regret in the years after their abortions.[19]

Whitehead had an abortion in 2001, just days before the 9/11 terrorist attack. In the following years, she attempted suicide, became addicted to drugs, and lived in a homosexual relationship even though she wasn't a lesbian. It wasn't until 2011 that Whitehead realized her abortion had been the "precipitating factor" of her self-destructive decisions: "I could trace it back to that event."[20]

17 "Mental Health and Physical Health Consequences of Abortion compared to Unwanted Birth," APHA Meetings: Online Program, American Public Health Association, accessed February 25, 2022, https://web.archive.org/web/20150605033351/https://apha.confex.com/apha/140am/webprogram/Paper263888.html. Research assistants in the Turnaway Study conducted phone interviews with about a thousand women who had sought abortions in twenty-one different states between 2008 and 2010, following up a week after seeking an abortion and then twice a year for five years.

18 David C. Reardon, "The Embrace of the Proabortion Turnaway Study: Wishful Thinking? or Willful Deceptions?" *The Linacre Quarterly* 85, no. 3 (August 2018): 204–5, https://dx.doi.org/10.1177%2F0024363918782156.

19 Pamela Whitehead, interview with author, January 15, 2020. See Corrine H. Rocca, "Emotions and Decision Rightness over Five Years following an Abortion: An Examination of Decision Difficulty and Abortion Stigma," *Social Science and Medicine* 248 (March 2020), https://doi.org/10.1016/j.socscimed.2019.112704.

20 Whitehead interview.

Few academics are interested in tracing those connections because it's an academic dead end. David Fergusson, an atheist and abortion advocate, researched the experience of young New Zealand women between ages fifteen and twenty-five. He hoped to prove that abortion had no negative mental health consequences. The results showed the opposite: those who had aborted a child had higher rates of mental health issues following the abortion than those who did not. Fergusson submitted his research for publication anyway. Four journals rejected him, which Fergusson said was unusual: "[W]e normally get accepted the first time." The New Zealand government's Abortion Supervisory Committee even asked him to withhold the results. The study eventually ran in the *Journal of Child Psychiatry and Psychology.*[21]

Despite the pro-abortion tilt of research funders and scientific journals, researcher David C. Reardon reviewed the literature on abortion and mental health and found "the consensus of expert opinion" is that "the abortion experience can directly contribute to mental health problems in some women," although preexisting mental health problems can also have a role, and no study can definitively determine the exact effect an abortion had on a specific mental health issue.[22]

As for the much-publicized Turnaway Study, Reardon said, the data was "meaningless" because more than 70 percent of women asked to participate said no, and half of those who did participate dropped out.[23]

---

21 David C. Reardon, "The Abortion and Mental Health Controversy: A Comprehensive Literature Review of Common Ground Agreements, Disagreements, Actionable Recommendations, and Research Opportunities," *SAGE Open Medicine* 6 (October 2018): 9–10, https://dx.doi.org/10.1177%2F2050312118807624; Ruth Hill, "Abortion Researcher Confounded by Study," *New Zealand Herald*, January 4, 2006, https://www.nzherald.co.nz/nz/abortion-researcher-confounded-by-study/3FYSQTNVHDEWTOTS4HKSEYG6GA/. Fergusson said, "The aim of our research was never political. . . . It was to say, 'The science in this area is not good. Let's add to it.'" (David M. Fergusson, "Abortion in Young Women and Subsequent Mental Health," *Journal of Child Psychology and Psychiatry* 47, no. 1 (September 2005): 16–24, https://doi.org/10.1111/j.1469-7610.2005.01538.x).
22 Reardon, "Abortion and Mental Health Controversy," 6, 8.
23 Reardon, "Abortion and Mental Health Controversy," 18–19.

Some pro-abortion activists link the negative mental health effects among women like Leslie Wolbert to negative stigma around abortion. In 2015, thirty-year-old Amelia Bonow's 153-word post about her own positive abortion experience went viral on social media: "Plenty of people still believe that on some level—if you are a good woman—abortion is a choice which should be accompanied by some level of sadness, shame, or regret. But you know what? I have a good heart and having an abortion made me happy in a totally unqualified way. Why wouldn't I be happy that I was not forced to become a mother?" That post spawned a #shoutyourabortion hashtag that appeared on social media more than a quarter million times in less than two months as many used it to celebrate their own abortions.[24]

Other organizations formed to fight abortion stigma. We Testify began training and supporting abortion storytellers to talk about their abortions so as to shift "the culture around abortion experiences." One such storyteller, Lexis Dotson-Dufault, stood in front of a microphone with balloons behind her and explained how her 2016 abortion changed her life. Yes, she felt some emotional turmoil after her abortion, but the abortion allowed her to live out her hopes and dreams, she said, and renewed her physical body.[25]

We Testify and Shout Your Abortion advocate using the word "abortion" in positive ways, but other groups have resorted to euphemisms.

[24] Lindy West (@thelindywest), "'The campaign to defund PP 'relies on the assumption that abortion is to be whispered about.' #ShoutYourAbortion," Twitter, September 19, 2015, 3:46 p.m., http://web.archive.org/web/20160402131119/https://twitter.com/thelindywest/status/645368432666374144?ref_src=twsrc%5Etfw; Caitlin Gibson, "How #ShoutYourAbortion Is Transforming the Reproductive Rights Conversation," *The Washington Post*, November 15, 2015, https://www.washingtonpost.com/lifestyle/style/how-shoutyourabortion-is-transforming-the-reproductive-rights-conversation/2015/11/13/aa64e68a-895f-11e5-9a07-453018f9a0ec_story.html.

[25] Dotson-Dufault spoke at an August 2021 event hosted by several pro-abortion groups in Charlotte, North Carolina. Watch it at Charlotte Reproductive Action Network, "My Abortion Story—Live Now!" Facebook video, August 10, 2021, https://www.facebook.com/charlottereproactionnetwork/videos/4357884647603429. See also "Announcing We Testify: Our Abortion Stories," News, National Network of Abortion Funds, posted August 1, 2016, https://sandbox.abortionfunds.org/announcing-we-testify/.

One favorite: "missed period pills." In 2020, researcher Wendy Sheldon found that 42 percent of all respondents, and 70 percent of the women who said they wouldn't be happy to know they were pregnant, expressed interest in missed period pills, abortive drugs to take before having a pregnancy test. (The official description: "uterine evacuation medications used for treatment of delayed menses without prior pregnancy confirmation.") Those taking the pill would never know whether they had aborted their children.[26]

Also in 2020, abortion provider Carafem advertised a "missed period pill" study and solicited women: "If you don't want to be pregnant, you may be eligible to use an early option to bring back your period with pills"—namely, mifepristone and misoprostol, and in the same doses as in the standard chemical abortion method.[27] In 2021 the University of California San Francisco started another missed period pill study, this time using only misoprostol.[28]

Does removing stigma solve the problem? Some women who posted their abortion stories on the Shout Your Abortion website said they were confident in their decisions but grieved the loss of children.[29] In August 2021, one woman wrote that believing she made the right decision "doesn't make it any easier. I grieve every day for my little one . . ."[30]

---

[26] Wendy R. Sheldon et al., "Exploring Potential Interest in Missed Period Pills in Two US States," *Contraception* 102, no. 6 (December 2020): 414–20, https://doi.org/10.1016/j.contraception.2020.08.014.

[27] "Missed Period Pill Study," Carafem, accessed March 7, 2021, https://web.archive.org/web/20210307000038/https://carafem.org/missed-period/; "Assessing Medical Menstrual Regulation in the United States," ClinicalTrials.gov, last modified March 24, 2021, https://clinicaltrials.gov/ct2/show/NCT03972358.

[28] "Missed Period Pill Study," Menstrual Regulation Studies, UCSF Clinical Trials, last modified October 26, 2021, https://clinicaltrials.ucsf.edu/trial/NCT04940013.

[29] "I Had Never Thought Twice about Having Children," Written Stories, Shout Your Abortion, last modified July 19, 2021, https://shoutyourabortion.com/writing/i-had-never-thought-twice-about-having-children/.

[30] "My Little Sesame Seed," Written Stories, Shout Your Abortion, last modified August 24, 2021, https://shoutyourabortion.com/writing/my-little-sesame-seed/.

46

Incremental vs. Radical

JANET FOLGER PORTER for two decades combined pro-life failures and small victories. She worked on a ballot initiative in South Dakota that failed twice. She testified on behalf of personhood bills that failed in committee. As Ohio Right to Life's legislative director in the 1980s and '90s, she helped pass informed consent and parental consent laws, laws to defund abortion, laws to regulate abortion, and a law banning partial-birth abortion.[1]

But those achievements seemed meaningless in 2010 when she found herself standing by the casket of Mark Lally, her former boss from Ohio Right to Life, and thinking he "worked his entire life to end abortion but never got to see it." She felt tired of standard bills that regulated abortion but didn't save many babies. At the wake, she found some pro-life friends and threw at them a radical idea: a bill to protect babies from abortions once they had heartbeats.[2]

At a hotel press conference across the street from the Ohio Statehouse just after Valentine's Day 2011, Porter announced the "Heartbeat Bill." Behind and in front of the podium were hundreds of red heart-shaped balloons that supporters later delivered to the state representatives in

---

1 Janet Folger Porter, *A Heartbeat Away* (Shippensburg, PA: Destiny Image, 2020), 29–30, Kindle.
2 Porter, *Heartbeat Away*, 29–30, 32.

their offices. The Ohio House of Representatives passed the bill easily but for five years the Ohio Senate blocked it. Porter blamed Republican lawmakers and other pro-life groups: "Suddenly, I was on the outside of the establishment and the outside of political favor that comes with asking those who represent us to merely manage abortion."[3]

The Ohio experience shows what Porter meant by "merely manage." The incremental approach had some success: Between 2011 and 2015 seven of the state's sixteen abortion businesses either closed or stopped providing surgical abortions.[4] The abortion rate also dropped from about eleven abortions for every one thousand women in 2011 to roughly nine in 2015.[5] But state officials and courts often refused to enforce regulations on abortion facilities, such as one in existence since the 1990s that requires every abortion center in case of emergency to have a written patient transfer agreement with a local hospital.

Ohio Department of Health actions to enforce that requirement did lead to the closure of Toledo's Center for Choice. A 2013 inspection showed the center had rusty and moldy equipment, expired medicine, blank prescription forms already signed by a physician—and no local hospital was willing to sign a transfer agreement.[6] Enforcing that requirement, after two years of administrative hassling, also stopped surgical abortions at a center near Cincinnati run by late-term abortionist Martin Haskell. He later closed the facility altogether.[7]

---

3 Porter, *Heartbeat Away*, 31, 33, 123–27.
4 Julie Carr Smyth, "Ohio Clinics Close, Abortions Decline amid Restrictions," Associated Press, May 3, 2015, https://apnews.com/article/369c2391530e41a8b351961edcdadf48.
5 John Paulson and Donna L. Smith, *Induced Abortions in Ohio* (Ohio Department of Health Statistical Analysis Unit Bureau of Vital Statistics, September 2021), 5.
6 For more on the closure of the Toledo Center for Choice, see Catherine Candisky, "Restrictions Forcing a Few Abortion Clinics to Close," *The Columbus Dispatch*, July 28, 2013, https://www.dispatch.com/story/lifestyle/health-fitness/2013/07/28/restrictions-forcing-few-abortion-clinics/23506645007/. See also Tom Troy and Kelly McLendon, "Center for Choice Closes after UT Dropped Pact," *The Toledo Blade*, June 11, 2013, https://www.toledoblade.com/State/2013/06/11/Kasich-won-t-say-if-he-d-veto-law-prohibiting-hospitals-from-engaging-in-transfer-agreements.html.
7 In his decision to revoke the Cincinnati-area facility's license, Ohio Department of Health Director Theodore Wymsyslo pointed to the facility's failure to request permission to add two doctors as their

But Haskell's Women's Med Center in Dayton maintained a long-running fight against the Ohio regulations. The state health department denied a transfer waiver in 2015 and moved to revoke the facility's license, which would have forced it to close—but years of court battles ensued. Summary of the back-and-forth: lawsuit, Ohio Supreme Court refuses to review the case, a loophole recommended by a pro-abortion Ohio Department of Health director in 2019 leads to a new license, a later director rejects another request for a transfer waiver, a judge bans enforcement. In mid-2022 the Women's Med Center was still open and offering surgical abortions.[8]

In Toledo, Capital Care Network also went to great lengths to circumvent Ohio regulations. In 2013 the University of Toledo president announced that his hospital system wouldn't renew its expiring transfer agreement with Capital Care Network, saying he wanted the school to remain neutral on the abortion issue. But Capital Care Network continued operating without a transfer agreement for five months and failed to seek a waiver of the requirement. It finally found a hospital partner 52 miles away: the University of Michigan Health System in Ann Arbor. But a 2013 law that codified the transfer

---

replacement for a transfer agreement as the main reason. He said those doctors had "credentialing and disciplinary issues" that "could have directly affected the ability to have back-up physicians available, without interruption, to admit patients in order to provide for the timely and effective continuity of care in the event of an emergency." See Cliff Peale, "State Orders Abortion Clinic to Close," *The Cincinnati Enquirer*, January 21, 2014, https://www.cincinnati.com/story/news/2014/01/21/sharonville-abortion-provider-one-step-closer-to-closing/4713611/. The Cincinnati-area building was for sale by October 2014 and, according to online listings, was vacant and still on the market by mid-2022. See Cheryl Sullenger, "Symbol of Victory: Haskell's Sharonville Abortion Building for Sale," Operation Rescue, October 7, 2014, https://www.operationrescue.org/archives/symbol-of-victory-haskells-sharonville-abortion-building-for-sale/; "11250 Lebanon Rd," LoopNet, accessed May 30, 2022, https://www.loopnet.com/Listing/11250-Lebanon-Rd-Cincinnati-OH/3683606/.

8 For a timeline of events and related official documentation about the Dayton facility, see "The Timeline," Wright State Abortion Connection, accessed March 23, 2022, https://www.wrightstateabortion.com/. For 2022 developments, see Laura Hancock, "Ohio Judge Temporarily Blocks Enforcement of Bill That Could Shutter Southwest Ohio Abortion Clinics," Cleveland.com, March 2, 2022, https://www.cleveland.com/news/2022/03/ohio-judge-temporarily-blocks-enforcement-of-bill-that-could-shutter-southwest-ohio-abortion-clinics.html.

agreement regulation into state law had stipulated the hospital must be local. So in 2014, the Ohio Department of Health decided 52 miles away wasn't "local" and revoked the facility's license.[9]

The abortion business appealed to the Lucas County Common Pleas Court, which found in its favor. When the state appealed to the Court of Appeals of Ohio, that court also ruled in favor of the abortion business. But the Ohio Supreme Court in January 2018 sided with the department of health and reversed the lower court ruling, forcing the abortion facility to stop performing surgical abortions.[10]

But in February 2018 the facility finally found a Toledo hospital willing to enter into a transfer agreement and received a new license. It then resumed surgical abortions until the facility changed owners in 2019, changed its name to Capital Care of Toledo, voluntarily relinquished its surgical license, and began providing chemical abortions only. In 2022, its owner and name changed again, this time to the Toledo Women's Center. It wasn't clear if the new owner would reapply for a surgical license.[11]

9 For more about the University of Toledo decision, see "Ohio Notifies Local Abortion Clinic License Could Be Revoked without a Hospital Transfer Agreement," *The Toledo Blade*, April 30, 2013, https://www.toledoblade.com/Medical/2013/04/30/Ohio-notifies-local-abortion-clinic-license-could-be-revoked-without-a-hospital-transfer-agreement.html; Jackie Borchardt, "Ohio Supreme Court Upholds State Order to Shut Down Toledo Abortion Clinic," Cleveland.com, February 6, 2018, https://www.cleveland.com/metro/2018/02/ohio_supreme_court_upholds_sta.html.

10 Robert Higgs, "Ohio Abortion Restrictions Unconstitutional, State Appellate Court Rules," Cleveland.com, July 26, 2016, https://www.cleveland.com/open/2016/07/ohio_abortion_restrictions_unc.html; *Capital Care Network of Toledo v. Dept. of Health*, 153 Ohio St. 3d 362, 2018-Ohio-440, https://www.supremecourt.ohio.gov/rod/docs/pdf/0/2018/2018-Ohio-440.pdf.

11 See "ProMedica Signs Agreement to Keep Toledo's Last Abortion Clinic Open," WTOL, February 13, 2018, https://www.wtol.com/article/news/promedica-signs-agreement-to-keep-toledos-last-abortion-clinic-open/512-703581e8-378f-443f-8933-c59fde9779af; Sabrina Eaton, "Surgical Abortions to Resume at Toledo Clinic Following Health Department Licensure," Cleveland.com, May 16, 2018, https://www.cleveland.com/metro/2018/05/surgical_abortions_to_resume_a.html; Laura Hancock, "Toledo Abortion Clinic Capital Care Network Changes Owners, Halts Surgical Abortions," Cleveland.com, September 18, 2019, https://www.cleveland.com/politics/2019/09/toledo-abortion-clinic-capital-care-network-changes-owners-halts-surgical-abortions.html; Ellie Buerk, "Toledo Abortion Clinic Fights for Compensation after Winning Anti-Abortion Legal Battle," *The Toledo Blade*, February 14, 2022, https://www.toledoblade.com/local/city/2022/02

Ed Sitter, director of Greater Toledo Right to Life, complained about the process: "Our concerns are why the laws aren't being enforced. . . . Administrations come and go every four, eight years. Directors of the Ohio Department of Health are appointed by the governor. They come and go." Unless something egregious makes headlines, Sitter said, it's nearly impossible to "make sweeping reform because there's too many layers."[12]

Ohio wasn't the only state having trouble with enforcement. By 2010 Pennsylvania had enacted a host of pro-life laws including required pre-abortion counseling, a twenty-four-hour waiting period, parental consent for minors seeking abortions, and a prohibition on abortions after twenty-four weeks. The law required abortion facilities to have at least one doctor certified by the American Board of Obstetrics and Gynecology and to have "ready for use" equipment and drugs needed for emergency resuscitation of patients. State law also required abortion facilities to have hallways, doors, and elevators wide enough to carry a patient through on a stretcher to a street-level exit.[13]

Detectives and FBI agents inadvertently found a Philadelphia abortion facility breaking all of those laws. The months-long investigation of the Women's Medical Society on Lancaster Avenue, run by the notorious Kermit Gosnell, started as a drug case. Evidence pointed to the facility as the source for illegal OxyContin prescriptions. Further digging uncovered reports of unsanitary conditions and a woman's death in 2009. The investigation culminated in a February 2010 raid.[14]

Officers who entered the facility were shocked by what they saw and smelled. A grand jury report released several months later noted bloody

---

/14/toledo-abortion-clinic-fights-for-compensation-after-winning-anti-abortion-legal-battle/stories/20220208110.

12 Ed Sitter, interview with author, February 10, 2022.

13 R. Seth Williams, *Report of the Grand Jury*, County Investigating Grand Jury XXIII (Misc. No. 0009901-2008), Court of Common Pleas First Judicial District of Pennsylvania Criminal Trial Division, January 14, 2011, 3, 21, 38, 75, 77, http://web.archive.org/web/20111003233309/http://www.phila.gov/districtattorney/PDFs/GrandJuryWomensMedical.pdf.

14 Williams, *Report of the Grand Jury*, 2, 19–20.

floors, the smell of urine, a flea-infested cat, cat feces, semiconscious women moaning in the waiting room, expired medications, and rusty equipment. Investigators opened up a refrigerator and found preserved body parts of dead babies. In a freezer lay a nineteen-week-old never-born child, the baby of Bhutani refugee Karnamaya Mongar, killed by Gosnell in 2009.[15]

I reported in chapter 43 the sparse coverage the national media gave the Gosnell story, even though it was full of sensational detail: Untrained and unlicensed Gosnell employees had overdosed Mongar with sedatives until she stopped breathing. The facility's defibrillator was broken and the junk filling the facility's narrow hallways and a padlocked emergency exit delayed the departure of the paramedics trying to get her to a hospital emergency room. Not even Gosnell knew where the key was.[16]

Gosnell was neither an OB/GYN nor board certified, in violation of Pennsylvania law. He ignored requirements regarding minors and offered abortions without the required twenty-four-hour wait. He trained staff to minimize the gestational age of the baby when doing measurements during pre-abortion ultrasounds. To "abort" these post-twenty-four-week babies, Gosnell's staff gave women drugs to induce labor. Then Gosnell took scissors and severed the spinal cords of the just-born babies.[17]

The jury in 2013 found Gosnell guilty of involuntary manslaughter in the case of Karnamaya Mongar, guilty in the murder of three babies born alive during abortions, and guilty of aborting twenty-one babies past Pennsylvania's twenty-four-week legal limit. Gosnell waived his right to an appeal in return for life imprisonment rather than execution.[18]

---

15 Williams, *Report of the Grand Jury*, 8, 20–21.
16 Williams, *Report of the Grand Jury*, 119–29.
17 Williams, *Report of the Grand Jury*, 3–4, 38.
18 Leigh Jones, "Gosnell Guilty of First-Degree Murder," *World*, May 13, 2013, https://wng.org/sift/gosnell-guilty-of-first-degree-murder-1617251998; Joseph Slobodzian, "Gosnell Won't Appeal; Gets Life, not Death," *The Philadelphia Inquirer*, May 15, 2013, https://www.inquirer.com/philly/news/20130515_Gosnell_avoids_death_penalty__won_t_appeal.html. During Gosnell's

The Gosnell case brought attention to the state health department. Before 2010, the department had last inspected Gosnell's facility in 1993, when pro-life Democrat Bob Casey, Sr., was governor. In 1995, Republican Tom Ridge became governor. His administration halted regular abortion facility inspections in 1999 because "officials concluded that inspections would be 'putting a barrier up to women' seeking abortions." Even complaints and reports of injuries and deaths were ineffective at initiating a review until the 2010 raid, months after Mongar died.[19]

Experience in Ohio and Pennsylvania showed how hard it is to enforce pro-life laws when courts, health department officials, and governors all play a role. It isn't surprising that Janet Folger Porter in Ohio remained convinced that real change required a different kind of law. She became known as the "architect of the pro-life Heartbeat Bill" as she and other Heartbeat supporters put up billboards, handed out bumper stickers, held prayer rallies, and gave legislators red roses and teddy bears with "beating" hearts. Porter ran unsuccessfully against a Republican state senator in the 2016 primary, citing her frustration with Senate Republicans' inaction on the Heartbeat Bill.[20]

The Ohio Senate passed the bill for the first time in December 2016, but Republican governor John Kasich vetoed it. At the same

---

2013 trial, those in the courtroom called the doctor's behavior strange. Philadelphia police officer Robert Flade, in an interview for the 2015 documentary *3801 Lancaster: American Tragedy*, said, "Every time the doctor would come into the court room, he was always smiling. He was always waving at somebody. He seemed excited to be in the court room." *World* magazine writer Andrée Seu Peterson, who covered the trial, said, "I never saw the curious Gosnell smile as cynical. I sat behind him for a month and he appeared to me to be genuinely clueless. I do not think he was being canny when he said in an interview after his arrest, 'If you are not making mistakes, you are not really attempting to do something; so I think that my patients are aware that I do my very best by them.'" See "An Epitaph to the Gosnell Trial," May 21, 2013, https://wng.org/articles/an-epitaph-to-the-gosnell-trial-1618211533.

19 Williams, *Report of the Grand Jury*, 9, 12, 147.
20 Porter, *Heartbeat Away*, 135–36, 415; Fr. Mark Hodges, "Heartbeat Bill Sponsor Running for State Senate in Ohio," LifeSite News, December 22, 2015, https://www.lifesitenews.com/news/heartbeat-bill-sponsor-running-for-state-senate-in-ohio/.

time, he signed a bill into law protecting babies from abortions after twenty weeks of pregnancy.[21] That set a pattern. Two years later, Kasich vetoed the Heartbeat Bill for a second time, simultaneously signing into law another bill banning a common method of abortion known as dismemberment abortion.[22]

The Heartbeat Bill divided Ohio pro-life groups. Ohio Right to Life, the state's National Right to Life affiliate, celebrated in a press release passage of the anti-dismemberment bill but said nothing about the Heartbeat Bill's veto. In previous years, Ohio Right to Life executive director Mike Gonidakis had expressed concerns that legal challenges against the Heartbeat Bill would endanger existing pro-life laws in the state. National Right to Life also opposed the bill.[23]

On the other hand, Dr. John "Jack" Willke, author of the 1971 *Handbook on Abortion* and a founder of both Ohio Right to Life and National Right to Life, supported Porter's legislation.[24] "I was Mr. Incremental," the 87-year-old Willke told the *New York Times* in 2011, talking about his past support of laws that minimally affected abortion access, "but after nearly 40 years of abortion on demand, it's time to take a bold step forward." He said Ohio Right to Life was not in tune with the "unrestrained enthusiasm" the Heartbeat Bill had caused among pro-lifers.[25]

21 Robert Higgs, "Gov. John Kasich Vetoes Anti-Abortion Heartbeat Bill, Signs 20-Week Abortion Ban," Cleveland.com, December 13, 2016, https://www.cleveland.com/open/2016/12/gov_john_kasich_vetos_anti-abo.html.
22 Jeremy Pelzer, "Gov. John Kasich OKs Tighter Abortion Restrictions, Vetoes 'Heartbeat' Bill and Pay Raises," Cleveland.com, December 21, 2018, https://www.cleveland.com/politics/2018/12/gov-john-kasich-vetoes-anti-abortion-heartbeat-bill-legislative-pay-raises.html.
23 "Dismemberment Abortion Ban Becomes Law," Press Releases, Ohio Right to Life, posted December 21, 2018, https://www.ohiolife.org/dismemberment_abortion_ban_becomes_law; Julie Carr Smyth, "Bill Advances in Ohio to Bar 'Heartbeat' Abortions," Associated Press, republished at *The Seattle Times* March 30, 2011, https://www.seattletimes.com/nation-world/bill-advances-in-ohio-to-bar-heartbeat-abortions/; Susan Olasky, "Strategic Battles," *World*, January 28, 2012, 38.
24 Olasky, "Strategic Battles," 38.
25 Erik Eckholm, "Anti-Abortion Groups Are Split on Legal Tactics," *New York Times*, December 4, 2011, https://www.nytimes.com/2011/12/05/health/policy/fetal-heartbeat-bill-splits-anti-abortion-forces.html.

While Gonidakis and other opponents of the bill feared the court battles the law could bring, that's just what supporters like Willke and Porter hoped for. "Our constitutional experts crafted the bill with the court challenge in mind. The Supreme Court has always been its destiny," wrote Porter in her 2020 book about the legislation. She described the passage of heartbeat bills across the country as messages "sent to the Supreme Court that the will of the people is to protect children from the moment we can hear their heartbeat."[26]

In 2018, Supreme Court Justice Anthony Kennedy announced his upcoming retirement. That fall, Justice Brett Kavanaugh took his empty seat. In December, the week after Ohio governor Kasich gave the Heartbeat Bill his second veto, Ohio Right to Life came out in support of it for the first time, citing the new makeup of the Supreme Court.[27]

When Ohio's new governor, Mike DeWine, signed the Heartbeat Bill into law in April 2019, Ohio Right to Life staff were among the thirty at the signing ceremony. Porter was notably absent. Some speculated that her track record of taking controversial positions on other issues and her unique lobbying tactics made her too polarizing. "Being disinvited to the bill signing by the governor, it stung," she told the Associated Press. "But I'm keeping my eye on the big picture. And the whole point of the last 10 years of my life was to bring the killing to an end."[28] In July, a federal judge blocked the state from enforcing the law.[29]

---

26 Porter, *Heartbeat Away*, 25, 40.
27 "Ohio Right to Life Supports a Pathway Forward for Ohio's Heartbeat Legislation," Press Releases, Ohio Right to Life, posted December 27, 2018, https://www.ohiolife.org/ohio_right_to_life_supports_a_pathway_forward_for_ohios_heartbeat_legislation.
28 Julie Carr Smyth, "Activist behind Anti-Abortion Heartbeat Bill Not at Signing," Associated Press, April 16, 2019, https://apnews.com/article/8b832c8f7b2e49c7bc31c8a438a6fbd9.
29 Corky Siemaszko, "Federal Judge Blocks Ohio's 'Heartbeat Bill,' Setting Up Legal Showdown over Abortion," NBC News, July 3, 2019, https://www.nbcnews.com/news/us-news/federal-judge-blocks-ohio-heartbeat-bill-setting-legal-showdown-over-n1026441.

47

The Abortion-Industrial Complex

IN 2007, James O'Keefe and UCLA sophomore Lila Rose (ages twenty-two and eighteen) entered two Planned Parenthood centers in Los Angeles. Rose pretended to be fifteen, impregnated by O'Keefe and desiring an abortion. With the camcorder hidden in her pocket, she videotaped a staff member at one facility telling her to provide a false birthdate and a staffer at another facility advising an abortion—but not reporting the presumed statutory rape, which California law requires. O'Keefe and Rose posted the videos on YouTube.[1]

The CEO of Planned Parenthood Affiliates of California later admitted the workers broke laws requiring them to report statutory rape. Nevertheless, the president of Planned Parenthood of Los Angeles sent Rose a letter demanding that she delete the videos and turn over the originals—or else face a lawsuit. After receiving the news, Rose said she sat on her dorm room bed and cried: "I was just, like, what is the world coming to when this tax-receiving, billion-dollar organization is coming after me, an 18-year-old girl, who just wants to see young girls protected?"[2]

Planned Parenthood has bullied older and bigger groups too. In 2012 Liz Thompson, president of the Susan B. Komen Foundation,

---

1 Lynn Vincent, "Silent Partners," *World*, June 9, 2007, 62.
2 Vincent, "Silent Partners," 62.

which funds breast cancer research and treatments, said Komen would no longer award grants to Planned Parenthood. Pressure from pro-life groups was proving a distraction from Komen's goal, and Planned Parenthood didn't even perform mammograms anyway—it only gave referrals. Komen hoped the breakup wouldn't be a big deal: the $680,000 Komen had been giving Planned Parenthood annually was less than 1 percent of Komen's grants, and a much smaller percentage of the abortion business's $1 billion in revenue. Komen encouraged pro-life groups not to make their celebrations public.[3]

Six weeks later, though, an AP story reported a "bitter rift" between the organizations. Planned Parenthood head Cecile Richards said, "It's hard to understand how an organization with whom we share a mission of saving women's lives could have bowed to this kind of bullying. It's really hurtful."[4] Planned Parenthood's supporters scolded Komen and replaced the lost money: New York City Mayor Michael Bloomberg gave $250,000.[5] But Komen ended up bowing to bullying. Komen grants continued: A 2018 press packet said Komen had just given Planned Parenthood $240,383.[6]

In 2015, pro-life activist David Daleiden's Center for Medical Progress (CMP) released undercover videos of Planned Parenthood executives discussing strategy for aborting babies and preserving their body parts to

---

3 Jill Stanek, "Komen and Planned Parenthood: Betrayed from Within, Part 2," LifeNews.com, October 1, 2012, https://www.lifenews.com/2012/10/01/komen-and-planned-parenthood-betrayed-from-within-part-2/; Marvin Olasky, "The Abortion Empire Strikes Back," *World*, March 24, 2012, https://wng.org/articles/the-abortion-empire-strikes-back-1620624121.
4 David Crary, "Planned Parenthood 'Reeling' after Losing Charity Funds," Associated Press, republished at NBC News January 31, 2012, https://www.nbcnews.com/id/wbna46209349.
5 Marvin Olasky, "Orchestrated Uproar," *World*, February 25, 2012, 5–6.
6 "Planned Parenthood 2018," Komen Materials, Susan G. Komen, accessed March 28, 2022, https://www.komen.org/uploadedFiles/_Komen/Content/About_Us/Media_Center/Newsroom/planned-parenthood-2018.pdf. Planned Parenthood announced receiving another Komen grant in a 2020 press release. See "Susan G. Komen® Greater Central and East Texas Awards Grant to Planned Parenthood of Greater Texas to Help Fight Breast Cancer," News, Planned Parenthood of Greater Texas, last modified July 17, 2020, https://www.plannedparenthood.org/planned-parenthood-greater-texas/newsroom/susan-g-komen-r-greater-central-and-east-texas-awards-grant-to-planned-parenthood-of-greater-texas-to-help-fight-breast-cancer.

sell for research. The first video, released on July 14, showed Dr. Deborah Nucatola, Planned Parenthood Federation of America's Senior Director of Medical Services, eating salad and sipping wine as she described how abortionists "crush below" and "crush above" to preserve particularly valuable parts of the unborn baby, like the heart, lung, and liver. Want to get an intact head? Make sure the baby comes out feet-first.[7]

In a press release with the first video, CMP said Nucatola's description of manipulating the baby to a feet-first position "is the hallmark of the illegal partial-birth abortion procedure." CMP noted that selling and purchasing human tissue is "a federal felony punishable by up to 10 years in prison and a fine of up to $500,000."[8] Planned Parenthood claimed the roughly $55 its affiliates made per "specimen" was just reimbursement for costs related to obtaining and storing the body parts.[9]

The videos energized efforts in some states to defund Planned Parenthood—and the organization pushed back. Eleven agents from the California Department of Justice, then headed by state Attorney General Kamala Harris, raided Daleiden's Huntington Beach apartment in April 2016. They seized four computers and "hundreds of hours of video footage."[10]

[7] See video at "Planned Parenthood Uses Partial-Birth Abortions to Sell Baby Parts," Center for Medical Progress YouTube video, July 14, 2015, https://youtu.be/jjxwVuozMnU.

[8] "Planned Parenthood's Top Doctor, Praised by CEO, Uses Partial-Birth Abortions to Sell Baby Parts," Press Releases, Center for Medical Progress, July 14, 2015, https://www.centerfor medicalprogress.org/2015/07/planned-parenthoods-top-doctor-praised-by-ceo-uses-partial-birth -abortions-to-sell-baby-parts/.

[9] Services Agreements between Stem-Ex, LLC, and Planned Parenthood affiliates (April 1, 2010, and May 15, 2012), cited in Memorandum from House Energy and Commerce Democratic Staff Re: Update on the Committee's Ongoing Investigation of Planned Parenthood Federation of America, September 9, 2015, 8, https://energycommerce.house.gov/sites/democrats.energy commerce.house.gov/files/Memorandum%20from%20Energy%20and%20Commerce%20 Committee%20Democratic%20Staff,%2009.09.2015.pdf. See also "How Planned Parenthood Profits from Fetal Tissue 'Donation,'" Human Capital Project, Center for Medical Progress, March 2, 2016, https://www.centerformedicalprogress.org/human-capital/how-planned-parenthood -profits-from-fetal-tissue-donation/.

[10] Daleiden and the Center for Medical Progress filed a lawsuit against Planned Parenthood, the National Abortion Federation, and the Attorney General of California in 2020. In that complaint, Daleiden's lawyers point to email exchanges and other correspondence between Planned Parenthood

For years, Daleiden has continued to face the possibility of jail time and crippling fines for allegedly recording the secret videos illegally, even though California law allows undercover reporting when investigating criminal activity.[11] The California Attorney General's office, under new leadership, even requested to withhold evidence that Daleiden's attorneys said proves his innocence: the evidence is a declaration of the former Orange County District Attorney Tony Rackauckas, who said he used evidence from Daleiden's investigations to bring civil action against two fetal tissue distributors for "illegal trafficking in fetal organs and tissues."[12]

The Daleiden videos helped many with pro-life sympathies to see what they're fighting for—and against. When the videos came out in 2015, thirty-four-year-old Terrisa Bukovinac worked in the San Francisco corporate offices of Louis Vuitton. She remembers taking a break from work one day to watch one of the videos when it debuted online: "It was just absolutely shocking, and then I had to go back to work and work for a luxury retailer and act like handbags were really important."[13]

---

staff and Harris's office and a March 2016 meeting between Harris and Planned Parenthood staff that suggest the abortion business had some influence in encouraging the April 2016 raid (*The Center for Medical Progress and David Daleiden v. Planned Parenthood Federation of America*, Case 8:20-cv-00891, doc. 1, filed May 12, 2020, in the United States District Court Central District of California). See also Jamie Dean, "Prosecutor and Persecutor," *World*, October 10, 2020, 42; Megan Cassella, "California Officials Seize Computers, Footage from Anti-Abortion Activist," Reuters, April 6, 2016, https://www.reuters.com/article/us-plannedparenthood-california-idUSKCN0X32GW.

11 Daleiden has had to post bond to secure the right to appeal unfavorable rulings but has not yet had to pay the multimillion dollar fines ordered by the courts as his cases work their way through the court system (Thomas More Society Vice President Peter Breen, interview with author, July 27, 2022).

12 Madeline Osburn, "California Prosecutors Attempt to Ban Exculpatory Evidence from Pro-Life Journalist's Criminal Trial," The Federalist, February 18, 2022, https://thefederalist.com/2022/02/18/california-prosecutors-attempt-to-ban-exculpatory-evidence-from-pro-life-journalists-criminal-trial/; Tony Rackauckas, January 18, 2022, in San Clemente, California, https://www.centerformedicalprogress.org/wp-content/uploads/2022/02/Declaration-of-Hon-Tony-Rackauckas-PPOSBCDV.pdf.

13 Terrisa Bukovinac, interview with author, February 25, 2022.

Bukovinac grew up in a family that was heavily involved in Herbert Armstrong's Worldwide Church of God. She doesn't remember her church or her family ever really talking about abortion, and she didn't have anything against the procedure: to Bukovinac, it was just removing a clump of cells. But when in her twenties her then-boyfriend showed her pictures of abortion procedures and unborn babies, it shocked her, and the images stuck in her mind. When she eventually adopted politically liberal views and later atheism, she held on to pro-life beliefs. She felt "an extreme sense of urgency" to fight for the rights of unborn babies, especially now that she no longer believed there was a heaven they could go to.[14]

Before Daleiden's videos came out in 2015, Bukovinac had mostly been involved with pro-life activism online with the group Secular Pro-Life, where she started volunteering in 2012. But in a 2022 interview, she said the videos were "extremely eye opening as to the reality that there was an industry behind this, looking to exploit and to profit. I feel like in a lot of ways, David's work did radicalize me and did kind of shock me to the point of wanting to get more involved than I had previously."[15]

Bukovinac started attending protests against Planned Parenthood. The next year, she started Pro-Life San Francisco—a bipartisan group with both atheist and Christian participants—and brought a homemade sign with her to one of Daleiden's court hearings. After that, Pro-Life San Francisco publicized the abortion industry's bullying in Daleiden's trial, and Bukovinac focused on ways to disrupt what she called "the abortion industrial complex."[16]

That phrase comes up a lot in Bukovinac's newest organization, the Progressive Anti-Abortion Uprising (PAAU), which she started

---

14 Mary Jackson, "Unconventional Ally," *World*, February 15, 2020, 67–68; Bukovinac interview.
15 Jackson, "Unconventional Ally"; Bukovinac interview.
16 Bukovinac interview. She said she got the term "abortion industrial complex" from her friend and fellow pro-lifer Herb Geraghty.

in October 2021. The PAAU website describes the group's stance on capitalism: "The Abortion Industrial Complex is the overlapping interests of government and industry that use fear, isolation, and violence to intensify the economic & societal inequalities that pressure people to abort when facing crisis pregnancies. Abortion is a powerful and coercive tool used by capitalists to benefit their own bottom line."[17]

Bukovinac said she's trying to target that money-making goal of the abortion industry with her work at PAAU: The idea for the group started when she was traveling around the country to Democratic debates and townhalls leading up to the 2020 election. She sat in the room wearing a "Democrats for Life" sticker and a shirt that said "WOMEN'S RIGHTS BEGIN IN THE WOMB" during then–Indiana Mayor Pete Buttigieg's January 2020 townhall in Des Moines, Iowa. She shook her red-bereted head as he made it clear the Democratic party had no room for pro-life liberals like her.[18]

To Bukovinac, the abortion industry's tight relationship with the Democratic party is the "main source of power for the abortion industrial complex."[19] In the 2020 fiscal year, Planned Parenthood received $618 million from government health services reimbursements and grants, up from $554 million in 2015, and performed 354,871 abortions, which could cost up to $1,000 each, according to a 2020 Planned Parenthood webpage.[20] Leading up to the 2020 presidential

17 "Stances: Capitalism," Progressive Anti-Abortion Uprising, accessed March 28, 2022, https://paaunow.org/stances-capitalism.
18 Terrisa Bukovinac (@terrisalin), "Thank you @foxnews for hosting . . ." Instagram, January 26, 2020, https://www.instagram.com/p/B7zm2rJlknw/; "Pete Buttigieg Asked about Abortion during Fox News Town Hall," Caffeinated Thoughts, YouTube video, January 27, 2020, https://youtu.be/_PedcUfbais.
19 Bukovinac interview.
20 "How Much Does an Abortion Cost?" For Teens, Ask the Experts, Planned Parenthood, posted June 29, 2020, https://web.archive.org/web/20200727151429/https://www.plannedparenthood.org/learn/teens/ask-experts/how-much-does-an-abortion-cost. A 2021 update to the Planned Parenthood webpage, originally posted in June 2020, increased the maximum estimated cost to $1,500. The page is no longer available on the Planned Parenthood website. "Planned Parenthood 2019–2020 Annual Report," and "Planned Parenthood 2014–2015 Annual Report," Planned

election, Planned Parenthood's political action committee pledged to donate $45 million to the campaigns of pro-abortion candidates, more than three times the amount it spent in the previous presidential election.[21]

Just as abortion pills are modernized versions of the abortion by ingestion (rather than surgery) practices of two centuries ago, so PAAU is a reminder that the pro-life movement of fifty years ago, before *Roe v. Wade*, had more liberal than conservative connections, and that Nellie Gray was surprised when it turned right rather than left.

Despite the stereotype of "pro-choice Democrats," some polling shows unequivocal support for abortion is more common among Democratic *politicians* than among Democratic *voters*. In Congress in 2021, Texas Representative Henry Cuellar was the only House Democrat to vote no when the chamber passed a bill that would have codified and expanded the current protections for legal abortion under *Roe v. Wade*. When it failed in the Senate the next year, West Virginia Senator Joe Manchin was the only Democratic politician in that chamber to vote

---

Parenthood, accessed March 28, 2022, https://www.plannedparenthood.org/uploads/filer_public/67/30/67305ea1-8da2-4cee-9191-19228c1d6f70/210219-annual-report-2019-2020-web-final.pdf and https://www.plannedparenthood.org/files/2114/5089/0863/2014-2015_PPFA_Annual_Report_.pdf.

21 Caroline Kelly, "Planned Parenthood's Political Arm to Spend $45 million on Electing Candidates Backing Reproductive Rights," CNN, October 9, 2019, https://www.cnn.com/2019/10/09/politics/planned-parenthood-2020-electoral-program/index.html.

At one time Planned Parenthood emphasized contraception rather than abortion, but in recent years its pro-abortion political priorities have become clearer. In 2019 Planned Parenthood ousted its president of eight months, Baltimore's Dr. Leana Wen, who had attempted to reframe abortion as a healthcare issue rather than a political one. A month later, reacting to President Donald Trump's new rule prohibiting recipients of Title X family planning funds from performing or referring for abortions, the organization decided to exit the program rather than cut off abortion "services." See Shane Goldmacher, "Planned Parenthood Ousts President, Seeking a More Political Approach," *New York Times*, July 16, 2019, https://www.nytimes.com/2019/07/16/us/politics/planned-parenthood-leana-wen.html; and Harvest Prude, "Planned Parenthood Forgoes Some Federal Funding," *World*, August 20, 2019, https://wng.org/sift/planned-parenthood-forgoes-some-federal-funding-1617395967.

against advancing the bill.²² And yet, 2021 data from Gallup shows one-fourth of Democratic voters identifying as pro-life.²³ Democrats for Life President Kristen Day said pro-lifers from strong Democrats for Life chapters in states like Colorado and Maryland have been testifying in their state capitals.²⁴

Bukovinac's organization in 2022 was still small, but it stood out from other largely religious pro-life organizations for its progressive political stances and aggressive "anti-capitalist" activism. She's been arrested for entering abortion facilities to hand out roses to patients and for "trespassing" by handing out pamphlets in front of a University of California San Francisco hospital to protest the university's participation in the fetal tissue trade. While awaiting arrest inside an abortion facility in Virginia, she and the other activists linked arms and sang a song she wrote calling for a "pro-life revolution": "A better world is possible / And it starts with us / We can end the suffering. . . ."²⁵

---

22 "Roll Call 295," September 24, 2021, https://clerk.house.gov/Votes/2021295; "On Cloture on the Motion to Proceed," February 28, 2022, https://www.senate.gov/legislative/LIS/roll_call_votes/vote1172/vote_117_2_00065.htm.
23 Megan Brenan, "Record-High 47% in U.S. Think Abortion Is Morally Acceptable," Gallup News, June 9, 2021, https://news.gallup.com/poll/350756/record-high-think-abortion-morally-acceptable.aspx. In other polling, 12 percent of Democrats said abortion should be illegal in all circumstances and 32 percent said it should be legal only in extreme cases such as rape, incest, and risk to the life of the mother (Julia Manchester, "Hill.TV Poll: Republicans Divided over Abortion," The Hill, September 6, 2018, https://thehill.com/hilltv/what-americas-thinking/405391-morning-consult-reporter-there-is-a-split-among-the-gop-on-roe).
24 Kristen Day, interview with author, March 26, 2022.
25 Lyrics from Terrisa Bukovinac, text message to author, November 3, 2021. PAAU (@PAAUNOW), "Activists singing @Terrisalin's song Pro-Life Revolution while awaiting arrest," Twitter, November 16, 2021, 2:18 p.m., https://twitter.com/PAAUNOW/status/1460688677202452494; Ryan Foley, "'We Will Not Be Silenced': Activist Declares She's Not Afraid of Racking Up Arrests in Effort to Save Lives," The Christian Post, November 24, 2021, https://www.christianpost.com/news/pro-life-activist-not-afraid-of-racking-up-arrests-to-save-lives.html.

48

A New Enforcement Mechanism

IN 2019 MARK LEE DICKSON, the thirty-three-year-old director of Right to Life of East Texas, was very familiar with the Hope Medical Group for Women in Shreveport, Louisiana. Sometimes he'd spend up to four—even eight—hours outside that abortion business, talking to women who had come to get abortions and offering them help. He should have welcomed the rumor that the facility might shut down.[1]

Except that Dickson had also run across a twenty-eight-year-old article written at a time when it looked like Louisiana would pass a law protecting unborn children except in cases of rape and incest. The headline in a small-town Texas newspaper was "Abortions at Border? Director Vows to Move Shreveport Clinic to Texas." The "Director" was abortion business director Robin Rothrock, promising to move her facility if the law went into effect: "We will just move our clinic 20 miles across the border into Waskom, Texas."[2]

The news back then didn't please the residents of Waskom, a small town with fewer than two thousand residents. "This area is very

---

[1] Mark Lee Dickson, interviews with author, March 25, 2020, and May 26, 2020.
[2] Dickson interviews. Anne Gillaspie, "ABORTIONS AT BORDER?" *Marshall News Messenger*, June 20, 1991, 1.

conservative and I don't know of a minister or a person who would condone an abortion clinic here," said Pastor Jim Walsh of the First Baptist Church of Waskom. The city's fire marshal agreed: "I don't feel people in Waskom will welcome this."[3]

The Louisiana law never did take effect, and Rothrock never moved her abortion facility across the border—but Dickson wondered if that threat in 1991 might become reality in 2019. He had been pro-life for a long time: His grandpa, Glenn Canfield Jr., had been the director of East Texas Right to Life and ran the organization's booth at the county fair, where Dickson held and examined the twelve-week-old baby models on display. He didn't want little Waskom, with its nine-acre park where visitors played tennis and volleyball and fished in the city pond, to become a destination for abortion tourism.[4]

Dickson pitched an idea to Waskom Mayor Jesse Moore: an ordinance prohibiting abortion within the city limits. Dickson drafted a version himself but hesitated to give it to the city council, fearing such a law would attract lawsuits that the small city couldn't afford. So he sought advice from pro-life state senator Bryan Hughes. Hughes knew just the person to help: Jonathan Mitchell, former law clerk for Supreme Court Justice Antonin Scalia and former Texas solicitor general.[5]

As solicitor general, Mitchell's job had been to defend in court the statutes passed by the Texas legislature. He learned that certain features made some laws easier to defend than others. So in 2013, when pro-life groups began crafting House Bill 2—limiting abortions after twenty weeks, requiring facilities to meet the standards of ambulatory surgery centers, and requiring doctors to have admitting privileges at local hospitals—Mitchell added a "severability clause." It told courts that if they disapproved some portions or specific applications of the

---

[3] Gillaspie, "ABORTIONS AT BORDER?"
[4] Dickson interviews; "The Residents and I Would Like to Welcome You . . ." From Mayor Jesse Moore, City of Waskom, accessed March 24, 2022, http://cityofwaskom.com/.
[5] Dickson interviews. Senator Bryan Hughes, interview with author, March 30, 2022.

law, the courts must preserve the remaining applications and allow the state to continue enforcing them.[6]

The test came soon enough: After the bill passed, Texas abortion providers sued over the admitting privilege and ambulatory surgical center requirements, arguing they would close many facilities and impose an undue burden on women seeking abortions. In 2016 the U.S. Supreme Court ruled in *Whole Woman's Health v. Hellerstedt* that the provisions were unconstitutional.[7]

Mitchell, by that time out of Texas government and working as a visiting professor at Stanford Law School, read Justice Stephen Breyer's take on his severability clause while in his home office: "The provisions are unconstitutional on their face: Including a severability provision in the law does not change that conclusion. . . . We reject Texas' invitation to pave the way for legislatures to immunize their statutes from facial review."[8]

For the next three years, Mitchell stewed over this frustrating pattern: pro-life legislatures passed laws that courts invariably blocked. In Mitchell's view, the courts don't hold veto-like power. The most they can do is to prohibit the executive branch of a government from enforcing the laws.[9]

So when Dickson contacted State Rep. Hughes and Hughes contacted Mitchell in 2019, Mitchell had been thinking deeply about a

---

6   Jonathan Mitchell, interview with author, January 25, 2022. Texas State Legislature, *Relating to the Regulation of Abortion Procedures, Providers, and Facilities; Providing Penalties*, HB 2, 83(2) legislative sess. Enacted 18 July 2013. https://capitol.texas.gov/tlodocs/832/billtext/pdf/HB00002F.pdf.

7   Erik Eckholm, "Abortion Providers in Texas Sue Over a Restrictive Rule That Could Close Clinics," *New York Times*, April 2, 2014, https://www.nytimes.com/2014/04/03/us/texas-abortion-providers-lawsuit.html.

8   Mitchell interviews, January 25, 2022, and February 10, 2022; *Whole Woman's Health v. Hellerstedt*, 136 S. Ct. 2292 (2016), 37–38.

9   Mitchell interviews. He even wrote a law review article debunking this idea of the court system's veto-like power. In the eighty-seven-page piece, he called it the "writ-of-erasure fallacy," clarifying that at most a court prohibits the executive branch of a government from enforcing the laws. Those laws are still laws, they're just unenforced. See Mitchell, "The Writ-of-Erasure Fallacy," *Virginia Law Review* 104 (April 2018): 933–1019, https://ssrn.com/abstract=3158038.

way for legislators to avoid unfavorable court rulings. He handed that solution to Dickson as a way to make sure Waskom wouldn't face lawsuits over its pro-life ordinance: a private civil-enforcement mechanism. Mitchell was so confident the mechanism would protect the city from lawsuits that he offered to represent the city in court, free of charge, if it did end up being sued.[10]

Here's how it worked: The ordinance declared it unlawful for people to "perform," "aid or abet" an abortion within the city limits but forbade any city official from actually enforcing the ordinance (adding, "unless and until the Supreme Court overrules *Roe v. Wade . . . and Planned Parenthood v. Casey*"). Instead, the ordinance left that job to "any private citizen." Any court's attempt to prohibit city officials from enforcing the statute wouldn't make a difference because the enforcement duties were up to the private citizens, and a court couldn't block all of those people: it would be anyone's guess as to which of Waskom's roughly two thousand residents would take legal action. It clarified that citizens could not sue the mothers of aborted children.[11]

On June 11, 2019, Dickson was in the unusually packed Waskom City Council chambers, wearing a suit jacket, jeans, and a backwards baseball cap, when five men sitting around the conference table in front of him raised their hands. With that, the city council voted unanimously to pass the sanctuary city ordinance.[12]

The success in Waskom energized Dickson. In the coming months, he spent weeks trekking across Texas in a 2008 white F-150 pickup sporting a Flash superhero sticker on the back window. His goal: to visit other Texas cities where residents had expressed interest in passing similar ordinances. Some city councils rejected the idea, some citing

---

10 Mitchell interviews.
11 Mitchell interviews; *Ordinance Outlawing Abortion within the City of Waskom, etc.*, Waskom, Texas, City Ordinance No. 336, June 11, 2019, 3–5.
12 Isaac Stanley-Becker, "East Texas Town with No Abortion Clinics Passes Ordinance Attempting to Ban the Procedure," *The Texas Tribune*, June 13, 2019, https://www.texastribune.org/2019/06/13/waskom-texas-city-council-votes-ban-abortion/.

concerns that they were too small to handle crippling legal fees, but by the end of 2020, seventeen Texas cities had passed similar ordinances.[13]

That year also saw the ordinances survive their first legal challenge. In February 2020, two abortion funding groups sued Waskom and six east Texas cities that had enacted sanctuary city ordinances. The lawsuit targeted one part of the ordinances: a provision that listed the two organizations and a handful of other abortion advocacy groups as "criminal," forbidding them from operating within the cities. The lawsuit did not challenge the abortion ban itself or its enforcement mechanism.[14]

Mitchell, who had agreed to represent the cities if such a challenge arose, saw an easy solution: remove that portion of the ordinances. Once that happened, the abortion advocacy groups dropped the lawsuit and claimed victory. So did Dickson, since the prohibition on abortion within city limits remained: "Now even the ACLU acknowledges that there is no basis for challenging these ordinances." Mitchell said that outcome emboldened him and reinforced his belief that the private enforcement mechanism would be immune from court challenge.[15]

13 Dickson interviews; "Sanctuary Cities," Sanctuary Cities for the Unborn, accessed March 24, 2022, https://sanctuarycitiesfortheunborn.org/sanctuary-cities-1. One of those seventeen cities (Omaha, TX) later walked back the ordinance and replaced it with a nonbinding resolution on the advice of the city attorney. In an interview on June 3, 2020, Omaha city attorney Wayne Paul Frank told me his concerns: "If you look at the ordinance, it purports to overrule *Roe v. Wade* and the other cases," he said. "That's just baiting someone into suing the city over that. At least that's the way I see it." Frank called himself pro-life and agreed that people need to fight against abortion, but he said small-town Texas is not the best place for that to happen. "These little cities don't have the resources to fight the battles like this. If you look at how much the state government has spent on the challenges, it's in the millions of dollars. . . . Cities like Omaha, they are trying to keep the water on and the septic system running and the police force going. . . . They can't afford to waste revenue and expenses on fighting these battles."
14 *Texas Equal Access Fund and Lilith Fund for Reproductive Equality vs. City of Waskom, Texas et al.* Case 2:20-cv-00055, doc. 1, Filed February 25, 2020, in the U.S. District Court for Eastern District of Texas, Marshall Division.
15 Mitchell interview; Daniel Friend, "ACLU Withdraws Lawsuit against Texas 'Sanctuary Cities for the Unborn,'" *The Texan* (Austin, TX), May 26, 2020, https://thetexan.news/aclu-withdraws-lawsuit-against-texas-sanctuary-cities-for-the-unborn/.

The ordinances faced a second challenge in 2020. In October, Planned Parenthood opened a facility in Lubbock, Texas. Meanwhile, pro-life residents gathered enough signatures to force the seven city council members to vote on a sanctuary city ordinance. When that failed, they forced a referendum. Of the 34,260 votes cast in May 2021, more than 60 percent were in favor of the ordinance. Lubbock became the biggest city to pass Dickson and Mitchell's ordinance—and the first with an existing abortion business to do so. Planned Parenthood wasn't happy.[16]

Planned Parenthood had been performing abortions in Lubbock for a month when the vote took place. The month before the ordinance went into effect, the group sued the city, claiming the ordinance violated the constitutional right to an abortion.[17]

The day the ordinance went into effect, a federal judge dismissed the lawsuit, ruling that Planned Parenthood could not sue the city of Lubbock because the city had no role in enforcing the ordinance. To challenge the constitutionality of the ordinance, the abortion business would have to first violate the ordinance and then wait for a lawsuit, which could be costly. So Planned Parenthood complied with the ordinance and halted abortions in Lubbock. Mitchell later noted that it

---

16 Mitchell interview; Grace Morris, "Planned Parenthood Opens Lubbock Clinic," Everything Lubbock, October 23, 2020, https://www.everythinglubbock.com/news/local-news/planned-parenthood-opens-lubbock-clinic/; Kaysie Ellingson, "Lubbock City Council Slams Down Sanctuary City for Unborn Ordinance 7-0," Texas Standard, November 19, 2020, https://www.texasstandard.org/stories/lubbock-city-council-slams-down-sanctuary-city-for-unborn-ordinance-7-0/; "Lubbock Validates Signature Petition for Proposed Ordinance Outlawing Abortion," Everything Lubbock, October 26, 2020, https://www.everythinglubbock.com/news/local-news/lubbock-validates-signature-petition-for-proposed-ordinance-outlawing-abortion/; Matt Dotray, "Lubbock Voters Say Yes to Sanctuary City for the Unborn Ordinance to Limit Abortion," Lubbock Avalanche-Journal, May 1, 2021, https://www.lubbockonline.com/story/news/2021/05/01/lubbock-voters-approve-anti-abortion-ordinance-municipal-election/4908890001/.

17 *Planned Parenthood of Greater Texas v. City of Lubbock, Texas*, Case 5:21-cv-00114-C, doc. 1, Filed May 17, 2021, in the U.S. District Court for the Northern District of Texas Lubbock Division. According to page 11 of the judge's order, the Lubbock Planned Parenthood began performing abortions on April 15, 2021.

was the first time since *Roe v. Wade* that an abortion ban had survived a court challenge.[18]

As this was going on in Lubbock, Mitchell and Hughes were talking again—this time about state-level legislation. Hughes wanted to enact a heartbeat law that would protect developing babies with detectable heartbeats from abortion. But Mitchell had seen what had happened to similar laws in states like Ohio, where Janet Folger Porter's heartbeat act was languishing under an injunction.[19]

Mitchell warned Hughes that courts would immediately declare unconstitutional any similar heartbeat law in Texas. Instead, he urged Hughes to pass a law using his private civil enforcement mechanism. Texas governor Greg Abbott signed a heartbeat act with Mitchell's private enforcement language on May 19, 2021. Like the local ordinances, it prohibited state officials from enforcing the law and gave private citizens the opportunity to collect money (under this law, at least $10,000) for successfully suing someone who performs or helps a woman access an abortion of a baby with a detectable heartbeat. The law gave citizens a four-year window to sue and, like the ordinances, shielded women who have the abortions from lawsuits.[20]

In July 2021 Texas abortion providers challenged the law, which was scheduled to go into effect on September 1. In August, the U.S. Court of

---

18 Gabriel Monte, "Federal Judge Dismisses Planned Parenthood Lawsuit against City of Lubbock," *Lubbock Avalanche-Journal*, June 2, 2021, https://www.lubbockonline.com/story/news/courts/2021/06/02/planned-parenthood-abortion-ordinance-lawsuit-against-city-lubbock-dismissed-federal-judge/7504804002/. "Planned Parenthood Stops Abortions in Lubbock, Except when Legally Permissible," KCBD, June 1, 2021, https://www.kcbd.com/2021/06/01/planned-parenthood-stops-abortions-in-lubbock-except-when-legally-permissible/. Mitchell interviews.

19 Mitchell interviews; Hughes interview.

20 Mitchell interviews; Paul J. Weber, "Texas Governor Signs Law Banning Abortions Early as 6 Weeks," Associated Press, May 19, 2021, https://apnews.com/article/texas-health-abortion-government-and-politics-ba02cd7c3f02b1eb5c87094257ee4db2; Texas State Legislature, *Relating to Abortion, Including Abortions after Detection of an Unborn Child's Heartbeat; Authorizing a Private Civil Right of Action*, SB 8, 87(R) legislative sess. Enacted 19 May 2021, 3–7, https://capitol.texas.gov/tlodocs/87R/billtext/pdf/SB00008F.pdf.

Appeals for the Fifth Circuit refused to halt enforcement of the law. On August 31, abortionists scrambled to abort as many babies as possible before the law went into effect at midnight. Abortion activists hoped the Supreme Court would rescue them, but a divided Court declined the abortion providers' request to prevent enforcement of the heartbeat ban, citing the novel private enforcement mechanism.[21]

The results in Texas were mixed. Some pregnancy centers saw more clients. Two centers in Houston performed a total of ninety-six ultrasounds between Monday and Saturday the week the law went into effect, about twice their normal number. "We're loving this," said Sylvia Johnson-Matthews, the CEO of the Houston centers. "This is what I've practiced for 36 years for."[22]

Heather Jones, the director at a small pregnancy center in Port Lavaca, Texas, was amazed that the law was actually in effect: "For now, for this season, the fact that abortion is illegal after a heartbeat is detected is something I don't know that I ever thought I'd see in my lifetime, and it's just—it's beautiful."[23]

A federal judge blocked enforcement of the law for two days in October in response to a lawsuit from the U.S. Department of Justice. Some abortion providers resumed aborting babies with detectable heartbeats during that short window, even though they could still be held liable

---

21 Heidi Pérez-Moreno, "Twenty Abortion Providers Sue Texas Officials over Law That Bans Abortions as Early as Six Weeks," *The Texas Tribune*, July 13, 2021, https://www.texastribune.org/2021/07/13/texas-heartbeat-bill-lawsuit/; *Whole Woman's Health et al. v. Austin Reeve Jackson, Judge, et al.*, Case 21-50792, doc. 00515998921, filed August 29, 2021, in the U.S. Court of Appeals for the Fifth Circuit; Alexandra Svokos, "How a Texas Clinic Raced to Provide Abortion Care before Law Went into Effect," ABC News, September 1, 2021, https://abcnews.go.com/US/texas-clinic-raced-provide-abortion-care-law-effect/story?id=79767646. *Whole Woman's Health et al. v. Austin Reeve Jackson, Judge, et al.*, 594 U. S. ___ (2021).

22 Sylvia Johnson-Matthews, text messages to author, September 4, 2021, and interview with author, September 2, 2021.

23 Heather Jones, interview with author, September 3, 2021. Not all Texas pregnancy centers saw an increase in clients. See Leah Savas, "Pro-Lifers Minister to Panicked Women in Texas," *World*, September 7, 2021, https://wng.org/roundups/pro-lifers-minister-to-panicked-women-in-texas-1631037402.

under the law. Later, two women represented by Jonathan Mitchell and lawyers at the Thomas More Society and the America First Legal Foundation requested depositions of two abortion fund directors who had admitted to helping women get abortions of babies with detectable heartbeats during that time. In March 2022, those funds sued the women and some of the lawyers, hoping to prevent them from eventually enforcing the heartbeat act.[24] As of mid-2022, Mitchell and the other lawyers were still working to depose the abortion fund directors, and the lawsuits filed by the abortion funds were ongoing.

San Antonio abortionist Alan Braid claimed in a September 2021 *Washington Post* op-ed that he had performed an abortion on a woman who was "beyond the state's new limit." He clearly intended the op-ed to bait a lawsuit that would allow him to challenge the heartbeat act. Three men took the bait, including two self-proclaimed pro-choice former lawyers from out-of-state who apparently wanted to challenge the law too. Braid countersued and argued in court documents that he didn't owe the $10,000 under the law because it "violates the United States Constitution." That case was still pending in mid-2022.[25]

By February 2022, the law had survived a number of court challenges. Its effect on abortion numbers was less clear. That month, the

---

24 Onize Ohikere, "Some Texas Centers Resume Abortions," *World*, October 8, 2021, https://wng.org/sift/some-texas-centers-resume-abortions-1633677843. Eleanor Klibanoff, "Anti-Abortion Lawyers Target Those Funding the Procedure for Potential Lawsuits under New Texas Law," *The Texas Tribune*, February 23, 2022, https://www.texastribune.org/2022/02/23/texas-abortion-sb8-lawsuits/. Caroline Kitchener, "Texas's Strict New Abortion Law Has Eluded Multiple Court Challenges. Abortion Rights Advocates Think They Have a New Path to Get It Blocked," *The Washington Post*, March 21, 2022, https://www.washingtonpost.com/politics/2022/03/21/texas-abortion-sb8/.

25 Alan Braid, "Opinion: Why I Violated Texas's Extreme Abortion Ban," *The Washington Post*, September 18, 2021, https://www.washingtonpost.com/opinions/2021/09/18/texas-abortion-provider-alan-braid/; Devin Dwyer, "2 Disbarred Attorneys outside Texas Sue Abortion Doctor under SB8," ABC News, September 21, 2021, https://abcnews.go.com/Politics/disbarred-attorneys-texas-sue-abortion-doctor-sb8/story?id=80147133; AJ McDougall, "'Cranky' Disbarred Lawyer Sues Texas Doc Who Broke Abortion Ban," *The Daily Beast*, September 20, 2021, https://www.thedailybeast.com/disbarred-arkansas-lawyer-files-texas-heartbeat-bill-suit-against-alan-braid-doctor-who-violated-abortion-ban; *Braid v. Stilley et al.*, Case 1:21-cv-05283, doc. 75, filed February 17, 2022, in the U.S. District Court Northern District of Illinois Eastern Division, 1.

state reported that abortions in Texas in September 2021 had fallen to 2,197, down from 4,511 the previous September.[26] But other reports showed requests to the European abortion pill website AidAccess had skyrocketed in September, as had the numbers of Texas women traveling to out-of-state abortion facilities. News outlets also told of abortion pill networks that helped women get abortion pills from Mexico.[27]

While Texas Right to Life celebrated the lives saved, other pro-lifers saw those stats and weren't convinced the law was that effective. When attorney Paul Linton, special counsel for the pro-life group Texas Alliance for Life, heard in September 2021 that Mitchell was encouraging lawmakers in other states to pass similar legislation, he advised against it, believing the laws would antagonize members of the U.S. Supreme Court, including justices whose votes could be crucial in the upcoming *Dobbs v. Jackson Women's Health* that pro-lifers hoped would help overturn *Roe v. Wade*.[28]

Even after the U.S. Supreme Court in December 2021 again declined to block enforcement of the law, Linton still thought the approach unwise. He pointed to Chief Justice John Roberts's dissent: "The clear purpose and actual effect of S.B. 8 has been to nullify this Court's rulings."[29] Other pro-life legal experts agreed that, despite the law's

---

26 "2021 Selected Characteristics of Induced Terminations of Pregnancy (Excel)," Induced Terminations of Pregnancy, Texas Health and Human Services, https://www.hhs.texas.gov/about/records-statistics/data-statistics/itop-statistics.

27 Abigail R. A. Aiken et al., "Association of Texas Senate Bill 8 with Requests for Self-Managed Medication Abortion," *JAMA Network Open* 5, no. 2 (February 2022): 2, doi:10.1001/jamanetworkopen.2022.1122; Kari White et al. "Out-of-State Travel for Abortion following Implementation of Texas Senate Bill 8," Texas Policy Evaluation Project at The University of Texas at Austin (March 2022), http://sites.utexas.edu/txpep/files/2022/03/TxPEP-out-of-state-SB8.pdf. See also "Inside Texas's Underground Abortion Pill Network," VICE News YouTube video, February 9, 2022, https://youtu.be/CR3uexqGgXo.

28 Paul Linton, interview with author, October 19, 2021.

29 Linton, email to author, March 18, 2022. The Texas Supreme Court dealt the final blow to that legal challenge in March, when it ruled the remaining defendants, all public officials, could not enforce the law, meaning the abortion providers' lawsuit against them was not valid. Abortion advocacy groups at the time said the ruling meant the Heartbeat Act would stay in place for the foreseeable future. See Paul J. Weber and Jamie Stengle, "Texas Clinics' Lawsuit over Abortion

unexpected months of success, it would be only a temporary victory in the long term—and perhaps an unnecessary solution should the Supreme Court rule to overturn *Roe* in the *Dobbs* case.[30]

John Seago, legislative director of Texas Right to Life, said in October 2021 that one benefit of the law was to demonstrate to the Court what a post-*Roe* scenario could look like: "Women want to access abortion, they go to another state. . . . We see that our hospitals are not filling up with women who are trying to do self-abortions and being harmed. I mean, all of the doomsday scenarios that the left puts out there about what happens if *Roe* is overturned, they're being disproven in Texas for the last month and a half."[31]

Ban 'Effectively Over,'" Associated Press, March 11, 2022, https://apnews.com/article/abortion-health-texas-0b4ed1808ed44d176bf6c86e6646a718. *Whole Woman's Health et al. v. Austin Reeve Jackson, Judge, et al.*, 594 U. S. ___ (2021), 4.

30 In a September 3, 2021, interview, Americans United for Life Chief Legal Officer and General Counsel Steven Aden told me he saw the law as "a victory in the short term," saying, "I don't believe the law will be found enforceable by Texas state courts." After months of the law remaining in force, Aden said in a March 22, 2022, interview that he stood by his earlier assessment: "It's my judgment that the law was designed to rely on the slow nature of the court system," he said, predicting that a court would eventually rule against the law, leaving it ineffective.

31 John Seago, interview with author, October 21, 2021.

49

Their One Person

DURING AN APPOINTMENT to get birth control, Hanah Wranosky learned that she was pregnant. She cried. The unmarried, twenty-one-year-old Texan was already the mother of a daughter, almost four, and a son about to turn one. Her second pregnancy had been difficult, and she didn't want to go through that again, but she initially thought abortion was off the table. It was August 2021, and Texas governor Greg Abbott earlier that year had signed the state's heartbeat bill.[1]

Wranosky thought the law had gone into effect immediately and made abortion illegal in the state. She was wrong. The doctor at the birth control facility told Wranosky abortion was still an option for her. The law allowing citizens to sue people who perform or help women obtain abortions of unborn children with detectable heartbeats would not go into effect until September 1. The doctor gave Wranosky a piece of paper with abortion information and recommended Alamo Women's Reproductive Services Clinic in San Antonio. She said it had the best reviews.

"I was relieved that it wasn't even like an option, and then to find out it was, brought on a whole nother level of difficult decision making,"

---

1 Hanah Wranosky, interview with author, September 4, 2021.

Wranosky said. "I wish it was illegal in the first place, honestly . . . so it wasn't an option for me at all."[2]

She said when her boyfriend found out, he wanted her to get an abortion. He was the father of Wranosky's son and of this new baby and didn't think they could afford another child. Wranosky, meanwhile, couldn't decide what she wanted to do: "I was so desperate to like try and fix the situation."[3]

The next day she went to the Pregnancy Center of the Coastal Bend in Corpus Christi. There, she had an ultrasound and talked with client advocate Aliyah Lawson about abortion and about the alternative services the pro-life center offered. They talked for more than ninety minutes. After her visit, Wranosky was leaning against abortion but was still unsure.[4]

Her boyfriend wasn't. She said he pushed her to make an appointment at the abortion facility: *If you don't want to go to the appointment, you don't have to but let's set it up so it's set up just in case you change your mind.* So Wranosky made an appointment for two weeks later at Alamo Women's. When the time came, she and her boyfriend made the 100-plus-mile drive for the morning appointment, a consultation that would precede the second appointment, when Wranosky would actually take the abortion pill. By then, it was the last full week in August. She was past six weeks pregnant.[5]

When she arrived, the waiting rooms were packed, the staff members rushed. She noticed they never asked her how she was feeling. She said yes when they asked if she would like to view the ultrasound. The image on the screen made her feel even more overwhelmed. Once she left, Wranosky told her boyfriend she didn't want to return for the abortion pill.[6]

[2] Wranosky interview.
[3] Wranosky interview.
[4] Aliyah Lawson, interview with author, February 2, 2022; Wranosky interview, September 4, 2021.
[5] Wranosky interview.
[6] Wranosky interview.

But the next day, she did return. She signed in on the iPad, filled out the paperwork, and handed in her $500 payment. Then she waited in a room with a group of fifteen or twenty other young women until the abortion facility staff passed out the pills to all of them at once, telling them to take them in front of the staff.[7]

Wranosky said none of the women made eye contact or talked to each other. Some were watching the TVs in the room. But Wranosky watched to see when most of them took the pill. She swallowed hers quickly so she could leave. She didn't really want to take it, but she had already paid and other women around her were taking the pill: "It's like, oh I'm very deep into this. I already paid them my money, so there is no turning back now."[8]

She was crying when her boyfriend picked her up. She cried during the long drive home. She had ultrasound images of the baby in her home and knew the due date. In the next twenty-four to forty-eight hours, she would have to take the second set of pills at home that would cause contractions to expel her baby. She had a lot of thinking to do in the meantime. On and off, she felt she had made the right decision and felt she had made a mistake from which she would never recover.

Wranosky that day discovered one complication of legal abortion. Advocates champion it as a woman's choice, but what if it's a choice the woman doesn't want to make? Having abortion as a legal option made it harder for Wranosky to say no to pressure from others. Some women who have had legal abortions say that they didn't doubt the decision since the procedure is legal. Others, like Wranosky, say they didn't want the abortion but felt they had to because friends or family encouraged it.

On September 1, the new Texas law went into effect. Esmie Fisher, nurse manager at the Corpus Christi center, said she had expected to see

---

7   An online two-star Google review of the facility written by "Katie" describes the staff following a similar routine in 2020.
8   Wranosky interview.

"an onslaught of women who would be very angry" that they couldn't get abortions. But, among the occasionally angry clients, Fisher was surprised to find women relieved to see a heartbeat during the ultrasounds she would perform.[9]

In September, Fisher performed an ultrasound on a woman with beautiful dark eyes and long lashes. She was in her early twenties and had another child not even a year old. According to Fisher, the woman's sister wanted her to get an abortion because they shared an apartment and one baby was enough: Her boyfriend also wanted her to abort. But as Fisher performed the ultrasound in the teal-walled sonogram room, the tiny flicker of an early heartbeat appeared on the screen. The woman didn't say anything when she saw it, but she smiled. Fisher said she later heard the woman sigh with relief as she was getting off of the paper-covered exam table and say under her breath, *Now I can get them off my back*.

Fisher recalled another woman who returned to the center repeatedly for ultrasounds until she could finally see a heartbeat on the screen. Fisher said a third woman who came in October began her appointment frustrated about the new time constraint of the law but giggled and laughed when she saw her baby's heartbeat on the ultrasound screen. Fisher averaged four to eight women per day leaning toward or planning abortion—but at least a couple each day took the news about the visible heartbeat better than she expected.

In September, as some Texas women responded to the heartbeat law by looking for out-of-state abortion facilities, pregnancy centers in neighboring states started getting more calls from Texas. Tabitha Dugas, director at New Life Counseling in Lake Charles, Louisiana, said her center initially received close to fifty calls each week from Texas women. Even though center staff tried to connect Texas callers with local pregnancy centers, Dugas said some women who called made

---

9 Esmie Fisher, interview with author, December 3, 2021.

hours-long drives to her center: "It was the number they called and it's the relationship they build." Dugas said many women just need to hear one person promise to support them in order to avoid abortion: She wants women to know, "We will be your 'one person.'"[10]

For Hanah Wranosky, that one person was Aliyah Lawson, the client advocate she had spoken with at the Corpus Christi pregnancy center. The day after Wranosky took the first drug in the abortion pill regimen, she still regretted it. She texted Lawson, *I followed through with the abortion, I got it yesterday, and I feel like I made a huge mistake. Is there anything I can do?*[11]

Wranosky had heard abortion pill reversal would lead to hemorrhage or death, but she trusted what Lawson told her: it was possible to stop the abortion. Wranosky hadn't yet taken the second set of pills, so progesterone treatment could reverse the effects of the mifepristone. Lawson gave Wranosky the number of Heartbeat International's Abortion Pill Reversal hotline so she could consent to the treatment. Wranosky returned to the center for an ultrasound and, after confirming that the baby was still alive, started taking progesterone pills picked up from a pharmacy and prescribed by a local doctor. By the end of the day Wranosky had taken two progesterone pills with instructions to continue taking them twice a day during the first trimester to halt the effects of the first abortion pill. At first, she was still scared and considered taking the misoprostol she had received from the abortion facility. But when her baby still had a heartbeat in an ultrasound a week later, she felt happy and more confident. At thirty-two weeks, both Wranosky and the baby were still healthy, and Wranosky said, "it's been like a normal pregnancy." Her daughter was born in early April 2022. She said her boyfriend at first had to adjust to her decision

---

10 Tabitha Dugas, interview with author, November 12, 2021. For more on Texas women traveling out of state in 2021, see Leah Savas, "Pregnancy Centers near Texas Respond to Abortion Tourism," *World*, November 22, 2021, https://wng.org/roundups/pregnancy-center-tourism-1637614870.

11 Lawson interview, February 2, 2022; Wranosky interview, September 4, 2021.

to keep the baby, but in May she said "he loves [the baby] very much and is so supportive."[12]

Abortion pill reversal is a newer service available at many pro-life pregnancy centers. The Corpus Christi pregnancy center, like others in recent years, offers obstetric ultrasounds, post-abortion counseling, and parenting classes. Clients attending the classes earn points toward free clothes, diapers, and other baby needs—a common model at pregnancy centers across the country.[13]

"Those voices are loud," said nurse Fisher of the people in women's lives who pressure them into getting abortions. "Many women do it only because they know that they're going to meet a lot of resistance from people around them. . . . It's their support people. And how is she going to buy diapers, and how is she going to support this baby? They feel that."[14]

Pro-life pregnancy centers typically help women during their pregnancies and for some time after a baby is born. The intent behind these services is to eliminate some of the reasons why women choose abortion, such as lack of financial and practical support. Jeanette Harvey,

---

12   Lawson interview; Wranosky interview; Hanah Wranosky, Facebook messages with author, February 14, 2022, and May 19 and 30, 2022. In her messages, Wranosky said she went to two appointments with a fetal medicine specialist to check on the baby because she had taken the abortion pill. But she said the baby looked healthy, so she proceeded with standard OBGYN visits after that. The National Institute for Health and Care Excellence (NICE) recommends progesterone treatments for women at risk of miscarriage (see Jacqui Wise, "NICE Recommends Progesterone to Prevent Early Miscarriage," *BMJ* [November 2021]: 375, https://doi.org/10.1136/bmj.n2896). Further studies of its ability to stop a chemical abortion are likely. According to Heartbeat International's director of medical impact Christa Brown, the Abortion Pill Rescue Network answers more than two hundred "mission-critical calls a month from women who regret their abortion decision" (Heartbeat International's Vice President of Communications and Marketing Andrea Trudden, email to author, March 21, 2022).

13   "WHY Pregnancy Center of the Coastal Bend," Pregnancy Center of the Coastal Bend, accessed February 15, 2022, https://hifriends4life.org/; Aliyah Lawson, text message to author, February 15, 2021; Mai Bean et al., *A Legacy of Life and Love: Pregnancy Centers Stand the Test of Time* (Arlington, VA: Charlotte Lozier Institute, 2020), 51. The Charlotte Lozier Institute estimated that U.S. pregnancy centers in 2019 provided $12,900,790 in free diapers and $9,150,809 in free baby clothes. See Bean et al., *Legacy of Life*, 16.

14   Fisher interview, December 3, 2021.

director of the pro-life Hope Women's Resource Clinic in Beaumont, Texas, has learned that "the crisis is not the pregnancy. The crisis is something else in their life that makes them think they shouldn't be pregnant now. Our goal is to figure out what the real crisis is and help them to resolve that."[15]

Lori Szala, national director of client services for the pro-life Human Coalition, said the group's hotline in early 2020 mainly heard from women concerned "about being able to pay for their existing children."[16] One woman found out she was pregnant the same week she lost her job and her insurance. She thought she needed an abortion in order to care for her other children. Human Coalition helped her find a job at Amazon and told her about local organizations that could assist her in paying for childcare and housing utilities. A guide prepared by Human Coalition staff gave the woman guidelines for what to look for when searching for a reputable daycare.[17]

The woman also felt squeezed in her current apartment, so a Human Coalition social worker helped her prepare a budget for a new apartment and local housing that would be a better fit for her family without being too expensive. The woman decided to give birth.[18] That was a common pattern: once women found job openings, insurance options, and other practical help, the perceived need to abort often diminished.

To reach more women both before and after a crisis, some centers have expanded services to include testing for sexually transmitted infections and disease, breastfeeding consultations, well-woman exams, and prenatal care. In 2019, 27 percent of pregnancy centers offered childbirth classes and 21 percent provided STI and STD treatments.[19]

Others have begun offering contraceptives. They hope to prevent unplanned pregnancies and thereby potential abortions. They see it

---

15 Jeanette Harvey, interview with author, April 10, 2020.
16 Lori Szala, interview with author, March 27, 2020.
17 Becky Gallagher, interview with author, March 17, 2022.
18 Gallagher interview.
19 Bean et al., *Legacy of Life*, 18.

as a way to attract women to pro-life centers so they're less likely to become regular clients at the local Planned Parenthood. CareNet's Vincent DiCaro, though, said that doesn't capture the entire mission of Christian pregnancy centers: "[W]e are here to prevent abortions, but we are also here to do other things, which is preach the gospel of Jesus Christ . . . and also to hold up God's standard for marriage and the family as God designed it."[20]

That debate is part of another question: How can pro-life centers help women who are alone, or feel they are, find new community? How can they help spiritually and psychologically, as well as materially? Some staff members are wary about discussing the need for Christ with women who come to them. Others see it as central to their conversations with needy women. Wanda Kohn, director of the Pregnancy and Family Care Center in Leesburg, Florida, said she speaks of the gospel with clients whenever she gets an opportunity: She calls abortion "a symptom of a problem with the heart."[21]

Tammy Hayward found out about Kohn's center through a Google search as she sat in the parking lot of an Orlando abortion facility in 2017. She had just driven an hour there to get the abortion pill only to find out the facility didn't accept Medicaid. Frantically looking for other places to get an abortion, Hayward called the Pregnancy and Family Care Center. Kohn answered and told her to stop by.[22]

In the center's counseling room, Hayward told her story: She already had three children more than ten years old. The pregnancy made her feel sick day and night, and she was struggling financially while trying to hold down an office job and a part-time position at Red Lobster. The baby's father was unemployed and addicted to drugs. Plus, she was

---

20 Mary Jackson, "Pro-Lifers Swallow the Pill," *World*, August 15, 2020, 54–57; Vincent DiCaro and Roland Warren, "Washington Post Questions Pregnancy Centers on Birth Control Policies," CareNet's *CareCast*, December 3, 2020, podcast, MP3 audio, 6:30, https://open.spotify.com/episode/6t0NqmW4SI58hUMC72V61q?si=f47e1517c02e4c23&nd=1.
21 Wanda Kohn, interview with author, August 25, 2020.
22 Kohn interview; Tammy Hayward, interview with author, September 8, 2020.

forty-one years old and afraid of having another miscarriage. In her mind, it was not a good time to have another baby.[23]

Kohn had had an abortion when she was seventeen. She saw in Hayward the same desperation that led Kohn and many others to abort their children: an inability to look beyond the present crisis and seek God's will. Kohn said she sees many women who don't want to be told what to do and don't want to be under anyone else's authority: "In a decision to end the life of their babies, these women are feeling like they're justified."[24]

During Hayward's visit, Kohn used low-tech methods to help her picture the child growing within her: she showed her a box of tiny rubber baby models illustrating the baby's stages of growth. She helped Hayward understand she was accountable to God for whatever she did. When she left the center, Hayward hadn't yet made a decision, but those baby models stuck in her mind. Even after her employer offered to pay for her abortion, Hayward ultimately decided not to abort. She joined a Bible study and started going to church with Kohn.[25]

Although Kohn gave Hayward help in the form of food, clothing, and a community of helpers, the biblical wisdom Kohn shared made the biggest difference to Hayward: "I wasn't looking for handouts. I was looking for direction. . . . She gave me enough to help me but also didn't give me something to make it easy. She made it to where I had to make decisions and make changes."[26]

Other changes came during the next five years. Hayward, still pregnant, moved her family to New England. In 2022 the girl she almost aborted turned four. Hayward loved her and also loved the job she was in, but family problems remained. Hayward was not going to church and had not yet found a new community.[27]

23 Kohn and Hayward interviews.
24 Kohn interview.
25 Kohn and Hayward interviews.
26 Hayward interview.
27 Hayward, text messages to author, February 7–14, 2022.

50

Egregiously Wrong

IN MAY 2021, the U.S. Supreme Court agreed to hear *Dobbs v. Jackson Women's Health Organization* (JWHO), a case concerning a Mississippi law that protected babies from abortion after 15 weeks. The court would consider the question, "Whether all pre-viability prohibitions on elective abortions are unconstitutional." At the center of the case was the state's last remaining surgical abortion facility, a pink-walled building in Mississippi's capital that mainstream media described as "bubblegum" and some pro-lifers said resembled Pepto-Bismol.[1]

The sidewalks on the other side of the black-tarp-covered fence surrounding JWHO had for years been the site of confrontations between pro-life sidewalk counselors, street preachers, and the Pink House Defenders, pro-abortion volunteers who came to distract patients from the pro-lifers. The tensions there were a microcosm of the nationwide conflict that, despite the urging of the Supreme Court Justices in *Casey*, had only increased since 1992.[2]

---

1 Pro-life activist Doug Lane frequented the sidewalk outside the "Pink House" and described the color as Pepto-Bismol to me in a September 30, 2021, interview. For a mainstream media description of the building and the news about the Supreme Court taking up the case, see Gabriella Borter, "Mississippi's 'Pink House' Becomes Ground Zero in U.S. Abortion Battle," Reuters, May 24, 2021, https://www.reuters.com/world/us/mississippis-pink-house-ground-zero-us-abortion-rights-fight-2021-05-23/.
2 For more on the conflict at the Pink House, see Leah Savas, "The Pink House Brawl," *World*, December 4, 2021, 40–45.

The JWHO battle intensified in 2017. That year, Jameson Taylor was the acting president of a small public policy group in Mississippi and a father of young children. He had a history of sidewalk counseling outside an abortion facility with his wife when they lived in Dallas, but he didn't frequent the Pink House sidewalks. His work was in lobbying, and late that year he began working with Mississippi lawmakers and a small group of lobbyists and lawyers on Mississippi's 15-week law.[3]

In a 2022 interview, he recalled their work to pass the 15-week bill: "It's not as if we're a bunch of geniuses in a room [who] sat down in late 2017 and thought about 'Okay, we're gonna reverse *Roe v. Wade.*'" In 2014, Mississippi had passed a law that protected babies from abortion after 20 weeks. It received no legal challenge. Taylor and his team thought protection at 15 weeks was the next best incremental step for Mississippi.[4]

Even when Mississippi petitioned the Supreme Court in June 2020 to take up the case after receiving unfavorable rulings from lower courts, the state assured the Court that the questions posed in the case "do not require the Court to overturn *Roe* or *Casey*. They merely [ask] the Court to reconcile a conflict in its own precedents."[5]

But, after the Court agreed to take the case, Mississippi Attorney General Lynn Fitch filed a brief at the Supreme Court in July 2021 that asked a bold question: "whether this Court should overrule" *Roe* and *Casey*. Her answer: "It should. . . . *Roe* and *Casey* are egregiously wrong. The conclusion that abortion is a constitutional right has no basis in text, structure, history, or tradition."[6]

---

3 Jameson Taylor, interview with author, October 22, 2021.
4 Jameson Taylor, interview with author, June 24, 2022.
5 *Petition for a Writ of Certiorari*, No. 19-1392 (2020), re. *Dobbs v. Jackson Women's Health Organization*, 5, https://www.supremecourt.gov/DocketPDF/19/19-1392/145658/20200615170733513_FINAL%20Petition.pdf.
6 *Brief for Petitioners*, No. 19-1392 (2021), re. *Dobbs v. Jackson Women's Health Organization*, 1–2, https://www.supremecourt.gov/DocketPDF/19/19-1392/184703/20210722161332385_19-1392 BriefForPetitioners.pdf.

Abortion advocates in Jackson saw the implications of the brief. "This time it's not just about keeping the doors open at JWHO," wrote the Pink House Defenders on their Facebook page on July 29, 2021. "It's about keeping the doors open across the country, completely changing abortion access as we know it."[7]

But Taylor wasn't banking on an overturn of *Roe*. He was optimistic the Court would use the case to allow states to regulate pre-viability abortions: If the Court intended to preserve the status quo, why would the justices take up the case? Taylor looked at how Mississippi had framed the question: "'Can states regulate pre-viability abortions?'" He predicted that the answer would be "Yes, but," and then asked: "What comes after the 'but'?"[8]

On the morning of Wednesday, December 1, 2021, about twenty pro-lifers stood praying in a circle near the parking lot of the Pink House as the Supreme Court gaveled in for two hours of oral arguments in the *Dobbs* case.[9]

Mississippi Solicitor General Scott Stewart renewed the demands of Mississippi's brief, encouraging the Court to "overrule Roe and Casey" and uphold Mississippi's law.[10] The justices, in their questioning, seemed at least open to upholding the state law. Chief Justice John Roberts asked, "If it really is an issue about choice, why is 15 weeks not enough time?" He said that cutoff in Mississippi's law matches standards set by most other countries. Under the viability standard, he noted, the United States was in company with countries like China and North Korea.[11]

---

[7] Pink House Defenders, "The Owner and Director of This Little Pink Building . . ." Facebook, July 29, 2021, https://m.facebook.com/PinkhouseDefenders/photos/a.235530613800455/8103 80466315464/.

[8] Taylor interview, October 22, 2021.

[9] This reporting from Stephanie Morton in Jackson, Mississippi, originally appeared in Leah Savas, "Pro-Lifers Hopeful 'Dobbs' Will Oust 'Roe,'" *World*, December 1, 2021, https://wng.org/round ups/supreme-court-weighs-its-own-precedent-on-abortion-1638399587.

[10] Supreme Court of the United States, Transcript of oral arguments in *Dobbs v. Jackson Women's Health Organization*, Heritage Reporting Corporation, 5–6, https://www.supremecourt.gov/oral _arguments/argument_transcripts/2021/19-1392_5if6.pdf.

[11] Transcript of oral arguments in *Dobbs v. Jackson Women's Health Organization*, 53–54.

The liberal justices echoed U.S. Solicitor General Elizabeth Prelogar's concern about maintaining previous court rulings. "Will this institution survive the stench that this creates in the public perception that the Constitution and its reading are just political acts?" asked Justice Sonia Sotomayor. "I don't see how it is possible."[12]

Justice Brett Kavanaugh, then seen by some as a wild card on the abortion issue, seemed inclined to buck precedent. He pointed to reversals in some major race-related cases: If the Court had upheld precedent in those cases, "the country would be a much different place."[13]

Justice Elena Kagan argued that nothing had changed since the *Roe* and *Casey* decisions: People today still disagree about those decisions for the same reasons they did decades ago. Kagan pointed to fifty years of decisions favoring a right to abortion: "This is part of the fabric of women's existence in this country."[14]

But the language of the oral arguments showed much *had* changed, partly through the proliferation of ultrasound technology. While *Casey* had tiptoed around the reality of unborn human lives, they took center stage in the *Dobbs* arguments. One pro-life attorney in *Casey* oral arguments had described unborn children as potential life, but Mississippi's Stewart, in his *Dobbs* argument, described them as "fully human" and able to recoil at an abortionist's tool "in the way one of us would recoil." The pro-abortion ACLU attorney in *Casey* had called the unborn "potential life," but pro-abortion attorneys in *Dobbs* never used the word "potential." In a telling slip, Prelogar even called an unborn child a "baby."[15]

The nation expected to hear the outcome of the case at the end of June, the standard timing for the Court to release decisions in its most controversial cases. But everyone got an early surprise when, on

---

12 Transcript of oral arguments in *Dobbs v. Jackson Women's Health Organization*, 15.
13 Transcript of oral arguments in *Dobbs v. Jackson Women's Health Organization*, 80.
14 Transcript of oral arguments in *Dobbs v. Jackson Women's Health Organization*, 34.
15 Transcript of oral arguments in *Dobbs v. Jackson Women's Health Organization*, 17–18, 86. See also Savas, "Advancing Arguments," *World*, December 25, 2021, 13–14.

the evening of Monday, May 2, *Politico* published a ninety-eight-page draft opinion authored by Justice Samuel Alito and dated February 2022. *Politico* cited an unnamed source who claimed Justices Clarence Thomas, Neil Gorsuch, Brett Kavanaugh, and Amy Coney Barrett had all joined Alito in the opinion, which *Politico* called a "full-throated, unflinching repudiation" of *Roe v. Wade*.[16]

"*Roe* was egregiously wrong from the start," wrote Alito in the draft, echoing the language of Mississippi's July 2021 brief. "Its reasoning was exceptionally weak, and the decision has had damaging consequences. And far from bringing about a national settlement of the abortion issue, *Roe* and *Casey* have enflamed debate and deepened division."[17] Under the language of the draft, states would have the power to legislate on abortion, allowing or prohibiting it as the elected representatives desired.

Within fifteen minutes of *Politico*'s publication of the story, protestors gathered outside the Supreme Court's white-pillared building under a black sky. They carried homemade signs and chanted "*Roe* cannot go!" and "Keep abortion legal." Capitol Police that night put up short fences around the building.[18]

The next day, the Supreme Court released a statement confirming the authenticity of the document but adding that it was not a final decision. Roberts announced an investigation of the leak.[19] Pro-abortion protestors at the Court shoved bullhorns into the faces of

---

16 Josh Gerstein and Alexander Ward, "Supreme Court Has Voted to Overturn Abortion Rights, Draft Opinion Shows," *Politico*, May 2, 2022, https://www.politico.com/news/2022/05/02/supreme-court-abortion-draft-opinion-00029473.

17 "SCOTUS Initial Draft," *Politico*, 6, https://www.politico.com/news/2022/05/02/read-justice-alito-initial-abortion-opinion-overturn-roe-v-wade-pdf-00029504.

18 Carolina Lumetta, "Bullhorns and Abortion Slogans at the Supreme Court," *World*, May 5, 2022, https://wng.org/roundups/bullhorns-and-abortion-slogans-at-the-supreme-court-1651783225; Associated Press, "Abortion Rights Demonstrators Rally Outside Supreme Court," published May 3, 2022, video, https://www.nytimes.com/video/us/politics/100000008331498/demonstrators-supreme-court-abortion-rights.html.

19 "05-03-22," Press Releases, Supreme Court of the United States, accessed July 9, 2022, https://www.supremecourt.gov/publicinfo/press/pressreleases/pr_05-03-22.

pro-lifers, grabbed their signs, and threw water on them.[20] Chanting groups showed up at the homes of justices, and officials replaced the fencing outside the Court with eight-foot, non-scalable fences and concrete barriers.[21]

Around the country, pregnancy resource centers and pro-life offices suffered broken windows and graffitied walls. Someone set on fire the Madison office of Wisconsin Family Action and scrawled a declaration on its wall: "If abortions aren't safe then you aren't either."[22] The pro-abortion group Jane's Revenge claimed responsibility for the arson and demanded "the disbanding of all anti-choice establishments" within thirty days.[23]

Within that month, vandals and arsonists targeted more than a dozen other pregnancy centers and pro-life groups across the country.[24] Jane's Revenge circulated another communique, promising "increasingly drastic measures [not] so easily cleaned up as fire and graffiti." The covert group called on supporters to "come out after dark" on the night of the final *Dobbs* decision to "make your anger known."[25]

Abortion had been mainly off newspaper front pages for years, but suddenly big headlines and florid articles predicted dire consequences.

20 For some examples, see Ford Fischer (@FordFischer), "VIDEO THREAD: Pushing Escalated . . ." Twitter, May 3, 2022, 9:17 p.m., https://twitter.com/fordfischer/status/1521660304316407808?s=21&t=lvTs9p26ZJUPe5dYn_3ZWA. See also Lumetta, "Bullhorns and Abortion Slogans."
21 Betsy Klein, "White House Warns against 'Violence, Threats, or Vandalism' after Protests outside Supreme Court Justices' Homes," *CNN*, May 9, 2022, https://www.cnn.com/2022/05/09/politics/abortion-protests-supreme-court-justices/index.html.
22 "Incident Report for Case #2022-171203," News & Data, Police, City of Madison, accessed July 9, 2022, https://www.cityofmadison.com/police/newsroom/incidentreports/incident.cfm?id=28881.
23 "First Communiqué," Jane's Revenge, posted on May 8, 2022, https://janesrevenge.noblogs.org/2022/05/08/first-communique/.
24 This count is based on an internal tally maintained by *World*, relying on local news reports and social media posts.
25 "Jane's Revenge: Another Communiqué," Jane's Revenge, posted on June 15, 2022, https://janesrevenge.noblogs.org/2022/06/15/janes-revenge-another-communique/; and "NIGHT OF RAGE," Jane's Revenge, posted on May 30, 2022, https://janesrevenge.noblogs.org/2022/05/.

Poll numbers reflected those concerns. Gallup polling within a week of the draft leak found 55 percent identified as pro-choice while 39 percent identified as pro-life, the largest pro-choice lead reflected in Gallup polls on abortion since the 1990s.[26]

Pregnancy centers expected increased violence following the official release of the final opinion. National pregnancy center groups advised centers on how to prepare for attacks, and many increased their security measures. A center in North Carolina installed more security cameras, bought pepper spray for employees, and purchased fire ladders to put in upper-story rooms.[27]

On June 24, 2022, the Supreme Court released its *Dobbs* ruling: 6 to 3 upholding the Mississippi law and 5 to 4 to overturn *Roe* and *Casey*. Mississippi's Jameson Taylor was on vacation with his family in Utah. He heard the news in their hotel room and gave his wife a hug, praising God for the victory. He asked her, *Hey, if I told you twenty years ago, when we first met, that I was going to reverse* Roe v. Wade, *what would you have done?* She laughed and said, *I probably would have thought you're crazy.*[28]

Taylor agreed. It wasn't just a victory for him, he said, but for "the millions of pro-lifers who . . . have worked their entire lives for *Roe v. Wade* to be reversed."[29]

The majority opinion, authored by Justice Alito, was largely the same as the draft that *Politico* had published more than a month earlier. Justices Thomas, Gorsuch, Kavanaugh, and Barrett had all joined

---

26 Lydia Saad, "'Pro-Choice' Identification Rises to Near Record High in U.S.," Gallup, June 2, 2022, https://news.gallup.com/poll/393104/pro-choice-identification-rises-near-record-high.aspx.

27 Hand of Hope Pregnancy Centers CEO Tonya Nelson, interview with author, June 17, 2022. See also Savas, "After Dobbs, Pregnancy Centers Brace for More Attacks," *World*, June 24, 2022, https://wng.org/roundups/after-dobbs-pregnancy-centers-brace-for-more-attacks-1656102951.

28 Taylor interview, June 24, 2022.

29 Taylor interview, June 24, 2022.

Alito in the majority.[30] Chief Justice Roberts had voted for upholding Mississippi's 15-week law but against overturning *Roe*.[31]

The majority found that the Constitution does not guarantee a right to abortion and that such a right is not grounded in the nation's history or tradition. Alito cited the case of Captain William Mitchell and Susan Warren that's central to chapter 2 of this book, but no other cases from American colonial times. Alito did state that common law considered abortion a crime at least post-quickening, and that many authorities condemned abortion before quickening as "unlawful."[32] (The Brooke case in ch. 3 shows that this was the "street-level" understanding as well.)

The majority also found that the due process clause of the Fourteenth Amendment did not imply a right to abortion, since at the time of its ratification three-fourths of the states made abortion a crime at all stages of pregnancy.[33] (Ch. 18 notes that legal situation and its grounding in public opinion.)

Rather than prohibit abortion altogether, the majority in *Dobbs* ruled to return the matter to the states: "The Constitution does not prohibit the citizens of each State from regulating or prohibiting abortion. *Roe* and *Casey* arrogated that authority. We now overrule those decisions and return that authority to the people and their elected representatives."[34]

---

30 CNN announced that the final version of the majority opinion had 125,290 characters (not counting footnotes or appendices), of which 24,188 (mostly responses to the dissent and to Justice Roberts's concurrence) were new. The majority had removed only 2,866 characters from the earlier draft, most of them minor changes in citation information. See John Keefe et al., "Track Changes between the Abortion Decision and the Leaked Draft," CNN, June 27, 2022, https://www.cnn.com/interactive/2022/06/us/supreme-court-abortion-dobbs-decision-changes/.

31 Roberts wrote, "The Court's decision to overrule Roe and Casey is a serious jolt to the legal system—regardless of how you view those cases. A narrower decision rejecting the misguided viability line would be markedly less unsettling, and nothing more is needed to decide this case" (*Dobbs v. Jackson Women's Health Organization*, 597 U.S. ___ (2022), ___, Roberts, C.J., concurring in judgment, 11, https://www.supremecourt.gov/opinions/21pdf/19-1392_6j37.pdf).

32 *Dobbs v. Jackson Women's Health Organization*, 597 U.S. ___ (2022), ___, Opinion of the Court, 17, 26-28.

33 *Dobbs v. Jackson Women's Health Organization* opinion, 5.

34 *Dobbs v. Jackson Women's Health Organization* opinion, 79.

As to other cases upon which *Roe* relied—such as the right to marry interracially, recognized in *Loving v. Virginia*, or the right to obtain contraceptives, recognized in *Griswold v. Connecticut*—the majority said that those decisions were totally different: "Abortion destroys what [*Roe* and *Casey*] call 'potential life' and what the law at issue in this case regards as the life of an 'unborn human being.' . . . None of the other decisions cited by *Roe* and *Casey* involved the critical moral question posed by abortion. They are therefore inapposite. They do not support the right to obtain an abortion, and by the same token, our conclusion that the Constitution does not confer such a right does not undermine them [i.e., cases including *Loving* and *Griswold*] in any way."[35]

Justices Stephen Breyer, Sonia Sotomayor, and Elena Kagan dissented. They opposed the majority's arguments about history and tradition and argued that the Court could on similar grounds dismiss the right to obtain contraceptives or to marry interracially: "Either the mass of the majority's opinion is hypocrisy, or additional constitutional rights are under threat. It is one or the other."[36]

The three dissenting justices asserted that the majority ruling would unleash a legal "upheaval" by throwing into doubt other acknowledged rights, dragging the Court into the minutia of issues related to abortion-like procedures and "life of the mother" exceptions.[37] They predicted an upheaval would also occur in society, since (they said) abortion had enabled women to take a more prominent role in society: "Indeed, all women now of childbearing age have grown up expecting that they would be able to avail themselves of *Roe*'s and *Casey*'s protections. . . . Taking away the right to abortion, as the majority does today, destroys all those individual plans and expectations. In so doing, it diminishes

---

35 *Dobbs v. Jackson Women's Health Organization* opinion, 31–32.
36 *Dobbs v. Jackson Women's Health Organization*, 597 U.S. ___ (2022), ___, Breyer, Sotomayor, and Kagan, JJ., dissenting, 5.
37 *Dobbs v. Jackson Women's Health Organization* dissent, 5, 35–37.

women's opportunities to participate fully and equally in the Nation's political, social, and economic life."[38]

But, as the majority's comments on the dissent pointed out, "The most striking feature of the dissent is the absence of any serious discussion of the legitimacy of the States' interest in protecting fetal life."[39]

State officials rapidly reacted to *Roe*'s demise. During the years leading up to *Dobbs*, thirteen states had passed conditional laws (known as "trigger bans") outlawing abortion—some outlawing it in all cases except to save the life of the mother, others also making exceptions for rape and incest. Legislators designed the laws to go into effect once a constitutional amendment or a decision from the U.S. Supreme Court overturned *Roe*.[40] Six minutes after the *Dobbs* decision came down, Missouri's attorney general announced on Twitter that he had signed an opinion putting the state's conditional law into effect, claiming Missouri therefore to be "the first in the country to effectively end abortion."[41]

Officials in other states also certified their conditional laws. In South Dakota, the conditional law went into effect immediately, requiring no certification. The next Monday, Mississippi's Lynn Fitch certified the state's law prohibiting all abortions except to save a mother's life or in cases of rape, starting a ten-day countdown to its July 7 effective date.[42] In some states, such as Wisconsin and West Virginia, pre-*Roe* laws that intervening legislatures had never repealed took effect, at least temporarily. Judges lifted injunctions on heartbeat

---

38 *Dobbs v. Jackson Women's Health Organization* dissent, 5, 48–49.
39 *Dobbs v. Jackson Women's Health Organization*, 597 U.S. ___ (2022), ___, Opinion of the Court, 37.
40 The tally of conditional laws, their exceptions, and their effective dates is based on an internal document from the National Right to Life Committee, shared with the author.
41 Attorney General Eric Schmitt (@AGEricSchmitt), "BREAKING Following the SCOTUS ruling . . ." Twitter, June 24, 2022, 10:16 a.m., https://twitter.com/AGEricSchmitt/status/1540338042413944832.
42 See Leah Savas, "Jackson's Abortion Pink House Fights to Reopen," *World*, July 12, 2022, https://wng.org/roundups/jacksons-abortion-pink-house-fights-to-reopen-1657654385.

laws in some states, including the one in Ohio for which Janet Folger Porter had fought (ch. 46).

Pro-abortion groups filed lawsuits in some states to try to halt or at least delay full enforcement of the laws. Mississippi's Pink House in Jackson put up a final fight to stay open, but owner Diane Derzis was one of many abortion facility owners nationwide who had already made plans to move operations to an abortion-friendly state.[43] Lawmakers in states like California and New York had long been exploring ways to expand abortion access and prepare for an influx of out-of-state abortion seekers. Now many other politicians and business owners also saw the opportunity for their states to become abortion destinations.[44]

But even majority pro-life states faced some after-effects of *Roe's* nearly 50-year tenure. States like Montana, Florida, and Kansas had to deal with State Supreme Court precedents that declared a *Roe*-style right to abortion in the state and stymied state-level legislative efforts. Those would have to go too, before thoroughly protective laws could take effect.[45]

States with pro-life laws faced enforcement problems that the country had not had to deal with since 1973. As soon as the Alito opinion circulated on June 24, 84 elected prosecutors released a joint statement announcing that "we decline to use our offices' resources to criminalize reproductive health decisions and commit to exercise our well-settled discretion and refrain from prosecuting those who seek, provide, or support abortions."[46]

43 Emily Wagster Pettus, "Scramble as Last Mississippi Abortion Clinic Shuts Its Doors," Associated Press, July 6, 2022, https://apnews.com/article/abortion-us-supreme-court-health-mississippi-06430712bf221d4da21e7fee7980b0ff.
44 For examples of how California and New York prepared to become abortion destinations, see Leah Savas, "New York, California Prep to Become Abortion Destinations," *World*, May 10, 2022, https://wng.org/roundups/new-york-california-prep-to-become-abortion-destinations-1652211964.
45 For more on the state-level versions of *Roe v. Wade*, see Leah Savas, "A *Roe* by Many Other Names," *World*, June 4, 2022, 46–51.
46 Zoë Richards, "Dozens of Elected Prosecutors Say They Will Refuse to Prosecute Abortion Care," NBC News, June 24, 2022, https://www.nbcnews.com/politics/politics-news/dozens-elected

By June 29, a total of 90 elected prosecutors had put their names on the statement. Many of the prosecutors were from states with few or no abortion restrictions, but more than twenty were in Georgia, Louisiana, Mississippi, Ohio, Missouri, and other states where pro-life officials were fighting to put into effect already-enacted laws protecting unborn children.[47]

In Wisconsin, the state attorney general—whose job is to defend state statutes—filed a lawsuit challenging his state's pre-*Roe* law.[48] Meanwhile, Wisconsin Family Action president Julaine Appling urged pro-lifers to turn out to vote abortion supporters out of office: "We need to be a good steward of [our votes] and say . . . it's time for us to get somebody else in there who will do their job, who will respect the sanctity of human life and uphold Wisconsin law."[49] Texas Right to Life championed the private civil enforcement mechanism in the state's Heartbeat Act as a way to work around the enforcement barrier posed by pro-abortion elected officials.[50]

Across the country, counselors and volunteers at pregnancy resource centers were gearing up for more clients. Leaders in adoption, foster care, and other compassionate groups were making their plans.

In Jackson, the Pink House performed its last abortions on Wednesday, July 6, the day before Mississippi's conditional law took effect. That day, pro-lifer Barbara Beavers, the former director of a pregnancy center in Jackson, was outside the Pink House with her husband. She said the facility was so busy that the dozen or so parking spots in the lot had filled up, forcing women to park on the street when they arrived for

---

-prosecutors-say-will-refuse-prosecute-abortion-care-rcna35305; "Joint Statement from Elected Prosecutors," Fair and Just Prosecution, last modified June 29, 2022, https://fairandjustprosecution.org/wp-content/uploads/2022/06/FJP-Post-Dobbs-Abortion-Joint-Statement.pdf.

47 "Joint Statement from Elected Prosecutors."
48 Todd Richmond, "Wisconsin's Democratic AG Sues to Block State's Abortion Ban," Associated Press, June 28, 2022, https://apnews.com/article/abortion-us-supreme-court-politics-wisconsin-donald-trump-2979751251868875a188e77b81eaac16.
49 Julaine Appling, interview with author, July 5, 2022.
50 Texas Right to Life Legislative Director John Seago, interview with author, July 5, 2022.

appointments. "Did we have to kill that many more babies till that place closes?" she said later. "Did we have to lose that many more lives?"[51]

The facility was still fighting a legal battle to reopen, but the closure became final later that month. Owner Diane Derzis told the Associated Press on July 18 that she had sold the building and moved the furniture and equipment to a new facility in Las Cruces, New Mexico. There, no laws prohibited abortion at any stage of pregnancy. The next day, the Pink House dropped the lawsuit and pro-lifers gathered near the Las Cruces building to protest its impending opening.[52]

Back in the 1980s, when Beavers's husband first started praying on abortion facility sidewalks, the state had about a dozen abortion facilities.[53] She said she and her husband used to pray outside four others that were once operating in Jackson. "We've seen them close one by one over the years," said Beavers. ". . . This was the last one. So it is a dream fulfilled."[54]

---

51 Barbara Beavers, interview with author, July 11, 2022.
52 Emily Wagster Pettus, "Owner: Mississippi Abortion Clinic Is Sold, Won't Reopen," Associated Press, July 18, 2022, https://apnews.com/article/abortion-us-supreme-court-health-jackson-state-courts-b7bf9ebeec9fa6c0083b40c060752bd4; Pettus and Leah Willingham, "Mississippi Clinic Ends Challenge of Near-Ban on Abortion," Associated Press, July 20, 2022, https://apnews.com/article/abortion-us-supreme-court-health-jackson-state-courts-5df14f3344a89d86eb2fb1272a21448c.
53 Elizabeth Arndorfer et al., *A State-by-State Review of Abortion and Reproductive Rights* (The NARAL Foundation/NARAL Legal Department, 1998), 70.
54 Beavers interview, July 11, 2022.

Epilogue

THE AMERICAN ABORTION DEBATE for fifty years suffered from a lack of imagination about what a world without *Roe v. Wade* would look like. Now, as some state governments give 100 percent support to abortion and others display 99 percent opposition, Americans are about to find out.

The Story of Abortion in America is a work of history, not prophecy, so I cannot forecast accurately the changes that will come in the first post-*Roe* decade. I can, though, list some fundamental things that will still apply. A kiss will still be a kiss. A sigh will still be a sigh. Some men with hearts full of passion, jealousy, and hate will pressure women to abort. Some pregnant women will take desperate measures in a case of do or die. The world will always welcome lovers, as time goes by[1]—but some churches won't, and some pastors who fear their congregations will be silent.

What this all means is that the need for compassionate help amid crisis pregnancies will remain. Some tiny humans will survive, but most who would have faced a death sentence will still face it, sometimes in New York, California, Illinois, or other abortion strongholds, sometimes in a lonely room where a desperate woman ingests a pill or potion, much as her predecessors in colonial America would have.

---

1 The reference here is to the 1942 movie *Casablanca*: worth seeing if you haven't seen it, worth seeing again if you have.

Life or death for unborn children will still depend on the willingness of their mothers to protect them.

Big media, as in the past, will be crucial, and street-level reporting will have more of an impact than suite-level pontificating. Sadly, initial press coverage of the *Dobbs* decision was largely hysterical. Fearmongers said governments would prosecute women and even use data from apps that millions of women use to track menstruation.[2] Journalists rarely told stories of an unexpected pregnancy enriching a life, rather than ruining it. On the other hand, some of my fellow pro-lifers were triumphalistic, foreseeing an era in which abortions vanish.

We need to remember the historical reality: Even when public opinion concerning abortion was more negative than it is now, enforcement of abortion bans was difficult. While millions of abortions occurred, only a tiny percentage of doctors did prison time. It was often hard to get police to arrest, juries to convict, or judges to support jury decisions and turn down appeals.

Activists on both sides should pay attention to a May 2022 *New York Times* column by pro-life doctor Matthew Loftus, and the reaction to it. Loftus described his "position on the political question of abortion: It should be illegal under nearly all circumstances to kill a baby in the womb because doing so deprives a human being of the right we afford to any other human being."[3] That, in itself, was unusual for the abortion-advocating *Times*.

---

2   Analysis of Justice Samuel Alito's opinion sometimes attempted to undermine his refutation of the history that underlay *Roe v. Wade*. On July 19, 2022, after I completed proofreading this book, a *Washington Post* headline declared, "Key Founders Saw Abortion as a Private Matter." The main evidence: Patrick Henry in 1792 defended two members of the wealthy Randolph clan after gossips said a young man had committed infanticide or a young woman had had an abortion. Accusations of adultery and incest were also part of the story. The *Post* article, though, did not take note of material in the papers of future Chief Justice John Marshall that render this abortion theory improbable. (See https://www.washingtonpost.com/made-by-history/2022/07/19/1792-case-reveals-that-key-founders-saw-abortion-private-matter; and https://rotunda.upress.virginia.edu/founders/default.xqy?keys=JNML-search-1-4&expandNote=on#match1.)

3   *New York Times*, May 20, 2022, accessed at www.nytimes.com/2022/05/20/opinion/abortion-doctor-pro-life.html.

Furthermore, Loftus did not make exceptions for rape, incest, or genetic findings. He wrote, "As devastating as pregnancies created by incest or sexual assault are, and as challenging as genetic malformations can be, the circumstances of one's conception are not used to justify ill treatment postnatally—so why would we discriminate prenatally? Rather, we assume that any disadvantages to a breathing child caused by poverty, violence or poor health are meant to be reckoned with by means of extra generosity and care."

But Loftus did describe the decision he had to make one day as he served the poor in Africa. A pregnant woman in her twenties had already lost about half of her blood before she arrived at the clinic. Loftus, another doctor, and the senior nurse on duty all agreed about the necessity of aborting the child to save her life, and with the consent of the woman and her husband they went to work. He mourned the need, in this extreme instance, to save one life by ending another, and said only his faith in Christ allowed him to get through the night and continue to view his medical work "as part of a battle against brokenness in the physical health of my patients, a battle whose tide was turned when Jesus Christ rose from the dead."

I tweeted that column and praised it. One reader responded by calling it "terrible" because Loftus took action rather than relying on "divine intervention" so as to save both mother and child. Then the reader sat in judgment, saying that although Loftus "talks about God, he does not believe in the God of the Bible who can and does do miracles. His guilty conscience is looking to justify his grisly deed so he felt compelled to write an opinion piece justifying himself before the world."

In one sense, such reaction was no surprise. Basketball is a contact sport, football a collision sport, and Twitter has aspects of both. Some abortion advocates screamed bloody murder and some pro-lifers said anyone against jailtime for women who abort is complicit in bloody murder. That is folly both ethically and practically. Social pressures both micro and macro—an irresponsible boyfriend, a society with many laws and economic imperatives that are not child-friendly—mean that many women are victims.

Leah has pointed out to me that women who have abortions aren't victims in the same way unborn children are. Women facing economic, social, or psychological pressure can choose not to give in. Here's where one compassionate friend (as chapter 49 notes) can be a lifesaver. How to assess degrees of responsibility is hard for me, but not for God: He knows what's in our hearts, and he shows mercy to millions. What I can say pragmatically is that arresting women is a sure way to arrest the progress of pro-life ideas in the twenty-first century.

American abortion history has also shown me that social and economic pressures are strong: When abortion pressure grows, the only fundamental thing stronger than that is love. Punitive attempts backfire. Harsh measures don't change hearts. Knowledge of fetal anatomy helps, and ultrasounds are great tools. Knowledge of the Bible helps, but many are resistant. Community pro-life sentiment is crucial not only in prevention but in enforcement as well: Without it, district attorneys won't prosecute and juries won't convict.

This doesn't mean law is irrelevant: Laws can reduce the supply of abortionists and affect beliefs about right and wrong. Laws will not end abortion but they can reduce the body count, similar to the way laws against drunk driving today cannot end the practice but can save lives. Child-friendly public policies and corporate practices can also help.

We can learn something from discussions of "structural racism" during the past several years: American society now has what I'd call "structural abortionism." The frequent corporate response to *Dobbs—we'll pay travel costs to legal-abortion states for employees in pro-life states*—shows abortion's economic role. We need more career and worktime flexibility. Governments and corporations should have child support stipends and generous maternity leave policies.

Besides those top-down changes comes the question of helping those who provide one-to-one help to women in crisis. States such as Missouri and Arizona are helping to reduce abortion demand by creating tax credits for contributions to pregnancy-resource centers. Tax credits could also help adoption nonprofits, but that will require more trust in God among women who sometimes choose abortion over "giving away" a child. As long as the only two choices for many women are abortion or becoming a single mom, pressure to allow abortions legally or illegally will remain.

Roe v. Wade poisoned children and poisoned American life. Leah and I hope the womb and the political arena will become safer places. Now that success on the supply side is possible, we hope pro-lifers will expand efforts on the demand side by helping more parents visualize their unborn children and by showing compassion in regard to material and spiritual needs. It's time for all of us to proceed, as Abraham Lincoln proposed in his second inaugural address, "With malice toward none, with charity for all."

Marvin Olasky
July 19, 2022

Bibliography

Books

Ackerman, Kenneth. *Boss Tweed*. New York: Carroll & Graf, 2005.

Acton, William. *Prostitution, Considered in Its Moral, Social, and Sanitary Aspects*. London: J. Churchill, 1857.

Adams, Grace, and Edward Hutter. *The Mad Forties*. New York: Harper & Brothers, 1942.

Adams, James Truslow. *Provincial Society 1690–1763*. New York: Macmillan, 1927.

Allen, Oliver E. *The Tiger: The Rise and Fall of Tammany Hall*. Reading, MA: Addison-Wesley, 1993.

Angle, Paul M., ed. *The Complete Lincoln-Douglas Debates of 1858*. Chicago: University of Chicago Press, 1991.

Anonymous. *The Life of Eliza Sowers, Together with a Full Account of the Trials of Dr. Henry Chauncey, Dr. William Armstrong, and William Nixon for the Murder of That Unfortunate Victim of Illicit Love: Containing the Examination of Witnesses, Verdict, &c. &c. at the Court of Oyer and Terminer, January Session, 1839*. Philadelphia: P. Augustus Sage, 1839.

Anonymous. *Madame Restell, With an Account of Her Professional Career, and Secret Practices*. New York: Charles, 1847.

Archives of Maryland. Baltimore: Maryland Historical Society, 1936.

"Aristotle." *Aristotle's Masterpiece, Or, The Secrets of Generation Displayed in All the Parts*. London: J. How, 1684.

Aristotle. *History of Animals*. Translated by Richard Cresswell. London: George Bell & Sons, 1902.

Atkinson, William. *Physicians and Surgeons of the United States*. Philadelphia: Charles Robinson, 1878.

Avery, Ephraim, and Richard Hildreth. *A Report of the Trial of the Rev. Ephraim K. Avery*. Boston: David H. Ela, 1833.

Ayer, Winslow. *The Great Crime of the Nineteenth Century and Perils of Child Life*. Grand Rapids, MI: Central Publishing, 1880.

Bailyn, Barnard. *The Barbarous Years: The Peopling of British North America: The Conflict of Civilizations, 1600-1675*. New York: Vintage, 2012.

Balkin, Jack, ed. *What* Roe v. Wade *Should Have Said*. New York: New York University Press, 2005.

Barnett, Ruth. *They Weep on My Doorstep*. Beaverton, OR: Halo, 1969.

Barrett, Robert South. *The Care of the Unmarried Mother*. Alexandria, VA: Florence Crittenton Mission, 1929.

Bates, Jerome, and Edward Zawadzki. *Criminal Abortion: A Study in Medical Sociology*. Springfield, IL: Charles C. Thomas, 1964.

Bean, Mai, Chuck Donovan, Moira Gaul, Jeanneane Maxon, and Genevieve Plaster. *A Legacy of Life and Love: Pregnancy Centers Stand the Test of Time*. Arlington, VA: Charlotte Lozier Institute, 2020.

Bennett, Sarah. *Woman's Work among the Lowly*. New York: American Female Guardian Society, 1877.

Blackstone, William. *Commentaries on the Laws of England*. Oxford: Clarendon, 1765. Reprint, Chicago: University of Chicago Press, 1979.

Blackwell, Elizabeth. *The Laws of Life, With Special Reference to the Education of Girls*. New York: Putnam & Sons, 1852.

Blackwell, Elizabeth. *Pioneer Work in Opening the Medical Profession to Women*. London and New York: Longman's, Green, 1895.

Bloom, Stephen G. *The Audacity of Inez Burns*. New York: Regan Arts, 2018.

Bowen, L. P. *The Days of Makemie: Or, The Vine Planted, A.D. 1680–1708*. Philadelphia: Presbyterian Board of Publication, 1885.

Bradford, M. E. *A Worthy Company: Brief Lives of the Framers of the United States Constitution*. Marlborough, NH: Plymouth Rock Foundation, 1982.

Britten, Emma Hardinge. *Modern American Spiritualism*. New York: Britten, 1870.

Brodhead, John, ed. *Documents Relative to the Colonial History of the State of New York*. Albany, NY: Weed, Parsons, 1855.

Brodie, Janet. *Contraception and Abortion in Nineteenth-Century America*. Ithaca, NY: Cornell University Press, 1994.

Browder, Clifford. *The Wickedest Woman in New York*. New York: Archon, 1998.

Brown, Slater. *The Heyday of Spiritualism*. New York: Hawthorn, 1970.

Brownson, Orestes. *The Spirit-Rapper*. Boston: Little, Brown, 1854.

Buchan, William. *Domestic Medicine*. London, 1769. Reprint, Sagwan Press, 2015.

Burnette, Patricia. *James F. Jaquess*. Jefferson, NC: McFarland, 2013.

Burns, John. *Observations on Abortion*. New York: Collins & Perkins, 1809.

Calderone, Mary, ed. *Abortion in the United States*. New York: Hoeber-Harper, 1958.

Callow, Alexander B. Jr. *The Tweed Ring*. London: Oxford University Press, 1965.

Campbell, Colin. *Towards a Sociology of Irreligion*. London: MacMillan, 1931.

Carmen, Arlene, and Howard Moody. *Abortion Counseling and Social Change, from Illegal Act to Medical Practice*. Valley Forge, PA: Judson Press, 1973.

Chambers, Talbot W. *The New York City Noon Prayer Meeting*. New York: Dutch Reformed Church, 1858. Reprint, Colorado Springs: Wagner, 2002.

Chernow, Ron. *Grant*. New York: Penguin, 2017.

Christian, S. Rickly. *The Woodland Hills Tragedy*. Westchester, IL: Crossway, 1985.

Cohen, Patricia Cline, Timothy Gilfoyle, and Helen Lefkowitz Horowitz. *The Flash Press: Sporting Male Weeklies in 1840s New York*. Chicago: University of Chicago Press, 2008.

Coke, Edward. *The Third Part of the Institutes of the Laws of England: Concerning High Treason, and Other Pleas of the Crown and Criminal Causes*. London: M. Flesher, 1648. Reprint, London: The Lawbook Exchange, 2001.

Conant, William C. *Narratives of Remarkable Conversions and Revival Incidents*. New York: Derby & Jackson, 1858.

Corry, Deloraine. *History of Malden, Massachusetts, 1643–1785*. Malden, MA: Self-published, 1898.

Coxe, A. Cleveland. *Moral Reform Suggested in a Pastoral Letter with Remarks on Practical Religion*. Philadelphia: J. B. Lippincott, 1869.

Crouthamel, James. *Bennett's New York Herald and the Rise of the Popular Press*. Syracuse, NY: Syracuse University Press, 1989.

Culpeper, Nicholas. *A Directory for Midwives*. 1651. Reprint, London: T. Norris, 1724.

Davis, Peter. *From Androboros to the First Amendment: A History of America's First Play*. Iowa City: University of Iowa Press, 2015.

Dayton, Cornelia Hughes. *Women before the Bar: Gender, Law, and Society in Connecticut, 1639–1789*. Chapel Hill: University of North Carolina Press, 1995.

Dean, Amos. *Principles of Medical Jurisprudence*. Albany, NY: Gould, Banks, 1850.

Denes, Magda. *In Necessity and Sorrow: Life and Death in an Abortion Hospital*. New York: Basic Books, 1976.

Derr, Mary Krane, Linda Naranjo-Huebi, and Rachel MacNair, eds. *Pro-Life Feminism: Yesterday and Today*. New York: Sulzburger & Graham, 1995.

Dodge, D. Stuart. *Memorials of William E. Dodge*. New York: Anson D. F. Randolph, 1887.

Dorr, Thomas Wilson. *A Report of the Examination of David Gibbs, Fanny Leach, and Eliza P. Burdick, for the Alleged Murder of Sally Burdick, at Coventry, R.I. on the 18th Feb. 1833*. Hartford, CT: Hanmer & Comstock, 1833.

Draper, Alexander C. *Observations on Abortion with an Account of the Means, Both Medicinal and Mechanical, Employed to Produce That Effect, Together with Advice to Females*. Philadelphia: Self-published, 1839.

Drury, Luke. *A Report of the Examination of Rev. Ephraim K. Avery, for the Murder of Sarah Maria Cornell*. Self-published, 1833.

Duden, Faye. *Serving Women: Household Service in Nineteenth-Century America*. Middletown, CT: Wesleyan University Press, 1983.

Dyer, Frederick. *Champion of Women and the Unborn: Horatio Robinson Storer, M.D.* Canton, MA: Watson, 1999.

Dyer, Frederick. *The Physicians' Crusade against Abortion*. Sagamore Beach, MA: Science History Publications, 2005.

Eidsmoe, John. *Christianity and the Constitution: The Faith of Our Founding Fathers*. Grand Rapids, MI: Baker, 1987.

Evans, Elizabeth. *The Abuse of Maternity*. Philadelphia: Lippincott, 1875.

Evenden, Doreen. *The Midwives of Seventeenth-Century London*. Cambridge: Cambridge University Press, 2000.

Fildes, Valerie, ed. *Women as Mothers in Pre-Industrial England*. London: Routledge, 2013.

Finch, Annie, ed. *Choice Words: Writers on Abortion*. Chicago: Haymarket, 2020.

Flamm, Jerry. *Hometown San Francisco*. San Francisco: Scottwall, 1994.

Forbes, Thomas. *The Midwife and the Witch*. New Haven, CT: Yale University Press, 1966.

Ford, Paul Leicester, ed. *The Works of Thomas Jefferson*, Federal Edition. Vol. 3. New York and London: G. P. Putnam's Sons, 1904–1905.

Forsythe, Clarke. *Abuse of Discretion: The Inside Story of Roe v. Wade*. New York: Encounter, 2013.

Foster, F. Apthorp, ed. *New England Historical and Genealogical Register*. Vol. 62. Boston: New England Historic Genealogical Society, 1908.

Friedan, Betty. *The Feminine Mystique*. New York: Norton, 1963.

Gallup, George Horace. *The Gallup Poll, Public Opinion 1935–1971*. New York: Random House, 1972.

Garrow, David. *Liberty and Sexuality*. Berkeley: University of California Press, 1994.

Gebhard, Paul, Martin Wardell, Clyde Martin, and Cornelia Christenson. *Pregnancy, Birth, and Abortion*. New York: Harper & Brothers, 1958.

Genovese, Vincent J. *The Angel of Ashland: Practicing Compassion and Tempting Fate: A Biography of Robert Spencer, M.D.* Amherst, NY: Prometheus, 2000.

Gilfoyle, Timothy. *City of Eros: New York City, Prostitution, and the Commercialization of Sex, 1790–1920*. New York: Norton, 1992.

Gleason, Rachel Brooks. *Talks to My Patients: Hints on Getting Well and Keeping Well*. 8th ed. New York: M. L. Holbrook, 1882.

Goodell, William. *Biographical Memoir of Hugh L. Hodge*. Philadelphia: Collins, 1874.

Gorney, Cynthia. *Articles of Faith: A Frontline History of the Abortion Wars*. New York: Simon & Schuster, 1998.

Grant, George. *Third Time Around: A History of the Pro-Life Movement from the First Century to the Present*. Brentwood, TN: Wolgemuth & Hyatt, 1991.

Griffith, R. Marie. *Moral Combat*. New York: Basic Books, 2017.

Grossberg, Michael. *Governing the Hearth: Law and the Family in Nineteenth-Century America*. Chapel Hill: University of North Carolina Press, 1985.

Guillimeau, James. *Childbirth, Or the Happy Delivery of Women*. London: A. Hatfield, 1612.

Hall, Kermit L., and Mark David Hall, ed. *Collected Works of James Wilson*. 2 vols. Indianapolis: Liberty Fund, 2007.

Hall, Mark David. *The Political and Legal Philosophy of James Wilson, 1742–1798*. Columbia: University of Missouri Press, 1997.

Halttunen, Karen. *Confidence Men and Painted Women: A Study of Middle-Class Culture in America, 1830–1870*. New Haven, CT: Yale University Press, 1982.

Hatch, Benjamin. *Spiritualists' Iniquities Unmasked*. New York: Hatch, 1859.

Hawes, Joel. *Lectures to Young Men on the Formation of Character*. Hartford, CT, 1828.

Hendershott, Anne. *The Politics of Abortion*. New York: Encounter, 2006.

Hening, William Waller. *The New Virginia Justice*. Richmond: T. Nicolson, 1795.

Hershkowitz, Leo. *Tweed's New York: Another Look*. Garden City, NY: Anchor/Doubleday, 1977.

Hilgers, Thomas W., Dennis Horan, and David Mall. *New Perspectives on Human Abortion*. Frederick, MD: University Publications of America, 1981.

Hodge, Hugh. *Foeticide, or Criminal Abortion: A Lecture Introductory to the Course on Obstetrics and Diseases of Women and Children. University of Pennsylvania, Session 1839–40*. Philadelphia: Lindsay & Blakiston, 1869.

Hodge, Hugh. *Memoranda of Family History*. Philadelphia: privately printed, 1903.

Hodge, Hugh L. *An Introductory Lecture*. Philadelphia: Collins, 1854.

Hoffer, Peter, and N. E. H. Hull. *Murdering Mothers: Infanticide in England and New England 1558–1803*. New York: New York University Press, 1981.

Hoffsommer, Don. *Minneapolis and the Age of Railways*. Minneapolis: University of Minnesota Press, 2005.

Hood, Mary G. *For Girls and the Mothers of Girls: A Book for the Home and the School Concerning the Beginnings of Life*. Indianapolis: Bobbs-Merrill, 1914.

Hopkins, Charles Howard. *History of the YMCA in North America*. New York: Association Press, 1951.

Horlick, Allen. *Country Boys and Merchant Princes: The Social Control of Young Men in New York*. Lewisburg, PA: Bucknell University Press, 1975.

Horn, James. *Adapting to a New World: English Society in the Seventeenth-Century Chesapeake*. Chapel Hill: University of North Carolina Press, 1994.

Hornberger, Eric. *Scenes from the Life of a City*. New Haven, CT: Yale University Press, 1994.

Howe, Daniel, ed. *Victorian America*. Philadelphia: University of Pennsylvania Press, 1976.

Howe, E. Frank. *Sermon on Ante-Natal Infanticide*. Terre Haute, IN: Allen & Andrews, 1869.

Hudson, Frederic. *Journalism in the United States from 1690 to 1872*. New York: Harper & Brothers, 1872.

Hunter, Robert. *Androboros: A Biographical Farce in Three Acts*. New York, 1715. Reprint, Franklin Classics, 2018.

Iseman, M. S. *Race Suicide*. New York: The Cosmopolitan Press, 1912.

Jennings, Louis. *Eighty Years of Republican Government in the United States*. London: John Murray, Albemarle Street, 1868. Reprint, San Francisco: Palala, 2015.

Jewett, Sarah Orne. *A Country Doctor*. Boston: Houghton, Mifflin, 1884. Reprint, New York: Penguin, 2005.

Jones, David Albert. *The Soul of the Embryo*. New York: Continuum, 2004.

Kasserman, David Richard. *Fall River Outrage: Life, Murder, and Justice in Early Industrial New England*. Philadelphia: University of Pennsylvania Press, 2010.

Keller, Alan. *Scandalous Lady : The Life and Times of Madame Restell, New York's Most Notorious Abortionist*. New York: Atheneum, 1981.

Kennedy, Annie. *The Heartsease Miracle*. New York: Heartsease, 1920.

Kersch, Ken. *Conservatives and the Constitution: Imagining Constitutional Restoration in the Heyday of American Liberalism*. London: Cambridge University Press, 2019.

King, Stephen. *Insomnia*. New York: Scribner, 1994.

Kopp, Marie. *Birth Control in Practice*. New York: Robert McBride, 1934.

Lader, Lawrence. *Abortion*. Indianapolis: Bobbs-Merrill, 1966.

Lader, Lawrence. *Abortion II: Making the Revolution*. Boston: Beacon, 1973.

Lader, Lawrence. *The Margaret Sanger Story: And the Fight for Birth Control*. Garden City, NY: Doubleday, 1955.

Larned, Ellen. *History of Windham County Connecticut, 1600–1760*. Self-published, 1874. Reprint, London: Forgotten Books, 2018.

Lispenard, William C. *Private Medical Guide*. Rochester, NY: J. W. Brown, 1854.

Long, Kathryn. *The Revival of 1857–58: Interpreting an American Religious Awakening*. New York: Oxford University Press, 1998.

Longchamp, Ferdinand. *Asmodeus in New York*. New York: Longchamp, 1868.

Lopez, Kathryn, ed. *Standing Athwart a Culture of Death*. New York: National Review Institute, 2018.

Lord, Daniel. *Address Delivered on the Opening of the Rooms of the New York Young Men's Christian Association*. New York: Theo. H. Gray, 1852.

Lynch, Dennis Tilden. *"Boss" Tweed: The Story of a Grim Generation*. New York: Boni & Liveright, 1927. Reprint, London: Routledge, 2017.

Makemie, Francis. *Life and Writings*. Edited by Boyd S. Schleither. Philadelphia: Presbyterian Historical Society, 1971.

Makemie, Francis, and William Livingston. *A Narrative of a New and Unusual American Imprisonment, of Two Presbyterian Ministers, and*

Prosecution of Mr. Francis Makemie One of Them, for Preaching One Sermon in the City of New-York. New York, 1755.

Malone, Dumas, ed. *Dictionary of American Biography.* New York: Scribner, 1935.

Manning, Kate. *My Notorious Life.* New York: Scribner, 2013.

Martin, Edward [James McCabe]. *The Secrets of the Great City.* Philadelphia: Jones Brothers, 1868.

Maternity Center Association. *How Does Your Baby Grow?* Florham Park, NJ: Gerber Products Company, 1939.

McCloskey, Robert. *The Works of James Wilson.* 2 vols. Cambridge, MA: Harvard University Press, 1967.

McDowall, John. *First Annual Report of the New York Magdalen Society.* New York: John T. West, 1831.

McDowall, Phoebe, ed. *Memoir and Select Remains of the Late Rev. John P. McDowall.* New York: Leavitt, Lord, 1838.

McIlwaine, H. R., ed. *Minutes of the Council and General Court.* Virginia State Library Board: Richmond, 1924.

Meigs, Charles. *The Philadelphia Practice of Midwifery.* Philadelphia: James Kay, 1842.

Melendy, Mary R. *The Ideal Woman for Maidens, Wives, Mothers.* Chicago: J. R. Peper, 1911.

Moerman, Daniel. *Native American Ethnobotany.* Portland, OR: Timber, 1998.

Mohr, James. *Abortion in America: The Origins and Evolution of National Policy, 1800–1900.* New York: Oxford University Press, 1978.

Montesquieu, Charles de Secondat, baron de. *The Persian Letters.* Cologne: Pierre Marteau, 1721. Reprint translated by John Ozell, Shrewsbury, MA: Garland, 1972.

Moore, James, ed. *The History of the Cooper Shop Volunteer Refreshment Saloon.* Philadelphia: J. B. Rogers, 1866.

Nathanson, Bernard. *Aborting America.* Garden City, NY: Doubleday, 1979.

Nathanson, Bernard. *The Hand of God: A Journey from Death to Life by the Abortion Doctor Who Changed His Mind.* Washington, DC: Regnery, 1996.

Nebinger, Andrew. *Criminal Abortion: Its Extent and Prevention.* Philadelphia: Collins, 1876.

Nevins, Allan and Milton Thomas, eds. *Diary of George Templeton Strong: The Turbulent Fifties, 1850–1859.* New York: Macmillan, 1952.

Newlin, W. H. et al. Regimental Reunion Association. *A History of the Seventy-Third Regiment of Illinois Infantry Volunteers.* 1890. Various reprint eds. available.

Nichols, Thomas. *Esoteric Anthropology.* New York: Nichols, 1853.

Nichols, Thomas. *Forty Years of American Life.* 2 vols. London: John Maxwell, 1864.

Nolen, William. *The Baby in the Bottle.* New York: Coward, McCann & Geoghegan, 1978.

Noonan, John. *A Private Choice: Abortion in America in the Seventies.* New York: The Free Press, 1979.

Oakley, Ann. *The Captured Womb: A History of the Medical Care of Pregnant Women.* Oxford: Basil Blackwell, 1984.

O'Connor, Richard. *Hell's Kitchen.* New York: Alvin Redman, 1958.

Odom, Lem. *Fifty Years in Rescue Work.* Cincinnati: Revivalist Press, 1938.

Olasky, Marvin. *Abortion at the Crossroads: Three Paths Forward in the Struggle to Protect the Unborn.* Brentwood, TN: Post Hill, 2021.

Olasky, Marvin. *Abortion Rites: A Social History of Abortion in America.* Wheaton, IL: Crossway, 1992.

Olasky, Marvin. *The Press and Abortion, 1838–1988.* Hillsdale, NJ: L. Erlbaum, 1988.

Olasky, Susan, and Marvin Olasky. *More Than Kindness: A Compassionate Approach to Crisis Childbearing.* Wheaton, IL: Crossway, 1990.

Omi, Michael, and Howard Winant. *Racial Formation in the United States.* 2nd ed. London: Routledge, 1994.

Pagan, John Ruston. *Anne Orthwood's Bastard: Sex and Law in Early Virginia*. New York: Oxford University Press, 2003.

Page, Marshall. *The Life Story of Rev. Francis Makemie*. Grand Rapids, MI: Eerdman's, 1938.

Parent-Duchâtelet, Alexandre-Jean-Baptiste. *De la prostitution dans la ville de Paris*. Paris: Balliere, 1837.

Paul, James C. N., and Murray Schwartz. *Federal Censorship: Obscenity in the Mail*. New York: Free Press, 1961.

Penrose, R. A. F. *Commemorative of the Life and Character of Hugh L. Hodge*. Philadelphia: Collins, 1873.

Perry, Lewis. *Childhood, Marriage, and Reform: Henry Clarke Wright, 1797–1870*. Chicago: University of Chicago Press, 1980.

Peters, Rebecca Todd. *Trust Women: A Progressive Christian Argument for Reproductive Justice*. Boston: Beacon, 2018.

Phillips, Daniel. *Griswold: A History*. New Haven, CT: Tuttle, Morehouse, & Taylor, 1929.

Population and the American Future. Washington, DC: Government Printing Office, 1972.

Porter, Janet Folger. *A Heartbeat Away*. Shippensburg, PA: Destiny Image, 2020. Kindle.

Pottinger, Stanley. *The Fourth Procedure*. New York: Ballantine, 1995.

Proceedings of the Free Convention. Boston: J. B. Yerrington & Son, 1858.

Rafferty, Philip A. *Roe v. Wade: Unraveling the Fabric of America*. Mustang, OK: Tate, 2012.

Rattenmann, Ferdinand. *Induced Abortion*. Philadelphia: Rudolph Stein, 1858.

Reagan, Leslie. *When Abortion Was a Crime: Women, Medicine, and Law in the United States, 1867–1973*. Berkeley: University of California Press, 1997.

Reed, James. *From Private Vice to Public Virtue: The Birth Control Movement in American Society Since 1830*. New York: Basic Books, 1978.

Riddle, John M. *Eve's Herbs: A History of Contraception and Abortion in the West*. Cambridge, MA: Harvard University Press, 1997.

Riggin, Lisa. *San Francisco's Queen of Vice*. Lincoln: University of Nebraska Press, 2017.

Roe, Clifford Griffith. *The Great War on White Slavery: Or, Fighting for the Protection of Our Girls*. Philadelphia: P. W. Ziegler, 1911.

Rogers, Ammi. *Memoirs*. Schenectady, NY: G. Ritchie, 1826.

Root, Hiram Knox. *The Lover's Marriage Lighthouse*. New York: Root, 1858.

Rosen, Harold, ed. *Therapeutic Abortion: Medical, Psychiatric, Anthropological, and Religious Considerations*. New York: Julian Press, 1954. Republished as *Abortion in America*. Reprint, Boston: Beacon, 1967.

Rosenberg, Charles. *The Cholera Years: The United States in 1832, 1849, and 1866*. Chicago: University of Chicago Press, 1987.

Rueff, Jacob. *The Expert Midwife*. London: E. Griffin, 1637.

Sanger, William. *The History of Prostitution*. New York: Harper Brothers, 1858.

Sass, Lauren R., ed. *Abortion: Freedom of Choice and the Right to Life*. New York: Facts on File, 1978.

Saur, Prudence B. *Maternity: A Book for Every Wife and Mother*. Chicago: L. P. Miller, 1889.

Schaeffer, Francis A. *How Should We Then Live?* L'Abri 50th Anniversary Edition. Wheaton, IL: Crossway, 2005.

Schaeffer, Francis A. *Whatever Happened to the Human Race?* Wheaton, IL: Crossway, 1983.

Schudson, Michael. *Discovering the News*. New York: Basic Books, 1978.

Schwarzlose, Richard. *The Nation's Newsbrokers*. Vol. 2. *The Rush to Institution, from 1865 to 1920*. Evanston, IL: Northwestern University Press, 1990.

Sears, Richard D. *Camp Nelson, Kentucky*. Lexington: University Press of Kentucky, 2002.

Semmes, Raphael. *Crime and Punishment in Early Maryland*. Baltimore: Johns Hopkins University Press, 1938.

Shapiro, Ilya. *Supreme Disorder: Judicial Nominations and the Politics of America's Highest Court*. Washington, DC: Regnery, 2020.

Sharp, Jane. *The Midwives Book, or The Whole Art of Midwifry Discovered*. 1671. Reprint, New York: Oxford University Press, 1999.

Shawyer, Joss. *Death by Adoption*. New York: Cicada, 1979.

Sinclair, Brevard. *The Crowning Sin of the Age: The Perversion of Marriage*. Boston: H. L. Hastings, 1892.

Smith, Matthew Hale. *Sunshine and Shadow in New York*. Hartford, CT: J. B. Burr, 1868.

Smith, Merril D. *Women's Roles in Seventeenth-Century America*. Westport, CT: Greenwood, 2008.

Smith, Page. *James Wilson, Founding Father, 1742–1798*. Chapel Hill: University of North Carolina Press, 1956.

Smith, William. *History of the Province of New-York*. London: Thomas Wilcox, Bookseller at *Virgil's Head*, 1757. Reprint, Cambridge, MA: Harvard University Press, 1972.

Solinger, Rickie. *The Abortionist: A Woman against the Law*. New York: Free Press, 1994.

Srebnick, Amy. *The Mysterious Death of Mary Rogers*. New York: Oxford University Press, 1995.

St. Clair, Augustus. *Guide to Rockaway Beach, with Illustration of the New Rockaway Beach Hotel, the Largest and Grandest Structure of Its kind in the World*. New York: Garland, 1880.

Stashower, Daniel. *The Beautiful Cigar Girl*. New York: Dutton, 2006.

Stephens, Mitchell. *A History of News*. New York: Viking, 1988.

Stockham, Alice B. *Tokology: A Book for Every Woman*. Chicago: Sanitary Publishing, 1883.

Storer, Horatio. *On Criminal Abortion in America*. Philadelphia: Lippincott, 1860.

Tappan, Lewis. *The Life of Arthur Tappan*. New York: Hurd & Houghton, 1870.

Taussig, Frederick J. *Abortion, Spontaneous and Induced*. St. Louis: Mosby, 1936.

Taussig, Frederick J. *The Prevention and Treatment of Abortion*. St. Louis: C. V. Mosby, 1910.

Tertullian, Quintus. *Treatise on the Soul*. Translated by Peter Holmes. Whitefish, MT: Kessinger Legacy Reprints, 2010.

Thomas, T. Gaillard. *Abortion and Its Treatment, from the Standpoint of Practical Experience*. New York: Appleton, 1890.

Thompson, Roger. *Sex in Middlesex: Popular Mores in a Massachusetts County, 1649–1699*. Amherst: University of Massachusetts Press, 1986.

Tietze, Christopher, and Stanley K. Henshaw. *Induced Abortion: A World Review*. 6th ed. New York: The Population Council, 1986.

Todd, John. *Serpents in the Doves' Nest*. Boston: Lee & Shepherd, 1867.

Tone, Andrea. *Devices and Desires: A History of Contraceptives in America*. New York: Hill & Wang, 2001.

Tracy, Stephen. *The Mother and Her Offspring*. New York: Harper & Brothers, 1853.

Treviso, John, trans. *On the Properties of Things: John Treviso's Translation of "Bartholomaeus Anglicus De Proprietatibus Rerum": A Critical Text*. Oxford: Oxford University Press, 1975.

Turner, E. S. *The Shocking History of Advertising*. New York: E. P. Dutton, 1953.

Ulrich, Laura. *A Midwife's Tale: The Life of Martha Ballard Based on Her Diary, 1785–1812*. New York: Random House, 1990.

Vice Commission of Chicago. *The Social Evil in Chicago*. Chicago: Vice Commission, 1911.

Vogel, Virgil J. *American Indian Medicine*. Norman: University of Oklahoma Press, 1970.

Von Baer, Karl Ernst. *Ovi Mammalium et Hominis Genesi*. Leipzig: Sumptibus Vossii, 1827. Google Books.

Wadsworth, Benjamin. *The Well-Ordered Family*. Boston, 1712. Reprint, Franklin Classics, 2018.

Warren, John H. Jr. *Thirty Years' Battle with Crime.* Poughkeepsie, NY: A. J. White, 1874.

Webster, Noah, and Associates. *An American Dictionary of the English Language.* Springfield, MA: G & C Merriam. 1864 edition.

Wells, Robert V. *Revolutions in Americans' Lives.* Westport, CT: Greenwood, 1982.

Werner, M. R. *Tammany Hall.* New York: Doubleday, 1928.

Wertz, Richard and Dorothy. *Lying-In: A History of Childbirth in America.* New Haven, CT: Yale University Press, 1989.

Wharton, Francis. *A Treatise on the Criminal Law of the United States.* Philadelphia: James Kay, Jun. & Brother, 1846. Reprint, Charleston, SC: Nabu, 2011.

Wharton, Francis, and Moreton Stille. *Treatise on Medical Jurisprudence.* 1855. Reprint, Arkose Press, 2015.

Wilkie, Laurie A. *The Archaeology of Mothering: An African-American Midwife's Tale.* Taylor & Francis, 2003.

Williams, Catherine Read. *Fall River, an Authentic Narrative.* Providence, RI: Cranston & Hammond, 1833.

Williams, Daniel K. *Defenders of the Unborn: The Pro-Life Movement before Roe v. Wade.* New York: Oxford University Press, 2016.

Wilson, Otto. *Fifty Years' Work with Girls, 1883–1933.* Alexandria, VA: National Florence Crittenton Mission, 1933.

Witt, John Fabian. *Patriots and Cosmopolitans: Hidden Histories of American Law.* Cambridge, MA: Harvard University Press, 2007.

Wolfe, Tom. *Radical Chic and Mau-Mauing the Flak-Catchers.* New York: FSG, 1970.

Wolff, Joshua. *Ministers of a Higher Law: The Story of the Clergy Consultation Service on Abortion.* New York: Self-published, 1998.

Wright, Henry Clarke. *The Unwelcome Child: The Crime of an Undesigned and Undesired Maternity.* Boston: Bela Marsh, 1858.

Selected Journal and Magazine Articles

Bacon, Charles. "The Duty of the Medical Profession in Criminal Abortion." Symposium before the Chicago Medical Society, November 23, 1904. *Illinois Medical Journal* 7 (1904).

Barbour, Judith. "Letters of the Law: The Trial of E. K. Avery for the Murder of Sarah M. Cornell." *Law, Text, Culture* 2 (1995): 118–33. https://ro.uow.edu.au/ltc/vol2/iss1/5.

Bartlett, Robert, and Clement Yahia. "Management of Septic Chemical Abortion with Renal Failure—Report of Five Consecutive Cases with Five Survivors." *New England Journal of Medicine* 281 (October 2, 1969): 747–53.

Blake, Judith. "The Supreme Court's Abortion Decisions and Public Opinion in the United States." *Population and Development Review* 3, no. 1 and 2 (1977): 45–62.

Butler, Sara. "Abortion Medieval Style: Assaults on Pregnant Women in Later Medieval England." *Women's Studies* 40, no. 6 (2011): 778–99. https://doi.org/10.1080/00497878.2011.585592.

Calderone, Mary Steichen. "Illegal Abortion as a Public Health Problem." *American Journal of Public Health and the Nation's Health* 50, no. 7 (July 1, 1960): 948–54.

Caplan-Bricker, Nora. "Planned Parenthood's Secret Weapon," *The Washington Post Magazine*, September 23, 2019. https://www.washingtonpost.com/news/magazine/wp/2019/09/23/feature/planned-parenthoods-woman-in-hollywood/.

Craddock, Joshua J. "Protecting Prenatal Persons: Does the Fourteenth Amendment Prohibit Abortion?" *Harvard Journal of Law and Public Policy* 40, no. 2 (2017): 539–71. https://ssrn.com/abstract=2970761.

Dayton, Cornelia Hughes. "Taking the Trade: Abortion and Gender Relations in an Eighteenth-Century New England Village." *The William and Mary Quarterly* 48, no. 1 (1991): 19–49. https://doi.org/10.2307/2937996.

DeWolfe, Elizabeth A. "Storytelling, Domestic Space, and Domestic Knowledge in the Murder of Berengera Caswell." *Storytelling: A Critical Journal of Popular Narrative* 6 (Winter 2007): 121–29.

Dorsett, Walter B. "Criminal Abortion in Its Broadest Sense." *Journal of the American Medical Association* 51, no. 12 (1908): 957–61. doi:10.1001/jama.1908.25410120001001.

Flanagan, Caitlyn. "The Dishonesty of the Abortion Debate: Why We Need to Face the Best Arguments from the Other Side." *The Atlantic*, December 2019. https://www.theatlantic.com/magazine/archive/2019/12/the-things-we-cant-face/600769/.

Francke, Linda Bird. "There Just Wasn't Room in Our Lives Now for Another Baby." *New York Times*, May 14, 1976.

Frazier, Carolyn, and Dorothy Roberts. "Victims and Villains in Murder by Abortion Cases from Turn-of-the-Century Chicago." *Triquarterly* 124 (2006): 63–78.

Gallup. In Depth: Topics A to Z. "Abortion." https://news.gallup.com/poll/1576/abortion.aspx.

Gillaspie, Anne. "ABORTIONS AT BORDER?" *Marshall News Messenger*, June 20, 1991.

Haldane, John, and Patrick Lee. "Aquinas on Human Ensoulment, Abortion, and the Value of Life." *Philosophy* 78, no. 304 (April 2003): 255–78. http://www.jstor.org/stable/3752047.

Hall, Kristin. "Selling Sexual Certainty? Advertising Lysol as a Contraceptive in the United States and Canada, 1919–1939." *Enterprise and Society* 14, no. 1 (March 2013): 71–98. http://www.jstor.org/stable/23701648.

Harris, Alisa. "Eyewitnesses." *World*, January 30, 2010.

Hentoff, Nat. "My Controversial Choice to Become Pro-Life." *Human Life Review*, Summer 2009. https://humanlifereview.com/9680-2/.

Holmes, Rudolph. "The Methods of the Professional Abortionist." *Journal of Surgery, Gynecology, and Obstetrics* (May 1910): 542–46.

Holz, Rose. "The 1939 Dickinson-Belskie Birth Series Sculptures: The Rise of Modern Visions of Pregnancy, the Roots Modern Pro-Life Imagery, and Dr. Dickinson's Religious Case for Abortion." *Journal of Social History* 51, no. 4 (June 2018): 980–1022.

Jackson, E. W., M. Tashiro, and George C. Cunningham. "Therapeutic Abortions in California." *California Medicine* 115, no. 1 (July 1971): 28–33. https://www.ncbi.nlm.nih.gov/pmc/articles/PMC1517904/.

Kennan, George. "The Sources of Soviet Conduct." *Foreign Affairs* 25 (July 1947): 566–82.

Lader, Lawrence. "Let's Speak Out on Abortion." *Reader's Digest*, May 1966.

Lader, Lawrence. "The Road from Buchenwald." *The New Republic*, September 20, 1948.

Lader, Lawrence, "The Scandal of Abortion—Laws," *New York Times Sunday Magazine*, April 25, 1965.

MacKay, Winnifred K. "Philadelphia during the Civil War, 1861–1865." *The Pennsylvania Magazine of History and Biography* 70, no. 1 (January 1946): 3–51. http://www.jstor.org/stable/20087800.

Maxwell, Joe, and Steve Hall. "Still-Silent Shepherds." *World*, January 25, 2014.

McCrummen, Stephanie. "A Maternity Ranch Is Born." *The Washington Post*, November 16, 2021. https://www.washingtonpost.com/nation/2021/11/16/evangelical-women-texas-abortion/.

Menard, Russell R. "The Maryland Slave Population 1658 to 1730." *The William and Mary Quarterly* 32, no. 1 (January 1975): 29–54. https://doi.org/10.2307/1922593.

Niles, Addison. "Criminal Abortion." *Transactions of the 21st Anniversary Meeting of the Illinois State Medical Society*, 98–101. Chicago, 1872.

Olasky, Susan. "Strategic Battles." *World*, January 28, 2012.

Ostler, Duane. "A Conversation about Abortion between Justice Blackmun and the Founding Fathers." *Constitutional Commentary* 167 (2014): 167–80. https://scholarship.law.umn.edu/concomm/281.

Parks, Casey. "What Happens when People in Texas Can't Get Abortions: 'Diapers Save a Lot More Babies Than Ultrasounds.'" *The Washington*

Post, November 13, 2021. https://www.washingtonpost.com/dc-md-va/2021/11/13/san-antonio-pregnancy-center-texas-abortion-ban/.

Pasulka, Nicole. "When Women Used Lysol as Birth Control." *Mother Jones*, March 8, 2012. https://www.motherjones.com/media/2012/03/when-women-used-lysol-birth-control/.

Paulsen, Michael. "The Plausibility of Personhood," *Ohio State Law Journal* 74, no. 14 (2012): 13–73. http://papers.ssrn.com/abstract=2254154.

Pendleton, Brian. "The California Therapeutic Abortion Act: An Analysis." *Hastings Law Journal* 19, no. 1 (November 1967): 242–55.

Pilarczyk, Ian C. "The Terrible Haystack Murder: The Moral Paradox of Hypocrisy, Prudery, and Piety in Antebellum America." *American Journal of Legal History* 41 (1997): 25–60. https://ssrn.com/abstract=1773022.

Powers, Kirsten. "Philadelphia Abortion Clinic Horror: Column." *USA Today*, April 11, 2013. https://www.usatoday.com/story/opinion/2013/04/10/philadelphia-abortion-clinic-horror-column/2072577/.

"A Protestant Affirmation on the Control of Human Reproduction." *Christianity Today*, November 8, 1968. https://www.christianitytoday.com/ct/1968/november-8/protestant-affirmation-on-control-of-human-reproduction.html.

Rafferty, Philip A. "Roe v. Wade: A Scandal upon the Court." *Rutgers Journal of Law and Religion* 7, no. 1 (2005): 1–84. https://parafferty.com/Documents/Rafferty_Roe_v_Wade-A_Scandal_Upon_the_Court_7_Rutgers_JL%20_Religion1_2005.pdf.

Reardon, David C. "The Abortion and Mental Health Controversy: A Comprehensive Literature Review of Common Ground Agreements, Disagreements, Actionable Recommendations, and Research Opportunities." *SAGE Open Medicine* 6 (October 2018): 1–38. https://dx.doi.org/10.1177%2F2050312118807624.

Reardon, David C. "The Embrace of the Proabortion Turnaway Study: Wishful Thinking? or Willful Deceptions?" *The Linacre Quarterly*

85, no. 3 (August 2018): 204–12. https://dx.doi.org/10.1177%2F 0024363918782156.

"Roe Warriors: The Media's Pro-Abortion Bias." Media Research Center, July 22, 1998. https://www.mrc.org/roe-warriors-medias-pro-abortion -bias.

Sauer, R. "Attitudes to Abortion in America, 1800–1973." *Population Studies* 28, no. 1 (March 1974): 53–67. https://doi.org/10.2307 /2173793.

Slobodzian, Joseph. "Teen Intern at Gosnell Clinic Recalls Hearing Aborted Fetus 'Screeching.'" *The Philadelphia Inquirer*, April 12, 2013. https:// www.inquirer.com/philly/news/20130412_Teen_intern_at_Gosnell _clinic_recalls_hearing_one_aborted_fetus__quot_screeching_quot_ .html.

Smyth, Julie Carr. "Ohio Clinics Close, Abortions Decline amid Restrictions." Associated Press, May 3, 2015. https://apnews.com/article/369c 2391530e41a8b351961edcdadf48.

Stout, David. "An Abortion Rights Advocate Says He Lied about Procedure." *New York Times*, February 26, 1997. A-12.

University of California San Francisco. "Abortion Onscreen." Advancing New Standards in Reproductive Health, accessed March 3, 2022. https://www.ansirh.org/research/ongoing/abortion-onscreen.

Vincent, Lynn. "Aborted Language." *World*, August 7, 2004.

Vincent, Lynn. "Climate Change." *World*, January 14, 2005.

Vincent, Lynn. "The Plots Thicken." *World*, January 12, 2008.

Westoff, Charles F., Emily C. Moore, and Norman B. Ryder. "The Structure of Attitudes toward Abortion." *Milbank Memorial Fund Quarterly* 47, no. 1 (January 1969): 11–37.

Witherspoon, James S. "Reexamining *Roe*: Nineteenth Century Abortion Statutes and the Fourteenth Amendment." *St. Mary's Law Journal* 17 (1985): 29–71.

Other Books by Marvin Olasky

On Abortion: *The Press and Abortion, 1838–1988. More Than Kindness: A Compassionate Approach to Crisis Childbearing* (with Susan Olasky). *Abortion Rites: A Social History of Abortion in America. Abortion at the Crossroads.*

On Journalism: *Prodigal Press. Telling the Truth: How to Revitalize Christian Journalism. Central Ideas in the Development of American Journalism. Reforming Journalism.*

On Fighting Poverty: *Freedom, Justice, and Hope: Toward a Strategy for the Poor and the Oppressed* (with Herbert Schlossberg). *The Tragedy of American Compassion. Renewing American Compassion: How Compassion for the Needy Can Turn Ordinary Citizens into Heroes. Compassionate Conservatism: What It Is, What It Does, and How It Can Transform America.*

On American History: *Philanthropically Correct: The Story of the Council on Foundations. Corporate Public Relations: A New Historical Perspective. Fighting for Liberty and Virtue: Political and Cultural Wars in Eighteenth-Century America. The American Leadership Tradition: Moral Vision from Washington to Clinton.*

On Contemporary Life: *Patterns of Corporate Philanthropy. Turning Point: A Christian Worldview Declaration* (with Herbert Schlossberg). *Whirled*

Views (with Joel Belz). *The Religions Next Door. The Politics of Disaster. World View: Seeking Grace and Truth in Our Common Life.*

Fiction and Memoir: *Scimitar's Edge. 2048: A Story of America's Future. Echoes of Eden. Unmerited Mercy: A Memoir, 1968–1996. Lament for a Father: The Journey to Understanding and Forgiveness.*

General Index

Abbott, Benjamin, 258–59
Abbott, Greg, 409, 415
ABC News, 358–59, 362, 410n21, 411n25
aborted babies
  descriptions of, 13, 27, 59, 80, 138, 341, 359–60
  discovery of, 8, 10–12, 173, 184
  remains of, 9–13, 119, 173, 245, 268, 390
  sale of, 396–98, 402
abortifacients
  ergot, 91, 101
  euphemisms for, 88, 103, 106n8, 114, 241
  Lysol, 3, 282–88
  Mifeprex, 378n10, 379n14
  mifepristone, 377–79, 383, 419
  misoprostol, 377–78, 383, 419
  morning-after pill, 375
  pennyroyal, 19, 90, 101, 192
  pills. *See* abortion pills
  Plan B, 375
  RU-486, 375
  savin, 46, 49, 91, 101
  tansy, 19, 90, 100–101
Abortion (Lader), 292, 301n12–13, 310
Abortion (O'Neill), 236
Abortion II (Lader), 293–94, 299n6, 301n13
abortion-industrial complex, 306, 395–402

abortion in film, 278, 365–72
abortion in the media
  attention to, 5, 65–66, 83, 100, 179, 357
  even-handed reporting, 321, 337, 357
  history of, xv–xvii, 5–12, 179, 439, 442
  pro-abortion bias, 105, 190, 299, 329, 331–37, 357–65
abortion pills
  early forms of, 100–02, 105–6, 115–16, 199
  euphemisms for, 383
  experience of, 375–79, 416–22
  mail delivery of, 260n15
  online sales of, 370, 412
  promotion of, 288n19, 401
  reversal of, 419–20
  See also abortifacients
abortion, procedure of
  danger to women in, 5, 38, 41, 55–60, 100–102, 111, 229, 281–88, 291, 376–77
  infection in, 58, 93, 102, 120, 228, 265, 277, 377–78
  proof of, 46, 72, 80–81, 202
  specialization in, 87, 93, 171, 229, 277
  tools of, 3, 57–58, 71, 95, 199, 268, 280, 282, 288n19, 428
abortion, topic in churches. *See* preaching: about abortion
"The Abortion Profiteers," 323–26

GENERAL INDEX

Abortion Rights Mobilization, 375
Abortion, Spontaneous and Induced: Medical and Social Aspects (Taussig), 256–57, 264n2
abortionists
  imprisonment of, 57, 59, 73–74, 81, 93, 115–17, 121, 179, 188, 191n13, 197, 229–30, 233, 250–51, 271, 277, 390, 397, 440
  lifestyles of, 165, 245–51, 271, 275, 397
  new-school abortionists, 171, 229, 243–51, 267–71, 273
  old-school abortionists, 171, 227–34, 243, 251, 270, 277
  prosecution of, 2, 20–22, 26n3, 46n10, 56n5, 81–85, 106, 117, 121, 153, 179, 183, 188, 201–2, 220, 223–25, 275–76, 359–60, 435–36
  specialized abortionists, 87, 171, 229, 277
Adams, Catherine Louisa, 119–20
Adams, James Truslow, 37
Adams, John, 64, 69
adoption
  alternative to abortion, 183, 215, 237–42
  backlash against, 280, 336
  support for, 334–36, 351, 368, 436, 443
adultery, 33, 43, 60, 130–31, 259, 264, 353, 440n2
advertising, 106–7, 111, 112n3, 114–116, 116n16, 163, 186, 219, 220, 221, 232, 243, 259, 284, 284n7, 383
Agency for International Development, 294
Ahern, Frank, 248–51
Aid Access, 378
Aikin, Nathan, 190–91
Alabama, 151n22, 152n23, 345
Alamo Women's Reproductive Services Clinic (San Antonio, TX), 415–16
Alaund, Katherine, 22
Albrecht, Pauline, 231

Alito, Samuel, 2–3, 429, 431–32, 435, 440n2
Alternatives to Abortion, 331
Amen, John, 275
America First Legal Foundation, 411
American Anti-Slavery Society, 128
American Association for the Study and Prevention of Infant Mortality, 225
American Board of Obstetrics and Gynecology, 389
American Civil Liberties Union (ACLU), 407, 428
American College of Surgeons, 263
American Dictionary of the English Language (Webster), 147
American Gynecological Society, 263
American Journal of Cancer, 264
American Law Institute, 291
American Medical Association, 139–40, 162, 205, 263, 284, 308
American Medico-Surgical Bulletin, 201–2
American Peace Society, 128
Americans United for Life, 306
Amherst College, 127
anatomy, fetal. *See* fetal anatomy
Anderson, Emily, 30
Andover Seminary, 127
Anglican church, 261
Anne, Queen, 51
antibiotics, 58, 93, 253, 267, 277, 285–86
anti-dismemberment bill, 392
anti-Semitism, 35
antiseptics, 91, 171, 228–32, 245, 267, 273, 277, 282–83, 287, 302
Appling, Julaine, 436
Aquinas, Thomas, 28–29
Archives of Maryland, 18–26, 30–31, 33–35, 39
Aristotle, 27–29
Aristotle (pseudonym), 53
Arizona, 279, 443
Arkansas, 345, 347
Arkansas Pregnancy Resource Center, 344
Arkansas Right to Life Committee, 319
Armstrong, Herbert, 399

GENERAL INDEX   471

Articles of Faith (Gorney), 305nn1–2, 306n3, 317n14, 326n9, 327n11, 331
Ascher, Dr. (Jacob Rosenzweig), 173, 178–79
Associated Press, 8, 11, 359, 362, 437
Association for the Study of Abortion, 291, 301, 310
atheism, 21, 267–68, 324, 381, 399
Atlanta, 223, 327, 349
The Atlantic, 281n1, 300n11, 361–62
Austin American Statesman, 336
Avery, Ephraim, 5, 82–85, 146

Bacon, Charles, 220, 228n4, 238n7
Baldwin, Mamie, 188–89
Ballard, Martha, 55
Ballard, Mildred Mason, 271
Bamberg, Justin, 354
Bangs, Isaiah, 79–80
Barnett, Ruth, 5, 273–77
Barnum, P. T., 259
Barrett, Amy Coney, 429, 431
Bartholomew the Englishman, 27–29
Barton, Frank, 161
Bates, Jerome, 286n13
Baxter, Delsie, 351n7, 356
Bean, Mary, 120
Beare, Eleanor, 57
Beautiful Cigar Girl (Stashower), 94–95
  See also Rogers, Mary
Beck, John Broadhead, 72
Bedford, Gunning, 112
Beersley, Hannah, 89–90
Beezer, Robert, 321
Belskie, Abram, 264–66
Bennett, Sarah, 78n19
Berkeley, William, 41
Bernstein, Nina, 311
Bethany Home for Unwed Mothers, 204–5
Bethlehem Baptist Church (Minneapolis), 349–51, 356
Bible
  belief in, 15, 18, 33, 56, 126, 131, 441
  centrality of, 27, 35–37, 64

  confusing verses in, 353–54
  imago Dei in, 352, 354–55, 356
  pro-life message of, 5, 35, 38–39, 47, 66, 77, 344, 351, 442
  study of, 213, 365–66, 423
  wisdom of, 58–60, 423, 442
  worldview of, 98–99, 111, 132–33, 328n13
Biden, Joe, 318
Bingham, John, 150
Birth Atlas (Dickinson), 266
birth control. *See* contraception
Bishopp, Jacob, 42–43
The Blacklist (TV show), 371
Blackmun, Harry, 22, 26, 66n10, 147, 306–10
Blackstone, William, 30, 65
Blackwell, Elizabeth, 205–6
"Blessed Be Abortion" (Dickinson), 264
Blood, Hannah, 46
Bloom, Stephen G., 243–51
Bloomberg, Michael, 396
Blunt, Samuel, 49
Bly, Nellie, 191
Bonow, Amelia, 382
Bork, Robert, 318, 320
Boston
  abortion culture in, 106, 133, 136, 158n10, 225, 253
  social conditions in, 123–24, 209, 217, 276
Boston Globe, 160, 177, 182–84, 187n2, 225, 323
Boston Medical and Surgical Journal, 121n6, 133n20, 135, 138–39, 191n14
Boston Post, 177n14, 184n10, 187
Boulton, Ann, 25
Bowlsby, Alice, 174
Bradford, Jay, 345
Bradford, M. E., 65n5
Braid, Alan, 411
Branch, Julia, 132–33
Breyer, Stephen, 322, 405, 433
Brisbane, Henry, 117–18
Britton, John, 328

Brodhead, John, 52n10, 54n14
Brokaw, Tom, 358
Bronson, Peter, 333–34
Brooke, Ann, 25, 30–31, 44, 432
Brooke, Francis, 25–26, 29–31, 33, 35, 432
Brooklyn Eagle, 121n6, 176–77, 182–83
Brooks, Gwendolyn, 4
Brown, Christa, 420n12
Brown, Edmund "Pat," 248–51, 275
Brown, James, 148
Brown, John, 327n10
Brown University, 55
Browne, Thomas, 66
Brownmiller, Susan, 267–68
Brownson, Orestes, 130
Brumberg, Joan, 237–38
Bryan, Pearl, 5, 199–201
Buchan, William, 66–67
Buckingham, Charles, 136
Buffalo Evening News, 303–4
Bukovinac, Terrisa, 398–402
Bulkley, Fannie, 271
Burdick, Sally, 80–81, 85, 127
Burger, Warren, 306, 308
Burke, James, 314
Burns, Ann, 178–79
Burns, C. C., 185–86
Burns, Inez Brown, 5, 243–51, 276n13, 277
Burns, John, 72
Bush, George H. W., 320–21
Bush, George W., 358, 368
Butler, Sara, 26n3
Buttigieg, Pete, 400
Byington, Mary, 175

Calderone, Mary, 285–87
California
    abortion culture in, 29, 244–51, 300, 342, 351, 377, 439
    abortion laws in, 151, 191, 242–46, 250, 287, 395–98, 435
    Therapeutic Abortion Act, 300
Calvin, John, 37
Calvinist, 84, 128

Canfield, Glenn, 404
Capital Care Network (Toledo, OH), 387–88
Capone, Al, 246–47
Carafem, 383
CareNet, vii, 328, 332, 346, 347, 422
    See also Christian Action Council
Carlson, Hannah, 230
Carothers, Robert, 199–200
Carpenter, Thomas, 80
Carson, Barbara, 42
Carson, Cary, 42
Casey, Bob, Sr., 391
Casey decision. See *Planned Parenthood v. Casey*
Casey, Richard, 359
Caswell, Berengera, 84n13, 120–21
Catholic Church
    contraception and, 259–62, 310
    funds for, 212n3
    opposition to, 261n20, 293, 300, 375
    pro-life leaders in, 158n10, 313–14, 315n7, 316–17
    pro-life organizations from, 211n3, 331
Catholic Conference of Bishops, 317
CBS, 278, 327, 357, 359, 362
Center for Choice (Toledo, OH), 386
Center for Medical Progress (CMP), 396–97
Center for Reproductive and Sexual Health (CRASH), 307
Charity Hospital (New Orleans), 142
Charleston Daily News, 176–77
Chaffee, John, 192–93
Charlotte Lozier Institute, 342n5, 379, 420n13
Chauncey, Henry, 90–93, 100n12, 106
Cher, 367
Chicago
    abortion culture in, 117, 181–82, 223, 225, 230, 302, 323–24
    pro-life organizations in, 211–12, 219–22, 238, 331
    social conditions in, 126, 192, 214, 236–38

GENERAL INDEX 473

Chicago Cubs, 219
Chicago Medical Examiner, 159
Chicago Medical Society
   Committee on Criminal Abortion, 219–22
   Committee on Midwives, 228
Chicago Sun-Times, 302, 323–26
Chicago Times, 192–93, 222, 323
Chicago Tribune, 117n20, 146–47, 181, 214, 220, 225n18, 226n19, 230nn6–7, 280n25, 321n21
Chicago Vice Commission, 237
Chicago World's Fair, 264
China, 278, 427
Chippewa tribe, 19
Christian Action Council (CAC), 316–17, 321, 332
   See also CareNet
Christian Advocate, 78, 159n14
Christian Family Care Agency, 334
Christian Legal Society, 317
Christian Maternity Home Association
Christianity
   evangelism in, 239–40, 422–23
   influence on early laws, 19–22, 26n3, 64–65
   influence on physicians, 14, 100, 137–39, 142, 207, 299–300, 341–42, 347–48
   influence on pregnancy centers, 218, 335, 347–48, 422–23
   influence on pro-life organizations, 7, 207n12, 316–21, 325n7, 364–67, 376–77, 399–402
   influence on social organizations, 122–25, 193, 205, 211n1, 218, 331–38, 363, 422
   media bias against, 192n15, 336–38
   opposition to, 18, 256, 261, 315
   preaching on abortion, 160–61, 349–52, 355–56
   pro-abortion influence on, 75, 354–55, 365–66
   revival of, 125–26, 137, 139, 142
Christianity Today, 299–300, 315, 324n4, 335n335

Christiansen, Sandy, 347–48
Choice Words (Finch), 4, 303n23
Church of England, 53–54
Cincinnati, 131, 185–86, 199, 386–87
Cincinnati Commercial, 150n18, 185n13–14, 186n15, 199–200
The Cincinnati Crime Book (Stinson), 199
Cincinnati Daily Times, 131
Cincinnati Enquirer, 150n19, 169n21, 184n10, 304, 387n7
City of Akron v. Akron Center for Reproductive Health, 319
civil rights, 292, 313–14, 326–27, 409n20
Civil Rights Act, 319
Civil War, U.S.
   destruction of records during, 45
   medicine during, 90n3, 141, 156, 181
   social changes of, 130, 152, 155n1, 159, 211
Clark, Jennie, 5, 183–84
Clark, Moses, 119–20
class inequality, 106–8, 158–59, 270, 277–78, 336
Claxton, Elizabeth, 26–31
Clay, Henry, 33
Clergy Advocacy Board (Planned Parenthood), 354–55
Clergy Consultation Service on Abortion, 298–99
Cleveland Daily Leader, 150
Clinton, Bill, 319, 321, 358
Clinton, Hillary, 369, 370n13
Closed: 99 Ways to Stop Abortion (Scheidler), 325–26
CNN, 361–62, 372, 401n21, 430n21, 432n30
Cohen, Jean, 231
Cohen, Patricia, 108n14
Coke, Sir Edward, 30, 65–66
Colden, Cadwallader, 26–27
Collamer, Jacob, 258
Columbia University, 227, 364
Comerfield, Judge, 231
Commentaries on the Laws of England (Blackstone), 30, 65n7

Committee on Criminal Abortion, 139–40, 219–21, 230
common law
 against abortion, 2, 17–23, 26, 30, 35, 64–66, 79, 118n21, 309, 432
 and common practice, 2, 17–23, 26, 65–66, 309, 432
 and common wisdom, 15, 23, 29–30, 35–36, 79
Commonwealth v. Follansbee, 201n19
Commonwealth v. Isaiah Bangs, 79nn1–2
Commonwealth v. Lumbrozo, 39
Communism, 270, 278, 289
community
 as deterrent to abortion, 5, 109, 332, 422–23
 breakdown of, 79, 111, 122–23, 223, 238n5
 pro-life sentiment of, 60, 115, 442
 protection of, for women, 15, 43–47, 51–52, 73
compassion movement, 331–38
Comstock Act, 259–60, 262, 309
Comstock, Anthony, 168, 258–61
Conant, William, 125nn15–16
Condon, Guy, vii, 332
Connecticut
 abortion laws in, 54, 56–61, 71–73, 106, 141, 148
 abortion stories in, 46n10, 56–59, 71–73, 94
 contraception laws in, 259–61, 309–10, 433
 first state law against abortion, 54, 73
 social conditions in, 107
consent
 age of, 108n14, 193–94
 informed, 309, 319, 385, 441
 parental, 319, 385, 389
Constitution, U.S.
 amendments against abortion, 314, 317, 319, 351, 434
 Fourteenth Amendment to, 2, 146–52, 320–21, 432
 persons in, 147–48, 150–52, 316
 pro-life views of signers, 63–69
 restrictions on abortion and, 313n1, 319, 388, 392, 425, 432–33
 rights guaranteed by, 2, 147–48, 308–12, 405, 408–11, 426–28, 432–33
Constitutional Convention, 64–65
contraception
 Catholic Church and, 261–62, 293, 310
 laws and, 259–62, 309–10, 433
 link with abortion, 253, 259–63, 284, 290–93, 309–11, 401n21, 433
 privacy and, 260, 309–10
 pro-life organizations and, 421–22
 Protestant churches and, 261–62, 298
 techniques for, 263, 284–85
Control of Conception (Dickinson), 263
Corman, Charles, 89
Cornbury, Lord, 51–52
Cornell, James, 82
Cornell, Sarah, 5, 81–85, 93, 121, 127
Cosgrove, Frank, 182–83
Cottrell, Jack, 315
Coxe, A. Cleveland, 158n10
A Country Doctor (Jewett), 203–4
court rulings on abortion
 colonial courts, 19–23, 25–30, 35, 42, 46–47, 50, 58
 difficulty of convictions, 195–200, 297, 391
 federal courts, 150, 262, 321, 327, 408, 410–11
 local courts, 120, 185–86, 190, 222, 408–9
 state courts
  California, 244
  Illinois, 230–31
  Maine, 121
  Maryland, 191, 228
  Massachusetts, 79–80
  Michigan, 190
  Mississippi, 436
  New Jersey, 188
  New York, 179, 197, 201
  Ohio, 387
  Pennsylvania, 359–62

GENERAL INDEX   475

Texas, 409–13, 436
Wisconsin, 190, 436
Supreme Court. *See* Supreme Court, rulings
Crawford, G. W., 185
Crawford, Mary, 60
Cree tribe, 19
Criminal Abortion: A Study in Medical Sociology (Bates), 286
Criminal Abortion: Its Extent and Prevention (Nebinger), 157–58
crisis pregnancy centers
  evangelism at, 239–40, 422–23
  lack of media coverage for, 239
  need for, 90, 107, 210–16, 331–38, 342, 347–48, 400, 439
  support from churches for, 212, 351
Critical Abortion Theory (CAT), 140
Crittenton, Charles, 217
Crittenton, Florence, 217
  See also Florence Crittenton Mission
Crouch, Sarah, 46–47
Cuellar, Henry, 401
Culpeper, Nicholas, 29n10, 53
Curtis, Annie, 186

D-and-C (dilation and curettage), 268
D-and-E (dilation and evacuation), 305–6, 357
Daily National Republican, 147
Daleiden, David, 396–99
Dalton, Daniel, 329
Dalton, Rex, 11–12
Darwinism, 267–68
Davidson, Geo L., 188–89
Davis, Albert, 250
Davis, Andrew Jackson, 131
Davis, Jefferson, 145
Davis, Lincoln, 368
Davis, Teri Ellen Cross, 4
Day, Kristen, 368, 402
Dayton, Cornelia, 56n2, 57, 58n7, 59n10, 61n13
Dean, Amos, 102
Death by Adoption (Shawyer), 336

death of mothers in abortion, 100–102, 113, 181–86, 196–200, 220n3, 228, 230–31, 278–79, 314, 351, 376
Deering, Minnie, 230
The Defenders (TV show), 278
DeJohn, Nick, 246–47
Delahoyde, Melinda, 332
Delaware
  abortion laws in, 45, 194, 237
Democratic National Convention, 370
Democratic Party
  pro-choice Democrats, 319, 322, 337, 354, 368–70, 401–2, 436n48
  pro-life Democrats, 314–19, 359–60, 368–69, 391, 400–402
Democrats for Life, 368, 400, 402
Denes, Magda, 13–14
Depp, Emma, 229
Derchow, Louise, 229
Derzis, Diane, 435
Detroit, 269–71, 295
Devices and Desires (Tone), 285
DeWine, Mike, 393
DeWolfe, Elizabeth A., 84n13, 120n4, 121nn5–6
DiCaro, Vincent, 346n18, 347n19, 422
Dickinson, Robert, 5, 263–67
Dickson, Mark Lee, 403–8
di Prima, Diane, 303
dismemberment, in abortions, 9, 392
Dobbs v. Jackson Women's Health Organization, 2–3, 152n24, 372, 412–13, 425–37, 440–42
doctors. *See* physicians
Dodge, William E., 122n8
Doe v. Bolton, 313n1, 373
Domestic Medicine (Buchan), 66–67
Donald, Ian, 342–43
Doolittle, Mary C., 177
Doolittle, William Augustus, Jr. *See* St. Clair, Augustus
Door of Hope, 218
Dories, Annie, 229
Dorsett, Walter B., 162, 221n7
Dotson-Dufault, Lexis, 382
Douglas, William, 310

Draper, Alexander, 100–102
Dred Scott v. Sandford, 139, 311n21, 318
due process clause, 147n6, 148, 432
Dugas, Tabitha, 418–19
Dunne, Finley Peter, 297
Dyer, Charles, 190

Eddy, Samuel, 81
Edelin, Kenneth, 323
Egbert, W. M., 93
Ehrlichman, John, 294
Eidsmoe, John, 65n5
Ekstrom, Kay, 335
Elkington, Norman, 248
Ely, Smith, 169
enforcement of abortion laws
    corruption and, 113, 158, 273, 275, 278
    difficulty of, 5, 185–92, 199, 219–26, 228–31, 273, 319, 384–91
    lack of, 87, 106, 116–18, 122, 156, 246, 278, 360
    private civil enforcement, 403–13, 436
    public opinion and, 1, 122, 158, 250, 435
Episcopal Church, 71, 158n10, 175, 211n1, 218, 263
Ericsson, Sam, 317–18
ergot, 91, 101
    See also abortifacients
Erring Women's Refuge, 211–18
Esoteric Anthropology (Nichols), 130–31
Esquire, 289
Ethical Society of St. Louis
eugenics, 132, 257, 261n20, 270n22, 314
euphemisms for abortion, 67–68, 105–6, 130–31, 161, 218, 280, 301, 382–83
    "missed period pills," 383
    "female irregularities," 105–6, 220
    "obstructed menses," 68, 106n8, 116
    "stoppage of the menses," 105, 106n8
euphemisms for birth control, 284
Euphoria (TV show), 370
evangelical churches, 299–300, 315–16, 332, 355, 364

Evangelical Theological Society, 300n9, 315–16
Evans, Elizabeth, 206n10
Evans, Thomas, 178–79
Evening World, 196–97
Evens, Thomas, 20
"The Evil of the Age" (St. Clair), 173, 176, 178, 192, 264
evolution, 268, 318
Ezell, Donna, 344–45

faith, Christian
    as deterrent to abortion, 19, 100, 126, 131, 422–23, 343–44
    of founding fathers, 65
    in Jesus, 240, 355, 441
Farnham, Eliza, 132–33
Federal Council of the Churches of Christ in America, 262
Federal Galaxy (Brattleboro, VT), 68
The Feminine Mystique (Friedan), 293–94
Feminists for Life, 332
Fergusson, David, 381
Ferris, Isaac, 122
    See also YMCA
fetal anatomy
    deterrent to abortion, 5, 111, 206–9, 267, 343, 344, 346, 348, 442
    early knowledge of, 26–29, 38, 47, 60
    increased knowledge of, 100, 137, 206, 267, 341
fetal tissue, selling of, 396–98, 402
feticide, 99–100, 186, 219, 316
fetus, use of the word, 11, 280, 316n10
Fieldstead Forum, 267n12, 313n2, 318n15, 321n21, 337n19
15-week bill, 425–27, 432
    See also *Dobbs v. Jackson Women's Health Organization (JWHO)*
Fifty Years in Rescue Work (Odom), 241–42
"final freedom," 292
Finch, Annie, 4nn10–12, 303n23
Finkbine, Sherri, 278–80, 291
Fish, Helen Mercy, 212
Fisher, Esmie, 417–18, 420

Fisk, Clinton, 145–46
Fisk, Jim, 166, 176
Fitch, Lynn, 426, 434
Fitzgerald, James, 197
Fitzpatrick, John Bernard, 158n10
Fitzsimmons, Ron, 358
Flamm, Jerry, 249
Flanagan, Caitlyn, 281–82, 285n10, 288
"flash press," 108
Florence Crittenton Mission, 194n22, 211n1, 217–18, 237n4
Florida
  abortion laws in, 151, 201, 237, 435
  abortion stories in, 328, 333, 422
foeticide. *See* feticide
Foeticide (Hodge), 99–100
forced abortions, 18, 26, 44, 79
Foreign Affairs, 276
For Girls and the Mothers of Girls (Hood), 208–9
Forsythe, Clarke, 306, 308n11
foster care, 240, 334–35, 436
Foster, John W., 181
Foster, William Z., 289
foundling hospitals, 183, 211n1
Foundlings' Home, 238
Fourteenth Amendment, 2, 146–52, 320–21, 432
Fox News, 361, 400n18
Francke, Linda Bird, 3–4
Freckleton, W. J., 231
Freedom of Access to Clinic Entrances Act (FACE), 328
Freiman, Michael, 305–6
French, Anna Densmore, 206
Friedan, Betty, 293–94

Gabler, Josephine, 277
Gallup polls, 262, 280, 294–95, 329n15, 369, 372–73, 402n23, 431
Garrow, David, 306, 308n11, 310n17
Gedicke, Herman, 187–88
Genovese, Vincent J., 268–69
George, Robert, xv–xvii, 152n24
Georgetown University, 308
Georgia
  abortion culture in, 223, 327, 349
  abortion laws in, 152n23, 223, 436
Gephardt, Richard, 314–15
Gerber Products Company, 265
Gething, Ellinor, 44
Gibbons, Maggie, 181
Gillett, Ron, 10
Gilmour, Addie, 243–44
Ginsburg, Douglas, 318
Ginsburg, Ruth Bader, 322
"girl reporters," 191–93
Girls' Protective League, 235
Gleason, Rachel Brooks, 206
Glover, Elizabeth, 33
Glover, Giles, 33
God
  blessings of, 36, 217n18, 431
  creative acts of, 35–36, 138, 316, 349–50, 355
  faith in, 19, 241, 325, 348, 355, 441, 443
  fear of, 37, 47, 58–59, 182, 423
  glory of, 350–51, 356
  grace of, 214–15, 356
  image of, 352, 354–55, 356
  law of, 36, 141, 262
  mercy of, 120, 442
  service to, 52
  standard of, 422
  unbelief in, 20, 133
  will of, 423
  wrath of, 160–61, 327, 329
Gonidakis, Mike, 392–93
Goodell, William, 98n5, 132n16
Goodrich, Caroline C., 184
Goodwin, Annie, 195–97, 201
Gore, Al, 319
Gorney, Cynthia, 305nn1–2, 306, 317n14, 326–27, 331
Gorsuch, Neil, 429, 431
Gosnell, Kermit, 359–62, 389–91
gospel (good news), 239–40, 349–51, 355–56, 422
Gould, John, 33–34
Gould, Margaret, 33–34
Grant, Christopher, 46

Grant, "Dr." *See* Thompson, Robert
Grant, Ulysses S., 258–59
Gratian, 27
Gray, Hannah, 69, 71
Gray, Nellie, 313–15, 325n7, 401
Great Awakening, 58–59
"great leap forward" (China), 278
Greater Toledo Right to Life, 389
Greeley, Horace, 94, 120n2, 130n9, 178
Green, H. L., 239
Greensburg Standard (Greensburg, IN), 185–86
Gregory, Benjamin, 186
Griffin, Michael, 328
Grindle, Madame H. D., 173, 178–79
Griswold v. Connecticut, 260n16, 309–10, 433
Grossberg, Michael, 117n19, 121n7, 191n14, 260n15
Grosvenor, Hannah, 57, 59
Grosvenor, Leicester, 56
Grosvenor, Sarah, 5, 56–60, 94
Grosvenor, Zerviah, 56, 58n7, 59
Grudem, Wayne, 353
Guillimeau, James, 29n10
guilt, after abortion, 14, 303, 334, 345, 369, 376
Gunn, David, 328
Guttmacher Institute, 287, 347n20

Hagenow, Lucy, 229–31
Hall, Robert, 301
Hallowell, John, 57–59
Hammond, John, 33
Handbook on Abortion (Willke), 392
Hannigan, Loretta, 201
Haring, Tere, 363
Harper's Weekly, 167
Harris, Kamala, 397–98
Harris v. McRae, 319
Harrison, Gus, 195
Hart, Gary, 337
Hart, H. L. A., xvi
Harvard University, 37, 127, 219, 236, 289, 318
Harvard Medical School, 135

Harvey, Jeanette, 420–21
Haskell, Martin, 386–87
Haskell, P. S., 142–43
Hathaway, Isaac, 7–10
Hatch, Benjamin, 130
Hatch, Orrin, 317
Hawes, Joel, 107–8
Hayward, Tammy, 422–23
HBO, 367, 370
Hearst, William Randolph, 183n6, 246, 249
heartbeat bills, 27n6, 354, 385, 391–93, 410, 415
Heartbeat International, 331, 419–20
Heartsease, 239–41
Heinrich, Bernard, 197
Hellman, Louis, 294
Hell's Kitchen, 163–64
Helms, Jesse, 38, 317
Hendricks, Agnita, 25
Hendrickson, Michele, 353
Henie, Sonja, 247
Henshaw, Stanley K., 287
Hentoff, Nat, 315n6, 324n4
Herod, 137, 157
Hershkowitz, Leo, 168n18
Hildreth, Richard, 85n16
Hill, Paul, 328
Hillabrand, John, 331
Hippocratic Oath, 27n6, 306
Hodge, Charles, 99
Hodge, Hugh, 5, 97–102, 135, 138, 156, 266
Hoff, Joe, 247
Hoffer, Peter, 46n10
Hoffman, Peter, 230
Hogan, Maggie, 216
Hollywood, 369, 374
  See also abortion in film
Holman, Lucy, 79–80
Holmes, Edward, 219
Holmes, Rudolph, 219–26, 230
Holmes, Sherlock, 3, 46n10
Homes of Mercy, 218
Hood, Mary Gould, 5, 204–9

Hope Medical Group for Women (Shreveport, LA), 403
Hope Women's Resource Clinic (Beaumont, TX), 421
Hopkins, Charles Howard, 123nn11–12, 124n13–14, 126n19
Horr, Oren, 141
Howard, Dorcas, 19
Howard, Jacob, 146–49
Howe, E. Frank, 152
How Should We Then Live? (Schaeffer), 316
Hubbard, Elizabeth, 91–92
Hudson, Stanton, 232–33
    See also Thompson, Robert
Hughes, Bryan, 404–6, 409
Hull, N. E. H., 46n10
Human Coalition, 421
Human Life Amendment, 314
Human Life Federalism Amendment, 317
Human Life Statute, 317
Hume, E. E., 162
Hunter, Robert, 52–54
Hyde Amendment, 319, 370
Hyde, Edward. *See* Cornbury, Lord

The Ideal Woman (Melendy), 208
If These Walls Could Talk (movie), 367
illegitimacy. *See* unwed mothers
Illinois
    abortion laws in, 73, 151, 190, 191n14, 222, 230–31, 237, 302, 411, 439
    abortion stories in, 9, 145–46, 153
The Illinois Medical Journal, 220n3, 236n1, 238
Illinois Right to Life Committee, 325
imago Dei, 352, 354–55, 356
indenture, 25, 41–44
informed consent, 309, 319, 385
Indianapolis News, 198–99, 312
Indianapolis Star, 303
infanticide, 46n10, 51, 72n4, 135, 152, 165, 192, 219, 352n9, 356, 440n2
    See also feticide

infections, in abortion, 58, 93, 102, 120, 227–28, 265, 277, 377–78
Ingenthron, Inez. *See* Burns, Inez Brown
Insomnia (King), 329
Institutes of the Laws of England (Coke), 30, 65–66
intra-uterine murder, 135
Iredell, James, 69
Iseman, M. S., 223

Jackson, Jesse, 314–15
Jackson, Scott, 5, 199–200
Jackson Women's Health Organization (JWHO), 2–3, 152n24, 372, 412–13, 425–37, 440–42
James, Cyrus, 80
Jane's Revenge, 430
Jaquess, James, 5
Jay, John, 64, 69
Jefferson, Mildred, 323
Jefferson, Thomas, 19
Jennings, Louis, 167, 176
Jesus
    faith in, 78, 216, 240, 355–56
    gospel of, 239–40, 349–51, 355–56, 422
    resurrection of, 441
    unbelief in, 18, 354
Jewett, Helen, 103–4
Jewett, Sarah Orne, 203–4
Jezebel, 288n19, 354
Jim Crow laws, 270
John the Scot, 22
Jones, Bob, 368n2
Jones, Flora, 150–51
Jones, Heather, 410
Journal of Child Psychiatry and Psychology, 381

Kagan, Elena, 428
Kan, Chris, 369
Kansas
    abortion laws in, 151, 435
    abortion stories in, 8–9, 334
Kansas City Times, 192
Kasich, John, 386n6, 391–93

Kavanaugh, Brett, 393, 428–29, 431
Kay, Herma, 310
Keemer, Edgar, 5, 269–71, 273
Keller, Tim, 36n9, 352–53, 355–56
Kelly, Dorothy, 261
Kelly, Patrick, 327
Kendall, John, 42–44
Kendall, William, 42–44
Kennan, George, 276
Kennedy, Annie, 239–41
Kennedy, Anthony, 320–21, 393
Kennedy, Ted, 313, 315, 318
Kentucky
  abortion laws in, 151, 200
  abortion stories in, 145–46, 162, 199, 307
Kerry, John, 368
Keys, Thomas, 306
Kimball, Daniel, 184
King, Stephen, 329
Kingsley, Mary, 91–93
Kinne, Theodore, 188–89
Kinsey, Alfred C., 263, 266–67
Knights of Columbus, 269, 373
Kohn, Wanda, 333, 422–23
Krause, Marshall, 310
Kuhn, Sophie, 230

Lader, Lawrence, 289–94, 297–302, 309–11, 324, 375
  Abortion, 292, 301nn12–13, 310
  Abortion II, 293–94, 299n6, 301n13
  The Margaret Sanger Story, 290–92
Ladies Christian Association, 125
Ladies Home Journal, 284
Lally, Mark, 385
Lamb v. State, 191
Landeau, Michele, 287
Lanphier, Jeremiah, 124
Lauer, Matt, 367
Law and Order: SVU (TV show), 370
The Laws of Life (Blackwell), 205
Lawson, Aliyah, 416, 419–20
Leach, Francis, 80–81
Leary, Mary Ellen, 247
Leavy, Zad, 310

LeCount, Caroline, 155
Lectures to Young Men (Hawes), 107–8
Lee, Robert E., 145
Lee, Sam, 326
Lenape tribe, 19
Leonard, Edward, 187
Leonard, John, 137
Levassy, Eliza Frances, 5, 185–86
Lewit, Sarah, 285
LGBTQ, 370
libel law, 191
liberty, definitions of, 3, 133, 138, 147–48, 260, 320–21
Library of Congress, 5, 109n16, 141–42, 157, 159n15, 212
Liby, Tibby, 198, 201
life before birth
  beginning of life, 3, 35–38, 137–38, 162, 206–9, 255, 265–66, 309, 311, 325
  biblical view of, 5, 35–38, 66, 99–100, 138, 161–62
  early understanding of, 28–29, 65, 72, 136–37
  rejections of, 72, 136, 142
  Roe v. Wade decision on, 22, 26, 147, 309–12
  ultrasounds show, 255–56n2, 288, 324–25, 339, 342–48, 367, 418, 428
The Life of Eliza Sowers, 90–94, 100n12
"life of the mother" exceptions for abortion, 74, 139, 279, 291, 295, 351, 373, 402n23, 433–34, 441
The LIGHT House, 334
Lincoln, Abraham, 1, 139, 146–47, 443
Lincoln Star, 231
Linton, Paul, 412
Lispenard, William C., 136
Lister, Joseph, 227
Lithwick, Dalia, 365
living conditions
  in Chicago, 126, 192, 214–15, 236–38
  in the colonies, 17–18, 35–36, 41–42, 47, 60
  in Minneapolis, 204–5

GENERAL INDEX   481

in New York City, 71–72, 102, 105, 161, 221
in Philadelphia, 108, 124, 155–56
LivingWell Clinic, 342
Loftus, Matthew, 440–41
Lohman, Anna, 104–6, 114–15
    See also Restell, Madame
Lohman, Charles, 104–6, 114–15
Long, William, 120
Longchamp, Ferdinand, 165
Lord, Daniel, 122–23
Los Angeles Times, 10–12, 232, 280, 292, 308, 328, 332, 337
Louisiana
    abortion laws in, 403–4, 418, 436
    abortion stories in, 346n18, 403, 418
Loving v. Virginia, 433
Lowy, Lottie, 231
Lubbock, Texas, 408–9
Lukens, Esther, 129
Lumbrozo, Elizabeth (née Weales), 33–35, 38–39
Lumbrozo, Jacob, 33–35, 38–39
Lydston, Bathsheba, 50, 60
Lysol, 3, 282–88

MacLeod, Jack, 337
Maddison, Lola, 230
Maeding, Weeseetsa, 371
Maginnis, Pat, 301
mail-order abortion businesses, 259–60, 379, 412
Maine
    abortion laws in, 60, 119, 121, 151
    abortion stories in, 55, 120, 141–42
Makemie, Francis, 51–52
Malcolm, Robert, 232–33
    See also Thompson, Robert
Mallory, James, 190
Malone, Dumas, 142
Manchin, Joe, 401–2
Manning, Kate, 102, 116n17
manslaughter, 81, 121, 151, 179, 197, 323, 368, 390
Marcantonio, Vito, 289
March for Life, 315, 353, 362–63

marriage
    anti-marriage movement, 127–29
    community pressure for, 31, 43, 45, 73, 236
    contraceptive use within, 259–62, 310
    false promises of, 42, 46, 60, 74, 182, 214, 241, 274
    forced, 34, 39, 41
    God's standard for, 422
The Married Woman's Private Medical Companion (Lohman), 114
Marshall, John, 440n2
Marshall, Thurgood, 308
Marshner, Connie, 315n7, 328
Martin, Nick, 10n9, 12
Maryland
    abortion stories in, 17–23, 25–31, 34–35, 39, 67–68, 347
    colonial abortion laws in, 22–23, 30–31, 34–35, 39, 72–73
    modern abortion laws in, 151, 191, 228, 237, 297, 309, 332, 402
Maryland Gazette, 67–68
Massachusetts
    abortion culture in, 37, 117, 120, 160
    abortion laws in, 46, 50, 79–81, 113, 151, 201
    churches in, 159–61
Mason, Melanie, 363
Masterson, Bridget, 231
Maternity: A Book for Every Wife and Mother (Saur), 207
Maternity Center Association, 264–66
maternity homes, 183, 335
Maternity Hospital (Minneapolis), 205
Mather, Cotton, 38
Mathewes-Green, Frederica, 332
Mauriceau, A. M., 114, 173
Mayo Clinic (Rochester, MN), 306
Mayo, Dwight, 133
McCabe, James, 164
McCloskey, Robert, 64nn2–4
McCrummen, Stephanie, 363–65
McDowall, John, 5, 75–78, 258
McDowall's Journal, 77–78
McGonegal, Henry, 195–97, 201

McGovern, Walter, 250
McKenzie, Lillian, 239
Means, Cyril, Jr., 22, 297, 309
Media Research Center, 358–59
Medicaid, 379, 422
Medical Society of Pennsylvania, 157–58
Meet the Press, 361
Meharry Medical College, 269
Melendy, Mary R., 208
Memphis Commercial Appeal, 303, 31n21
Memphis riots, 148–52
men
    double standard for, 59, 191, 236, 242, 371
    pressure for abortion from, 44, 56, 76, 417, 420, 439
    promiscuity of, 45, 76–77, 83, 101n14, 106–8, 122–24, 129, 191–94, 205n6, 214
    "reputed fathers," 50, 58, 85
    responsibility of, 43–45, 50, 60–61, 85, 94, 193, 212
mental health
    effects of abortion on, 380–82
    as reason for abortion, 278, 307
    See also therapeutic abortion
Meric, Victor, 261
Mexico City policy, 321–22
Michael, David, 350–51
Michaelson, Judith, 10
Michigan
    abortion laws in, 151, 190–91, 295
    abortion stories in, 190, 269–71
Midtown Pregnancy Support Center, 369
midwives
    in colonial society, 51
The Midwives Book (Sharp), 21nn13–14, 28–29, 36
Miller, Amy Hagstrom, 365
Miller, Ray, 108
The Militant, 270
Milwaukee Journal, 311
Minneapolis
    churches in, 349–51, 355–56
    living conditions in, 204–5
    pro-life organizations in, 204–5, 217

miscarriage
    Bible references to, 300n9, 353–54
    later effect of abortion, 265, 376, 422
    misnaming abortion as, 20, 34, 378–79
    result of abortive techniques, 57, 59, 113, 277, 301
    synonym for abortion, 20, 26, 54, 67, 73, 131n10
    treatment for, 420n12
misprision, 65–66
Mississippi
    abortion laws in, 425–29, 431–37
    See also Jackson Women's Health Organization (JWHO)
    See also Pink House
Missouri, 73, 151, 319, 434–36
Mitchell, James, 161
Mitchell, Jonathan, 404–12
Mitchell, Michael, 249n21
Mitchell, William, 17–30, 35, 432
Mohegan tribe, 19
Mongar, Karnamaya, 390–91
Montana, 376–77, 435
Montesquieu, Charles-Louis de Secondat, 66
Moody, Howard, 298–99, 302
Moore, Jesse, 404
Moorecocke, Elizabeth, 19–20
morning-after pill, 375
Morning Joe (MSNBC), 287n16, 362
"The Mother" (Brooks), 4
The Mother and Her Offspring (Tracy), 137
Mother Jones, 285n10, 335n14, 361
Mottard, Henry, 239
MSNBC, 287n16, 362
Myers, Lonny, 302
Myers, Will, Jr., 5, 185–86
My Notorious Life (Manning), 102, 116
The Mystery of Marie Roget (Poe), 94

Nathanson, Bernard, 293n13–14, 294, 307, 324–25
National Abortion Federation, 335, 397n10
National Abortion Rights Action League (NARAL), 293n15

GENERAL INDEX 483

National Association for the Advancement of Colored People (NAACP), 270
National Association of Evangelicals, 355
National Association for the Repeal of Abortion Laws (NARAL), 22, 293–94, 302, 437n53
National Coalition of Abortion Providers, 358
National Institute of Family and Life Advocates (NIFLA), 346
National Institute for Health Care Excellence (NICE), 420n12
National Organization for Women, 294, 320, 326
National Police Gazette, 112–13, 114n9
National Public Radio, 3, 288n17
National Review, 287n15, 300n10, 336n15
National Right to Life Committee (NRLC), 316, 323, 358n3, 373, 392, 434
Native American tribes, 19
nativism, 140–41
Nazi Germany, 30n13, 305
NBC, 357–59, 362–63, 370–71, 393n29, 396n4, 435n46
Nebinger, Andrew, 5, 156–59
Nebraska, 151, 231
Nebuchadnezzar, 161
Neuharth, Al, 89
New Age beliefs, 137
New England Journal of Medicine, 284–85, 325
New England Non-Resistance Society, 128
New Hampshire, 120, 139, 320
New Hampshire Journal of Medicine, 139
New Jersey
  abortion laws in, 151–52, 188
  abortion stories in, 187–89, 358
New Life Counseling (Lake Charles, LA), 418
Newman, Melanie Roussel, 371
New Orleans
  abortion reporting in, 78, 114, 174, 178
  massacre in, 149–52
  pro-life organizations in, 142
Newsboy Home (Minneapolis), 205
new-school abortionists, 171, 229, 243–51, 267–71, 273
  See also Barnett, Ruth; Burns, Inez; Keemer, Edgar; Spencer, Robert
New York Call, 260
New York City
  abortion culture in, 104–9, 111–17, 164–68, 182, 206, 223, 233, 240, 269, 286, 291, 298, 307, 367, 396
  anti-abortion culture in, 51–54, 76–78, 122–27, 217–18, 238–39, 258–59, 324–25, 367
  living conditions in, 13, 53, 73–78, 94–95, 102, 163–65, 204, 221
  World's Fair in, 263–66
New York Children's Aid Society, 238
New York City Board of Education, 206
New York Daily News, 233
New York Express, 111, 112n2
New York Herald, 103–6, 111, 114, 117, 125, 182
New York Post, 299
New York Society for the Suppression of Vice, 258
New York State, abortion laws in, 51–54, 72, 76, 106, 113–17, 164–66, 179, 197, 201, 307, 435
New York Sun, 104–5, 106nn7–8, 166, 175
New York Times
  abortion stories in, 7–10, 13, 120, 167–69, 173–79, 181, 187–88, 192, 195–97, 280, 323, 358, 361–62
  legal stories in, 260n15, 392, 405n7
  political stories in, 38n14, 313, 401n21, 440
  pro-abortion bias in, 3–4, 289n1, 299, 301–2, 311, 335n14, 337, 346, 367, 380
  religion stories in, 125n16, 131–32, 301–2

New York Tribune, 94, 113n8, 114, 120nn2–3, 178
New York World, 191, 201n17
New Zealand, 381
Nichols, Thomas, 130–31
Nightingale, Abigail, 56–57, 59
Niles, Addison, 159–60
Nilsson, Lennart, 267
Nixon, Richard, 294–95
Nixon, William, 89–91
Noel, Mary, 190
Noonan, John, 295n18
Northern California Civil Liberties Union, 310
Northwestern Hospital, 204
Northwestern University, 226
Norwich Courier (Norwich, CT), 72
Nucatola, Deborah, 397

Observations on Abortion . . . Together with Advice to Females (Draper), 100–101
Obvious Child (movie), 369
O'Callaghan, Peter, 236
O'Connor, Anne, 347n19
O'Connor, Sandra Day, 318
O'Keefe, James, 395
O'Neill, Eugene, 236
O'Toole, Kitty, 5, 189–90
Odom, Lem, 241–42
Ohio
  abortion laws in, 150–51, 152n23–24, 385–89, 391–93, 409, 435–36
  abortion stories in, 195, 199–200, 207
  pro-life organizations in, 78, 385, 391–93
Ohio Right to Life, 385
Ojibwe tribe, 19
Olasky, Marvin
  Abortion at the Crossroads, 327n10
  "The Abortion Empire Strikes Back," 396n3
  Abortion Rites, 109n16, 133n18, 218n19
  Fighting for Liberty and Virtue, 52n8
  "Frontline Dispatches," 333n7
  More Than Kindness, 334n10–11, 335n13, 336n17
  "Opposing Abortion Clinics," 175n5
  "Orchestrated Uproar," 396n5
  The Press and Abortion, 105n5, 116n16, 169n20, 298n3, 323n1, 324n2, 335n14
  Prodigal Press, 192n15
  The Tragedy of American Compassion, 238n6
  "The Village's Pro-Life Voice," 324n4
  "The War on Adoption," 336n15
Olasky, Susan, 332n3, 335n12
  More Than Kindness, 334n10–11, 335n13, 336n17
  "Strategic Battles," 392n23–24
old-school abortionists, 171, 227–34, 243, 251, 270, 277
Old South First Presbyterian Church (Newburyport, MA), 160
Oles, Margaret, 35
Omaha World-Herald, 302–3, 312
"On the Property of Things" (Bartholomew), 27
Operation Rescue, 326–8, 331, 387n8
Oregon, 151, 273–77
Oreman, Jennie, 207–8
Orlando Sentinel, 312, 333
Orthwood, Anne, 5, 18n3, 41–46, 112n2
Orton, C. H., 5, 189–90
Orwin, George, 19
ovariectomy, 140
Oxford English Dictionary, 147
OxyContin, 389

Packwood, Bob, 38
Padawer, Ruth, 358
Parade, 289, 290n3
parental consent, 103, 385, 389
Paris, 94, 109
Park, John, 149
Parks, Casey, 363
partial-birth abortion, 357–58
Partial-Birth Abortion Ban, 358
Pasteur, Louis, 227
Patterson, Holly Marie, 377–78

Paul, Daniel, 50
Pease, Elizabeth, 128
Pelley, Scott, 327
Pence, Mike, 362
Pendleton, Brian, 300n10
Penitent Female's Refuge (Boston), 217
Pennsylvania
　abortion laws in, 141, 155, 158, 319, 389–91
　abortion stories in, 68, 157, 223, 267–68, 359, 362
　pro-life groups in, 335n13
　See also Philadelphia
pennyroyal, 19, 90, 101, 192
　See also abortifacients
Penrose, R. A. F., 100n11
personhood, of the unborn, 147–48, 150–52, 316
Peters, Rebecca, 7n1
Pew Research Center, 371–72
Pharaoh (Egypt), 161
Philadelphia
　abortion cases in, 359–61, 389–91
　abortion stories in, 7–8, 89–94, 103, 106, 359–61
　living conditions in, 108, 124, 155–56
　pro-life efforts in, 69, 98–100, 124–25, 157–59
Philadelphia Almshouse Hospital, 98
Philadelphia Inquirer, 7n3, 68nn17–18, 157n7, 159n11, 169n21, 223n14, 359–60, 390n18
The Philanthropist, 193–94
Phoenix, 278–79, 334
physicians
　female, 203–9, 302, 342, 371
　pro-abortion, 223–25, 229–32, 263–64, 270
　pro-life, 99, 137, 139–42, 156, 205, 219–26, 238, 299, 302, 342
　specialized in abortions, 87, 93, 171, 221, 229, 276–77, 286, 307–9
Pickering, Charlie, 329
Pierce, Nina, 231
Pilpel, Harriet, 297, 300

Pink House. *See* Jackson Women's Health Organization (JWHO)
Pink House Defenders, 425, 427
Pio Nono College, 142
Piper, John, 349–51, 355–56
Plan B, 375–76
　See also abortifacients
Planned Parenthood
　abortions at, 375–76, 408–9
　Clergy Advocacy Board, 354–55
　demonstrations at, 332, 349, 353, 399
　financial support for, 396–97, 400–401
　illegal actions of, 395–98, 408–9
　leadership of, 129, 266, 273, 285, 297, 327
　media bias for, 333–34, 369–74
Planned Parenthood v. Casey, 2, 133n19, 320–21, 406, 425–33
Playboy, 301–2, 336–37
Poe, Edgar Allen, 94
Politico, 429, 431
Pope Pius XI, 261–62
population control, 140–41, 292, 294–95, 301n12, 314
Porter, Janet Folger, 385–86, 391–93, 435
Post, Emma, 117
post-partum psychosis, 140
post-*Roe* effects, 285–88, 321, 413, 439–43
"potential life," 428, 433
Pottinger, Stanley, 337
Powell, Lewis, 318
Powers, Kirsten, 360–61
preaching
　about abortion, 158–60, 191, 296, 349–52, 355–56
　about the gospel, 349–51, 355–56, 422
　about sexual ethics, 75
Preformationists, 137
Pregnancy and Family Care Center (Leesburg, FL), 422
Pregnancy Center of the Coastal Bend (Corpus Christi, TX), 416, 420n13
pregnancy help centers. *See* crisis pregnancy centers

pregnancy resource centers. *See* crisis pregnancy centers
Prelogar, Elizabeth, 428
prenates, 7
Presbyterian churches, 51–52, 98, 122, 159–61, 352
The Prevention and Treatment of Abortion (Taussig), 255
Prince, Nan, 203
Princeton University, 97, 352
privacy issue, 3, 260, 306n4, 310–11, 314–15n6, 440n2
private civil enforcement, of abortion laws, 402–11, 436
Progressive Anti-Abortion Uprising (PAAU), 399–400
Pro-Life Action League, 325
pro-life Democrats. *See* Democratic Party
pro-life physicians. *See* physicians
pro-life pregnancy centers. *See* crisis pregnancy centers
Pro-Life San Francisco, 399
ProLove Ministries, 380
prostitution, 76–77, 103–9, 123, 205, 212, 237, 258, 276
Protestant churches
 abortion, view of, 298–301, 351
 contraception, view of, 262, 298
 pro-life organizations from, 211–12, 218, 331
 revival in, 125–26, 137, 139
Provincial Court of Maryland, 20, 23, 26, 30, 35
public funds for abortion, 320–22
public opinion
 anti-abortion, 151, 167–69, 233, 369, 372
 effect on judicial opinion, 1, 201, 432, 440
 pro-abortion, 294, 372
Pufendorf, Samuel, 66
Pulitzer, Joseph, 183n6, 191, 196
Puritans, 46, 71–72
Putnam, May, 230

Queen, Lavinia, 250
Queen Mother's Maternity Hospital (Scotland), 343
quickening
 abortion before, 45, 206–7, 309, 432
 definition of, 21, 26n4, 65
 legal precedence and, 25–26, 29–30, 73, 118n21, 151, 156–58
 life before, 99, 139, 142, 207–9, 253
 proving pregnancy before, 21, 34, 80, 121, 201

racism, 140–41, 151–52, 155, 269–71, 336, 442
Rackauckas, Tony, 398
Rafferty, Philip A., 22–23nn16–17, 26n4
Rand, Madeline, 245
Random House, 337
Rattenmann, Ferdinand, 136
Ravenholt, Reimert, 294–95
Reader's Digest, 292
Reagan Democrats, 315
Reagan, Leslie, 141n20, 162n21, 269n19, 276–78
Reagan, Ronald, 12, 300n10, 317–18, 324n4
Reardon, David C., 380n18, 381
Reddy, Mary, 43
Redeemer Presbyterian Church (New York City), 352
Reed, John, 256
Rehnquist, William, 2n3, 318
Republican party
 divided over abortion, 316–18, 402n23
 inaction on abortion laws, 152, 259, 386, 391
 pro-life support from, 294, 314–15, 320, 368, 386
"reputed fathers," 50, 58, 85
Restell, Madame, 5, 103–9, 111–17, 164–69, 173, 206n8, 246, 277
Restellism, 106
Revolutionary War, 59n10, 63
Rhode Island
 abortion laws in, 45, 59, 80–81

abortion stories in, 55, 80–85, 127, 137, 346n18
Richards, Alice, 229
Richards, Cecile, 396
Ridge, Tom, 391
Right to Life of East Texas, 403–4
Riis, Jacob, 240
Ritchie, Lauren, 333
Roberts, John, 412, 427, 429, 432
Roberts, Troy, 357
Robinson, Richard, 103–4
Rockefeller, John D., III, 294, 301, 314
Rockefeller, Nelson, 314
Roe, Clifford Griffith, 237
Roe v. Wade
　common law and, 22–23, 26
　Fourteenth Amendment and, 2, 147–51
　influences on, 22–23, 26, 257, 260, 297, 300, 309
　decision of, 22, 306–8, 313–14
　legal challenges to, 317, 318–22, 339, 371–73, 401–2, 406–13
　post-*Roe* effects, 285–88, 321, 413, 439–43
　privacy and, 3, 260, 306n4, 310–11, 314–15n6, 440n2
　reversal of, 1, 320, 426–37
Roger the Spicer, 22
Rogers, Ammi, 71–76, 148
Rogers, Mary, 94, 106
　See also *Beautiful Cigar Girl*
Romper Room (TV show), 278
Root, Hiram Knox, 131n10
Rose, Lila, 395
Rosen, Harold, 286
Rosenzweig, Jacob, 178–79
Rothrock, Robin, 403–4
Roush, Jack, 198
Rowland, Levi, 124
RU-486, 375–77
　See also abortifacients
Ruiz, Viva, 354
Rush, Benjamin, 69, 92
Rush, Jacob, 69
Rush, James, 92–93

Rush Medical College, 219, 226
Russian roulette, 55
Rutland Convention, 132–33

Saad, Lydia, 373, 431n26
Salvation Army, 218
Sammis, Cora, 5, 181–83
sanctity of life, xiv–xv, 349–51, 355–56, 436
Sanctity of Life Sunday, 349–51, 355–56
San Francisco
　abortion laws in, 245–50, 275
　abortion stories in, 229, 232, 243–51, 303, 377
　pro-life organizations in, 399, 402
San Francisco Chronicle, 303
San Francisco Examiner, 232, 243, 283
Sanger, Margaret, 260–62, 273, 286n13, 290–92
Sanger, William, 108–9
Sass, Lauren R., 311–12
The Saturday Evening Post, 89nn1–2, 157n5, 289, 290n3
Saur, Prudence, 207–8
Savas, Leah
　"Advancing Arguments," 428n15
　"After Dobbs, Pregnancy Centers Brace," 431n27
　"Calling on a Fighter to Fight," 371n17
　"Jackson's Abortion Pink House," 434n42
　"New York, California Prep to Become Abortion Destinations," 435n44
　"The Pink House Brawl," 425n2
　"Pregnancy Centers near Texas Respond," 419n10
　"Pro-Lifers Fight to Protect Women from Dangerous Drugs," 377n6
　"Pro-Lifers Hopeful 'Dobbs' Will Oust 'Roe,'" 427n9
　"Pro-Lifers Minister to Panicked Women in Texas," 410n23
　"A Roe by Many Other Names," 435n45
savin, 46, 49, 91, 101
　See also abortifacients

Scalia, Antonin, 318, 404
Scarborough, Joe, 362
Schaeffer, Francis A., 316
Schwarzlose, Richard, 112n2
Scheidler, Joe, 325–26
Schlackman, Aubrey, 363–65
Schulz, William, 335
Seago, John, 413, 436
Sears, Richard D., 146
Secular Pro-Life, 399
Seiling, J. H., 223–25
self-administered abortions, 130, 214, 288, 413
self-esteem, 109, 129, 354
Semmes, Alexander, 142
sermons. *See* preaching
Sessions, Alexander, 57
Sessions, Amasa, 5, 56–60
Sessions, Nathaniel, 56–60
Sessions, Silence, 57
Severance, Sadie, 187–88
Sex in Middlesex (Thompson), 46–47, 49n1, 50nn1–2, 51n5
Sexual Behavior in the Human Male (Kinsey), 266
sexually transmitted disease (STD), 421
sexually transmitted infection (STI), 421
Shafer, Brenda Pratt, 357
Shannon, Gloria, 249
Shannon, Mamie, 201
Shannon, Shelley, 328
Shannon, Warren, 248
Sharp, Jane, 5, 21nn13–14, 28–29, 36
Shaw, Fannie, 196
Shawyer, Joss, 336
Sheldon, Wendy, 383
Sheltering Arms Home (Minneapolis), 205
Sheridan, Joe, 247
Shields, Barney, 275
"Shout Your Abortion," 4, 354n16, 382–83
Shrill (TV show), 370
"Shun the Aborting Woman," 4
"Siege of Atlanta," 327
The Silent Scream (movie), 325

sin
 abortion as, 23, 46n11, 59, 159–60, 195, 206, 344, 422–23
 adultery as, 51, 131
 community response to, 51, 258
 confession of, 58–59
 contraception as, 259–62
 forgiveness of, 239–40, 350
 preaching about, 77, 160–61
Sinclair, Brevard, 160–61
Singer, Peter, 352
Sitter, Ed, 389
Sioux tribe, 19
Slate, 365
Slaughter of the Innocents, 161, 173, 255
slavery
 anti-slavery movement, 127–30, 142, 145, 155
 indentured servants, 41–45
 similarities with abortion, 63, 132n16, 140–43, 159, 237n3, 298, 314–15n6, 316n11, 355–56
 treatment of slaves, 52–53n10
Slobodzian, Joseph, 359–62, 390n18
Smith, Asenath, 71
Smith, James, 120–21
Smith, Kirby, 145
Smith, Rose, 26, 29–30
Smith, William, 51–52
Snow, Tony, 337
socialism, 267, 270, 289
Socialist Workers Party, 270
Society for Humane Abortion, 301
Society of Magazine Writers, 289–90
Society for the Moral and Religious Improvement, 75
Solinger, Rickie, 273–74, 275nn7–10
Sotomayor, Sonia, 428, 433
Souter, David, 320–21
South Carolina, 8, 78, 354
South Dakota, 385, 434
Southern Baptist Convention (SBC), 351
Soviet abortarium, 256
Sowers, Eliza, 5, 89–94, 98, 100n12, 103, 106
Sparrow House, 334

Spencer, Robert, 267–69, 273
spiritism, 130–33
Sprague, A. W., 133
Sproul, R. C., 355
Spruch, Caren, 369
Srebnick, Amy, 94n19
Stalin, Joseph, 256, 270, 289
Stanford Law School, 405
St. Clair, Augustus, 173–78, 193, 264
Staubach, Roger, 316
Stehman, Ella, 223
Steinem, Gloria, 371
Stevens, Thaddeus, 148
Stewart, Scott, 427–28
Stickney, Elizabeth, 127
Stiles, Ezra, 55
Stimson, George, 199
Stockham, Alice Bunker, 207
Stokes, Edward, 176
Stokes, Kenny, 351n7
Stolk, Hank, 12
Storer, David, 135–36
Storer, Horatio, 117n18, 118n21, 136–42, 256
street-level reporting, 75, 276, 308, 311, 389, 432, 440
Strong, George, 131
Strong, William, 258
structural abortionism, 442
structural racism, 151–52, 155, 270–71, 442
Students for Life, 353
Suffolk District Medical Society (Boston), 136
Sunshine and Shadow in New York (Smith), 109, 125n15
Sununu, John, 320
supply and demand of abortion, 75–76, 116–17, 122, 158, 171, 202, 442–43
Supreme Court, Justices
  Alito, Samuel, 2–3, 429, 431–32, 435, 440n2
  Barrett, Amy Coney, 429, 431
  Blackmun, Harry, 22, 26, 66n10, 147, 306–10
  Breyer, Stephen, 322, 405, 433
  Burger, Warren, 306, 308
  Douglas, William, 310
  Eddy, Samuel, 81
  Gorsuch, Neil, 429, 431
  Iredell, James, 69
  Jay, John, 64, 69
  Kagan, Elena, 428
  Kavanaugh, Brett, 393, 428–29, 431
  Kennedy, Anthony, 320–21, 393
  Marshall, John, 440n2
  Marshall, Thurgood, 308
  Rehnquist, William, 2n3, 318
  Roberts, John, 412, 427, 429, 432
  Scalia, Antonin, 318, 404
  Sotomayor, Sonia, 428, 433
  Strong, William, 258
  Thomas, Clarence, 320, 429, 431–32
  Wilson, James, 63–69, 71
Supreme Court, rulings
  City of Akron v. Akron Center for Reproductive Health, 319
  Dobbs v. Jackson Women's Health Organization, 2
  Doe v. Bolton, 313n1, 373
  Dred Scott v. Sandford, 139, 311n21, 318
  Griswold v. Connecticut, 260n16, 309–10, 433
  Harris v. McRae, 319
  Loving v. Virginia, 433
  Planned Parenthood v. Casey, 2, 320–21, 406, 425–33
  Roe v. Wade. See *Roe v. Wade*
  Thornburgh v. American College of Obstetricians and Gynecologists, 319
  Webster v. Reproductive Health Services, 319
  Whole Woman's Health v. Jackson, 410n21, 413n29
  Whole Woman's Health v. Hellerstedt, 405
Susan B. Komen Foundation, 395–96
Swamidass, Geeta, 341–44, 347
Swan, Eva, 232–33
Szala, Lori, 421

Talks to My Patients (Gleason), 206
tansy, 19, 90, 100–101
  See also abortifacients
Tappan, Lewis, 77, 458
Tapper, Jake, 361–62
Taussig, Florence, 256
Taussig, Frederick, 5, 255–57, 262–64, 285, 307–8
Taylor, Darius, 120
Taylor, Jameson, 426–27
Taylor, Justin, 350n2
Taylor, Robert, 201–2
Taylor, Zachary, 258
Tehachapi Women's Prison, 250
Ten Commandments, 30
Ten Days That Shook the World (Reed), 256
Tenny, John, 121
Terry, Cindy, 326
Terry, Randall, 326–28
Tertullian, Quintus, 58
Texas
  abortion cases in, 297
  abortion laws in, 151n22, 354, 403–13
  abortion stories in, 396n6, 408–10, 415–18
  pro-life stories in, 260n15, 363–65, 401, 410–13, 417–23, 436–37
  See also private civil enforcement, of abortion laws
Texas Alliance for Life, 412
Texas Right to Life, 404, 412–13, 436
thalidomide, 278–79
"Thank God for Abortion" (Ruiz), 354
therapeutic abortion, 257, 277–78, 286n13, 292, 299–300, 368
Therapeutic Abortion Act, 300
Thimmesch, Nick, 12
13 Reasons Why (TV show), 370
Tietze, Christopher, 285–87
Timanus, George, 277
Time, 257, 336
Thomas, Clarence, 320, 429, 431–32
Thomas, Gary, 321, 332
Thomas More Society, 398n11, 411
Thomas, T. Gaillard, 227–29

Thompson, Liz, 395–96
Thompson, Robert, 232–33, 243
Thompson, Roger, 46–47, 49–50nn1–3, 51n5
Thornburgh v. American College of Obstetricians and Gynecologists, 319
Tiller, George, 328
Todd, John, 159–60
Todd, Monroe, 223
Todd, Samuel, 60
Tokology: A Book for Every Woman (Stockham), 207
Tone, Andrea, 285
Tracy, Stephen, 137–39, 266
Traveler's Aid Committee, 235
Trotsky, Leon, 270
Tucson Citizen, 231n10, 333–34
Tufts, James, 49–50
Turnaway Study, 379–81
Tushnet, Mark, 308
"trigger bans," 434
Trumbull, Jonathan, 59
Trumbull, Lyman, 148
Trump, Donald, 371, 401n21
"trunk murder," 174, 181, 183–84, 232
"trust the woman," 50, 60
Tweed, William "Boss," 163–69, 175–76, 192
Twitter, 365, 382n24, 402n25, 430n20, 434, 441
two patients, in abortion, 97–102, 113, 135–36, 181–86, 228, 245, 303–4, 376

ultrasounds
  as deterrent to abortion, 255–56n2, 288, 324–25, 339, 342–48, 363n22, 367, 416, 418, 428, 442
  fetal knowledge before, 200, 264, 344
  legal requirement for, 319, 345–47
unborn children
  personhood of, 147–48, 150–52, 316
  protection of, 207, 316, 324, 334, 426, 433
Unitarian Universalist Association, 335

University of California San Francisco
    (UCSF), 347n19, 370, 379–80,
    383, 402
University of Michigan, 125, 209
University of Pennsylvania, 64, 97–98,
    100, 156
University of Texas at Austin, 2, 412n27
University of Toledo, 387–88
University of Virginia, 125
unwanted child, 127–34, 183, 291,
    295n18, 380
unwed mothers, 44, 50–51, 53, 204–5,
    236–38
unwelcome child. *See* unwanted child
The Unwelcome Child (Wright), 129
USA Today, 89, 335, 360–61
U.S. Food and Drug Administration
    (FDA), 279n21, 377–79
U.S. Post Office, 260–61
U.S. Congress, 38, 146–50, 257–59, 289,
    314–22, 328, 357, 401–2

Van Bunckle, Henry, 177
Van Buskirk, Madame, 173, 178
Van Cleve, Charlotte, 205
Vermont
    abortion laws in, 151
    abortion stories in, 68, 82, 175
    spiritism conference in, 132
Vesey, William, 54
viability of fetus, 319, 321, 425, 427,
    432n31
Village Church (Dallas, TX), 364
Village Voice, 268n15, 324
Vincent Memorial Hospital (Boston), 208
Virginia
    abortion laws in, 37, 45, 50–52,
        151n22, 433
    abortion stories in, 19–20, 41–45, 402
Von Baer, Karl Ernst, 137
Von Schultz, Ida, 229

Wadsworth, Benjamin, 37
Wagner, Richard, 247
waiting period, for abortion, 319, 389
Wall Street Journal, 337, 361

Wallace, Dewitt, 292
Walling, Alonzo, 199–200
Walsh, Jim, 404
Waltke, Bruce, 300n9, 315–16
Wanamaker, John, 124
Ward, Thomas, 33
Wardleworth, Thomas, 101–2
Warren, John, 109
Warren, Susan, 17–23, 25, 30, 44, 432
Waring, Maria, 128
Washburn Home (Minneapolis), 205
Washington, DC
    abortion culture in, 147, 223, 305, 316
    pro-life culture in, 313n2, 316, 353,
        362
Washington, George, 64–65, 69
Washington Post
    pro-abortion bias, 280, 287, 292, 301,
        361–65, 369, 380, 382n24, 411,
        440n2
    pro-life coverage, 306, 331, 363–65,
        422n20
Washington Times, 361, 377n9
Washington v. Glucksberg, 2n3
Waskom, Texas, 403–7
Waters, Matt, 328
Waters, William, 43
Wattleton, Faye, 327
We Testify, 382–83
Webb, John, 41–42
Webster, Noah, 147
Webster v. Reproductive Health Services,
    319
Weales, Elizabeth, 34–35, 39
Wells, Elizabeth, 49–50, 60
Welter, Elizabeth, 231
West, Eugene F., 243–44
West Germany, 279n21
West, James J., 192–93
Westervelt, Jacob, 117, 166
West Virginia, 434–35
Wexler, Natalie, 69n19
Wharton, Francis, 118n21
Whatever Happened to the Human Race?
    (Schaeffer), 316
Wheel of Fortune, 105

Wheeler, Anna, 56–57
When Abortion Was a Crime (Reagan), 141n20, 162n21, 269n19, 276–78
White Cross Society, 193
Whitefield, George, 58–59, 98, 160n17
Whitmer, James, 266
Whole Woman's Health, 365
Whole Woman's Health v. Jackson, 410n21, 413n29
Whole Woman's Health v. Hellerstedt, 405
Wichita (Kansas), 327–28
Wilkes, George, 112–14
Willkie, John "Jack", 392–93
Wills, John, 43
Williams, Catherine, 82–84
Williams, Daniel K., 297n1
Williams, Louisa C., 145–46, 153
Wilson, Henry, 258
Wilson, James, 63–65, 69, 71
wire hanger, 3, 282, 288n19
Wisconsin
    abortion laws in, 117–18, 434, 436
    abortion stories in, 187, 189–90, 430
Wisconsin Family Action, 430, 436
Witherspoon, James S., 151nn21–22
Wodlake, William, 22–23
Wolbert, Leslie, 375–77, 382
The Woman Rebel (Sanger), 260–61
Woman's Boarding House (Minneapolis), 205
Woman's Christian Association, 205
Women's Christian Temperance Union, 193, 218
woman-to-woman education, 203–9, 260
Women's March, 362–63
Women's Medical Center (Dayton, OH), 387
Women's Medical College of Pennsylvania, 204
Women's Medical Society (Philadelphia), 389

women's suffrage movement, 256
Woods, Helen, 212–17, 239
World's Fair, 1933 (Chicago), 264
World's Fair, 1939 (New York City), 263–66
World (magazine), 359
    Olasky, Marvin, 333n7, 396nn3–5
    Olasky, Susan, 392n23–24
    Savas, Leah, 4, 371n17, 377n6, 410n23, 425n2, 427n9, 428n15, 431n27, 434n42, 435nn44–45
    reporting on abortion, 314nn5–7, 328n14, 346–47n18, 349n1, 358n4, 359, 368–69, 377nn6–9, 390–91n18, 395n1, 398n10, 399n14, 401n21, 411n24, 419n10, 422n20, 429n18, 430n24
World War II, 248, 267, 270, 289, 342
Worldwide Church of God, 399
Wranosky, Hanah, 415–20
Wrigley, William, 219
Wright, Henry, 127–30, 132–33

Yale University, 71, 75, 125
Yard, Molly, 320
YMCA, 122–26, 258
    See also Ferris, Isaac
Youngblut, John, 200
Young, Curtis, 316–18
Young, John, 69
Young Men's Christian Association. *See* YMCA
Young Women's Christian Association. *See* YWCA
youth culture, 105
YWCA, 125

Zawadzki, Edward, 286n13
Zeh, Katey, 355
Zogby poll, 368

Scripture Index

Genesis
1 36
1:26–27 352
2 36
3 36
4 36
9:6 .... 37, 37n10
9:7 37
17 36
25:1–4 .... 37n11
29 36
30 36

Exodus
book of 36
21:22 315
21:22–23 .... 38, 300n9

Leviticus
book of 36

Numbers
5:27 353–354

Deuteronomy
book of 36
32:35 .... 328n13

1 Samuel
book of 36

2 Samuel
book of 36

2 Kings
8:12 .... 36n8
15:16 .... 36n8

1 Chronicles
book of 36

Job
book of 35, 355
31:15 .... 35n7

Psalms
book of 35, 355
113 36
127 36
139 36
139:13 .... 35n7

Proverbs
24:11–12 350

Isaiah
book of 35
44:24 .... 35n7
49:1 .... 35n7
49:5 .... 35n7

Jeremiah
book of 35

1:5 .... 35n7

Hosea
13:16 .... 36n8

Amos
1:13 .... 36n8

Matthew
book of 36, 355

Luke
book of 35, 355
1:15 .... 35n7

John
book of 36
19:30 .... 14n20

Acts
book of 36

Romans
book of 355
3:23 60
12:19 .... 328n13

Galatians
book of 35
1:15 .... 35n7

Hebrews
book of 36
10:30 .... 328n13

1 Peter
book of 355